WITHDRAWN

Irresistible Dictation

Writing Science

EDITORS *Timothy Lenoir and Hans Ulrich Gumbrecht*

Irresistible Dictation

GERTRUDE STEIN AND THE CORRELATIONS
OF WRITING AND SCIENCE

Steven Meyer

STANFORD UNIVERSITY PRESS
STANFORD, CALIFORNIA

Stanford University Press
Stanford, California

© 2001 by the Board of Trustees of the
Leland Stanford Junior University

Printed in the United States of America
On acid-free, archival-quality paper

Library of Congress Cataloging-in-Publication Data
Meyer, Steven
    Irresistible dictation : Gertrude Stein and the
correlations of writing and science / Steven Meyer.
        p. cm. — (Writing science)
    Includes bibliographical references and index.
    ISBN 0-8047-3328-7 (alk. paper)
        1. Stein, Gertrude, 1874–1946—Knowledge—
Science.   2. Literature and science—United
States—History—20th century.   3. Science in
literature.   4. Authorship.   I. Series.
    PS3537.T323 Z73   2001
    818'.5209—dc21   00-049266

Designed by Janet Wood
Typeset by TypeWorks in 10/13 Sabon

Original Printing 2001

Last figure below indicates year of this printing:
10   09   08   07   06   05   04   03   02   01

CONTENTS

ILLUSTRATIONS

Quotations from Gertrude Stein's works are identified by abbreviated title and page number. Complete citations can be found in the Works Cited, pp. 401–29.

ABT	*The Autobiography of Alice B. Toklas*
AF	"An American and France"
ALL	"American Language and Literature"
BTV	*Bee Time Vine and Other Pieces*
CE	"Composition as Explanation"
EA	*Everybody's Autobiography*
FE	*Fernhurst, Q.E.D., and Other Early Writings*
FIA	*Four in America*
GCA	"Genuine Creative Ability"
GHA	*The Geographical History of America*
GMP	*Matisse Picasso and Gertrude Stein with Two Shorter Stories*
GP	*Geography and Plays*
HTW	*How To Write*
HWW	*How Writing Is Written*
LCA	*Lucy Church Amiably*
LIA	*Lectures in America*
LOP	*Last Operas and Plays*
MA	*The Making of Americans*
MES	"Message from Gertrude Stein"
MGS	"More Grammar for a Sentence"
MOT	*Motor Automatism*

N	*Narration*
OP	*Operas and Plays*
PC	"Possessive Case"
PCW	*Picasso: The Complete Writings*
PF	*Paris France*
PL	*Painted Lace and Other Pieces*
PP	*Portraits and Prayers*
RAB	*Reflection on the Atomic Bomb*
RM	"The Radcliffe Manuscripts"
SIM	*Stanzas in Meditation and Other Poems*
SR	*A Stein Reader*, ed. Dydo
SVV	*The Letters of Gertrude Stein and Carl Van Vechten*, ed. Burns and Dydo
T	*Two: Gertrude Stein and Her Brother and Other Early Portraits*
TACF	"Thoughts on an American Contemporary Feeling"
TB	*Tender Buttons*
TBr	[Comment accompanying reprint of *Tender Buttons* in *transition*]
TI	"A Transatlantic Interview 1946"
TL	*Three Lives*
UK	*Useful Knowledge*
WAM	"What Are Masterpieces And Why Are There So Few Of Them"
WIHS	*Wars I Have Seen*

In addition, the following works have also been abbreviated for convenience:

AI	Whitehead, *Adventures of Ideas*
BABF	Edelman, *Bright Air, Brilliant Fire: On the Matter of the Mind*
BC	James, *Psychology: Briefer Course*
CBM	Taylor, *William James on Consciousness Beyond the Margin*
DCE	James, "Does 'Consciousness' Exist?"
EL	Emerson, *Essays and Lectures*
EM	Varela, Thompson, and Rosch, *The Embodied Mind*
ENQ	Whitehead, *An Enquiry Concerning the Principles of Natural Knowledge*

EPR	James, *Essays in Psychical Research*
FF	Gallup, ed., *Flowers of Friendship*
HGS	Skinner, "Has Gertrude Stein a Secret?"
INT	Bolinger, *Intonation and Its Parts: Melody in Spoken English*
LB	Wordsworth and Coleridge, *Lyrical Ballads*
M	Langer, *Mind: An Essay on Human Feeling*
ML	James, *Manuscript Lectures*
MT	Whitehead, *Modes of Thought*
NHI	Emerson, *Natural History of Intellect and Other Papers*
NM	Changeux, *Neuronal Man: The Biology of Mind*
NS	Barker, *The Nervous System and Its Constituent Neurones*
PBE	James, "The Physical Basis of Emotion"
PI	Wittgenstein, *Philosophical Investigations*
PR	James, *The Principles of Psychology*
PRE	Wordsworth, *The Prelude: 1799, 1805, 1850*
PRO	Whitehead, *Process and Reality*
RPP	Wittgenstein, *Remarks on the Philosophy of Psychology*
SMW	Whitehead, *Science and the Modern World*
SW	Eliot, *The Sacred Wood: Essays on Poetry and Criticism*
TK	Maturana and Varela, *The Tree of Knowledge*
VAR	James, *The Varieties of Religious Experience*
WIM	Toklas, *What Is Remembered*

In a conversation with John Hyde Preston that appeared in *The Atlantic Monthly* shortly after she concluded her six-month lecture tour of the United States in 1934 and 1935, Gertrude Stein responded to Preston's confession of just how "miserable, despairing, self-doubtful" he still felt about his writing. Drawing on half a century's experience in her chosen medium, she counseled him to write

> without thinking of the result in terms of a result, but think of the writing in terms of discovery, which is to say that creation must take place between the pen and the paper, not before in a thought or afterwards in a recasting. Yes, before in a thought, but not in careful thinking. It will come if it is there and if you will let it come, and if you have anything you will get a sudden creative recognition. You won't know how it was, even what it is, but it will be creation if it came out of the pen and out of you and not out of an architectural drawing of the thing you are doing. (p. 188)

These remarks may well appear unexceptional, for Stein is articulating a version of the Romantic commonplace that some two decades later—already forty-five years ago—M. H. Abrams would term "the expressive theory of art." According to Abrams, such theories hold that "poetry is the overflow, utterance, or projection of the thought and feelings of the poet; or else (in the chief variant formulation) poetry is defined in terms of the imaginative process which modifies and synthesizes the images, thoughts, and feelings of the poet" (pp. 21–22). Stein's subsequent comment to Preston that "when one has discovered and evolved a new form, it is not the form but the fact that *you are the form* that is important" would seem to confirm that her theory of art is expressive and none too original at that. Still, there is something peculiar going on here, as Stein's example of James Boswell—she calls him "the greatest biographer who ever lived"—demonstrates. She is not speaking of self-expression, of the writer expressing himself or herself, but of the expression of someone or something apart from oneself. It is this phenomenon that she had in mind when she spoke of her writing, as she often did, as a form of portraiture. The writing comes "out of you" and "out of the pen," yet it is neither you nor the pen; nor does it merely reflect, phenomenologically, the consciousness of the individual portrayed. Hence Boswell, in his *Life of Johnson*, "discovered [Samuel] Johnson's real form which Johnson never knew." Stein doesn't stop with this provocative claim, however, but concludes the conversation with Preston by remarking:

> The great thing is not ever to think about form but let it come. Does that sound strange from me? They have accused me of thinking of nothing else. Do you see the real joke? It is the critics who have really thought about form always and I have thought about—writing! (p. 194)

With that retort, Preston observes, "Gertrude Stein laughed enormously and went [back] into the hotel with the crowd"—"a modern and post-modern Medusa," as Catharine Stimpson has aptly characterized her in the context of this exchange ("Humanism and Its Freaks," p. 316).

Not only does Stein substitute *writing* for *form* in this aperçu; she replaces the Romantics' (and Abrams's) emphasis on poetry with a corresponding emphasis on writing, as I shall do as well in examining the complex interweaving of writing and science in her compositional practices. In this way the traditional nineteenth- and twentieth-century "contradistinction . . . of Poetry and Matter of Fact, or Science," as Wordsworth put it, is elided (LB, p. 254). No serious literary work, whether a composition by Stein or by Wordsworth, permits an exclusively formal reading, isolating it from "matter of fact." On the contrary, any reading that befits the text involves situating it in a larger textual context, that is to say, in an important and illuminating part of the textual nexus from which it has emerged. Consequently, my invocations of Wordsworth and Sterne, and George Eliot and Pater, in the first two chapters of the present study are not just readings of these figures; they are also readings of Stein's writing in relation to texts that form the contours of her compositional practices and bear a more than analogical relation to her own writing. Stein's compositions are especially interesting in this regard because she so successfully rid them of overt literary allusions, among other forms of referentiality. I have endeavored here neither to produce a source study nor to situate Stein in a context, or series of contexts, only externally related to what she was actually doing in her writing. Instead, I have sought to show how she queries various sources that remain implicit in her texts, making them over in her own image, as it were. It is this emphasis on the active transformations involved in her compositional practices which distinguishes my readings both from traditional source studies and from a good deal of contemporary cultural studies. The basis for my own practice of reading, then, is a conviction that texts exist in relation to other texts or they do not exist at all, and that it is in uncovering these relations that the activity of reading proceeds. More purely formal readings are in fact instances of what Alfred North Whitehead called "misplaced concreteness," relying no less on such nexuses but abstracted from them, and in this sense idealizing the work of writing as well as the work of reading (SMW, p. 3). I try to keep the historical development of a work's formal significance always in mind, that is, its origins within a temporal framework that it partly creates—perhaps an impossible task but surely a useful methodological aim. One may ask whether on the basis of such an account one can ultimately distinguish Stein's writing from other writing. In an ultimate sense, the answer is probably no; as poets have always done, Stein renders features of writing explicit that are ordinarily ignored yet present. Where her writing differs from other writing is the extent she requires the reader, and herself, to be conscious of such compositional features in order to understand and enjoy the writing as fully as possible.

In Stein's case, the textual context of her work is not just literary (Laurence Sterne et al.) but also philosophical (Emerson, Whitehead), psychological (William James, Ludwig Wittgenstein), and neurophysiological (Lewellys Barker, Gerald Edelman, Francisco Varela). Of course, these categories themselves overlap; with the exception of Barker, associate professor of anatomy during Stein's first years of graduate study at Johns Hopkins, each writer fits comfortably under several headings. It is this circumstance that compels an interdisciplinary and comparative study both of them and of Stein. Nonetheless, the various writers differ according to the primacy of one or another category in their work; and Stein differs from the others, as I argue, largely in the extent to which the four categories function in tandem in her writing. In order to read James, for example, one can readily bracket the literary aspects of his philosophical and psychological studies (with "literary" understood broadly as marking explicit references to writing as well as implicit self-consciousness with respect to one's writing practices); in order to read Wordsworth one can ignore the neurophysiological basis of the plotting of his poems. Something is lost, yet one's reading remains relatively unaffected by the loss. I have attempted to demonstrate that Stein's compositions, by contrast, demand equal attention to all four components. That she herself often emphasized the literary aspects of her writing needs to be understood in a historical context in which first her brother Leo, then prospective publishers, and finally reviewers insisted that it wasn't writing at all. It is only because the inevitable first question posed by readers of her work is

"Is it writing?" that it is reasonable, although certainly not necessary, that the literary, philosophical, psychological, and neurophysiological contexts of the writing be addressed by someone whose principal training has been in literature. Yet I also believe that the practice of reading is never restricted to any particular field, and always occurs between fields. Consequently, I have tried to draw connections among these domains of knowledge, connections that writers ranging from Emerson and Eliot to Whitehead and Donna Haraway have already made, in their own ways, implicitly and explicitly.

In the course of this broad reevaluation of Stein's career, I situate her both within the lineage of such Romantic poet-scientists as Wordsworth, Goethe, and Shelley, and in an important line of speculative thinkers that extends from Emerson to James and Whitehead, emerging today in figures as disparate as the bioaesthetician Susanne Langer, neuroscientists like Varela and Edelman, and Haraway, doyenne of contemporary science studies. These two lines share the perspective that James designated *radical empiricism*. In Chapter 1, I review the multiple points of contact between Stein's evolving writing practice and radical empiricism in its more traditionally scientific as well as poetic guises. I then examine in Chapter 2 the ways in which the formulation of the neuron doctrine in the 1890s motivated her subsequent "autopoietic," or self-organizing, writing, premised on and exemplifying an organicism divorced from traditional notions of organic form. This nonvitalist organicism is similar to that analyzed by Haraway in her 1976 study *Crystals, Fabrics, and Fields: Metaphors of Organicism in Twentieth-Century Developmental Biology*, and serves as the hallmark of the neurophysiological imagination exhibited by all these figures. In the next two chapters, loosely tied together under the heading "The New Organism," I am especially concerned with the correlations between Stein's understanding of writing and the speculations of Emerson, Whitehead, and Varela on the mechanisms of life and of consciousness. From here I proceed to four linked chapters (Chapters 5–8) that focus on Stein's literary practice in light of its development from James's physiological psychology as well as from his studies in psychical research. I argue that the radical reconceptualization of consciousness articulated by James in his 1904 essay "Does 'Consciousness' Exist?" proved decisive for Stein's writing; even so, a full range of differences emerged between Stein and her mentor with respect to automatic writing, the relation writing bears to consciousness, the extent to which the act of writing is reducible to subsequent acts of reading, and the nature and desirability of self-consciousness. In the next-to-last chapter of this section I juxtapose Stein's perspective on these and related matters with that of the Anglo-Austrian philosopher Ludwig Wittgenstein, for whom, rather unexpectedly, James's speculations also played a central role. Finally, in an extended analysis of a 1935 recording of Stein reading her work aloud, I offer a material overview of the phenomenon I am calling, after Emerson, "irresistible dictation."

The key difficulty I have faced from the outset of this project has been that of talking about Stein in a way that doesn't reduce her to a version of some other writer, while still focusing on her correspondences with, and ties to, a wide range of figures. It would be misleading to begin the book, for example, with the portrait of Emerson I sketch in "The New Organism" (which emphasizes the radical empiricism that replaced his early naturalistic idealism), because it is crucial for my study that he be read in the context provided by Stein no less than that he contextualize Stein. This would be all but impossible were I to open with him. I have attempted to resolve this difficulty by invoking, at the outset, the broadest possible context in which to address the relation between science and literature while at the same time remaining true to Stein's own experience: hence the movement in Chapter 1 between Sterne and Wordsworth, on the one hand, and contemporary neuroscience on the other, with James's radical empiricism providing a way station. Then, in Chapter 2, I proceed to Stein's more immediate context of Pater and George Eliot as well as her extensive training at Johns Hopkins in laboratory technique. Only after I have established these histories, broad and narrow, do I introduce the pair of chapters concerned with the Emersonian background, foreground, and prospects of her writing: that is, with Emerson himself, with Whitehead, and with the Emersonian biology theorized by Varela. These chapters in place, it becomes possible to address the details of Stein's relation with James without either getting lost in them or falsely generalizing from them.

Although my emphasis on James's radical empiricism accords with his own sense of things, it has been overshadowed in the twentieth century by two complementary reductions: James as father of a distinctively American psychology and midwife of the equally American philosophy of pragmatism. My work is part of a current reassessment, in literary studies due largely to the efforts of Richard Poirier, and outside literary studies attested to in superb recent works on James's psychological investigations by Eugene Taylor and Edward Reed. These authors portray James the radical empiricist rather than James the pragmatist. To be sure, Poirier tends to speak of James as a pragmatist, but the pragmatism he has in mind is radical empiricist through and through. (As James insisted, and as the "new pragmatism" of the 1980s and 1990s amply testifies, pragmatism may take many forms, not all of them radical empiricist.) It is here, in the context of Stein's scientific training and the Emersonian/Whiteheadian strain of radical empiricism, as well as of the literary tradition of a science consistent with poetic values, that my study most directly revises current Stein scholarship, since I am concerned to demonstrate the ways in which she developed a more radical empiricism than James was able to, owing to her greater concentration on her compositional practices.

In the work that has ensued, I place greater emphasis on what might be termed Stein's poetics than on individual works of poetry (often composed, in her case, in prose). Although I tend to focus on discrete paragraphs in my readings of particular compositions—the paragraph offering, according to Stein, the minimum unit of composition in prose, an aspect of her poetics I discuss in Chapter 7—there are extended readings of individual works as well, as in the treatment, in more or less chronological order, of "Two" (in Chapter 1), "Old and Old" (Chapter 2), *Matisse Picasso and Gertrude Stein* (Chapter 3), "Mrs. Emerson" (Chapter 4), "Wherein the South Differs from the North" (Chapter 6), and "More Grammar for a Sentence" (Chapter 7). My aim is principally to make the reading of texts like these a more manageable undertaking for other readers, not to do their reading for them. The first order of business, then, is to clarify a number of Stein's more gnomic statements about her writing (statements that often appear transparent at first glance), by juxtaposing them with her literary practices or by calling attention to the literary qualities they display. This has the double function of demonstrating not just what she meant but also that she really did know what she was doing.

In fact, my study has two complementary motives: to explicate Stein *and* to bring Emerson, James, Whitehead, and Wittgenstein, as well as aspects of late nineteenth-century physiological psychology and late twentieth-century neuroscience, "into focus through the lens of Stein's writing," as one of the anonymous readers of the manuscript aptly phrased it. If, along the way, I propose that the neuron doctrine played a crucial, and among major American writers unique, role in the development of Stein's compositional practices, I am not thereby arguing that experimental writing, Stein's or anyone else's, *reflects* experimental science nor that in her writing Stein automatically (that is to say, unthinkingly) applied the scientific doctrines she was exposed to as a young woman. Her writing no more reflects the neuron doctrine than it reflects particular psychosocial or psychosexual discursive formations—or any of her exquisite verbal portraits of Picasso can flatly be said to be "about" her great friend. (Nor, of course, does this last observation imply that "If I Told Him. A Completed Portrait of Picasso" could just as well be a portrait of Matisse as of Picasso, or that when you've read one work of Stein's you've read them all.) Such assertions attribute too passive a role to Stein's compositional practices, which are experimental in a way that other experimental writing isn't. Instead of being modeled on scientific experimentation, her writing turns out to be a form of experimental science itself. It is not just that her ideas about writing were influenced by science; she reconfigured science *as* writing and performed scientific experiments *in* writing.

I recognize that this is a provocative claim, and it is the burden of my first two chapters to justify it. Here I will remark that Stein spent her first decade of sustained intellectual and emotional independence—from the age of twenty to twenty-eight—doing experimental work in the leading psychological laboratory and then in the leading medical school in the United States, and only subsequently turned from a scientific to a literary career. This is the fact that animates my study, not the neuron doctrine per se; the question I ask is, what constitutes this shift? What role, or more exactly roles, did Stein's scientific training, first at Harvard and then at Johns Hopkins, play in her compositional practices in the ensuing decades? I find answers in the works she composed, works that, in proving to be more than these answers, remain opaque although not unintelligible. My use of the term *opaque* may seem puzzling, for I regard it as a positive quality, and aim in my readings to respect the integrity, or opacity, of these dense texts. Too often, readers of Stein have attempted to render her compositions transparent, to crack the code. Such interpretations merely invert the mistaken accusation that her writing lacks any sense at all. Operating in another register than ordinary communication with its ideal of transparency, these autopoietic compositions function as what James called "irreducible and stubborn facts." No less than James in his psychology or Whitehead in his philosophy, Stein displayed a "passionate interest in the *relation* of general principles to irreducible and stubborn facts"; only in her case the objects of radical empiricism were extended to the words on the page (SMW, p. 3, emphasis added). Consequently, in my readings I focus on this relation, so as to convey both the process and the results of Stein's rigorous meditations, concluding, as she does, with principles and facts still in play, neither reduced to the other. As I asserted at the outset, I am concerned here with meanings that emerge between texts and not with the endeavor, entirely appropriate in other contexts, to fix the meaning of particular texts.

My investigations of this great writer's compositional practices have taken me much further afield than I expected to venture when, a dozen years ago, I started to assemble material for a dissertation on the role of autobiography (or, as I liked then, and still like, to think of it, *auto-*, *bio-* and *graphē*) in shaping the work Stein produced over the course of more than fifty years of determined writing. In addition to the studies collected in the present volume, I have found myself returning time and again to her exemplary reconfigurations of narrative, and hope shortly to bring out a companion volume on this topic. All in all, it has been quite an adventure, and here I would like to acknowledge the institutional and personal support that has made it possible. Thanks first to the trio of professors who encouraged me to write on Stein in my final year of coursework at Yale—Alan Trachtenberg, Harold Bloom, and Jacques Derrida. Thanks to John Hollander for his great learning and great appreciation of Stein in his capacity as adviser, a capacity that continues to this day; to Richard Poirier for the fine editorial pen he wielded when I sent him a draft of the first chapter I *thought* I had completed, for subsequently publishing a much-revised version, and for continuing encouragement; to Marjorie Perloff for her unfailing enthusiasm for all manner of Steiniana, in particular for an afternoon of spirited conversation in Maine and for her sponsorship of an MLA panel I proposed on Stein and Wittgenstein; to the other participants on the panel, Jacques Lezra, Charles Altieri, and Linda Voris, and to the editors of *Modernism/Modernity* for so swiftly publishing the papers presented at that gratifyingly well-attended session; to Ulla Dydo, Stein scholar par excellence, both for her example and her encouragement; especially to my colleagues in the Washington University English department, who have supported this project in countless ways; to my colleague across the courtyard in Philosophy, Bill Gass, and his great love and understanding of Stein; to my students, graduate and undergraduate, at Washington University and at Yale, for the education they have permitted me; to Anthony Cascardi and Charles Altieri again for inviting me to participate in an NEH Institute on Ethics and Aesthetics in the summer of 1993, where I found myself thinking untoward thoughts about convergences between Stein and Wittgenstein; to the Whitney Humanities Center at Yale, and its directors David Bromwich and David Marshall, for awarding me a Richardson Fellowship for the 1994–95 academic year, which enabled me to begin to address the significance of Stein's neuroanatomical studies for her experimental writing; to Washington University for providing leave support that year as well as Faculty Research Grants in 1994, 1996, and 1998; to my colleagues at the Center for creating such an engrossingly interdisciplinary environment, and in particular to Katherine Kearns and Langdon Hammer, fellow teachers and students of twentieth-century poetry, and to the historians of medicine Mark Micale and Sherwin Nuland; to the editorial board of the *Yale Journal of Criticism* for soliciting and accepting "Writing Psychology Over" while I was in residence; to the various audiences at talks I have given on Stein at Washington University, at Yale, at the MLA, at the Society for Literature and Science, at Stanford, and at Berkeley; to Helen Tartar of Stanford University Press for her continuing support, and in particular for her vast store of patience the last four years; to Ann Klefstad for doing such a great job copyediting the manuscript, and to Nathan MacBrien for shepherding it through the Press; to Patricia Willis, curator of the Yale Collection of American Literature, to Donald Gallup, former curator, and to the Beinecke Library staff, for making the library a home away from home all this time. Thanks all along to my family, with whom I visited Stein's summer home at Bilignin fifteen or more years ago, before I had made the acquaintance (so far as I knew) of a word of her writing. Thanks to Karen, who has given me the courage and the occasion to complete this study.

CREDITS

Portions of this book are reprinted here by permission of the publishers. Chapter 3 appeared in earlier form as "Emerson and Stein," in *Raritan* 10 (Fall 1990): 87–119; Chapter 5 as "Writing Psychology Over: Gertrude Stein and William James," in *The Yale Journal of Criticism* 8 (Spring 1995): 133–163; and Chapter 7 as "'The Physiognomy of the Thing': Sentences and Paragraphs in Stein and Wittgenstein," in *Modernism/Modernity* 5 (Winter 1998): 99–116.

Irresistible Dictation

PART ONE

The Neurophysiological Imagination

CHAPTER ONE

Ecstatic Science: Natural History of the Soul

As a student at the Harvard Annex (rechristened Radcliffe College at the end of her freshman year), Gertrude Stein worked closely with William James and Hugo Münsterberg at the Harvard Psychological Laboratory. Her early exposure to the new science of physiological psychology was supplemented by a summer at the Woods Hole Marine Biological Laboratory in 1897, followed by four years, and part of a fifth, of further study at Johns Hopkins Medical School. This thorough training in experimental science played a crucial role in Stein's subsequent development as perhaps the twentieth century's preeminent "experimental" writer. Among modern American writers, William Carlos Williams and Marianne Moore each possessed extensive acquaintance with contemporary biology, and scientific models of knowledge permeated the literary and social criticism even of High Church modernists like T. S. Eliot and Ezra Pound, yet Stein's scientific training was unique, as were its ramifications in her writing.[1] This does not mean, however, that in her compositional practice she unreservedly accepted what Jacques Loeb, early in the century, termed the "mechanistic conception of life."[2] In fact, she was much more critical of mechanistic science than has generally been supposed by scholars who have addressed her scientific background—with her criticism, constructive as well as deconstructive, emerging principally in her experimental writing.[3]

Certainly, Stein's understanding of science was initially mechanistic; thus in *The Making of Americans*, written between 1902 and 1911, she attempted to describe the precise mechanisms of human personality in great detail, with the ultimate aim of describing every possible kind of human being. The following passage, which she selected for a recording made at Columbia University in 1935, conveys a sense both of her empirical method and of the ecstatic tone she attributed to her narrator, the sense of "wonder" that scientific investigation is capable of producing. It occurs about a third of the way through the novel:

Slowly every one in continuous repeating, to their minutest variation, comes to be clearer to some one. Every one who ever was or is or will be living sometimes will be clearly realised by some one. Sometime there will be an ordered history of every one. Slowly every kind of one comes into ordered recognition. More and more then it is wonderful in living the subtle variations coming clear into ordered recognition, coming to make every one a part of some kind of them, some kind of men and women. Repeating then is in every one, every one then comes sometime to be clearer to some one, sometime there will be then an orderly history of every one who ever was or is or will be living. (p. 284)

Careful attention to repetition, with its capacity for "minutest variation," supplied Stein at this stage of her career with a methodology appropriate in equal measure to her research and her writing. Yet with *Tender Buttons*, composed the year after she completed her monumental novel, she embraced a vigorously nonmechanistic outlook. In this collection of prose poetry, and in hundreds of pieces, large and small, written over the next twenty years, she endeavored to portray consciousness in terms of the experience of writing, as she moved to a more fully "organic" sense of composition. Stein's new perspective corresponded to an Emerson-inflected naturalism as well as to Whitehead's "philosophy of organism." Although she characterized the shift as a wholesale rejection of science, it actually only represented a disillusionment with the dominant vision of science, science understood as devoted exclusively to what James, in *The Principles of Psychology*, called "knowledge-about" or descriptive knowledge.

Whitehead devised his "theory of organic mechanism" in order to "bridg[e] the gap," as he proposed in his 1925 Lowell Lectures, *Science and the Modern World*, between "science and the fundamental intuition of mankind which finds its expression in poetry and its practical exemplification in the presuppositions of daily life," namely, the "organic view of nature"— whereby natural phenomena are regarded as "ends in themselves" that possess "intrinsic reality" (SMW, pp. 80, 93–95). As I shall argue in Chapter 4, Whitehead's analysis of what he initially called "rhythm," and subsequently referred to as "vibrating pattern" or "vibratory organism," provides a scientific framework for understanding Stein's claims to recreate, and not merely represent, individuals in her post-1911 compositions. Her "fundamental intuition" remained scientific, despite the fact that her expression of a non-Cartesian, non-Newtonian, "organic view" radically failed to conform to traditional scientific writing practice; indeed, one may say that she applied the autopoietic premises of Whitehead's redescription of science to the practice of writing itself. Consequently, her own frequent claims that her writing represented a fundamentally twentieth-century rejection of science need to be qualified by the recognition that she made these claims with what she herself would have described as a characteristically nineteenth-century conception of science in mind.

The "one thing" she had "completely learned" from James, Stein remarked in her 1934 lecture "The Gradual Making of The Making of Americans," was that

> science is continuously busy with the complete description of something, with ultimately the complete description of anything with ultimately the complete description of everything. (LIA, p. 156)

More recently, Jean-Pierre Changeux invokes the same traditional conception of science when, in *Neuronal Man: The Biology of Mind*, he suggests that in order to get away from the idea of "a 'genetic program' controlling the development of the embryo in time," a notion that inaccurately yet inevitably "implies a single control center," scientists need to "abandon" altogether the metaphor of "the organism as a cybernetic machine," replacing it with "an *exhaustive description* of properties, elements, geometry, and a communication network." Changeux's alternative model of an "embryo system" which "can be broken down naturally into automatonlike elements represented by the embryonic cells" requires, if only provisionally, the reification of its minimal elements, which, "automatonlike," lack significant internal organization and even metaphorical agency (pp. 191–92). It was this dependence of all projects of "complete description" on an atomistic and ultimately materialistic and deterministic model that Stein, in the course of writing *The Making of Americans*, came to distrust. To the practical question of the ultimate completion of any such description—"if this can really be done the complete description of everything," she asked herself, "then what else is there to do"—she responded that one might try to stop "continuing describing everything" (LIA, pp. 156–57). This seeming tautology is easier said than done. When some lines later Stein rewrote her question in the form of the more brutal and rhetorical, "If it can be done why do it," she was offering a motive both for discontinuing the scientific project of *The Making of Americans*, which she had become convinced could in fact be accomplished, and for beginning a new project of "stop[ping] describing everything," about which she was not certain at all.

The shift from writing in what Stein termed her "first manner" to the Mannerism of *Tender Buttons* (from "It is a simple thing to be quite certain that there are kinds in men and women. It is a simple thing and then not any one has any worrying to be doing about any one being any one" to "Suppose it did, suppose it did with a sheet and a shadow and a silver set of water, suppose it did") occurred because James's scientific psychology, as she understood it, had ceased to interest her (GMP, pp. 23, 114; cited in LIA, pp. 154, 156).[4] "Being at last really convinced that a description of everything is possible it was inevitable that I gradually stopped describing everything" (LIA, p. 157). In her new "portraiture," as she called it, description was replaced by compositional procedures designed to convey what James had called "knowledge of acquaintance" in *The Principles of Psychology*.[5] "I am acquainted," he proposed there, "with many people and things, which I know very little about, except their presence in the places where I have met them. . . . *About* the inner nature of these facts or what makes them what they are, I can say nothing at all. I cannot impart acquaintance with them to someone who has not already made it himself. I cannot describe them" (PR, pp. 216–17).[6] Stein in her writing attempts to do what James says can't be done: impart acquaintance to someone who hasn't already experienced it. In order to do this she replaces acquaintance *without* description with what she would term, in 1926, "an acquaintance with description."[7] The story of the "gradual making" of *The Making of Americans* was consequently the story of Stein freeing herself from James's beneficent influence—from the dictates, that is, of his descriptive psychology, the limits of his science.[8] It was in the course of this prolonged struggle with what she identified as her most compelling nineteenth-century intellectual inheritance that she laid the groundwork for her ecstatic science.

THE EMPIRICAL LIMITS OF EMPIRICISM

A recent article in *Time* magazine concerning divergent approaches to modeling consciousness in computer science cites MIT professor Rodney Brooks on the "mind" of the self-programming robot he calls Cog, a "vaguely person-shaped concoction of metal, plastic and silicon, with cameras where its eyes should be and eight 32–bit microprocessors for a brain." The robotic mind—Brooks had once considered naming his creation Psyche before settling on the cognomen Cog—is merely "a collection of loosely coordinated digital reflexes scattered among its eight processors, with no place to point to as the seat of intelligence. 'There's no there there,' notes Brooks with a touch of pride" (Dibbell, p. 57).[9] Needless to say, when Gertrude Stein coined the phrase Brooks uses here to characterize Cog's mind, she was referring not to the attributes of mind but to Oakland, California. "We went across the bay on a ferry," she recalled in *Everybody's Autobiography*, her account of the six-month lecture tour she made of the United States in 1934 and 1935. "That had not changed but Goat Island might just as well not have been there, anyway what is the use of my having come from Oakland it was not natural to have come from there yes write about it if I like or anything if I like but not there, there is no there there" (p. 298). The remark has often been taken as a joke at Oakland's expense, a way of distinguishing it from other cities by drawing attention to a lack of distinctive character, much as the terms of Stein's dictum—those three little *theres*—seem to blend into one another. Yet Stein wasn't in an especially jocular frame of mind on this occasion, and the phrase marks her own discomfort at returning to the place where she had lived between the ages of six and eighteen, years of steadily increasing self-consciousness.

Although the neighborhood where she'd lived between 1881 and 1885 looked much as it formerly had, little remained even there of the Oakland she had known so well:

> I asked to go with a reluctant feeling to see the Sweet School where I went to school and Thirteenth Avenue and Twenty-fifth Street which I described in The Making of Americans. Ah Thirteenth Avenue was the same it was shabby and overgrown the houses were certainly some of those that had been and there were no bigger buildings and they were neglected and lots of grass and bushes growing yes it might have been Thirteenth Avenue when I had been. Not of course the house, the house the big house and the big garden and the eucalyptus trees and the rose hedge naturally were not any longer existing, what was the use. (p. 298)

What was the use of returning to Oakland, let alone of having come from there? The person returning was a different person, the place a different place. "If I had been I then my little dog would know me but it had not been I then." The dog wouldn't recognize in the girl of eleven the woman in her sixties; nor would "that place," which she had known fifty years earlier, "be the place" she "could [now] see" (p. 300). There was no there in Oakland because Stein's memories (of whom she had been, what she had done, what, growing up, she had experienced) prevented her from experiencing the actual quiddity of the present-day city, the sense of being there *now*. By contrast, it was this sense of immediacy, of herself caught up in her surroundings, that she regularly experienced elsewhere in the U.S. and which she valued most about her tour of the nation. As she observed several pages after the remark about Oakland, "I did like being everywhere everywhere where I was I never very much wanted to be any other place than there" (p. 304). No doubt, Oakland's embarrassing "shabbiness" contributed to her sense of alienation—particularly against a backdrop of Parisian sophistication—as did the decided ambivalence Stein felt concerning her family; yet the proposal that "it was not natural to have come from there" wasn't merely a defensive gesture, an unnatural denial of natural ties. For upwards of three decades she had endeavored in her writing, and as much as possible in her daily life, to live deliberately in the present moment, in a "continuous present," as she put it. "What [was] the use of . . . having come from Oakland" if Oakland, home of the Stein parents and children, proved the place where she could least be herself—be herself, that is, as she had come to be, almost preternaturally receptive to the present occasion?

The discrepancy that Oakland impressed on Stein between past and present experience, or more exactly, between the seemingly inevitable discontinuities of one's experience of the past as such and the ordinary seamlessness of present experience, served as the principal subject of the meditative study she began composing shortly after her return from the U.S., entitled *The Geographical History of America or the Relation of Human Nature to the Human Mind*. Rodney Brooks's transference of the description of Oakland into the context of the late-twentieth-century understanding of mind as an emergent property of the brain (the autopoietic Cog having been devised to provide experimental evidence for this still controversial thesis) becomes less far-fetched when viewed in light of Stein's own speculations concerning the human mind. These occupied her for much of the year between the extended tour of the U.S. and her narrative account of it; indeed, in *Everybody's Autobiography* she insisted that the meditations were the upshot of her unhappy visit to Oakland. After complaining that she hadn't liked "the feeling" she experienced there, nor "anything that was happening" during her fraught homecoming, she added that "all [of] that went to make The Geographical History of America that I wrote, what is the use of being a little boy if you are going to grow up to be a man" (p. 300).

In the final chapter of *Everybody's Autobiography*, ironically titled "Back Again"—back home, that is, in France—she described beginning to compose her *Geographical History*. Having "settled down" in the manor in eastern France where she and Alice Toklas had passed part of each year since the late 1920s (which, with its terraced garden overlooking a valley, and its "flowerbeds shaped in geometric patterns by low boxwood hedges," presented a striking contrast to the vanished garden, eucalyptus trees, and rose hedge of the hilltop Oakland house), she "became worried about identity and remembered the [line from] mother goose I am I because my little dog knows me" (Mellow, p. 397; EA, p. 306).[10] Yet, she added, perhaps "that only proved the dog was he and not that I was I." "To get this trouble out of my system," she continued,

I began to write the Geographical History of America or the Relation of Human Nature To The Human Mind and I meditated as I had not done for a very long time not since I was a little one about the contradiction of being on this earth with the space limiting and knowing about the stars in an unlimited space that is that nobody could find out if it was limiting or limited . . . I meditated a good deal about how to yourself you were yourself at any moment that you were there to you inside you but that any moment back you could only remember yourself you could not feel yourself and I therefore began to think that insofar as you were yourself to yourself there was no feeling of time inside you you only had the sense of time when you remembered yourself and so I said what is the use of being a little boy if you are to be a man what is the use. (pp. 306–7)

Remarkably, in describing the contrary experiences of time passing and of a self-consciousness that takes the form of feeling that "you [are] there to you inside you," a contrariety she had already uncovered in her deconstructive reading of the Mother Goose nursery rhyme, Stein bridges the abyss between herself and the child she once had been. She does so on the basis of a common awareness of the gap—an awareness from either side, as it were. Earlier in *Everybody's Autobiography* she had recalled the experience of first reading the Old Testament as a child, and it is to this youthful occasion of independent reading and thinking that she refers here. "Brought up not a Christian but in Christian thinking," and hence in a cultural climate where the notion of personal immortality would have seemed as natural as the Oakland air she breathed, she could "remember being very excited" to find that in the Old Testament "they never spoke of a future life." It was then that "the contradiction of being on this earth with the space limiting and knowing about the stars in an unlimited space" first pressed itself on her. As she put it with respect to the "little one's" midrash on the Old Testament: "There was a God there was eternity but there was no future life and I found how naturally that worried me, that there is no limit to space and yet one is living in a limited space and inside oneself there is no sense of time but actually one is always living in time" (p. 250).

When, in the extended meditation on "the nineteenth century feeling about science" that frames this recollection of her first, excited reading of the Old Testament, Stein concludes that "naturally science is not interesting," she does so from the perspective of someone for whom scientific investigation initially seemed otherwise, seemed to provide a means of addressing, without prematurely resolving, the contradiction that concerns her here (WIHS, p. 61; EA, p. 251). Despite the fact that the investigator was necessarily "living in a limited space" as well as "in time," such investigation appeared to accord with the sense of ever-widening possibility that derived from the twin convictions that "space had no limitation" and that "inside oneself there is no sense of time." By contrast with philosophy and religion, which sought "satisfaction with a solution," science encouraged one to regard a solution as "a way to a problem." "As Carl [Van Vechten] said of Mabel Luhan," Stein remarks of the subject of her 1912 "Portrait of Mabel Dodge at the Villa Curonia," "a marriage for her is but a springboard to a higher life. That was what science was every solution was an opening to another problem." This, at least, was what Stein, as a creature of the nineteenth century, "a natural believer in science[,] a natural believer in progress," was inclined to believe. In *Everybody's Autobiography* she traced her disillusionment to William James's suggestion that, in her phrasing, "science is not a solution and not a problem it is a statement of the observation of things observed and perhaps therefore not interesting perhaps therefore only abjectly true" (pp. 250–51). As a "statement of observations," it merely served to distract one from the brute fact of one's human nature, one's mortality, even as it denied that there really was any more to life than "the struggle for existence" and "the will to live."[11] Nineteenth-century science, which had seemed to promise endless new vistas, turned out to be quite as limited and limiting as contemporary philosophy and religion. Darwin's theory of evolution may have "opened up the history of all animals vegetables and minerals, and man," yet "at the same time [it] made them all confined, confined within a circle." The result was that "there was no longer any beyond[,] . . . no excitement of creation any more" (WIHS, p. 61).

Initially, evolutionary science had seemed to provide an explanatory framework for novelty or creation which exemplified the very creativity it served to explain. It was this impression, Stein suggested in her 1938 study of Picasso, which encouraged the nineteenth-century "faith in what the eyes were seeing, that is to say the belief in the reality of science," and, as an expression of this belief, "the ecstasy of things seen, only seen" (pp. 38–39). The ecstatic nature of Darwin's new science derived from the apparent coincidence, in Emerson's phrasing, of "the axis of vision . . . with the axis of things," the sense of being at one with the universe (EL, p. 47). The continental divide between subject and object seemed finally to have been crossed, and consequently, as Stein observed, "there was nothing more interesting in the nineteenth century than little by little realizing the detail of natural selection in insects flowers and birds and butterflies and comparing things and animals and noticing the protective coloring nothing more interesting" (WIHS, p. 17). Each detail served to confirm the evolutionary "principle which was the basis of all this" (PCW, p. 38). Yet even as the principle was reaffirmed, it diminished in interest; the two axes became fixed, anchored in place, therefore producing a coincidence characterized by stasis rather than by the ecstatic sense of unlimited possibility. Evolutionary science, with its mechanism of natural selection, may have looked as if it were attending closely to the "sweet . . . lore which nature brings," so as to avoid "misshap[ing] the beauteous forms of things," yet it too, like the empirical science of Wordsworth's day, regularly "murder[ed] to dissect" (LB, p. 106).

In her 1935 audio recording at Columbia, Stein brought home the disparity between the impression of disinterested wonder experienced in "little by little realizing the detail of natural selection" and the "misshapen" motives informing the relentless pursuit of such knowledge. Reading from *The Making of Americans*, she juxtaposed the passage cited above concerning the "wonder" produced by "subtle variations coming clear into ordered recognition" with an account two hundred pages later of a boy's desire to "make a collection of butterflies and beetles." In this allegory right out of Wordsworth, the youth's father questions whether it "is not a cruel thing that you are wanting to be doing, killing things to make collections of them." The son, "at last . . . convinced that it was a cruel thing,"

> said he would not do it and his father said the little boy was a noble boy to give up pleasure when it was a cruel one. The boy went to bed then and then the father when he got up in the early morning saw a wonderfully beautiful moth in the room and he caught him and he killed him and he pinned him and he woke up his son then and showed it to him and he said to him "see what a good father I am to have caught and killed this one," the boy was all mixed up inside him and then he said he would go on with his collecting. (pp. 489–90)

Wordsworth's dissection in "The Tables Turned" of eighteenth-century empiricism—turning the tables on science, as it were, analyzing the analyst with his own instruments—holds for any empiricist method, including that of evolutionary science, because ordinary empiricism, unlike radical empiricism, requires that one divorce the pursuit of knowledge from one's emotional investment in the procedures one has come to follow.

James coined the phrase *radical empiricism* in the preface to his 1897 collection *The Will to Believe*, published during Stein's final semester at Radcliffe. There he observed that were he "obliged" to name the "philosophical attitude" expressed in his essays, he would call it "radical empiricism":

> I say "empiricism" because it is contented to regard its most assured conclusions concerning matters of fact as hypotheses liable to modification in the course of future experience; and I say "radical" because it treats the doctrine of

monism itself as an hypothesis, and, unlike so much of the half-way empiricism that is current under the name of positivism or agnosticism or scientific natural-ism, it does not dogmatically affirm monism as something with which all experi-ence has got to square. (p. 447)

The radical empiricist is unwilling to conform philosophical or scientific investigation to limits that satisfy the positivist, who holds that "we must always wait for sensible evidence for our beliefs" and consequently refuses to admit speculation concerning any "portion of the total universe" which, "stretch[ing] beyond this visible world," takes the form of "an unseen world of which we now know nothing positive" (pp. 497, 495). It was this dog-matic positivism that James rejected as an unexamined inheritance of con-temporary science from "naive empiricism," with its "epistemological model," as Susanne Langer has expressed it, of a "mosaic of pure sense data linked by a sort of magnetic process, association, into compound entities" (M, pp. 324, 25).

James proposed to treat the intermediate, magnetic processes as them-selves partaking of the same order of experience as the "purely 'given'" sense-data (M, p. 25). (In physiological terms this suggests, as Langer has observed, that for any "intuitive perception" which seems, at least "on the empirical level of knowledge," to be given directly, it nonetheless "take[s] a highly elaborated nervous system to create such an apparently direct pre-sentation" [p. 355]. The mind's associative processes are no less embodied than are the sense-data.) "To be radical," James posited in "A World of Pure Experience,"

> an empiricism must neither admit into its constructions any element that is not directly experienced, nor exclude from them any element that is directly experi-enced. For such a philosophy, *the relations that connect experiences must them-selves be experienced relations, and any kind of relation experienced must be accounted as "real" as anything else in the system.*

"Like that of Hume and his descendents," the radical empiricist's "*Weltan-schauung*" is "essentially a mosaic philosophy, a philosophy of plural facts" that neither "inhere" in "Substances" nor are created by "an Absolute Mind," as alternate forms of rationalism would have it. Yet it "differs from the Humian type of empiricism in one particular." Whereas "ordinary em-piricism, in spite of the fact that conjunctive and disjunctive relations pre-sent themselves as being fully coordinate parts of experience, has always shown a tendency to do away with the connections of things"—as in "Hume's statement that whatever things we distinguish are as 'loose and separate' as if they had 'no manner of connection'"—a genuinely radical empiricism "*does full justice to conjunctive relations*, without, however, treating them as rationalism always tends to treat them, as being true in some supernal way, as if the unity of things and their variety belonged to different orders of truth and vitality altogether" (pp. 1160–61).

Radical empiricism is empiricism divorced from the idea of the primacy of sense-data; instead it stresses the decisive role of processes and procedures, of conjunctive as well as disjunctive relations, in the composition of experience. Both empiricisms ground themselves in experience, and thereby differ from rationalist abstraction, yet radical empiricism's conception of experience is much broader than that traditionally associated with empiricism. (As Stanley Cavell puts it, "what is wrong with empiricism is not its reliance on experience but its paltry idea of experience"—rephrasing Emerson's "late prayerful remark [in] his essay on 'Experience' [that] 'far be from me the despair which prejudges the law by a paltry empiricism'" ["Thinking of Emerson," p. 126].) Radical empiricism demonstrates that ordinary empiricism's notion of experience is itself, inevitably, an abstraction. When Stein observed of Oakland that "there is no there there," she was articulating an attitude that comes readily to dogmatic empiricism. She was so removed from the child she had been, and therefore from the child's experience of the city's vitality, that present-day Oakland only existed for her as a collection of sense-data. Her past amid that grid of streets and hills and views couldn't be ignored, precisely because she had put it so far behind her, rendering any appreciation of the actual city impossible. If "'places' are not geographical regions but pragmatic entities, locations of felt events," as Langer has argued (perhaps against positivist common sense, yet certainly in conformity with most persons' sense of things), then Oakland was no place (M, p. 194). For in order to be experienced as actually "there," a place requires emotional resonance in addition to spatiotemporal coordinates, what Stein called "a sense of movement of time included in a given space" (LIA, p. 224). Of course, no self-respecting empiricist will recognize in Stein's Oakland the contours of actual laboratory or field experience. The conviction that there really is *a there there* is a function of one's long-term investment in intimately experienced investigative procedures; and it is these procedures that enable one to perceive the object of study as naturally an object and not, as the radical empiricist would insist, a fellow participant in the "conjunctive relations" that lend those familiar abstractions, observer and observed, their vitality.

VARIETIES OF COGNITIVE EXPERIENCE

The first of Stein's *Lectures in America*, "What Is English Literature," opens with the statement, "One cannot come back too often to the question what is knowledge and to the answer knowledge is what one knows" (p. 11). Throughout her lectures, Stein regularly returns to this paired question and answer.[12] Why? Perhaps because the answer ("knowledge is what one knows") doesn't exactly function as a solution to a specific problem ("what is knowledge"), nor is it merely tautological. Rather, it provides just the sort of "opening to another problem" that nineteenth-century science had failed to deliver. In defining knowledge as "what one knows," Stein emphasizes that knowledge does not exist apart from a knower. There is no such thing as knowledge in the abstract; it is always the possession of an individual, some "one." Yet, in itself, this recognition does not generate another problem, a novel challenge. The new problem arises because in the English language the phrase "what one knows" retains the ambiguity of the term "knowledge." "There are two kinds of knowledge," James observed in *The Principles of Psychology*. "We may call them respectively *knowledge of acquaintance* and *knowledge-about*. Most languages express the distinction; thus, γνῶναι, εἰδέναι; *noscere, scire; kennen, wissen; connaître, savoir*" (pp. 216–17).[13] Most languages may express this distinction with two different terms, but English does not; and in order to articulate it in his native tongue James had to resort to phrases like "knowledge of acquaintance" and "knowledge-about." Consequently, when Stein defines knowledge as "what one knows," she leaves herself, and her listeners and readers, with the problem of deciding just which kind of knowledge it is that one knows. To solve *this* problem one must know the difference between knowledge of acquaintance and knowledge-about as well as how they are related. This presents a particularly knotty problem, made even more so by the inevitable reflexivity of its formulation: One has to *know*, after all, just what knowledge-about, knowledge of acquaintance, and their disjunctive and conjunctive relations come to.

It is certainly neither incidental nor coincidental that the English term *science* derives from the Latin *scientia*, roughly equivalent to "knowledge-about." One way to solve the problem at hand is peremptorily to declare that "science is essentially 'knowledge about,'" as Langer does, and to add, as she does not, that scientific knowledge is really the only kind of knowledge that counts (M, p. 24). This is the empiricist's solution, a dogmatically reductive solution much like that which I. A. Richards appeared to propose in his 1926 study *Science and Poetry*, when he famously suggested that words in poems functioned as "pseudo-statement," or like the "heterophenomenological" account of consciousness promoted by Daniel Dennett in his 1991 manifesto *Consciousness Explained*. What, the radical empiricist wonders, is one to make, then, of the sort of experience described by James in "The Place of Affectional Facts in a World of Pure Experience":

Let the reader arrest himself in the act of reading this article now. *Now* this is a pure experience, a phenomenon, or datum, a mere *that* or content of fact. *"Reading" simply is, is there*; and whether there for some one's consciousness, or there for physical nature, is a question not yet put. At the moment, it is there for neither; later we shall probably judge it to have been there for both. (pp. 1209–10)

Does this experience involve real knowledge or doesn't it? Is it beyond the purview of science or not? And what of the perfectly ordinary experience described by Nicholas Humphreys in his recent *History of the Mind*: "When I feel a pain in my toe, the sensation is there for me as the sensation that it is, without my having to do any kind of mental work to classify it" (p. 138). Is it possible to account scientifically for the experience of pain without explaining it away—as if, at bottom, it were nothing more than knowledge-about?[14]

Moreover, what of the experience invoked by Stein when, in one lecture, she characterized "the best writers" as "the writers who feel writing the most," or her description in another lecture of "the physical something that a writer is while he is writing" (LIA, p. 89; N, p. 56)? In the latter instance she elaborates that, as long as the writer is writing, "that physical something by existing does not connect him with anything but concentrates him on recognition." The act of *recognition* that occurs while the writer is directly engaged "in the act of writing what he is writing" is surely a form of knowledge; yet one may still wonder what relation it bears to knowledge-about and to science. This is the problem that Stein faced in *The Making of Americans*, when, in attempting to overcome the double legacy of positivist science and realist fiction bequeathed to the United States by nineteenth-century England, she found herself confronted by the epistemological discrepancy between "acquiring [one's] knowledge gradually," in the form of knowledge-about, and subsequently coming to possess a "complete conception . . . of an individual . . . at one time" (involving a sense of acquaintance). "A great deal of The Making of Americans," she later proposed, was "a struggle . . . to make a whole present of something that it had taken a great deal of time to find out, but it was a whole there then within me and as such it had to be said" (LIA, p. 147). Finally, one might adduce the experience of *reading* Stein's compositions, as the young philosopher Ralph Church characterized it in a 1928 "Note" for the avant-garde journal *transition*. Stein's writing, he proposed, was "like affection" in that it was "given without suggestion, reference, or style. Miss Stein registers on paper what she realizes, and makes that appear with all the unmediated finality of a pain or an intense pleasure" (p. 168).[15]

Without disputing Church's attribution of "all the unmediated finality of a pain or an intense pleasure" to Stein's writing, one may still question his statement that her writing is "given," any more than affection is, sans "suggestion, reference, or style." In the course of making, as she put it in 1946, "innumerable efforts to make words write without sense," Stein came to understand not only that this outcome was impossible but that her endeavors were no less valuable on account of their impossibility, because they demonstrated that pure knowledge of acquaintance was as much an abstraction as pure knowledge-about (TI, p. 18). In English, the term *knowledge* may itself be ambiguous; yet whatever one's language, the experience of knowledge is always hybrid. Beginning with her "Studies in Description" of 1912 (subsequently published in *Tender Buttons* under the heading "Food") and then in the hundreds of experimental works that followed, Stein set out to investigate the many ways in which knowledge of acquaintance and knowledge-about interact. In a brief overview prepared on the occasion of her return to the United States in 1934, she commented that her lectures were "to be a simple way to say that if you *understand* a thing you *enjoy* it and if you *enjoy* a thing you *understand* it" (emphasis added). "I always say in my lectures," she continued, "knowledge is what you know, and I do want you to have knowledge and to know this that understanding and enjoying is the same thing."[16] No thought exists without feeling, nor any human feeling without some kind of thought. By the same token, all description requires "an acquaintance with description," and, conversely, all knowledge of acquaintance involves some degree of knowledge-about, at least for any creature capable of descriptive knowledge. It is the recognition of this co-implication of knowledge of acquaintance and knowledge-about that marks radical empiricism in both its poetic and its more straightforwardly scientific forms.

James, in distinguishing knowledge of acquaintance and knowledge-about, suggested that "the words *feeling* and *thought* give voice to the antithesis. Through feelings we become acquainted with things, but only by our thoughts do we know them." All "elementary natures," he added, as well as "the kinds of relation that subsist between them," either are not "known at all, or known in this dumb way of acquaintance without *knowledge-about*." Stein refused to concede that such acquaintance was necessarily "dumb" or incommunicable: that, as James put it, "at most, I can say to my friends, Go to certain places and act in certain ways, and these objects will probably come" (PR, p. 217). Beginning with "Melanctha," composed in the winter and early spring of 1906, she endeavored to impart acquaintance with particular persons or things by obliging her reader, and herself, to attend to what she would later call "the continuous present" formed in the process of writing and reading her words and sentences. In this way present experience might be conveyed in language without losing the quality of "being in the present" (CE, p. 31). Yet in order to do so, one would have to regard feelings of acquaintance, and in particular the experience of "feeling writing," as something more than "the germ and starting point of cognition," with "thoughts the developed tree" (PR, p. 218).

By 1904 James was himself criticizing this earlier, too restrictive conception of feeling in print, as "for seven or eight years past" he had been doing in the classroom. The dualist distinction between "the subject or bearer of . . . knowledge" and "the object known" did not correspond to what he called, in "Does 'Consciousness' Exist?", "realities of experience" (pp. 1141–42). Instead of "the 'I think' " which "Kant said must be able to accompany all my objects," an "I breathe" (the awareness, however indistinct, that one is breathing) accompanies the objects of one's thought. Furthermore, James proposed, "philosophers ha[d] constructed the entity known to them as consciousness" on the basis of this sense of breathing, perhaps combined with "other internal facts" such as the sensation of "muscular adjustments" in one's head. "Thoughts in the concrete are fully real," he acknowledged; yet he took this to mean that they are "made of the same stuff as things are," rather than out of an alternative "mind-stuff" (pp. 1157–58). "I mean only to deny that the word [*consciousness*] stands for *an entity*," James explained in a sentence cited by Whitehead as exemplary of the "entirely alter[ed] lighting" that resulted from the new perspective—adding that he still "insist[ed] most emphatically that it [stood] for *a function*" (p. 1142; SMW, p. 143). There was "no aboriginal stuff or quality of being, contrasted with that of which material objects are made, out of which our thoughts of them are made; but there is a function of experience which thoughts perform, and for the performance of which this quality of being is invoked. That function is *knowing*" (p. 1142). Whether in the form of knowledge-about or knowledge of acquaintance, thoughts remain embodied and as such are experienced as feelings, that is, as a function of the body.

With her emphasis on "acquaintance with description," Stein stood in relation to James's radical empiricism much as T. S. Eliot, diagnosing modern culture as displaying an unmistakable "dissociation of sensibility," stood in relation to the "logical atomism" of Bertrand Russell's 1914 *Our Knowledge of the External World*.[17] In this work, based on the Lowell Lectures Russell delivered the semester Eliot studied with him at Harvard, and even more explicitly in works such as "Knowledge by Acquaintance and Knowledge by Description" (1910–11) and "On the Nature of Acquaintance" (1914), Russell set himself flatly against James's radical empiricism, asserting a determination "to preserve the dualism of subject and object in my terminology, because this dualism seems to me a fundamental fact concerning cognition." Russell's principal interest, as he acknowledged in the earliest of these studies, was with "the nature of our knowledge concerning objects in cases where we know that there is an object answering to a definite description, though we are not acquainted with any such object" (pp. 210, 214). Here he readily dissociates thought from feeling as both James and Stein refused to do, and as Eliot, in the 1921 essay on the Metaphysicals in which he used the phrase *dissociation of sensibility* to such effect, did with reluctance and on an apparently historical and contingent basis rather than as logically incontrovertible. Russell, by contrast, enthusiastically sought to remove emotion from science, so as to base scientific procedure on emotionless cognition, "knowledge by description" with whose object one remains unacquainted.

Russell's astonishing claim was that empiricism, if it was to be practiced in a truly scientific manner, had to be grounded in logic rather than knowledge of acquaintance. In this respect his perspective complements that of radical empiricism. Both derive from a vivid recognition of the inadequacies of traditional empiricism: whereas the radical empiricist reconceives empiricism in terms of knowledge of acquaintance and its relation to knowledge-about, Russell focused on the logical construction of "our knowledge of the external world." His logical atomism may have been superseded in the late 1920s by the "logical positivism" (or "logical empiricism") of the Vienna Circle, yet the pursuit of this chimera dominated Anglo-American academic philosophy in the middle years of this century (Carnap, p. 302).[18] It is only within this context that Robert C. Marsh, editor of Russell's 1956 collection *Logic and Knowledge*, might remark, with some truth if little justice, that "Russell would have left a stronger mark on the Harvard philosophic faculty than Whitehead" did. Russell's teacher at Cambridge University, and co-author with him of the three-volume *Principia Mathematica*, Whitehead arrived at Harvard in 1924, where, according to Marsh, his "speculative thought ceased to be influential . . . within a short time after his retirement [in 1936] and has now [as of 1951] seemingly vanished without a trace." By contrast, Russell's ideas "had a relevance to contemporary American thought which Whitehead's cosmology had never possessed" (p. 126).[19] It is part of the object of the present study to demonstrate that this disheartening claim remains true only if one radically circumscribes "contemporary American thought." Yet for a time modes of thought associated with Russell did give the impression of having dealt a decisive blow to the pragmatist, radical empiricist lineage in American philosophy. Even Langer, herself solidly in the radical empiricist camp, credits Russell with having formulated the distinction between knowledge of acquaintance and knowledge-about which he actually derived from James. "We all have direct knowledge of feeling," she writes—" 'knowledge by acquaintance,' as Bertrand Russell has called it"—and "very little of what he termed 'knowledge by description,' or knowledge *about* feeling" (M, p. 24).

More recently, Russell's logical empiricist perspective has been translated from the domain of speculative physics ("the central problem by which I have sought to illustrate method," he writes in *Our Knowledge of the External World*, "is the problem of the relation between the crude data of sense and the space, time, and matter of mathematical physics") into the realm of experimental neurophysiology in *A Vision of the Brain*, Semir Zeki's remarkable study of how the brain constructs knowledge of the world through vision (pp. 10–11). Zeki substitutes biological for logical operations, replacing a "philosophical" account of knowledge-about with "a physiological and neurological one"; yet in other respects his vision matches Russell's (p. 2). Although the scope of *A Vision of the Brain* is limited to the operations of sight, Zeki "hold[s] the view that the problem of vision is the problem of knowledge, knowledge about the external world acquired through the sense of vision" (p. 4). "These are philosophical questions in a sense," he observes, "but the more plausible answers to them and to many other questions like them do not come from philosophical speculation alone but rather from the hard science of experimentation" (p. 345).[20] The flip side of this emphasis on experimentation is a thoroughgoing skepticism concerning ordinary experience and knowledge by acquaintance, a distrust Zeki finds expressed by T. S. Eliot in the passage from *Four Quartets* that serves as the volume's epigraph:

> There is, it seems to us,
> At best, only a limited value
> In the knowledge derived from experience.
> The knowledge imposes a pattern, and falsifies,
> For the pattern is new in every moment
> And every moment is a new and shocking
> Valuation of all we have been.

In his epilogue Zeki accords a similarly "limited value" to "knowledge derived from experience":

> The brain strives to acquire knowledge about the permanent, invariant and unchanging properties of objects and surfaces in our visual world. But the acquisition of that knowledge is no easy matter because the visual world is in a

continual state of change. Thus, the brain can only acquire knowledge about the invariant properties of objects and surfaces if it is able to discard the continually changing information reaching it from the visual environment. (p. 355)

Color vision, on this account, serves as "a system for acquiring knowledge about certain unchanging physical properties of objects, namely their reflectance for lights of different wavelengths" (p. 346). What Zeki, following Russell, refers to as "our knowledge of the external world" is composed exclusively of "constant properties" which the brain "reconstruct[s] . . . from the information reaching it which, itself, is never constant" (p. 234).[21] In Zeki's capable hands this "biological empiricist" perspective, as one might call it, has proven immensely fruitful within its self-appointed limits, yet it is far removed from radical empiricism generally, and from the perspective of Stein's ecstatic science in particular.

Consider the alternative perspective articulated by Gerald Edelman in *Bright Air, Brilliant Fire: On the Matter of the Mind*, his 1992 account of "how we know" (p. xiii). For the biological empiricist, consciousness, or knowledge of acquaintance, is an unavoidable and error-prone avenue of ingress for "permanent, invariant and unchanging" knowledge-about, an avenue whose "new and shocking / valuation[s]" the brain must continually correct for. By contrast, for Edelman it is a process that scientific explanation requires in order to exist at all. He and Zeki agree that "knowledge cannot be acquired without consciousness," yet, unlike Zeki, Edelman does not abstract the processes he is concerned to describe from his own experience in seeking to describe them (Zeki, p. 346). The difference between the two scientists is that Edelman tries seriously to scrutinize his own "vision," seeking to understand its limits as part of his account of knowledge. Zeki, however, limits his scrutiny to vision's own limitations. For Edelman, knowledge-about and knowledge of acquaintance proceed in a necessarily conjunctive relation. Science, as he conceives it, remains unable to "describe individual or historical experience adequately," since ordinary experience, as a function of knowledge of acquaintance, cannot be described nonreductively in terms of knowledge-about; nevertheless, science "does provide a satisfactory (indeed, the best) description of the *constraints* on experience" (BABF, p. 163). These constraints, the correlative features of embodiment that in each individual "lead to consciousness," are open to science in a way that experience is not, because they are reproducible and hence available to analysis, which aims to develop elegant, pragmatically useful models of "the formal correlations of properties" (pp. 136, 138). Yet if science can describe such constraints—one might say this is all it describes—it is also subject to them. "After a certain point," Edelman suggests, "the mind lies beyond scientific reach," because the constraints on consciousness are themselves constrained by the unique "forms of embodiment that lead . . . in each individual" to consciousness (p. 136). Scientific knowledge is consequently open-ended, because actual forms of embodiment, unlike the reconstructed "properties of objects and surfaces" in Zeki's "visual world," are not "permanent, invariant and unchanging." The difference between Edelman's and Zeki's perspectives, then—like Whitehead's and Russell's, and Stein's and Eliot's—comes down to "that slightest change of tone" that, in Whitehead's formulation, "yet makes all the difference" (SMW, p. 2). Sharing a definition of science as knowledge-about derived from experimentation, they differ in their respective senses of the relation that exists between knowledge of acquaintance and knowledge-about. For Edelman the relation is conjunctive; for Zeki it is disjunctive.

Although Edelman offers an exemplary radical empiricism, his is not the only strain. Complementing this straightforwardly scientific version is another that predates it.[22] The scientific practice of Wordsworth or Shelley or Stein differs from Edelman's more traditional one chiefly with respect to the medium in which they perform their experiments. Writing, ordinarily treated in science as a means whereby experiments are reported and analyzed, itself becomes the medium for experimentation in these writers' hands. As a result, the hybrid nature of scientific practice, which in fact always combines knowledge of acquaintance and knowledge-about, albeit in different proportions and different relations, is rendered explicit in a way that the protocols of scientific writing actively discourage. Certainly, science *is* knowledge-about, but it is always something else as well; and in poetic science (which emerges historically as a corrective to what the poet-scientist perceives as the inadequacies of ordinary science, inadequacies stemming from its embrace of an extreme empiricism), the something else takes the upper hand. By the same token, poetic science may serve, as a good deal of Shelley's verse does, or William Empson's in this century, to investigate the traces of radical empiricism already present in scientific knowledge, although scientists have chosen to ignore it.[23]

I. A. Richards, in distinguishing poetic from scientific description, comments that "in its use of words most poetry is the reverse of science":

Very definite thoughts do occur, but not because the words are so chosen as logically to bar out all possibilities but one. They are not; but the manner, the tone of voice, the cadence and the rhythm play upon our interests and make *them* pick out from among an indefinite number of possibilities the precise particular thoughts which they need. This is why poetical descriptions often seem so much more accurate than prose descriptions. Language logically and scientifically used cannot describe a landscape or a face. To do so it would need a prodigious apparatus of names for shades and nuances, for precise particular qualities. These names do not exist, so other means have to be used. The poet, even when, like Ruskin or De Quincey, he writes in prose, makes the reader pick out the precise particular senses required from an indefinite number of possible senses which a word, phrase or sentence may carry.

This is very aptly observed; yet when Richards goes on in *Science and Poetry* to affirm that "it is never what a poem *says* which matters, but what it *is*," since "the poet is not writing as a scientist," he overstates his case (pp. 32–33). Some poetry makes use of the resources of poetic description in order to extend the domain of science, complementing traditional scientific practice rather than setting itself up as an alternative creed. Works of this kind provide knowledge of acquaintance with what Whitehead called "organic mechanisms" (which traditional science can only describe, and empirical science describe reductively) in the process of analyzing them. If the analysis is thereby obscured, the obscurity exists in the eye of the beholder who insists on dissociating the two aspects of cognitive experience—insists, as James was doing in 1890 but no longer by 1904, and as Church did in his description of Stein's writing, that knowledge of acquaintance and knowledge-about be viewed as discrete forms of experience.

SENSUOUS THOUGHT

The radical empiricist perspective articulated by James in "Does 'Consciousness' Exist?" takes up the theory of "emotional consciousness" that he had first proposed twenty years earlier in an article entitled "What Is an Emotion?" and extends it to all cognitive experience (PBE, p. 346). That initial account had been fleshed out in *The Principles of Psychology*—in a chapter on "The Emotions" that reprinted most of the earlier article, although in substantially reorganized form—and then again in the 1894 article "The Physical Basis of Emotion." "My thesis," James wrote in 1884 (and reiterated in 1890, merely substituting *theory* for *thesis*), "is that the bodily changes follow directly the perception of the exciting fact, and that our feeling of the same changes as they occur *is* the emotion" (p. 247; PR, p. 1065 [BC, p. 352]).[24] This thesis, popularly known as the James-Lange theory because "Professor Lange of Copenhagen and the present writer published, independently of each other, the same theory," took its point of departure from the influential account of the mechanisms of emotional expression that Darwin had proposed just a decade earlier (PBE, p. 346).

In "What Is an Emotion?" James observed that whereas "books on Expression" had traditionally been "written mostly from the artistic point of view," so that only "the signs of emotion visible from without" were considered,

> Sir Charles Bell's celebrated *Anatomy of Expression* noticed the respiratory changes; and Bain's and Darwin's treatises went more thoroughly still into the study of the visceral factors involved,—changes in the functioning of glands and muscles, and in that of the circulatory apparatus. But not even a Darwin has exhaustively enumerated all the bodily affections characteristic of any one of the standard emotions. (pp. 250–51)

In heeding the "clear distinction" drawn by Herbert Spencer between emotions and sensations ("the latter being 'generated in our corporeal framework,'" the genesis of the former remaining an open question), Darwin had refused to equate emotional "states of mind" with bodily sensations (*Expression*, p. 27). James was less hesitant; or perhaps one should say that he was more so, as he was able, on the basis of his radical empiricism, to address the question of how emotional consciousness was related to its corporeal expression without having either to reduce the one to the other or to keep them clear and distinct. He did this by attributing the experience of "emotional consciousness" to its "so-called 'expression,'" thereby reversing the viewpoint implicit in the characterization of certain movements as "expressions" of emotion. Emotional consciousness was "not a primary feeling, directly aroused by the exciting object or thought, but a secondary feeling indirectly aroused" by "the organic changes, muscular and visceral, of which the so-called 'expression' of the emotion consists" (PBE, p. 346).

Whereas Darwin had focused on the causal mechanism linking *sensation* and *movement* in emotional experience, with bodily movement identified as an emotional expression of a prior sensation, an "immediate reflex," James proposed that *movement* and *emotion* were related causally as well (PBE, p. 346). An initial sensation, S_1, leads to "the perception of the exciting fact," thereby causing the body to move in response. The movement is registered in turn by the body as a second sensation, S_2, and it is this auto-sensation (the body feeling itself move in response to S_1) that is experienced as emotion. The "general seizure of excitement" that makes up the emotion consists of "additional sensations" such as these, "secondary" feelings accompanying the "sensible quality" that initiated the bodily movement in the first place. "Often hard to describe," they are nonetheless "usually easy to identify," since they are "localized in divers parts of [one's] organism" (PBE, pp. 358–59). Does all experience therefore involve emotions? Apparently not. It is only second-order experiences, the feeling not so much of feelings as of the motor effects of feelings, motions resulting from sensations, that we characterize as emotional. A decade later, James would term such experiences "appreciations," and would propose that they exist somewhere in between physical experiences (the "general group of experiences that *act*," involving "'real' objects" to which "consequences always accrue") and mental or "conceptual" experiences, which don't have physical consequences. "Mental fire," as he put it, "is what won't burn real sticks; mental water is what won't necessarily (though of course it may) put out even a mental fire." Appreciations, by contrast, as "esthetic, moral and otherwise emotional experiences," form "an ambiguous sphere of being." In mental as well as physical contexts, they "affect their associates actively, though in neither quite as 'strongly' or as sharply as things affect one another by their physical energies" (DCE, pp. 17–19). James's point is that one's mental state, in emotional experience, is never exclusively mental but has physical consequences, just as one's physical state has mental consequences. Appreciations may therefore readily be figured, in Marianne Moore's memorable phrasing, as "imaginary gardens with real toads in them" ("Poetry," p. 267).[25]

Whitehead provocatively compared "Does 'Consciousness' Exist?" to Descartes' *Discourse on Method* on the basis that each "expressed definitively and in decisive form what was already in the air of his period" (SMW, p. 143). Indeed, in his own speculative philosophy Whitehead generalizes James's "appreciations": All actual experience, he suggests, involves their equivalent, which he calls "prehensions." There is no purely mental or purely physical experience; rather, all seemingly unmixed experiences are abstractions from actual experience, and any actual experience is a second-order experience involving some degree of appreciation, the auto-sensation of some bodily activity, whether visceral or somatic. James would no doubt agree, at least in principle, for this is the basis of his radical empiricism, however vaguely he delineates the "stubborn facts." (It is this inexactness, and the resulting suggestiveness of his examples, that makes him such an "adorable" genius [pp. 2–3].) Langer, Whitehead's student at Harvard, phrases her mentor's speculative emendation of James in more expressly physiological terms: "The percept," she observes, is "a hybrid of sense impression and dreamlike image" (M, p. 292).[26] *All* perception consequently consists of imaginary gardens with real toads in them; for, "as everyone recognizes today," percepts "are not the pure sense data that naive empiricism assumed; they are, quite literally, what we make of the sensations that impinge on our receptors" (p. 324). Paradoxical as it may seem, sensation pure and simple, S1, is not experienced. Experience requires a bodily response and a recognition, however diffuse, of that response: S2.[27]

James has often been criticized for his reliance on procedures of introspection as an investigative strategy, as when he claims, in "The Physical Basis of Emotion," that his "theory of emotional consciousness" is based on "no theoretic grounds, but because of the introspective appearances exclusively" (pp. 346, 358). In *The Embodied Mind*, Francisco Varela and his coauthors, Evan Thompson and Eleanor Rosch, offer the following dismissive account of introspective psychology:

> Introspectionism as a school of psychology, made popular by the nineteenth-century psychologist Wilhelm Wundt, failed definitively to provide a basis for experimental psychology. . . . Each laboratory began with a theory that experience was decomposable into certain kinds of elements, and subjects were trained to decompose their experience in that fashion. A subject was asked to look at his own experience as an outside observer would. This is, in fact, what we usually think of as introspection in daily life. This is the very essence of what Merleau-Ponty and Heidegger called the abstract attitude of the scientist and the philosopher. [One might] say that the introspectionists were not actually aware of mind at all; they were just thinking about their thoughts. (p. 32)

Yet to what extent does this account apply to James? His practice of introspection, particularly as his radical empiricism became more entrenched, certainly did not take the usual form of a mental inventory of thoughts, memories, and empiricist "ideas." Instead, it assumed the more prehensive form of "localiz[ing] the various elements" of his "organic excitement when under emotion" in order to determine how the internal activity of his body felt to him (PBE, p. 361). This is hardly "the abstract attitude of the scientist and the philosopher."

No doubt, in composing "The Physical Basis of Emotion," James "thought about his thoughts," and about his feelings, in devising arguments to support the previously formulated "theory of emotional consciousness" summarized in the essay. Even so, his actual practice of introspection can't adequately be characterized in terms of such second-order or reflective thinking. The stream of thought that he investigated was in fact not a stream (at least not in the sense of a current moving in a particular direction), nor was it composed of thoughts. Instead, it was a body of sensations. Hence in describing the "general seizure of excitement" characteristic of emotions, he might report that

> whenever I myself have sought to discover the mind-stuff of which such seizures consist, it has always seemed to me to be additional sensations often hard to describe, but usually easy to identify, and localized in divers portions of my organism. In addition to these sensations I can discern nothing but the "objective

content" (taking this broadly so as to include judgments as well as elements judged), together with whatever agreeableness or disagreeableness the content may come tinged by. (pp. 358–59)

The second and third categories here, "objective content" and "pleasantness or painfulness of the content," may seem unlikely candidates for sensory processes; yet, according to James, this is exactly what they are. In the first place, the "objective qualities" are the "results of sensation": They are "*sensible* qualities." Moreover, whether one attributes the agreeable (or disagreeable) "tone of feeling" to the "process in the [affected] nerve of sense" or to "additional specific nerves," in either case it "seems due to afferent [incoming] currents" of the "neural processes" in question (p. 354). "Such organic sensations," James reiterated in reference to both sensible qualities and feeling-tones, being "presumably due," like the sensations that comprise the emotion, "to incoming currents, the result is that the whole of my consciousness . . . seems to me to be outwardly mediated by these. This is the length and breadth of my 'theory'" (pp. 359–60). From this introspective or inward-looking perspective, no outwardly perceptible aspect of emotional consciousness remains unaccounted for. There is no mentalistic remainder.

Although James was certainly no slouch in the production of all manner of theses, and the Harvard Psychological Laboratory he founded in 1875 actually preceded Wundt's famous laboratory at Leipzig by several years, the account of introspective theory in *The Embodied Mind* caricatures his practice.[28] Despite distinguishing among several forms of sensation, he does not "decompose" emotional experience into clear and distinct elements, as Darwin did; nor is his perspective that of "detached, unemotional, exact intellectual scrutiny of one's condition, conducted in the way a scientist would conduct a piece of research," to cite Martha Nussbaum on the pursuit of "knowledge of the heart by intellectual scrutiny" (p. 262). James's introspective procedure shares the same basic mechanism, involving the sensation of bodily movement, with the object of his introspection; thus in "The Physical Basis of Emotion" he describes "the horror" that remains upon "waking from nightmare" as "largely composed of an intensely strong but indescribable feeling in my breast and in all my muscles, especially those of the legs, which feel as if they were boiled into shreds or otherwise inwardly decomposed" (p. 357). One might ask whether these sensations of bodily decomposition are themselves an aspect of how the emotion feels to him (serving, together with the "indescribable feeling" in his breast, to "compose" the sense of horror) or whether the emotion only feels *like* this, and only upon introspection. Yet James may also be regarded as challenging such strict demarcations between emotional and introspective experience. After all, he's describing the feeling of decomposition here, not decomposing feeling. Moreover, far from beginning with a hard-and-fast theory that is then mechanically applied to experience in a laboratory setting, the theory that ultimately emerged from his experience of introspection explicitly disputed "the usual view" that "we can separate" the state of consciousness from its content by some form of "mental subtraction." James concluded, rather, that experience "has no such inner duplicity; and the separation of it into consciousness and content comes, not by way of subtraction, but by way of addition"—by supplying contexts for one's experience, with the result that different contexts abstract different features (DCE, pp. 6–7). Through the process Whitehead would term the "fallacy of misplaced concreteness," the sense of concreteness that actually inheres in the experience is falsely attributed to the abstractions derived from it, *consciousness* and *content* (SMW, p. 51).[29]

When, later in the same essay, James extended the perspective he had derived from the auto-analysis of emotions to the auto-analysis of thought, he described himself quite literally as being what the authors of *The Embodied Mind* characterize as "mindful of the breath" rather than, in classic introspective fashion, thinking "about the breath" (p. 24). "Let the case be what it may be in others," he proposed; "I am as confident as I am of anything that, in myself, the stream of thinking (which I recognize emphatically as a phenomenon) is only a careless name for what, when scrutinized, reveals itself to consist chiefly of the stream of my breathing" (DCE, p. 19). By contrast with the perspective expressed in *The Principles of Psychology*, where he tended to treat the stream of thought as a concrete entity and not "a careless name" of his own invention, James's later introspective practice stressed knowledge of acquaintance ("sensations often *hard to describe*, but usually easy to identify," "an intensely strong but *indescribable* feeling") in conjunction with more readily communicable knowledge-about. Concerning the radical empiricist outlook articulated in "Does 'Consciousness' Exist?" he could with considerable justice have applied Stein's 1908 self-description to himself: "[the] aesthetic has become the whole of me."[30] Even in Stein's case, however, this recognition (in theory) of the basis of her own experience, and of human experience generally, in the organic mechanisms of *appreciation* didn't fully carry over into her compositional practices for another four years. Only in 1912, with her "studies in description," did she radically extend the range of conjunctive relations operating within and between words and sentences which she permitted herself to investigate. In doing so, she substituted, or perhaps more exactly supplemented, a self-conscious sensitivity to her writing processes for James's sensitivity to the physiology of his emotional processes. "I found myself plunged," she recalled in 1944, "into a water of words, having words choosing words liberating words feeling words" (ALL, p. 231).[31] Plunged, that is to say, not into the stream of thought but into a still more free-flowing "water" composed of words. If James's introspective investigations were limited by the difficulty of describing the internal activity he was feeling in the correlational terms of traditional science, Stein was able to record her investigations of at least one form of feeling—"feel[ing] writing"—by rendering it visible, and hence verifiable, yet without subjecting it to the inevitable inaccuracies of ordinary scientific description.

The shift that occurred in Stein's writing style as she "plunged into [the] water of words" is registered graphically in a number of transitional texts composed between late 1911 and early 1913, each between seventy-five and a hundred and fifty printed pages in length. In these works, written concurrently, she gradually replaced the complexly patterned sentences of *The Making of Americans* with the startlingly free-form sentences and paragraphs of the pieces later collected in *Tender Buttons*. Indeed, in reading the twenty years of radically experimental writing that ensued, one often feels as if one has been "plunged into a water of words" with nothing to hold on to; yet this appearance of omnipresent dissociation is deceptive. As Stein observed in a notebook entry written around the time she completed *The Making of Americans*, the "only way to unconventionalize is by the power of experiencing"; and the only way to *realize* the conjunctive relations of her liquid writing is to approach it in the spirit of radical empiricism in which it was composed (NB-M, p. 26). This means principally that one resist dissociating intellect from feeling, whether by abstracting knowledge-about from one's experience (as in different ways both rationalist and empiricist hermeneuts do) or, conversely, by abstracting knowledge of acquaintance, as mysticism requires. It is in this context that Stein's transitional work "Two" takes on particular significance, for in it she portrays a pair of individuals, modeled on her brother Leo and her sister-in-law Sally (married to the eldest of the Stein siblings, Michael), who represent, in strikingly pure form, the extremes of intellect dissociated from feeling and feeling dissociated from intellect.

In a March 1912 letter Stein described herself as "working on four books now," one of which she characterized as "a study of two a man and woman having the same means of xpression and the same emotional and spiritual xperiences with different quality of intellect" (Everett, p. 51).[32] Whereas Sally was "more capable of first hand experience from sensitiveness but with that her intellect does not in any way connect," Leo "thinks thinkingly and analytically but he does not present the object to his thought," as "his experiencing power is too limited" (NB-N, p. 1, and NB-M, p. 26). It may seem improbable that two individuals whose "quality of intellect" is so different should still have *the same means of expression* and *the same emotional and spiritual experiences*; yet it was this unlikely conjunction that Stein chose to investigate in "Two." How might contrary valuations of intellectual analysis nonetheless be correlated with similar features of expression and experience? "The sound there is in them comes out from them," the double portrait begins:

> Each one of them has sound in them. Each one of them has sound coming out of them. There are two of them. . . . There has always been sound in them in each one of them. There is always sound in them in each one of them. There always will be sound in them, in each one of them. (p. 1)[33]

Over the next 87 pages of the 142-page text Stein patiently teases out the differences in intellectual "quality" that accompany the resemblances in her sister-in-law's and brother's means of expression—principally their comparable need, in the context of their shared "emotional and spiritual experiences," to express themselves through "sound coming out of them," in a continuous stream of talk. (In one note Stein attributed this emotional equivalence to a common absence of "immediate passion"; they "believe too little believe too much," respectively, in the "effect of appreciations on actions, both because there is no immediate passion.")[34] Such intellectual differences, differences not in opinion but in the role that intellect plays in one's experience, come to the fore in passages like the following, from the work's opening pages:

> *There are not two of them. There is one of them, and there is one of them.* There are sometimes two of them, the one and another one. . . . *They are not alike, the sound each one of them is having come out of them is sounding different from the sound coming out of the other one.* They are alike in having the sound changing meaning as they are going on being living. *They are not alike in one being one hearing something and making a sound then and the other being one hearing himself and making a sound then.* They are alike in making sounds that have more meaning than beginning. . . .
>
> They were both of them having noise come out of them. *They were very different the one from the other one of them. They were each of them thinking that thing thinking they were very different the one from the other one of them.* (pp. 1–4, emphasis added)

James's introspective scrutiny revealed his own stream of thinking to "consist chiefly of the stream of my breathing"; Stein, from the more traditional third-person perspective of empirical science, elicits streams of thought from streams of speech.[35]

What distinguished Stein's science from the preliminary observations and note-taking of ordinary scientific description, a great deal of which still entered into the composition of "Two," was the concern to portray the ways her brother's and sister-in-law's differences emerged in conjunction with their similarities; too great an emphasis on likeness would necessarily serve to obscure this interplay. Leo and Sally might each think the same thing (that "they were very different the one from the other one of them"), yet the constitutive role of intellect in their thought varied greatly. Despite the descriptive nature of her own language, Stein was determined not to limit herself merely to *analyzing* or *describing* behavior, treating experience from the exclusively intellectual perspective she attributed to Leo: "Sound was coming out of him. Sound had been coming out of him. He was *thinking about* this thing. Sound had come out of her, sound had been coming out of her, he was *thinking about* that thing." Nor did she wish, like Sally, to dissociate herself from intellect: "She had sound coming out of her. She was *knowing that thing*. She had had sound coming out of her, she was *knowing that thing*. He had had sound coming out of him, she was *knowing that thing*. He had sound coming out of him, she was *knowing this thing*" (p. 5, emphasis added). Consequently, while retaining the language of shared, generalizable features (with difference understood as different degrees of likeness), Stein conveyed a more individuated sense of difference as well, through the continuous syntactical play of her prose. This syntactic movement enabled her to breach the limits of traditional science and approximate the movements of her brother's and sister-in-law's thought processes, thereby portraying how it felt to think as they did. At the same time her description of the content of their thought involved the application of a well-practiced empiricist technique to the sounds they uttered.

The first four of the seven notebooks in which Stein composed the manuscript of "Two" (through page 87 in the published version) offer an extraordinarily concentrated meditation on the relation between the emergence of "sound" and the role of intellect. With the beginning of the fifth manuscript notebook, however, the emphasis on sound recedes, replaced by a new focus characterized by Stein in manuscript notes as the subjects' "religion" and "spirituality" (pages 87 to 91).[36] This leads to considerations of their "integrity" (91 to 97) and "inconsistency" (97 to 99) and, after a brief "contrast between the two" (99 to 100), an extended portrayal of what Stein called, again in her notes, their respective expressions of "Romance Legend Ideal" (100 to 109). The abrupt removal of the motif of sound seems to have coincided with Stein's and Toklas's departure from Paris in early May to spend the summer in Spain, with the immediate consequence that Stein ceased to be exposed to the streams of speech emanating from her brother and sister-in-law. When she returned to the composition in Spain, now physically removed from her subjects, she began to concentrate instead on some of the more abstract features organizing their modes of expression.[37]

In Leo's case, his "religion" (which Stein understood generally as the circularity of reasoning that makes conviction dependent on belief rather than on argumentative logic) took the form of his constant anticipation of great things for himself. "He was changing quite changing everything. He was hoping"—hoping, that is, to change everything. At a minimum, this self-religion took the form of "hoping that he would be hoping." The circularity of Sally's own scrupulousness, by contrast, enabled her to "say that what she was she saw and what she saw she heard and what she heard she knew and what she knew she said," a self-confirming quality expressed even more clearly in the very next sentence in "Two":

> She did say that what she said she felt and what she felt had come and having come it would be that and being that she would not ask and not asking she would know and knowing she would hear and hearing she would work and working she would express and expressing she would be helping and helping she would come and coming she would speak and speaking she would smile and smiling she would rest and resting she would save and saving she would have and having she would have what she could have what she had had what she must have. (p. 87)

Several pages later, in a manuscript note, Stein observes that Sally "can have what she wants[,] don't [sic] know what she hasn't." Here was the crux of the matter. Leo's and Sally's respective ignorance of what they did not know wasn't just a failure to know something. It involved a determination not to know, an act of dissociation or repression compelling them continually to justify their preferred forms of knowledge: knowledge-about in Leo's case, knowledge of acquaintance in Sally's. The "integrity" of each was founded on "inconsistency," with Leo backing his reliance on analytic knowledge— he seemed incapable of "leav[ing] the slightest subject without critical analysis," his close friend Hutchins Hapgood commented—with the extra-analytic conviction that this was all anyone needed (Rewald, p. 68). Sally, on the other hand, argued continually for a position that couldn't be defended coherently, since she did not admit the legitimacy of rational argument, based as it was on the abstractions of knowledge-about.

Between Sally and Leo there really wasn't any satisfactory choice, and in "Two" Stein chose neither, or rather both, blending Leo's emphasis on knowledge-about, his "measured way"—the "regular way" of "measuring being dividing and describing," the "way of talking, english, french, and german"—with Sally's emphasis on knowledge of acquaintance, a "way that denies the way that has the way that accepts the way . . . the way that was encircled when there was not an object that would be missing" (pp. 104, 108–9). "To show it," Stein concluded, "this is the way to do it"; and among the things that Leo, despite himself, enabled her to demonstrate, was that, as the last lines of the text declare, "[a] belief that has translation is not all there is of exaltation. He has all of any of that use" (pp. 140, 142). "Two" is as much about the parting of the ways of Stein and her brother as it is about the differing "qualit[ies] of intellect" of Leo and Sally; and in the bound typescript of the work Stein made this theme explicit when, at some later date, she added the subtitle "Gertrude Stein and her brother." This reference has caused some confusion among commentators on "Two," yet it can readily be accounted for by distinguishing the story that the work *tells*, which concerns the correlations between Leo and Sally, and the story *shown* by the seismic shift in Stein's own means of expression. This latter story (from descriptive study to "study in description," from a radical empiricism still modeled on abstract reasoning to poetic science's heightened attention to one's means of expression) is the story of the steadily increasing distance Stein put between herself and her brother, to whom she had once displayed a "singular devotion," as Hapgood recalled of the early years of his acquaintance with them—"admir[ing] and lov[ing] him in a way a man is seldom admired and loved" (Rewald, p. 71). At the same time, it is important to recognize that if Stein shared with her sister-in-law a deep appreciation for knowledge of acquaintance, the transformation in compositional procedure that "Two" displayed did not correspond to a shift from Leo's to Sally's characteristic form of abstraction. Sally, whose "impermeability" Stein addressed at some length in the work, was no more attentive than Leo to her own means of expression.[38] This, in the end, was what it meant to lack "immediate passion," and, late in "Two," Sally's failure as a painter as well as her turn to Christian Science are both attributed to her relative insensitivity to the complex forms of motion and variation at work in her immediate surroundings: "If the rain that occupied all the day began early she was not feeling that the wetter was drying. She had not that perception. . . . She had not any of all there is of that climate. She did not have any of all there is of any climate" (p. 135).[39] By contrast, Stein aligned herself with those for whom, as she described them in *The Making of Americans*, "spirituality and idealism have no meaning excepting as meaning completest intensification of any experiencing": radical empiricists all, for whom "any conception of transcending experience" was meaningless (MA, p. 779).[40]

In different ways Leo and Sally insisted that the only way really to know experience was to transcend it, whether by dissociating intellect from feeling or feeling from intellect. Such unselfcritical dissociation wasn't exactly what T. S. Eliot had in mind when, a decade after Stein completed *The Making of Americans* and began "Two," he diagnosed a "dissociation of sensibility" which had "set in" sometime in the seventeenth century. This condition was unrelated to the inevitably "chaotic, irregular, fragmentary" experience of "the ordinary man," who, according to Eliot, "falls in love, or reads Spinoza, and these two experiences have nothing to do with each other, or with the noise of the typewriter or the smell of cooking." By contrast, in the mind of Eliot's thoroughly Emersonian poet "these experiences are always forming new wholes" (*Selected Prose*, p. 64). Just two weeks after the publication of the review of Herbert J. C. Grierson's *Metaphysical Lyrics and Poems of the Seventeenth Century* in which he made these assertions, Eliot informed Richard Aldington that a famous "nerve man" had "satisfied" him that his own "nerves" were "a very mild affair, due not to overwork but to an aboulie [the loss or impairment of the ability to decide or act independently] and emotional derangement which has been a lifelong affliction" (*The Waste Land*, p. xxii). "Nothing wrong with my mind," he added. Subsequently, Eliot decamped to the Swiss clinic where, his mind untouched, he completed "The Waste Land." The poet's mind, he had written in the *Times Literary Supplement*, ceased "to be perfectly equipped for its work" after Donne and Chapman, because a particular form of experience, namely, abstract thought, was no longer available to it. Poets weren't able to "feel their thought as immediately as the odour of a rose" (*Selected Prose*, p. 64). Or, as he had earlier phrased the matter, "the intellect" was no longer "immediately at the tip of the senses" (*Sacred Wood*, p. 129). Even in the poet's hands, feeling and thought had become dissociated, and poetry rarely, if ever, displayed "the quality of sensuous thought, or of thinking through the senses, or of the senses thinking" (p. 23). The poet's intellect having turned anaesthetic, the capacity to render abstract thought in the natively sensuous terms of poetry had been lost.

Within its self-appointed limits Eliot's argument may convince; nonetheless, the same limits function as severe limitations. On his account, philosophy after Donne falls exclusively into the Cartesian tradition, and science becomes irresistibly Newtonian. As Whitehead argued several years after Eliot's review appeared, philosophy and science in these seventeenth-century modes required the very dissociation lamented by Eliot. One may wonder, however, whether post-"Metaphysical" poetry was as thoroughly divorced from modern science, in spirit and in fact, as Eliot imagined. Did science after Galileo's "new philosophy," source for Donne of a great many of the "heterogeneous ideas" he "yoked together" with the "violence" that so offended Samuel Johnson's sensibilities, offer such an impoverished account of experience that poetry, taking its cue from Hume, could only set itself in opposition to it (Hardy, p. 12)?[41] Eliot seems to have assumed that *sensuous thought* might be construed as scientific only to the extent that it fed off previously formulated scientific speculations, which it then incorporated, like "the smell of cooking," into "new wholes." Even in Donne's case, science merely provided ideas and experiences that the poet's mind conjoined with nonscientific experiences. The poetry was *about* the science, not the thing itself. Yet was poetry really so incapable of providing a medium for original scientific experimentation and speculation in its own right, of cooking up new smells and new meals, even novel knowledge-about? What is one to make, for instance, of the medium with which Wordsworth worked in his poems on the growth of the poet's mind—compositions concerned, like Stein's, with the conjunctive relations between sensory-based (that is to say, sensorimotor) experience and the intellect?

ROMANTIC SCIENCE

Wordsworth and Stein

In the preface to the 1802 edition of *Lyrical Ballads*, Wordsworth imagined a time "when what is now called Science . . . shall be ready to put on, as it were, a form of flesh and blood." If "the labours of men of Science should ever create any material revolution, direct or indirect, in our condition, and in the impressions which we habitually receive," he prophesied, the poet "will be ready to follow the steps of the Man of Science, not only in those general indirect effects, but he will be at his side, carrying sensation into the midst of the objects of Science itself." "The remotest discoveries of the Chemist, the Botanist, or Mineralogist," Wordsworth added,

> will be as proper objects of the Poet's art as any upon which it can be employed, if the time should ever come when these things shall be familiar to us, and the relations under which they are contemplated by the followers of these respective sciences shall be manifestly and palpably material to us as enjoying and suffering beings. (pp. 259–60)

Wordsworth addresses chemist, botanist, and mineralogist here, but not the scientist who most directly challenges the poet's dominion over the sensations responsible for making relations "manifestly and palpably material to us as enjoying and suffering beings." In fact, it was only in the same year, 1802, that the term *biology* was coined, in Jean-Baptiste Lamarck's *Hydrogeology* and, independently, in the *Biologie oder Philosophie der Lebenden Natur für Naturforscher und Ärtze* of Gottfried Reinhold Treviranus. In both cases, as Georges Canguilhem has commented, "the concept of biology was invented to characterize, in retrospect, a discipline that had not yet broken with its past." On the one hand, Lamarck's evolutionary biology (which involved "modification in the organs through force of habit and under the influence of changing environmental conditions") was "explicitly intended to reestablish 'the very order of nature' beyond the lacunae and discontinuities in the system of classification proposed by naturalists" (Canguilhem, "Normality," p. 126). Despite its evolutionary component, Lamarckian science was a variant of the transcendental biology epitomized by Goethe in his poems and essays on the metamorphosis of plants and animals as well as by Coleridge's "Theory of Life"—a biology that had yet to break with the idealist and Aristotelian strains in natural history.[42] Treviranus, on the other hand, was "limited by the traditional association of the standpoint of the naturalist with that of the physician, that of the investigator with that of the healer" (p. 127).[43] *His* biologist was a man of medicine whose investigations were explicitly guided by normative aims, hence not strictly a "Man of Science."

Ernst Mayr makes the same point when he observes that "the coining of the *word* 'biology' did not create a *science* of biology. . . . What existed was natural history and medical physiology. The unification of biology [that is, the unification in one field of these hitherto discrete scientific domains] had to wait for the establishment of evolutionary biology and for the development of such disciplines as cytology," the branch of biology concerned with the formation, structure, and function of cells (p. 108). Although Mayr is quite right in postponing the creation of the more familiar modern form of biology until later in the century, I want to suggest that by the time Wordsworth wrote the lines cited above, he had already created a complementary form of biological science in his poetry, one also uniting natural history and physiology. In ordinary biology the unification occurred at the phylogenetic level (leading, in the 1930s, to the "evolutionary synthesis" that linked modern genetic theory and such "major evolutionary phenomena" as speciation, evolutionary trends, the origin of evolutionary novelties, and the entire systematic hierarchy, or taxonomy, of species). In contrast, Wordsworth's poetic science joined natural history and physiology at the ontogenetic level, that is, at the level of the individual rather than of the species (p. 119).

In conjunction with the "lyrical ballads" of the late 1790s, drafts of *The Prelude*, the long autobiographical work Wordsworth would describe several years later as "a poem . . . on my earlier life, or the growth of my own mind," served as the principal experimental laboratory in which he mapped the parameters of his new science (PRE, p. 533). If the 1802 preface conjured a future poet working alongside the scientist, Wordsworth already provided a model in his poetry of the poet working *as* a scientist. Not only did he "carry sensation into the midst of the objects of Science"—in this case, into the categories of the empiricist psychology of the day, *sensation* chief among them—but in discursive works like "The Two-Part Prelude" (1798–99) and "Lines Written a Few Miles above Tintern Abbey" (1799), he also analyzed his experience using a vocabulary derived from empiricist psychology. In the process he revised the empiricist terms, and thereby the science they articulated, within the radical empiricist framework of his own characteristic dialectic of mind and nature.

In devising his Romantic science in the late 1790s, Wordsworth combined the penetrating physiological self-analysis pioneered by Laurence Sterne a generation earlier with the rigorous training in natural history that Coleridge recalled undertaking with the Wordsworths when they moved to Alfoxden to be near him, in July 1797.[44] Shortly after that date, Dorothy Wordsworth began composing the first of the journals for which she is justly renowned. Her deft, artless-seeming observations required months of preliminary training, both in attending to the phenomena "immediately" before her and in articulating them in carefully descriptive language. Traces of this ongoing training in natural history are still present at the outset of the Alfoxden journal, as in the third entry, dated January 22, 1798, when she remarks: "Walked through the wood to Holford. The ivy twisting round the oaks like bristled serpents. The day cold—a warm shelter in the hollies, capriciously bearing berries. *Query: Are the male and female flowers on separate trees?*" (p. 3, emphasis added). The journals record the empirical work, involving both human beings and the environments they inhabit, which formed the basis of her brother's poetic science—although, unlike the journals, the poetry testifies to that "vehement and passionate interest in the relation of general principles to irreducible and stubborn facts" which is the hallmark of radical empiricism.

Wordsworth's poems, like Stein's compositions, may be regarded as experiments (or, in the case of both "The Two-Part Prelude" and *Tender Buttons*, linked sequences of experiments) designed to convey and in the process account for individual phenomena of human consciousness in terms of more general principles or mechanisms.[45] The form of explanation that emerges in the experimental writing of Wordsworth and Stein differs from ordinary mechanistic accounts in that it is characterized by what Whitehead called "organic mechanisms," involving an element of unpredictability or individuation absent from thoroughly mechanical explanations such as those provided by Newtonian physics. Although organic explanation (or "composition as explanation," in Stein's phrasing) remains implicit in poetic science, it may nonetheless be deduced and made explicit from the compositional features of particular experiments. For instance, in Wordsworth's writing, two such organic principles operate in tandem. The first is a conception of present temporality allied to Stein's notion of "the continuous present" or "complete actual present." The second is a synesthetic conception of consciousness, somewhat along the lines of Stein's characterization, in 1928, of *Tender Buttons* as her "first conscious struggle with the problem of correlating sight, sound and sense" (or, as she put it four years later, of "express[ing] the rhythm of the visible world" [LIA, pp. 104–5; TBr, p. 13; ABT, p. 119]). This correspondence testifies to the convergence of the two writers' ecstatic sciences, which differ principally in Stein's extension of the range of "manifestly and palpably material" objects addressed by the poet-scientist from Wordsworth's "sensations" to her own "lively words" (LIA, p. 209).[46]

Geoffrey Hartman has suggested that, instead of "us[ing] synaesthesia," Wordsworth's "typical intensities are those in which he is 'now all eye and now / All ear,'" and cites half a dozen lines from the poem "There Was a Boy" as evidence of the process whereby "ears counteract eyes" and so "restore touch to visible things by picking up vibrations" (pp. 24–25; PRE, p. 423). Composed in 1798 or 1799, the poem describes the boy listening intently to "pauses of deep silence." "Then, sometimes, in that silence," Wordsworth continues, "a gentle shock of mild surprise / Has *carried far into his heart* the voice / Of mountain torrents, or the visible scene / Would *enter unawares into his mind* / With all its solemn imagery," including, spread out before the child, "that uncertain heaven, *receiv'd / Into the bosom* of the steady lake" (LB, p. 134, emphasis added). "Hearing seems to mediate touch," Hartman acutely observes; yet is this experience of tactility due to the counteraction, or the conjunction, of sight and sound? Repeatedly in his poetry Wordsworth investigates the costs exacted by too great a reliance on any single sense, whether sound or sight, along with the corresponding increase in liveliness and intensity of consciousness that results from "the merging of the senses," as Barry E. Stein and M. Alex Meredith have titled an important recent study of the neural bases of "multisensory integration" (p. xii).[47] Indeed, the "solemn[ity]" that accompanies the child's vision of an "uncertain heaven received into . . . the steady lake" marks the experience as auditory and motor as well as visual.

In his own account of "There Was a Boy" in the preface to the 1815 *Poems*, Wordsworth stressed this "sensory convergence" (to use another phrase of Stein's and Meredith's) by directly incorporating the term "tranquilliz-ing" into the epithet "solemn imagery." Of "the series of Poems placed un-der the head of Imagination," inaugurated by "There Was a Boy," he had

> begun with one of the earliest processes of Nature in the development of this
> faculty. Guided by one of my own primary consciousnesses, I have represented
> a commutation and transfer of internal feelings, cooperating with external acci-
> dents, to plant, for immortality, *images of sound and sight* in the celestial soil
> of the Imagination. The Boy, there introduced, is listening, with something of a
> feverish and restless anxiety, for the recurrence of the riotous sounds which he
> had previously excited; and, at the moment when the intenseness of his mind is
> beginning to remit, he is surprised into a perception of *the solemn and tranquil-*
> *lizing images* which the Poem describes. (p.190, emphasis added)[48]

The images may alternately be aural ("the voice / Of mountain torrents") and visual ("that uncertain heaven [reflected in] the steady lake"), yet the process whereby they are "planted" in the imagination, and so contribute to the imagination's own "development," combines the two sensory regis-ters. For Wordsworth, then, the imagination was a natural, and naturally synesthetic, phenomenon (a "celestial soil"). Still, the synesthetic principle of sensory convergence does not suffice to explain the functioning of the neurophysiological imagination, which requires a second organic principle, a "space of time," in Stein's phrasing, within which motor processes can op-erate with a degree of impunity, connecting sensory processes to one an-other (LIA, p. 161).

"The sensible present has duration," James observed in *The Principles of Psychology*. "Let anyone try, I will not say to arrest, but to notice or attend to, the *present* moment of time," and "one of the most baffling experiences occurs":

> Where is it, this present? It has melted in our grasp, fled ere we could touch it,
> gone in the instant of becoming. . . . It is only by entering into the living and
> moving organization of a much wider tract of time that the strict present is
> apprehended at all. It is, in fact, an altogether ideal abstraction, not only never
> realized in sense, but probably never even conceived of by those unaccustomed
> to philosophic meditation. Reflection leads us to the conclusion that it *must*

exist, but that it *does* exist can never be a fact of our immediate experience. The only fact of our immediate experience is what Mr. E. R. Clay has well called "the specious present." (p. 573 [BC, p. 266])[49]

James may readily have embraced Clay's terminology of a *specious present*, yet "the practically cognized present" which he then went on to describe was anything but specious (p. 574). If, from an exclusively analytic perspective, it seemed to involve, as Gerald Myers has put it, "a constant slipping into the past while yielding to the future," and so was never "strictly present," James countered that as "a synthetic datum" it could only be "decompose[d]" through a retrospective, rather than genuinely introspective, procedure (*Life and Thought*, p. 144; PR, pp. 574–75).

By contrast with the "living and moving organization of the much wider tracts of time" characteristic of the "spots of time" investigated by both Wordsworth and Stein, it is the strict present, the instantaneous point of time to which the present is reduced as a function of linear temporality, that is specious. Although Wordsworth, in "The Two-Part Prelude," referred to "spots of time" as "moments . . . seem[ing] to have their date / In our first childhood," he clearly meant *intervals*, like those described by James: spaces of time "which with distinct pre-eminence retain / A fructifying virtue, whence, depressed / By trivial occupations and the round / Of ordinary intercourse, our minds— / Especially the imaginative power— / Are nourished and invisibly repaired" (PRE, pp. 8–9 [Part I, ll. 288–96]). Because these occasions display the synthetic quality possessed by experience at any particular moment, and hence are felt to be self-contained, continuous wholes despite being anything but momentary, they convey the impression that time has been suspended, replaced by what Emerson, on one occasion, called "the strong present tense" (EL, p. 481). Time, in the sense of linear time, seems not to pass or, to put it another way, one seems to have stepped out of time into an "eternal" realm, in which the oppressive "round / Of ordinary intercourse" dissolves into the child's "unconscious intercourse / With the eternal beauty" (PRE, p. 11 [Part I, ll. 394–95]).

James and Stein each offered a thoroughly naturalistic account of this ahistorical present, and Wordsworth already delineated a comparable account in his poetic science, in which the "spots of time" touched by eternity were conceived quite naturalistically as "given space[s] of time," involving sensory convergence and "filled, always filled with moving" (LIA, 160–61). From the perspective of eighteenth-century empiricism, with its mechanical ("associationist") model of the coordination of externally derived sense-data, Wordsworth's investigation of the experience of suspended time may seem to depend on what Paul de Man once characterized as "more than . . . natural" premises ("Time and History," p. 93). Yet if one reads Wordsworth as implicitly experimenting with a radical empiricist perspective, it becomes clear that the occasions of hanging or suspension that so frequently signal suspended time in his writing serve to direct one's attention inward: to the motions that course through the body when to all external appearances, as in "There Was a Boy," it remains motionless. *Then, sometimes, in that silence, while he hung / Listening, a gentle shock of mild surprize / Has carried far into his heart.* The intensity of visual and auditory perception in such intervals—their literally *ecstatic* nature, the sense of being driven out of, and beyond, one's senses—occurs because one's eyes and ears are focusing inward as well as outward.[50] Although the body may have fallen physiologically into a trance state ("with an eye made quiet by the power / Of harmony," as Wordsworth put it in "Tintern Abbey"), it retains the character of a "living soul" due to its internal activity, and in particular the ongoing coordination of internally derived sense-data (LB, p. 114 [ll. 47–49]). Indeed, neuroscientists now hold, in line with Wordsworth's observations, that the proprioceptive sense of bodily "harmony" or balance involves both eye and ear turned inward rather than outward, as organic components of the body's vestibular system, which is responsible for "the maintenance of body orientation in space" (Gacek, p. 41).

Sterne and Stein

I have already suggested that Wordsworth, who observed to a correspondent in 1791 that his "incursions into the fields of modern literature" had hitherto been limited to "three volumes of *Tristram Shandy*" (along with "two or three papers of the *Spectator*"), may well have been indebted for the development of his radical empiricism to Sterne's investigations of physiological self-analysis (De Selincourt, I, p. 56). In an essay coauthored with the poet Louis Zukofsky in 1930, William Carlos Williams proposed that Stein's writing might similarly be likened to Sterne's.[51] "Let it be granted," the essay opens, "that whatever is new in literature the germ of it will be found somewhere in the writings of other times; only the modern emphasis gives work a present distinction" (p. 113). As for "the work of Gertrude Stein," its germ could be traced, according to Williams, to the following passage from *Tristram Shandy*, some two-thirds of the way into the novel. "The verbs auxiliary we are concerned in here," Tristram's father remarks,

> are, *am; was; have; had; do; did; make; made; suffer; shall; should; will; would; can; could; owe; ought; used;* or *is wont.* . . . Now, by the right use and applica-

tion of these, continued my father, in which a child's memory should be exercised, there is no one idea can enter his brain how barren soever, but a magazine of conceptions and conclusions may be drawn forth from it.—Did'st thou ever see a white bear? cried my father, turning his head round to *Trim*, who stood at the back of his chair;—No, an' please your honour, replied the corporal.—But thou could'st discourse about one, *Trim*, said my father, in case of need?—How is it possible, brother, quoth my uncle *Toby*, if the corporal never saw one?—'Tis the fact I want; replied my father,—and the possibility of it, is as follows.

A WHITE BEAR! Very well. Have I ever seen one? Might I ever have seen one? Am I ever to see one? Ought I ever to have seen one? Or can I ever see one?

Would I had seen a white bear! (for how can I imagine it?). . . .

If I never have, can, must or shall see a white bear alive; have I ever seen the skin of one? Did I ever see one painted?—described? Have I never dreamed of one?

Did my father, mother, uncle, aunt, brothers or sisters, ever see a white bear? What would they give? How would they behave? . . .

—Is the white bear worth seeing?—

—Is there no sin in it?—

Is it better than a BLACK ONE? (p. 307)

Concerning this grammatical catechism Williams comments:

> In this manner ends Chapter 43 [and Volume 5] of *The Life and Opinions of Tristram Shandy*. The handling of the words and to some extent the imaginative quality of the sentence is a direct forerunner of that which Gertrude Stein has woven today into a synthesis of its own. It will be plain, in fact, on close attention, that Sterne exercises not only the play (or music) of sight, sense and sound contrast among the words themselves which Stein uses, but their grammatical play also. (p. 115)

"It would not be too much to say," Williams concludes, "that Stein's development over a lifetime is anticipated completely with regard to subject matter, sense and grammar—in Sterne."

This is exactly right; yet Williams remained unaware of just how right it was. In stating that "it is simply the skeleton, the 'formal' parts of writing, those that make form, that [Stein] has to do with, apart from the 'burden' which they carry," he articulated a sense of her writing identical with Ralph Church's understanding of it, and subject to the same limitations (p. 115). This parallel can hardly have been due to chance, given that he alludes to the description appended by the editors of *transition* to their 1928 reprint of *Tender Buttons*, which appeared in the same issue as Church's article on Stein. The magazine, the editors noted, was happy to re-publish *Tender Buttons*. This epochal work which first appeared in 1914 has been out of print for many years and only a few copies are still extant. Concerning it Miss Stein says: "It was my first conscious struggle with the problem of correlating sight, sound and sense, and eliminating rhythm; some of the solutions in it seem to me still alright, now I am trying grammar and eliminating sight and sound." (TBr, p. 13)

In his article, Williams cites Stein's remark a page *after* the comment that so obviously relies on it, namely, that Sterne "exercises not only the play (or music) of *sight, sense and sound contrast* among the words themselves which Stein uses, but their *grammatical play* as well." However, in applying Stein's analysis of her own writing to Sterne, Williams collapses her careful distinction between the parameters established in *Tender Buttons* and those of the works subsequently collected in *How To Write*, between "studies in description" that concentrate on "the problem of correlating sight, sound and sense, and eliminating rhythm" and more recent investigations involving "grammar and eliminating sight and sound."

Stein testified to Williams's astuteness in recognizing the "germ" she seems to have found in Sterne, particularly with regard to grammatical or formal concerns, when she decided to have the published version of *How To Write* look, as Toklas recalled in 1963, "like an eighteenth-century copy of Sterne which she had found once in London, bound in blue and white paper on board" (WIM, p. 136).[52] Yet Williams went too far in proposing that Stein's investigations, even in *How To Write*, were exclusively formal in the way that Walter Shandy's exposition was. In his enthusiasm, Williams made the mistake of confusing the sentiments of Shandy *père* with Sterne's own. For Sterne was parodying Walter Shandy's reasoning, not promoting it, and explicitly set his own persona, Yorick, off to one side: "*Yorick* listened to my father with great attention; there was a seasoning of wisdom unaccountably mixed up with his strangest whims, and he had sometimes such illuminations in the darkest of his eclipses, as almost attoned for them" (p. 305). Williams even repeated Walter Shandy's principal error, of treating phrases like *a white bear* as purely formal counters. Hence he instructed the reader to "note" how, in the lines *If I never have, can, must or shall see a white bear alive; have I ever seen the skin of one? Did I ever see one painted?—described? Have I never dreamed of one?*,

> the words *alive, skin, painted, described, dreamed* come into the design of these sentences. The feeling is of words themselves, a curious immediate quality quite apart from their meaning, much as in music different notes are dropped, so to speak, into repeated chords one at a time . . . for themselves alone.

"Compare this," he added, "with the same effects common in all that Stein does. See *Geography and Plays*, 'They were both gay there' " (p. 114).

Although in the work to which Williams alludes, the pre-*Tender Buttons* sketch "Miss Furr and Miss Skeene," Stein doesn't use *gay* primarily with reference to homosexual pleasures, the reference is not entirely absent, any more than one might erase the suggestion of *fur* and *skin* from the title of the piece. "They were both gay there," Stein wrote, "they were regularly working there both of them *cultivating their voices* there, they were both gay there" (GP, p. 17, emphasis added). The cultivation of one's voice is a *gaya scienza*, a form of knowledge in which the subject serves as its own object, hence a science of "self-fashioning" or autopoiesis. If the referent of *gay* remains uncertain, this is because the act of reference is itself gay or lively, not because there is none. Similarly, Walter Shandy may wish to use such terms as *alive, skin, painted, described*, and *dreamed* "apart from the 'burden' which they carry," yet he only partially succeeds in doing so. Even Williams, despite emphasizing the purely formal qualities of Shandy's terminology, spotlights a pentad of terms that, taken together, summarize the conjunction of aesthetics and radical empiricism found not just in Stein, and in James and Wordsworth, but in Sterne as well. If ever there was a literary character whose "skin," both bodily and textual, was truly "alive," it has to be Sterne's surrogate, Yorick, participant-observer in *A Sentimental Journey* and possessor of a sensibility perpetually in motion. The work that Yorick pens consists of a series of thought experiments designed to challenge the perspective articulated by Walter Shandy, while continuing to respect the "seasoning of wisdom" mixed in with the elder Shandy's "strange whims."[53]

Instead of the abstract connective tissue that language becomes in Walter Shandy's hands, Sterne insists that linguistic composition isn't just concrete but is concretely *physiological*. It is this explicitly physiological sense of writing that he shares with Stein, a sense that remains implicit in Wordsworth and emerges in James's work only as a figure of speech (most famously in his grammatical account of the stream of consciousness). As a result, Stein's investigations in *Tender Buttons* and *How To Write*, like Sterne's in *A Sentimental Journey* and *Tristram Shandy*, differ from the ecstatic science of their fellow radical empiricists in that they directly apply what James called the "generalized conclusion" of radical empiricism (that "the parts of experience hold together from next to next by relations that are themselves parts of experience") to the activity in which they are most immediately engaged as they write (*Meaning of Truth*, p. 826). To the extent that one fails to include one's own trials with language among the facts demanding a more radical empiricism, one is less likely to regard the linguistic relations connecting "white bears" (and "real toads") to other "parts of experience" as them-selves derived from experience.[54] Here James and Walter Shandy resemble each other more than either resembles Stein or Sterne. Despite starting at opposite ends of the philosophical spectrum, their investigations stall at the same spot. On occasion, James may complain of the difficulty of composing sentences adequate to the "stubborn facts" of human psychology, yet in *his* ecstatic science he neglects to treat such composition as a stubborn fact in its own right. Walter Shandy's formalism may require an account of lan-guage as, in James's words, an "*extraneous* trans-empirical connective sup-port," yet his impassioned conjugation of the "verbs *auxiliary*" gives the lie to these putatively disembodied abstractions (*Meaning of Truth*, p. 826).[55]

Whereas for Sterne (as distinct from Tristram's *pater grammaticus*) writ-ing provides a medium for the expression of physiological experience chiefly at the level of punctuation marks, for Stein it is the written words, and not just the marks framing them, which function physiologically. The difference is summed up in the resonance displayed by her signature phrase "tender buttons," in sharp contrast with a line in *Tristram Shandy* that could easily have served as its catalyst: "Button-holes!——there is something lively in the very idea of 'em—" Tristram makes this observation shortly after re-counting an exchange between his father and the family maid, Susannah, on the occasion of his own christening. Walter Shandy, having "fastened [his breeches] through haste with but a single button, and that button through haste only half into the button-hole," inquires after his wife:

> —And how does your mistress? As well, said *Susannah*, as can be expected—
> Pish! said my father, the button of his breeches slipping out of his button-hole.—So that whether the interjection was levelled at *Susannah*, or the button-hole,—whether pish was an interjection of contempt or an interjection of modesty, is a doubt, and must be in doubt till I have time to write the three following chapters, that is, my chapter of *chamber-maids*—my chapter of *pishes*, and my chapter of *button-holes*. (pp. 216–17)

Tristram anticipates "much merry work with my button-holes—I shall have 'em all to myself—'tis a maiden subject—I shall run foul of no man's wis-dom or fine sayings in it," yet he never does get to discourse on button-holes; and a century and a half later Stein would fill the breach with her own more fully realized "tender buttons."[56] The juxtaposition of words like *tender* and *buttons*, from such divergent semantic registers, loosens them from their dictionary meanings and in the process enables them to function as something like tender buttons themselves. By contrast, Sterne's "favored dashes" serve as *lively button-holes*, framing his words (Conrad, p. 364).

The only exception in this passage is the interjection *Pish!*, which, despite being expressly defined in terms of its context of utterance, remains semantically indeterminate. The ejaculation's exceptional liveliness underscores the buttoned-down referentiality (however lively or lewd the referent) of the rest of Sterne's terminology: his *chamber-maids* and *button-holes*, *interjection of contempt* and *interjection of modesty*, *haste* and *half*.

Both Stein and Sterne conceive of the "connective support" holding their words together as neither "extraneous" nor "trans-empirical." In Stein's writing, however, it is internalized in the very words, as a product of their conjunction, whereas in Sterne the connections are still marked externally. When Williams proposed, in his essay on Stein, that it was "simply the skeleton, the 'formal' parts of writing, those that make form, that she has to do with, apart from the 'burden' which they carry," his metaphor of writing's "skeleton" conforms more closely to Sterne's masterful manipulation of punctuation than to Stein's own compositional practices. Distinguishing the skeleton from the "soft parts," and "the composition of the words" from the "dead weight of logical burdens," Williams unhesitantly places Stein on the "formal" side of the ledger even as he argues that the basis of this distinction, in the "scholastic" idea of a "logic" or meaning "supposed to transcend the words," is ultimately untenable (pp. 115–17). Needless to say, he misjudged the breadth of Stein's radical empiricism. Just as Yorick is both skull ("Alas, poor Yorick!") and skin, Stein collapses the hard and soft "parts" of writing in her *tender buttons*, which are at once soft (because tender) and hard as buttons: skeleton *and* tissue.

Throughout *A Sentimental Journey* Yorick's skin mediates inside and outside, and it is in terms of a strikingly similar experience of mediation that Stein has Toklas, in the *Autobiography*, describe the transition in her lover's writing that occurred in 1912:

> We enjoyed Granada, we met many amusing people english and spanish and it was there and at that time that Gertrude Stein's style gradually changed. She says hitherto she had been interested only in the insides of people, their character and what went on inside them, it was during that summer that she first felt a desire to express the rhythm of the visible world. (p. 119)[57]

"It was a long tormenting process," Toklas adds. Stein "looked, listened and described. She always was, she always is, tormented by the problem of the external and the internal," the problem, that is, of tactile sensitivity or what Susanne Langer has termed *cutaneous aesthesis* (p. 119; M, p. 252). As examples of Romantic science, both *Tender Buttons* and *A Sentimental Journey* investigate varieties of activity that are neither exclusively a function of external behavior nor of internal activity described phenomenologically; they exist on the interface of third- and first-person perspectives. Sense-data impinge on the cutaneous organ as a result of internal as well as external processes, and the second-person acquaintance that ensues when an organism exists in a self-consciously conjunctive relation to its environment requires the coordination of both forms of activity. Moreover, such acquaintance is not dependent on its being mutual; on the contrary, it presumes an acknowledgment of the environment's relative indifference in addition to its more-than-merely-relative difference. As Stein proposed in one of her *Lectures in America*, "the landscape does not have to make acquaintance. You may have to make acquaintance with it, but it does not with you, *it is there*" (p. 122, emphasis added). A "natural phenomenon," or "thing existent in itself," the landscape isn't determined exclusively by its relations and hence cannot fully be grasped from the external perspective of traditional science—that is, in terms of its associations or resemblances (ABT, p. 224).

"Phenomena of nature," as Stein understood them, are *phenomenal* in both senses of the term.[58] Like Wordsworth's landscapes, they are subject to natural law, hence "natural," yet at the same time they are exceptional or singular, seeming to possess independent, unpredictable lives. In "Composition as Explanation" (itself composed in the winter of 1926, while she was working on her extended study "Natural Phenomena") Stein characterized the shift in her writing in 1912 as involving a change in emphasis from the first to the second of these aspects, from a concentration on "everything being alike" to the sense of "everything being simply different," which she labeled "romanticism" (p. 35). "Everything is the same," she explained, "except composition and as the composition is different and always going to be different everything is not the same" (p. 34). Over the years, her investigations of such compositionally based differentiation took many forms, yet she always focused on specific compositional features as constraints for the experiments in question. She might thus distinguish the works written in St. Rémy in 1922–23 (among them "Four Religions, Capital Capitals, Saints in Seven and a great many other things") from the works of her Spanish period, a decade earlier, on the grounds that they involved distinct, albeit complementary, constraints. Having set herself the task that "amusing" summer in Granada of investigating sensory convergence, Wordsworth's first principle of organic experience, by the "long winter in Saint-Remy" her experiments had come to be dominated by the second of his principles, the emergence of "spots of time" due to the conjunction of sensations by motor processes (ABT, pp. 156, 209). In seeking, as she put it, to "concentrate the internal melody of existence" which, in Spain, she "had learned in relation to things seen . . . into the feeling I then had there in Saint Remy of light and air and air moving and being still," she was investigating how the motor activity that joined sensations together produced second-order sensations of the motor activity itself. It was this process that enabled one to experience "natural phenomena" as such (LIA, p. 197). Susanne Langer, similarly arguing for the correspondence between bodily consciousness and the bodies one is conscious *of*, has observed, "Body feelings may be the first thing man projected, and thus, all unwittingly, imputed to everything he objectified as material bodies in his world. The very existence of 'things' is modeled on his own inward expectation of strains, directions, and limitations of his felt actions; the wholeness and simplicity of molar objects is that of his own soma" (M, p. 321).

During that winter in St. Rémy, Stein first conceived of landscape "as a play" with its own internal motor processes (the currents of "air moving and being still") in addition to the more terrestrial dimensions that form a relatively immotile background against which to measure the movements of actors (ABT, p. 209). Only by experiencing one's environment, whether ecological or cultural, as "a complete other a romantic other another that stays there where it is," Stein would observe more than a decade later in "An American and France," might one possess "in it" the "freedom inside [one]self" necessary for creative activity (p. 63). These remarks sketch the irreducible or heterogeneous dialectic at the core of James's and Whitehead's radical empiricist accounts of experience, the same dialectic exhibited, in its turn, in Wordsworth's poetry.[59] The romantic setting "is *there* but it does not continue it has no time it is neither past nor present nor future"; consequently it provides the sense of a "complete actual present" which enables one to regard oneself as an autopoietic agent, rather than as a being determined exclusively by historical and environmental forces (WAM, p. 64, emphasis added; LIA, p. 105).

In an early essay on "The Sentiment of Rationality," James associated this "sort of anaesthetic state" with the "ecstasy" experienced by Walt Whitman at "such moments of energetic living" when "logic fails" yet "the peace of rationality" persists (p. 318). The seemingly irreconcilable combination of anaesthesia and "energetic living" marks the sense of peace or calm as ecstatic, involving a break in the customary organization of time along sequential grids of—in Stein's phrasing—"past present and future" or "beginning middle and end" (AF, p. 64). "Even the least religious of men," James asserts, "must have felt with Walt Whitman, when loafing on the grass in some transparent summer morning, that 'swiftly arose and spread round him the peace and knowledge that pass all the argument of the earth'" (p. 324). In the juncture of internal and external landscapes investigated by Stein in works ranging from *Tender Buttons* to *Four Saints in Three Acts*, scientific description becomes poetic and poetic description scientific; writing proves to be more than a transparent *means* ideally falling away to reveal a "'peace and knowledge that pass all the argument of the earth,'" in James's biblical phrasing. As so often with James, his figuration is premised on a sense of the desirability of transcending the opacity and embodiment of writing or its equivalent, a lingering idealism in the midst of his radical empiricism which Stein sought to correct. The ecstatic sense of disembodiment, with its thorough blurring of the boundaries between inside and outside and its self-conscious dissolution of self into environment, remained an embodied, natural phenomenon for Stein, "made out of real earth the way it was done to make Adam," as the narrator of *The Making of Americans* has it (p. 544). Broadening the context for such embodiment from the human soma, with its unceasing internal activity, to the experience of writing recorded in her manuscript notebooks set Stein's ecstatic science off from that of James and brought it more in line with Sterne's.

In *The Principles of Psychology* and again, a dozen years later, in *The Varieties of Religious Experience*, James embraced the traditional aim of science to collect and organize knowledge-about, albeit in an unconventional hybrid form that might be termed *knowledge about "knowledge of acquaintance."* An ecstatic science like his, treating "the relations that connect experiences" as *objects* of knowledge on a par with the experiences they connect, necessarily remains at a remove from the "experienced relations" as such. Consequently, it is set off from the correspondences that exist between the compositional or autopoietic features of such relations as well as from any correspondences involved either in relating them to one another or in *relating* a sufficiently nuanced account of their features ("World of Pure Experience," p. 1160). By contrast, poetic science, in reversing the relative emphases placed on the two varieties of knowledge, seeks to convey *knowledge of acquaintance of "knowledge-about,"* or acquaintance with the conjunctive relations that make discrete knowledge-about possible. In her shift from the procedures of systematic description employed in *The Making of Americans* to the self-consciously synesthetic portraiture of *Tender Buttons*, from description to "acquaintance with description," Stein exchanged James's more obviously scientific brand of ecstatic science for its poetic counterpart, and in the process transformed the object as well as the method of her inquiry. Yet, as I shall argue in Chapter 2, it was precisely her exposure to the new procedures and "quasi-objects" of late nineteenth-century biological science, particularly in her extensive studies in descriptive neuroanatomy at Johns Hopkins, which distinguished Stein's poetic science from that of her predecessors.[60]

SCIENCE

DIAGNOSIS: *The Doctor Makes An Analysis of Gertrude Stein*

For years Gertrude Stein has confounded literary critics. Few felt justified in charging her with duping the public. Most hesitated to credit her with founding a new school of writing. Thus with little critical help Stein readers have had to muddle their own way through such sentences as: "A meal in mutton mutton why is lamb cheaper, it is cheaper because so little is more."

Last week Morris Fishbein, shrewd editor of The Journal of The American Medical Association, made an editorial suggestion. After watching Stein antics in Chicago and reading her book of poetry "Tender Buttons," he believed she might be suffering from palilalia.

Palilalia is a frequent hangover from encephalitis, better but less correctly known as "sleeping sickness." Sufferers from it repeat words and phrases more and more rapidly until they dwindle finally into an inaudible hum.

"It is interesting in surveying the writings of Gertrude Stein," Dr. Fishbein observes, in commenting on an article by B. F. Skinner in The Atlantic Monthly, "to find that (she) worked at Radcliffe with Munsterberg (famous Harvard professor of psychology) and that she wrote a paper . . . 'Normal Motor Automatism.' In their experiments . . . they (Miss Stein and Leon M. Solomons, another student) were successful . . . to the extent of being able to perform many acts, such as writing or reading aloud, in an automatic manner while carrying on at the same time some other activity. Miss Stein reported that spontaneous automatic writing soon became easy.

"Thus she said: 'A phrase would seem to get into the head and keep repeating itself at every opportunity . . . The stuff written was grammatical, and the words and phrases fitted together all right, but there was not much connected thought. The unconsciousness was broken into every six or seven words by flashes of consciousness, so that one cannot be sure but what the slight element of connected thought which occasionally appeared was due to these flashes of consciousness. But the ability to write stuff that sounds all right, without consciousness, was fairly well demonstrated by the experiments.'"

Dr. Fishbein's conclusions: "Obviously, therefore, the writing of Miss Gertrude Stein . . . is quite the same as she developed when experimenting with spontaneous automatic writing . . . The ordinary reader cannot infer from this writing that the author possesses any consistent point of view, because there is seldom, if any, intelligent expression of opinion. Her writing seems to be the result of a stream of consciousness of a woman without a past—a personality without any background, intellectual opinions, or emotions . . ."

•

MEDICINE: *Why Does Rainbow Woman Act Like a Chameleon?*

Human skin is almost as susceptible to color changes as the vacillating hide of the chameleon. Bruises will produce black, blue, and green effects. Cold will cause a blue tinge and nausea a green. High on "hospital hill" in Kansas City's Municipal General Hospital last week lay a woman who was making national news with her color changes.

Nov. 20 when 32-year-old Edith Perry was taken to the rambling, four-story hospital from her drab West 12th Street hotel, her skin was faintly bluish. Rapidly this changed to a deep purple, then to red and brown.

The hospital's staff has seen Mrs. Perry before. A year ago she presented herself. Her skin was a bright red. Placed in a scarlet fever isolation ward, she refused tests to determine her illness. When doctors insisted, she left the hospital.

Several months ago another woman patient in General Hospital sprang to national fame by crying "tears of blood." Deliberately she provoked this phenomenon by holding her nose and forcing air into nasal passages. The pressure was so great that blood oozed into tear ducts. She hoped the publicity she might gain would bring her wandering husband home.

In Mrs. Perry's case hospital authorities are not so mystified as Associated Press men report. The medical staff privately believes that Mrs. Perry "took something each time to cause the condition—but this time took too much."

Circus "blue men" generally induce their condition by taking silver salts. One of the symptoms of poisoning from large doses of arsenic and various arsenic compounds is the skin's changing color every few hours. Peasants in Styria, Austria, swallow arsenic constantly to improve their wind for mountain climbing. Regular dosage develops in them an "arsenic tolerance" which prevents their changing color.

Persons who treat mucous membrane infections with such silver compounds as neo-silvol and argyrol develop an "after shaving" blue skin cast after years of continued applications.

Mrs. Perry last week had a competitor for publicity laurels. A quack doctor in Ohio offered to cure her free of charge if hospital authorities would allow her to be shipped to his institution. He knew, just as Kansas City doctors knew, that the fair skin covering her plump body would return to its normal color without any treatment.

INTERNATIONAL   WIDE WORLD

Figure 1. "The Doctor Makes an Analysis of Gertrude Stein." (*Newsweek*, December 8, 1934. © 1934 Newsweek, Inc. Reprinted by permission.)

CHAPTER TWO

Beyond Organic Form: Gertrude Stein and Johns Hopkins Neuroanatomy

They do quote me, that means that my words and my sentences get under their skins although they do not know it.

— GERTRUDE STEIN, *The Autobiography of Alice B. Toklas*

Photographs of a doctor and his (involuntary) patient illustrate the Science column of the December 8, 1934, issue of *Newsweek*, accompanied by the caption, "Dr. Morris Fishbein, Who Suggested That Gertrude Stein (Right) Might Be Suffering From Palilalia" (see Figure 1). Stein had just completed the first month of her lecture tour of the United States, a tour designed both to publicize her writing and, through the series of six interconnected lectures that she delivered across the nation, to help readers understand the concerns that led her to write in so notoriously opaque a manner. Yet both the columnist and the good doctor chose to ignore the author's own account. "For years Gertrude Stein has confounded literary critics," the column begins:

> Few felt justified in charging her with duping the public. Most hesitated to credit her with founding a new school of writing. Thus with little critical help Stein readers have had to muddle their own way through such sentences as: "A meal in mutton mutton why is lamb cheaper, it is cheaper because so little is more."

"Last week," however, "Morris Fishbein, shrewd editor of The Journal of The American Medical Association, made an editorial suggestion," upstaging the hesitant literary critics. "After watching Stein antics in Chicago and reading her book of poetry 'Tender Buttons,'" Fishbein concluded that "she might be suffering from palilalia . . . a frequent hangover from encephalitis, better but less correctly known as 'sleeping sickness.'" Victims of this condition, the *Newsweek* columnist explains, "repeat words and phrases more and more rapidly until they dwindle finally into an inaudible hum" ("Diagnosis," p. 24).[1]

Aside from the elision of several commas, the anonymous columnist correctly cites the penultimate sentence of Stein's prose poem "Mutton" (which, like the preceding poem in *Tender Buttons*, "Roastbeef," is explicitly concerned with the "tender[ness]" of meat and by extension of living flesh). Yet the columnist neglects to observe that the self-descriptive sentence with which the poem ends, "Lecture, lecture and repeat instruction," parodies equally the programmatic analysis of the literary critic and the time-honored formula of medical prescription, as well as pointing to the severe doubts that Stein continued to have two decades later about the rationale for lecturing (TB, p. 41). As she observed at the University of Chicago, several months after Fishbein's remark: "The actual physical presence that connects the audience to [the lecturer] in a way destroys the physical something that a writer is while he is writing, because while he is writing that physical something by existing does not connect him with anything but *concentrates* him" (N, p. 55, emphasis added). Such concentration made possible the form of recognition that she took to be the *sine qua non* of writing, namely, "recogniz[ing] what you write as you write," or as she put it later in the same lecture, "achieving recognition of the thing while the thing [is] achieving expression" (pp. 53, 60). "A recital, what is a recital," she had asked herself in "Roastbeef," "it is an organ and use does not strengthen valor, it soothes medicine" (TB, p. 38). No less than medical prescription or musical recital, lecturing is essentially instrumental and serves as a means to a desired effect on audience or patient, rather than as an end in itself. "Organ," after all, derives from the Greek *organon*, meaning "instrument."[2] In the columns of *Newsweek* and the *Journal* of the AMA, medicine *was* being soothed. The disruptive or diffractive nature of Stein's writing, due in large part to the difficulty of saying just what it meant, was smoothed over by a diagnosis that functioned as a species of "magic lantern," in T. S. Eliot's phrasing, which by "thr[owing] the nerves in patterns on a screen" removed any opacity of meaning. Stein's writing proved meaningless, rather than confoundingly subtle, because it was the product of an individual who lacked full control of her senses and hence of her wits. To be sure, Eliot's striking image in "The Love Song of J. Alfred Prufrock" merely expresses the futility experienced by Prufrock in attempting to "say just what I mean," by whatever means, medical or verbal (*Collected Poems*, p. 6).[3] The neurological pattern spells out an utterance which, some lines earlier, the hesitant lover, "pinned and wriggling on the wall," has already imagined himself saying. "That is not what I meant at all. / That is not it, at all" is replaced with its mirror image, "That is not it at all, / That is not what I meant, at all" (pp. 5–7). Eliot's point is that the quandary confonted by Prufrock is metaphysical, not physical ("I should have been a pair of ragged claws / Scuttling across the floors of silent seas," with the emphasis on *silent*). Fishbein's point, by contrast, was that Stein's writing possessed an exclusively physical significance, lacking any meaning that might be attributed to conscious intent. With no discernible emphasis, not even on silence, the words and phrases "dwindle finally into an inaudible hum."

In one respect, however, Fishbein was being shrewder than he knew, for the invocation of encephalitis (a generic term for inflammation of the brain, derived from the Greek *enkephalos*, "[marrow] in the head," from *en-*, in + *kephalē*, head) poses the question of the relation between Stein's writing and the functioning, whether proper or improper, of the human brain. Fishbein's answer may be grossly reductive because he ignores Stein's own grasp of neurophysiology; nevertheless, the question is crucial for understanding her writing, particularly the more radically experimental work composed between *Tender Buttons* and *Stanzas in Meditation*. The suggestion that Stein exhibited the aftereffects of encephalitis was absurd, yet the pathology of that condition, closely linked to the pathology of Parkinson's disease (*paralysis agitans*), is in fact directly connected to her earlier training as a medical student. According to Stanley Finger, the suggestion was already being made in 1895, two years before she matriculated at Johns Hopkins, that the substantia nigra (a structure in the midbrain which "contain[s] a [melanin-] pigmented group of neurons," hence *nigra*, or black) provided the "anatomical substratum" for Parkinson's disease. "It was not until 1919," Finger adds,

> when Constantin Tretiakoff studied the substantia nigra in patients with *paralysis agitans*, that the importance of the *locus niger de Soemmerring* began to be appreciated. Tretiakoff . . . also saw nigral lesions in his cases showing Parkinson's symptoms in association with *encephalitis lethargica*, the sleeping sickness that became epidemic in Europe in 1915. (p. 227)[4]

Studies of viral encephalitis in the wake of this outbreak contributed significantly to an understanding of the mechanisms of sleep as involving the "isolat[ion of] the brainstem from higher parts of the nervous system," a process often termed *deafferentiation* (p. 251). The relevance of these clinical investigations of sleeping sickness to Stein's writing is twofold. In the first place, in 1899 she published a description of the neuroanatomy of the nucleus of Darkschewitsch, a small collection of nerve cells adjacent to the substantia nigra, which is the largest nucleus in the midbrain. Second,

Stein's compositional procedures in the dissociative writing she produced between 1912 and 1932 involved a form of meditation that, although it certainly did not result in sleep, and was voluntary rather than involuntary, induced a form of rest or withdrawal from the anxieties of daily living that might readily be confused with such neurasthenic symptoms of *encephalitis lethargica* as "apathy, double vision, and extreme muscular weakness" (*American Heritage Dictionary*, p. 451). The principal question I shall address here is how to construe the relation between these two facets of Stein's career, her early neuroanatomical training and her subsequent literary practice. Is it possible to understand the latter as *building* upon the former, rather than as either *divorced* from it, as Stein herself tended to suggest, or as *dictated* by it, merely a set of procedures and a perspective inherited from her scientific training? A sketch of the broader context of scientific and literary relations within which Stein's dissociative practices emerged should prove helpful in answering this question.

THE MODERN SPIRIT

In his 1951 *Autobiography*, the physician-poet William Carlos Williams proposed that the "distinguishing" characteristic of "the modern" might be found in its attention to the "tactile" qualities of words, by contrast with what thirty years earlier, in *Kora in Hell*, he had termed "associational or sentimental values," the "loose linking of one thing with another" (*Autobiography*, pp. 300–301; *Imaginations*, pp. 14, 18). In setting tactility against associative linkage Williams was revising the contrast, traditional at least since Coleridge, between organic and mechanical theories of literary composition, by substituting organic qualities modeled on the nervous system for Coleridge's vegetative model. Implicit in this emphasis on the tactile is a sense of the intimate correspondence between the experience of writing (in Stein's phrasing, "the physical something that a writer is while he is writing") and the operations of the nervous system, especially given that the body's nervous structures, including the eyes and ears, possess "the same embryonic source as the skin," the ectoderm, or outermost of an embryo's germ layers (M, p. 162). With an intensity and directness unparalleled among English-language writers, Stein investigated this correspondence in compositions in which her own neuroanatomical researches at the turn of the century continued to play a critical role.

Stein's psychological studies as an undergraduate at Harvard have been much remarked on. These consisted principally of three years spent working closely with Münsterberg and James, during which she served, for instance, as an experimental subject in research on the saturation of colors reported in the state-of-the-art journal *The Psychological Review*, in addition to publishing articles in the same journal on normal and cultivated motor automatism.[5] By contrast, her broader scientific training has received scant attention, although she was taking a full load of science courses by her senior year. Besides two semesters of the graduate "Psychological Laboratory," her schedule that year included one course in chemistry (in which she did poorly); another in botany, covering the "morphology, histology (with special reference to the technique of the microscope), and physiology of the flowering plant"; and three in zoology—one on the "comparative anatomy of vertebrates," another on "the nervous system and its terminal organs, central nervous organs and terminal organs of efferent [that is, outwardly directed] nerves," and the third on the "embryology of vertebrates."[6] The following summer, she took an advanced course on vertebrate embryology at the Woods Hole Marine Biological Laboratory before starting at Johns Hopkins, where she was enrolled at the Medical School between 1897 and 1901 and continued to conduct research until 1902. "Practical medicine did not particularly interest her," she observed on the dust jacket of her 1922 collection *Geography and Plays*, in an inaugural effort at the third-person mode of autobiographical composition perfected a decade later in *The Autobiography of Alice B. Toklas*, "and soon she specialized in the anatomy of the brain and the direction of brain tracts." By 1903, Stein had moved to Paris, and for the next eight or nine years, in the midst of "an art movement of which the outside world at that time knew nothing," she continued to regard her investigations as largely scientific in nature (ABT, p. 28). The perspective articulated in her writing of this period is predominantly mechanistic or deterministic, and only with the completion of the 925-page *Making of Americans* in 1911 were the procedures of systematic description employed in it replaced by the "studies in description" of *Tender Buttons*. This, she suggested, marked the end of her scientific investigations.

Yet, instead of leaving science behind, Stein merely rejected the dominant model of science of the period, exchanging a practice rooted in James's physiological psychology and his subsequent research on "extraordinary mental states" (which culminated in the "Science of Religions" outlined in his Gifford lectures of 1901 and 1902) for a practice more akin to the poetic science of writers like Emerson and Whitman, and prior to them, Wordsworth and Sterne. Stein's exposure to the new procedures and "quasi-objects, quasi-subjects" of late nineteenth-century science distinguished her science from that of her predecessors even as it set her apart from contemporaries like D. H. Lawrence, who in his 1923 tract *Fantasia of the*

Unconscious called for a "science which proceeds in terms of life" (Latour, p. 51; Lawrence, p. 12). Arguing that "biology never considers life, but only mechanistic functioning and apparatus of life," Lawrence invoked a "subjective science" that certainly sounds something like the poetic science Stein had already been practicing for a decade, at least in contrast with what he termed the "objective science of modern knowledge," a "science of the dead world" that "concerns itself only with phenomena . . . in their cause-and-effect relationship." All the same, despite his keen sense of the rhythms of living creatures, Lawrence's acquaintance with contemporary biology was woefully inadequate compared to that of Stein. Hence his embarrassing localization, for instance, of the two forms of "dynamic knowledge," sympathetic and voluntary—"I am I" because "I am at one with the universe" and "I am I" because "I am other than all the universe"—in the nerve centers of the solar plexus and the lumbar ganglion respectively (pp. 12, 35).[7] Hence also the temptation posed for him by *social* organicism, as against the more strictly biological organicism that informed Stein's writing, as well as the tendency to a Bergsonian vitalism, so widespread in the early decades of the century and from which Lawrence, in particular, suffered greatly.[8]

Stein's training at Johns Hopkins, by contrast, enabled her to develop an organic perspective that avoided the temptations to totalization (aesthetic and political) to which organicism since Coleridge has so frequently been subject. Although modernist practice is often regarded as antithetical to organicism, substituting a twentieth-century New Mechanism for the organicist tendencies of the nineteenth century, this account is vastly oversimplified. Organicist and mechanistic perspectives compete not just between writers but within individual writers; the hero of James Joyce's *Stephen Hero* may assert that "the modern spirit is vivisective," yet neither Stephen Dedalus nor Leopold Bloom is fully "modern" in this sense (p. 185).[9] Perhaps, as the contemporary historian and philosopher of science Bruno Latour argues, the modern spirit has never actually been fully modern—or perhaps it has never been fully vivisective, for Western thought since the mid-eighteenth century has been characterized by a conflict between vivisectionist and what I propose calling *neuraesthetic* perspectives. An ever-more-detailed anatomizing of the human body (Wordsworth's "meddling intellect / Misshap[ing] the beauteous forms of things") is matched by an increasingly neurophysiological sense of the not-merely-anatomical phenomena traditionally categorized as *spirit* (LB, p. 106). Although the body's spirits and humors have presumably been neurophysiological all along, only in the past two-and-a-half centuries have human beings acquired a conceptual framework that permits us to confront this fact of life head-on.

Gerald Edelman cites several remarks of Diderot's Dr. Bordeu, for instance, which already express a recognizably modern attitude. "There is only one centre of consciousness," Bordeu proposes in *D'Alembert's Dream* (1769):

> It can only be at one place, at the common centre of all the sensations, where memory resides and comparisons are made. Each individual thread [or nerve] is only capable of registering a certain number of impressions, that is to say sensations one after the other, isolated and not remembered. But the centre is sensitive to all of them; it is the register, it keeps them in mind or holds a sustained impression, and any animal is bound, from its embryonic stage, to relate itself to this centre, attach its whole life to it, exist in it. (p. 210; cited in BABF, p. 21)

Bordeu acknowledges grave limitations in his ability to observe directly how the "centre of the network" manages to register and coordinate the sensations conducted to it by individual threads, yet he remains convinced that experiences traditionally attributed to noncorporeal spirit ("manifestations [of] reason, judgement, imagination, madness" and so forth) are in fact the expression of neurophysiological processes (pp. 210–11). As it happens, Diderot was a great admirer of Sterne, who in 1762 arranged for him to receive several volumes of *Tristram Shandy*, which Diderot described as "the craziest, wisest, and gayest of books" (Cash, p. 139).

For contrastive purposes, one might set this modern perspective against that of Johannes Kepler who, at the beginning of the seventeenth century, "broke with tradition by suggesting that the problem of the retinal inversion," the formation of inverted and reversed images on the retina, "did not belong to the realm of optics," since, as he expressed the matter, "the armament of opticians does not take them beyond [the] first opaque wall encountered within the eye" (Finger, p. 74). "How the image or picture is composed by the visual spirits that reside in the retina and the nerve," he wrote,

> and whether it is made to appear before the soul or the tribunal of the visual faculty by a spirit within the hollows of the brain, or whether the visual faculty, like a magistrate sent by the soul, goes forth from the administrative chamber of the brain into the optic nerve and the retina to meet this image, as though descending to a lower court—this I leave to be disputed by the physicists. (cited in Finger, p. 74)

Early traces of the development from this overburdened society of spirits to Bordeu's speculative nervous system—from premodern to modern worldviews—may be found in several observations made by Antonie van Leeuwenhoek later in the seventeenth century. Having examined the optic nerves of several cows with the newly invented microscope, Leeuwenhoek reported in 1674 that he "could find no hollowness in them" such as "some Anato-mists" had claimed to observe, "through which they would have the Ani-mal spirits, that convey the visible species, represented in the eye, pass into the Brain." Instead, the nerves were "composed and conjoined of globuls, and wound about again with particles consisting of other transparent globuls." A year later he proposed that the mechanism whereby the image on the retina "pass[ed] into the Brain" was similar to that operating in "a tall Beer-glass full of Water," when, the water having been

> touch'd on its Surface with the Finger, [the] Contact of the Water made by the Finger cannot be said to touch and move only on the Surface of the Water, but we must also grant, that all the Water in the Glass comes to suffer, and to be more pressed by it, than it was before the Finger touched the Water, and that also all the Parts of the Water are moved thereby.

Given the initial "Motion of a visible Object . . . upon the soft Globuls, that lie at the End of the Optick Nerve of the Eye," these "Globuls do commu-nicate the like Motion to the other Globuls so as to convey it to the Brain" (cited in Finger, p. 77). The transition from a spirit-based metaphorics, and metaphysics, to an Age of Sensibility had begun, with the dual perspective that the term *sensibility* suggests: of the self-effacing ratios of reasonable-ness, on the one hand, alternating with hypersensitivity and its self-drama-tizing emotions, on the other.

Stein and Pater

Merely to assert that the modern spirit, in being at once vivisectionist and neuraesthetic, differs from the worldview hitherto dominant in the West, of spirits and bodies unselfconsciously interpenetrating (satirized so acutely in the early eighteenth century by Pope in his perfectly turned *Rape of the Lock*), is of course no more precise a statement than Bordeu's explanation of memory as the "specific sense" of a hypothetical nerve center (Diderot, p. 210). It still leaves one with the problem of reconciling the two halves of modern self-consciousness, or of demonstrating how they have failed to be reconciled, or even how the figuration of self-division and reconciliation may be part of the problem, not part of the solution. Yet at least it sets the terms of the problem. The second of these terms, *neuraesthetic*, is in fact a neologism, which I use to refer to the general condition of sensitivity to the physiological operations of one's own nervous system, of which neurasthe-nia (nervous exhaustion) is one pathologized state, as, in the vast arsenals of the symptomology of modernity and modernism, is the shell shock experi-enced by veterans of the First World War.[10] In certain contexts, however, heightened states of what in the last chapter I called *auto-sensation*, sensitivity to one's own nervous condition, have been represented as desirable, and it is to keep this Paterian alternative open that I have substituted *(a)esthesia*, or "the ability to feel or perceive" (a back-formation from *anesthesia*, which in turn derives from the Greek *an-*, "without" + *aisthēsis*, "feeling"), in place of *asthenia*, meaning "loss or lack of bodily strength," and derived from the Greek *a-*, "without" + *sthenos*, "strength."[11]

When Pater asserts in the "Conclusion" to *The Renaissance* that we still "have an interval," he is defending the neuraesthetic perspective against anatomical reductiveness, regardless of whether such reduction is construed in third- or first-person terms: that is, with respect to "*our physical life*" (as when science reduces processes like "the passage of the blood, the wasting and repairing of the lenses of the eye, the modification of the tissues of the brain by every ray of light and sound" to "simpler and more elementary forces") or to the "continual vanishing away" that characterizes "*the inward world* of thought and feeling" ("that strange, perpetual weaving and unweaving of ourselves"). Against the seemingly irrefutable argument of "analysis" that "those impressions of the individual mind to which, for each of us, experience dwindles down, are in perpetual flight," so that even the "single moment" is "gone while we try to apprehend it"—vanishing in the twinkling James would subsequently term *the specious present*—Pater sets the neuraesthetic: "For our one chance lies in expanding that interval, in getting as many pulsations as possible into the given time," and thereby experiencing a "quickened sense of life" (pp. 150–53). Stein is perhaps at her most Paterian in her lecture "Poetry and Grammar," when she insists that "a sense of movement of time included in a given space" is "a definitely American thing," and that "an American can fill up a space in having his movement of time by adding unexpectedly anything and yet getting within the included space everything he had intended getting." That her "definitely" American aesthete turns out to be the "engine-driver" of a train merely confirms just how native to America the aesthetic or neuraesthetic perspective is, extending to the soul of the machine (LIA, pp. 224–25).

Stein did not start out a full-blooded Paterian, however. Several months after his death in 1894, she ventured the following analysis of *Marius the Epicurean*, a novel of "sensations and ideas" in which Pater "dealt more fully . . . with the thoughts suggested" by his "brief 'Conclusion,'" as he himself remarked in a note appended to *The Renaissance* (p. 150). "In the last few books of Marius the Epicurean," she wrote for a sophomore composition class,

> I felt a decided falling away in strength and truth. In trying to analyse the cause, insofar as it concerned the delineation of the character of Marius himself, it occurred to me that Pater gave us two decidedly antagonistic elements in the process of conversion.
>
> On the one hand he discourses on the suddenness of the change, the deep impression that here was a revelation, a something utterly different and shows us that the spirit was the same and the ritual largely that of his old faith. Soon, however, I felt that this far from leading in the direction I supposed forced me to quite a contrary conclusion, and showed a clear insight in the order of influence necessary to produce not a violent conversion, but the quite slow-working change that took place in Marius.
>
> I now found that my dissatisfaction consisted rather in the purely emotional flavor of this new belief. It seemed hardly probable that this student of philosophy would so completely throw all his systematic thought to the winds and rely on the emotional wave alone. (RM, p. 131)[12]

Pater, in introducing the conversion (which occurs when Marius witnesses a Christian service for the first time), writes, "It was not in an image, or series of images, yet still in a sort of dramatic action, and with the unity of a single appeal to eye and ear, that Marius . . . found all his new impressions set forth, regarding what he had already recognised, intellectually, as for him at least the most beautiful thing in the world" (II, p. 128). The *order of influence* established here by Pater begins with the statement, "To understand the influence upon [Marius] of what follows the reader must remember that it was an experience which came amid a deep sense of vacuity in life," when "Marius saw for the first time the wonderful spectacle—wonderful, especially, in its evidential power over himself, over his own thoughts—of those who believe" (II, pp. 128, 130). Then follows a description of the service, its ritual being, as Stein noted, "largely that of his old faith": from "the people, answering one another, somewhat after the manner of a Greek chorus," to the priest chanting "like some new sort of *rhapsodos*," to "a sacrifice, it might seem, like the most primitive, the most natural and enduringly significant of old pagan sacrifices," with an accompanying consecration of "bread and wine[,] . . . pure wheaten bread, the pure white wine of the Tusculan vineyards" (II, pp. 132, 136–37). As a result of these manifold correspondences, "the natural soul of worship" in Marius "had at last been satisfied as never before" (II, p. 140).

Far from undercutting the apparent "suddenness of the change" by dwelling on familiar elements in the experience, Pater actually displayed an acute sense of the causes that enable "slow-working change" to come to a head in "a violent conversion." In remarking this, Stein expressed what forty years later she would characterize as a typically nineteenth-century satisfaction with the ways that past experiences condition present ones. It was this perspective to which James alluded when, in a talk he gave in 1896 at a Harvard reception for the American Society of Naturalists, he suggested that "the causal elements and not the totals are what we are now most passionately concerned to understand" ("Louis Agassiz," p. 15). The difficulties Stein encountered over the next decade and a half in rendering an adequately *neuraesthetic* sense of "the totals," using instruments designed principally for registering "causal elements" *anatomically*, persuaded her, in the end, to recalibrate her writing procedures. To convey an adequate sense of individuals as totals, the medium would itself have to be experienced neuraesthetically, thereby foregrounding what Williams termed the *tactile* qualities of words.

Her initial diagnosis having unexpectedly demonstrated evidence of a genuinely analytic temperament on the part of the author of *Marius the Epicurean*, Stein then made a second effort to account for her impression of the novel's "falling away in strength and truth." Pater may have exhibited great independence of mind in his handling of the episode, yet in the process he transformed Marius from a "student of philosophy" and "systematic" thinker into someone "rely[ing] on the emotional wave alone." Stein judged the transformation "hardly probable," especially by contrast with the way Marius's formerly "intellectual" appreciation was represented as taking on the form of a "dramatic action" in the course of his conversion. At this stage, Marius hadn't yet "throw[n] his systematic thought to the winds," and Pater could still write that unlike "the old pagan worship," where "there had been little to call the understanding into play," here "the utterance, the eloquence, the music of worship conveyed, as Marius readily understood, a fact, or series of facts, for intellectual reception" (II, p. 138). These were facts in the root sense of the Latin term *factum*, or "deed," including lessons and readings as well as the narrative of Christ. Within the expanded interval of his conversion, Marius remained a systematic thinker, yet the true believer's reliance on what Stein termed the *emotional wave* of "utterance, . . . eloquence, [and] the music of worship" to provide food for thought ("to call the understanding into play") foreshadowed a very different fate. The active quality of Marius's mind during the conversion-experience differed sharply from the state of "intellectual reception" awaiting him. Whether there was indeed nothing in his past experience, nothing in the "deep sense of vacuity in life" he brought to "the wonderful spectacle," to motivate *this* transformation, it may still strike one as *under-* if not exactly *un*determined. However, the representation of Marius's post-conversion experience rang false for Stein chiefly in another respect. It was one thing to demonstrate how an intellectual appreciation might be fleshed out, bringing anatomical and neuraesthetic perspectives together "in the unity of a single appeal to eye and ear." It was quite a different thing summarily to replace an anatomical with a neuraesthetic perspective, "throw[ing] . . . all systematic thought to the winds and rely[ing] on the emotional wave alone"—or, to invoke James's corresponding distinction, to embrace *knowledge of acquaintance* while choosing to ignore and consequently repress descriptive, systematized knowledge, irrespective of the system of *knowledge-about* involved.

Stein and Eliot

Appearances to the contrary, Stein never sacrificed knowledge-about at an altar to knowledge of acquaintance: hence her insistence that emotion should never "be the cause of poetry or prose" as well as the distinction she drew between the "mystical basis" of Juan Gris's sense of "exactitude" and her own "pure passion for exactitude," the "necessity" of which was "intellectual" rather than emotional or mystical (ABT, p. 211). Unlike the obscurities native to both mystic and aphasic expression, the dissociative compositions of the middle years of Stein's career do not involve the dissociation of knowledge-about from knowledge of acquaintance. Nor was she prepared in these works to sacrifice knowledge of acquaintance, and the corresponding experience of "feeling-tone," at an altar to systematic knowledge, resulting in inexactness in the "reproduction of either an outer or an inner reality" due to insufficiently contextualized processes of abstraction—misplaced concreteness, as Whitehead called it (ABT, p. 211). Unlike Pater, or Maggie Tulliver in George Eliot's *The Mill on the Floss*, Stein did not promote an aesthetic of sacrifice. This is not to say, however, that in the initial, explicitly scientific stage of her career, she did not *practice* such an aesthetic, even as she resisted it. The sadomasochistic dynamic implicit in her divided engagement is fully on display in the first of the compositions she prepared for her sophomore writing course, "a first-person account of a hallucination experienced by a young woman afraid of madness and aware of strong sado-masochistic tendencies within herself" (Moers, p. 65). The thematic of self-sacrifice is already registered in Stein's title, "In the Red Deeps," as Ellen Moers comes close to acknowledging in her 1976 study, *Literary Women*:

> Perhaps to be expected as characteristic of the period—the 1890s—are the morbidity, perversity, and decadence of [the composition]; but wholly unexpected is its title—for "In the Red Deeps" is George Eliot. It is the title she used for Chapter 1, Book V of *The Mill on the Floss*. (p. 65)

In appropriating George Eliot's title, Stein sacrificed her own self-identity to "destiny," whether this is figured, following Moers, as "the one thing about a woman that does not change[,] her anatomy," or as a function of discipleship, of "being still under the influence of George Eliot," as Stein herself once remarked of this uncharacteristic choice of title (EA, p. 157).

The metaphor Stein "found in George Eliot" was "the kind that Freud found in [a] dream," Moers remarks in the concluding chapter of *Literary Women*. "'The complicated topography of the female genital parts,' he said, 'makes one understand how it is that they are often represented as *landscapes*.'" (This citation comes from the tenth of Freud's *Introductory Lectures on Psychoanalysis*.) "Most men," Moers adds, "know almost nothing of that 'complicated topography,' but Freud was a doctor; he would have been as capable as Gertrude Stein of perceiving the distinctively female *landscape* 'In the Red Deeps'" (p. 253). "An insignificant rise of ground crowned by trees," Eliot writes:

> Insignificant . . . because in height it was hardly more than a bank: but there may come moments when Nature makes a mere bank a means towards a fateful result. . . . Just where this line of bank sloped down again to a level, a by-road turned off and led to the other side of the rise, where it was broken into very capricious hollows and mounds by the working of an exhausted stone-quarry—so long exhausted that both mounds and hollows were now clothed with brambles and trees, and here and there by a stretch of grass which a few sheep kept close-nibbled. (*The Mill on the Floss*, p. 274)

Moers observes that "what most matters here," and "set[s] off the Red Deeps from other places, is its location in *The Mill on the Floss*":

> The most difficult moment of Maggie Tulliver's adolescence has come, the break between girlhood and growth, the choice between brother and lover. The Red Deeps are a place of seclusion that Maggie loves, and where she agrees to carry on a series of clandestine meetings with the sensitive hunchback Philip Wakem, whom her brother Tom forbids her to know, and toward whom Maggie feels affection but no physical attraction. There Maggie's sexual existence is born, abortively. "Ah, Maggie," says Philip, "you would never love me so well as you love your brother." (*The Mill on the Floss*, p. 282; Moers, pp. 253–54)

This may be what matters most in *The Mill on the Floss* as well as to the twenty-year-old Stein, but it is not what mattered to the author of *Everybody's Autobiography* some forty years later.

Moers, who credits Stein not just with having directed her to this metaphor of female anatomy but also with having taught her "to listen as women writers do to each other's voices in literature—many voices of different rhythms, pitches, and timbres to which they have always listened with professional sensitivity for an echo to answer their own"—directs her own reader to Stein's "reminisce[nce] about her literary beginnings" in *Everybody's Autobiography* (pp. 65–66). "When I wrote my first story," Stein recalled,

> I called it Red Deeps out of George Eliot, one does do that, and since well since not, it is a bad habit, American writers have it, unless they make it the taken title to be a sounding board to send back the sound that they are to make inside, that would not be too bad. (EA, p. 290)[13]

Moers reads this passage less as an acknowledgment of the "sense" she believes Stein to have shared with other women writers, "of encountering in another woman's voice what they believed was the sound of their own" (if only a common "sense of the surrounding silence" and of "deaf ears"), than as pointing to a stylistic resemblance between Stein's writing and that of other "great ladies who also wrote queer." Among these ladies, Moers numbers Queen Victoria, whose letters Stein "read . . . aloud to Alice Toklas," and Teresa of Avila, for whom both Stein and Eliot shared a marked "enthusiasm." "St. Teresa's autobiography in particular," she asserts, "is full of echoes of what Gertrude Stein called 'the sound inside'" (p. 66). Whether or not this experience of internal sound is marked by gender to the same degree that one's anatomy inscribes one's sex, it undeniably serves as a useful image for Stein's sense of her writing process—echoing, as it were, her description in *The Autobiography of Alice B. Toklas* of one of her principal compositional procedures in the "early restless years after the war." Among the "most successful" of "these experiments," in which she would "set a sentence for herself as a sort of tuning fork and metronome and then write to that time and tune," was a work she titled "Mildred's Thoughts" (ABT, pp. 206–7). Composed in 1922, this portrait of the thoughts of Mildred Aldrich, close friend of Stein and author of the best-selling *A Hilltop on the Marne*, offers a clear example of what it might mean for Stein to "reproduce" the "inner reality" of another woman writer.

Recreating someone else's inner reality was not to be confused, however, with actually "enter[ing] into" that person's mind through some form of telepathic channel. "Mildred's Thoughts" does not comprise Mildred Aldrich's actual thoughts (whatever these might have been) but reproduces her innermost sense of things on the basis of the thoughts she actually articulates. It is an "intellectual recreation" of Aldrich's neuraesthetic experience, informed by careful attention to the manner in which she expresses her thoughts (LIA, p. 238).[14] "Nobody enters into the mind of someone else,"

Stein once observed, "not even a husband and wife. You may touch, but you do not enter into each other's mind. Why should you?" (TI, p. 30). In the same interview, she reiterated: "Nothing can be the same thing to the other person. Nobody can enter into anybody else's mind; so why try? One can only enter into it in a superficial way. You have slight contacts with other people's minds, but you cannot enter into them" (p. 34). Experience, which from an analytic standpoint is "already reduced," in Pater's words, "to a swarm of impressions," is further "ringed round for each one of us by that thick wall of personality through which no real voice has ever pierced on its way to us, or from us to that which we can only conjecture to be without. Every one of those impressions is the impression of the individual in his isolation, each mind keeping as a solitary prisoner its own dream of a world" (*The Renaissance*, p. 151). Still, the skepticism expressed here by Pater is not Stein's, at least not in the radically experimental writing of her middle period. *Nothing can be the same thing to the other person, so why try?* This isn't the skeptic's lament but the realist's shrug, the same realist who might comment that taking a title from another author "is a bad habit," because it suggests an illusory continuity between what she means, for example, in titling her composition "In the Red Deeps" and what Eliot meant with the same title. This is a bad habit, not just because Stein regards *all* writing habits as bad insofar as they save one from thinking, nor because it is illusory and premised on a category mistake—same words, same meaning—but because it promotes the murderous aesthetic of self-sacrifice that culminates, in *The Mill on the Floss*, with the "hideous triumph" of the watery deeps that sweep Maggie Tulliver and her brother to their deaths. The only consolation experienced by a grieving Philip Wakem is that afforded by "the trees of the Red Deeps, where the buried joy seemed still to hover—like a revisiting spirit" (pp. 485–86). Yet is this residual spiritualism consolation or torture, further evidence of Philip's own sadomasochistic tendencies to self-sacrifice, complementing Maggie's? The practice of quotation exemplified by Stein's title is a decidedly bad habit *unless* one is able to redirect it, so that it doesn't irresistibly point back to the writer from which it has been "taken" but instead serves, as Stein says, as "a sounding board to send back" to oneself (that is, to the writer in the process of writing) the sound one is "*to make* inside." The near future, rather than the distant past, informs this expanded interval.

As it happens, a particularly striking example in Stein's corpus of this alternative form of quotation involves another Eliot title, this time from *Middlemarch*. "Old and Young," the second book of Eliot's masterpiece, possesses obvious thematic overtones in the context of any consideration of influence, literary or otherwise; but instead of using the title of her 1913 composition "Old and Old" to point back to Eliot and thereby to associate her writing with that of the earlier author, Stein used it to sound out the direction that her own composition would take, much as the title of "Mildred's Thoughts" functioned almost a decade later. If Stein didn't entirely dissociate her composition from Eliot's, she did avoid the logic of subordination ordinarily associated with allusive quotation, which typically provides the basis for its significance. Yet, unlike the title of "Mildred's Thoughts," that of "Old and Old" doesn't recur in the body of the text that follows, even if Stein never loses sight of the topic of aging. Instead, the phrase reverberates chiefly at the level of phonetic play, often involving terms that rhyme with *old* or, more exactly, serve as variations on a base of *-old*: "old and [-old]." Among these, the dominant term is probably *cold*, operating, in conjunction with *old and old*, "as a sort of tuning fork," as in this set of examples from the first of the work's seven sections, entitled "Conditions": "in *loud coal* bust . . . in *hold hot*"; "*Crowd a col*lection with large layers, ages, *ages and ages*"; "*Hold* up. Saw a case *cool*"; "sudden *and a pole* mischurch, miss *ol*ives, miss *old age col*lars *and* cuffs *and* rhubarb"; "The high arrangement which makes *colds*"; "A g*r*and st*a*nd a real *old* gr*a*nd st*a*nd *and* . . . "; "*Cold* wets *and cold* woods *and cold* cow harness *and cold* in the stretch"; "a way both *heat*, a way they *heat cold*"; "a *coat*, a *collided* blotter" (pp. 221–22). "Old and Old" concerns the degeneration of the body, as Stein registers the debilitating effects of the passage of time, as it confines one initially to the house—the first section opens on the discouraging note of "House plants"—and then, in the second section, "Treatment," to one's bed: "It is so hold," a voice sniffles in the "bedroom" (pp. 221, 223). "A cold state, a kind of stable life, a kind of boiler," the fifth section, "Widows," begins: "Cold wet nurses and cold wet noises, cold wet noses, cold wet nurses" (p. 227). Yet the term *wet nurse*, defined by the *American Heritage Dictionary* as "a woman who suckles another woman's child," should give one pause. What is this word doing here, among these "widows"? Is "It is so hold" the slurred speech of someone with a cold or fever, or is it a portmanteau phrase? *It is so cold, hold (me)?* The title of the last section, "Cut Indians," similarly plays on the title of the first—cut *conditions* and it bleeds *Indians*—and the section opens by welcoming the reader *in*: "Come in little cubicle stern old wet places. Come in by the long excuse of more in place of bandages which send a little leaf to cut a whole condition with a pan, all the can all that can see the pen of pigs wide" (p. 229). One may be reminded here of Mina Loy's "Pig Cupid his rosy snout / Rooting erotic garbage," and the association proves pertinent as Stein, putting "all this in bedding," concludes the section, and the composition, in what she calls "the perulean repetition of amalgamated recreation of more integral and less solidifying rudeness," namely, sex on the page (*Lost Lunar Baedeker*, p. 53; "Old and Old," p. 230). Or is it perhaps more exactly a matter of moving one's bowels? "Baby mine, baby mine, have a cow come out of have a cow come out of baby mine have a cow come out with time . . ." (p. 230).[15] "Old and Old" is a play—Stein included it in her 1932 collection *Operas and Plays*—and the playwright insists on playing even with the inevitable inroads of time. No mere houseplant she.

Stein's youthful familiarity with George Eliot's writing is indisputable; evidence of it frames her career, from the title of her first story to an overt allusion in the last work she composed, the "Message from Gertrude Stein" which introduces the posthumously published *Selected Writings*.[16] There, in commenting on her desire "to be historical, from almost a baby on," Stein recalls, "When I was almost fourteen I used to love to say to myself those awful lines of George Eliot, May I be one of those immortal something or other, I havent the poem here and although I knew then how it went I do not now" (p. vii). (A decade earlier, in *Everybody's Autobiography*, she still remembered the lines: "When I was adolescent I read a poem of George Eliot I cannot often remember poetry but I can remember that. May I join the choir invisible of those immortal dead who live again" [p. 119].) Yet, by contrast with the fairly obvious thematic concerns shared by Stein and Eliot in their respective versions of "In the Red Deeps"—let alone by Eliot in her secular hymn "O may I join the choir invisible" and Stein in her last "Message," contemplating the body of her writing retrospectively and her own imminent mortality—the reader of "Old and Old" is actively discouraged from distinguishing thematic strands in the tissue of the work. Even if, on the basis of the title, one reads the work as a meditation on aging and mortality, this wouldn't suggest any specific connection to Book II of *Middlemarch*. In fact, it would seem to point to a more direct connection with Book III, "Waiting for Death." Still, there *is* a direct connection, however slant, between Stein's and Eliot's works. Nineteenth-century neuroanatomical research, which, as I am arguing, played so decisive a role in the development of Stein's *compositional* procedures, proves to be a primary *thematic* concern of "Old and Young" as well. To what extent, then, does Eliot's suggestion of an analogy between the scientific investigation of "certain primary webs, or tissues, out of which the various organs . . . are compacted" and the investigation of the social body of Middlemarch (an investigation that takes the form of "unravelling certain human lots [in] this particular web," so as to see "how they [are] woven and interwoven") shed light on the relation between Stein's compositional practices and her research in neuroanatomy (pp. 177, 170)?

Book II of *Middlemarch* contains the memorable encounter of Dorothea Brooke, "a Saint Theresa, foundress of nothing," with Rome, "city of visible history" (pp. 26, 224). An equally compelling, if not quite so monumental, encounter of "old and young" also occurs between the science of natural history, exemplified by Camden Farebrother ("I am going on both with the fauna and flora; but I have at least done my insects well"), and the new medical science of Tertius Lydgate, with its overriding concern with structure (p. 202). "I have never had time to give myself much to natural history," Lydgate testifies: "I was early bitten with an interest in *structure*." Having opened "an old Cyclopaedia" by chance to a page "under the heading of Anatomy," he, or more precisely "his eyes," were drawn to a "passage . . . on the valves of the heart." This "startl[ed] him with his first vivid notion of finely adjusted mechanism in the human frame"—"for anything he knew his brains lay in small bags at his temples"—and "from that hour Lydgate felt the growth of an intellectual passion" (pp. 202, 173). Yet, as Eliot's narrator acknowledges in a remarkable account of the state of medicine in the 1820s, Lydgate's new science, and in particular his search for a "primitive tissue," had long since become dated by the time *Middlemarch* was composed in the 1870s: "What was the primitive tissue? In that way Lydgate put the question—not quite in the way required by the awaiting answer; but such missing of the right word befalls many seekers" (p. 178).

"We are apt to think it the finest era of the world," Eliot writes, "when America was beginning to be discovered, when a bold sailor, even if he were wrecked, might alight on a new kingdom; and about 1829 the dark territories of Pathology were a fine America for a spirited adventurer." Then follows an encapsulated account of the exploration of these "dark territories," and of their appeal to Lydgate:

> The more he became interested in special questions of disease, such as the nature of fever or fevers, the more keenly he felt the need for that fundamental knowledge of structure which just at the beginning of the century had been illuminated by the brief and glorious career of Bichat, who died when he was only one-and-thirty, but like another Alexander, left a realm large enough for many heirs. That great Frenchman first carried out the conception that living bodies, fundamentally considered, are not associations of organs which can be understood by studying them first apart, and then as it were federally; but must be regarded as consisting of certain primary webs, or tissues, out of which the various organs—brain, heart, lungs, etc.—are compacted . . . No man, one sees, can understand and estimate the entire structure or its parts—what are its frailties

and what its repairs, without knowing the nature of the materials. . . . This great seer did not go beyond the consideration of the tissues as ultimate facts in the living organism, marking the limits of anatomical analysis; but it was open to another mind to say, have not these structures some common basis from which they have all started. . . . Here would be another light, as of oxy-hydro-gen, showing the very grain of things, and revising all former explanation. Of this sequence to Bichat's work, already vibrating along many currents of the European mind, Lydgate was enamored. . . . What was the primitive tissue? (pp. 176–78)[17]

Eliot suggests, moreover, that Lydgate's infatuation with medical science was strongly reinforced by his disenchantment with Madame Laure, a French actress who, having, as he thought, innocently murdered her actor-husband on the stage, informs him that, on the contrary, she "did not plan: it came to me in the play—I meant to do it." "I do not like husbands," she adds, "I will never have another." Lydgate takes this dismissal to heart. "Three days afterwards [he] was at his galvanism again in his Paris chambers, believing that illusions were at an end for him. . . . [H]enceforth he would take a strictly scientific view of woman, entertaining no expectations, but such as were justified beforehand" (pp. 182–83).

So, what do pathology's "need for [a] fundamental knowledge of structure" and Lydgate's corresponding "strictly scientific view of woman" have to do with Stein's compositional practices? "Old and Old" begins within the diagnostic framework of medical science, with the initial section, "Conditions," followed by an appropriate "Treatment," as the second section is called. Yet if one chooses to look *inside* the frame—

1. Conditions.

House plants.
Cousin to cousin the same is a brother.
Collected tumblers.
Pretty well so called, pretty careful and going all the detention.
Hopping.
Pretty well Charlie, pretty sour poison in pears, pretty well henny pretty soon most soon bent.
Collect.
In do pot soon, in loud coal bust, in do pot soon, in chalk what . . .

—one finds that Stein rigorously adheres to Madame Laure's denial of premeditation, continually upsetting the reader's painstakingly assembled expectations (p. 221).[18] The absence of any "plan" gives the lie to the claim that "structure" is "fundamental." For if, according to the "strictly scientific view" expressed by Lydgate, structure provides the basis for medical science, enabling one to "entertain no expectations, but such as are justified beforehand" (surely the ideal of diagnosis), what is one to make of the dual assertion that "I did not plan" yet "I meant to do it"? "My foot really slipped," Madame Laure tells Lydgate (p. 182). Accident, rather than plan, is experienced as deliberate action. Clearly, the perspective expressed by Madame Laure is either delusional (or, what amounts to the same thing, merely willful) or it refers to an aspect of experience that the diagnostic or determinist framework cannot accommodate. Instead of proving "fundamental," structure turns out to be composed of externally derived rules of the sort that husbands are often said to impose on wives, a charge that the subsequent Mrs. Lydgate, née Rosamond Vincy, bitterly, and somewhat unjustly, directs at her husband. The much-vaunted structure is an abstraction, not an essence; and the limits of structure correspond to the limits of anatomy per se—anatomy abstracted from the physiology that conditions it.

Even as George Eliot, at least in the guise of her narrator, extends the range of the living organism in *Middlemarch* from the individual to society at large ("Middlemarch, in fact, counted on swallowing Lydgate and assimilating him very comfortably"), she remains an anatomist at heart. This is aptly demonstrated in her appropriation of Lydgate's microscope, "which research had begun to use again with new enthusiasm of reliance," for her own figurative purposes (pp. 183, 178). Having imagined the failure of "a careful *telescopic* watch" to detect "any ingenious plot, any hide-and-seek course of action" which might be attributed to the local busybody, Mrs. Cadwallader (who always displays "the same unperturbed keenness of eye and the same high natural colour"), the narrator changes instrument:

> Even with a microscope directed on a water-drop we find ourselves making interpretations which turn out to be rather coarse; for whereas under a weak lens you may seem to see a creature exhibiting an active voracity into which other smaller creatures actively play as if they were so many animated tax-pennies, a stronger lens reveals to you certain tiniest hairlets which make vortices for these victims while the swallower waits passively at his receipt of custom. In this way, metaphorically speaking, a strong lens applied to Mrs. Cadwallader's match-making will show a play of minute causes producing what may be called thought and speech vortices to bring her the sort of food she needed.

Training this figurative microscope on the voracious Mrs. C. reveals, in Eliot's sublime phrasing, "a mind, active as phosphorus, biting everything that came near into the form that suited it" (pp. 83–84). It reveals, in other words, the mind of one anatomizer (Mrs. Cadwallader) as seen from the perspective of another (George Eliot). Inevitably, in *Middlemarch*, the individual mind is reduced to an anatomical feature by one stunning metaphor or another; at the same time, individual neuraesthetic experience proves to be a function of either genealogical or interpersonal relations (or some combination of these), and ultimately of that larger network, the Middlemarcher social body.

Eliot observes of Lydgate that his search for a "primitive tissue" was misguided, and that the material of which "the various organs—brain, heart, lungs, etc.—are compacted" turned out to be organized according to a very different principle than the "primary web, or tissue," he imagined as "the common basis" of an organism's multiform structures. Yet Eliot does not herself utter the word missed by Lydgate (*cell*), and she certainly does not describe the discontinuous cellular structure which "gained immediate acceptance for all organs except the nervous system" once the cell theory was articulated by Theodor Schwann in the late 1830s (Shepherd, p. 4). Eliot's silence in *Middlemarch* is no doubt justified, given her penchant for historical accuracy; any mention of cellular structure in the novel would have been anachronistic. All the same, the conceptual scheme that enabled her so graphically to distinguish anatomy (including mind) from neuraesthetic experience (typically figured in terms of heart and will) was premised on a fundamental uncertainty in cell theory in the mid-nineteenth century regarding the cellular organization of the nervous system. As Gordon Shepherd remarks, "two basic problems were encountered" in determining the nervous structure:

> One was the difficulty, with the microscopical methods then available, to determine whether all nerve fibres arise directly from nerve cells, or whether some might exist independently of the cells. The other problem was that it could not be seen whether the long and thin branches arising from nerve cells and nerve fibres have definite terminations, or whether they run together with neighboring thin branches to form a continuous network. A great deal was at stake in this controversy, not only the cellular basis of nervous organization but also whether that basis differed fundamentally from the way all other organs of the body were constructed.

These "difficulties in establishing the relations between nerve cells, nerve fibres, and terminal branches delayed the application of the cell theory to the nervous system for half a century," a delay that enabled Eliot to continue to imagine nervous organization on the model, or metaphor, of tissue (and even to extend the "continuous diffuse networks" of the nervous system beyond the anatomical boundaries of individual bodies) even as she modeled the minds and bodies of her characters anatomically in accordance with post-1839 cell theory, with cells functioning as the atoms of the body (Shepherd, p. 4).

I have already suggested that the distinctively modern spirit of the last couple of centuries is characterized by a perspective at once anatomical and neuraesthetic. Alongside various reductive stances (mechanistic-materialist and vitalist-spiritualist), others have emerged that enable one to conceive of anatomical features, on the one hand, and neuraesthetic experience, on the other, as forming, in Stein's phrasing, "not a contradiction but a combination" (LIA, p. 93). Necessarily tied conceptually to the neuroscience of the day, although sometimes, as in the poetry of Wordsworth and Shelley, foreshadowing the neuroscience of a later era, these stances organize neuraesthetic experience in at least partly anatomical terms, without, however, reducing neuraesthesis to anatomy. Hence the significance of the heart and sense of touch in Sterne; of sight- and sound-based synesthesia in Wordsworth and Shelley; of pulsations in Pater, and connective tissue in Eliot; and, as I shall argue, of the neuron doctrine in Stein. In addition, stances tied to outdated neuroscience continue to thrive long after the scientific basis has been revised away, as in Moers's division between the "fatedness" of anatomy, its fixed nature, and the neuraesthetic "sound inside" which translates so readily into the "many voices of different rhythms, pitches, and timbres." This distinction may have had some scientific basis in Eliot's day, but it can only be read metaphorically today.

How, then, did Stein move from a sense of individual self-division like that expressed in *The Mill on the Floss* and *Middlemarch* (a self-division framed by Eliot in terms of a *social* organicism, that is, a social *organism* in which neuraesthesis and anatomy combine without contradiction) to the autopoietic perspective that informs the experimental writing of Stein's middle period? Or, to rephrase the question somewhat: How did compositions like *Tender Buttons* and "Old and Old" emerge from the same hand that penned "Melanctha" just seven years earlier, a work that at once allegorizes and literalizes the antinomy experienced by Maggie Tulliver between anatomy and neuraesthesis? Maggie, who "direct[s] her walk to the Red Deeps . . . on the first day she [is] free to wander at her will—a pleasure she loved so well, that sometimes, in her ardours of renunciation, she thought she ought to deny herself the frequent indulgence in it"; Melanctha, who, initially "wander[ing] on the edge of wisdom," "come[s] to see very clear . . . what it is that gives the world its wisdom" and begins to "wander very widely," wanting "something that would move her very deeply, something that would fill her fully with the wisdom that was planted now within her, and that she wanted badly, should really wholly fill her" (*Mill on the Floss*, p. 275; TL, pp. 70, 73, 76). In Stein's more radically experimental writing, neuraesthetic experience (the "expanded interval" of Pater's "individual in his isolation") continues to be viewed as a function of anatomy; yet instead of anatomy proving to be fate, so much food for the cemetery, it is reconceived as a function, in its own turn, of physiological processes, and hence of life. At the close of the nineteenth century and the beginning of the twentieth, Johns Hopkins neuroanatomy offered the young writer-to-be a vigorous new scientific account of this Wordsworthian sense of anatomy as a function of physiology (as, in effect, a function of biological functioning), an account nonetheless at odds with the biases built into the very instruments being used to investigate it.

THE NEW BIOLOGY

In 1924, Mina Loy compared Stein to Marie Curie in the verse epigraph that headed her ten-page missive to *the transatlantic review* on the subject of Stein and modern letters:

> Curie
> of the laboratory
> of vocabulary
> she crushed
> the tonnage
> of consciousness
> congealed to phrases
> to extract
> a radium of the word (p. 305)

Hence Stein as chemist. More often, Stein's writing has been likened to the New Physics, a connection she herself made "on the inside cover of a notebook for 'Sentences' (1929)," where, according to Ulla Dydo, she "played with two words—two names—or perhaps it is one: 'Caesar Onestone / Mr. Einesteine.'" "No time, no space, no center, standard, or authority," Dydo remarks. "Stein wrote in a world changed by Einstein and even more by Heisenberg and Schrödinger. She knew she was one of them, constructing for words what they had constructed for quantum mechanics." Dorothy Dudley Harvey, writing to Stein in 1928, compared her to the new physicists described by Bertrand Russell. "Nowadays," Russell suggested in the *Saturday Review of Literature*, "physicists, the most hard-headed of mankind . . .

have embodied in their technique this insubstantiality which some of the metaphysicians have so long urged in vain." "In connection with grammar," Harvey proposed, "I thought at once of you, and wondered, knowing little about them, if you have not been one of the metaphysicians as an artist, with whom the physicists have just caught up" (SR, pp. 2–3). Hence Stein as physicist.

Yet correspondences like these are only persuasive to the extent that the sciences in question posit a world that operates in terms of organicist principles—on the basis, that is, of what Whitehead called "organic mechanisms." Jacques Loeb (who taught the physiology seminar at Woods Hole the summer Stein attended the embryology seminar) may have sought to reduce biology to the mechanical operations of classical physics, but several decades later Whitehead would provide the New Physics with a theoretical basis in organicist, and hence biological, processes. A broad distinction may nonetheless be drawn between the biological and the physical (that is, physics-derived) sciences on the basis of the relative adequacy of mechanical or computational explanations to account for purely physical phenomena by contrast with biological phenomena. Donna Haraway and Evelyn Fox Keller have argued that biology in the twentieth century has itself alternated between frameworks that subordinate it to physics and others that represent it as an area of study (and, by extension, a domain of reality) distinct from although not entirely divorced from physics. Haraway thus demonstrates in *Crystals, Fabrics, and Fields* that in the 1930s, while Stein was lecturing on "lively words" and being subjected to textbook diagnoses by psychologist and physician alike, developmental biologists like Ross Harrison, Joseph Needham, and Paul Weiss were conducting embryological and morphogenetic studies on the basis of a model of "nonvitalist organicism" irreducible to the inorganic mechanisms of physical science. (This model was derived in large part from the "philosophy of organism" articulated by Whitehead the previous decade.) More recently, in *Refiguring Life*, Keller has described the rise in the aftermath of World War II of a reductionist frame of analysis within biology, and in particular in molecular biology, as well as subsequent challenges to this genetics-centered perspective that have accompanied a renewed interest in developmental biology. Even so, important recent studies of the influence of scientific doctrine on modern literature by Gillian Beer (*Open Fields: Science in Cultural Encounter*), Daniel Albright (*Quantum Poetics: Yeats, Pound, Eliot, and the Science of Modernism*), and Ira Livingston (*Arrow of Chaos: Romanticism and Postmodernity*) concur, despite great differences among them, in mapping modern literature along coordinates derived chiefly from the New Physics, whether in terms of late nineteenth-century wave theory, or the quantum theory contemporaneous with Stein, or the physics-inflected chaos theory of our own day. In this context Stein's extensive exposure to the New Biology offers an invaluable opportunity to consider the influence on literature of modern *biological* theory, with its distinctive experimental praxis, as well as the related question of the extent to which literature may be regarded as an appropriate, and perhaps inevitable, domain for physiologically based scientific experimentation.

Stein moved from Radcliffe to Johns Hopkins in order to acquire the hands-on physiological training that James deemed necessary for further study in psychology.[19] At Johns Hopkins she was soon working in the Anatomical Laboratory with the great anatomist and embryologist Franklin Mall. "She delighted in Doctor Mall, professor of anatomy, who directed her work," she recalled thirty-five years later, and "always quotes his answer to any student excusing him or herself for anything. He would look reflective and say, yes that is just like our cook. There is always a reason. She never brings the food to the table hot. In summer of course she can't because it is too hot, in winter of course she can't because it is too cold, yes there is always a reason." Mall also "believed in everybody developing their own technique . . . [and] remarked, nobody teaches anybody anything, at first every student's scalpel is dull and then later every student's scalpel is sharp, and nobody has taught anybody anything" (ABT, p. 81).

The Medical School, which had opened its doors only four years earlier when several Baltimore women contributed half a million dollars on the condition that women be admitted on equal terms with men, was already, as one historian of experimental medicine has put it, "the model institution for new medical science and medical teaching in the United States" (Pickstone, p. 738).[20] In conjunction with "purely mechanical" brain modeling for Mall, Stein also studied the histology of the central nervous system with Mall's assistant, Lewellys Barker.[21] In his influential textbook on *The Nervous System and Its Constituent Neurones*, published in 1899, Barker cited a description by Stein of the appropriately named nucleus of Darkschewitsch, an obscure collection of nerve cells situated near the top of the midbrain (see Figures 2 and 3; also see Figure 8 below).[22]

Just above the oculomotor nucleus, the nucleus of Darkschewitsch serves as one of three accessory oculomotor nuclei, along with the interstitial nucleus of Cajal and the nucleus of the posterior commissure.[23] (The oculomotor nucleus derives its name from its key role in eye movement, as well as in covert changes in visual attention, and it appears that the nucleus of Darkschewitsch, like the other accessory nuclei, has a related function,

MIDBRAIN: UPPER LEVEL.

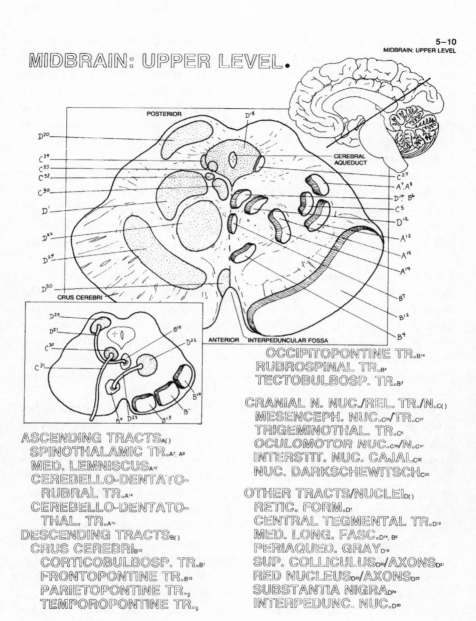

OCCIPITOPONTINE TR.B14
RUBROSPINAL TR.B4
TECTOBULBOSP. TR.B7

CRANIAL N. NUC./REL. TR./N.C( )
MESENCEPH. NUC.C29/TR.C27
TRIGEMINOTHAL. TR.C5
OCULOMOTOR NUC.C30/N.C31
INTERSTIT. NUC. CAJAL C32
NUC. DARKSCHEWITSCH C33

OTHER TRACTS/NUCLEI D( )
RETIC. FORM.D1
CENTRAL TEGMENTAL TR.D12
MED. LONG. FASC.D14, B6
PERIAQUED. GRAY D18
SUP. COLLICULUS D20/AXONS D21
RED NUCLEUS D22/AXONS D23
SUBSTANTIA NIGRA D24
INTERPEDUNC. NUC.D30

ASCENDING TRACTS A( )
SPINOTHALAMIC TR.A7, A6
MED. LEMNISCUS A12
CEREBELLO-DENTATO-
RUBRAL TR.A14
CEREBELLO-DENTATO-
THAL. TR.A15
DESCENDING TRACTS B( )
CRUS CEREBRI B12
CORTICOBULBOSP. TR.B1
FRONTOPONTINE TR.B13
PARIETOPONTINE TR.g
TEMPOROPONTINE TR.g

Figure 2. Midbrain, upper level, with nucleus of Darkschewitsch indicated ("c33"). (From Diamond, Scheibel, and Elson, *The Human Brain Coloring Book*, Plate 5-10. © 1985 Coloring Concepts, Inc. Reprinted by permission of Harper-Collins Publishers, Inc.)

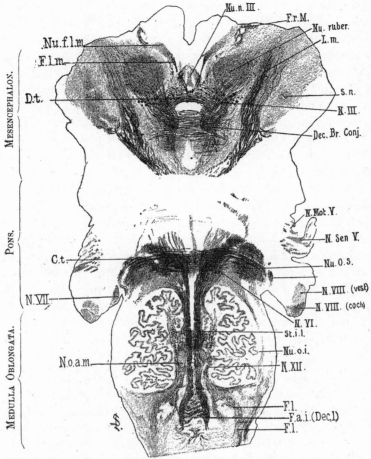

Fig. 462.—Horizontal section through the medulla, pons, and midbrain of new-born babe. Level of stratum interolivare lemnisci, corpus trapezoideum and nucleus ruber. Weigert-Pal staining. (Series iii, section No. 136.) *C.t.*, corpus trapezoideum; *Dec.Br.Conj.*, decussatio brachii conjunctivi; *D.t.*, decussatio tegmenti ventralis (ventral tegmental decussation of Forel); *F.a.i.(Dec.l.)*, fibræ arcuatæ internæ (decussatio lemniscorum); *F.l.*, fibres continuous with the funiculus lateralis of the spinal cord; *F.l.m.*, fasciculus longitudinalis medialis; *F.r.M.*, fasciculus retroflexus Meynerti; *L.m.*, lemniscus medialis; *N.III.*, radix N. oculomotorii; *N.Mot.V.*, motor root of N. trigeminus; *N.Sen.V.*, sensory root of N. trigeminus; *N.VIII.(coch.)*. radix N. cochleæ; *N.VIII.(vest.)*, radix N. vestibuli; *N.VI.*, radix N. abducentis; *N.VII.*, radix N. facialis, pars secunda; *N.XII.*, radix N. hypoglossi; *Nu.f.l.m.*, nucleus fasciculi longitudinalis medialis, or nucleus commissuræ posterioris (*oberer Oculomotoriuskern* of Darkschewitsch); *Nu.n.III.*, nucleus N. oculomotorii; *Nu.o.a.m.*, nucleus olivaris accessorius medialis; *Nu.o.i.*, nucleus olivaris inferior; *Nu.o.s.*, nucleus olivaris superior; *Nu.ruber*, nucleus ruber; *St.i.l.*, stratum interolivare lemnisci; *S.n.*, substantia nigra. (Preparation by Dr. John Hewetson.)

Figure 3. Horizontal section through the medulla, pons and midbrain, with nucleus of Darkschewitsch indicated ("Nu.f.l.m."). (From Barker, *The Nervous System and Its Constituent Neurones*, p. 723.)

although there is still considerable uncertainty as to its precise function.) "Peculiarly puzzling," Barker observed, are "the relations of the fasciculus longitudinalis medialis at its anterior extremity. . . . One has only to read the descriptions in the various text-books and in the original articles dealing with this topic to appreciate the confusion which exists with regard to it." "Especially conflicting," he added, "are the views which have been held concerning the relations to the nucleus of Darkschewitsch," which is adjacent to the fibers of origin and termination of the medial longitudinal fasciculus. "I shall restrict myself, therefore, in the main, to a mere statement of the results of my own studies, and of those of Miss Sabin and Miss Stein, who have especially studied this region" (p. 721).[24]

Definitions of several terms of direction should prove helpful in following Stein's description: "The back of the brain and spinal cord is *posterior*. In the case of the brain stem and spinal cord (as well as the body in general), the term *dorsal* is used synonymously with *posterior*. . . . The front of the brain and spinal cord is *anterior* . . . [and] the term *ventral* is used synonymously." In addition, "when comparing two structures, the structure closer to the midline is said to be *medial* to the other, which is *lateral*," whereas "the terms *proximal* and *distal* refer to relative distances from a reference point, proximal being closer and distal being farther" (Diamond, Plate 1–5). Here, then, is the passage from *The Nervous System and Its Constituent Neurones*:

> Miss Gertrude Stein, who is now studying a series of sagittal sections through this region from the brain of a babe a few weeks old, describes the nucleus of Darkschewitsch as follows: "The nucleus is more or less conical in shape. It lies dorso-medial from the red nucleus, being about as thick in a dorso-ventrical direction as is the dorsal capsule of the red nucleus in which it lies. At this period of medullation [or *myelinization* as the process is more commonly known—the layering around axons of the fatty substance myelin, which serves to increase the rate at which impulses travel] the commissura posterior cerebri, considered simply topographically (that is, as a medullated fibre-mass without particular reference to the course of the fibres), appears as a dorso-ventral bundle, solid in the middle, subdivided dorsally into an anterior (proximal) portion and a posterior (distal) portion, while ventrally it expands in the form of a hollow pyramid, which rests directly upon the nucleus of Darkschewitsch." As to the bundle of fibres described above as being situated ventral to the nucleus, and passing forward and ventralward, Miss Stein in the brain she is studying can follow the fibres only as far as the fasciculus retroflexus. (pp. 725–26)[25]

Forty years later in his autobiography, Barker recalled Stein as having been among the first batch of medical students to whom he taught "modern neurological histology," or the neuroanatomical structure of animal and plant tissue, and acknowledged that he had "often wondered whether my attempts to teach her the intricacies of the medulla oblongata had anything to do with the development of the strange literary forms with which she was later to perplex the world" (*Time and the Physician*, p. 60).

At the outset of *The Principles of Psychology*, James had provided a summary of the "nerve-physiology" with which his reader needed to be acquainted in order to follow the work's general argument concerning the physiological basis of psychology. The principal difference between James's understanding of neurophysiology at the beginning of the decade and the instruction Stein received first at Radcliffe and then at Johns Hopkins, as the decade wore on, stems from the articulation in 1891 of what has come to be known as "the neuron doctrine," which amounts to the claim, as Shepherd has characterized it, that "the nerve cell is the anatomical, physiological, metabolic, and genetic unit of the nervous system" (p. 4).[26] The difference that this assertion makes can be summed up as follows: Before 1891 it was intellectually respectable for a neuroanatomist to argue for the reticular theory of neural organization, that is, for the existence of a continuous network of branches connecting nerve cells. After 1891, it was widely recognized that nerve cells, like all other types of cells, are discontinuous from one another. As Barker put it in *The Nervous System and Its Constituent Neurones*, a work in which, as he subsequently observed, "for the first time, the conduction paths of the central and peripheral nervous system were comprehensively and systematically described from the standpoint of the neurone doctrine": Nerve branches "often enter into close proximity to other nerve cells . . . but nowhere could any evidence . . . be found of actual union." "The interrelations of the nerve elements," he concluded, depend "entirely upon contact or contiguity, not upon organic connection" (*Time and the Physician*, p. 61; NS, p. 22).

Furthermore, in 1897, the year Stein entered medical school, the English neurophysiologist Charles Sherrington introduced the concept of the synapse as "an anatomical and functional explanation for the mechanism by which the individual neuronal units could communicate with each other" (Shepherd, p. 5). Hence Stein, in her first two years at Johns Hopkins, much of the time spent conducting laboratory research, found herself in the midst of a paradigm shift if ever there was one. The crucial thing to note here is that in taking neurons, as described by the neuron doctrine, as paradigmatic of organic life (and thereby presuming that nerve cells, like other cells, don't form "actual unions," or organic unities, but are only exceptional in that they "do something very different from other cells of the body," namely, they "process information"), it becomes necessary to reconceive organicism as a function of contact or contiguity, rather than of organic connection (Shepherd, p. 292). It was this perspective that Stein brought to her experimental writing, although it didn't come fully into play until a decade after she left medical school, when she began writing her "studies in description." Here is "A Long Dress," from the "Objects" section of *Tender Buttons*:

> What is the current that makes machinery, that makes it crackle, what is the current that presents a long line and a necessary waist. What is this current.
> What is the wind, what is it.
> Where is the serene length, it is there and a dark place is not a dark place, only a white and red are black, only a yellow and green are blue, a pink is scarlet, a bow is every color. A line distinguishes it. A line just distinguishes it. (TB, p. 17)

Writing like this might be characterized, in properly radical empiricist fashion, as *studies of exchanges at word junctions and across word membranes*, designed *to show the ways in which words join together into functional multi-word units*.

In describing "A Long Dress" in this way, as a collection of words that functions after the manner of a collection of neurons in the brain, I have actually appropriated Jane Maienschein's characterization of biological research of the last half-century on cellular organization, merely substituting the term *word* for *cell*. "The most serious weakness of the cell theory," Maienschein writes,

> is its inability in itself to explain cell-to-cell interaction or [the] organisation of many cells. . . . Especially since the Second World War[,] . . . studies of exchanges at cell junctions and across cell membranes have begun to show the ways in which cells join together into functional multi-cellular units. ("Cell Theory," p. 370)

However, I could just as well have cited Stein directly, in remarks concerning the composition of *Tender Buttons* which she made in an interview shortly before her death in 1946. "I took individual words," she noted,

> and thought about them until I got their weight and volume complete and put them next to another word, and at this same time I found out very soon that there is no such thing as putting them together without sense. I made innumerable efforts to make words write without sense and found it impossible. Any human being putting down words had to make sense out of them. (TI, p. 18)

Half a century earlier, in *The Principles of Psychology*, James had already observed that "*subjectively*, any collocation of words may make sense—even the wildest words in a dream—if one only does not doubt their belonging together." Yet Stein is not concerned here with the "feeling of rationality" that one may experience while writing (or reading) what is, objectively speaking, sheer nonsense. Because she isn't seeking rational or "abstract" knowledge in the first place, she doesn't *fail* to abstract her thought processes from her compositional practices, as occurs with rational-seeming nonsense like James's example of a 784-page "volume . . . lately published in Boston" entitled "*Substantialism; Or, Philosophy of Knowledge*, by 'Jean Story.' "

This work, James observes, is entirely "composed of stuff like this passage picked out at random":

> The flow of the efferent fluids of all these vessels from their outlets at the terminal loop of each culminate link on the surface of the nuclear organism is continuous as their respective atmospheric fruitage up to the altitudinal limit of their expansibility, whence, when atmosphered by like but coalescing essences from higher altitudes,—those sensibly expressed as the essential qualities of external forms,—they descend and become assimilated by the afferents of the nuclear organism.

"Take the obscurer passages in Hegel," James continues, "it is a fair question whether the rationality included in them be anything more than the fact that the words all belong to a common vocabulary, and are strung together on a scheme of predication and relation,—immediacy, self-relation, and what not,—which has habitually recurred." Even so, he adds, "there seems no reason to doubt that the subjective feeling of the rationality of these sentences was strong in the writer as he penned them, or even that some readers by straining may have reproduced it in themselves" (PR, pp. 254–55).[27] By contrast, Stein is thinking autopoietically, and neuraesthetically, in the course of "thinking about" the relations that emerge when the words are "join[ed] together in functional multi-word units." Hence in compositions like "A Long Dress," as she observed in 1928, she "correlated sight, sound and sense," attempting, as she was already proposing four years earlier, to achieve "completed composition . . . through the study of the relation of words in meaning sound and volume."[28] This sense of the *volume* of words, reiterated more than twenty years later, suggests that she conceived of words, like cells, as existing in three-dimensional space rather than two-dimensionally on the page or the microscope slide.

Stein's writing practice may thus be viewed as a form of laboratory science, descending, by way of the psychological and anatomical laboratories at Harvard and Johns Hopkins, from the medical laboratory described several decades earlier by Claude Bernard in his *Introduction to the Study of Experimental Medicine*. In *her* laboratory she experimented with words in an attempt to articulate her sense of their life. For Bernard, the intellectual rigor of physiology treated "as an experimental subject" was based on the possibility of controlled experiments in which "the animal suffers all but the single interference in question, so allowing the experimenter to separate the specific effect from others which the whole procedure may involve." Through "the careful regulation of experimental procedure," the phenomenon in question might "be controlled at will," although such control required both a "determinism of physiological phenomena, in the sense that experimentalists could produce and reproduce them in specified ways," and the relative freedom of these phenomena from external constraints. Bernard accounted for this last feature with his notion of the *milieu intérieur*, or internal milieu, whereby "the constancy of bodily fluids in higher animals" served as a "precondition of their sophisticated functions and their relative independence of external factors such as temperature" (Pickstone, p. 735). Stein, in characterizing her experimental writing in *Tender Buttons* as involving a "conscious struggle with the problem of correlating sight, sound and sense, and eliminating rhythm," and further proposing that "some of the solutions . . . seem to me still alright," clearly regarded her writing as consonant with Bernard's model (TBr, p. 13).

"The role of the [experimental] scientist," Sally Shuttleworth has observed, "was not simply to record and observe, but actively to construct experiments, to bring about, as Bernard observed, 'the appearance of phenomena which doubtless always occur according to natural laws, but in conditions which nature has often not yet achieved'" (p. 22; cited from Bernard, p. 18). The question, of course, is the extent to which Stein's literary experiments are *controlled* in the sense that other experimentalists might "produce or reproduce them in specified ways." Would such reproduction require original experimental writing, or might analysis of Stein's writing in terms of the constraints she set herself, and "the specific effects" she produced, suffice? What about reading in the manner attributed to Toklas in the *Autobiography*? "I always say," one reads / Toklas says / Stein writes, "that you cannot tell what a picture really is or what an object really is until you dust it every day and you cannot tell what a book is until you type it or proof-read it. It then does something to you that only reading never can do." Again: "Correcting proofs is, as I said before, like dusting, you learn the values of the thing as no reading suffices to teach it to you" (pp. 113, 217). In typing or proofreading, the reader experiences a composition as it has already been experienced by the writer, acquiring a sense of it as an "object," with "weight and volume." The dissociative writing of Stein's middle period differs from ordinary writing (and even from *The Making of Americans*, the immediate subject of these remarks on correcting proof and typing manuscripts) in that works like "A Long Dress" and "Old and Old" and "Mildred's Thoughts" render conventional reading practices self-evidently inadequate to the task at hand. To prevent one's experience of reading from "dwindl[ing] into [the] inaudible hum" which seems to have been Morris Fishbein's experience, certainly not Stein's, the reader is obliged to reproduce the recursive act of reading which, in line with the parameters under investigation, was part and parcel of the original process of writing. Such *experimental reading*, as it were, is not a matter of reductively decoding Stein's writing word for word or phrase for phrase but of neuraesthetically reproducing her "stud[ies] of the relation of words in meaning sound and volume" in ways specified by the compositions themselves. That only some of Stein's experiments may have succeeded ("*some* of the solutions seem to me still alright") does not make them any less scientific; after all, every successful experiment leaves behind it a trail of false turns. "Experimenting," as Stein observed in one of the lectures she gave in Chicago several months after Fishbein's "editorial suggestion," is "trying to do some thing in a way that may produce a result which is a desired result by the person doing it" (N, p. 31). By the same token, in failing to conform to the desired result, the outcome may oblige one to reformulate one's objectives. An apparent failure turns out to have the makings (supposing one to be broadminded enough, and sufficiently radical an empiricist) of a desired solution, at least at the level of the experiment's parameters if not within the framework delineated by them.

DELIBERATE ERROR

A particularly ignominious failure capped Stein's association with Johns Hopkins, when the faculty decided not to award her a degree despite four years of courses and, as she put it, a "reputation for original scientific work" (ABT, p. 82). Even before Barker's departure for the University of Chicago at the end of the third year, her coursework had begun to slide. The first two years' grades ranged, on a scale of 1 (best) to 4 or lower (failure), from a 1 in anatomy to a 2.5 in physiological chemistry, with a pair of 1.5's in normal histology and in pathology and bacteriology, as well as 2's in physiology and in pharmacology and toxicology. In her third year, by contrast, they dropped almost a full point to a 2 in medicine, a 2.5 in surgery, and three 3's, in clinical microscopy, neurology and obstetrics. Then, her last year, dedicated to clinical practice, they slipped another point, with out-right failures in four areas—5's in obstetrics and in laryngology and rhinol-ogy, 4's in dermatology and in ophthalmology and otology—as well as a 2 in gynecology, a pair of 2.5's in psychiatry and surgery, and a 3 in medicine.[29] As Dorothy Reed Mendenhall, an acquaintance of Stein at Johns Hopkins and the aunt of Edmund Wilson, told her nephew: "At medicine [by con-trast with experimental study], she worked only in a half-hearted way," and consequently "her grades were always poor" (*Upstate*, p. 63).[30] Stein had not gone to medical school to become a clinician, and she wasn't about to become one.

"The last two years at the medical school," Stein herself noted in *The Autobiography of Alice B. Toklas*, "she was bored, frankly openly bored" (p. 81). The professors "would ask her questions from time to time and as she said, what could she do, she did not know the answers and they did not believe that she did not know them, they thought that she did not answer because she did not consider the professors worth answering. It was a diffi-cult situation. . . . It was impossible to apologise and explain to them that she was so bored she could not remember the things that of course the dullest medical student could not forget." As a result, one of these "big men" determined that "she should be given a lesson": "He refused to give her a pass mark and so she was not able to take her degree" (p. 82). Ac-cording to Mendenhall, this was Stein's professor of obstetrics, John Whit-ridge Williams, "an aristocrat and a snob," who "couldn't stand her marked Hebrew looks, her sloppy work, and her intolerance—so he flunked her" (*Upstate*, p. 63). In the *Autobiography*, Stein added that Williams later "asked her to come to see him. She did. He said, of course Miss Stein all you have to do is to take a summer course here and in the fall naturally you will take your degree." "You have no idea how grateful I am to you," she re-sponded, "I have so much inertia and so little initiative that very possibly if you had not kept me from taking my degree I would have, well, not taken to the practice of medicine, but at any rate to pathological psychology and you don't know how little I like pathological psychology, and how all med-icine bores me" (pp. 82–83).

In all likelihood, this exchange represents what in 1932 Stein believed she should have said to Williams thirty years before. Yet, according to Mendenhall, she actually was given another opportunity to graduate, and made an effort (perhaps not every effort) to comply. "Dr. Franklyn [sic] Mall, professor of Anatomy, felt that she should have another chance," Menden-hall informed Elizabeth Sprigge, author of an early biography of Stein. "So he told her that if she would make a model of an embryo human brain, which he gave her from his own collection, he would see if he could make the medical faculty change their mind" (p. 40). As Mendenhall remarked to Wilson,

> Dr. Mall set her a problem similar to one Dr. Sabin had completed successfully in her fourth year. This was the sectioning of an embryo human brain and its reconstruction, and a study of the development of the centers in the brain and the tracts leading from them. She worked on it for weeks and finally handed her reconstruction to Dr. Mall in the hope that it would be credited to her instead of obstetrics and allow her to graduate. Some days after, Dr. Mall—the greatest living anatomist at the time—came to Dr. Sabin and said, "Either I am crazy or Miss Stein is. Will you see what you can make out of her work?" (p. 63)

To Sprigge, Mendenhall gave the following account of what ensued, which she had directly from her "intimate friend . . . Dr. Florence Sabin":

> Dr. Mall brought the model in to [Sabin] one morning and said that it was beyond him to see what Miss Stein had done. Dr. Sabin, the best woman ever graduated at J. H. Medical and afterwards head of one of the Rockefeller Institute departments, spent hours working over the model and finally decided that Gertrude had bent the spinal cord under the head of the embryo so that every section contained cells of the cerebral cortex and of the cord, so that the reconstruction was fantastic. Dr. Mall listened to the explanation of what Dr. Sabin *thought* had happened and chucked the entire model into the waste basket. (p. 40)[31]

So much for Stein's degree.

Besides judging Stein's work, Florence Sabin also set the standard against which it was judged. Classmate of Dorothy Mendenhall and a year ahead of Stein at Johns Hopkins, she "has been hailed as the outstanding woman scientist in the medical field in the first half of this century" (Farnes, p. 274).[32] In the authoritative biography of Franklin Mall that she brought out in 1934, Sabin observed that "the course in neurology, given in his laboratory, was for many years the most extensive one on this subject given in America" and "formed the basis of the book on the Nervous System, published in 1899 by Dr. Barker," who was the course director at the time. Mall, having "realiz[ed] that the structure of the brain stem was obscure," asked "one of the students [to] make a model of the tracts of the brain stem as far as they were medullated at birth." Sabin neglects to identify the student, who was of course herself, although she does add that the model continued to be used in the course "until newer work in comparative anatomy, that is, the study of the determination of the function of each tract as it developed in lower forms [of animal life,] provided a simpler and better basis for an understanding of the nervous system" (pp. 166–67).

Already in a review of Barker's textbook in the December 1899 issue of the *Johns Hopkins Medical Bulletin*, attention was being drawn to Sabin's contribution:

> All through the book references are made to Miss Sabin's reconstructions of tracts and nuclei. This is a recent and valuable mode of studying the central nervous system, and Miss Sabin has been one of the most active workers in this field. We have an excellent proof of the value of this work in the picture of the lower olive given on page 958. A picture like this conveys a better idea of the convolutions of this body than can be obtained from a study of microscopical sections. This reconstruction demands time and care, and we read therefore with some surprise the numerous references to the extensive work Miss Sabin has accomplished. (p. 235)

The next year, Sabin's "Model of the Medulla, Pons and Midbrain of a New Born Babe" would be included in volume 9 of the *Johns Hopkins Hospital Reports*, followed soon after by its independent publication, with very slight modifications, as the *Atlas of the Medulla and Midbrain*.[33] In fact, the plate mentioned in the *Johns Hopkins Medical Bulletin* is reproduced in both versions of Sabin's atlas as well as in Barker's textbook (see Figure 4). This plate illustrates an elongated structure on the surface of the medulla oblongata, called the lower olive or inferior olivary nucleus, because it "resembles olive-shaped rumpled sacs with partially pulled drawstrings" (Diamond et al., plate 5–6).

In 1947, the year following Stein's death, Sabin recalled that, even if "Gertrude did not seem to care a rap, . . . we women felt pretty badly" about her failure to graduate. "She said she would have had more respect for those who had passed her if they too had given her failing marks for she didn't know any more about those subjects than the ones in which she had actually failed. Also she said that she didn't care a rap about the degree." Even so, Sabin continued, "Dr. Mall, who liked independence, and thought [that Stein's] attitude of not caring for the degree showed a good spirit, welcomed her back" the following fall (Wineapple, pp. 149–50). That August, Mall was already informing Barker that, despite having "failed to graduate with us last June," Stein "comes up again next Feb. After that I will do all in my power to make her round out her work started with you." By October, he was confidently asserting that she would soon "be back and [would] devote the whole year to the brain. I will tell her what you said regarding her work & will urge her to go to Chicago. I know you would like to finish it!!" (Wineapple, p. 144). Several weeks later, Stein returned to Baltimore and resumed her research, not yet ready to give up on the elusive degree.

Lateral Surface.

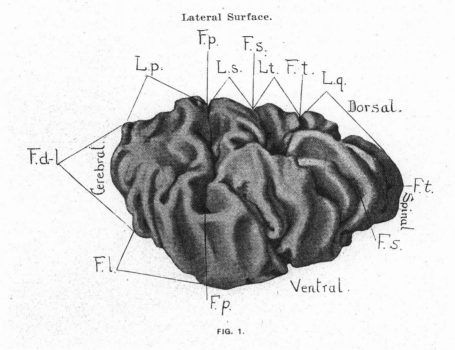

FIG. 1.

Ventral Surface.

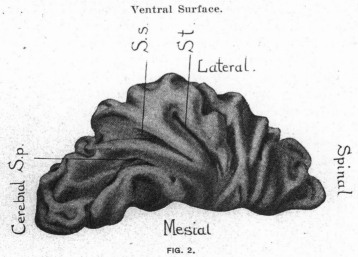

FIG. 2.

Figure 4. Inferior olive. (From Florence R. Sabin, *An Atlas of the Medulla and Midbrain: A Laboratory Manual*, Plate I.)

Recently, Brenda Wineapple has clarified Stein's aim in pursuing the degree. The previous year she had made arrangements to do postgraduate work with Adolph Meyer, at the time chief neuropathologist at the Massachusetts State Hospital for the Insane and subsequently professor of psychiatry at Johns Hopkins and director of the Henry Phipps Psychiatric Clinic there. "In conjunction with Clark University," over which William James's estranged student G. Stanley Hall had already presided for more than a decade, the Massachusetts State Hospital for the Insane served as "a training school for the study of nervous diseases" (p. 140). Meyer, who was active in the mental hygiene movement from its inception in 1908 (actually coining the phrase "mental hygiene" to designate the use of psychiatry and psychology in promoting mental health), treated psychiatric problems in light of the patient's total personality, under the general rubric of psychobiology. "I was not able to complete the work I had begun under Dr. Mall," Stein wrote him in mid-June, after she had failed to get her degree. "So I will have to remain in Baltimore another year. This will defer the work that I meant to do with you until the following year when I hope to be able to come to Worcester." As Wineapple observes, Stein's "implication was clear: in due course she would have her degree" (pp. 143–44). Exactly as Stein proposed thirty years later, she would then have gone on, if not "to the practice of medicine, . . . at any rate to pathological psychology."

By early November, with her fifth year at Johns Hopkins safely under way, Mall informed Barker that "Miss Stein is diligent[ly] at work with her model," adding that she needed "the brain of a child 6 months old . . . in order to connect her work with Miss Sabins." "Can you not supply it?" he inquired (Wineapple, p. 150). It remains unclear whether in these remarks Mall was referring to the model meant to "change [the faculty's] mind" concerning Stein's qualifications for the degree (although, according to Mendenhall, this model involved the sectioning of an *embryo* brain, not that of a six-month-old child), or whether, as seems more likely, she had undertaken to produce a second model in the course of research related to Sabin's work on "the tracts of the brain stem." In the former case, the model would have required sectioning an entire brain and "reconstruct[ing its] tracts and nuclei," presumably according to the procedures described by Sabin in her *Atlas*.[34] This model proved "fantastic," as Mendenhall reported, due to elementary errors in the preparation of the sectional series. The result was that Stein's second chance at a degree came to naught. The research "connect[ing her] work" with Sabin's investigations of the brain stem, however—the object of Mall's remark to Barker that he would "do all in my power to make her round out [the] work started with you," of which only the material on the nucleus of Darkschewitsch survives—had nothing to do with the medical degree.

A sequence of letters between Barker and Stein, and Barker and Henry Knower (instructor in anatomy at Johns Hopkins and editor of Sabin's *Atlas*), further illuminates the nature and extent of Stein's research.[35] In a letter dated January 30, 1902, Barker reported to Stein that he had only "gone through [the] second part" of a batch of material she had recently sent him, because he had "studied these sections more thoroughly than the other set," and was therefore "more familiar" with them. Presumably, the microscopical sections Stein was working with had been prepared at some earlier date, whether by her or, as is more likely, by some third party; even Sabin hadn't used her own sections but instead relied on serial sections "prepared by Dr. John Hewetson in the Anatomical Laboratory of the University of Leipzig" (*Atlas*, p. 13). In his letter, Barker continued:

> I do not think you have included too many drawings from section. It seems to me that these are necessary in order to give a clear idea to the reader. Do you think that one drawing of the model will suffice? Dr. Mall's advice on that point will be valuable.

He also referred to "photographs of the brains showing the planes of sections," which would be "of special value to any research worker who wishes to identify convolutions," and suggested bibliographical as well as stylistic improvements for a final draft. After noting that Stein was "soon to get off to Europe," he closed by inquiring whether she would "continue [to] work on the nervous system," remarking that "it would seem a pity not to, now that you have gone so far in this line of work and have so good a background" (FF, p. 24).

By this date, it had become clear to Stein (and no doubt to Barker as well) that she was not going to be awarded her degree. Despite having shelved her plans to work with Adolph Meyer, she still managed to submit an article detailing her research on the brain stem to the *American Journal of Anatomy*. Both Mall and Barker were on the editorial board of the year-old journal, and Knower served as its secretary, or managing editor. In a letter to Barker dated April 7, 1902, accompanying "some manuscript and sixty-three drawings from Miss Stein, . . . now presented for press, except for minor revision," Knower described himself, together with "Professor Mall [and] Dr. Sabin," as "unfavorably impressed with the paper." Still, they left the final decision concerning publication up to Barker. Because the study included roughly twenty-five pages of text as well as "seven pages more of line figures or sections, in addition to the half tone page," it was "expensive" to publish. Knower questioned the appropriateness of "print[ing] such data before they are sifted more and worked up into a new or better mental picture." By the time he made this remark, near the end of the letter, he had in fact assumed a fairly conciliatory tone, acknowledging, for instance, that "a good paper [could] be made of the elements here presented" and that "a serious thoughtful additional effort should produce new descriptions which would be well worth while." Yet, early on, he had been rather more critical, allowing that the paper struck him as

> unfinished, and lacking in constructive thought. The materials for building are corrected and ready for use but only here and there can one see a bit of new structure. I am disappointed to find the author's efforts discontinued just at the point where she seems to have completed preparations to begin the serious work of construction from the data before us.

"As a rule," he concluded, "it is difficult to relate the structures described[,] in the setting drawn for them."

In order to demonstrate this "unfinished" quality, Knower turned to Stein's data on "the medial Lemniscus," an important structure in the medulla oblongata which extends the pathway concerned with proprioceptive or kinesthetic phenomena (as well as with the experience of "well-localized and refined touch," so-called "epicritic" phenomena) from the spinal cord into the farther reaches of the brain. At the uppermost level of the medulla, this bundle of fibers is *medial*—that is to say, closer to the midline—with respect to the inferior olive, which Sabin had reconstructed to such effect (Diamond et al., sections 5–5 and 5–6). According to Knower, Stein "locates the fibers . . . in a number of sections which illustrate more or less satisfactorily their course, but when this is done very little new is added to our knowledge. We have no clearer conception of the bundle considered. It remain[s] for her to go further and give a clearer or fuller new account." Moreover, he noted, Stein's "incompletely reconstructed model . . . lack[s] in its median relations which seem so essential." (These are the relations neuroanatomical structures bear to the median plane, which divides the brain along its longitudinal axis into left and right halves.) Nor had an "adequate attempt" been made "to relate [the model's] structure to known landmarks," with the consequence that "the average reader" wouldn't be able "to make out what is represented or what she is driving at, without following her from section to section as has been done before by others" (cited in Schoenberg, pp. 254, 256).

Barker replied two days later. Although he didn't have time to undertake the "very careful study of the bibliography [as well as of the] drawings and descriptions, and possibly of the original preparations," warranted by such severe criticism, he remained "convinced of the great value of the material." Nonetheless, he did express surprise

> to learn from your letter that so much of it has already been published. I am certainly not familiar with publications which cover the embryological series. I should be glad to have references to them. The adult series seems to me to be inadequately represented in the sketches. It is a question in my mind whether such rough diagrams should be published when we have for the adult sample illustrations such as those of von Kolliker and von Monakow.

"Under the circumstances," Barker continued, he was "unwilling to pass the paper" without "more elaborate study"—he seems to have had no thought of rejection—and therefore proposed that Knower "leave" it with him, in order that he might "take it up as soon as I conscientiously can" (Schoenberg, pp. 256–57).

Remarkably, responses to this stalemate, penned by each of the three parties, have survived. "Thanks for your satisfactory letter as to Miss Stein's work," Knower replied a week after Barker had written him: "It seems best, as you say, that she wait until later. I feel sure that a fine paper can be made from the valuable material she has before her." However, in the same letter, dated April 15, Knower took issue with the "idea that I imply 'that so much of the work has been published before.'" He had not meant to suggest "that all, or much, has been published already," but simply "that Miss Stein does not succeed in bringing out the valuable results which evidently lie in the material." "In rereading the letter which I wrote you," Knower added, "I do not see that I have implied more than that she has dropped the subject before finishing the task, and writing it up in a thorough, well-considered manner. She has stopped too soon." Knower was so touchy, of course, because Barker *had* caught him out. In remarking that "very little *new* is added to our knowledge"; that "it remain[s] for her to go further and give a clearer or fuller *new* account"; that the data still needed to be "worked into a *new* or better picture"; that "a serious thoughtful additional effort should produce *new* descriptions which would be well worth while"; that "only here and there can one see a bit of *new* structure," Knower *had* implied that much of the material "had already been published." This insistence on the lack in Stein's paper of new (that is to say, unfamiliar, unpublished) material is a far cry from his suggestion to Barker, in the April 15 letter, that "it is impossible to *weed out the new from the old* or to *follow* the author into a satisfactory *new* conception." Knower professed himself no less "convinced of the great value of the material" than Barker was; it was just that Stein had failed to *bring out the valuable results which evidently lay in the material.* Evidently, Knower was determined not to give Stein any credit for her own work in rendering the value of the material self-evident.

Barker proved of another mind. A year and a half after the original exchange, he sent Mall the following note, presumably having given the paper the "more elaborate study" he had promised. It is dated October 23, 1903:

> Dear Dr. Mall:
>   I am sending you by express today Miss Stein's paper, which I think ought to be published as it is in the *Journal of Anatomy*. If however, on looking it over again, you should feel that it is not suitable for the *Journal of Anatomy*, will you please send it to the *Journal of Comparative Neurology*.
>
>   Yours sincerely,
>   LEWELLYS F. BARKER (cited by Schoenberg, p. 257)

Hence, before Stein's paper summarily vanished—this is the last record of it—Barker had given it a clear vote of confidence. In the meantime, however, its author had exchanged the life of a scientist for that of a creative writer, coincidentally completing her first significant work of fiction, *Quod Erat Demonstrandum (Q.E.D.)*, the very next day, October 24.

One might argue that the multiple failures Stein experienced at Johns Hopkins were due to constraints on creativity built into a genre of writing modeled on analytic geometry (that is, as a matter of "bringing out the valuable results which evidently lie in the material," *Q.E.D.*) and no less centrally built into the anatomical perspective itself. More exactly, it was Stein's resistance to these constraints that accounted for the failures, the same resistance that fueled her subsequent experimental writing. The letter she wrote to Barker in response to Knower's criticism suggests the solution that she ultimately arrived at concerning the delineation between *object of knowledge* and *increasingly knowledgeable investigator*, which lies at the heart of the anatomical perspective (see Figure 5). Although the letter is undated, Stein was clearly responding to a summary Barker had sent her of his remarks to Knower. Her "aim in writing this article," she observed, was "not so much to give new matter but to make confusion clear"—adding that she did not "feel that Dr. Knower is a good judge of this matter because he does not know the region and its confusion." To Barker's own concern as to whether "such rough diagrams should be published when we have for the adult sample illustrations such as those of von Kolliker and von Monakow," she replied: "My drawings are of course very much more diagrammatic than Von Kolliker's but it seems to me that they tell a clear story."

Early in the account of Stein's education in *The Autobiography of Alice*

B. Toklas, the reader is informed that Stein had "never been able" nor did she have "any desire to indulge in any of the arts. *She never knows how a thing is going to look until it is done*, in arranging a room, a garden, clothes or anything else. She cannot draw anything. She feels no relation between the object and the piece of paper." Hence at medical school, when "she was supposed to draw anatomical things she never found out in sketching *how a thing was made convex or concave*" (p. 76, emphasis added). Clearly this ignorance would pose difficulties in modeling neuroanatomical structures in three dimensions, as Sabin, for instance, had represented the convolutions of the inferior olive. It would pose difficulties, that is, if Stein had actually aimed to portray three-dimensional *objects*. In her letter to Barker, she suggests that this was not what she was after:

> The whole point of the adult series to me is not so much that there is very definite new material although there is some of that but that as far as I have been able I have endeavored to expres[s] a very clear image which exists in my own mind of a region which the existing literature of the subject leaves in a hopeless mess. My drawings are of course very much more diagrammatic than Von Kolliker's but . . . they clear away the underbrush and leave a clear road.

"I had so much difficulty," she explained, "in understanding the conditions that I felt such a clarifying process to be much needed. Not that the books do not tell the truth as I know it but that they tell so much more that one is confused. By my series of recapitulations and a pretty careful selection of sect[i]ons I felt that I had to a certain extent accomplished this." "Of course," she added, "of such a matter I am not the best judge." "My object," she reiterated, "has been to save the next man from a long p[re]lim[i]nary work."

The "very clear image" Stein possessed in her "own mind" was of the *region*, rather than of particular objects in it, a region which the "existing literature," presumably including Sabin's work, had left "in a hopeless mess" because the textbooks "t[old] so much more" than one needed in order to "understand the conditions" of the region as such. How, then, are we to judge Stein's dismissal of Knower as being unfit to judge her on the basis that "he does not know the region and its confusion"? Is this anything other than a brazenly presumptuous gesture on her part? Knower, after all, in his preface to Sabin's *Atlas*, had extolled that work for succeeding exactly where Stein's paper did not—as "a valuable and new remedy" for the "hazy ideas" students typically acquired of this "important central relay-station of the brain." In particular, he commended Max Broedel's "excellent drawings of [Sabin's] reconstruction" which "show[ed] for the first time accurately

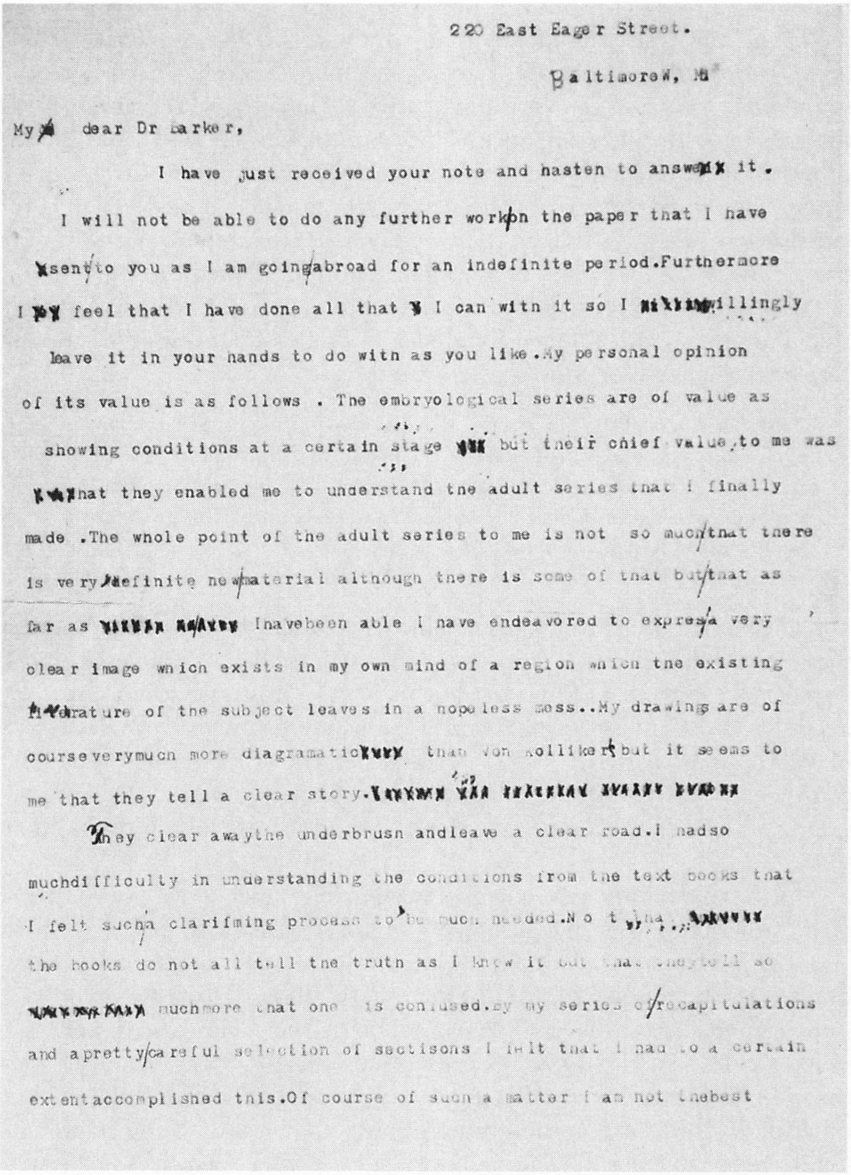

220 East Eager Street.

Baltimore, Md

My dear Dr Barker,

I have just received your note and hasten to answer it.

I will not be able to do any further work on the paper that I have sent to you as I am going abroad for an indefinite period. Furthermore I feel that I have done all that I can with it so I willingly leave it in your hands to do with as you like. My personal opinion of its value is as follows. The embryological series are of value as showing conditions at a certain stage but their chief value to me was that they enabled me to understand the adult series that I finally made. The whole point of the adult series to me is not so much that there is very definite new material although there is some of that but that as far as I have been able I have endeavored to express a very clear image which exists in my own mind of a region which the existing literature of the subject leaves in a hopeless mess.. My drawings are of course very much more diagramatic than von Kolliker but it seems to me that they tell a clear story.

They clear away the underbrush and leave a clear road. I had so much difficulty in understanding the conditions from the text books that I felt such a clarifying process to be much needed. Not that the books do not all tell the truth as I knew it but that they tell so much more that one is confused. By my series of recapitulations and a pretty careful selection of sections I felt that I had to a certain extent accomplished this. Of course of such a matter I am not the best

Figure 5. Letter from Stein to Lewellys Barker, 1902. (Photograph courtesy of The Alan Mason Chesney Medical Archives of the Johns Hopkins Medical Institutions.)

judge but my aim in writingthis article has been not so ~~much~~ much
to give the matter but to make confusion clear.I do not feel thatDr.anower
i/a good judge of this matter because he does not know the region and its
confusion.My object has been to save the next man from a longp
~~x~~ perlimanrywork.§§

As I have said I will not have the time nor do I feel that I can
makemany changes.I have done with it all that I can and the rest
must remain with you.Ido not expect to do any neuroliogical work for
s ometime to come .In biddingyou good by I want to thankyou for
your manykindnessesand to hope that my workwill be of some
service toyou you.

Sincerely yours

Gertrude Stein .

and satisfactorily *structures to be studied*" (see Figures 6, 7, 8). The student needed only to "compare his own sections" with the *Atlas*'s four dozen illustrations ("of sections cut into two planes and drawn to resemble actual preparations") in order to "find the parts there clearly designated and explained" (p. 5). In turn, Sabin credited Knower with having initially suggested that she put the material published in the *Johns Hopkins Hospital Reports* "into a more convenient form for the student." He had overseen the changes required by the new edition, such as "fuller references," "a rearrangement of contents," and "a full index" (*Atlas*, p. 7).

The question, as far as Stein was concerned, was whether Knower's familiarity with Sabin's *Atlas* readily translated into familiarity with the "conditions" of the brain stem; and if it didn't, as she implied, then just how did the familiarity she sought to convey in her paper ("the truth as I know it") differ from the sense of familiarity the *Atlas* was designed to supply? The *Atlas* may provide the student with a clearly articulated model of the "structures to be studied"—Knower's criterion for success—yet it entirely fails to convey any sense of the actual conditions in which these structures exist—any sense, that is, of their physiological conditions, from which the anatomy of any living organism is only an abstraction. I don't mean to suggest that Stein imagined the two series of sliced dead brain stem described in her paper to be the equivalent of a single living brain stem observed over time; I *am* proposing that the "truth" she sought to express, the confusion she sought to clarify, concerned the region's *interconnectedness*, its existence *as a region* rather than as a set of interlocking structures. No doubt, abstracted from physiology, the brain stem *is* nothing but a collection of structures; and when Stein proposed that "Dr. Knower . . . does not know the region and its confusion," she was implying that, from his perspective, the crucial facts that one needed to know were limited to the region's structures. For Knower, "the serious work of construction from the data" remained "unfinished" in Stein's paper, because as matters stood, "the structures described" could only be "relate[d]" with "difficult[y] . . . in the setting drawn for them." Stein, by contrast, in judging his incapacity to judge her work, placed the emphasis on the last words of her sentence: Knower did not know "the region *and its confusion.*" Not to acknowledge this confusion was not to know the region.

The difference between Stein's and Sabin's projects—Knower obviously took them as having the same objective—comes down to the differences between the pairs of serial sections that they used. Sabin constructed the model in her *Atlas* on the basis of a "series of *horizontal* sections passing [longitudinally] through the medulla, pons, and midbrain of a new-born

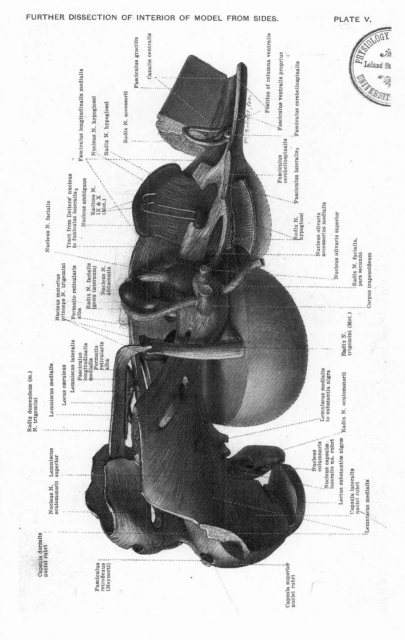

Figure 6. Interior of model of medulla and midbrain. (From Florence R. Sabin, *An Atlas of the Medulla and Midbrain: A Laboratory Manual,* Plate V.)

PLATE VII.

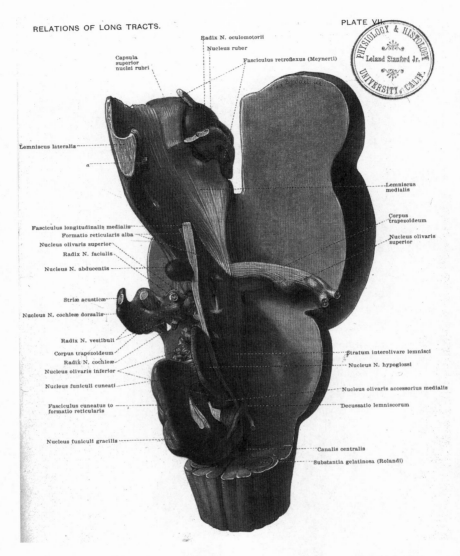

Figure 7.   Relations of long tracts in model of medulla and midbrain. (From Florence R. Sabin, *An Atlas of the Medulla and Midbrain: A Laboratory Manual*, Plate VII.)

babe." A second set of sections, cut transversally, or perpendicular to the first set, represented "almost the same stage of medullation" and served "as a check upon every point of the model" (p. 13). One may compare this with Stein's account, in the letter to Barker, of her two series, which she gives along with her "personal opinion of [the paper's] value":

> The *embryological series* are of value as showing conditions at a certain stage but their chief value to me was that they enabled me to understand the adult series that I finally made. The whole point of *the adult series* to me is not so much that there is very definite new material although there is some of that but that as far as I have been able I have endeavored to express a very clear image, etc.

Sabin's second series served to check the first, merely confirming the translation of neuroanatomical structures from two-dimensional sections to a three-dimensional model, with the temporal dimension remaining constant. In contrast, Stein's two sectional series showed conditions at different stages. She used the earlier series to clarify the rather more complex relations exhibited at the later stage of development. (Recall that Mall was still writing Barker in November to find out if he could supply "the brain of a child 6 months old," in order to "connect" Stein's work "with Miss Sabins." The paper Stein ultimately produced, correlating embryo and adult series, wasn't so readily subordinated to Sabin's work.) Admittedly, there is some ambiguity in Stein's phrasing as to whether the confusion that needed clarifying existed in the literature on the subject, or whether it was to be found in the region itself (as when she spoke of "the region and its confusion"), or whether it was located in her own mind ("they all tell so much more that one is confused"). Indeed, one may find oneself feeling a little dizzy in trying to distinguish the *mind* of the observer from the slices of *brain* she is observing as well as from the *textbooks* she has read and which have supplied her with knowledge of this region of the brain, not to mention the relation between brain and mind. Perhaps these entities are harder to distinguish than *the anatomical perspective built into Stein's instrument of choice at the turn of the century, the microscope,* would have one believe. *Resistance, then, to the dictates* of this perspective, a resistance that derailed the medical career the early successes at Harvard and Johns Hopkins had seemed to promise, at the same time started Stein on a literary career of deliberate error.

Deliberate error, as I use the phrase here, should not be mistaken for *deliberate failure,* although this is certainly what many of Stein's literary experiments look like when measured against an anatomical yardstick. If a sentence like "A meal in mutton . . ." can't be explained away etiologically

PLATE VIII.

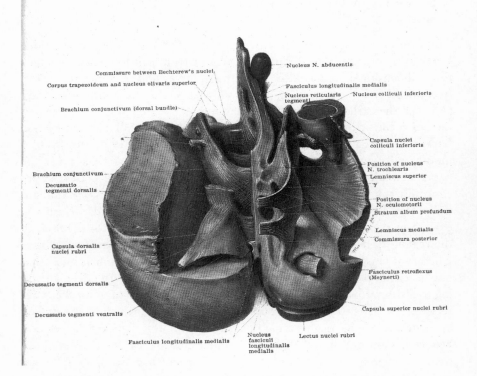

Figure 8. Model of the midbrain from above, with nucleus of Darksche-witsch indicated ("Nucleus fasciculi longitudinalis medialis"). (From Florence R. Sabin, *An Atlas of the Medulla and Midbrain: A Laboratory Manual*, Plate VIII.)

(that is, as a function of palilalia, aphasia, split personality, depression, even repression), then from this perspective it demonstrates a willful failure, on Stein's part, to respect grammatical rules. Indeed, her final run at Johns Hopkins seems almost to demand that it be judged as one deliberate failure after another: the "fantastic" model, the paper "lacking in constructive thought," the sole surviving letter to Barker, announcing that she did not "expect to do any *neuroliogical* work for *s ometime   to   come.*" Up to now, I have avoided looking at Stein's letter, but, of course, its format is the first thing one notices about it. The typing isn't just atrocious but flamboyantly (some might say pathologically) so. How is one to account for this mess? The ready answer is that it demonstrates a correspondingly confused internal, or mental, state. Certainly, at the time she composed the letter Stein had reason enough to be upset. She was deeply embroiled in the lesbian triangle that, a year later, found expression in *Quod Erat Demonstrandum*; eight years of hard work had just gone down the drain with her failure to get a medical degree; the value of her research on the brain stem was in doubt. This left her with little more than vague literary ambitions to fall back on—and judging from the manner in which the letter in question was composed, her literary prospects can't have seemed especially secure.

To an eye raised on the typewriter and word processor, the large quantity of misplaced and crossed-out letters registers provocatively. It looks as if Stein is saying to Barker (without putting it in so many words) that he and his kind can go to hell; she's not going to bother neatening up for him. Furthermore, to an eye educated in Stein's subsequent literary experiments, it may seem obvious that the letter offers a preview of the exceptional sensitivity she would display in coming years to the material conditions of language. How can the fact that the composition is in such a hopeless mess possibly be irrelevant to the story Stein wants to tell about a region she found in a similar state? *I XX feel that I have done all that X I can with it so I XXXXXXwillingly leave it in your hands* probably doesn't strike the reader as a wholly unproblematic expression of willingness. All that's left of the partly erased *XXXerature* are traces of literature's self-deconstruction. No caption is needed to spell out the pictorial logic of *it seems to me that they tell a clear story. XXXXXXX XXX XXXXXXXX XXXXXX XXXXX. / They clear awaythe underbrush* and of *I felt sucha clarifming process to be much needed.N o t that XXXXXXX the books do not all tell the truth as I know it.* And what of *my aim in writing this article has been . . . to make crnfusion clear*? As for the restatement of Stein's object as having been *to save the next man from a longp X perlimanar y work,* "the next man" appears right on cue in the middle of *preliminary*.

However, both of these accounts (emotional and literary) prove flawed. The extended double entendres, for instance, are readily explicated without assuming that Stein deliberately composed them. It is hardly surprising, given the overlap between the concerns she expressed with regard to her research and the concerns that one is likely to experience in composing a letter (at a minimum, issues of clarity, reading, identity, will), that some degree of *crnfusion* might have ensued, particularly in combination with the fairly primitive typewriters of the day and Stein's well-documented dislike of typing. And even this appearance of confusion is misleading. For Stein's corrections are just that, corrections, painstakingly etched, letter by letter. The markings that interrupt the phrase *as far as XXXXXX XX/XXXX I havebeen able* in fact suggest that there was more than one stage of correction. She seems first to have separated words mistakenly run together (*aa/aaaa*) and only subsequently crossed them out (XX/XXXX). By contrast, the final paragraph *looks* clean, although by that point she had simply stopped correcting her typos. Why? As she writes of her neuroanatomical research: "I will not have the time nor do I feel that I can make many changes."[36]

Appearances to the contrary, the letter is a remarkably clearheaded document. No doubt such clarity was taxing, just as it cannot have been easy for Stein to close: "In bidding you good by I want to thank you for your many kindnesses and to hope that my work will be of some service *toyou you*. / Sincerely yours / Gertrude Stein." It cannot have been easy, but that doesn't mean that there were two Gertrude Steins composing the letter—matching the double *you*—one clearheaded and the other brokenhearted. Instead, the informality of address ("*My dear* Dr. Barker," not "Dear Dr. Barker") suggests that, in the rush of departure, Stein felt comfortable enough with Barker to send him what amounts to a rough draft. For surely that is what this is; and Stein seems not to have misjudged her recipient and his readiness, as a reader, to distinguish between the roughness of her manner and the integrity of the point of view she expressed.

On her own testimony, Stein was no better equipped constitutionally for typing than she was for anatomical drawing. The faulty typing of the letter to Barker is important, but not because it tells us something dark and hidden about Stein's psyche; on the contrary. In *The Autobiography of Alice B. Toklas* we are informed that soon after she completed *Three Lives*, Stein "asked her sister-in-law to come and read it. She did and was deeply moved." Sally Stein had "always meant a great deal in [Stein's] life but never more than on that afternoon. *And then it had to be typewritten.*" No pause, no transition—this is the crux of the matter. "Gertrude Stein had at that time a wretched little portable typewriter which she never used," the account continues. She "tried to copy Three Lives on the typewriter but *it was no use, it made her nervous*, so Etta Cone came to the rescue. The Miss Etta Cones as Pablo Picasso used to call her and her sister." Four years had passed since the farewell letter to Barker; Stein was ensconced in Paris, introducing Matisse and Picasso to each other, et cetera, et cetera, yet she hadn't exactly left Baltimore behind. The second of the "Miss Etta Cones" was the formidable Dr. Claribel Cone, who taught medicine at the Women's Medical College of Baltimore and had contributed a paper on gastric tuberculosis to the same volume of the *Johns Hopkins Hospital Reports* that contained Sabin's original *Model*. In any case, "Etta Cone offered to typewrite Three Lives and she began." Then comes the twist: "Baltimore is famous for the delicate sensibilities and conscientiousness of its inhabitants. It suddenly occurred to Gertrude Stein that she had not told Etta Cone to *read* the manuscript before beginning to *typewrite* it. She went to see her and there indeed was Etta Cone *faithfully copying the manuscript letter by letter* so that she might not by any indiscretion become conscious of the meaning. Permission to *read the text* having been given the typewriting went on" (pp. 52–53, emphasis added).

This literal-mindedness might be dismissed as the mild eccentricity of a delicate inhabitant of Baltimore, except that the rather indelicate Toklas, hardy California perennial, who soon took over Etta Cone's role as Stein's faithful amanuensis, confirms its appropriateness for acquainting oneself with Stein's compositions. "I always say," Toklas observes in the *Autobiography*, in one of a pair of passages already cited, which nonetheless bear repeating, "that you cannot tell what a picture really is or what an object really is until you dust it every day and you cannot tell what a book is until you type it or proof-read it. *It then does something to you that only reading never can do.*" A hundred pages later, she reiterates: "Correcting proofs is, as I said before, like dusting, you learn *the values of the thing* as *no reading* suffices to teach it to you" (pp. 113, 217, emphasis added). Typing the letter to Barker, by contrast, possessed no such value for Stein; nor did Knower's abstract form of knowledge, which remained abstract precisely because its objects (discrete neuroanatomical structures like the medial lemniscus or the inferior olive) were divorced both from the physiological conditions of their existence (the complex circuitry of brain function) and from the neurophysiological imagination of the observer. Value of the sort that Toklas no less than Etta Cone finds in Stein's writing proves to be a function of what William James called *knowledge of acquaintance*, capable of bringing an obscure region of the brain *to life* in one's mind, just as it possesses the capacity to bring any old object to life when "you dust it every day." Stein makes a similar point in *The Geographical History of America*, with an anecdote confirming the consanguinity of the attention her writing demands and that required by her microscopical research. She has found, she reports,

> that any kind of a book if you read with glasses and somebody is cutting your hair and so you cannot keep the glasses on and you use your glasses as a magnifying glass and so read word by word reading word by word makes the writing that is not anything be something.

"Very regrettable but very true" (p. 115). As with Etta Cone's fastidious *non*reading ("letter by letter"), reading "word by word" makes "something" of the writing, even as it prevents the reader from actually putting the words together and thereby making sense of them.

In typing up a manuscript, as in proofreading, the reader acquires a sense of the composition as an object, with its own values; yet the two activities share another feature as well, namely, that the typist, like the proofreader (and indeed like the grammarian), is more than ordinarily sensitive to error. Surely, it isn't too much to say that the conscientious typist, in seeking to avoid error, and the proofreader, in ferreting it out, are both haunted by nondeliberate error, as well as by the possibility of their failing to distinguish between deliberate and nondeliberate error.

In Stein's hands, such deliberate error—always distinguishable from nondeliberate error, although often not by very much—served as the basic compositional device for her experimental writing. A particularly graphic example of how this works is supplied in an exchange of letters, twenty years after the correspondence with Barker, with another inhabitant of Chicago. In early 1922, Sherwood Anderson sent Stein an introduction he had written, at her request, for her collection *Geography and Plays*. Not only did he seem genuinely to grasp the way she "work[ed] with words," but for the first time in her career a major writer had come forth who was willing to sing her praises in public (GP, p. 6). For this reason, she was quite ready to put up with the fact that his remarks inevitably would serve as a misleading example for the reader, since Anderson's good sense about her writing was flatly contradicted by the way he said it, marshaling his words to get the point across. In a superb passage at the end of the same letter in which she acknowledged that the introduction was "just what it should be," Stein demonstrated the very different attention her work actually required. In his last letter she had come across some words that were quite as opaque as any of hers. "I am sending this to your permanent address," she wrote, "which is very nearly permanently *illisible* [that is, illegible] as the French say with this kind of an address . . . *I did a solid concentration and the light came,* I hope it came rightly" (White, p. 18). Anderson's hastily scribbled address offered Stein a perfect example of what she was after in her writing. The difference between his "Permanent address / Critchfield & Company / Brooks Bldg. / Chicago" and her own scrambled writing was, of course, that the effect of opacity was wholly deliberate on her part, whereas Anderson would have wanted nothing less than to have the address reach her as garbled nonsense (p. 14). He sent it to facilitate communication between them; what delighted Stein was that, as written, it made communication all but impossible. Yet not entirely impossible; the correct meaning might prove available if one "concentrated solidly" enough. This is the difference, then, between the two forms of error: Deliberate error is error that may nonetheless be correct, error, that is, with the means for correction built into it. If such error requires deliberation, it also rewards it.

In her 1934 lecture "Poetry and Grammar," Stein distinguished verbs and adverbs from nouns and adjectives on the basis that the former "can be so mistaken," whereas the latter "never can make mistakes can never be mistaken" (LIA, p. 211). "A name is adequate or it is not" (p. 210). By contrast, "it is wonderful the number of mistakes a verb can make . . . both as to what they do"—functioning as a past participle, conditional, or whatever—"and how they agree or disagree with whatever they do," that is, according to person and number (pp. 211–12). On another occasion, discussing her earliest innovations with grammar in *The Making of Americans,* Stein remarked that in "trying to get this present immediacy [the sense of acquaintance she was after] without trying to drag in anything else," she "had to use present participles, *new constructions of grammar. The grammar-constructions are correct, but they are changed,* in order to get th[e] immediacy" that one experiences when one *"feels anybody else"* (HWW, p. 155, emphasis added). This is the perspective of a grammarian, not an anti-grammarian, the perspective of someone for whom grammar is not fixed but malleable. "Then comes the thing," she continued in her anatomy of the parts of speech, "that can of all things be most mistaken and they are prepositions." These "can live one long life being / really being / nothing / but absolutely nothing / but mistaken."[37] "That makes them irritating if you feel that way about mistakes but certainly something that you can be continuously using and everlastingly enjoying" (LIA, p. 212).[38] As sources of irritation or enjoyment, whether construed as something to be corrected or something to be used, these terms of positioning (and pre-positioning) demand careful attention: even "the stolid word 'about,'" which James held responsible for "engulfing[,] . . . in its monotonous sound," all the "delicate idiosyncracies" of otherwise "anonymous psychic states" (PR, p. 239). Like verbs and adverbs, and like articles and conjunctions, prepositions are "lively," Stein remarks, because "they all do something and as long as anything does something it keeps alive" (LIA, p. 214). From this perspective, anatomy proves a function of physiology, and grammar, in Geoffrey Hill's phrasing, "transfigure[s] syntax," and it is all gist—and grist—for deliberate error ("Intelligible Structure," p. 17).

LIVELY WORDS

> I see I have a trained eye I do microscopic work
>
> —GERTRUDE STEIN, "Possessive Case"

Stein's experimental writing between 1912 and 1932 is both premised on and exhibits an organicism divorced from traditional notions of organic form and organic unity, an organicism that can accommodate the most disjunctive work of this most disjunctive of writers as well as make sense of her trajectory from student of neuroanatomy in the late 1890s to lecturer in the 1930s on the life that words possess. Repeatedly, in the lectures she delivered across the United States in 1934 and 1935, Stein articulated a sense of the liveliness of words which it is plainly reductive to call metaphorical. "I like the feeling," she observed in one lecture, "of words doing as they want to do and as they have to do when they live where they have to live / that is / where they have come to live / which of course they do do" (N, p. 15). Elsewhere in the same lecture she proposed that "words that in the English were completely quiet or very slowly moving began [in the hands of American writers] to have within themselves the consciousness of completely moving, they began to detach themselves from the solidity of anything, they began to excitedly feel themselves as if they were anywhere or anything" (N, p. 10). In another lecture, "What Is English Literature," she noted that in English writing of the Elizabethan period, unlike the more settled writing of the nineteenth century, "there was . . . constant choice constant decision and the words have the liveliness of being constantly chosen" (LIA, p. 25). These words are "gaily and happily alive" (N, pp. 12–13).

Similarly, periods "might come to have a life of their own / to commence breaking up things in arbitrary ways." In her lecture on "Poetry and Grammar," she explained that "they could begin to act as they thought best and one might interrupt one's writing with them that is not really interrupt one's writing with them but one could come to stop / arbitrarily stop at times in one's writing and so they could be used and you could use them. Periods could come to exist in this way and they could come in this way to have a life of their own" (LIA, p. 218). As an example of such lively punctuation, she promised to read an excerpt from "a poem . . . called Winning His Way," but at least in the published version of the lecture she never did. Here is a brief excerpt from the 50-page composition:

> And so. Now. A poem.
> Is in. Full swing.
> A narrative poem. Is commencing.
> A poem. Entitled.
> Winning his way.
> A poem. Of poetry.
> And friendships.
>
> (SIM, p. 166)

Like so much of Stein's writing this needs to be read aloud, yet it can't be. By this I mean that it requires reading at two different levels: at the level of ordinary, relatively consecutive speech ("And so now a poem is in full swing. A narrative poem is commencing, a poem entitled 'Winning His Way,' a poem of poetry and friendships") and, in counterpoint to this norm, at the palpably more complex level of the syntactic and semantic instructions suggested by the words' juxtaposition on the page. "And so," the passage, itself a sequence of passages, begins. *And so (on)*. And then? "Now." Now? *Now* . . . Unlike Stein's description of the nucleus of Darkschewitsch, where the difficulty a reader may experience is due principally to the relative unfamiliarity of the terminology (so that decoding the linguistic record takes the form of a mechanical exercise because the words' meanings are fixed beforehand), here the words are themselves "in full swing" and the reader must join in the dance to get anywhere with them.

The sense that words, in certain circumstances, possess a life of their own "invites an analogy," as Frank Kermode has observed, "with unconscious organic life." There are at least three respects, however, in which Stein's characterization differs from the sort of thing Kermode had in mind. In the first place, her words are not unconscious. They "excitedly feel themselves." Second, Kermode is concerned with "the notion of a work of art as having a life of its own," whereas Stein says nothing about works of art. She is describing the liveliness of words rather than of any particular form they may take in finished works. Finally, in terms of the "organicist theory of art" that Kermode is elucidating, the living thing to which the work of art is likened, a "thing with a life of its own, with all its parts in some organic relation," isn't just any living organism but is more specifically a tree or plant. The work of art, Kermode observes, "is not susceptible to ordinary intellectual analysis any more than you can describe a tree by cutting it up" (pp. 92–93). Whatever form of life Stein was imagining when she called words "gaily and happily alive," it was not that native to a tree (although it might be native to leaves).

"It is astonishing," M. H. Abrams observes of Coleridge, codifier of organicism in the English tradition, "how much of [his] critical writing is couched in terms that are metaphorical for art and literal for a plant" (p. 169; cited by Kermode, p. 93).[39] In this respect, Coleridge's speculations stand in direct contrast to Stein's brand of organicism (contrasting as well, I would add, with the organicism exhibited in Wordsworth's poetry).[40] As an account of what Pater called "the act of creation" in "the greater works of art," the horticulturalist perspective requires the dissociation of the actual process of creation from the organic "growth" the artwork is said to exhibit. If this is what it means for a poem to be organic, then it follows that the poet (like the author of Coleridge's "Kubla Khan") is an automaton. As Pater observed, in what Harold Bloom has called his "pioneering" rejection of "the Organic Analogue":

> What makes [Coleridge's] view a one-sided one is, that in it the artist has become almost a mechanical agent: instead of the most luminous and self-possessed phase of consciousness, the associative act in art or poetry is made to look like some blindly organic process of assimilation. The work of art is likened to a living organism. That expresses truly the sense of a self-delighting, independent life which the finished work of art gives us: it hardly figures the process by which such work was produced. (pp. xxvii, 152)

The artist, on this account, proceeds not by "conscious invention" but, as Pater puts it, by "self-surrender to the suggestions of an abstract reason or ideality in things . . . evolved by the stir of nature itself." Shakespeare's "hand moving freely" is "curved round as if by some law of gravitation from within," with the result that "the constraining unity of effect, the ineffaceable impression," of *Hamlet* or *Macbeth* "intervenes," and "an energetic unity or identity makes itself visible amid an abounding variety." The "waywardness" in "capricious detail" so characteristic of Shakespeare, "a waywardness that plays with the parts careless of the impression of the whole," is supervened in Coleridge's account by the emerging unities of the plays themselves—unities figured as much by the "ineffaceable impressions" of a Hamlet or a Macbeth as by the "constraining unities of effect" of the works that bear their names (p. 151).

With her emphasis on lively words, Stein refused to subject Shakespeare's freely moving hand to the greater good. It was the "waywardness that plays with the parts" which so delighted her and which she addressed in her lecture on "Plays." "I remember Henry the Sixth," she recalled of her adolescent experience of dramatic literature,

> which I read and reread and which of course I have never seen played but which I liked to read because there were so many characters and there were so many little bits in it that were lively words. In the poetry of plays words are more lively words than in any other kind of poetry and if one naturally liked lively words and I naturally did one likes to read plays in poetry. I always as a child read all the plays I could get hold of that were in poetry. Plays in prose do not read so well. The words in prose are livelier when they are not a play. I am not saying anything about why, it is just a fact.

Stein may not have explained the basis of her assertion concerning the greater liveliness of nondramatic prose—perhaps it is due to an inconsistency between the sentential rhythms of prose and the "play," the give and take, appropriate to the treatment of words in a more dramatic context—but she did provide an account of what makes poetry "connected with a play" livelier than poetry that is not. No doubt, the homology between the lineation of verse and the distribution of lines among different characters in a play contributed to her sense of the words' liveliness; yet the increase was primarily due to the circumstance that in plays, by contrast with the relatively continuous forms of nondramatic poetry, the words were broken into "a great many bits that were short and sometimes . . . only a line" in length (LIA, p. 111).[41] In this way, as she said of her use of periods in a correspondingly lively manner, they "might come to have a life of their own to commence breaking up things in arbitrary ways." In acting "as they thought best," these concatenations of words enabled the reader (and writer) to "interrupt" the relentless forward motion of reading or writing, and thereby to display the "waywardness" Pater characterized as a matter of "*play[ing] with the parts* careless of the impression of the whole." These parts were not related to one another, and to the whole that they make up collectively, as "the parts of a growing plant" are—not at least if the plant is regarded as anatomically continuous, so that its parts possess, in Cleanth Brooks's phrasing, "a closer relation to each other than do the blossoms juxtaposed in a bouquet" ("Irony," p. 232).

In an important essay on "Form and Intent in the American New Criticism," Paul de Man criticized claims for organic unity in poetry, observing that "this sense of the unity of forms" is "supported" by an "analogy between language and a living organism." According to de Man, the New Critics, in pushing the interpretative process as far as they did, caused the metaphor to "explode," and thereby confirmed, however unintentionally, "the absence of the unity [they] had postulated." De Man's account of the New Criticism's self-deconstruction turns out to be just as unselfcritical as the object of his critique, since he postulates that the living organism remains a unity, imbued with "the coherence of the natural world," and that "the language of poetry" alone constitutes "a discontinuous world of reflective irony and ambiguity." In thus practicing his own form of "unitarian criticism," de Man leaves open the possibility of conceiving of an organism as coherent yet discontinuous, and of a poem as discontinuous yet coherent, and so restoring the analogy between language and life (p. 28).[42]

This, I would like to suggest, is how Stein conceived of the matter; although, I would add, she did not end up restoring the analogy. Rather, she demonstrated that to the extent that any utterance, and in particular any piece of writing, is experienced as *lively* and therefore, paradoxical as it may sound, as something *concrete* (so that, like the language of poetry, it requires explicit attention to its compositional features in order for one to grasp how it functions "as explanation"), this autopoietic entity isn't just like a living organism. It is every bit as much a living organism as a living organism is.

In a 1935 address to the students of the Choate School, Stein distinguished the nineteenth century—"the Englishman's Century," she called it—from "the American Century" that succeeded it. "Instead of having the feeling of beginning at one end and ending at another," of somehow "muddling through," the United States

> had the conception of assembling the whole thing out of its parts, the whole thing which made the Twentieth Century productive. The Twentieth Century conceived an automobile as a whole, so to speak, and then created it, built it up out of its parts. It was an entirely different point of view from the Nineteenth Century's. The Nineteenth Century would have seen the parts, and worked towards the automobile through them.

"This idea of a whole thing" ("a whole made up of its parts" as distinct from "pieces put together to make a whole") might be illustrated in terms of the contrast between the conception of the "automobile as a whole," which made Henry Ford's assembly line so "productive," and the piecemeal invention of self-propelled vehicles over the course of the nineteenth century—from the initial development of steam-driven carriages in France and England around 1800 to Benz and Daimler's introduction of the internal-combustion engine in 1885.

Alternately, Stein's own "conception of the whole paragraph" might serve to exemplify the general change in method, as the "new conception" emerged in the course of composing *The Making of Americans*. Or, as she observed to her audience of high school students, the poetry of Walt Whitman might do:

> In the Twentieth Century you feel like movement. The Nineteenth Century didn't feel that way. The element of movement was not the predominating thing that they felt. You know that in your lives movement is the thing that occupies you most—you feel movement all the time. And the United States had the first instance of what I call Twentieth Century writing. You see it in Walt Whitman. He was the beginning of the movement. He didn't see it very clearly, but there was a sense of movement that the European was much influenced by, because the Twentieth Century has become the American Century. (HWW, pp. 152–54)

The "sense of movement" articulated by Whitman in the title of the ever-expanding and oft-reconfigured "whole" of his poetry, *Leaves of Grass*, corresponds to the "rhythm of the visible world" Stein began to investigate in *Tender Buttons*. Indeed, "leaves of grass" may be regarded as a figure, however much more vague and unfocused than Stein's own "tender buttons," for the composition of the nervous system as it was established by the neuron doctrine in the 1890s, a resolution Whitman foresaw in his poetry of the 1850s and 1860s but which he did not live to see with the dawning of the New Biology.

The nervous system as characterized by the neuron doctrine is anatomically discontinuous and physiologically or functionally continuous, and as such it offers a model for an organicism that combines discontinuity and coherence. The sense of a whole, the overarching sense of *acquaintance* displayed in Stein's dissociative practices, may not correspond to any particular anatomical, or subanatomical, structure, yet it is itself a function of a properly functioning nervous system. Consequently, Stein avoids the need to posit preformative mechanisms like those that Coleridge, with his transcendental organicism, substituted for the mechanistic automatisms and habit-formation of late-eighteenth-century associationist psychology. A tissue- or plant-based model of the nervous system like his (in which, to cite Barker again, "the interrelations of the nerve elements" depend "entirely upon . . . organic connection" rather than upon "contact or contiguity") cannot account for growth or development without a teleological principle, without the "latent purposes" of what Pater, paraphrasing Coleridge, called "the reasonable soul antecedent" in nature (p. 150).

Although James certainly didn't sell growth short in his psychology, the inadequacies of his physiology emerge most clearly when considerations of growth come into play. Compared to the Austrian brain anatomist and psychiatrist Theodor Meynert (under whose supervision, as it happens, Freud conducted microscopical studies that, like Stein's at Johns Hopkins, involved the nerve tracts in the medulla oblongata), James displayed an understanding of epigenesis and the functional organization of the nervous system that no doubt represented a considerable improvement. The "lower centres" of the nervous system, such as the midbrain, "are more spontaneous," he proposed, and "the hemispheres . . . more automatic" than the Meynert scheme would allow (PR, p. 80). For "the plain truth is that neither in man nor beast are the hemispheres the virgin organs which [Meynert's] scheme called them. So far from being unorganized at birth, they must have native tendencies to reaction of a determinate sort." These "are the tendencies which we know as emotions and instincts." For purposes of education, or the modification of such "native" tendencies, "the hemispheres do not need to be *tabulae rasae* at first, as the Meynert scheme would have them; and so far from being educated by the lower centres exclusively, they educate themselves" (p. 83–84).[43]

This is not the place to go into the complex relation between Freud and Stein in terms of their respective neuroanatomical training, but several remarks are perhaps in order.[44] First, with his concept of the unconscious, Freud remained entirely within the framework of the Meynert scheme, premised as it was on an absolute distinction in kind between the hemispheres of the brain, on the one hand, and the "lower centres," on the other. Second, Stein's insistence (which I discuss in detail in Chapter 5) that in the act of writing she was conscious of her so-called unconscious processes should be evaluated within the context of James's less rigid scheme, in which the lower nervous centers aren't "wholly automatic," rather than in terms of Meynert's strict dichotomy. Third, the prominent mesencephalic structure near the nucleus of Darkschewitsch which Barker refers to when he comments that "Miss Stein in the brain she is studying can follow the fibers only as far as the *fasciculus retroflexus*" happened to be named for Meynert. In addition to citing a description by Sabin of the "*fasciculus retroflexus Meynerti*" in relation to the nucleus ruber, or red nucleus, Barker also provides an illustration of these two structures based on "a reconstruction by Miss Florence Sabin, Baltimore, 1898" (pp. 777–79).[45]

The problem with James's modification of Meynert's (and Freud's) scheme is that it stops at exactly the point where it begins, namely, with the question of just how the hemispheres come to be "organized at birth," the question, that is, of embryology. James's bracketing of the actual physiology of the matter—resorting to talk of "native tendencies" and "emotions and instincts" rather than "nerve-tracts" and "loop-lines"—is due not to any particular inadequacy in the contemporaneous state of knowledge about embryogenesis but rather to the basis of his psychology in studies of pathological, or degenerative, physiology. Broca's discovery in 1862 that, as Oliver Sacks has put it, "a specific language defect, aphasia, could be ascribed to damage of a specific part of the brain," inaugurated modern physiological psychology ("Scotoma," pp. 173–74). As Sacks suggests, neurology began with this discovery as well, but unlike psychology, neurology isn't obliged to make general claims about the human *mind*. The only neurophysiological facts that, at least in the case of human beings, could directly be correlated with psychic or mental states were thus facts involving degenerate physical states. This was because the only persons whose brains were accessible to surgeons were persons who for one reason or another had been deemed degenerate, or who were dead.

Clearly, the challenge for a physiological psychology like James's lay in devising experiments that could build on the results of descriptive neurology without requiring invasive brain surgery; and it was exactly this sort of training that Stein acquired in her work at the Harvard Psychological Laboratory, as her 1896 and 1898 studies of character and automatic writing demonstrate. (These are also discussed in Chapter 5 below.) The further challenge, which James did not address but which came to concern Stein more and more, was how any physiological psychology could ultimately be distinguished from pathological psychology, given that the basis for the physiology was so unavoidably pathological. Today, at the outset of the twenty-first century, it has perhaps finally become possible, both conceptually and technologically, to extend James's speculations concerning neurological self-education *after* birth into the sphere of *prenatal* development, as well as to view the brains of ostensibly normal, healthy persons through techniques of brain imaging. A hundred years ago this was inconceivable. Yet this is the only kind of physiological psychology that could possibly have satisfied Stein; and one may argue that in her most experimental writing she aims to record the characteristic brain activity of individuals who haven't yet been slated for surgery. She also models her writing on neurological self-education, which is most pronounced at the embryological and neonatal stages.

In the mid-1930s, Stein summed up her mature perspective with a pair of distinctions between human nature and the human mind, and identity and entity. Human nature was a function of identity, constructed over time and experienced in temporal terms. "You know who you are because you and others remember anything about yourself." By contrast, "when you are doing anything essentially you are not that," for human activity cannot be understood exclusively in terms of identity or memory (WAM, pp. 83–84). Any identity is an abstraction, the *identification* of two distinct states of activity, and consequently less concrete, less "real," than activity as such. Like so many modern writers, Stein recoiled at the naturalistic vision of inexorable forces determining every motion and emotion—the other shoe of the characteristically nineteenth-century conviction regarding progress' inevitability, which, as she remarked in *Everybody's Autobiography*, she still shared when she "began to write," having grown up "a natural believer in science a natural believer in progress" (p. 251). Unlike T. S. Eliot, however, Stein never replaced the ideology of progress with an ideology of loss; nor did she replace it, as Yeats did, with a sense of the rigorous cyclicality of history. Her early writing was generally naturalistic—one has only to think of *Q.E.D.*, with its geometric interpretation of human relations, or the deterministic color scheme of "Melanctha," and the single-minded concentration on "bottom natures" in *The Making of Americans*. Later, however, as she suggested in the pair of lectures, "An American and France" and "What Are Master-pieces," she emphasized those aspects of her writing that removed it from the dictates, respectively, of place and time. Although she may thereby appear to reinstate an old-style idealism, with the focus on the human mind seeming to confirm this impression, Stein actually does nothing of the kind. Instead, she substitutes a duality of function for the Cartesian dualism of substance. Writing, no less than the human mind—or any entity for that matter—is an activity, not a substance; accordingly, it is made, in James's phrasing, of the same *non*substantial—neither substantial nor insubstantial—"stuff as things are."

"Words are said that serve as bread," Stein wrote in "Mildred's Thoughts," and then added, chewing over her own words: "That is to say they are indigestible. Bread is the staff of life and so are words" (pp. 667–68). It is in their indigestibility that words, or more exactly, combinations of words, come to life, functioning on their own terms and not just as means to a determinate end. This is *life* understood on the model of the nervous system, as in the following passage from the 1934 lecture "Portraits and Repetition." Here Stein is describing what she calls "the essence of genius" (of being, as she says, "most intensely alive") in terms of self-consciously "being one who is at the same time talking and listening." "It is necessary," she proposes, "if you are to be really and truly alive / it is necessary to be at once talking and listening / doing both things, not as if there were one thing, not as if they were two things, but doing them, well if you like, like the motor going inside and the car moving, they are part of the same thing" (LIA, p. 170). An automobile may not actually be a living organism but it nonetheless catches the spirit of the thing, as the very name *automobile*, "self-moving," suggests. Stein seeks the engine's movement in her portraiture, "the current that makes machinery crackle," as she put it in "A Long Dress": what it is that "inside any one, and by any one I mean every one" is "intrinsically exciting" (p. 183). It is this internal movement that, like Bernard's internal milieu in the living organism, distinguishes the functioning of language from "external factors," and makes controlled experiments of individual neuraesthetic experience possible, at least in a milieu composed of words.

"Language *as a real thing*," Stein wrote in "Poetry and Grammar," "is not imitation either of sounds or colors or emotions it is an intellectual recreation and there is no possible doubt about it and it is going to go on being that as long as humanity is anything" (LIA, p. 238, emphasis added). In other words, in its capacity as "an *intellectual* recreation," language isn't exclusively a creature of its environment, merely serving to register external factors. Like an automobile, it is self-moving and functions independently (at least so long as humanity remains in the driver's seat). Stein made this observation in the context of criticizing the "invention" of words, whether by coining new terms or by "imitating movements and emotions in sounds," as in the way that, in "the german language . . . what the words mean sound too much like what they do." This "has really nothing to do with language," she added, nothing to do, that is, with language experienced "as a real thing" instead of as an instrument, a means of getting from one place to another, with the destination set in advance. "Every one must stay with the language their language that has come to be spoken and written and which has in it all the history of its intellectual recreation" (p. 238).

Of her own efforts at "inventing words," in the early stages of investigating the interface of Bernard's external and internal milieus (with both milieus reconceived in neuraesthetic as well as anatomical terms), she observed that "she soon gave that up. The english language was her medium and with the english language the task was to be achieved, the problem solved. The use of fabricated words offended her, it was an escape into imitative emotionalism" (ABT, p. 119). In saying this, she didn't have in mind the tuneful nonsense of "Hey nonny nonny no," surely part of the "language that has come to be spoken and written," but lines like these from her 1913 composition "Bee Time Vine": "No poe, coop ham. / Leaf as not. / Ixtact, lime. / Co hie" (BTV, p. 36). "The problem of poetry," which for

Stein had begun with *Tender Buttons* the year before, was to "realize . . . anything" in such a manner that she "could *recreate* that thing" (LIA, p. 238, emphasis added). The problem, to put it bluntly, was not to confuse imitation with recreation.

One might consider, in this light, the striking concatenation that concludes "Bee Time Vine": "Way mouth, soph, chive, bee, so, it, any, muse, in, lee, vie" (p. 36). On the occasion of the work's initial publication, in 1953, Virgil Thomson cited a passage from *Four Saints in Three Acts* which echoed the title—"Will be there all their all their time there be there vine there be vine time there be there time there all their time there"—and acutely observed that this "second version . . . is simply a hymn about the future life" (OP, p. 44; BTV, p. 35). "Bee Time Vine" itself is, more broadly, a hymn to life: life understood not along vitalist lines but as a function of the sort of play that, bracketing time, extends the present moment, just as "bee" and "vine" bracket "time" in the title of this work. Such play with words corresponds to the sexual play at the end of "Old and Old," characterized by Stein as "the perulean repetition of amalgamated recreation of more integral and less solidifying rudeness." "Perulean" is the adjectival form of *perule*, which in botany means "the cover of a seed" (as well as "the covering of a leaf-bud formed by scales" and "a projection in the flower of the orchids formed by the enlargement of two lateral sepals"), and no doubt the "amalgamation" recreated here in the co-evolutionary play of bee with vine portrays the mutual pleasuring of oral sex as well.[46] *Way mouth, soph, chive, bee, so, it, any, muse, in, lee, vie.* A mouthful of words, concluding with *vie*: French for "life"; alternatively, the English verb meaning "to contend" or "strive for victory." It is all the more "integral" in literally being so much less "solidifying," *vine* with the *n* removed.

It was to the human mind that Stein attributed the self-conscious experience of an extended or continuous present, a sense of oneself that wasn't limited by the dictates of an ever-advancing and ever-retreating time as well as a deterministic human nature. Yet she no more conceived of the mind as a substance, along vitalist or idealist lines, than James did the phenomenon of consciousness. The human mind no more precedes or *causes* human activity than emotions determine their apparent symptoms. Instead of requiring a dualistic explanation, mental and emotional experience might be understood as operating in terms of the nonvitalist organicism articulated in Stein's automobile simile, not as "a contradiction but a combination." The important thing about the simile is that in it Stein refuses to decouple the internal movement of the car (the motions of the motor) from the external movement (registered in terms of the car's passage through the environment, and against its backdrop). The experience of being "most intensely alive" involves the coordination of heterogeneous parts, one environmentally defined, the other not, yet each "part of the same thing." Human *nature* is a matter of how one identifies oneself, or finds oneself identified, against a background (whether of family or generation, social or cultural group, whether constructed on the basis of skin color, economic status, sexual orientation, nationality, or psychological type), much as a car is seen to move only in terms of the background it moves across. By contrast, the human *mind* operates inside one, invisibly, like the car's engine, or more exactly like the brain or nervous system in one's body. What, Stein inquired, is *the current that makes machinery*, as distinct from *the current that machinery makes*? What current flows when one juxtaposes "long" and "dress," for instance, transforming the diverse dimensions of sight and sound and meaning into a three-dimensional "object" which crackles, possesses volume, shapes time? The human mind turns out to be nothing less than the human brain, continually becoming what it is, emerging autopoietically—as occurs most dramatically in neonates and in the course of embryological development but also in "studies in description" like "A Long Dress."

Stein's writing itself proves to be the offspring of what it is that moves her and what it is that moves the person or personlike object she is portraying: "personlike" because, as in her "completed compositions," something exists in the object, moving inside, enabling it to move and be moved.[47] This may not be the sort of nervous system that vertebrates possess, yet it is no less a nervous system. "In anyone," Stein insisted, "I must / or else I must betake myself to some entirely different occupation and I do not think I will, I must find out what is moving inside them that makes them them, and I must find out how I *by the thing moving excitedly in me* can make a portrait of them" (LIA, p. 183, emphasis added). Stein's writing consequently needs to be understood as consistent with the sort of imaginative leap that the visionary geneticist Barbara McClintock made in her work on maize, a leap that required, in McClintock's terms, a "feeling for the organism" as something more than its parts, more than its past, more than its purely mechanical features, as an embodiment of that which makes the earth itself, as Stein's narrator puts it in *The Making of Americans*, "complete and fructifying" (p. 574).[48]

PART TWO

The New Organism

Introduction: Irresistible Dictation

It so happens that Emerson's essay "Fate" opens with several sentences that invoke chance rather than the *necessity* of the title: "It chanced . . ."; "By an odd coincidence . . ."; "It so happened . . ." More is in the air than the "theory of the Age," or "Spirit of the Times," that the denizens of Boston, New York, and London have lately been "bent on discussing" (EL, p. 943).[1] In the words of the introductory poem, "Delicate omens traced in air / To the lone bard true witness bare" (p. 941). These delicate omens are at odds with the discourse of the cities, as in the archaic spelling *bare*, with its suggestion of unadorned witness, antithetical to the city's busyness and the indelicacies of a world driven by practical considerations—a world, Emerson had written a decade and a half earlier, "which I converse with in the city" and, not to draw too fine a distinction, "in the farms," by contrast with "the world I think" (p. 491). How then, with the oxymoronically "Civil" War looming, is Emerson to bear witness in turn to his fellow citizens, to "chant" these "undeceiving things" that have been chanted to him (p. 941)? The answer lies perhaps in the undersong of his lecture, which sets the tone for the essays that succeed it in *The Conduct of Life*: the "coincidence" of an uncommon manner of expressing himself and a subject matter shared with so many other public speakers, whereby this essayist, this *poet*, combines what I have been calling, after James, *knowledge of acquaintance* and *knowledge-about*. Necessity is realized, in short, in the "chance" of a chant.

" 'Tis fine," the same paragraph concludes—Emerson concluding as well, as does the reader in a corresponding gesture—"for us to speculate and elect our course, if we must accept an irresistible dictation." The bitter irony of this statement derives from nothing having been left to chance. The "irresistible dictation" even dictates that we accept it. Yet what is the nature of this acceptance? Returning to his newly coined phrase, Emerson speculates:

> If there be irresistible dictation, this dictation understands itself. If we must accept Fate, we are not less compelled to affirm liberty, the significance of the individual, the grandeur of duty, the power of character. This is true, and the other is true. (p. 943)[2]

What Emerson calls *irresistible dictation* here, Stein, in the title of her first public lecture, called *composition as explanation*. Instead of trusting the tale and not the teller, as D. H. Lawrence cautioned, one must go a step further, to the composition of the tale, indeed to the tale of the composition. The teller, the narrator, the person behind the tale has to be explained in terms of the act of composition and not the other way around. All the same, it isn't enough merely to assert this neat inversion. In the first place, the inversion is not as neat as one may desire. The claim that words are given substance by humans (by human desires, designs, actions, thoughts, emotions, what have you) requires the corresponding recognition that human beings are themselves composed of, and by, the words they use. Yet simply privileging words over persons will not do. Bare assertion is necessarily insufficient in this case, for the act of assertion supposes the very transparency of the terms being used that the assertion, at the level of idea rather than act, resists. For all Emerson's assertiveness in his essays, it remains difficult to grasp just what he is saying and even to characterize the speaker hazarding, *essaying*, these often contrary remarks. ("This is true, and the other is true.") The identity of Emerson as interlocutor proves indeterminate, or multiple. This cannot be said, however, of the individual *writing* all these sentences and paragraphs. If Emerson typically seems to be trying to say too many things at once, and so failing to make determinate sense, Stein often gives the impression of failing to complete or get to the point of any assertion, and consequently to be saying too little. She refuses to convey the illusion, as she sees it, that there is a still center to her writing, or to any piece of it, which, once found, will serve synecdochically as the key to what one has just read, the point around which everything else coalesces, a theory of everything. The only adequate explanation of a piece of her writing is that realized in the act of composition itself, in the autopoietic process whereby the composition "understands itself."

Particularly with respect to the dissociative writing of her middle period, Stein's reader is obliged to reproduce self-consciously, neuraesthetically, the recursive act of reading inherent in any act of writing. Despite the fact that all reading requires scansion—that is to say, the rereading of what one has already read in order to make sense of what one is currently reading before passing on to the next word or sentence or line—such processes tend to be latent, with the reader remaining unaware of them except in the event that the "smoothness" of the activity is interrupted. By contrast, as William Carlos Williams observed, much twentieth-century writing is characterized by the attention required of both writer and reader to the tactile qualities of the words, an alertness to what Frank Bidart more recently has called "the thing that lives" in a poem and which "has often lived in this century by violation, juxtaposition, disjunction—not a process that feels 'organic,'" at least if one imagines organic process to be characterized by "a smooth feeling with no vibration," no resistance in it, as Stein described the experience of "words com[ing] out" which lack any "recognition as [they] are forming[,] because the recognition had already taken place" (Bidart, p. 16; N, p. 55). To Thornton Wilder she commented, to much the same effect, "Before you write it must be in your head almost in words, but if it is already in words in your head, *it will come out dead*" (*Journals*, p. 45, emphasis added). With her "lively words" she created compositions that differed from other poetic or autopoietic works primarily in the degree of self-consciousness they demanded and, at the same time, made possible—in other words, in both the range and explicitness of the organic mechanisms they exemplified.

Emerson's reiteration of the phrase *irresistible dictation* provides a convenient example of one such mechanism in operation. Through a process that combines knowledge of acquaintance and knowledge-about, the phrase's turn back on itself—its doubling and redoubling—graphically demonstrates that "if we must accept Fate, we are not less compelled to affirm liberty." With the new emphasis, and the new measure that it introduces, Emerson breaks the hold of "Beautiful Necessity" no less firmly, if no less temporarily, than when he chants at the end of his essay:

> Let us build altars to the Blessed Unity . . .
> Let us build altars to the Beautiful Necessity. . . .
> Let us build altars to the Beautiful Necessity, which secures that all is made of one piece . . .
> Let us build to the Beautiful Necessity, which makes man brave in believing that he cannot shun a danger that is appointed, nor incur one that is not. (EL, pp. 967–68)

The slight variations here in the repeated phrasing—what Stein called "insistence" or "emphasis"—make all the difference between a deadening determinism and a determined freedom. When Ralph Church, in the article he published at Stein's urging in *transition*, described her writing as "selfcontained" (adding that "what it says is given in no tenuous references to an external subject, but in the presented character of the writing itself"), he was describing a form of irresistible dictation as well as glossing her definition of *composition* as "explanation" (p. 165). Unlike "discourse," or writing that is "about something not given in the writing itself," a composition of Stein's possessed "all the unmediated finality of a pain or an intense idea"; it was, in a word, irresistible (pp. 166, 168). If it didn't thereby prove irresistible to the casual reader, as Stein remained all too painfully aware, this was because it functioned not as the sort of "irresistible dictation" that, in Emerson's original formulation, "we must accept," but rather as a dictation that, in his reformulation, "understands itself." In obliging us to "accept Fate" and, in the same breath, "affirm liberty"—a double compulsion that not only determines the lives we lead but also distinguishes life from its absence—such dictation is directed essentially at itself and only incidentally at us. Consequently, we may remain unaware of the ways it functions in our lives, at least to the extent that awareness is measured by *what* we say to one another irrespective of *how* we say it.

Stein aimed in her writing to map the contours and operations of such dictation, and thereby to understand it as it "understands itself." As she said of diagramming sentences, which she recalled as the only "really completely exciting thing" from her school days and which "ever since" had remained "the one thing that has been completely exciting and completely completing":

> I like the feeling the everlasting feeling of sentences as they diagram themselves. / In that way one is completely possessing something and incidentally one's self. (LIA, p. 211)

It is both the assumption and the argument of the present study that in tracing Stein's highly self-conscious, although no less contextually sensitive, compositional practices, one may better understand not just the organic mechanisms that operate in her own compositions but also those investigated by several generations of radical empiricists in very different, yet not altogether different spheres.

The radical empiricism of such figures as Emerson, James, Whitehead, Langer, Edelman, Haraway, and Varela is characterized by a redefinition of "entity" in terms of process, and hence as a function of both conjunctive and disjunctive relations. Because conjunction operates at a different level of concreteness (or abstraction) than disjunction, any organic mechanism—that is to say, any process in which the two forms of relation are dynamically or dialectically linked—will operate on the basis of what, sixty years ago, Gregory Vlastos described, with reference to Whitehead's "theory of

organic mechanism," as "a *heterogeneous* dialectic." By contrast with Hegelian dialectic, "the second term of the triad [thesis, antithesis, synthesis]
cannot be generated from the first term by negation, nor the third from the
second" (Vlastos, p. 159).[3] Consequently, Whitehead's reinscription of *mechanism* as *organic* against the full weight of the atomistic and anatomizing
tendencies of scientific materialism (with the objective of both exposing and
correcting what he called the "radical inconsistency at the basis of modern
thought," a "scientific realism, based on mechanism[,] . . . conjoined with
an unwavering belief in [a] world . . . composed of self-determining organisms") exactly corresponds both to Emerson's understanding of irresistible
dictation as at once deterministic and self-determining *and* to Stein's assertion concerning "the essence of genius," already cited in Chapter 2—that
"if you are to be really and truly alive it is necessary to be at once talking
and listening, doing both things, not as if there were one thing, not as if they
were two things, but doing them, well if you like, like the motor going inside and the car moving, they are part of the same thing" (SMW, p. 76; LIA,
p. 170). Whether the heterogeneous dialectic in question is called "correspondence" (Emerson), "organic mechanism" (Whitehead), or a "difference"
that turns out to be "a combination and not a contradiction" (Stein), and
whether it serves to link, in a continuous present, "the world I converse
with" and "the world I think," or "talking and listening," or what Whitehead in his account of symbolism termed "presentational immediacy" and
"causal efficacy," it is the stuff of which organisms are made. Hence "the
new organism"—not a new thing under the sun but a new way of regarding
all the old things.

In the pair of chapters that follow, I examine the correlations between
the heterogeneous dialectics investigated by Emerson, Whitehead, and Stein,
and between the organisms created in the image of these mechanisms. Of
the organisms in question, at once autopoietic and exhibiting what Maturana and Varela refer to as a "necessary structural congruence" with the
"medium[s] that constitute [their] ambience," Stein's experimental compositions are exemplary insofar as they are experienced as "objects" with
"weight and volume," capable, as she writes, of "do[ing] something to you
that only reading never can do" (TK, p. 95; ABT, p. 113). "The world built
up by tactual means," Langer has observed, is "not filled with completely
given or imagined forms, analogous to visual shapes, at all. Distances and
directions, terrain and the location of things are its framework, but 'things'
are not simple sensuous presentations in any mode"—are never presented,
that is, in a single sensory modality (M, p. 252). "All the sensory reactions
of the skin and underlying structures," Langer adds, "are engaged in the

tactual perception of substances: feelings of pressure and release of pressure, of warm and cold impingements, pin-pointed encounters with resistance, oiliness, wetness, and mixtures like sliminess, hairiness, stickiness. The result is that we have not only a report of surface and edge but of volume imbued with multimodal, often nameless qualities," what Whitehead characterized as "the sense of unseen effective presences" (M, p. 251; *Symbolism*, p. 43). Clearly, Stein's portraits of "objects," "food," and "rooms" in *Tender Buttons* are modeled less on the abstractions of visual shapes and more on such concrete, if incompletely given, tactual presences.

Emerson's and Whitehead's speculations concerning the new organism are premised, like Stein's, on a keen sense of the neuraesthetic functioning of the human body. Obviously, this may be said of James as well, who among these four figures was most explicitly, and consistently, concerned with the biological basis of consciousness.

Consider, for instance, the parenthetical remark I elided in Chapter 1, in citing James's assertion that the "whole of [his] consciousness" seemed to him "outwardly mediated" by organic sensations due to incoming currents: "*whatever its inner contrasts be*" (PBE, pp. 359–60, emphasis added). Here James was referring to the internal relations among the sensations that made up his emotional consciousness, and in particular to relations between "visceral and muscular sensibility" and "the higher senses" such as sight and hearing. He did not pretend he could account, on the basis of his method of introspection, for the "strong contrast within consciousness" between "receptive and . . . reactive states of mind," which more than half a century later Langer would distinguish as *impacts* and *acts*, "felt sensory impingements" and "felt impulses" (M, p. 185).

Introspectively, he could localize feelings, but he was incapable of mapping the pathways of the nerve currents that triggered them. At this level of analysis he had to rely on knowledge-about rather than knowledge of acquaintance; and as he observed, the state of descriptive knowledge in 1894 concerning the operations of physical currents in the nervous system was insufficient to determine whether the contrast between impulses and impingements, the former felt to be directed outward, the latter inward, were "mediated" by "outgoing nerve-currents" and "currents passing in" or whether, as James supposed, the "inner contrast" was brought about despite "the similarity of direction of [the] two physical currents" (PBE, pp. 355–56).

By 1906, James's surmise had achieved the status of fiat. Sherrington, in *The Integrative Action of the Nervous System*, published that year, remarked in the course of a discussion of the absence of "reflex action or sensation" after "excitation of the spinal end of [a] severed motor root," that

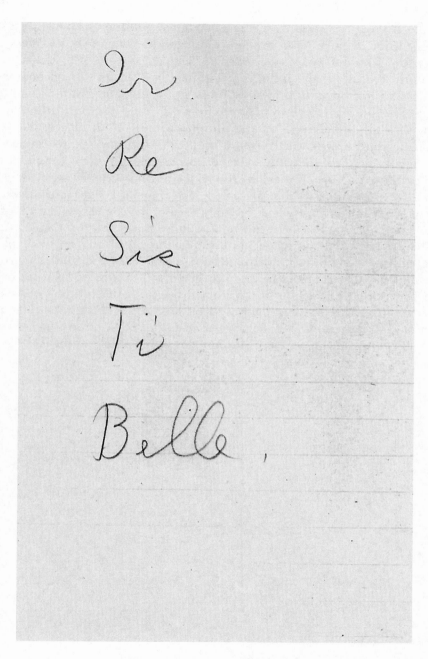

Figure 9. Gertrude Stein, page from manuscript *carnet*. (Box 35, Folder 727, Gertrude Stein and Alice B. Toklas Papers, Yale Collection of American Literature, Beinecke Rare Book and Manuscript Library.)

"this is the special case which forms the first foundation of the law that conduction in the neural system proceeds in one direction only, *the 'law of forward direction' (W. James, 1880)*." (The reference is to "The Feeling of Effort," which includes James's earliest published remarks on innervation and "ideo-motor action"; parts of the essay were reprinted in the chapter on "Will" in *The Principles of Psychology*.) "Evidently," Sherrington concluded, "the central nexus between afferent channel and efferent [incoming and outgoing nerve currents] is of a kind that, although it allows conduction from afferent to efferent, does not allow it from efferent to afferent" (p. 38, emphasis added). Particularly from mid-1912 on, Stein investigated the organic mechanisms whereby sensations were conjoined, and consciousness experienced, by introspecting (in James's sense) the complex pathways of somatic and visceral activity. Where she differed from other practitioners of "methodical ascetic discipline," in James's phrasing, is that she left an external record of her introspective activity, as the feelings she introspected were those that accompanied the act of writing.[4] A written composition may in fact be regarded as a quintessentially radical empiricist "entity," from one perspective functioning as a material object, from another as a meaning located neurophysiologically in someone's consciousness. In Stein's hands, this paradigmatic *new organism* comes irresistibly to life (see Figure 9).[5]

CHAPTER THREE

Line of Divergence: Emerson and Stein

Writing on "Intellect" in his first collection of essays, Emerson observed: "Gladly would I unfold in calm degrees a natural history of the intellect, but what man has yet been able to mark the steps and boundaries of that transparent essence?" (EL, p. 417). By 1848, with renewed exposure to English and French science during his second visit to Europe, he had begun to formulate how one might make an "enumeration . . . of the laws and powers of the Intellect" similar to "the exhaustive accuracy of distribution which chemists use in their nomenclature and anatomists in their descriptions," only "applied to a higher class of facts." And "why not?" he asked. "These powers and laws are also facts in a Natural History" (NHI, pp. 3–4). Among the set of lectures he offered in London that spring, three concerned the "Natural History of the Intellect," a subject to which he would return in 1849, 1850, and 1858, again in 1866 after the conclusion of the Civil War, and in the university course he taught at Harvard in 1870 and 1871.[1] His own contribution to the science of mind, he suggested, would be "simply historical. I write anecdotes of the intellect; a sort of Farmer's Almanac of mental moods . . . *Mémoires pour servir* toward a Natural History of Intellect" (pp. 10, 14).[2]

AN EMERSONIAN BIOLOGY

"Natural History of Intellect," in many respects Emerson's *Prelude*, remained unpublished until 1893, more than a decade after his death and only a few months after Stein matriculated at the Harvard Annex as a special student. A century later, after the *Decade of the Brain*, the text may appear quaint, a collection of anecdotes that have failed to lead anywhere, certainly not toward the sort of biological account of consciousness which has emerged of late in the speculations of figures such as Edelman and Varela. Yet the "mental moods" articulated by Emerson aren't merely the jottings of an aged Transcendentalist, products of a "later idealistic naturalism" (Detweiler, p. 427). Here are several of them:

> 1. I cannot myself use that systematic form which is reckoned essential in treating the science of the mind. . . . The inward analysis [of metaphysics] must be corrected by rough experience. Metaphysics must be perpetually reinforced by life[,] . . . must be biography,—the record of some law whose working was surprised by the observer in natural action. . . . It will one day be taught by poets [insofar as they see whole and avoid the pitfalls of analysis]. (pp. 10–13)

> 2. If you cut or break in two a block or stone and press the two parts together, you can indeed bring the particles very near, but never again so near that they attract each other so that you take up the block as one. That indescribably small interval is as good as a thousand miles, and has forever severed the practical unity. Such is the immense deduction from power by discontinuity. The intellect that sees the interval partakes of it, and the fact of intellectual perception severs once for all the man from the things with which he converses. Affection blends, intellect disjoins subject and object. (pp. 40–41)

> 3. The grasp is the main thing. Most men's minds do not grasp anything. All slips through their fingers. . . . As a talent Dante's imagination is the nearest to hands and feet that we have seen. He clasps the thought as if it were a tree or a stone, and describes it mathematically. (pp. 44–45)

The "grasp"—or prehension, in Whitehead's terminology—"is the main thing." This is the sentiment of neither the "solid men" nor the "idealist" invoked by Emerson in his late essay "Poetry and Imagination," with its Stevensian dispute between "the solid men complaining that the idealist leaves out the fundamental facts" and "the poet complain[ing] that the solid men leave out the sky." "You must have the eyes of science," Emerson continues, "to see in the seed its nodes; you must have the vivacity of the poet to perceive in the thought its futurities" (p. 474). Like Wordsworth, whose "genius," with Swedenborg's, he counts "as the agent of a reform in philosophy," Emerson seeks to "bring poetry back to nature,—to the marrying of nature and mind, undoing the old divorce in which poetry had been famished and false, and nature had been suspected and pagan" (p. 469).

In a late work like "Poetry and Imagination," Emerson's poets are as likely as not to be scientists and to write in prose. Every good reader, he advises, "will easily recall expressions or passages in works of pure science which have given him the same pleasure which he seeks in professed poets." As an example, he cites a sentence by the paleontologist Richard Owen: "All hitherto observed causes of extirpation point either to continuous slowly operating geologic changes, or to no greater sudden cause than the, so to speak, spectral appearance of mankind on a limited tract of land not before inhabited" (p. 461).[3] Well before the 1860s, Emerson's enthusiasm for the topic of poetry per se had begun to flag, and what excited him instead was the prospect, already suggested in Wordsworth, of science as poetry and poetry as science. "Is not poetry the little chamber in the brain," he asks rhetorically in "Poetry and Imagination," "where is generated the explosive force which, by gentle shocks, sets in action the intellectual world"—much as "the spectral appearance of mankind," in Owen's statement, operates quite as efficaciously as do "continuous slowly operating geologic changes" in bringing about the extinction of species (p. 468). Owen's sentence conforms to what, elsewhere in the essay, Emerson characterizes as "our best definition of poetry," which he attributes to "the Chaldean Zoroaster," Nietzsche's Zarathustra. According to Zoroaster, in Thomas Taylor's translation (dating from the 1790s), "Poets are *standing transporters*, whose employment consists in speaking to the Father and to matter; in producing apparent imitations of unapparent natures; and inscribing things unapparent in the apparent fabrication of the world." "In other words," Emerson explains, "the world exists for thought: it is to make appear things which hide: mountains, crystals, plants, animals, are seen; that which makes them is not seen: these, then, are 'apparent copies of unapparent natures'" (p. 447).[4] Poetry (that is, the poetic experience of the world) sets thought in motion by portraying "new possible enlargements to [one's] narrow horizons," as when, impelled by the "gentle shocks" generated by Owen's sentence, one begins to contemplate, beneath the long, allegorical shadow cast by "continuous slowly operating geologic changes," the effects and, more portentously, the causes of mankind's "spectral appearance on a limited tract of land not before inhabited" by human beings (p. 450).

Combining poetry and science functions to keep them, and oneself, intellectually honest; neither is idealized, abstracted from the other. Moreover, in producing his own variant of poetic science in the form of "anecdotes of the intellect," Emerson expresses the distinctive radical empiricism that had already replaced his early transcendental idealism by the time he composed "Experience" in 1844.[5] Nevertheless, the biological features of Emerson's radical empiricism are more apparent in his figuration than in his thematics—more implicit, that is, than explicit. What, then, might a contemporary view of biology look like that could properly be labeled Emersonian? Take the approach to cognitive science advocated in recent years by Francisco Varela. By contrast with the perspectives that have dominated cognitive science since the Second World War—*cognitivism*, which holds that cognition is a function of information processing through the "rule-based manipulation of symbols," and *connectionism*, according to which cognition is due to "the emergence of global states in a network of simple components," states often referred to as "emergent properties"—Varela's *enactive* approach supposes that cognition, as the product of a "history of structural couplings that brings forth a world," operates "through a network consisting of multiple levels of interconnected, sensorimotor subnetworks" (EM, pp. 21–22, 41–42, 99, 206).

With his colleagues Eleanor Rosch and Evan Thompson, Varela explains enaction or "embodied action" in the following manner:

> By using the term *embodied* we mean to highlight two points: first, that cognition depends upon the kinds of experience that come from having a body with various sensorimotor capacities, and second, that these individual sensorimotor capacities are themselves embedded in a more encompassing biological, psychological, and cultural context. By using the term *action* we mean to emphasize once again that sensory and motor processes, perception and action, are fundamentally inseparable in lived cognition. Indeed, the two are not merely contingently linked in individuals, they have also evolved together.

"The overall concern of an enactive approach to perception," the authors of *The Embodied Mind* continue, "is not to determine how some perceiver-independent world is to be recovered; it is, rather, to determine the common principles or lawful linkages between sensory and motor systems that explain how action can be perceptually guided in a perceiver-dependent world" (pp. 202–3). Perception is fate, as Emerson insisted in "Self-Reliance" and again in "Natural History of Intellect," where he wrote: "Every new impression on the mind is not to be derided, but is to be accounted for, and, until accounted for, registered as an indisputable addition to our catalogue of natural facts. *The first fact is the fate in every mental perception,*—that my seeing this or that, and that I see so or so, is as much a fact in the natural history of the world as is the freezing of water at thirty-two degrees of Fahrenheit" (pp. 37–38, emphasis added).[6] Here "the science of the mind," in Emerson's phrasing, becomes neuroscience, since, as embodied action, the linkage "between sensory and motor systems" is a function—indeed, *the* integrative function—of the nervous system. To be sure, neuroscience is not the only operational level of an enactive cognitive science. Hence Varela posits "multiple levels or units of selection working in parallel" in evolution, from "DNA short sequences, genes, whole gene families, the cell itself," on to "the entire species . . . the ecosystem of actually interacting species, and the global biosphere." Each unit possesses "unique self-organizing qualities, and so . . . its own emergent status with respect to other levels of description" (EM, pp. 192–93). All the same, neuroscience remains a privileged domain for Varela and his colleagues, since cognitive science is principally concerned with the linkage of perception and action, and hence of the sensory and motor processes of the individual organism.

To the extent that the organic network that has evolved, consisting of "multiple levels of interconnected, sensorimotor subnetworks," continues to operate smoothly, "the role of the environment as a source of input recedes into the background." Conversely, as Varela notes, the environment "enters in explanations only on those occasions when systems undergo breakdowns or suffer events that cannot be satisfied by their structures" (EM, pp. 206–7). This biology is perfectly consistent with the perspective articulated by Emerson in the early 1840s in "Self-Reliance" and "Circles" and further developed by him in works ranging from the essays on Swedenborg and Goethe in *Representative Men* through "Natural History of Intellect." As Varela and the neurobiologist Humberto Maturana explain in *The Tree of Knowledge: The Biological Roots of Human Understanding*, "what is distinctive [about living beings] is that their organization is such that their only product is themselves, with no separation between producer and product" (pp. 48–49). Through such "autopoietic organization," living beings "become real and specify themselves at the same time," thereby acquiring autonomy (p. 43). Still, if each organism is born with "an initial structure," it is also born into "a particular place" or "medium that constitutes the ambience in which it emerges and in which it interacts" (pp. 48–49). The medium in question, as Maturana and Varela remark, may "appear to have a structural dynamics of its own, operationally distinct from the living being," yet "there is a necessary structural congruence" between it and the living "unity" (pp. 95–96). This is what enables the organism to survive in the environment—and hence the assertion in "Natural History of Intellect" of the "perfect correspondence" that exists between man and muskrat.

The muskrat, Emerson writes,

> is only man modified to live in a mud-bank. A fish in like manner is man furnished to live in the sea; a thrush, to fly in the air; and a mollusk is a cheap edition with a suppression of the costlier illustrations, designed for dingy circulation, for shelving in an oyster-bank or among the sea-weed. (p. 20)

To the extent, then, that the autopoietic unity (man, muskrat, or mollusk) avoids entering into "destructive interaction with its environment, we as observers will necessarily see between the structure of the environment and that of the unity a compatibility or congruence" (TK, p. 99). Structural changes in the living being "will appear to an observer as having been 'selected' by the environment," even if the environment doesn't actually "determine what happens to the living being" (p. 103). Rather, "the structure of the [disturbed] system determines its interactions by specifying which configurations of the environment can trigger structural changes in it" (pp. 95–96). By the same token, "the interactions of the nervous system" within its ambience "continually trigger in it the structural changes that modulate its dynamic of states"; instead of "'pick[ing] up information' from the environment," the nervous system "brings forth a world by specifying which patterns of the environment are perturbations and what changes trigger them in the organism" (pp. 135–36, 169).[7]

This autopoietic account of the operations of a muskrat's or a human being's nervous system is entirely consistent with Emerson's philosophy of self-reliance; yet, to judge from the paucity of references to neurology in his essays, Emerson seems to have found less that was properly poetic in accounts of neurological processing than in perhaps any other scientific field. As the nineteenth century unfolded, physiologists acquired ever greater abilities to localize neurological functions, from the "separation of sight and hearing from muscular movement" effected by Pierre Flourens to Johannes Müller's "subdivision and specialization of the human sensory apparatus" on the basis of "the doctrine of specific nerve energies" (Crary, pp. 82–83, 89–90). Despite this expanding capability, however, neurology served only to confirm Emerson's conviction that the fixed senses "imprison us" in merely collecting "the surface facts of matter" ("Poetry and Imagination," p. 449). "This plague of microscopes," he shuddered in his essay on Goethe—grotesquely adding that, despite having managed to "strike the harp with a hero's strength and grace," Goethe still "seems to see out of every pore of his skin" (*Representative Men*, p. 183). What makes the image of sight seeping from flesh so grotesque is that it is felt to be unnatural. Had Emerson possessed an understanding of the nervous system like that proposed by Varela, he would probably have viewed matters differently.

"The soul raised over passion," he wrote in 1841, "beholds identity and eternal causation, perceives the self-existence of Truth and Right, and calms itself with knowing that all things go well" (EL, p. 271). For such a soul, having transcended bodily desires, "fear and hope are alike beneath it. . . . In the hour of vision, there is nothing that can be called gratitude, nor properly joy." Even so, the soul raised above the desiring self is itself grounded in an "aboriginal Self." In the same essay, the famous "Self-Reliance," Emerson apostrophizes "the sense . . . which in calm hours rises, we know not how, in the soul," of being "not diverse from things, from space, from light, from time, from man, but one with them," and which proceeds "obviously from the same source whence their life and being also proceed" (p. 268–69). This sense of well-being, of present continuance and of *the present* continuing, is nothing less, I want to suggest, than a sense of internal bodily equilibrium, in which one's activities cease to be driven by one's passions. The experience entails a corresponding harmony between oneself and one's environment, and in this respect "all things go well," nothing is amiss. This is, admittedly, a naturalistic account of what Emerson describes in quasi-supernatural or mystical fashion (much as James did in the allusion to Whitmanian "loafing" cited at the end of Chapter 1). Yet, even at the height of his Transcendentalist phase, even when he is emphasizing the mysterious nature of out-of-body experience ("we know not how"), Emerson imagines it in bodily, rather than extracorporeal, terms. "Here are the lungs of that inspiration which giveth man wisdom," he writes: "We lie in the lap of immense intelligence, which makes us receivers of its truth and organs of its activity" (EL, p. 269). Like the paradigmatically mystical experience recounted half a dozen years earlier in *Nature* ("I become a transparent eyeball . . . the currents of the Universal Being circulate through me"), the individual self, in surmounting passions it might call its own, becomes "part or parcel" of a nervous system that incorporates it, much as an organ or a nerve cell functions as part of a larger organism (EL, p. 10).

THE AMERICAN CHARACTER

That there is always another person in *The Autobiography of Alice B. Toklas* may simply be a way of saying that this is a work that functions as the autobiography of two distinct individuals. The marvelous thing, then, is the way the book suggests these two, Stein and Toklas, living together; it is the story of a life shared, of converging, complementary lives. Yet it is also a book that can be counted on to produce another person, a person whom the reader is likely already to have heard of, and whose name therefore represents something in its own right, on almost every page. "Another person," for example, "who turned up during that week was Bertrand Russell" (p. 151). These cameo appearances, supplementary lives, serve to refine, occasionally even to redefine, one's sense of the two autobiographers—especially of Stein, the one writing. This is why there is always another person like Russell turning up, to turn the heat up again. Stein, writing as Toklas, listens to herself respond:

> Gertrude Stein, to divert everybody's mind from the burning question of war
> or peace, introduced the subject of education. This caught Russell and he
> explained all the weaknesses of the American system of education, particularly

their neglect of the study of greek. Gertrude Stein replied that of course England which was an island needed Greece which was or might have been an island. At any rate greek was essentially an island culture, while America needed essentially the culture of a continent which was of necessity latin. . . . She grew very eloquent on the disembodied abstract quality of the american character and cited examples, mingling automobiles with Emerson, and all proving that they did not need greek. (pp. 151–52)[8]

No, they did not need Greek, these eloquent Americans. They might choose to learn it, as Emerson did; then again, they might not. Thus Donald Sutherland, author of an important early "biography" of Stein's writing, taught classics at the University of Colorado for many years; yet Stein, who had been tutored in Latin at Radcliffe (in order to pass an entrance exam), herself knew no Greek. Not only was such neglect entirely benign, she insisted, it pointed to a peculiarly American strength which had its source in what she called, in the passage above, "the disembodied abstract quality of the american character." But the language here is so disembodied and abstract itself that something more is obviously needed to flesh it out. The disembodied abstract nature of Russell's work on the foundations of mathematics with Alfred North Whitehead (who, as it happens, was host to Russell and Stein on the occasion of their dispute) cannot be what Stein had in mind.

Take away the Greek, and with it the island mentality, and it develops that a "disembodied abstract quality" means something very different for the American character, and for Stein, than it would when applied to an Englishman, even one as uncharacteristic as Russell, with his very public objections to English participation in the First World War. In the series of lectures she gave at the University of Chicago in 1935, Stein asserted that the English in the nineteenth century were characterized by the fact that they "lived their daily life every day" (N, p. 9). She meant by this that they had generally arranged things so that life was predictable and conformed to established patterns. As a result, they could "live their daily life" relatively unselfconsciously, without concerning themselves overmuch with the circumstances that made such a settled life possible, and without fearing disruption. Yet not only were they settled; their language was settled, and it was with this language that Americans like Emerson had to express an entirely different reality, one in which the norm was not a settled life but an unsettled one.

Consequently, words, which Stein regarded not merely as tools crafted by humans but potentially as persons, conscious actors in their own right, "began to have within themselves the consciousness of completely moving"

(N, p. 10). In contrast to the British, Americans and their words were relatively easily abstracted from their circumstances and might wander off in any direction, whether on the page or around the country. Automobiles, as one of Stein's examples of a native strain of abstraction, certainly facilitate this movement, and what she called their "series production" offered an entirely American model of the process (PF, p. 23).[9] Henry Ford's perfection of the assembly line, and with it of a distinctly American capitalism, successfully completed the abstraction of the finished product from the individual assembly worker (with the corresponding alienation of the worker from the product). The worker, no less than the Model T, was interchangeable; and Stein would insist that this form of abstraction was even more fundamentally American than it was capitalist. It could already be found in the work of the prophet of Concord a half century before industrial capitalism had moved its center of operations from England to a relatively democratic America.

Although Washington Irving and James Fenimore Cooper both crop up in her meditations on writing, Stein tended to set Emerson at the head of her personal canon, as she did lecturing at Chicago:

> Those same words that in the English were completely quiet or very slowly moving began to have within themselves the consciousness of completely moving, they began to detach themselves from the solidity of anything, they began to excitedly feel themselves as if they were anywhere or anything, think about American writing from Emerson, Hawthorne Walt Whitman Mark Twain Henry James myself Sherwood Anderson Thornton Wilder and Dashiell Hammitt [sic] and you will see what I mean. (N, p. 10)

As the words were detached from the solidity of things, and from the British environment in which they had acquired their significance, they inevitably became disembodied and abstract. Moreover, such abstraction or detachment clearly went hand in hand with an Emersonian individualism that proclaimed the individual's freedom to be anywhere and to do anything. The cost of this detachment was, on the one hand, Emerson's apparent coldness—what Stein elsewhere called "the New England tradition with its aridity and its sterility, but also with its individuality"—and, on the other hand, the loss of the traditional crafts, with the opportunity they provided of performing a determinate, even personalized, function in the workplace, although usually anonymously (ABT, p. 218).

In reading Stein's list of American writers, one immediately notices the lack of punctuation, only to dismiss it as the sort of thing one has come to expect from her. But in order to get the point of her writing, one needs to rid oneself of such expectations. So attentive herself to the difference the slightest distinctions make, Stein requires that her readers also, in Emersonian fashion, forget everything they know. Each grammatical and rhetorical choice must be felt to pose questions, must be understood as having been a choice at all, to keep it from being automatically registered and thereby dismissed. The way of ignorance, the *negative* way of understanding something by beginning with one's lack of knowledge and not from what one already knows, is often the best way to address Stein. For she was the least automatic of writers, despite the resemblance her writing unquestionably bears to the automatic writing of the psychologists and the surrealists. The difference between what she observed in her studies of automatic writing as an undergraduate at Radcliffe (which I discuss in detail in Chapter 5) and her literary experiments in Paris is rather like that between the English language in English and in American hands. The writing either moves quietly in fixed patterns, which is hardly to move at all, or it acts unpredictably, individually. The difference is between a kind of free association that is not the least bit free because it is entirely grounded on past experience, whether remembered or not—and which consists ultimately of mere offshoots of "daily life"—and a process of dissociation that is free precisely because it is willful and not automatic, and is thereby "detached from the solidity of anything," particularly from patterns of association. When, in the *Autobiography*, Stein has Toklas say that the only way really to read writing like hers is to proofread it, the idea is to dissociate the reading as thoroughly as possible from any context of associations and expectations. (With Emerson too, because it is so difficult to read him consecutively, one tends to compensate by reading him moment by moment—perhaps even more so in the essays than in the journals—without worrying too much about the connections. They will come, or they do not. This is *not* to say that they are unimportant; quite the opposite.) Thus in the list of American writers from Emerson to Hammett, Stein's willful use of a comma after *Emerson* changes the sense of the sentence: from a simple collection, constructed merely on the basis that all these writers were American, to the assertion that a line of American writers, in which Stein squarely set herself, found its origin in Emerson, and descended from him. Giving Emerson pride of place in American literature is hardly an original gesture in itself; what is interesting is, first, that Stein should have done it at all and, second, how indirectly she did it. She made the grammar make her point.

The American tradition is most decidedly not an anonymous one, a fact we probably have Emerson to thank for as much as anyone. Yet aside from her sometimes extravagantly high self-regard, Stein would appear to have little in common with him. Her writing, in sheer diversity and inventiveness of form, may well be the most radical that America has produced, whereas his, much more regular generically, was limited to gnomic verse, lectures, and a voluminous journal. But they both wrote for the "lustres" and were equally unwilling to impose conventional order on what they had written.[10] If American writing is generally less tidy than its British counterpart, that of Emerson and Stein was particularly so. Still, we do not find Stein drawing such comparisons between herself and Emerson. The only one of her predecessors she seems to have acknowledged with more than a passing reference was Henry James, whom, according to Alice Toklas, she liked to call "the precursor" (*Staying on Alone*, p. 86).[11] Yet even about him she was less than candid. It has often been observed, for instance, that despite her assertion in the *Autobiography* that she had not read James during her "formative period," she can already be found quoting from *The Wings of the Dove*, published in 1902, in her first completed work of fiction, *Quod Erat Demonstrandum*, which dates from 1903.

Stein's denial of James's influence is even more duplicitous, however, than it first appears. "She contends," the passage in the *Autobiography* begins,

> that Henry James was the first person in literature to find the way to the literary methods of the twentieth century. But oddly enough in all of her formative period she did not read him and was not interested in him. But as she often says one is always naturally antagonistic to one's parents and sympathetic to one's grandparents. The parents are too close, they hamper you, one must be alone. So perhaps that is the reason why only very lately Gertrude Stein reads Henry James. (p. 78)

Yet if anyone "was the first person in literature to find the way to the literary methods of the twentieth century," it was Emerson (of the generation of Stein's grandparents) and not James; and Stein did herself something of a disservice by so stressing the uniqueness of her own writing that she has been all too often taken at her word, as sui generis, instead of being, as she also insisted and as she genuinely was, a central figure in the Emersonian line of American writing. Of course, it was Emerson himself who argued for the importance of keeping up at least the appearance of self-reliance, if for no other reason than that it was the only way one was likely to get anything of lasting interest done.

When Stein chose to discuss James's literary method, as in her 1934 lecture "What Is English Literature," she described it not as some radical break with the past but instead as typically American, "what American literature had always done." By this, she meant that he wrote essentially after the manner of Emerson. His—James's—

> whole paragraph was detached what it said from what it did, what it was from what it held, and over it all something floated not floated away but just floated, floated up there. . . . And so this makes it that Henry James just went on doing what American literature had always done, the form was always the form of the contemporary English one, but the disembodied way of disconnecting something from anything and anything from something was the American one. The way it had of often all never having any daily living was an American one.
>
> Some say that it is repression but no it is not repression it is a lack of connection, of there being no connection with living and daily living because there is none, that makes American writing what it always has been and what it will continue to become. (LIA, pp. 53–54)

Although it can be said of James that he wrote in discrete paragraphs, this description is much more germane to Emerson's method of composition, which was generally to select paragraphs from his journal and then more or less forcibly to combine them. In this way, the paragraphs dictated the rhythm, so often discontinuous, of his essays.

Whatever James's paragraphs are, they are not about the "daily" lives of his perfectly extraordinary Americans; they are detached, as Stein said, from everyday life. What they may "say" about such lives has little or nothing to do with what he was "doing" in writing such elaborate prose. Stein starts from the fairly obvious point that James's style was greatly in excess of what was needed to describe life naturalistically, and then carries the point two steps further. First, she stresses that James, like all the writers in Emerson's tradition, was never particularly interested in representing any kind of settled, daily life per se. He would introduce "foreign" elements that disturbed the hard-won equilibrium in the same way that his own writing, and that of the other Americans, revised the British equivalent. Second, like all these writers, what kept him writing, and what his writing was meant to suggest if not describe, was a higher reality that transcendentally floated above the individual paragraphs. Between this transcendental function and anything one might be able to gloss about daily existence, there was simply no connection.

"I know that the world I converse with in the city and in the farms," Emerson wrote in the essay he called "Experience," "is not the world I *think*. I observe that difference, and shall observe it. One day I shall know the value and law of this discrepance" (EL, pp. 491–92). The tone here, as most often in Emerson, is that of someone who, although a participant, keeps his wits about him, remaining dispassionate, even objective. As with

Stein, not only did this discrepancy—and detachment—underwrite both the work and the life, it was the sole guarantee of any continuity between the two. The connection, then, was the "lack of connection," and American writing from Emerson to Stein, if not written in the image of American life, still conveyed its negative image—not, however, as the representation of a repressed other, but as the thoughts of a disconnected, liberated self.

The Aboriginal Self

As a Harvard- and Johns Hopkins–educated American of the last quarter of the nineteenth century, Stein would have encountered Emerson's ideas everywhere; more unexpectedly, we now encounter her everywhere in his work. "Illusion, Temperament, Succession, Surface, Surprise, Reality, Subjectivity," he wrote, and he might have been describing Stein's own writing,

> —these are threads on the loom of time, these are the lords of life. I dare not assume to give their order, but I name them as I find them in my way. I know better than to claim any completeness for my picture. I am a fragment and this is a fragment of me. (EL, pp. 490–91)[12]

When Emerson says that he listed his "lords of life" as he did because it was the order he found them "in his way," he is being literally accurate, and having a joke at his own expense. The lines open the magnificent closing section of "Experience," and he had discussed the seven ideas in exactly this order in the preceding pages.

All the same, these "lords of limit," as Auden called them, organized Stein's thought and writing even more thoroughly than they did Emerson's.[13] Whereas he retained a commitment to at least the pretense of objectivity, which he could never keep up, she learned to do without it and to rely entirely on the kind of subjectivism he expressed when he observed, in the same essay, that "thus inevitably does the universe wear our color, and every object fall successively into the subject itself" (EL, p. 489). They both conceived of their first writing as largely scientific in nature, with Emerson preferring the guise of a naturalist, and Stein, perhaps more judiciously, presenting herself as a psychologist. She rid herself more easily of the objective standards of a nonhuman universe and an impersonal language, because the object of her study was always the human subject.

Stein and Emerson both found the rhetoric of science amenable to the transformations they imposed on it: Stein initially with her immense lists of what she called people's "bottom natures," which turned on the minute differences that could be discerned in basically repetitive behavior, and Emerson in the reports he issued of his observations of nature and man. Although he insisted that he lacked any kind of systematic understanding of human experience, Emerson often did sound as if he were making absolute claims. The rhetorical nature of these was foregrounded, however, in the breaks in argumentation for which his essays, many presented initially as public lectures, have become renowned. The claims were made with some effect, not some absolute truth, in mind.

An undercurrent of pathos is produced by a recurring conflict in Emerson's writing. There is, on the one hand, his strong desire for a knowledge of what William James was to call, after him, "the stream of consciousness," along with the desire to redirect the flow and bring the past, dead and done, back to life. But, against this, he possessed an equally strong disillusionment and sense of personal powerlessness. Stein experienced both the desire and the disillusionment in the early period of her writing, which included "Melanctha" and *The Making of Americans*, yet in the decades that followed, when she produced her most original work, Emerson's particular pathos faded away. While she continued to write by the rules he had formulated for himself, she made even the discontinuous style of his essays look conventional. At the same time, she embraced his much-maligned optimism, with its disburdenment of constraints and general "abandon," more fully than he had ever been able to. His pessimism, which even he sometimes overlooked, had severely limited the range of his style. It assured that in the writing after *Nature*, his conscience, always near to hand, took the form either of his fearing that he might have been abandoned by something, God perhaps, which ought to have loved him, or alternatively, that he might abandon, might already have abandoned, something or someone he ought always to love and cherish—his dead son, wife, brother, his possibly dead language.

From Emerson's observation that "our life seems not present so much as prospective," it quite naturally followed that any formulation was sufficient for the moment only insofar as it would have to be changed to suit the next (EL, p. 486). The *continuous present* that Stein aimed at in her writing was only a more generous interpretation of the same recognition. Their writing styles could be unashamedly, although unequally, fragmented because they both held "abandonment"—what Emerson, in other moods, would also call transition, discontinuity, detachment—to be the law of writing as much as it was the unwritten law of life. It was the negative ground for the seven disembodied lords, or lords of disembodiment, in whatever guise they appeared.

That Emerson tended to say the same thing over and over, only rewritten for different occasions, was not a failure on his part to think of something new to say, or a clever way of dressing up and merchandising the few things he did have to say; it was the invention of what, at least in America, was a new rhetoric. It was the kind of "abuse" of language that becomes necessary when people are obliged, in order to distance themselves from communities they find culturally, economically, or socially oppressive, to use the same language as their oppressors. What made this rhetoric so new and powerful in Emerson's hands was that he directed it against a literary tradition that, however much it was his own, was even more so another nation's—a nation America had famously declared its independence from. As Stein would insist a century later, in *Wars I Have Seen*, the English language had presented America with a peculiarly literary "difficulty in proving itself American which no other nation had ever had" (p. 258). Emerson, with his fragmentation of British literary models, his principled stand against "good form," began to break the hold England still had on the language of America. This hold was utterly broken only with Stein's twentieth-century transgressions of all such sense and sensibility.

Emerson was considerably more than just a literary theorist, however, and Stein, who shared all his central literary concerns—originality, power, genius, language—followed him in translating these into more general psychological terms. Human subjectivity, and with it one's sense of possessing an inner life, was not exclusively the domain of writing, and both thinkers desired to examine its operations in the broadest possible light. One would then see more completely and nonreductively how writing actually did figure in it. Emerson's great theme, of course, was the experience of the individual confronted by and confronting, in a single embrace, the self and the universe—the self in the universe, the universe in the self. Nevertheless, his was not a psychology of the "self," if for no other reason than that the word *self* seems to have played only a marginal, almost incidental, role in the expression of his thought. He rarely used the term apart from emphatic pronouns like *himself* and compound nouns like *self-reliance*. This has been obscured for us by such extraordinary readers of his work as Freud and William James, who have made the term so indispensable within the current intellectual climate.[14] It was Emerson, to be sure, who made the term indispensable for them in his essay on "Self-Reliance." But what are we to do with the fact that this is his single use of *self*, naked and exposed, in the essay:

> What is the aboriginal Self, on which a universal reliance may be grounded?
> What is the nature and power of that science-baffling star, without parallax,
> without calculable elements, which shoots a ray of beauty into trivial and
> impure actions, if the least mark of independence appear? (EL, p. 268)

What are we to make of this? What does it make of us?

First, it is true that Emerson possessed a host of other terms that corresponded with various ways of understanding what we call the self. These would include, in this one essay, "man," "the soul," "genius," "mind," "human nature," "consciousness," "my nature," "my constitution," "a great soul," "every pure and wise spirit," "his will," "his being," "character," "humanity," "something godlike in him," "my giant," "essential man." All of these, different as they are, contribute to the remarkable definition Emerson proposed for the power that transforms "self-reliance" from self-possession or mere confidence into a way of acting among others: as "that which relies, because it works and is" (p. 272). Certainly this is the self, but Emerson would refuse to name it here precisely because, as he had suggested a few sentences earlier in what are among his most famous lines, "life only avails, not the having lived. Power ceases in the instant of repose; it resides in the moment of transition from a past to a new state, in the shooting of the gulf, in the darting of an aim" (p. 271). To name the self is to kill it off, deactivate it, put it to rest; and one might say that the strength of Emerson's psychology—perhaps of what he was like as a human being, certainly of what he had to say about it—resided in an accommodation of restlessness that was summed up in his refusal to call a self a *self*.

If in spite of this refusal, he still did conjure up a "Self" (capitalized like a proper name, and echoing "sylph," its opposite number, ether to its earth), it would be fair to say that at least there is nothing of the psychological in this "aboriginal" ground, this ground of all originality. In categorizing the "Self" as a "science-baffling star," Emerson distanced himself from the lines of Beaumont and Fletcher he used as an epigraph to the essay: "Man is his own star; and the soul that can / Render an honest and a perfect man, / Commands all light, all influence, all fate; / Nothing to him falls early or too late. / Our acts our angels are, or good or ill, / Our fatal shadows that walk by us still" (p. 257).[15] These lines, with their astrological imperatives, become a commentary on Emerson's own quasi-scientific figuration ("without parallax, without calculable elements"), yet remain merely in orbit around his "science-baffling" questions. They offer up a weak, because human-centered, reading of what is essentially a negative, originating, denaturing, even unmanning gesture on Emerson's part. "The moment he acts from himself, tossing the laws, the books, idolatries and customs out of the window, we pity him [man] no more but thank and revere him"—for it is only in such acts that "the least mark of independence" appears, and that we can testify that someone has been genuinely touched by the negative, nonscientific (at least insofar as the science in question is incapable of addressing Emerson's questions constructively) and nonpsychological mark of the individual. The moment someone "acts [apart] from himself," he participates in an "aboriginal Self," which has nothing to do with daily existence and a personal self—with one's sense of "identity," as Stein called it, as distinct from a sense of being a "thing in itself" or "entity." It is a sign of Emerson's independence, and of the crucial element of negation in it, that he should call this aboriginality by the name of exactly that which it is not.

After her immensely successful six-month lecture tour of the United States in the mid-1930s (much as Emerson had lectured across America in the 1850s and 1860s), Stein chose to describe the country she had just revisited for the first time in thirty-one years in categories that exactly corresponded to Emerson's distinction between dependent and independent human existence. Her terms, *human nature* and *human mind*, were as disembodied and abstract, even as undistinctive, as she could make them, but in the course of the extended meditation she wrote during the summer of 1935, on "the geographical history of America," she gave them a twist that was not only distinctly American but enabled her to redefine them strictly with regard to America. ("We use the same words as the English do," she wrote some years later, "but the words say an entirely different thing" [WIHS, p. 259].) She determined that the lie of the land in America, its geographical situation, was the plumb line of the mind—of Emerson's "aboriginal self." It was always seen as if from above, flattened out, whereas in other countries it took on the features of human nature and daily existence. America was thus uniquely transcendental, with the disembodiment of Americans and of their writing embodied, as it were, in the land.

In other words, America was even more a state of mind than were other countries; and this is quite obviously true. Americans, for example, might claim the country as theirs to make over only by forgetting the "aboriginal" claims of the native populations they were in the process of murdering and disenfranchising. With their transcendentalisms, both Emerson and Stein responded to the simultaneous impossibility and necessity of living with the blood of genocide on one's hands and one's writing. This was the true "lie" of the land. The saving grace as well as a large part of the horror was that it was so easy not to acknowledge the brutal facts and to imagine a "virgin America" that bore no relation to the actuality—that, as Stein said of James's paragraphs, "just floated, floated up there."[16] Stein, providing in *The Geographical History of America* an analysis of the American writing that she and Emerson and like-minded peers have invented and reinvented, pointed to the relation between it and the awful blank of American geographical history. The lines at the bottom of the first page tell all: "In the United States there is more space where nobody is than where anybody is. That is what makes America what it is" (p. 17).

The Abstract Subject

When Emerson described man, he did not talk of the person one might meet anytime or anyplace—whether in 1836 or 1936, Concord, Massachusetts, or Cheyenne, Wyoming—but focused on the individual removed from what Stein called the "daily life every day," during those moments when a person appeared to transcend him- or herself. It was in such discontinuous moments that man (as Emerson chose to call this generic as well as transcendent human being) was truest to himself, not only to his nature but to nature: when in becoming one with nature, he contained all nature within him. Only then did one fully possess a sense of oneself, a consciousness of one's self, as something entirely different from one's workaday existence. Beginning with the equations of man and nature in his first book, *Nature*, Emerson grounded his idea of nature so thoroughly in his idea of humanity, that in effect there was no nature for him that did not have reference to man. Wilderness, as nature not subject to human encroachment, signified nothing for Emerson (other than perhaps as an irrelevant historical detail), because he would not countenance a "slovenly" sprawling nature without the touch of a human being on it, no Tennessee, that is, without its Stevensian jar.

The extent that nature did sprawl was just another sign, however pathetic, of man's inescapable presence. Despairing of much that he had formerly championed but still fortified in his central equation, Emerson could thus ask in "Fate," "Why should we fear to be crushed by savage elements, we who are made up of the same elements?" (EL, p. 967). A nonhuman universe might pose the threat of irreconcilable difference; for, being human, we sometimes forget that we are also nonhuman. Alternately, we might feel threatened by the similarity: it would mean that we too were not human. In either case, the only sufficiently human response to such a threat would be to embrace it, not in the manner of Christ but after Jacob wrestling at Peniel. Nature, whether human or nonhuman, Emerson insisted, was the same as man, whether human or nonhuman, and it was only armed with this equation, with its absence of "calculable elements," that one might hazard the unknown and the hitherto unknowable. William James's transformation of psychology from philosophical colony to independent science; his brother's arduous, unsettling, masterful novels of consciousness; Gertrude Stein's reinvention of America (and Americans) in the name of a distinctly

American language—each was an expression of the same bravado. They are all variations on Emerson's bitter, brave question.

If Emerson was continually prophesying man, Stein had merely to point to herself. Although she too combined a profound suspicion of the self with an unrepentant individualism, she could write about herself more readily than Emerson did. However discontinuous her sense of self, she still knew that she was completing his prophecies. In calling for "liberating" poets, Emerson had in effect liberated the poets, and Stein could thus afford to be less disinterested in her language than either Emerson or William James, because she had learned from them the full extent that language had its ways—both as something to be made use of, and as something that often, unavoidably, makes use of us (EL, p. 462).

Primarily in the powerful discontinuities of his rhetoric, and in the ways these contribute to the intensity of his writing, Emerson came closest to having the sense Stein had of language as a living, moving, acting entity. One had to come to terms with it almost as if it were another person. When in one of his rare and, as always, displaced uses of the term *self*, Emerson called the poet's songs his "new self," he certainly meant to suggest something of this. He went on, though, to idealize the poet's relation to language, characterizing the poetry as the poet's "progeny," and a heavenly progeny no less (EL, pp. 457–58).[17] Emerson's relation to his own language, inasmuch as the essays are a kind of prose poetry, is actually much better served by Stein's description of poetry than by his own, on which hers was based. "The poet," he explained, "is the Namer or Language-maker, naming things sometimes after their appearance, sometimes after their essence, and giving to every one its own name and not another's" (pp. 456–57). This is all very well, but it tells us remarkably little about what the experience of such naming might be like. The experience, as we see it etched everywhere in Emerson's own writing, was concerned, Stein announced in *Lectures in America*, "with using with abusing, with losing with wanting, with denying with avoiding with adoring with replacing the noun" (p. 211). One has only to examine Emerson's daily waltz with the self to see how this works.

It was the way that writing worked in Stein's life, the life she wrote about, that made her autobiographical project so much like Emerson's. There is more to this resemblance than the peculiarly unfinished styles and the seemingly incomplete nature of their works; more even than the fact that they developed similar critiques of the unitary self at the same time that they constructed whimsical yet often deadly serious authorial selves. What they chiefly have in common is a particular relation of the life to the work. Where they differ is in the way this relation is generally understood. While

Emerson's work has been elevated to the status of a necessary myth, dwarfing his life, Stein's own work is rarely read, yet her life is gigantic, sheer, overwhelming. It has been said of Emerson that no biography can be written of him because he lived so much in the mind.[18] What this means is that no account of the events of his life can begin to do justice to the strength and strangeness of his writing; or, rather, the events that count in the life of the writing are the acts of writing themselves. The writing is alienated from the life as it is normally and narrowly understood. The sole biography that would live up to the standards of Emerson's own work would be one that not only acknowledged that his writing was always a kind of autobiography, but which insisted that what he had to say about himself—whether directly or indirectly—was always about himself as a man writing, *homo scribens*. The writing must not be reduced to psychodrama, whether Freudian or otherwise, if we are going to do justice to either the man or his work. One importance of Emerson lies at least in part in the way he makes us recognize both the strength of our psychologizing tendencies and the necessity of restraining them.

Still, not all psychologizing is of a piece. There are both subjective and objective kinds. "Peter," Emerson once observed in an essay whose very title, "Natural History of Intellect," Stein echoes in *Geographical History of America*, "is the mould into which everything is poured like warm wax, and be it astronomy or railroads or French revolution or theology or botany, it comes out Peter" (p. 53). The exhilarating thing about such subjectivism is that, as Emerson noted in the same essay, "every man is a new method and distributes things anew"; but because what is new quickly loses its novelty when it is repeated, this particular form of individuality needs always to be accompanied by the denial of system if it is to remain original (p. 27). It takes method to restrain method, and in this case only a fragmentary style will remove the personal from the methodical. The personality of the observing subject is thereby consumed, leaving what Emerson elsewhere called one's character in full possession of the field. When on the occasion of an early lecture on Francis Bacon he praised Bacon's "detached observations," Emerson meant by this to praise their fragmentary, nonsystematic nature, and also to suggest that there was no objectivity—no way of "sequestering one object from the embarrassing variety" (this is from the 1841 lecture "Art") and "looking at it as somewhat foreign" (from "Natural History of Intellect")—that was not fragmentary ("Lord Bacon," p. 335; EL, p. 432; NHI, p. 35).[19]

For both Stein and Emerson, the true test of character, and of one's resistance to a subjectivity that identified everything as one's own and lay behind all forms of systematizing, was linguistic. Only at the grammatical level of "putting words next to each other" and "shoving the language around" (which, Stein observed in her late autobiographical text *Wars I Have Seen*, was what enabled the Americans to appropriate the English language for themselves and finish the business of revolution) might one partake of an alternative subjectivity that resisted any conceivable fixing of identity (p. 259). In "Poetry and Grammar" Stein explained that the only activity she had found "completely exciting and completely completing" in school had been the diagramming of sentences, which had provided her with the sense of "completely possessing something and incidentally one's self" (LIA, p. 231). It was this contingent grounding of the self in language, and more exactly in the concreteness of language, that constituted her entirely Emersonian response to Emerson's own quietly astonishing description of thought as a stream in "Natural History of Intellect," which James would put to such good use. "In my thought," Emerson wrote,

> I seem to stand on the bank of a river and watch the endless flow of the stream, floating objects of all shapes, colors and natures; nor can I much detain them as they pass, except by running beside them a little way along the bank. But whence they come or whither they go is not told me. Only I have a suspicion that, as geologists say every river makes its own valley, so does this mystic stream. It makes its own valley, makes its banks and makes perhaps the observer too. (p. 15)

To understand what Stein was doing with the incidental self she presented as an author, one should think of it not as something structured by her language—that is, as exclusively grammatical—but along more Emersonian and rhetorical lines, as activated by it. She was always a moving target, crossing over and under bridges made of words. More readily than the Emerson of the public writings, although not of the twenty-volume journal, she lends herself at one and the same time to psychological accounts of literature and to accounts that would substitute language or writing for the author, because her writing is always about herself and about ways of removing herself from it.

Besides such varieties of psychologizing that emphasize one's subjectivity, there is also the more literally objective case: wherein everything can be seen as if it were a version of oneself. It was this form of making the world over that Emerson had in mind when he wrote, in an oblique commentary on the title of "Natural History of Intellect," that "from whatever side we look at Nature we seem to be exploring the figure of a disguised man" (NHI, p.

21). Such anthropomorphism presented the obvious danger that nature might be understood not merely as a disguised man but as a much-simplified version of man. Emerson's insistence on complicating any idea we might have of ourselves, and on drawing new circles instead of resting with any particular idea of the self, was meant to safeguard us against this prospect. The model of nature as a "disguised man" requires that there be no limit to the disguises of man.

The corollary, that there are necessary limits to what one can know, obliged Emerson to posit ignorance as constitutive of the self: and this held for Stein too. When she confessed in *Wars I Have Seen* that "I always take it for granted that people will know who I am and at the same time at the last moment I kind of doubt," it is the combination of so much self-assurance with the lingering self-doubt, and the remarkable precision of her expression (in the composed and utterly deflating movement from "always" to "at the same time" and then "at the last moment," at the very last moment of the sentence, a "kind of doubt") that marks her as Emersonian (p. 245). "An intellectual man," Emerson wrote in "Natural History of Intellect," or, as Stein must have read it, an intellectual woman

> has the power to go out of [her]self and see [her]self as an object; therefore [her] defects and delusions interest [her] as much as [her] successes. [S]he not only wishes to succeed in life, but [s]he wishes in thought to know the history and destiny of a [wo]man. (p. 36)

It was this desire to know, and even to prophesy, their own histories and destinies that caused Stein and Emerson to go out of themselves and to write their histories, their destinies, their representative lives, their own biographies, themselves; yet, except perhaps in the matter of degree, this alone is not sufficient to distinguish them from other intellectual men and women with the same need to know and to write.

"And I said there was Emerson," Stein recalled in an essay she wrote for *Cosmopolitan* about her visit to America—it had the modest title "I Came And Here I Am"—"and there was Hawthorne and there was Edgar Poe and there was Walt Whitman and there was, well, in a funny way there was Mark Twain and then there was Henry James and then there was—well, there is—well, I am" (HWW, p. 72). In this account of her literary genealogy, Stein illustrates the chief lineaments of Emerson's legacy. "Then there was—well, there is—well, I am." The fragmentary nature of this, the obvious discontinuity of the syntax and the diction, the abstractness of it—these all play a part, but the essential aspect is, first, the replacement of the past by the present ("there was" won't quite work), and then, along with this, a doubt as to the very existence of the self ("there is" won't do), coupled with a strong assertion of the individual ("I am" it must be).

In the course of acknowledging her indebtedness to a line of American writers, Stein nevertheless manages to foreground the absolute discontinuity between herself and them. As she relegates them to the past and, in the same gesture, irons out their considerable differences with the repetitive formula *there was . . . and there was . . .* , they drop off into a writer's oblivion, leaving their strengths for her to assume as she will. Emerson, somewhere in that oblivion, would have been proud of his pupil, although as the original Emersonian he would have had to be prouder of himself for having produced such a wonder, and at the same time rendered anxious by the suspicion that he might have learned something from her.

THE INDIVIDUAL, ABSOLUTE?

In her variously autobiographical writings Stein positioned herself directly against the strongly anti-Emersonian, anti-individualist theory of literary production that found its classic expression in T. S. Eliot's "Tradition and the Individual Talent." In this essay, Eliot located what he called "the effect, the dominant tone," of a poem in the combination of a "structural emotion" (which the entire "dramatic situation" of the work provided) with "a number of floating feelings" that the writer attached to "particular words or phrases or images" (SW, pp. 57, 54). Eliot aimed, in his "Impersonal theory of poetry," to "divert interest from the poet to the poetry," and consequently chose to minimize the importance for the writer of the "particular events in [her] life" (pp. 53, 59, 57). It was only a short step from this to the anti-intentionalist line developed by W. K. Wimsatt and Monroe Beardsley a generation later, and it is precisely this Coleridgean divorce of the writer from the writing that, as the alternative emphasis in Stein's work suggests, was meant to serve as a way of limiting both the writing and the variety of selves that might be entertained in the writing to something more manageable, something altogether less individual.

When Wimsatt made the perfectly reasonable claim in his essay "Genesis: An Argument Resumed" that the motives of past moments become less and less clear as time passes, it was in order that he might the better "discriminate between the cogently organized artistic structure" of a work of literature and "the particularities of personal moments" (p. 37). It was just this discrimination that Stein, in more than forty years of writing, made a little harder to make, as she tried to do away with—or do without—both the "cogently organized artistic structure" and the sense that the "particularities of personal moments" could be dismissed as merely transitory and minor. Instead she wanted to organize artistic structure on the basis of the particularities of the personal moment, looking for what one might well call cogently organized structures of disorganization, or cogently disorganized constructions of selfhood, as being truer to her sense of the difficulties an Emersonian individualism (the Emerson of "our moods do not believe in each other") would come up against in the twentieth century (EL, p. 406).

Often the difficulties the reader is confronted with in Stein's work are enough, however, to send one back for relief to the more familiar complexities of our own late- and post-twentieth-century lives; and it was to counter retreats like this from her "terrible simplicities" (Emerson's phrase, from "The Poet") that Stein provided various accounts, beginning with "Composition as Explanation," of why she wrote the way she did—of what it was that, as she often said, was "bothering" her at different times.[20] If these accounts do not exactly provide a foundation on which to build—Stein was not in the business of providing foundations—they do serve the function of showing that interpretation is possible. They get one over a threshold that threatens to nip even the prospect of interpretation in the bud; and that is about all they can do with this writing that is so foreign to the conventions of both literary and everyday language.

On the subject of the related unconventionality of Matisse and Picasso, Stein wrote in *Lectures in America* that a genuine familiarity with oil painting makes it impossible to deny that a painting, no matter how shocking, actually is a painting.[21] When Matisse's "La femme au chapeau" (the first of his works that Stein and her brother Leo bought) was exhibited in 1905, at the autumn salon in Paris, "it infuriated the public, they tried to scratch off the paint." It "was not attractive," Stein observed, precisely because it was so original, just as the early Picassos were "awful," "ugly" (ABT, pp. 34, 23). They were much more difficult to grasp, and therefore accept, than prettier, more derivative work. The paintings were a "bother," but they did not present the artist with "the bother of a refusal" (LIA, p. 80).

Stein, however, repeatedly experienced such refusals with her writing. Whereas no one seriously denied that Matisse and Picasso were painters, crude or garish as their work might appear, when Stein sent the manuscript of *Three Lives* to a vanity press to get it published—since no commercial press would take it—she found herself confronted with the following situation, as she recalled it in the *Autobiography*:

> One day some one knocked at the door and a very nice very american young man asked if he might speak to Miss Stein. She said, yes come in. He said, I

have come at the request of the Grafton Press. Yes, she said. You see, he said slightly hesitant, the director of the Grafton Press is under the impression that perhaps your knowledge of English. But I am an american, said Gertrude Stein indignantly. Yes yes I understand that perfectly now, he said, but perhaps you have not had much experience in writing. I suppose, said she laughing, you were under the impression that I was imperfectly educated. He blushed, why no, he said, but you might not have had much experience in writing. (p. 68)

It proved all too easy for people to refuse Stein's writing by leveling such ad hominem attacks on her somehow obvious ignorance. Among the most vicious of these was the review of *Composition as Explanation* that appeared in *The Calendar of Modern Letters*, a short-lived but highly intelligent and provocative British periodical, in which Stein was described as possessing "an intellect so cloudy as to be literally defective" (Holms, p. 187). Her response to the "very nice very american" young man in the *Autobiography* is, to the contrary, so decisive that it asks to be read not just as one incident in a book comprising many such incidents but as a declaration of her own independence as a writer, once and for all. "It's alright," she said to the young man, "I will write to the director and you might as well tell him also that everything that is written in the manuscript is written with the intention of its being so written and all he has to do is to print it and I will take the responsibility" (p. 68).

Stein's insistence here that her independence and her composition (the conscious manipulation of her language) be respected could well have been Emerson's; but he did not confront the same obstacles she did. First, as a woman, she could count on less intellectual respect, among both Americans and Europeans, than a male American writer would receive even in provincial England. Emerson, on the other hand, was given a great deal of benefit of the doubt, both at home and abroad, with the consequence that his intentions were often wildly misconstrued. Yet at least he was read and respected. Moreover, Stein was mistaken when she proposed that the form of American writing "was always the form of the contemporary English one." Much as this had certainly been true of Emerson's writing, it was not true of her own, which had more in common with the paintings of Picasso and the assorted postmodernisms of the past thirty years than it had with the work of British contemporaries like Edith Sitwell, Virginia Woolf, and Wyndham Lewis.[22] Other American writers resembled the British, but not Gertrude Stein.

Her alliance with Emerson comes across particularly clearly in the compositional history of some works that are among the most "imperfectly" written, the pieces she collected in *Matisse Picasso and Gertrude Stein with Two Shorter Stories*. This was one of five books that she and Toklas published under the Plain Edition imprint with the proceeds from the sale of an early Picasso, "Woman with a Fan." Although published shortly after Stein wrote the *Autobiography*, the three pieces in *Matisse Picasso and Gertrude Stein* dated back to 1911 and 1912. They were written around the time she completed *The Making of Americans*, when she embarked on what was to be an even longer work, optimistically named *A Long Gay Book*. Simultaneously, as she recalled in *Lectures in America*, she "began several shorter books which were to illustrate the Long Gay Book, one called Many Many Women another Five, another Two and another G.M.P., Matisse Picasso and Gertrude Stein" (p. 148). In her initial conception of *A Long Gay Book*, as in the bulk of *The Making of Americans*, Stein's concerns had been explicitly scientific as well as literary. In keeping with an ideal of "complete description," she wanted to describe "every possible kind of human being" in *The Making of Americans*, and in the subsequent works "the way every kind of human being acted and felt in relation with any other kind of human being" (LIA, pp. 156, 150).²³ But instead, *A Long Gay Book* turned into "A Long Gay Book," which was published together with "Many Many Women" as the two shorter stories of the Plain Edition volume.²⁴

Stein began writing "A Long Gay Book" and "Many Many Women" near the end of 1910, during a break in the composition of *The Making of Americans* which continued until the next summer. At the same time she began to compose brief portraits of acquaintances—among the first, one of Alice Toklas, who in September had moved into the apartment Stein shared with her brother Leo. The portraits that Stein wrote early in 1911, mainly of artists she knew, included those of Matisse and Picasso subsequently published by Alfred Stieglitz in his journal *Camera Work*. In these Stein tried to portray the attitudes of her subjects toward themselves—what they looked like to themselves—by conveying the relation between what they were saying and how they were saying it. In *Lectures in America*, she described her technique: "I said what I knew as they said and heard what they heard and said until I had completely emptied myself of all they were that is all they were in being one hearing and saying what they heard and said" (p. 178).

These portraits, and the challenge they presented to her scientific project, in fact enabled Stein to complete *The Making of Americans* later that year, although in a new mode she would come to call philosophical. Philosophy, as she said in her lecture on "The Gradual Making of The Making of Americans," began where science ended, when "one stop[ped] continuing describing everything" in relation to other things and began to focus on each discrete moment—when, like Emerson, one tried to portray objects or states of consciousness instead of merely describing them (LIA, p. 157). (As James counseled in 1909, "Philosophy should seek [a] living understanding of the movement of reality, not follow science in vainly patching together fragments of its dead results" [*Pluralistic Universe*, p. 751].) Near the end of the novel, in the course of the extraordinary portrait of the dying protagonist that Stein wrote in the summer and early fall of 1911, her narrator suggests that what distinguishes one person from another is "the way of experiencing anything and expressing that thing" (MA, p. 783). The earlier portraits were an ingenious solution to the problem of conveying a person's innermost nature, for they did not require Stein to claim that one could somehow enter into another person's consciousness as one might with a fictional character. In portraying the experience of someone talking and listening, Stein merely had to claim that the simultaneous expression of that experience might be caught in the movements of the talk itself. These portraits were quite literally verbal portraits, portraits of others' words (or more precisely, of their relations to words) as well as portraits in Stein's own words.

Through the fall and winter of 1911–12 Stein continued to work on her group portraits. There was an inherent tension, however, between her general concern to describe "what any one feels acts and does in relation to any other one," as she later characterized it, and her recent successes in individual portraiture (LIA, p. 150). The tension was resolved in "Many Many Women" only by ending the work. The last paragraph offers a model of her dilemma: It consists of a string of "ones" initially related in one form or another ("Any one and any one, one and one and two, and one and one and one, and one and many, and one and some, and one and any one . . ."), yet ending on an affirmation of individuality ("The one who is the one who is that one, any one and any one is one, one is one, one is that one, and any one, any one is one and one is one, and one and one, and one and one and one and one" [GMP, pp. 197–98]). Stein perfected the remarkably abstract and disembodied language of these portraits in order to rid the words of her private associations and of any obvious reference to her life. Nevertheless, Leo Stein's criticism, as she reported it in *Everybody's Autobiography*, is still trenchant. "He said it was not it it was I. If I was not there to be there with what I did then what I did would not be what it was. In other words if no one knew me actually then the things I did would not be what they were" (p. 60). Stein is certainly correct when she insists that this was not entirely true, and that one does not need to know what the writing originally referred to in order to get a good deal out of it; still, she was unable to remove the traces of the removal. One reads these pieces, not in the absence of referentiality, but knowing full well that someone has removed the local references. The demand for embodiment has not been quieted.

It was because these portraits still had to be filtered through Stein's own consciousness that she decided, in the summer of 1912, to use words that ideally had nothing in them of what she later called the "quality of description" (LIA, p. 191). As long as the words continued to function at all descriptively, not only would the object or individual state of consciousness be removed from the present moment, it would necessarily be described as it appeared to her instead of being portrayed as it was in itself. For Stein, no less than for Emerson, a person was a mode of being—in particular a mode of making and getting one's way—and an adequate portrait would have to convey the individual's tendency or direction without objectifying it, that is, without equating it with what was already known. That Stein wanted to do something that seemed impossible, since she could no more enter the consciousness of another person than abandon her own, was no objection. Its impossibility was precisely what interested her. After all, as she explained in her lecture on *The Making of Americans*, she had stopped "describing everything" only when she was "at last really convinced that a description of everything [was] possible" (LIA, p. 157). Just as Emerson wrote "whim" on the lintels of his doorpost, Stein might have nailed up the sign, "If it can be done why do it," to give prospective readers some idea of the uncompromising and hardy transcendentalism they would find in her writing (LIA, p. 157).[25]

THE EXPERIENCE OF THE UNKNOWN

The portraits composed in early 1911 not only enabled Stein to complete *The Making of Americans* that year but also opened up the way for the technical innovations of 1912 and 1913, most notably in her portraits of "Objects," "Food," and "Rooms" in *Tender Buttons*. Rather than choosing words for their descriptive value, she began to compose with them in much the same way that Matisse and Picasso composed with color and line. "In hundreds of ways," she recalled in one of her *Lectures in America*, "I related words, then sentences then paragraphs to the thing at which I was looking" (p. 192). Words, she felt, could be made to possess meaning in their grammatical, rhetorical, and metrical aspects, rather than as concepts per se or representations.

The analogy to Matisse and Picasso is not incidental. Although Stein had known the two artists, and with her brothers collected their works, since

1905—she introduced them to each other—they were especially on her mind during this transitional period in her writing. In February 1912, the portraits she had composed of them were accepted for publication by Stieglitz, who proposed to print a special number of *Camera Work* with, as he put it in a letter dated February 26, "a few Picasso's and a few Matisse's reproduced as illustrations to accompany your text." He added: "You have undoubtedly succeeded in expressing Matisse and Picasso in words, for me at least" (FF, p. 57). *Three Lives* had been published in 1909, yet it had been at Stein's own expense; this was the first acceptance of her work for publication, after years of rejections, and Stieglitz was accepting her on equal terms with Matisse and Picasso.

Sometime that spring, Stein began work on the piece she called "G.M.P." Although she referred to it in one letter as "the long one about the whole Paris crowd," it was more precisely an account of, and an accounting for, the relative accomplishments of the three leaders of the art world as she viewed it—Matisse, Picasso, and herself (Everett, p. 171). Her faith, along with that of Toklas, in her own genius was a rather lonely affair in Paris, unpublished and unread in a country whose native tongue was not English and where she did not move in a particularly literary circle. (If she had, she would have fared no better; women were not encouraged to write in the French avant-garde.)[26] Stieglitz's recognition was a much-needed boost, and Stein made the most of it. That same spring she also bought her first painting by Picasso independently of Leo, "The Architect's Table," a late work of high Analytic Cubism (see Figure 10). Picasso had painted her calling card into the composition after she had left it at his studio "as a joke" (ABT, p. 111). His appropriation of her signature, however, was no joke.

In the first place, the signature was in the lower right-hand corner of the oval painting, which suggested that she might have painted it. Was it a representation of any work of hers? Of what her work might become? (As when people questioned the likeness of his early portrait of her, and he said that she would come to look like it?) Was any of her writing as superb as this? Was this the best she could do? Alternatively, he could be seen as defining her in terms of her social relation to him rather than as a fellow artist— the kind of woman who left her calling card, had a salon, might buy his paintings. Moreover, hers was one of two women's names in the painting, the other being "Ma Jolie."[27] In the *Autobiography*, the juxtaposition is hastily defused with a referential appeal: "As we went away Gertrude Stein said, Fernande is certainly not ma jolie, I wonder who it is. In a few days we knew. Pablo had gone off with Eve" (p. 111). The rather crude joke is that Stein certainly wasn't *ma jolie* either. But if *ma jolie* could be decoded as

Figure 10.   "The Architect's Table," by Pablo Picasso (early 1912). Oil on canvas, mounted on oval panel, 28⁵/₈ × 23¹/₂″ (72.6 × 59.7 cm). (© 2001 Estate of Pablo Picasso / Artists Rights Society, New York. Photograph © 2001 The Museum of Modern Art, New York, William S. Paley Collection.)

Picasso's new mistress—Eve to his Adam—then who did "Miss Gertrude Stein" refer to? Who, Gertrude Stein might ask, *was* Miss Gertrude Stein? Was she the signatory of an already considerable body of literature? Was she the close friend of this protean artist? Of Picasso's 1905–6 portrait of her, she would write in the *Autobiography* that, after leaving it unfinished in the spring, he "painted the head in" when he returned to Paris that fall, "without having seen Gertrude Stein again"—"out of *his* head," like Zeus giving birth to Athena (p. 57).[28] (See Figure 11.) In her 1938 book on him, she observed: "I was and I still am satisfied with my portrait; for me, it is I, and it is the only reproduction of me which is always I, for me" (p. 34). Now he had painted a portrait of her signature.

It was with this threat to her individuality—and to her originality, for if he could reproduce her so readily, was she perhaps merely copying Picasso's techniques?—along with the challenge she had received from Stieglitz and her dissatisfaction with her abstract writing style for the ambitious program of portraiture she was contemplating, that Stein left Paris, to spend the summer with Toklas in Spain. She wanted to make portraits that approached self-portraits; whether they were of other people or of what she called "the rhythm of the visible world," she aimed to present what was seen or heard in the way that "it" saw itself (ABT, p. 119). She had therefore to begin by actively refusing—which was not at all the same as refuting—whatever she might know, through a willful negation of such knowledge. "I would not know what I knew about everything what I knew about anything," she asserted in *Lectures in America* and immediately followed this with an example of how the positive negation she had in mind operated:

> And so the Long Gay Book little by little changed from a description of any one and everything there was to be known about any one, to what if not was not not to be not known about any one about anything. (p. 158)[29]

"What / if not / was not / not to be / not known about . . ." By this succession of negatives, the writing was transformed into the expression and the experience of the unknown: what is not, never was, and never will be known. This was something that was entirely a matter of supposition ("what if") and by the same token, absolutely irrefutable. Perhaps it only existed in the writing; certainly it was an experience of some kind, yet as different from ordinary experience as the world of Emerson's thoughts was from that of everyday conversation. All the same, it was Stein's quite literal concentration on the negative that, in purely formal terms, served to liberate her style from the monumental and quasi-scientific rhythms of *The Making of Americans* and made possible later that summer and fall the delicate miracles of *Tender Buttons*.

Figure 11. Pablo Picasso, "Portrait of Gertrude Stein" (1905–6). (The Metropolitan Museum of Art, Bequest of Gertrude Stein, 1946. © 2001 Estate of Pablo Picasso / Artists Rights Society, New York.)

The works that Stein carried with her to Spain—"Two," "Jenny, Helen, Hannah, Paul and Peter," "A Long Gay Book" and "G.M.P."—all flesh out the quintessentially Emersonian "moment of transition from a past to a new state." They are transitional both literally and figuratively, instances of it and stances toward it. Like Picasso's portrait of her as well as his 1907 "Desmoiselles," they aim to study change, tease it out—to portray movement without resorting to the illusion, the repose, of either narrative sequence or the new medium of the motion picture. A few pages after the new synesthetic style is introduced in "A Long Gay Book" with the "gentle little tinkle" of "A tiny violent noise is a yellow happy thing," along with the increasing quantity of negations, Stein comments, "She could not be saying that authorising something was believing that she was not having what she was having" (GMP, pp. 82, 87). This indirect, almost indeterminate note on her writing is followed by a correspondingly decisive statement on its own writing: "Now I have it. Now I see. This is the way. Not that way. The other way is not the way." It is a tangible moment of self-recognition, when Stein sees her way and sees herself already on it. The next sentence, which opens a new paragraph, completes this local study of transition: "A lively way to call is to run and call and a lively way to stand is to stand" (p. 87).[30]

One of the effects of the shift in style in these pieces is that it becomes increasingly hard while reading them to attend to the "author." It is not that the writing takes on an impersonal veneer. On the contrary, it appears that much more subjectively and obviously "written," even as the sense of a stable, consistent author goes out the window. Some kind of "individual force" undoubtedly remains, to distinguish the "actual creation" from what Stein in the *Autobiography* characterized as "the sensitiveness of the hysteric"—if nothing more than the outrageous conceit that yoked the styles together in the first place (p. 228). Yet Stein was able here to cut her writing loose, so that it was no longer anchored in either the personality or the impersonality of the author. She was probably noting this herself when she wrote in "A Long Gay Book" that "largely additional [the earlier style?] and then completely exploding [the later one?] is one way to deny authorisation" (GMP, p. 98).

The point was not to deny the author's existence, but to deny the claims made for any "authorisation" (which could be grounded as readily in a cult of impersonality as in a personality cult). It was the sense that there might be an authoritative version of anything, an authorized biography, for instance, that Stein utterly rejected. Another way of denying such authorization—and another way of reading her formula—can be seen in her manipulation of the title of the collection in which "A Long Gay Book" and

"G.M.P." appeared: alternately *Matisse Picasso and Gertrude Stein* and *G.M.P.* The three titular figures are reduced literally to their initial "characters," and the order of these is shifted. This is surely an "explosion," a complete fragmentation, of what was initially additive. What made for the thoroughness of Stein's anti-authoritative stance was not, however, that the one title was reduced to the other but that the two titles continued to exist in tandem, just as Stein's name appeared both in the title and on the title page. Any such distancing of herself from what still had to be called her self—whether accomplished as it was here or in a work like the third-person *Autobiography*—raised doubts about the self and about any authority derived from it that Eliot's stress on impersonality refused to admit. Again, it was not that Stein did away with the self, or even rejected it, but that by exploiting a formal discrepancy between the two wildly diverging styles in *Matisse Picasso and Gertrude Stein*, she was able to get away from it, at least in pieces like these.

Her doubts about the self were in fact inextricably linked with the set of doubts that characterized Matisse's and Picasso's own work. Matisse, she explained in her study of Picasso, "began to doubt what his eyes could see," and Picasso carried this even further in his "long struggle / not to express what he could see / but / not to express the things he did not see, that is to say the things everybody is certain of seeing, but which they do not really see" (pp. 22, 47).

Emerson made the same point when he observed in "Self-Reliance" that "there are roses under my window that make no reference to former roses or to better ones; they are for what they are; they exist with God to-day" (EL, p. 270).[31] To see things as they are, and not merely to observe what is anticipated or remembered, one has to rid oneself, empty oneself, of everything one already knows—one has to get out of "the habit," as Stein put it, "of knowing what one is looking at" (P, p. 47). Stein understood so clearly what Picasso was doing because he was, in his painting, Emerson all over again. The hysterical blindness that Emerson experienced as a student at the Harvard Divinity School left its mark on his transcendentalism, with the result that his own "self-doubts," as any glance at his writing will show, were always tied up with doubts as to what, and whether, his eyes could see.

"Matisse, Pablo and I," Stein observed in a notebook she kept during the writing of *The Making of Americans*, "do not do ours with either brains or character, we have all enough of both to do our job but our initiative comes from within a propulsion which we don't control, or create" (PCW, p. 107). Here again Stein's artistry, in this respect so like Emerson's, is exhibited in her use of the more formal characteristics of her writing to convey ideas that are quite explicitly expressed in the writing—often suggesting turns of thought, in addition, that go beyond what merely gets "said." In this sentence, for example, the ellipsis of a comma propels one element of an apposition ("our initiative comes from within") directly into the other ("a propulsion which we don't control") in an almost bodily collision. Although it might be argued that Stein in fact did "control," and even "create," this propulsion—having removed the comma in the first place—it is precisely her own "initiative" that remains indeterminate, and quite happily so. As long as we are unable to decide whether she chose not to use the comma or whether she involuntarily neglected it, the sentence provides a self-reflexive, nonreductive portrait of the spontaneity at its own heart—the spontaneity coming from within, from "a propulsion which we don't control, or create." Stein's addition of a comma at the end of the sentence was equally inspired, both as a counterweight to the ellipsis and as a way of giving equal weight to both elements of the nonappositive pair, "control" and "create." This is a genuinely wandering comma, propelled from the first location to the second by the merest slip of a pen.

The spontaneity or instinct or intuition—all Emerson's words—that Stein recognizes in her works as well as in those of Matisse and Picasso is another version of the "aboriginal Self," only invoked in a terminology better suited to the twentieth century; it is the same "deep force" that is addressed in "Self-Reliance," to which all "involuntary perceptions" are due and which paradoxically guarantees one's individuality by insuring that one's perception of anything is "as much a fact as the sun" itself (EL, p. 156). "Place yourself in the middle of the stream of power and wisdom which animates all whom it floats," Emerson preached in the essay he called "Spiritual Laws," "and you are without effort impelled to truth, to right, and a perfect contentment." Your "constitution," he added, would then "organize" itself "as do now the rose, and the air, and the sun" (EL, pp. 309–10). Stein shared these convictions, but what he proposed as a way to live, she developed as a way of writing.

With Emerson, the stress is on writing as a part of life, whereas Stein was much quicker to incorporate the minute particulars of life into her own writing. Yet for both of them, if life was essentially something that was written, it also had less to do with the peripheral and particular activity of writing than they would have liked. It is finally this alternatively diverging and converging movement between life and writing, rather than any distinct concept of life or writing, that they shared and which makes for the commerce between them. The lack of connection between life and writing was not, they both rather desperately hoped, a sign of a deeper repression—of a deeper yet still too shallow connection—but simply a consequence of the impermanence of any connection one might make. It was not that there were none, but that every connection was temporary, a placeholder. The essential thing was the making of connections, not the connections themselves. The best explanation of what one was doing in writing was therefore to be found in the writing itself. By taking the "composition" as its own explanation, as Stein suggested, both the reader and the writer were freed to make their own connections and to draw their own conclusions. But they could only exercise this freedom within the constraint of trying to understand how the composition might be explained in its own terms, how it would explain itself; and the impossibility of ever getting this explanation exactly right was what enabled the writing to live on in any particular account of it.

The writer's experience in the act of composition, the reader's in construing such an act—these were alternative explanations of the "finished" composition itself, something that although it had no existence independent of these activities, at the same time transcended them, and, remaining distinct from them, "just floated, floated up there." For Stein, as for Emerson, a theory of life was necessarily indistinguishable from a theory of writing, and if to a more British, more orderly mind, this must signify a "cloudy" intellect, for Emerson, as for Stein, it was the clouds—literally, figuratively, above everything—that spoke most profoundly of the life of things, and of the permanent flux, and of the writing on both sides of the wall. "Crossing a bare common, in snow puddles, at twilight, under a clouded sky. . . ." (EL, p. 10).

CHAPTER FOUR

At the Whiteheads': Science and the Modern World

Early in July 1914, as storm clouds gathered over Europe in the fast-ebbing twilight of the nineteenth century, Stein and Toklas crossed the Channel to make arrangements for the publication of an English edition of *Three Lives*. One evening, at a dinner party in Cambridge, the visiting Americans were introduced to Alfred North Whitehead and his wife, Evelyn, and Toklas "met [her] third genius" (ABT, p. 145). "Only three times in my life," the Toklas of the *Autobiography* would comment,

> have I met a genius and each time a bell within me rang and I was not mistaken, and I may say in each case it was before there was any general recognition of the quality of genius in them. The three geniuses of whom I wish to speak are Gertrude Stein, Pablo Picasso and Alfred Whitehead. I have met many important people, I have met several great people but I have only known three first class geniuses and in each case on sight within me something rang. In no one of the three cases have I been mistaken. (p. 5)

Invited to spend "the last week end in July with them in their country home," Stein and Toklas were visiting the Whiteheads in Lockeridge when war broke out. The weekend over, they told Evelyn Whitehead that they would have to leave. "But you cannot get back to Paris now, she said. No, we answered, but we can stay in London. Oh no, she said, you must stay with us until you can get back to Paris" (p. 147). Aside from brief visits to London to inquire as to when they might go back, Stein and Toklas remained in Lockeridge for the next eleven weeks; only in mid-October, in the company of Mrs. Whitehead, did they return to Paris.

Toklas's remark on the shared "quality" of genius possessed by Stein, Picasso, and Whitehead needs to be read, like all such comments concerning Stein in the *Autobiography*, as commentary by Stein about herself.[1] Lately, the concept of genius has fallen out of favor as a term of general approbation, in part due to a sense that its use privileges an inherently elitist individualism and thereby perpetuates an overly sharp division between the

165

individual and society. In addition, the term is strongly gendered—although for this reason alone it might be viewed as a stroke of genius for Stein to attribute the quality to herself. A widespread interest in the operations of the unconscious has replaced the earlier, relatively unselfconscious concern with genius, a shift already suggested in Logan Pearsall Smith's essay "Four Romantic Words," from his 1925 collection, *Words and Idioms: Studies in the English Language*. Pearsall Smith, an important expatriate critic and prose writer who lived in England from 1888 until his death in 1946, was a student of William James's and a friend of both Stein and her brother Leo. His sisters married Bernard Berenson and Bertrand Russell, and Stein first met Russell when she and Leo visited the Pearsall Smiths—parents, siblings, in-laws—near Greenhill-Fernhurst in 1902.

The meanings of the four terms *originality*, *creative*, *imagination*, and *genius* had been "much enriched," Pearsall Smith wrote,

> by the modern conception of the unconscious self. Although many psychologists would not now accept, without considerable qualifications, the earlier notion of the Unconscious as the abiding place of genius, and the source of inspiration, yet they would probably all agree that something analogous to the conscious processes of thought, which may go on beneath awareness, and reveal itself to it in a sudden uprush, probably plays an important, and possibly a dominant, role in what we call inspiration and the creative activity of genius. (p. 118)[2]

Stein resisted the equation of genius and the unconscious, however, instead emphasizing the more traditional identification of genius with a *heightened* state of consciousness. What exactly did she have in mind, then, in calling herself a genius and linking herself in that capacity to Picasso and, in particular, to Whitehead? She certainly didn't mean what Robert McAlmon did when he titled his account of 1920s expatriate life *Being Geniuses Together*. In her 1963 memoir, *What Is Remembered*, Toklas recalled that Whitehead "had a most benign sweet smile and a simplicity that comes only in geniuses" (p. 83). Although *simplicity* might not seem a defining attribute of genius, Stein characterized it as exactly that in her monograph on Picasso. The surrealists, she proposed,

> still see things as every one sees them, they complicate them in a different way but the vision is that of every one else, in short the complication is the complication of the twentieth century but the vision is that of the nineteenth century. Picasso only sees something else, another reality. Complications are always easy but another vision than that of all the world is very rare. That is why geniuses are rare, to complicate things in a new way that is easy, but to see things in a new way that is really difficult, everything prevents one, habits, schools, daily

life, reason, necessities of daily life, indolence, everything prevents one, in fact there are very few geniuses in the world. (pp. 79–80)[3]

Picasso, Stein suggests here, saw the present in its own terms rather than through the lens of the past century and hence refracted through "habits, schools, daily life," even "reason." He was "contemporary with the things" he saw, and it is this immediate perception of the present (whether that of Picasso or Whitehead, or her own acknowledgment of the actual present) that Stein attributed to "genius" and Toklas characterized as being "simplicity" itself (PCW, p. 80).[4]

In this respect, the quality linking Toklas's three "first class geniuses" is closer to what Stein elsewhere referred to as a "simply complicated" normality than to the more "obvious" complications of either abnormal psychology or surrealism (ABT, p. 83). Nonetheless, for Stein, as for Emerson, there was more to genius than a "really difficult" simplicity. These further elaborations (for example, the suggestion that genius takes the form of simultaneous "talking and listening," or the observation, in *Everybody's Autobiography*, that it is a matter of "existing without any internal recognition of time") need to be understood as reformulations of the Romantic conception of genius and in particular of Emerson's frequent invocations of a "solitary, grand, secular" genius (LIA, p. 170; EA, p. 251; NHI, p. 52).[5] Indeed, Stein seems to have associated Whitehead quite directly with Emerson. Not only does the single mention of Emerson in the *Autobiography* occur during the account of the extended visit at Lockeridge (on the occasion of the dispute with Russell concerning "the american character"), but that summer she composed a work, "Mrs. Emerson," whose title, as I shall presently argue, alludes to Evelyn Whitehead.

"Walk[ing] endlessly around the country" with her host, "talking about all things" and "philosophy and history" in particular, Stein would have discovered a striking correspondence between the Cambridge don's thought and that of Emerson—all the more striking as Whitehead had coauthored, with Russell, the monumental *Principia Mathematica*, which aimed to place mathematics on a firm logical footing (ABT, p. 148). "It was during these days," Stein noted in the *Autobiography*, that she "realised how completely it was Doctor Whitehead and not Russell who had had the ideas for their great book" (p. 153). Needless to say, Whitehead is principally recalled today, when he is recalled at all, as the lesser half of the composite author *Russell/Whitehead*, who wished to demonstrate that all knowledge of the world—and not just that provided by mathematics—conformed to the patterns of logic.[6] Although this caricature might hold for Russell, at least during the part of his career when he was developing his philosophy of logical atomism, it never held for his teacher and mentor. Instead, Whitehead brought a mind deeply versed in logic to bear on matters that he always recognized as fundamentally irreducible to the categories of logical analysis. Stein would have been forcefully struck by the British logician's expression of an understanding of "Nature and Life," as he titled a pair of lectures delivered twenty years later at the University of Chicago, so similar to Emerson's perspective and her own.

TRANSFORMATIONS OF GENIUS

Whitehead opened the Chicago lectures (which he delivered in 1933, a year or so before Stein embarked on her American lecture tour) with the observation, "Philosophy is the product of wonder" (MT, p. 127). "The effort *after* the general characterization of the world around us," he continued— that is to say, "the aim *at*," rather than the aim *of*, "philosophic understanding"—"is the *romance* of human thought" (pp. 127, 169, emphasis added).[7] Some years earlier, in *Process and Reality*, he had put this the other way around, suggesting that his thought might be viewed as "a transformation of some main doctrines of Absolute Idealism onto a realistic basis" (p. xiii). In either formulation, Whitehead's sense of the romance of philosophy, philosophy understood as continually *aspiring* to some form of general understanding, corresponds to Emerson's open-ended conclusion in "Experience" that "the true *romance* which the world exists to realize, will be the transformation of genius into practical power" (EL, p. 492, emphasis added).[8]

Stein, for her part, contemplated similar alchemical transformations in the "Advertisement" to her 1928 collection *Useful Knowledge*. After positing that "in America the best material is used in the cheapest things because the cheapest things have to be made of the best material to make them worth while," she proposed that the very idea of the "best material [making] the cheapest thing" is what, however fleetingly, "mak[es] into living . . . the *romance* of human being" (UK, p. i, emphasis added). It was this transformation of *genius* (the quality of being "the very best material") into *practical power* (with even "the cheapest things" proving "worth while") which Stein aimed at in her collection of "Useful Knowledge or Americana," as she referred to her new "book of . . . American things" (SVV, I, p. 161). In asserting that "romance is Useful Knowledge," she was suggesting that all romance, any impression that the true action is really taking place elsewhere, contains the potential of being transformed into "practical power," with the action occurring *right now, right here* (UK, p. i). Romance is *useful* knowledge because it inspires one to act, to turn there into here and here into there, even if, as Emerson did not hesitate to remind himself, we "have not found that much was gained by manipular attempts to realize the world of thought" (EL, p. 492).[9]

"Intellect," Emerson proposed in his 1841 essay on the topic, "lies behind genius, which is intellect constructive," both "the thought and its publication" (EL, p. 417). In itself, he explained, thought is

> revelation, always a miracle, which no frequency of occurrence or incessant study can ever familiarize, but which must leave the inquirer stupid with wonder. . . . But to make it available, it needs a vehicle or art by which it is conveyed to men. . . . The thought of genius is spontaneous; but the power of picture or expression [implies] a certain control over the spontaneous states, without which no production is possible.

"Yet the imaginative vocabulary seems to be spontaneous also," he continued. "Not by any conscious imitation of particular forms are the grand strokes of the painter executed, but by repairing to the fountain-head of all forms in his mind" (EL, pp. 422–23). In "Natural History of Intellect," he made the same point, writing that "genius is *a delicate sensibility* to the laws of the world, *adding the power to express them again* in some new form. . . . [It] is not a lazy angel contemplating itself and things. It is insatiable for expression. Thought *must* take the stupendous step of passing into realization" (pp. 39–40, emphasis added).

Nevertheless, in distinguishing thought from expression, Emerson did not suppose that thought could ever be entirely abstracted from expression. On the contrary, he readily spoke of a "language of the intellect," and would no doubt have accepted Whitehead's careful qualification of the claim that "language is not the essence of thought" (EL, p. 489; MT, p. 35). As Whitehead observed, "the denial that language is of the essence of thought" is not equivalent to "the assertion that thought is possible apart from the other activities coordinated with it," activities that together comprise "the expression of thought." Emerson's agreement that "pure thought in abstraction from all expression is a figment of the learned world" is vividly demonstrated by his use of imagery that complements Whitehead's own (MT, pp. 35–36).

"In my thought," Emerson wrote, in a passage already cited, "I seem to stand on the bank of a river and watch the endless flow of the stream. . . . Whence [the floating objects] come or whither they go is not told me. Only I have a suspicion that, as geologists say every river makes its own valley, so does this mystic stream. It makes its own valley, makes its banks and makes perhaps the observer too" (NHI, p. 15). Nearly a century later, Whitehead would also rely on the figure of water to convey his impression of this driest of elements. Thought, as he conceived it,

> is a tremendous mode of excitement. Like a stone thrown into a pond it disturbs the whole surface of our being. But this image is inadequate. For we should conceive the ripples as effective in the creation of the plunge of the stone into the water. The ripples release the thought, and the thought augments and distorts the ripples. In order to understand the essence of thought we must study its relations to the ripples amid which it emerges. (MT, p. 36)

Whitehead's subject, no less than Emerson's, was the "stupendous step" that all thinking, including thought that lacks the "grand strokes" of genius, must take in "passing into realization." Moreover, even as Whitehead and Emerson addressed this process of realization, they exemplified it in their own *passages*, which in this respect function as instances of "intellect constructive," thought expressed in such a manner that it becomes "communicable" (EL, p. 422). Genius, by this account, differs from thought per se only to the extent that the medium in which a thought is conveyed is "of [that thought's] essence." The reader of Emerson's and Whitehead's lines, for instance, doesn't merely decipher their meaning; instead, the ideas are actively realized in the act of reading, much as the writers would have experienced them in the first place.

The dual sense of *realize* is exactly to the point. In each passage, the author *realizes* (in the sense of "embodies," "gives form to") an occasion of *realization* (in the sense of "recognition," "coming to awareness") that occurs in the process of composition. As a more or less spontaneous turn, in, by, and on the writer and his language, such realization has an effect comparable to that of ripples in "the creation of [a] plunge." Emerson's recognition that his image has swept him up with it, like Whitehead's recognition that an "inadequate" image may be transformed into one more appropriate to his thought, is an occasion of genius because it conveys not just a particular thought but the experience of *having* that thought. It is this communicable form of self- or double consciousness (whereby the conscious subject both experiences and communicates an immediate awareness of the medium and so combines knowledge of acquaintance and knowledge-about in one gesture) that Stein had in mind when, in "Portraits and Repetition," she equated genius with "being one who is at the same time talking and listening" (LIA, p. 170).

Emerson, having observed that "the world I converse with in the city and in the farms is not the world I *think*," added that if he couldn't yet account for "this discrepance," he would someday "know [its] value and law" (EL, pp. 491–92). In her 1934 lecture, Stein provided the basis for just such an account with her substitution of "talking and listening" for his "*thought* of genius." Appearances to the contrary, she did not thereby collapse the two spheres into a single conversational modality. It was exactly such confusion that she was concerned to avoid—suggesting that "the trouble with a great many so called intelligent people" is that "they mix up remembering with talking and listening":

> As a result they have theories about everything. . . . Although they talk as if they knew something [they] are really confusing, because they are so to speak keeping two times going at once, the repetition time of remembering and the actual time of talking.

Instead of "talking and listening, that is talking being listening and listening being talking . . . they always are remembering" (LIA, pp. 179–80). The past is substituted for the present even as the speaker professes to be addressing the immediate occasion.

It is this failure to acknowledge the difference between present activity ("the actual time of talking") and the remembered present (the present as it is filtered through memory)—a failure, essentially, to distinguish between "action" and "repetition"—that causes "many eager persons," in Emerson's words, to "attempt to realize the world of thought" and, in doing so, to "make themselves ridiculous" (LIA, p. 180; EL, p. 492). Instead of *genius* being transformed into *practical power*, both genius and practical power are diminished, and active transformation, or creativity, ceases. Those who believe that "invitations from heaven to try a larger sweep" may be addressed by practical-minded "concentration on the moment and the thing to be done" end up talking mindlessly (NHI, p. 53). As Stein put it: "Although they are clearly saying something they are not clearly creating something" (LIA, p. 180).

In *Everybody's Autobiography* she offers a particularly telling example of how "concentration on . . . the thing to be done" requires the use of memory (in this case, the deliberate translation of the present occasion into something *to be remembered*), with the consequence that one remains deaf to the "invitation from heaven" that the moment might otherwise convey, unaware of its full potential. "I got very interested in reporters," she reports:

> [These] are mostly young college men who are interested in writing and naturally I was interested in talking with them. I always knew that of course they would say what it was the habit for newspapers to say I said and yet I did like

talking with them. Once it may have been in Cleveland or Indianapolis, I was talking there were two or three of them and a photographer with them and I said you know it is funny but the photographer is the one of the lot of you who looks as if he were intelligent and was listening now why is that, you do I said to the photographer you do understand what I am talking about don't you. Of course I do he said you see I can listen to what you say because I don't have to remember what you are saying, they can't listen because they have got to remember. (EA, p. 224)

As Stein describes it here, the photographer's listening functions as a mode of talking. For, in listening as he does, he displays an *expression* of understanding, the only "one of the lot of you who looks as if he . . . understand[s] what I am talking about." The response he then makes ("I can listen to what you say because I don't have to remember what you say") confirms the impression that he really has been listening and thinking— with his thought taking the form of the *heightened consciousness of the medium* he shares with Stein, of "listening and talking, the two in one and the one in two" (LIA, p. 180).[10]

The photographer was able, without confusion, to characterize the feature of the interview format that promoted confusion, because unlike the reporters he was not implicated in that format. His removal from the governing discursive mode made it possible for him to concentrate on the medium, and consequently on "the actual time of talking," without being distracted by a concern for what was "to be done" with Stein's comments. Elsewhere in *Everybody's Autobiography*, Stein attributes to herself an equivalent freedom from the confusions and conventions built into a related mode of public discourse, that of college teaching. Following a class she had taught at the University of Chicago with Robert Hutchins and Mortimer Adler, inaugurators of the Great Books of the Western World series, Hutchins (who was the university's chancellor and a major figure in twentieth-century American education) observed that the students "all talk[ed] more than we can make them and a number of them talked who never talked before." "You see why," Stein responded:

> [It] is that I am like them I do not know the answer, you you say you do not know but you do know if you did not know the answer you could not spend your life in teaching but I I really do not know, I really do not, I do not even know whether there is a question let alone having an answer for a question. To me when a thing is really interesting it is when there is no question and no answer, if there is then already the subject is not interesting. (pp. 219–20)[11]

Definite answers, like newspaper reporting, limited the range of thought by substituting "concentration on . . . the thing to be done" (here, the question to be answered) for "concentration on the [present] moment" as possessing interest and value in itself, apart from past or future considerations.[12] Genius, as the expression of the latter form of concentration, consequently "exist[ed] without any internal recognition of time." "After all," as Stein observes, "if you ask a question unless not even then when you are very little is the answer interesting, if there is an answer why listen to it if you can ask another question, listening to an answer makes you know that time is existing but asking a question makes you think that perhaps it does not" (pp. 251).[13]

The world that interests Stein, like the world that Emerson thinks, is a world in which each moment is valuable in itself rather than as a means to an end. With regard to this world, a question is better than an answer; better yet is a question as to whether there really is any question to be asked; best of all is the absence of questions and answers altogether. It is this world that "the poetic view of nature" expresses, a world "permeate[d] through and through" by "the element of value, of being valuable, of having value, of being an end in itself, of being something which is for its own sake"—in sum, a world composed of "unities" possessing "intrinsic reality." This characterization of "the poetic rendering of our concrete experience" is neither Emerson's nor Stein's, however, but Whitehead's, who aimed in his philosophy, as he put it, to "bridg[e] the gap between science and that fundamental intuition of mankind which finds its expression in poetry and its practical exemplification in the presuppositions of daily life" (SMW, pp. 93, 95).

Agreeing with Emerson that "science was false by being unpoetical," Whitehead concluded that the only way to heal "the discord between the aesthetic intuitions of mankind and the mechanism of science" was to "transfer . . . to the very texture of realisation in itself . . . that value which we recognise so readily in terms of human life"—namely, the intrinsic reality attributed, if not always quite so readily, to the persons with whom we "converse in the city and in the farms," that "element of value" which exists apart from all conversational ends ("Poetry and Imagination," p. 443; SMW, pp. 87, 93). The object of Whitehead's philosophy, then, was to conceptualize the role of value in the "emergence into actuality," the *realization*, of anything, and consequently to understand how intrinsic reality serves as the engine of the "irresistible mechanism of nature" (SMW, p. 75). If "the materialistic concepts of the orthodox scientific theory" failed to accord with "full concrete experience"—with "experience drunk and experience sober," as he characterized it in *Adventures of Ideas*,

> experience sleeping and experience waking, experience drowsy and experience
> wide-awake, experience self-conscious and experience self-forgetful, experience

intellectual and experience physical, experience religious and experience scepti-
cal, experience anxious and experience care-free, experience anticipatory and
experience retrospective, experience happy and experience grieving, experience
dominated by emotion and experience under self-restraint, experience in the
light and experience in the dark, experience normal and experience abnormal—

then a scientific scheme capable of providing a fuller account of such "naive
experience" was called for (SMW, pp. 88, 81; AI, p. 226; SMW, p. 89).

It is here that Whitehead's perspective may seem most at odds with that
of Stein. Whereas he argued for the necessity of *transforming* the scientific
view of "nature and life" (by "basing nature upon the concept of organism,
and not upon the concept of matter," and consequently introducing considerations of value into science), she suggested that her writing was the product of a gradual disillusionment with science and hence represented an attempt to move *beyond* a scientific worldview (SMW, p. 75). "I began," she
observed in *Everybody's Autobiography*,

> when evolution was still exciting very exciting. . . . Science meant everything
> and any one who had an active mind could complete mechanics and evolution,
> philosophy was not interesting, it like religion was satisfaction in a solution
> but science meant that a solution was a way to a problem. . . . That was what
> science was every solution was an opening to another problem and then
> William James came that is I came to him and he said science is not a solution
> and not a problem it is a statement of the observation of things observed and
> perhaps therefore not interesting perhaps therefore only abjectly true. (pp.
> 249–50)

Here Stein describes the loss of a sense of romance, as a form of inquiry that
seemed to appeal to the active mind—for which solutions are neither interesting nor satisfying except insofar as they serve as provocations to further
thought, Emerson's "thought of genius"—is transformed into the "statement
of observation" and, as such, the sort of thing "that can be taught" (EA, pp.
251, 220).

A NEW REALISM

At the beginning of *Science and the Modern World*, Whitehead alluded to
William James as an example of the "new mentality" that the "quiet growth
of science" had produced. The "vehement and passionate interest" exhibited by James "in the relation of general principles to irreducible and stubborn facts" made for a "new tinge in modern minds." "All the world over
and at all times," Whitehead explained,

there have been practical men, absorbed in "irreducible and stubborn facts": all the world over and at all times there have been men of philosophic tempera- ment who have been absorbed in the weaving of general principles. It is this union of passionate interest in the detailed facts with equal devotion to abstract generalisation which forms the novelty in our present society.

"Previously," he added, "it had appeared sporadically and as if by chance" (pp. 2–3). This characterization of modernity closely resembles Emerson's speculations concerning modes of understanding customarily designated "nominalist and realist," as he titled an 1844 essay in which he revisited the dispute in medieval philosophy between the Nominalists (who, like "young people[,] admire talents or *particular* excellences") and the Realists, for whom "the *genius* is all," and who, as occurs when one "grow[s] older," "value *total* powers and effects" (EL, p. 576, emphasis added). The truth of the matter, Emerson proposed, was that "we are amphibious creatures, weaponed for two elements, having two sets of faculties, the particular and the catholic" (p. 577). On the one hand, "Nature will not be Buddhist: she resents generalizing, and insults the philosopher in every moment with a million of fresh particulars" (pp. 580–81). On the other hand, "we are very sensible of an atmospheric influence in men and in bodies of men, not ac- counted for in an arithmetical addition of all their measurable properties" (p. 577). "Every man is a partialist," and "every man is a universalist also" (pp. 585–86).

Emerson argues in "Nominalist and Realist" that each person possesses two mutually exclusive perspectives: "Life is made up of the intermixture and reaction of these two amicable powers, whose marriage appears be- forehand monstrous." "We must reconcile the contradictions as we can," he counsels, "but their discord and their concord introduce wild absurdities into our thinking and speech" (p. 585). Whitehead, generally in agreement with Emerson, nonetheless insisted that with the rise of modern science (and with the ever-increasing technological applications of science in the nineteenth century), a mode of understanding had emerged that took a "ve- hement and passionate interest in the *relation* of general principles to irre- ducible and stubborn facts," and didn't merely oscillate between a realist in- terest in the principles and a nominalist valuation of the facts. Consequently, the task he set himself, as a product of his times, was to make sense of the absurdities that Emerson claimed we are irresistibly led to utter since "no sentence will hold the whole truth, and the only way in which we can be just, is by giving ourselves the lie." "Speech is better than silence" *and* "si- lence is better than speech." "All things are in contact" *and* "every atom has a sphere of repulsion." "Things are, *and* are not, at the same time" (p. 585, emphasis added). To do justice to the feelings expressed in these gnomic utterances, while at the same time removing the absurdity of the expression, Whitehead retained the realist emphasis of Emerson's definition of human cognition but replaced the nominalist half with an alternative sense of *realism* that flourished in English-language philosophy in the first decades of this century.[14] The new mentality analyzed, and exemplified, by Whitehead was not "nominalist and realist" but instead combined two distinct varieties of realism, which contrasted respectively with nominalism and with philosophical idealism.

Although the realist/idealist distinction is usually characterized in terms of the view that "material objects exist externally to us and independently of our sense experience" (realism) or alternately that "no such material objects or external realities exist apart from our knowledge or consciousness of them" (idealism), Whitehead insisted that "the distinction between realism and idealism does not coincide with that between objectivism and subjectivism" (Hirst, p. 77; SMW, p. 90).[15] "Both realists and idealists," he argued,

> can start from an objective standpoint. They may both agree that the world disclosed in sense-perception is a common world, transcending the individual recipient. But the objective idealist, when he comes to analyse what the reality of this world involves, finds that cognitive mentality is in some way inextricably concerned in every detail. This position the realist denies. (p. 90)

For the objective or absolute idealist, cognitive mentality persists all the way down, even if what one perceives isn't merely "the outcome of the perceptive peculiarities of the [individual] subject enjoying the experience" (p. 88).

Whitehead faulted nineteenth-century idealism, whether absolute or pluralistic, objective or subjective, on the grounds that in "find[ing] the ultimate meaning of reality in mentality that is fully cognitive," such idealism remained "too much divorced from the scientific outlook" and consequently "swallowed the [dominant] scientific scheme [of the day] in its entirety" (SMW, p. 63).[16] In accepting without question that the prevailing "scientific materialism" was "the only rendering of the facts of nature," the various "idealistic schools . . . conspicuously failed to connect, in any organic fashion, the facts of nature with their idealistic philosophies" (pp. 91, 64). In other words, "philosophic idealism" was notably out of sync with the modern "interest in the relation of general principles to stubborn facts." In his own "objectivist philosophy," Whitehead offered "a further stage of provisional realism" in lieu of idealist complacency (pp. 63, 89, 64). Acknowledging the facts' irreducibility to "fully cognitive . . . mentality," he "recast" the scientific scheme in a manner that made it more responsive to "the concrete experience of mankind" than classical materialism had proven to be (pp. 50, 89).

Whitehead's "organic philosophy of nature" was premised on an understanding of wholes as being greater than the sums of their parts, and of general concepts (*pace* nominalism and in this respect agreeing with idealism) as not being entirely reducible to names or words but instead as possessing "a real, objective existence" (SMW, p. 120; Hirst, p. 77). At the same time, in accordance with the "new tinge in modern minds," itself largely the product of the science he wished to put on a new footing, his theory of nature was neither idealistic nor merely realistic in the medieval sense of the term, since it held that "the things which lie around us," the "simple immediate facts" which "are the topics of interest" of poetry as well as of science, were not ultimately reducible to cognitive mentality (SMW, p. 15). "I would term the doctrine of these lectures," Whitehead observed in *Science and the Modern World*, "the theory of *organic mechanism*. In this theory, the molecules may blindly run in accordance with the general laws, but the molecules differ in their intrinsic characters according to the general organic plans of the situations in which they find themselves" (p. 80). Such a "philosophy of organism" contrasted with "the extreme doctrine of materialistic mechanism," which argued that "each molecule blindly runs. The human body is a collection of molecules. Therefore, the human body blindly runs, and therefore there can be no individual responsibility for the actions of the body" (PRO, p. xi; SMW, p. 78). As Whitehead noted, "if you once accept that the molecule is definitively determined to be what it is, independently of any determination by reason of the total organism of the body, and if you further admit that the blind run is settled by the general mechanical laws, there can be no escape from this conclusion" (p. 78).[17]

Whitehead, like Stein, was a single-substance realist. As Richard Rorty has argued, it was this feature of his thought that distinguished him from Descartes, for whom "subjects enjoying conscious experiences" were "substances" of a kind that was radically different from the material substratum, and which allied him with Aristotle, who held that there was only one "primary substance" (Rorty, "Subjectivist," p. 134; cited from PRO, p. 159).[18] For Whitehead, as for Aristotle, intellect was not "an added extra ingredient."[19] "The Achilles heel" of the post-Cartesian "scheme of scientific ideas," Whitehead suggested, was to be found in "the concepts of life, organism, function, instantaneous reality, interaction, order of nature," which all fell "in between [Descartes's] fundamental duality, with *material* on the one hand, and on the other hand *mind*" (SMW, p. 57). Individuals who, like Stein and Whitehead, "ha[d] it in them," in the words of the narrator of *The Making of Americans*, "to be certain that everything in a way is made out of real earth the way it was done to make Adam," confronted the corresponding difficulty of how to account for "what as experience" seemed to be "without any [material] condition," namely, thought or self-directed action or even life itself (pp. 544, 780). Could these phenomena be understood without either reductively "leav[ing] out something" or, alternatively, falling back on a Bergsonian notion of Vital Spirit or *élan vital*, the idea that "be[ing] a live one" requires something "inspiriting" (pp. 779, 583)? In other words, did a sense that all "things have really ordinary materially existing being," as Stein's narrator puts it, condemn one to a crude materialism (p. 596)?

The Making of Americans provides an account of the evolution of the narrator's worldview from a "doctrine of materialistic mechanism" (with individual character understood as a mix of inherited characteristics and environmental factors) to the sort of "theory of organic mechanism" displayed in the definition of individuality that the narrator arrives at late in the work, a definition of one's sense of self, one's present unity, as the product of a "way of experiencing anything" that is also a way of "expressing that thing" (p. 783).[20] In effect, Stein was making the same argument in her portrayal of this change of perspective that Whitehead would put forward almost fifteen years later concerning the inadequacy, with respect to "the ordinary stubborn facts of daily life," of "a doctrine of materialistic mechanism" as well as the need to replace it with a "theory of organic mechanism" (PRO, p. xiii). The difference between them was that whereas Stein limited her attention, at least in *The Making of Americans*, to human beings, Whitehead aimed for a more complete cosmology. Nevertheless, the general principles in terms of which they accounted for the stubborn facts were identical.

At the core of the organic mechanism / materialistic mechanism contrast in *Science and the Modern World* was an earlier distinction between rhythm and pattern that Whitehead had proposed in his first extended work of philosophy, *An Enquiry Concerning the Principles of Natural Knowledge*. Published in 1919, the *Enquiry* had been "thought out and written amid the sounds of guns," as Whitehead acknowledged in his preface; it was "the product of intervals of leisure amid pressing occupation, a refuge from immediate fact" (p. viii). Indeed, Bertrand Russell testified in his *Autobiography* that "before the war started Whitehead had [already] made some notes on our knowledge of the external world"—notes that Russell himself used in the Lowell Lectures he delivered in Boston in the spring of 1914 (p. 101).[21] These lectures (an "attempt," as Russell put it, "to show, by means of examples, the nature, capacity, and limitations of the logical-analytic method in philosophy") were published later that year as *Our Knowledge of the External World*, and in the preface Russell recorded his debt to Whitehead, "to whom [were] due almost all the differences between the views advocated here and those suggested" in the 1912 volume *The Problems of Philosophy* (p. 10). In particular, he credited Whitehead with having made him "aware of the importance" of the "central problem" to which he applied the new method, "the problem of the relation between the crude data of sense and the space, time, and matter of mathematical physics." "I owe to him," Russell continued,

> the definition of points, the suggestion for the treatment of instants and "things," and the whole conception of the world of physics as a *construction* rather than an *inference*. What is said on these topics here is, in fact, a rough preliminary account of the more precise results which he is giving in the fourth volume of our *Principia Mathematica* [the first three volumes having been published in 1910, 1912, and 1913]. It will be seen that if his way of dealing with these topics is capable of being successfully carried through, a wholly new light is thrown on the time-honoured controversies of realists and idealists, and a method is obtained of solving all that is soluble in their problem. (pp. 10–11)

Whitehead never completed the fourth volume of the *Principia*, however, which was to have addressed the logical foundations of geometry. Instead, he turned his attention to the consequences of "the modern theory of relativity" for "geometry as a physical science," substituting an "enquiry concerning the *principles of natural knowledge*" for the projected concluding volume of the *Principia Mathematica* (ENQ, p. v).

In a letter to Russell composed early in 1917, Whitehead explained his refusal to share his most recent thinking on the subject with his former collaborator:

> I don't want my ideas propagated *at present* either under my name or anybody else's—that is to say, as far as they are at present on paper. . . . My ideas and methods grow in a different way to yours and the period of incubation is long and the result attains its intelligible form in the final stage,—I do not want you to have my notes which in chapters are lucid, to precipitate them into what I should consider as a series of half-truths. I have worked at these ideas off and on for all my life, and should be left quite bare on one side of my speculative existence if I handed them over to some one else to elaborate. . . . I am sorry that you do not feel able to get to work except by the help of these notes—but I

am sure that you must be mistaken in this. . . . I will send the work round to you naturally, when I have got it into the form which expresses my ideas. (cited in Russell's *Autobiography*, pp. 100–101)

During the summer and early fall of 1914, Stein and Whitehead no doubt discussed these still nascent ideas, at least in general outline, during their "endless" walks together. Already that spring Whitehead had delivered a paper in Paris on "the relational theory of space," which contained "the first presentation of a logical technique [he] later called the method of extensive abstraction," elucidated at great length in the *Enquiry*.[22] As Patrick Hurley has observed, this method "consists of an application of the logical apparatus of *Principia Mathematica* to spatial concepts for the purpose of providing a link between material objects and geometrical entities and, in a later application, a link between the content of perception and the concepts of science" ("Whitehead's *Relational Theory*," p. 743). Hurley also notes that, although *The Relational Theory of Space* is, "as the title implies, a work about space," Russell recalled on at least one occasion that "Whitehead had, as of its writing, extended the method of extensive abstraction to time, even though he did not include this treatment in the published version" ("Time," p. 92).[23] Any hint of Whitehead's subsequent speculations on rhythm would have struck a particularly resonant chord in Stein, who some years later described the pieces collected in *Geography and Plays* (among them one titled "Mrs. Whitehead") as "translat[ing] the rhythm of the spoken personality as directly as possible, using every form that she can invent to translate the repeated story of everybody doing what, what they are being."[24] Obviously, this objective differs from that of the portraits in *Tender Buttons* (none of them of persons per se), in which she sought, as she put it in the *Autobiography*, "to express the rhythm of the visible world"; yet in either case her writing was to be understood as an expression of rhythm (p. 119).

Although the *Enquiry* was a study of "speculative physics" and, as such, not concerned with the biological aspects of "physical phenomena," Whitehead nevertheless presented an account of how "nature includes life" in the closing chapter, on "Rhythms" (ENQ, pp. v, 3, 195). He began by defining a *pattern* as an object the whole of which is equal to the sum of its parts. "An object," he observed,

is a characteristic of an event. Such an object may be in fact a multiple relation between objects situated in various parts of the whole event. In this case the quality of the whole is the relationship between the parts, and the relation between the parts is the quality of the whole. The whole event being what it is, the parts have thereby certain defined relations; and the parts having all the relations which they do have, it follows that the whole event is what it is. *The whole is explained by a full knowledge of the parts as situations of objects, and the parts by a full knowledge of the whole.* Such an object is *a pattern.* (p. 195, emphasis added)

To perceive an event entirely as "a multiple relation between objects situated in various parts of the whole event" is to objectify the event as pattern. "Specific recognizable liveliness," on the contrary, "is the recognized character of [an] object to the event which is its situation" (p. 196). *Liveliness,* then, is a function of the relation between object and event, whereas *pattern* is a function of the "multiple relation between objects" situated in a common event.

"We have therefore to ask," Whitehead continued, "what sort of events have life in their relations to objects situated in them, and what sort of objects have life in their relations to their situations?" "A life-bearing object," he proposed,

is not an "uniform" object. Life (as known to us) involves the completion of rhythmic parts within the life-bearing event which exhibits that object. (p. 196)[25]

In other words, an event's temporal duration is of the essence to the life that both it and any object situated in it may "bear" or "express" (p. 195). "There is no such thing as life 'at one instant,'" because there is no such thing as rhythm at one instant; each of the "rhythmic parts" is no more instantaneous, or uniform, than is the event as a whole, since each part, insofar as it is related to the event and not just to the other parts, functions as "the same object of life" as every other part and carries the rhythm of the whole "unbroken" (p. 196). For this reason, "a rhythm is too concrete to be truly [or merely] an object" and "refuses to be disengaged from the event in the form of *a true object* which would be *mere pattern*" (p. 198, emphasis added).

The simplest "Way of Rhythm," Whitehead remarked a decade later, is structured as "a round of experiences, forming a determinate sequence of contrasts attainable within a definite method." As with a train of waves, "the end of one such cycle is the proper antecedent stage for the beginning of another such cycle" (*Function*, p. 17).[26] In this instance, "the cycle is such that its own completion provides the conditions for its own mere repetition." Yet, "at the level of human experience," he added, cyclical repetition of this minimal form produces "fatigue" or loss of vividness—decay that can only be obviated by a procedure that combines the "preservation of the fundamental abstract structure of the cycle [in effect, its pattern] with the variation of the concrete details of succeeding cycles." As a result, "the Rhythm of *life*," in circumventing decay, "is not merely to be sought in simple cyclical recurrence. The cyclical element is driven into the foundation, and variations of cycles, and of cycles of cycles, are elaborated" (p. 17, emphasis added). Stein made a similar point in her 1934 lecture "Portraits and Repetition," when she suggested that "what makes *life*" is "that the insistence is different, no matter how often you tell the same story if there is anything alive in the telling the emphasis is different. It has to be, anybody can know that" (LIA, p. 167, emphasis added). As she proposed in another lecture, "the only time there is repetition is when somebody tells you what he has learned" (HWW, p. 159).

Still, it hadn't always been so clear to Stein that a story's vitality resided in the telling rather than in what it was about—that the rhythm, and never the pattern alone, was the source of liveliness. "Everybody," the narrator of *The Making of Americans* comments at the start of the hundred-page methodological interlude that opens the second part of the book, "is a real one to me, everybody is like some one else too to me" (p. 289). This dual perspective informs the entire work, which is at once a general analysis of human character in terms of likeness and human kinds—an analysis, that is to say, in terms of *pattern*—and an attempt to understand how persons "come together in them to be [each] a whole one," essentially a consideration of the role of *rhythm* in the formation of human personality (p. 382). Stein had begun writing *The Making of Americans* with what she regarded as the scientific "idea that I could get a sense of immediacy if I made a description of every kind of human being that existed until really I had made a description of every [possible] human being." In constructing and implementing her categories, she used "rules for resemblances" and anything else that proved helpful, including "new constructions of grammar" (HWW, pp. 155–56).[27] Yet even after she had become convinced that description (or pattern) couldn't adequately convey immediacy (or rhythm), she continued to experience difficulty in articulating her acquaintance with individual rhythms without reducing them to more or less general patterns. In "The Gradual Making of The Making of Americans," she described the situation that ensued:

> When I was up against the difficulty of putting down the complete conception that I had of an individual, the complete rhythm of a personality that I had gradually acquired by listening seeing feeling and experience, I was faced by the trouble that I had acquired all this knowledge gradually but when I had it I had it completely at one time. Now that may never have been a trouble to you but it was a terrible trouble to me. And a great deal of The Making of Americans was

a struggle to do this thing, to make a whole present of something that it had taken a great deal of time to find out, but it was a whole there then within me and as such it had to be said.

"That then and ever since," she proposed, "has been a great deal of my work" (LIA, p. 147). Or, as she reiterated more expansively in "How Writing Is Written": "From that time on I have been trying in every possible way to get the sense of immediacy, and practically all the work I have done has been in that direction" (p. 155).

At the beginning of what I have termed the methodological interlude in *The Making of Americans*, the narrator describes the gradual accumulation of knowledge in similar terms, although apparently without any awareness yet of the "terrible trouble" that lies ahead:

> Each one slowly comes to be a whole one to me. Each one slowly comes to be a whole one in me. Soon then it commences to sound through my ears and eyes and feelings the repeating that is always coming out from each one, that is them, that makes then slowly of each one of them a whole one. . . . Sometimes it takes many years of knowing some one before the repeating that is that one gets to be a steady sounding to the hearing of one who has it as a natural being to love repeating that slowly comes out from every one. Sometimes it takes many years of knowing some one before the repeating in that one comes to be a clear history of such a one. (p. 291)

Had human character been the sort of thing that might adequately be summed up, as Emerson put it, by "an arithmetical addition of all [its] measurable properties," Stein wouldn't have encountered the more perplexing *qualitative* difficulty, as distinct from the *quantitative* one described here. Without a sense of a whole, no sense of immediacy would have arisen, demanding "to be said" or "put down" in writing. Yet character *is* experienced as more than the sum of its parts; the whole *is* present on every occasion that it is expressed, not simply when viewed *sub specie aeternitatis*, and as such it takes the form of a rhythm rather than a pattern. "Really listen to the way you talk," Stein counseled, "and every time [that you say the same thing] you change it a little bit. That change, to me, was a very important thing to find out. You will see that when I kept on saying something was something or somebody was somebody, I changed it just a little bit until I got a whole portrait" (HWW, p. 159). The idea was that "the complete rhythm of a personality" could no more be determined solely from the words of a single utterance than from a snapshot; rather, it might only be determined comparatively, from changes in expression occurring over time— "variations of cycles, and of cycles of cycles." By the same token, neither a person in a catatonic state nor an automaton could be said to possess personality; in each case expression remains constant, and the rhythm is merely that of cyclical repetition.

The principal difference between Whitehead's realism and that of Aristotle comes down to the distinction, as Rorty has phrased it, "between a realism built around the notion of . . . process" and one "built around the notion of stasis" ("Matter and Event," p. 511). Indeed, Whitehead's characterization of "the new physics" as "substitut[ing] the notion of *forms of process*" for "the Aristotelian notion of the *procession of forms*" applies to his own philosophy as well (MT, p. 140).[28] In this respect, Stein differed from him only to the extent that, instead of limiting herself to formal analysis of the properties of process, or transition, she sought to "*translate* the rhythm of the spoken personality" and "to *express* the rhythm of the visible world"—that is, to put the characters expressed by other persons and the character of the visible world into her own words. Rather than elucidating the general patterns of rhythm as Whitehead, ever the mathematician, did, she aimed in her portraiture to express the particular rhythms that she experienced around her. Even so, accurate portrayal of *rhythms* required close attention to *pattern*; and as Stein observed of herself in the *Autobiography*, "her work [was] often . . . compared to that of mathematicians" on account of the "intellectual," and hence "pure," "passion for exactitude" that she shared with those who, like Whitehead, practiced the science of patterns (p. 211).[29]

THE LIFE OF THINGS

"Life," Whitehead concluded in the *Enquiry*, "is the rhythm as such." Whereas the living organism "preserves its expression of rhythm and its sensitiveness to rhythm" in the whole as well as in the parts, any truly uniform physical object constitutes "an average of [molecular] rhythms which build no rhythm in their aggregation." Consequently, in "the macroscopic aggregate . . . matter [really] is lifeless." The corollary of this claim is that "wherever there is some rhythm, there is some life" (p. 197). Events only impress us with their liveliness when their rhythms are "more complex" and "subtler . . . than those whose aggregate is essential for [a uniform] physical object"; thus molecules may be "non-uniform objects and as such exhibit a rhythm," yet because the rhythm is "of excessive simplicity," the aggregate takes an exclusively patterned rather than a rhythmic form (pp. 197, 199). By comparison, "living bodies exhibit rhythm of the greatest subtlety within our apprehension," while objects on the scale of "solar systems and star clusters exhibit rhythm of a simplicity analogous to that of molecules" (p. 197). Concerning this distribution of rhythmic complexity, Whitehead commented in the aftermath of a war that had left his youngest son dead, that "it was impossible not to suspect that the gain in apparent complexity at the stage of our own rhythm-bearing events is due rather to our angle of vision than to any inherent fact of nature" (p. 199). Suspicious, like Stein, of all dualisms that absolutely sundered life and nature, he insisted on distinguishing *nature lifeless* (nature as it was characterized by scientific materialism) from *nature alive*.[30]

Of the work he calls "Wordsworth's greatest poem . . . by far, the first book of *The Prelude*," Whitehead asserts that it is "pervaded by [a] sense of the haunting presences of nature," of *nature alive* (SMW, p. 83).[31] If the "brooding, immediate presences of things are an obsession to Wordsworth," they are no less so to Whitehead, whose objectivist doctrine, as he remarked in *Science and the Modern World*, is "extremely consonant with the vivid expression of personal experience" found in Wordsworth's nature poetry (p. 92). Suppose "you are in a certain place perceiving things," Whitehead explained:

> Your perception takes place where you are, and is entirely dependent on how your body is functioning. But this functioning of the body in one place, exhibits for your cognisance an aspect of the distant environment, fading away into the general knowledge that there are things beyond. If this cognisance conveys knowledge of a transcendent world, it must be because the event which is the bodily life unifies in itself aspects of the universe. (p. 92)

By *transcendent world*, Whitehead means "a common world which transcends knowledge, though it includes knowledge" (p. 89). It is this haunted, transcendent sense of *things beyond*, a sense expressly tied to the "functioning of [one's] body" in the place one happens to be, that Wordsworth articulated so vividly in his poetry.

Even if Whitehead's phrasing leaves open the possibility of limiting bodily functioning to the soma's movements in and through its immediate environment, his example of Wordsworth makes it clear that such functioning must be understood in a *physiological* as well as a *physical* sense. The characteristic personal experience investigated by Wordsworth in his nature poetry involves the dual perspective already remarked on in Chapter 1—at once bimodal and bidirectional, with the individual's eyes and ears focused inward as well as outward. This experience is strikingly portrayed in the famous passage in "Tintern Abbey," apostrophizing

> that serene and blessed mood,
> In which the affections gently lead us on,
> Until, the breath of this corporeal frame,
> And even the motion of our human blood
> Almost suspended, we are laid asleep
> In body, and become a living soul:
> While with an eye made quiet by the power
> Of harmony, and the deep power of joy,
> We see into the life of things.
>
> (ll. 42–50; LB, p. 114)

These lines may appear to argue for the soul's transcendence of the body, and the dissolution of self in the external world, yet this impression stems from reading the words too hastily, with an insufficiently "quieted" eye. The poet speaks of breathing and "the motion of our human blood" as "*almost* suspended"; and we prove able to "see into the life of things" only because, in being "laid asleep" (not, euphemistically, laid to rest), we synesthetically experience the *quiet* of the eye, in both the auditory and motor senses of the term.

This is the sort of self-consciousness Whitehead had in mind when he proposed that Wordsworth, "to the height of genius, expresses the concrete facts of our apprehension, facts which are distorted in scientific analysis" (SMW, p. 84). Eighty years earlier, in an essay on "Character," Emerson expressed a similar recognition: "Man," he wrote, "ordinarily a pendant to events, only half attached, and that awkwardly, to the world he lives in, in these examples appears to share *the life of things*, and to be an expression of the same laws which control the tides and the sun, numbers and quantities." Among his examples, Emerson included Iole's explanation of how she immediately knew Hercules to be a god: " 'When I beheld Theseus, I desired that I might see him offer battle, or at least guide his horses in the chariot-race; but Hercules did not wait for a contest; he conquered *whether he stood, or walked, or sat, or whatever thing he did*' " (EL, pp. 495–96, emphasis added). Incapable, even when motionless, of appearing incapacitated, Hercules participates in "the life of things" no less than Wordsworth does in expressing "the concrete facts of our apprehension"—or, for that matter, than Saint Therese stationed "half in doors and half out of doors" in Stein's 1927 opera *Four Saints in Three Acts*, and the entire assembly of saints in "Saints and Singing," "A Saint in Seven," and "Talks to Saints Or Stories of Saint Remy," all works dating from the winter of 1922–23 (OP, p. 15).

A saint "shouldn't do anything," Stein remarked in the wake of the phenomenal success of *Four Saints* in the mid-1930s. "The fact that a saint *is there* is enough for anybody" (HWW, p. 158, emphasis added). Still, the *concrete fact* of a saint's, or a god's, self-sufficiency (Therese's *there is*, or that of Hercules) does not suffice to transform such otherworldly creatures into *things*, any more than "an organism [is ever] really a thing" (Langer, "Living Form," p. 47). The organism's "individual, separate, thing-like existence," Langer explained four decades ago, is actually "a pattern of changes," and "its unity . . . a purely functional unity." As such, it is "indescribably [more] complex and intimate and profound" than "the self-identity of the most permanent material concretion, such as a lump of lead or a stone" (p. 47). Those exceptional occasions when even stones come to life occur because the stones have been caught up in a "pattern of changes" more "complex and intimate and profound" than they possess in themselves, at least as they are ordinarily viewed from "our angle of vision." They have been "entrained" in a rhythm that acts as a "pacemaker" (M, p. 144). For example, in Wordsworth's early poem, "The Ruined Cottage," the "loose stones that cover the highway" are incorporated into the transcendent world of an aged wanderer, gifted with an "ear which deeply felt / The voice of Nature in the obscure wind, / The sounding mountain and the running stream" (ll. 77–79; *Selected Poetry*, p. 7). "To every natural form, rock, fruit, and flower, / Even the loose stones that cover the highway, / He gave a moral life, and *saw them feel / Or link[ed] them to some feeling*" (ll. 80–83, emphasis added). In gathering the stones synesthetically into his own life, the pedlar comes to "share the life of things."

Like Whitehead, Langer distinguished two kinds of rhythm. The general definition that she used, *a functional involvement of successive events*, allows for minimum satisfaction in instances of "periodic succession" (the "succession of similar events at fairly short, even intervals of time") as well as more complex rhythms which, despite failing to conform to periodicity, still satisfy the criterion that "the completion of one distinct event appears . . . as the beginning of another" ("Living Form," pp. 50–52). These two varieties are equivalent to Whitehead's "cyclical repetition of [a] minimal form" and "variations of cycles, and of cycles of cycles," although Langer made a crucial emendation when she applied his "philosophy of organism" directly to *physiological* phenomena. In *Science and the Modern World*, Whitehead had argued that the "new aspect" of modern science, "neither purely physical, nor purely biological," was due to "the rise of physiology" in the nineteenth century (pp. 103, 147). All the same, he was content to limit his own discussions of scientific explanation to *physical* phenomena (with *physics* understood as devoted to modes of inquiry that concern "the concrete aspects" of organisms "in so far as their *effects on patterns and on locomotion* are expressible in *spatio-temporal terms*"), while giving physiology only the most cursory treatment (p. 132, emphasis added). "The effect of physiology" may have been, as he acknowledged, "to put mind back into nature." Yet, even as the "change of tone" stemming from the new "physiological instinct" among psychologists such as William James resonated throughout his speculations, he devoted just a single sentence in *Science and the Modern World*, and another in *Process and Reality*, to the neurological investigations of mind concurrent with his own philosophical investigations of organic function (p. 147).[32]

Perhaps the most important feature of Langer's foundational "attack on the problem of mind in the context of natural history," in the three-volume *Mind: An Essay on Human Feeling*, consists in her meticulous unfolding of the physiological logic of the philosophy of organism in terms supplied by neurological investigations of the first three-quarters of the twentieth century (p. xi).[33] Whitehead, by contrast, merely sought to ground the revolutionary notions of the New Physics in a perspective that remained consistent with the New Physiology, attempting, as he remarked in a letter to his son North, "to evolve one way of speaking that applies equally to physics, physiology, and to our aesthetic experiences" (cited in Lowe, II, p. 223).[34] In proposing to return the romance to science (and the science to romance), he interpreted modern science in a manner that would have appealed no less to Stein than to Wordsworth. "The philosophy of organism," he wrote in *Process and Reality*, "is a cell-theory of actuality. Each ultimate unit of fact [that is, each "actual occasion"] is a cell-complex, not analysable into components with equivalent completeness of actuality." "The cell," he added, "can be considered genetically and morphologically," with the caveat that neither approach completely accounts for its capacity as a complex, or compound, entity any more than they fully explain the living cell in biology (p. 219). The genetic analysis Whitehead undertook in Part III of *Process and Reality* ("The Theory of Prehensions") is essentially an analysis of the nature of *rhythm*, of how the cell "appropriate[s] for the foundation of its own existence . . . the various elements of the universe out of which it arises," whereas the morphological approach of Part IV ("The Theory of Extension") involves the analysis of *pattern* or "logical relationships" (pp. 219, 139). As Stein full well understood, these perspectives were complementary rather than contradictory; rhythm no more existed independently of pattern than (to return to James's terms) knowledge of acquaintance might exist without knowledge-about.

In addition to anchoring the philosophy of organism more firmly in the physiological realm, Langer also sought to extend it into the third arena earmarked by Whitehead, that of *our aesthetic experiences*. Owing to the influence of her earlier books, *Philosophy in a New Key* and *Feeling and Form*, Langer is probably best known as an aesthetician; yet inadequate attention to the language arts occasionally mars her aesthetic speculations, both generally and for the study of literature in particular.[35] Here Stein offers an especially telling corrective to her as well as to Whitehead. In proposing that "verbal conception and discursive forms of thought" possess "inherent . . . limitations" which make language *"peculiarly unsuited"* for "the symbolization of vital and emotional experience," Langer followed Whitehead's insistence that great poetry like Wordsworth's somehow transcends common speech instead of working with resources implicit in ordinary usage (M, pp. 69, 38, emphasis added). Where "our powers of analysis [and] of expression" are concerned, Whitehead wrote in *Adventures of Ideas*, "language is *peculiarly inadequate*" in addressing those "elements . . . on the fringe of consciousness," which, "barely discriminated," nevertheless "massively qualify our experience"; still, he does allow that "meanings beyond individual words and beyond grammatical forms" are "miraculously revealed in great literature" (pp. 163, 226, emphasis added). Wordsworth's characteristic "theme," after all, concerned "that mysterious presence of surrounding things, which imposes itself on any separate element that we set up as an individual for its own sake." "He always grasps the whole of nature as involved in the tonality of the particular instance" (SMW, p. 84).

Aside from proposing that in such writing the reader "enjoy[s] flashes of insight beyond the meanings already stabilized in etymology and grammar," flashes available to "all men" if not often realized in ordinary life, Whitehead seems to offer no concrete suggestion as to how these literary miracles work linguistically. This contrasts sharply with the care he took in detailing how philosophy ought to go about "finding linguistic expressions for meanings as yet unexpressed," an end it shared with literature and indeed with all the "special sciences" (AI, pp. 226–27). "The very purpose of philosophy," he insisted, "is to *delve below the apparent clarity of common speech*," in order to analyze, for instance, "the ambiguities of words expressive of conjunctions," whose logical inconsistencies are responsible for the paradoxes of "ancient and . . . modern logic" (AI, p. 222, emphasis added; MT, pp. 53–54). As unambiguously as possible, Whitehead asseverated that words like *and* and *together* "are the death traps for accuracy of reasoning" (MT, p. 53). They are death traps, that is to say, *except* when they are used in literature. For the difference between common speech and great literature (or, if one prefers, uncommon usage of common speech) is surely this: that the latter expressly attends to logical inconsistencies, thereby freeing itself from dependence on them, while the former, in generally ignoring its own illogic, remains trapped by it.

If Whitehead neglected to draw this conclusion, having little or nothing to say on the matter, he did intimate in his important 1927 study of "symbolic reference" how he imagined language to function in literary miracles. As he understood it, such reference was not limited to literature or art; instead, as he put it in *Process and Reality*, where "human experience is in question, 'perception' almost always means 'perception in the mixed mode of symbolic reference'" (p. 168). The mode is mixed, because it combines "the two pure [perceptual] modes" he termed *presentational immediacy* and *causal efficacy*. Still, works of art, or more exactly, one's experiences of them, offered exemplary instances of symbolic reference. At one stage in his unfolding argument, Whitehead took as his text "the inscription on old sundials in 'religious' houses," *Pereunt et imputantur*, or "The hours perish and are laid to account"—remarking that "'pereunt' refers to the world disclosed in immediate presentation, gay with a thousand tints, passing, and intrinsically meaningless" (*Symbolism*, p. 47). By contrast, "'imputantur' refers to the world disclosed in its causal efficacy, where each event infects the ages to come, for good or for evil, with its own individuality." If, as he also suggested, "the contrast between the comparative emptiness of Presentational Immediacy and the deep significance disclosed by Causal Efficacy is at the root of the pathos which haunts the world," then in this inscription (which, not coincidentally, closely resembles the memento mori structure favored by Wordsworth) the two contrary modes of perception are joined in a manner that recreates the experience of pathos for the reader (p. 47). Similarly, the pathos in the final stanza of Keats's "Eve of St. Agnes" derives "from the imagined fusion of the two perceptive modes by one intensity of emotion"; and, in a final example of such literary conjunction, several lines cited by Whitehead from *The Winter's Tale* are said to "fuse" the two modes "by exhibiting the infectiousness of gay immediacy" (p. 48). (*Gay immediacy* refers here to the element of presentational immediacy, while *infectiousness* introduces the complementary strain of causal efficacy, as in "events *infecting* the ages to come.") In each passage, the two modes are experienced as logically distinct, hence not subject to the critique Whitehead leveled at the merely "apparent clarity" of common speech. At the same time, they are *fused together*, examples of a *confusion* due not to "logical inconsistency" but experiential complexity.

In her 1957 essay on "Living Form," Langer interpreted a comparable confusion in a lyric of William Blake as a device that served exclusively to increase the reader's impression of organic-seeming interconnectedness among the elements comprising the work's "fabric." On her reading, the poem revealed the metaphorical status of any claim that works of art "must be organic"; and, certainly, in denying digestive and circulatory functions to a poem (even one titled "Love's Secret"), the philosopher is on unassailable ground (p. 44). Yet one might still ask whether this argument really is sufficient to show that the work possesses *no* biological or physiological functions more distinctive than a presumed inviolability and a broad-ranging interconnectedness. As Whitehead demonstrated in his account of *Pereunt et imputantur*, the heterogeneous dialectic at the heart of his philosophy of organism was no less implicated in the life of certain concatenations of words than it was in the lives of their authors. Langer inadvertently confirms this very point in her analysis of Blake's "perfect little poem," as well as Stein's related point concerning the definitive role of logical or grammatical imperfection—*deliberate error*, as I termed it in Chapter 2—in verbal liveliness (p. 56).

With regard to the "erratic shift of thought" that occurs in the poem's opening quatrain ("Never seek to tell thy love, / Love that never told can be; / For the gentle wind doth move / Silently, invisibly"), Langer remarks that the transition is "logically, of course, a complete *non sequitur*" (pp. 56–57). "The word 'for,'" which introduces the shift, functions in these lines to "create the feeling of rational connection where literally there is none." Attributes qualifying the activity of the wind are transferred from the second pair of lines to the first, and "transform[ed] . . . at a stroke into metaphors for [love's] ineffable nature," so that, rightly understood, love proves as silent and invisible as the wind's movements (p. 57). On the basis of this uncontroversial elucidation, Langer concludes that the work's *life-likeness*, its "*semblance* of life," derives principally from the "many-sided involvement of every element with the total fabric" (pp. 53, 57, emphasis added). Despite insisting on the illogical nature of the vehicle responsible for all this activity—the little word *for*—Langer neglects to ask whether the poet might have chosen to use it deliberately, that is, whether the non sequitur as such possesses any significance for one's reading of the poem. On her account, the fact that the quatrain's third and fourth lines don't follow from the first two isn't just irrelevant to the poem's import; it is something that the poem, insofar as it is felt to possess a "semblance of organic structure," obliges one to overlook (p. 57). In order for the metaphor to work, one must repress any recognition of its basis in a non sequitur.

Obviously, the presence of this "complete *non sequitur*" makes it rather awkward to assert, as Langer goes on to do, that, "like living substance, a work of art is inviolable; break its elements apart, and they are no longer what they were—the whole image is gone" (p. 57). A work that possesses a non sequitur at its heart can hardly be said to be "inviolable," and consequently for Langer to locate the work's "semblance of life" in such inviolability requires her to ignore both the non sequitur and the logical inconsistency in her own reading. By contrast, Stein's literary practices suggest that the *liveliness* of Blake's writing, as distinct from its *lifelikeness*, is actually due to the proper functioning of the device in question. The non sequitur that structures the stanza makes Blake's sentence into a *portmanteau sentence*. Such sentences (which I discuss further in Chapter 7) may be logically incoherent, yet they function as emotional wholes, due to the recursively structured reading process they require in order to be read at all meaningfully. As such—and in line with James's account of emotional experience as minimally structured S1–M–S2: sensation, movement, auto-sensation—they serve to recreate, in the reader, the emotional rhythm the author wishes to suggest. The sentence, turning in on itself as a result of the non sequitur, obliges the reader to return to the first half in order to make sense of the conjunction. What Langer describes as merely lifelike really *is* merely lifelike, yet by the same token it doesn't come near to exhausting the concrete reality of the sentence.

Nor was Blake's impulse iconoclastic, any more than Stein's was—contrary to the charge of literary destructiveness leveled by Whitehead on the occasion of Radcliffe's Fiftieth Anniversary Jubilee in 1929. Talking on the subject of "historical changes," he proposed that "the iconoclastic impulse which is so prominent in the literary school today has done its work. It is not rejected. It is not shocking anybody. But its preoccupations have ceased to interest the creative ability under thirty, still more that under twenty-five years of age." Whitehead doesn't name names, yet the reference to a certain Radcliffe alumna is unmistakable. The "spectacle" of "middle-aged destructive vehemence," he continues, is unlikely to appeal to "the young," especially those who concern themselves "with the beauty derived from artistic finish of workmanship, with style, with restraint, with balance," as he characterizes the present generation of young adults ("Historical Changes," p. 205). Only a month after these remarks appeared in a special segment on "Women and History" in the *Radcliffe Quarterly*, Stein herself published an essay on "Genuine Creative Ability," offering a creative response to the allegation of iconoclasm. Composed in the form of a letter to her old friend the art critic Henry McBride (who solicited it for the journal *Creative Art*, which he edited), the essay begins with the articulation of "a scheme of study": "There are several subjects about which I can write. First Basket, then paragraphs, then Tonney, then three. . . . And then me" (GCA, p. 104). Needless to say, the proposed scheme is immediately revised, as Stein starts (instead of concluding) with herself: "I have just changed my mind. I have just had that experience. Listen to me." In changing her mind, she has, indeed, just had the experience of listening to herself; and it is this experience—the experience, it will be recalled, of *genius*, and as such a pretty good indicator of creative ability—that she is concerned to register in her writing.

The next sentence—"He looks like a young man grown old"—elicits the fairly innocuous-looking commentary: "That is a sentence that they could use." Stein had already asserted, at the outset of the essay, that "genuine creative ability" served as the principal criterion for awarding "the Guggenheim prize," and the implication is that this sentence, a particular favorite of hers, exhibits the required creativity. By contrast, the prize's administrators "cannot use" sentences such as "I was overcome with remorse" or "It was my fault that my wife did not have a cow" (where *cow* equals *feces*), because these sentences concern someone's feelings about a situation, but don't actually communicate anything about the state of mind in which they were uttered or written (p. 104). Either of these statements might be correlated with any number of different states; and the only way to convey, or determine, the actual state of mind involved—the motivation, as one might say of an actor—is through some form of creative activity expressed in the very composition of the sentence.[36] By registering a *change of mind* (some "erratic change of thought," in Langer's phrasing), the writing renders the mind visible. This is hardly iconoclastic, unless one's idea of images or likenesses (and consequently of image-making and image-breaking) is limited to static forms. Whitehead may have been the leading twentieth-century philosopher of "forms of process," as against "processions of forms," yet, in failing to appreciate a corresponding shift in aesthetic composition (at least in works whose immediate aesthetic aim was the *portrayal of creativity* rather than the *creation of beauty*), he displayed what Stein would have characterized as a conventionally nineteenth-century, and British, bias. A year later, again in *Creative Art*, she could not refrain from remarking on the tendency of "those who concern themselves with aesthetic things critically and academically" to be "several generations behind themselves"—in the process reiterating the position she had taken several years back in "Composition as Explanation" (TACF, p. 160). "May I quote myself," she now inquired, playfully citing an allusion in the Oxbridge lecture to a prior quotation (" 'For this reason as in quoting Lord Grey . . .' "), all in the name of contemporaneity (p. 159).

"MRS. EMERSON"

It was certainly not lost on Stein that the contemporary cinema presented an analogue to her investigations of images of movement. "Any one is of one's period and this our period was undoubtedly the period of the cinema and series production," she acknowledged in 1934 (LIA, p. 177). Motion pictures "offered a solution" similar to the one she had initially devised in response to the problem of recreating "the rhythm of anybody's personality" and so conveying a sense of *acquaintance*: "By a continuously moving picture of any one there is no memory of any other thing and there is that thing existing, it is in a way if you like one portrait of anything not a number of them." In her early portraiture she had done "what the cinema was doing," by "making a continuous succession of the statement of what that person was until I had not many things but one thing" (pp. 174, 176–77). Nor was the analogy lost on her readers. In June 1927, Kenneth Macpherson sent Stein a copy of the inaugural issue of *Close Up*, a monthly journal devoted to "films from the artistic, psychological and educational points of view," which he was editing with the assistance of Winifred Bryher.[37] "Greatly increasing numbers of people," he proposed in his cover letter, were "coming to regard films as a medium for the possible expression of art in its most modern and experimental aspects." As, in his opinion, Stein had "done more toward the advancement of thought in art than almost any other writer," he wondered "if perhaps some time you would send a poem or article for *Close Up* in which this development of experimental art is concerned." "The most modern tendency," he continued, "seems so linked up in this way and the kind of thing you write is so exactly the kind of thing that could be translated to the screen that anything you might send would be deeply appreciated" (FF, pp. 208–9). The work that Stein promptly sent to Macpherson, and he no less promptly printed, was "Mrs. Emerson," composed thirteen years earlier on the occasion of her visit with the Whiteheads.

Undoubtedly, the portrait displayed a "most modern tendency," but this was *not* the tendency linking the "continuous succession" of motion pictures with the periodic style of *The Making of Americans* (which Bryher's former husband, Robert McAlmon, had published only two years earlier). Despite beginning with an extended meditation on periodicity, or "the regular way," the portrait quickly turns on itself and its own forceful syntactic regularities:

The regular way of instituting clerical resemblances and neglecting hazards and bespeaking combinations and heroically and heroically celebrating instances, the regular way of suffering extra challenges, the regular way of suffering extra changes, the regular way of suffering extra changes the regular way of submitting to examples in changes, the regular way of submitting to extraordinary celebrations, the certainty, because keep centre well half full whether it has that to close when in use, no not repeatedly, he has forgotten. (RAB, p. 44)[38]

By the end of this one-sentence paragraph *the regular way* has suffered a severe shock to the system—something like a frame of film burning up, collapsing in on itself, and in this respect severer than that caused by wartime *challenges*, which, in calling forth responses of *heroism*, *suffering*, and *submission*, are rendered bearable to the individual by the very regularity with which they are endured. Stein suggests that this regularity provides the basis, in turn, for a rational-seeming *certainty*, much as the regularity of the sun's rising makes it something one can count on. It is a settled activity in the midst of an otherwise unsettled world, which, "celebrating *instances*" rather than *regularities*, routinely throws "extra challenges" at one. Needless to say, these challenges are not experienced as routine but as "extra changes" or "examples in changes" or "extraordinary celebrations," celebrations of matters not ordinarily celebrated.

From *regularity*, then, to *certainty*; and then, in the next turn of the sentence, to the acknowledgment of underlying causal efficacy articulated in the syntagma *A because B*. Here *A* is the regular way of this and the regular way of that and the certainty of it all, and *B* is, well, *B* is something that refuses to accommodate itself to syntactic regulation. It is about "keep[ing the] centre well half full," about "whether it has that to close," about "when in use." In other words, it raises questions of location and degree of preparedness, questions concerning closure, questions concerning use, even the question of just what vague instructions like these can possibly have to do with one another. Finally, in the closing phrases of the sentence, Stein sets *B* directly against the *repetitive* core of regularity ("no *not repeatedly*"), concluding that the resistance in question is a matter of *not* following through, *not* moving straight ahead, *not* knowing something, not even knowing *what* one is doing, at least for the time being: "He has forgotten." It doesn't necessarily follow, of course, that *B* is to be construed negatively, any more than that war is necessarily a bad thing. In the early days of the war, for instance, the Whiteheads found themselves regularly arguing for the merits of British entry—against Russell, and despite the mobilization of their eldest son. As Stein recalled, she introduced the topic of American education into the ongoing discussion at Lockeridge the very day "North

Whitehead left for the front," her idea having been to "divert everybody's mind from the burning question of war or peace" (ABT, p. 151). According to Whitehead's biographer, this would have been August 21. What *does* follow is that in the portrait's opening sentence B does *not* follow from A, nor does A follow from B. This is a non sequitur writ large, and as such much harder to ignore than the one Langer brought to the attention of Blake's readers.

"Now then," Stein continues, needing just these two words, framed as a discrete utterance, to equate present with past and join presentational immediacy and causal efficacy in the mixed mode Whitehead suggested was both native to human perception and responsible for the experience of pathos. Then (that is to say, now), the third paragraph, like the first two made up of a single odd sentence, shining a spotlight on itself and perhaps on someone or something else. "Now then shining, now then shining." Is that: If it's *now*, *then* it's *shining*? Or: *Now* and *then*, it's *shining*? Or does the repetition of *Now then shining* serve rather to convey, no less concentratedly than the initial expression of pathos, how, in circumstances like those investigated in "Mrs. Emerson," a Paterian insistence on "expanding [the] interval" may transform seemingly irreversible pathos (*Now then*) into the liveliness of "Now then *shining*," as one might say of someone strikingly full of life, or of a smile breaking dazzlingly through beclouded melancholy?

The composition's next paragraph (the last I shall address here, only the fourth of seventy-five, many of which are a line or less in length and altogether filling just over four printed pages) departs from the newly established ratio of one sentence per paragraph with its four short sentences: "Mrs. Evangeline Henderson went in. She said that the morning. She said that in listening. No I will not be funny" (p. 44). Now, just what is so "funny" here? Did "she," whoever this may be, say something *about* "listening"? Or did she, more creatively, say something "*in* listening"? Is it something about "Mrs. Evangeline Henderson," something one might see in the name, something Mrs. Evangeline Henderson sees in her own name? Or rather, that Stein sees in her, in so naming her? *Evangeline*: from *evangel*, which in turn derives from the Greek *euangelos*, the bringing of good tidings. (Despite everything, the sun still shines this morning.) And what relation does the aforenamed Mrs. Henderson bear to the titular Mrs. Emerson—"Mrs. *Henry* Emerson," as the name is written out in the manuscript of the text, although not in the printed versions? Is this "*Evangeline Hen*derson," as in *Evelyn* White*head*? "*Evangeline Henderson*" (initials: *E.H.*), as in "*Henry Emerson*" (initials: *H.E.*)? And, stirring somewhere in the background, *Alfred North Whitehead*, as in *Ralph Waldo Emerson*? What of *Mrs. Henry Whitehead*, Evelyn Whitehead's real-life sister-in-law? How, indeed, is one to determine whether "Mrs. Emerson" is the portrait of one Mrs. Whitehead or the other?

In *The Autobiography of Alice B. Toklas* Stein recorded the following impression of the wife of Alfred North Whitehead's elder brother Henry, longstanding Anglo-Catholic Bishop of Madras. "Mrs. Bishop," as Toklas disparagingly refers to her, insisted that, given Stein's status as "an important person in Paris" and as "a neutral," she ought to "suggest to the french government that they give us Pondichéry." "It would be very useful to us," the Bishop's wife added. Stein "replied politely that to her great regret her importance such as it was was among painters and writers and not with politicians. But that, said Mrs. Bishop, would make no difference." After lunch, Toklas reports, Stein asked "under her breath": "Where the hell is Pondichéry" (p. 152). Mrs. Henry Whitehead supposes that all matters of import are coterminous—that Stein's position in Paris gives her access to everyone of significance, and that as "an important person" herself she may be assumed to recognize the import of Pondichéry. In opening "Mrs. Emerson" with "the regular way of instituting clerical resemblances and neglecting hazards," Stein may well have had this Mrs. Whitehead in mind; yet with the syntax's increasing irregularity as one moves from *A* to *B*, it becomes clear that a much freer spirit than "Mrs. Bishop" is being portrayed.

The nominal play of *Evangeline Henderson* establishes that this composition is in some sense a portrait of *Evelyn* Whitehead, complementing the companion piece from the long stay at Lockeridge, the austerely (and ambiguously) titled "Mrs. Whitehead." Near the end of that work, Stein also plays with Evelyn Whitehead's name when she writes, "Please ocean spoke please Helen" and "I saw a spoken leave leaf"—echoing *Evelyn* in *Helen* and then again in the "spok*en leave*" read back to front: "*eavel/len*" (GP, p. 156). Admittedly, this last bit of play may strike one as something of a stretch on Stein's (or her reader's) part, even if the section of "Mrs. Whitehead" which contains the lines *is* subtitled "Next stretching," and begins "Next for that leaf stretching" (in the process, stretching two words to fit five).[39] However, these are the kind of questions Stein asks one to put to her creations, questions about the "things that are really most entirely exciting" in composing sentences as well as in one's life apart from such composition, questions "bespeaking combinations" and consequently addressing themselves to the *life* of things (*leaves stretching, a spoken leaf*). The crucial matter, as Stein explained in her 1934 lecture "Plays," following several pages of inquiries directed no less at herself than at her audience, was that the questions be asked, since "in asking a question one is not answering but one is as one may say *deciding about knowing*" (LIA, p. 102, emphasis added). Implicit in the very act of posing a series of questions (with the questions emerging one from the other, not questions and answers in quick succession), the determination is made that "there *is* knowledge," even if "there is no one who answers these questions" (p. 102). Recall, for instance, Walter Shandy's grammatical catechism, likened by Williams to Stein's compositions. This was designed to show that one can readily "discourse about" a white bear without ever having actually seen any such beast. In letting his questions unfold themselves so seamlessly, Mr. Shandy communicated that here there *was* knowledge to be had, without misleadingly claiming that he *really* knew what he was talking *about*.

"I said I knew America," Stein writes in "Mrs. Emerson," presumably alluding to her recent dispute with Russell at the Whiteheads as well as to earlier conversations with him on the same topic the last time she had visited the English countryside, in 1902 (RAB, p. 44).[40] Both in the Lockeridge discussion and in "Mrs. Emerson," Stein portrayed an America defined contextually—that is to say, in relational terms, and principally in relation to England (ABT, p. 152). The premium placed, according to Stein, on movement and transition by a typically American, twentieth-century sensibility *coexisted*, in both cases, with the English or nineteenth-century emphasis on regularity it served to critique. Consequently, she found parallels not only between her own experience in the early days of the war (as an American confined to England's "island culture") and Emerson's experience as a mid-nineteenth-century American seeking to break free of the hegemonic cultural and linguistic environment of his day, but also between Emerson, herself, and Evelyn Whitehead.

The following anecdote, supplied just before Russell made his entrance onto the *Autobiography*'s stage, suggests a basis for the parallel:

> There were a great many people coming and going in the Whiteheads' home and there was of course plenty of discussion. First there was Lytton Strachey[, who] came one evening to see Mrs. Whitehead. [They] discussed the possibility of rescuing [his] sister who was lost in Germany. [Mrs. Whitehead] suggested that he apply to a certain person who could help him. But, said Lytton Strachey faintly, I have never met him. Yes, said Mrs. Whitehead, but you might write to him and ask to see him. Not, replied Lytton Strachey faintly, if I have never met him. (p. 151)

Evelyn Whitehead's advice here to the author of *Eminent Victorians* bears the mark of a decidedly untypical Englishwoman (at least insofar as Strachey is understood to represent the English type), an impression highlighted a page later by the anecdote already cited about the much more conventional wife of Henry Whitehead.[41] Indeed, according to Alfred North Whitehead's biographer and former student, Victor Lowe, Evelyn Whitehead's "delight in," and emphasis on, "the uniqueness of every human occasion," a delight entirely unknown to her political-minded sister-in-law, was responsible for her husband arriving at "the opinion he held in his Harvard years, namely, that every occasion is unique, and so transcends . . . general rules" (II, p. 142). On this account, Whitehead's radical empiricism, his unacknowledged Emersonianism, derived in no small part from his wife's influence.[42]

In possessing a capacity to imagine change and to appreciate creative irregularities far beyond that available either to "Mrs. Bishop" or to Lytton Strachey, Evelyn Whitehead presented Stein with an opportunity to continue the conversation with Russell about America, only on her own terms: in a manner that enabled her to take full advantage of the recursive mechanisms of writing for investigating experiential matters, in "talking and listening" all "at once" (LIA, p. 170). Already in the concluding sentences of "Mrs. Whitehead," Stein had begun to meditate explicitly on the limits of the regularity she associated with Russell, a concern that, together with the persistent nameplay, she carried over from "Mrs. Whitehead" into the first paragraph of "Mrs. Emerson." "I cannot deny," she wrote in the earlier work, that

> Bertie Henschel is coming tomorrow. Saturdays are even. There is a regular principle, if you mention it you mention what happened.
> What do you make of it.
> You exceed all hope and all praise. (GP, p. 156)

Bertrand Russell, B*ertie Hen*schel—meet Mrs. *Hen/r/y* Emerson. As Stein intimated with this wordplay, an accurate portrait of Alfred North Whitehead's wife would need to accommodate the role Russell played in her life, and she in his.

According to Victor Lowe, Russell had fallen in love with Evelyn Whitehead a dozen years earlier, when, by his own account, he fell out of love with his wife, Alys. At the time, in 1902, the Russells were living at the Whiteheads, "in a new bedroom . . . paid for with money Russell had supplied" (I, p. 246).[43] Early the previous year, Russell and Whitehead had begun to collaborate on the investigations that resulted in the *Principia Mathematica*, and Russell had also witnessed an apparent heart attack of Mrs. Whitehead's, which he experienced as a revelation.[44] In his *Autobiography* he recalled that she seemed cut off from everyone and everything by walls of agony, and the sense of the solitude of each human soul suddenly overwhelmed me. Ever since my marriage, my emotional life had been calm and superficial. I had forgotten all the deeper issues, and had been content with flippant cleverness. Suddenly the ground seemed to give way beneath me, and I found myself in quite another region.

Nothing could penetrate such solitude, he realized, "except the highest intensity of the sort of love that religious teachers have preached." At least in hindsight, he credited this recognition with transforming his worldview: "Having been an Imperialist, I became during those five minutes a pro-Boer and a Pacifist" (cited in Lowe, I, p. 239).

Over the course of the extended stay at Lockeridge, punctuated by visits from Russell arguing the Pacifist line against the woman who had inspired it in him, Stein can't but have observed his passion for his mentor's wife, encouraged but not reciprocated by her.[45] The concluding line of "Mrs. Whitehead," *You exceed all hope and all praise*, exactly conveys "the sort of love that religious teachers have preached," even as it underscores the division afflicting Russell's perspective, between an emotional life drawn to excess and an intellectual life that embraced rationality and "regular principles." The initial allusion to Russell, by name, is followed by a parody of his rationalism, with its unreflective desire to reduce everything to regular principles and arithmetical relations. "Saturdays are *even*," presumably because they fall on the sixth day of the week (on the principle that the week begins on Monday rather than on Sunday). *There is a regular principle, if you mention it you mention what happened*: Here Stein articulates the basic rationalist assumption, that whatever happens happens by grace of regular principles. At the same time, in framing the claim as she does, she belittles it, suggesting that the regularity is merely associative or correlative, akin to gossip ("if you *mention* it you *mention* what happened"), rather than explanatory and principled (if you *invoke* it, you *explain* what happened). Had she stopped with this, Stein might readily be classed as a Humean skeptic, leveling the usual empiricist critique at rationalism. However, she continues: "What do you make of it." Not only does she suppose that something is made of the mentioning; the mentioning is itself a making, a creative act. As such, it serves as an opportunity for recreation (with *what is happening* suggesting *what happened*), and not just as a vehicle for describing past events (with the conveyance abstracted from that which it conveys). Russell's rationalism proved unable to account for such creativity— thereby failing to do justice to the full range of his own experience, and ultimately to any experience per se. Whitehead, by contrast, attempted to elucidate the principle of irregularity expressed in forms of process or patterns of change: the heterogeneous dialectic operating in what, in the last chapter, I termed "cogently organized structures of disorganization." His wife, as Stein recognized, represented this principle of life for him no less than she did for Russell. Yet, unlike Whitehead, Russell remained content in his philosophy, if not in his life, to precipitate regularities from irregularities.

A common interest in organic mechanisms, and therefore in creativity (as they understood it), led Stein and Whitehead to an appreciation of the essential role of irregular, aperiodic rhythms in life. In turn, each came to believe that the actual world, "nature alive," was ultimately a function of "vibratory existence" and composed, at bottom, of "entit[ies] constituted by . . . vibrations," or *vibratory organisms*, in Whitehead's phrasing (SMW, p. 36). "On the organic theory of nature," he explained in *Science and the Modern World*, "there are two sorts of vibrations which radically differ from each other. There is vibratory locomotion [of a given pattern as a whole] and there is vibratory organic deformation," or "vibratory change of pattern" (p. 131). Changes of the latter sort distinguish vibratory organisms from mere patterns in motion, and it is exactly such *vibratory organic deformation* that Stein had in mind in a memorable description of Francis Picabia. Despite having been put off for many years by what she regarded as the Cubist and Dadaist painter's "delayed adolescence," she nevertheless concluded that he was possessed by "an idea that has been and will be of immense value to all time" (ABT, p. 134). According to Stein, Picabia had "conceived and is struggling with the problem that a [painted] line should have the vibration of a musical sound and that this vibration should be the result of conceiving the human form and the human face in so tenuous a fashion that it would induce such vibration in the line forming it" (p. 210). Only in this way was it possible to conceive of *actually painting* "the human being"—of portraying an individual's distinctive "vibratory existence" on canvas (p. 119).

In her own literary portraiture, from 1912 on, Stein attempted to compose similarly "vibrant lines," working in a medium that she conceived of in essentially visual terms (p. 210). To Toklas's inquiry early in their acquaintance, for instance, as to whether she ever "read french," Stein replied: "No, . . . you see I feel with my eyes and it does not make any difference to me what language I hear, I don't hear a language, I hear tones of voice and rhythms, but with my eyes I see words and sentences and there is for me only one language and that is english" (p. 70). Like Picabia, she sought to compose lines that possessed "the vibration of a musical sound" without relying on tone of voice or speech rhythms—as, for instance, when she "set a sentence for herself as a sort of tuning fork and metronome and then [wrote] to that time and tune" (p. 206). By contrast with her earliest portraits (many of them of painters) in which, as she explained in 1935, she tried to "make a cinema," with each sentence "just infinitesimally different from the one before," she sought in subsequent works to "condense" the writing "as much as possible and change it around, until you could get the movement of a human being" (HWW, pp. 158–59). In the hands of someone who happened to hear "more pleasantly with the eyes than with the ears," such changing around, informed by the physiological mechanisms of visual feeling, produced the sort of vibratory organic deformation one finds in "Mrs. Emerson" (EA, p. 90). Stein was certainly not claiming that considerations of sound were entirely absent from the composition of such a work; after all, within a year of its appearance in *Close Up*, she was describing the compositions collected in *Tender Buttons* as investigations of "the problem of correlating sight, sound and sense." Even in the course of asserting that hearing (with one's ears) "plays [too] large [a] part in everything," she was still prepared to observe in *Everybody's Autobiography* that "as I write [these sentences] the movement of the words spoken by some one whom lately I have been hearing sound like my writing feels to me as I am writing." "That," she remarked, "is what led me to portrait writing" (p. 91). If, on a personal level, her argument was with the all-too-common allegation that her compositions "appeal[ed exclusively] to the ear and to the subconscious," on a more general level it was directed at the potential for speech rhythms to *dictate* how one apprehends writing, in the process drowning out any visually oriented compositional rhythms (ABT, p. 75).

Elsewhere in *Everybody's Autobiography* Stein recalled some remarks of Charlie Chaplin's concerning a similar problem in his chosen medium. Introduced at a dinner in Beverly Hills, the two celebrities "naturally talked about the cinema, and he explained something":

> He said naturally it was disappointing, he had known the silent films and in that they could do something that the theatre had not done they could change the rhythm but if you had a voice accompanying naturally after that you could never change the rhythm you were always held by the rhythm that the voice gave them. (p. 291)[46]

In this respect, silent film encouraged one to "hear with one's eyes" in a manner that the new talkies actively discouraged; and, instead of increasing the potential for the cinema to function, in Macpherson's words, as "a medium for the possible expression of art in its most modern and experimental aspects," the new technology (introduced in 1927, as it happens, in *The Jazz Singer*) created an illusion of *regular* movement that made the medium less amenable to investigations of the sort that most interested Stein—of patterns of change and images of movement. In 1934, she remarked that, in considering how the *cinema* had "changed from sight to sound, and how much before there was real sound how much of the sight was sound or how much it was not," she "suppose[d] one might have gotten to know a good deal" about such matters as whether, in a *theatrical* performance, "the thing heard replace[s] the thing seen," or whether it "help[s]" or "interfere[s] with it," and vice versa. The cinema, she continued, "undoubtedly had a new way of understanding sight and sound in relation to emotion and time," a perspective that was expressed in the "inevitable experiments" carried out by figures like Chaplin, and which she attributed to "the same impulse to solve the problem of the relation of seeing and hearing" that lay behind her own experiments (LIA, pp. 103–4).

Aside from the introduction of talk (which, Stein predicted to Chaplin, would result in "the films . . . becom[ing] like the newspapers just a daily habit and not at all exciting or interesting"), "the trouble with cinema" was that "it is after all a photograph, and a photograph continues to be a photograph" (EA, pp. 291–92; LIA, p. 117). In other words, films all too readily conveyed the impression that depth and movement were illusions, built up out of static, two-dimensional units—tricks the mind played on the body, and the body on the mind.[47] This was the same problem she had confronted with her initial, cinemalike, portraits, and which she only resolved by loosening up the strict grammatical patterning of her sentences.[48] "And yet," Stein wondered, concluding her cinematic musings on a characteristically hopeful note, "can it [the photograph] become something else," just as her sentences had become something else? "Perhaps it can," she allowed, "but that is a whole other question. If it can then some one will have to feel that about it" (LIA, p. 117).[49] After all, Picabia's own aggressively counterintuitive sense that "painting should not be painting," and that "anything should not look like anything even if it did and that really it did not," could itself be traced back, according to Stein, to the fact that his grandfather had been "a French scientist and one of the inventors of photography" (EA, p. 59).

Bryher, in her 1963 memoir *The Heart to Artemis*, painted a considerably bleaker picture, looking back on "the golden age of what I call 'the art that died' because sound ruined its development" (p. 247). In addition to having furthered a "popular internationalism" by offering "a single language across Europe," the silents supplied "richer . . . material," because they "had to suggest rather than state" (pp. 248, 261). When Stein, in her conversation with Chaplin, compared "the sentiment of movement" that he had "invented" in his silent films with the "sentiment of doing nothing" she had "invented" in *Four Saints in Three Acts*, she was addressing the potentialities for *suggestion* that they had each investigated in their respective media. These were possibilities capable of producing "real excit[ement]" insofar as the true "interest" possessed by the works was autopoietic in nature, emerging from their status as "inevitable experiments" with the media in question, rather than as determined by a principle of regularity like that laid down in the talkies, of a colloquy of voices lending coherence to a sequence of images and so shaping the viewer's experience of the work (EA, p. 292).

Consider the semi-cinematic line, *He looks like a young man grown old.* This sentence, a sort of one-line picture of Dorian Gray, clearly complements the sentence fragment cited in Chapter 1, *What is the use of being a little boy if you are to be a man what is the use.* Yet, unlike the latter, the former is logically (although not grammatically) a non sequitur; not only does it describe someone who looks both young and old, prematurely old or preternaturally young, but it also presumes to capture the passage of time ("grown old") in a slice of time ("He looks like"). As such, it conveys the pathos, derived from the potent combination of causal efficacy and presentational immediacy, which Whitehead located in the "miraculous revelations of great literature"—in which "the whole of nature" is "grasped . . . as involved in the tonality of the individual instance." At the conclusion of the *Enquiry Concerning the Principles of Natural Knowledge* Whitehead returned to literature in order to articulate his sense of the rhythmic foundation of life, and for solace. For solace, one is compelled to recognize, is what he required in order to complete this work dedicated to his youngest son. "TO / ERIC ALFRED WHITEHEAD," the dedication runs:

ROYAL FLYING CORPS
November 27, 1898 to March 13, 1918

Killed in action over the Forêt de Gobain
giving himself that the city of his vision
may not perish.

The music of his life was without discord,
perfect in its beauty.

Here, then, is the work's concluding section:

64.91   Thus the permanence of the individual rhythm within nature is not absolutely associated with one definite set of material objects.* But the connection for subtler rhythms is very close.** So far as direct observation is concerned all that we know of the essential relations of life in nature is stated in two short poetic phrases. The obvious aspect by Tennyson,

> "Blow, bugle, blow, set the wild echoes flying,
> And answer, echoes, answer, dying, dying, dying."

Namely, Bergson's élan vital and its relapse into matter.
And, Wordsworth with more depth,

> "The music in my heart I bore,
> Long after it was heard no more." (pp. 199–200)

These three brief paragraphs comprise an ode in mixed prose and verse, effectively *prehending* the distinctive shape and concerns of Wordsworth's immortal Intimations Ode. In them, Whitehead expresses a keen sense that the music of his son's life need not perish with the "relapse" of the élan vital into matter. The vibratory organism remains, even if the living body does not.

It is such *individual* rhythms, audible to the "eye made quiet by the power / Of harmony, and the deep power of joy," which Whitehead sought to delineate in his philosophy of organism, and which Stein no less sought to recreate in her portraits, matching the visionary music of her subjects' lives, their distinctive vibratory existences, with the visionary music of her writing, the way it "feels to me as I am writing." In the end, to be sure, the little boy may fail to grow into a man; but at least he hasn't grown old before his time. For Stein, as for Whitehead (and no less for Wordsworth or Emerson), that would be the greater tragedy, inasmuch as it substitutes a facsimile of life, the equivalent of a "talkie," for the real thing. "The problem of problems," Whitehead wrote on April 8, 1928, to Rosalind Greene (whom Victor Lowe calls Evelyn Whitehead's "most intimate friend"), concerning the difficulties he was encountering in preparing his Gifford lectures,

> is the real transitoriness of things—and yet!!—I am equally convinced that the great side of things is weaving something ageless and immortal: something in

---

* As occurs, for example, with "stray rhythms which pass over the face of nature utilising physical objects as mere transient vehicles for their expression." To a degree, Whitehead notes in the previous section, "this is the case in living bodies, which exhibit a continual assimilation and rejection of material" (ENQ, p. 199).

** Hence living bodies, which "exhibit rhythm of the greatest subtlety within our apprehension . . . appear to require a certain stability of material" (p. 199).

which personalities retain the wonder of their radiance—and the fluff sinks into its utter triviality. But I cannot express it at all. No system of words seems up to the job. (cited in Lowe, II, p. 245)

Kurt Gödel's 1931 "incompleteness theorem," demonstrating, as Whitehead subsequently put it, "the foundation of logic on the notion of inconsistency," would lead one to expect that no *system* of words could possibly describe the processes involved in "weaving something ageless and immortal," without at one level or another falling into a non sequitur; yet does this mean that Gödel must be given the last word (MT, p. 52)? For when a linguistic system, unlike a purely logical one, encounters a non sequitur, it indulges in some pretty immortal weaving of its own—suggesting, in a *visual* medium, the experience of a *voice*, and consequently recreating *the wonder of a personality's radiance*, in Whitehead's terms, or communicating *knowledge of acquaintance*, in William James's. "Word-systems" don't in fact operate on exclusively rational principles; however systematic the application of non sequiturs (and Stein's were nothing if not systematic), they remain non sequiturs.[50] Such "systems" may not be nervous systems *tout court*, but who is to say that they aren't extensions of nervous systems? In turning now to the third, and final, part of the present study, I shall examine this question from several angles suggested by James with respect to physiological psychology and psychical research, and addressed by Stein in her investigations of the writing process.

Stein and William James

Introduction: The Will to Live

In wartime, Stein recalled William James as having "said he always said there is the will to live without the will to live there is destruction, but there is also the will to destroy, and the two like everything are in opposition, like wanting to be alone and when you are alone wanting to have company and when you have company wanting to be alone and like wanting eternity and wanting a beginning and middle and ending and now in 1943 the thing that we know most about is the opposition between the will to live and the will to destroy" (WIHS, pp. 63–64). Almost a decade earlier, Stein had remarked in "Portraits and Repetition" that "it is not possible *while anybody is alive* that they should use exactly the same emphasis." "Anybody," she continued, "can be interested in a story of a crime because no matter how often the witnesses tell the same story the insistence is different. That is what makes life that the insistence is different, no matter how often you tell the same story if there is anything alive in the telling the emphasis is different. . . . No matter how often what happened any time any one told anything there was no repetition. This is what William James calls *the Will to Live*. If not nobody would live" (LIA, pp. 167, 169, emphasis added). Although Stein is addressing issues of self-expression and narration here, her repeated invocation of *life* isn't merely rhetorical; rather she is describing a feature of discourse that links it quite directly with biological evolution as well as with the sense, discussed above in Chapter 2, of words and punctuation coming "to have a life of their own." In all such insistences and emphases, including Stein's own in composing these sentences, repetition is *repetition with a difference*.

In *Everybody's Autobiography*, Stein directly invoked the context of "excitement" that "evolution and James' the Will to Live" had supplied in her youth. Even in that context, however, the excitement was somewhat dulled by the seeming inevitability of death, no matter how great one's desire to live. "There is the will to live," she noted, "but really when one is

completely wise that is when one is a genius the things that make you a genius make you live but have nothing to do with being living that is with the
struggle for existence." "Really," she continued, "genius that is the existing
without any internal recognition of time has nothing to do with the will to
live, and yet they use it like that." In other words, although one may speak
of life both in relation to genius *and* in relation to "the will to live" (or
"struggle for existence"), these two forms of life prove incommensurable
(EA, pp. 250–51). The latter leads ultimately, if not immediately, to death
and as such remains in the purview of traditional science, amenable to description and hence to a form of explanation rooted in description. ("After
all," Stein remarked of *The Making of Americans*, "description is explanation" [LIA, p. 142].) The former, by contrast, leaves open the possibility of
experiencing what she once called the "everlasting feeling" of an unbroken
world, a feeling "killed" for some—here she may have had herself in
mind—by their awareness of having "been a baby" once, "helpless" and
with "*no conscious feeling in them, . . . without anything to know inside
them or around them.*" "Their having been so little once and knowing
nothing makes it all a broken world for them that they have inside them."
Short of positing an immortal soul or vital principle, one might try to recover this sense of everlastingness by "making a baby to make for [oneself]
a new beginning and so win . . . a new everlasting feeling" (GMP, p. 13, emphasis added; cited in LIA, p. 149). Alternatively, one might *write*. As Stein
explained more than twenty years after she made these observations in
"Matisse Picasso and Gertrude Stein," in a passage I have already cited several times:

> Other things may be more exciting to others when they are at school but to me
> undoubtedly when I was at school the really completely exciting thing was
> diagramming sentences and that has been to me ever since the one thing that
> has been completely exciting and completely completing. I like the feeling *the
> everlasting feeling* of sentences as they diagram themselves. (LIA, p. 211,
> emphasis added)

Composition as explanation in lieu of *description as explanation*; and
instead of explanation in terms of direct causation, explanation, as Langer
phrased it, "in terms of motivation," the "much more complicated causal
relationship" suggested by a "conceptual frame of acts and motivating situations" (M, pp. 359, 159). Indeed, it was Stein's extraordinary sensitivity to
the "indirect causation of acts via the prevailing dynamic situation" (in
short, by "alter[ing] the organic situation that induces acts" rather than directly by "the simple transmission of motion, heat, or other physical quan-

tity from one body to another") that made B. F. Skinner's behaviorist account of her writing so inappropriate (M, p. 111).

At this point, by way of introducing the following linked set of chapters, I shall adduce two more of the themes that Stein wrote for her sophomore composition course at Radcliffe. The first, dated December 19, 1894, and titled "In a Psychological Laboratory," graphically displays the inadequacies of late nineteenth-century psychophysics, with its desiderata of strict causation, for investigating the *much more complicated indirect causation of acts*.[1] "One is indeed all things to all men in a laboratory," the twenty-year-old Stein wrote:

> At one moment you find yourself a howling mob, emitting fiendish yells, and explosive laughter, starting in belligerent attitudes hammer in hand and anon applauding violently.
>
> Before long this vehement individual is requested to make herself a perfect blank while someone practices on her as an automaton.
>
> Next she finds herself with a complicated apparatus strapped across her breast to register her breathing, her finger imprisoned in a steel machine and her arm thrust immovably into a big glass tube. She is surrounded by a group of earnest youths who carefully watch the silent record of the automatic pen on the slowly revolving drum.
>
> Strange fancies begin to crowd upon her, she feels that the silent pen is writing on and on forever. Her record is there she cannot escape it and the group about her begin to assume the shape of mocking fiends gloating over her imprisoned misery. Suddenly she starts, they have suddenly loosened a metronome directly behind her, to observe the effect, so now the morning's work is over. (RM, p. 121)[2]

Already, Stein is understandably ambivalent about the impoverishment of experience so characteristic of this environment.[3] By 1914, twenty years on, she will have developed a variety of compositional practices permitting her to resist the sensation of a "silent pen" relentlessly "writing on and on forever" and confining her with its "silent record." Yet if she resisted a dictation that took the form of automatic writing, this doesn't mean that she believed, any more than Emerson did in "Fate," that there was no irresistible dictation or that it could be successfully avoided. Here she differed profoundly from James, who at twenty-eight famously asserted in his diary, after a year of near-suicidal depression (and the same week that Emerson, his godfather, began the course of lectures at Harvard on the natural history of intellect), that "my first act of free will shall be to believe in free will" (Perry, II, p. 323). In saying this, he took a directly contrary stand to that expressed by Emerson in a work such as "Fate," where instead of being free to believe in free will, one is *obliged* to believe in it. Stein was no less skeptical than Emerson was with respect to purely psychological matters—recall her statement that "nobody enters into the mind of someone else, not even a husband and wife"—yet she also believed, again like Emerson, that a propitious combination of psychology and writing could produce *liberties, individuals, duties, characters* that one wouldn't hesitate to affirm even if one was, after all, compelled to do so (TI, p. 30).

Directly following his chapter on "The Sick Soul" in *The Varieties of Religious Experience*, James invoked a distinction between "the two ways of looking at life which are characteristic respectively of . . . the healthy-minded, who need to be born only once, and of the sick souls, who must be twice-born in order to be happy" (p. 166). Among exemplars of healthy-minded optimism, he listed Emerson. Common as the impression is, here James was mistaken; for Emerson doesn't conform to either half of the distinction in question. *Initially* "once-born" or "healthy-minded," he was so far set back by the death of his son (following those of his wife and brother) that he had to be "born again," not "in order to be happy" but not to be overwhelmed by unhappiness. Much the same may be said of Whitehead, especially by contrast with more conventionally "twice-born" radical empiricists such as James and Stein. James actually delivered a lecture on the topic "Is Life Worth Living?" near the end of Stein's sophomore year at Harvard, and we know that she was in the audience because she composed her theme that evening in response:

> Is life worth living? Yes, a thousand times yes when the world still holds such spirits as Prof. James. He is truly a man among men; a scientist of force and originality embodying all that is strongest and worthiest in the scientific spirit; a metaphysician skilled in abstract thought, clear and vigorous and yet too great to worship logic as his God, and narrow himself to a belief merely in the reason of man.
>
> A man he is who has lived sympathetically not alone all thought but all life. He stands firmly, nobly for the dignity of man. His faith is not that of a cringing coward before an all-powerful master, but of a strong man willing to fight, to suffer and endure. He has not accepted faith because it is easy and pleasing. He has thought and lived many years and at last says with a voice of authority, if life did not mean this, I don't know what it means.
>
> What can one say more? He is a strong sane noble personality reacting truly on all experience that life has given him. He is a man take him for all in all. (RM, pp. 146–47)

Discoursing on "that metaphysical *tedium vitae* which is peculiar to reflecting men," James anticipated in "Is Life Worth Living?" the much better-known lecture he delivered a year later on "the will to believe," when he cautioned that "the part of wisdom as well as of courage is to *believe what is in the line of your needs,* for only by such belief is the need fulfilled" (*Writings 1878–1899*, p. 485).[4]

"The will to *believe*" is about as close as James gets to the expression "the will to *live*" in print. One doesn't have to look far to see why he was unlikely to avail himself of the phrase, despite Stein's assertions to the contrary. As Michel Henry observes in his definitive study of the intellectual origins of the Freudian unconscious, the will to live served as the "central concept" in the pessimistic, dualistic philosophy of Arthur Schopenhauer, who used it to refer to "the instinctual life of the body, the ceaseless and monotonous repetition of its pulses and desires" (p. 134; Crary, p. 77). It was *this* "will to live" that Stein associated with "the struggle for existence," and a quite distinct "will to live" to which she attributed enlivening variations in emphasis (by contrast with the "monotonous repetition" of Schopenhauer's usage). As it happens, James summed up the more positive usage in another important lecture dating from this period, when he stated, in "On a Certain Blindness in Human Beings" that "wherever a process of life communicates an eagerness to him who lives it, there the life becomes genuinely significant" (*Writings: 1878–1899*, p. 843). No less than the phrase "the will to live," however, this remark remains ambiguous; for, with his use of the term *communicate*, James leaves open the possibility that instead of being *produced* by the living individual (as, in effect, a by-product of the "process of life"), the "eagerness" is *transmitted* by means of this process, from some unknown source to "him who lives it."[5] As I shall argue in the following chapters and particularly in Chapter 6, Stein and James chiefly differed concerning the implications of these alternative mechanisms of communication. Is such communication autopoietic and therefore better understood in terms of motivation or *composition as explanation* (Stein)? Or does it function within a more traditionally causative framework, however untraditional the agents operating in that framework may turn out to be (James)?

CHAPTER FIVE

Writing Psychology Over:
Toward a More Radical Empiricism

At the beginning of *Science and the Modern World*, Whitehead invoked William James as a representative modern man, exemplary of the "quiet growth of science" that had "practically recoloured our mentality so that modes of thought which in former times were exceptional are now broadly spread through the educated world" (p. 2). "Perhaps my metaphor of a new colour is too strong," Whitehead continued:

> What I mean is just that slightest change of tone which yet makes all the difference. This is exactly illustrated by a sentence from a published letter of that adorable genius, William James. When he was finishing his great treatise on the *Principles of Psychology*, he wrote to his brother Henry James, "I have to forge every sentence in the teeth of irreducible and stubborn facts."

In a few broad strokes, Whitehead sketched a climate in which radical empiricism could flourish—a climate in which "a vehement and passionate interest" existed "in the *relation* of general principles to irreducible and stubborn facts." "Devotion to abstract generalization" and "passionate interest in the detailed facts" were put mutually into play, without either attachment, whether for rationalist or empiricist procedures, taking precedence (pp. 2–3).

Because the "change of tone" exemplified by James's radical empiricism has "recoloured our mentality" does not mean, however, that the abstract generalizations whereby modern scientists explain their practices to themselves necessarily express a radical empiricist perspective. On the contrary, in much of his speculative philosophy Whitehead was concerned to demonstrate the fallacious reasoning that scientists exhibit when they base accounts of their own research on empiricist, and hence insufficiently empirical, grounds. Jean-Pierre Changeux offers an especially clear instance of this when, near the end of *Neuronal Man*, he sums up the perspective expressed in his study:

> To consider mental processes as physical events is not to take an ideological
> stand but simply to adopt the most reasonable and, more important, the most
> generative working hypothesis. . . . The combinatorial possibilities provided by
> the number and diversity of connections in the human brain seem quite suffi-
> cient to account for human capabilities. There is no justification for a split
> between mental and neuronal activity. What is the point of speaking of "mind"
> or "spirit"? It is only that there are two "aspects" of a single *event*, which one
> may describe in terms taken from the introspective language of the psychologist
> or from the language of the neurobiologist. (p. 275)

This is a radicalized empiricism, not radical empiricism, although echoes of
the latter can certainly be heard, both in the emphasis on connectivity and
in Changeux's recognition that mental and neuronal activity are "two 'aspects' of a single event." The difference between the two empiricisms is
principally a matter of tone, as Whitehead said, with the tone in this case
being registered by the quotation marks around the term *aspects*. These are
not really distinct aspects but related ways of describing just one aspect.
The psychologist's introspective language and the neurobiologist's language
of "combinatorial possibilities" are mirror-images, alternative " 'aspects' " of
"naïve empiricism." Instead of consciousness and neurophysiology being put
into play, as radical empiricism aims to do, they are reduced to isomorphic
descriptions: that is, each is constructed on the model of "behavior visible
to the outside world," which is the hallmark of empiricism (NM, p. 274).[1]

The differences in tonality of ordinary and radical empiricism may be
seen in a distinction Varela and his coauthors make in *The Embodied
Mind*. Concerning "two very different senses that the term *empirical realism* can have," they observe that

> it might mean that our world will continue to be the familiar one of objects and
> events with various qualities, even if we discover that this world is not pregiven
> and well grounded. On the other hand, it might mean that we will always
> experience this familiar world as if it were ultimately grounded, that we are
> "condemned" to experience the world as if it had a ground, even though we
> know philosophically and scientifically that it does not. This latter supposition
> is not innocent, for it imposes an a priori limitation on the possibilities for
> human development and transformation. (p. 218)

Radical empiricism insists on the open-ended quality of human experience,
what Whitehead referred to as the world's "creative advance" into novelty,
rather than affixing experience to the empiricist construction of an ultimate
ground given once and for all (PRO, p. xiv). Only on the basis of the latter
assumption can one profess to believe, for instance, that it will someday be

possible to determine everything one needs to know about butterflies and beetles from physicochemical analysis of the genetic makeup of a few specimens, neatly killed and pinned. The first sense of *empirical realism* is perfectly consistent with Varela et al.'s radical empiricism (involving "the back-and-forth communication between cognitive science and experience," as they characterize it), whereas the second sense articulates the limits of an empiricist realism, empiricism of the sort that Stein attributed to nineteenth-century science and which still dictates the rationale of much research in molecular biology (EM, p. 237).[2] A *reductio ad absurdum*, this latter version of empirical realism supposes the empiricist perspective to be hard-wired into human physiology, and that consequently the scientific or philosophical refutation of empiricism can only produce a tragic dissociation between knowledge of acquaintance (the world as we are condemned physiologically to experience it) and knowledge-about (scientific descriptions of what the world is really like). The radical empiricist disputes this characterization of knowledge of acquaintance and knowledge-about as well as of the relations, or absence of relation, between them.

EXPERIENCE AS A KIND OF WRITING

By 1904 James could observe in the essay "Does 'Consciousness' Exist?" that "for twenty years past I have mistrusted 'consciousness' as an entity; for seven or eight years past I have suggested its non-existence to my students" (p. 1141). Stein, his student between 1895 and 1897, would have witnessed this pedagogical shift. Experience, he had come to believe, "had no such inner duplicity" as that between content and consciousness. Divisions along these lines resulted from "the addition, to a concrete piece of [experience], of other sets of experience," which caused the same piece to be taken in two different ways. This could be illustrated with some paint, as James explained:

> In a pot in a paintshop, along with other paints, it serves in its entirety as so much saleable matter. Spread on a canvas, with other paints around it, it represents, on the contrary, a feature in a picture and performs a spiritual function. Just so, I maintain, does a given undivided portion of experience, taken in one context of associates, play the part of knower, of a state of mind, of "consciousness"; while in a different context the same undivided bit of experience plays the part of a thing known, of an objective "content."

Dualism, he observed, "is still preserved in this account, but reinterpreted, so that, instead of being mysterious and elusive, it becomes verifiable and

concrete. It is an affair of relations, it falls outside, not inside, the single experience considered, and can always be particularized and defined" (pp.
1144–45).[3]

James's was a *radical* empiricism because it required that both content
and consciousness be recognized as epiphenomena and as essentially relational.[4] At the cost of denying substantiality to either form of substance,
material or mental, he was able to counter reductive monisms with a "pluralistic universe."[5] Dualism was not all that was reinterpreted in this account of experience, however; James also reinterpreted the experience of es-
trangement that Emerson had so powerfully expressed in the essay he chose
to call "Experience." "We fancy," Emerson had written,

> that we are strangers, and not so intimately domesticated in the planet as the
> wild man, and the wild beast and bird. But the exclusion reaches them also. . . .
> [They too] are just such superficial tenants of the globe. Then the new molecular
> philosophy shows astronomical interspaces between atom and atom, shows that
> the world is all outside: it has no inside. (EL, pp. 480–81)

Yes, James responded, there is no inside per se; but that does not empty us
and our categories of all meaning.

James proposed to treat pieces of experience the way the poet and literary critic William Empson would later treat pieces of writing: as meaning
different things in different "contexts of associates" and as such becoming
"an affair of relations." (The resemblance to Empson is not arbitrary; Empson's mentor, I. A. Richards, was trained as a psychologist and like James
was fascinated by the mechanics of reading.) Rather than defining consciousness in terms of categories, say, that could either be filled or emptied—a model in which all activity occurs *within* the categories—James
reinterpreted it here as one way of contextualizing "undivided" bits of experience, which had necessarily to be taken up from the outside. This pluralism, enabling him as it did to equate the "state of mind" of the knower
with the "thing known," would form the rationale for Stein's project (and
projection) of a portraiture that recreated the object instead of merely describing it. Yet, as James would have been the first to recognize, his conception of representation remained inadequate for so ambitious a project.

As a second example of the pluralism he had in mind, James described an
experience he could be sure all his readers shared. "Let [the reader] begin
with a perceptual experience," he instructed, "the 'presentation,' so called,
of a physical object, his actual field of vision, the room he sits in, with the
book he is reading at its centre" (p. 1145). Aside from the insistent "he"
(and the unlikely event that anyone reading *The Journal of Philosophical,*

Psychological and Scientific Methods, where the article first appeared, would be lying down or out of doors), this would seem to define James's common reader, who could be defined with certainty only in terms of the experience of reading the article James was currently writing. The book or journal that contained the article would simultaneously be at the center of the room and in the reader's mind—not to speak of all of this also being in James's mind and in the center of the room he was sitting and writing in. Typically, however, James did not address the Pandora's box of self-reflexivity he opened here with his gesture to the very words he was writing as he was imagining the reader reading them. He left it up to the reader to make the connection between the reading of the article and its writing. All that really mattered, as far as James was concerned, was the reading. For him, and certainly for most of his readers as well, books may often have been the objects closest to hand; yet he did not consider, as Emerson would have, what effect this was having on his philosophy.[6] (The effect of this curious failure of curiosity, or nerve, on James's writing was obvious: the famous clarity of style survived intact.) He left it for Stein to ponder the effect on his thought.

Part of the inadequacy of James's theory of representation lay in its oversimplification. "A given undivided portion of experience," he had written, "taken in one context of associates, play[s] the part of a knower, of a state of mind, of 'consciousness'; while in a different context the same undivided bit of experience plays the part of a thing known, of an objective 'content.' " Yet in writing, as even more obviously in his example of painting, the content is not unidimensional. There is the physical paint and there are the objects painted; there are the words and there is what the words are about. It would seem that in the analogy with painting James had only the material— the paint on the canvas, the words on paper—in mind as "content." "There is no self-splitting," he would say a few pages later of "experience per se," "into consciousness and what the consciousness is 'of' "; but the "of" here self-splits (DCE, p. 1151). In a painting of a person reading a book, or in a written description of such a person, is one not conscious of the person as well as of the words and paint?

The same nonmaterial item that would seem so readily to operate as content—the representation of someone reading, for example—can also be taken as performing a further "spiritual function." The viewer of the painting might, and in all probability would, begin to contemplate what "state of mind" of the painter's was expressed in the representation of the reader. Thus, at least in the experience of writing and painting, a third item appears to partake of the double-edged nature that James attributed to experience generally. James was so concerned to stress the "undivided" nature of experience that he quite radically oversimplified the doubleness of ordinary experience. If, for example, one were to take literally his comments about the pot of paint, one would have to attribute to the paint on the canvas the part of a knower, of "consciousness." This could only be asserted within a much more complicated story than the one he was prepared to tell.

Even if this oversimplification were corrected, James's representational scheme would still remain inadequate. Although writing certainly counted as a representational act for him, it was wholly reducible to the act of reading. He was always ready to mistake the act of writing for all the acts of reading that followed from it, as neither Emerson nor Stein was. The account of representation he relied on was essentially interpretative; representation involved different "contexts of associates" whereby "undivided" pieces of experience appeared in different forms, with different meanings. The writing, pragmatically speaking, was what one made of it, not what went into its composition; in itself it was assumed to be just another undivided piece of experience. The enemy was opacity of meaning, whether the experience in writing of inspiration—of the writing running ahead of consciousness, of one having meant more than one could know—or the experience of indeterminacy, of the impossibility of getting down to the bottom of what something might mean. Either such opacity was interpretable, or there was nothing interesting one could say about it.[7] Ultimately this model of representation depended on an unexamined notion of "undivided." In exposing the ill-considered "divisions" of experience, James too readily assumed that actual experience could not be examined directly. "The instant field of the present," as he called the domain of undivided experience, was by definition inaccessible to any kind of analysis, although one continually acted in response to it (DCE, p. 1151).

Emerson provided a contrary model for Stein in his own example—as someone who, although he too refrained in his lectures and essays from directly discussing the experience of writing, nevertheless faced up to it in the act of composition. (When he addressed writing per se, he stood at some remove and retreated into either an idealized or a demonized version of it—writing as originality or as threat to originality.) Whereas James talked about "undivided" pieces of experience and let them go at that, Emerson elaborated, as in the lines quoted above from "Experience": "undivided" meant that "betwixt atom and atom" there were "astronomical interspaces." It was these "astronomical interspaces," only between word and word, that James left out of his picture; Stein would spend her career, especially the period between 1912 and 1932, examining them with what she called in *The Autobiography of Alice B. Toklas* "the intellectual passion for exactitude in the description of inner and outer reality" (p. 211). This was the same passion that she attributed to Emerson in a 1935 interview when she observed that he "might have been surprised if he had been told that he was passionate. But Emerson really had passion; he wrote it; but he could not have written *about* it because he did not know about it" (Preston, p. 192). The passion he wrote, but could not write about, was, like Stein's, a passion for writing.[8]

James, as it happened, left unrepresented in his theory of representation the exacting form of "concentration" that Stein practiced: the kind of concentration—the word is Stein's, from her lectures of 1934 and 1935, and harkens back to Emerson's riveting figure of concentric circles—which consists in exploring the inter-, not inner, spaces of words.[9] He accepted too uncritically the notion that representation was always in some manner a *re*-presenting, and thus that the "present" lay beyond examination. Although for both Stein and Emerson it was impossible to get behind the present (there was nothing "behind" it or inside it, it was all outside) or beyond it (the present was always present in our experience of everything as "outside," in our estrangements), it was certainly not itself beyond examining. In one's acts of writing, it was what was most immediately there to have its measure taken. It was the writing as it was being written. Stein, like Emerson, might exult in this fact; she might despair of it. James, by keeping his distance from his own writing—keeping a hands-off attitude toward it, even as he was so hands-on with respect to the reader—allowed himself no such direct experience of it.

It is here too that William Empson stops looking so much like William James. To be sure, Empson was most concerned with the effects that "pieces of writing" had on readers—hence his elaborate mapping of the ways words themselves self-split and, through the lines of force he alternately called "ambiguity" and "equation," produce significance, or as he preferred to think of it, impose doctrines on readers. He insisted nonetheless that there was more to writing than these effects; thus, early in *Seven Types of Ambiguity*, he made room for "the poet's sense of the nature of a language," which was to be distinguished from a poet's or anyone's sense of language. The latter determined how successfully one achieved the effects one was after; it was one's way with words, one's ability to have one's way with words. The sense of a language was nothing like that. It involved recognizing any word "as a member of the language" rather than as "a solid tool" for the production of meaning.[10]

The examples Empson gave, in 1930, of writers with this sense of "language as such" were Racine, Dryden, and "Miss Stein." More than likely, Empson had been in the Cambridge audience four years earlier when Stein presented the first of her public lectures, "Composition as Explanation." Writing like hers, he noted, was not susceptible to his method of analysis, for it was not "about" something of which the reader was supposed to be convinced. "The mode of action" of the language was not directed toward the reader; rather, it was directed toward the language, toward the writing itself (*Seven Types*, pp. 6–7).

AUTOMATIC WRITING

The difference between James and Stein on the subject of writing, and particularly on the relation writing bears to consciousness, is exhibited most clearly in their attitudes toward automatic writing. While an undergraduate at Harvard, Stein conducted experiments in automatic writing under James's supervision.[11] "The first automatic writing I ever saw," James recalled in 1909, the year Stein's *Three Lives* was published, "was forty years ago." "I unhesitatingly thought of it as deceit," he continued, "although it contained vague elements of supranormal knowledge. Since then I have come to see in automatic writing one example of a department of human activity as vast as it is enigmatic. Every sort of person is liable to it, or to something equivalent to it" (EPR, p. 372). Stein, in contrast, some thirty-five years after her first encounter with automatic writing, would insist that it did not exist, that it was a delusion. This is how she put the matter in a letter she wrote a month or so after having completed *The Autobiography of Alice B. Toklas*. Addressing "the xperiments that [Leon] Solomons reported"—Solomons, a brilliant graduate student of James and close friend of Stein, published an account in *The Psychological Review* of a set of experiments he and Stein jointly conducted—she observed that these

> were not cases of automatic writing, they were xamples of a certain amount of distraction of attention entered into deliberately to ease the act of creation. That is as I understood it. He and I did not agree in this matter. Later on I carried on xperiments of my own in automatic writing with students and I came to the conclusion that there are no real cases of automatic writing, there are automatic movements but not automatic writing. Writing for the normal person is too complicated an activity to be indulged in automatically.[12]

Yet Stein's disagreement was with James as well as with Solomons. Everyone, James said, wrote automatically or did something like it; for Stein, nobody did, least of all herself.

In this comment and others like it Stein was responding to accusations that culminated in a 1934 article by B. F. Skinner titled "Has Gertrude Stein a Secret?" Interestingly enough, some months after this article appeared in *The Atlantic Monthly*, Skinner found himself "set[ting] forth the principal arguments of behaviorism" to Stein's old friend Alfred North Whitehead at a dinner of the Harvard Society of Fellows. Skinner recalled this exchange two decades later in *Verbal Behavior*, his classic analysis of the "functional relations . . . govern[ing]" language use, where he reported that "Professor Whitehead" had been

> equally in earnest—not in defending his own position, but in trying to understand what I was saying and (I suppose) to discover how I could possibly bring myself to say it. Eventually we took the following stand. He agreed that science might be successful in accounting for human behavior provided one made an exception of *verbal* behavior. Here, he insisted, something else must be at work. He brought the discussion to a close with a friendly challenge: "Let me see you," he said, "account for my behaviour as I sit here saying, 'No black scorpion is falling upon this table'." (pp. 10, 456–57)

"The next morning," Skinner added, "I drew up the outline of the present study."[13]

Despite acknowledging that the "set of circumstances" in which the remark was uttered had "long since" been "largely forgotten," and that any present "suggestion" therefore amounted to nothing more than a "mere . . . guess," Skinner offered to take up Whitehead's challenge in the epilogue to *Verbal Behavior* devoted to the work's origin: "Just as the physicist may suggest various explanations of the drop of temperature" which may have taken place during their conversation, "in order to show that it could be explained in lawful terms, so it is not entirely beside the point to make a guess here. I suggest, then, that *black scorpion* was a metaphorical response to the topic under discussion. The black scorpion was behaviorism" (pp. 457–58). According to Skinner, Whitehead was implicitly asserting that there had to be "a brighter side," that "on *this* pleasant and stimulating table no black scorpion had fallen"—despite the fact that Skinner's "radical behaviorism" was designed to leave "no originating control inside the skin" nor apparently any "opening for human responsibility and creativeness" (p. 459, emphasis added). Skinner may well have hit the nail on the head in decoding *black scorpion* as he did. Nevertheless, he overreached himself when he went on to suggest that the determinist doctrine he was propounding (that "men will never become originating centers of control, because their behavior will itself be controlled") shouldn't have offered Whitehead any "cause for alarm," as the "role [of human beings] as mediators may be extended without limit," and that consequently "no black scorpion *has* fallen upon this table" (pp. 459–60).

Unlike Skinner, Whitehead wouldn't complacently have invoked "the growth of man's place in nature," and the ever "more rapid" increase in "man's power" due to behaviorism, as evidence of the new science's "compatib[ility] with a sense of dignity" (p. 460). And unlike Skinner, he did not view terms such as "personal freedom" and "responsibility" (and "creativity," for that matter) merely as "bywords" that would make way for others, which, "as is the nature of bywords, will probably prove satisfying enough" (p. 460). Nor did he believe, on the model of the classical physics that underwrote Skinner's psychophysics, that once the "circumstances" of an utterance were "largely forgotten," any suggestion as to its significance amounted to mere guesswork—not, at least, in the case of sufficiently self-conscious, autopoietic uses of language. Nor, finally, would he have accepted Skinner's reasoning that the "stimulus which evoked the response *black scorpion falling upon this table*" (namely, "the topic under discussion," behaviorism, to which the "*black scorpion* was a metaphoric response") might be said to have led "in turn . . . to the autoclitic *No*" (p. 458). *Autoclitic*, a neologism of Skinner, refers to a verbal response stimulated by prior verbal behavior of the same agent. Whitehead's use of *no* was, in fact, no afterthought; rather, the so-called substantive—the scorpion—was the afterthought, even if Skinner failed to recognize this.

Whitehead's point was not, as Skinner believed, that the reference, "taken, as it were, out of the blue," represented a phenomenon which was "*not* obviously controlled by a present stimulus" (p. 458). The choice of a black scorpion might readily be attributed to an external factor; yet could the ability to respond *negatively*, to express what Whitehead elsewhere termed a "negative prehension," be explained away quite so readily (PRO, p. 41)? Whence the resistance to the present stimulus, to the "plausible account of human behavior as part of a lawfully determined system"? Surely this was not due, *contra* Skinner, to the beguilements of "traditional concepts which assign spontaneous control to the special inner self called the speaker" (p. 460). For Whitehead wasn't asserting an ability to come up "spontaneously" with a counterexample—at will, as it were. Instead, he was asking *Skinner* to account, within the limits of a stimulus-response mechanics, for the remarkable ability possessed by humans to imagine something that was *not* present (and so didn't take the form of a present stimulus), without peremptorily concluding that the ability in question was itself an illusion. Whitehead's challenge was a variant of that posed by Laurence Sterne with respect to Walter Shandy's catechism; only in this case it was a matter of knowing that something was not present (*a black scorpion*) rather than being able to discourse about something which, so far as one's own experience or that of one's acquaintances was concerned, had never been present (*a white bear*). Supposing that one did wish to class this ability as an illusion, wouldn't one then be obliged to account for the corresponding ability to be so deluded (that is, to imagine something *not* present *as present*) without willy-nilly assuming the validity of the illusory ability (of imagining what is not present *as not present*)? Yet how is one to argue that *something not present has mistakenly been thought present* without believing oneself capable of registering its absence, hence of making the same sort of discrimination one started out by denying? Here the behaviorist falls victim to the vicious circle that awaits all insufficiently radical empiricisms—internal contradictions due to the investigator's inadequately nuanced attention to context and to the subtler forms of interrelatedness, such as those ignored by Skinner in his article for *The Atlantic Monthly*.[14]

In "Has Gertrude Stein a Secret?" Skinner asserted that Stein was trading on techniques of automatic writing that she had learned as a psychology student and passing them off as literary innovations. His argument was twofold. First, she had become accomplished in automatic writing in the series of experiments at the Harvard Psychological Laboratory. Second, in her later "experimental writing" she used these techniques to construct a secondary personality, the "hypothetical author" of these works, as he phrased it—although a singularly immature one, "intellectually unopinionated," "emotionally cold," with "no past" and "unread and unlearned beyond grammar school" (HGS, pp. 67–68).[15] The writing, then, rather than being the significant construction of art that it was sometimes taken for, merely entailed the construction of a "superficial" author. If it seemed meaningless, this was because the "inferential author" had an inadequate conception of meaning, not because the meaning was difficult; it was not a reflection on any inadequacies on the part of the reader (p. 68).[16] Skinner offered his analysis ingeniously as nothing more than a diagnosis of the failure, in his eyes, of Stein's experimental writing to mean anything. It was not directed at Stein or at, as he put it, "the finer work of a very fine mind" (p. 71). The writing was only as superficially related to Stein as its "hypothetical" author was and as easily and painlessly removed. It was a mistake perhaps but not a very serious one.

Skinner's argument was itself premised on a series of factual and interpretative mistakes. Stein and Solomons, he would have read in the *Autobiography*, "together worked out a series of experiments in automatic writing under the direction of Munsterberg."[17] "The result of her own experiments," the passage continued, "which Gertrude Stein wrote down and which was printed in the *Harvard [sic] Psychological Review*, was the first writing of hers ever to be printed" (pp. 77–78). Skinner took this publication to be an article entitled "Normal Motor Automatism" which appeared in the September 1896 issue of the *Review*. In fact, the first publication that Stein composed herself, and the one she was referring to, was "Cultivated Motor Automatism; A Study of Character in Its Relation to Attention," published in May 1898. The earlier study had been written entirely by Solomons, although Stein was credited as coauthor. It had been Solomons's project; Stein had assisted and with him served as one of the two subjects, but she had not written a word that was not "automatic." Indeed, as she later noted, she had her doubts about whether any of the writing was genuinely automatic.

Both sets of experiments were designed to test the extent of what could be considered "automatic" actions in "normal" persons. In the first series, with Solomons, the aim was to show that actions which in hysterical patients were usually taken as having been performed by "secondary personalities" could, nonetheless, be performed by "ordinary people" as automatic actions—performed, that is, without consciousness of the action. Hysterics, suffering from a particularly extreme form of neurosis, often exhibited what was termed an *anaesthesia* in the sensibility of parts of the body. From no apparent physical cause, the hysteric would lose sight in an eye, for example, or sensation in an arm.[18] Emerson's hysterical blindness during his months at the Harvard Divinity School took this form; often the anaesthesia would persist much longer than it did in his case. It had already been observed by clinical psychologists in the late 1880s that such lack of consciousness or sensibility was often accompanied by a distinct "sensibility to the anaesthetic parts," as James put it in *The Principles of Psychology*, which took "the form of a secondary consciousness entirely cut off from the primary or normal one, but susceptible of being tapped and made to testify to its existence in various odd ways" (p. 201). If it might be shown that the "normal subject" could write automatically or unconsciously, as the hysteric did, then the hypothesis of some kind of split in consciousness—the hypothesis upon which the notion of a "secondary personality" was premised—would be superfluous. Solomons's experiment was thus meant to disprove the construct of the kind of secondary personality to which Skinner wanted to attribute the writing of works like *Tender Buttons*.

In the experiments Stein conducted on her own she shifted the emphasis of inquiry from this earlier concern with the different kinds of actions that "normal" persons could be shown to perform automatically (in which the normal, nonhysterical, subjects were assumed to be a homogeneous mass) to the differing capabilities of individuals to perform particular automatic actions. As Stein observed in *Everybody's Autobiography*, she had been led to doubt the validity of the original experiments by the fact that there had been only two subjects. This was not merely because there were just the two of them, self-proclaimed normal, but because of the artificiality of the experiments and the extreme self-consciousness of the experimenters:

> Solomons reported what he called his and my automatic writing but I did not think that we either of us had been doing automatic writing, we always knew what we were doing how could we not when every minute in the laboratory we were doing what we were watching ourselves doing, that was our training. (p. 231)

In her own article Stein still talked in terms of automatic writing, but the writing consisted of "circles, the figure eight, a long curve, or an m-figure," movements "of a decidedly rhythmic character" (MOT, p. 28). The so-called automatic writing of the Solomons experiment (with Stein, for example, coming up with "When he could not be the longest and thus to be, and thus to be, the strongest") was, on the contrary, never automatic (MOT, p. 21).[19]

It should be added, all the same, that Skinner's hasty indictment of Stein was not entirely a trap of his own making. In *The Autobiography of Alice B. Toklas*, unlike her other statements on the subject, Stein did not explicitly dissociate herself from Solomons's description of their experimental writing as automatic. She spoke of the "series of experiments in automatic writing" and "the result of her own experiments" without observing that the point, and interest, of her work was the way it illustrated that if movements were automatic they would not produce writing and if, on the other hand, they did produce writing they were not automatic. Moreover, when she noted in the *Autobiography* that "the method of writing to be afterwards developed in Three Lives and Making of Americans already shows itself," she unhelpfully conflated her writing in the Solomons piece (the examples of so-called automatic writing) with what she actually had in mind: the *mode of analysis* that she used in writing up her later experiments at Harvard (p. 78). Skinner, however, chose to interpret each ambiguity in such a way as to prop up the weak, uneducated secondary personality he had unearthed, a personality that he hastened to add was not "a true second personality" but "a literary second personality," not a conscious self but merely the expression of an arm that Stein periodically set in motion (HGS, pp. 70–71).[20]

Stein never denied the obvious link between the writing in her work with Solomons and the experimental writing she began to compose after *The Making of Americans*; thus in describing the writing produced at the Harvard Laboratory as "xamples of a certain amount of distraction of attention entered into deliberately to ease the act of creation," she deliberately left room for the later acts of "creative" writing as well. What she objected to was the characterization of any of this writing as automatic and hence—this is the crux of the matter—both unconscious and meaningless. No writing was meaningless, she countered, and her compositions were certainly not unconscious. On the contrary, she insisted that her writing, no less in the experiments with Solomons than in works like *Tender Buttons*, be recognized as conscious and the product of a rational mind; that it not be taken as a simulacrum of the unconscious writing of a hysterical woman—as little more, and perhaps much less, than the work of female hysteria.[21] This consideration made all the difference. To Ellery Sedgwick, the editor of *The Atlantic Monthly*, which between May and August of 1933 had published four large excerpts from the *Autobiography*, she wrote in response to Skinner's piece: "No it is not so automatic as he thinks. . . . If there is anything secret it is the other way. . . . I think I achieve by xtra consciousness, excess."[22]

There are two equally valid ways of understanding Stein's categorical rejection of any attempt to explain her writing as somehow "tapping" her unconscious—as James might have said had he found the notion of an unconscious, or even subconscious, useful in relation to normal life, which he did not.[23]

In the first place, she quite reasonably associated claims made for unconsciousness with attributions of hysteria. The experimental psychology of her college days would have confirmed her in this, and just as she later observed that abnormal psychology "frightened" her, she shifted the emphasis in her experiments at Harvard from the psychology of the abnormal hysteric (which was what intrigued Solomons) to that of the normal college student (EA, p. 229). "The subjects used in this experiment," one reads in "Cultivated Motor Automatism," "were members of Harvard University and Radcliffe College[,] 41 male subjects [and] 50 female subjects" (MOT, pp. 28–29). "She always says she dislikes the abnormal," Stein had Toklas comment about her, "it is so obvious. She says the normal is much more simply complicated and interesting" (ABT, p. 83). This insistence on normality extended to Stein's characterization of herself in the second installment of her life story, which was concerned primarily with the reception of the first, and was framed as the autobiography of an ungendered Everybody instead of the life of a particular woman. The same refusal to make a public issue of her personal negotiations with gender (and in so refusing, making it all the more an issue for any serious consideration of her writing) entered as well into her delighted self-identification with the middle class, whose mores she flaunted but never rejected.[24] Clearly her embrace of what she called in the first draft of *The Making of Americans* the "material middle class" derived in part from a fear of losing control, or more precisely, of her control—her ability to call her life and writing her own—being taken away from her (FE, p. 144). Within a page of expressing a decisive interest in the "simply complicated," she might confess that "Dickens had always frightened her," and note, without missing a beat, that "as she says anything can frighten her" (ABT, p. 84). If she could so readily acknowledge the fear, she already had it well under control. The middle class, which provided protection and a certain camouflage, at the same time presented the greatest threat to a person's independence; the refuge in normality has to be understood as a response to the common labeling of nonconformist tendencies in women as signs of "hysteria." The best disguise, as Poe—favorite of Stein and an important early theorist of hysteria—so clearly spelled out in "The Purloined Letter," was one that looked like no disguise at all.[25]

Besides this political explanation of Stein's refusal to accept a role for the unconscious in her writing (with the unconscious representing a mode of putting, or keeping, women and others who challenge the dominant social order in their place), one can also observe a second, less partisan motive. The unconscious was not merely situated on one side of a dividing line—it was itself divisive. In addition to being, by definition, invisible, it could at any time prevent what one saw in the normal course of things from being accurately registered. Stein, like contemporaries as different from her and from each other as William Carlos Williams, Robert Frost, and Marianne Moore, chiefly concerned herself in her writing with possible (possibly impossible) constructions of the ordinary, what was normally seen and heard and said and done. She aimed to remove all distortions from the writing and thereby rid it, as she said of Picasso's similar art, of "the things everybody is certain of seeing, but which they do not really see" (PCW, p. 47).

The notion that some form of dynamic unconscious was unavoidable implied a skepticism that put all perceptions, and any supposed relation of the self and world, into question; and Stein's experimental portraiture from late 1910 on served to counter, if not exactly refute, a comparable skepticism that had informed her previous work. Thus the elegiac ending of *The Making of Americans*, from 1911, is among other things a representation of the death that this skepticism, embodied in the melancholy of David Hersland, drives inexorably toward. At the same time, in allowing Hersland to die, Stein can be said to have freed herself from her own skeptical frame of mind. The skepticism—what Stein referred to, in lines from "A Long Gay Book" already cited in Chapter 1, as "any worrying to be doing about any one being any one"—had operated in conjunction with a desire, indeed a faith, that "the complete description of everything" was possible. "It is a simple thing," as she put the matter in *The Making of Americans*, "to be quite certain that there are kinds in men and women." With the shift from description (of *kinds*) to portraits (of *individuals*, and occasionally of groups of individuals), the skepticism, at least its force, dropped out of the picture. It had to be overcome, or transcended, as one might say, for the shift to be possible at all. Yet it could only be overcome in the course of the move it-self; hence the back-and-forth movement, the extended period of transition, which was carried out *in*, as well as carried over *into*, so many different works of Stein's between 1910 and 1913.

When, in an anthology of American writing called *Americans Abroad* that appeared in 1932, Stein proposed that "I take things in and they come out that way independent of conscious process," she was distinguishing such independence from any kind of dependence on an unconscious process. "All this foolishness," she continued, "about my writing being mystic or impressionistic is so stupid. Every word I write has the same passionate ex-actness of meaning that it is supposed to have. Everything I write means ex-actly what it says" (Neagoe, p. 418). She was not claiming to have absolute control over her writing, but she was not willing to acknowledge any other entity as possessing such control over her. She was not, in other words, will-ing to divide herself up into a consciousness and an unconscious of any kind. Skinner in his exposé might talk unconcernedly about "the two Ger-trude Steins"; Gertrude Stein was having none of that (HGS, p. 68).[26]

NON-AUTOMATIC WRITING

"There is no good nonsense without sense," Stein concluded in her letter to Hubbell, "and so there cannot be automatic writing" (YCAL). She agreed with Skinner that the only sign of automatic writing in nonhysterical cases was its meaninglessness. There was no other way of registering that the re-quired degree of disengagement had been achieved. Skinner was too hasty, however, in attributing such meaninglessness to her own work. "I found out very soon," she observed in lines already cited with respect to her neur-aesthetic experience of composition, "that there is no such thing as putting [words] together without sense. I made innumerable efforts to make words write without sense and found it impossible. Any human being putting down words had to make sense out of them" (TI, p. 18). At a minimum, this meant that automatic writing was impossible for anyone who was not clinically hysterical.

Stein's dismissal of automatic writing, and more generally of the notion that a dynamic unconscious was somehow necessary to human life and writing—her "refusal," as she said in *The Autobiography of Alice B. Toklas*, "of the use of the subconscious"—was not a gesture of repression but on the contrary a liberating act for her (p. 50). Any attempt to ally her with the subconscious, she insisted, was nothing other than a repressive gesture itself. She could even cite James on this. "Gertrude Stein," begins an account in the *Autobiography* of what emerges as an attempt to deny her her individuality, and her conscious participation in it,

> never had subconscious reactions, nor was she a successful subject for automatic writing. One of the students in the psychological seminar of which Gertrude Stein, although an undergraduate was at William James' particular request a member, was carrying on a series of experiments on suggestions to the subconscious. When he read his paper upon the result of his experiments, he began by explaining that one of the subjects gave absolutely no results and as this much lowered the average and made the conclusion of his experiments false he wished to be allowed to cut this record out. Whose record is it, said James. Miss Stein's, said the student. Ah, said James, if Miss Stein gave no response I should say that it was as normal not to give a response as to give one and decidedly the result must not be cut out. (p. 79)

Part of what being normal meant for Stein was that it legitimated responses of hers that were exceptional; she might or might not be the exception that proved the rule but she *was* the rule that proved to be an exception. No matter how far out of line she appeared, she still had to be taken seriously.

In *Everybody's Autobiography* some of the details of the experiment in question are given: "Sidis was interested in studying sub-conscious reactions but being a Russian he naturally expected us to do things and we did not do them. He would have a table covered with a cloth and one of us sat in front of it and then when he pulled off the cover there was a pistol underneath it, I remember I naturally did nothing after all why should any one do anything when they see a pistol uncovered and there is no danger of anybody shooting. We all of us were somewhat discouraging to all of us" (p. 230).[27] Instead of acting automatically or, as one might say, emotionally, and starting at the sight of a gun, Stein acted with equanimity. She quite reasonably refused to delude herself and forget the context of the experiment. She was not in the Wild West or a Dostoevsky novel but in the Harvard Psychological Laboratory.

The unconscious might be, in Emily Dickinson's pointed phrase, "a Loaded Gun," but in certain contexts its potential for good or ill, destruction or defense, makes no difference; or rather, the fact that this makes no difference makes all the difference.[28] Sidis, like Solomons, tried to ignore the laboratory context of their experiments. Stein distinguished herself from them by her self-consciousness, her awareness of what she liked to call the "training" that went into the work, which for example enabled her to recognize that a gun in a laboratory no longer functioned as a gun: that it was as good as painted and perhaps even less effective than a painting might be. Moreover, a refusal to attend to something, such as the actions of one's writing hand, required a great deal of concentrated attention. Stein may well have only just begun to appreciate this in the early experiments, but by 1932, after thirty years of writing with precisely that degree of concentrated attention, she knew that any attempt not to credit her claims of rigor and "passionate exactness of meaning" was, however innocently, an attempt on her life and on her life's work. "Automatic" writing, produced in a laboratory context, required the same degree of attention that one needed to write a book which, like *Three Lives*, contained long stretches that reworked the broken, or hybrid, English of German immigrants as well as the dialect of American English spoken in the African-American community of Baltimore. Stein's critics, of course, would still insist that the transcendence of her own habitual, highly educated, patterns of speech was merely a matter of inattention or even ignorance. In her writing through *The Autobiography of Alice B. Toklas* Stein responded to these accusations with increasingly novel examples of her powers of inattention.

Ultimately dictating the experiments with automatic writing at the Harvard Laboratory was William James himself, who made the initial proposal to Stein and Solomons that they work with a planchette, the kind of small, mobile board with a pencil attached that Spiritualists used to spell out messages from the spirit world.[29] "William James added a planchette," Stein recalled in *Everybody's Autobiography*, "he liked a planchette" (p. 230). More than that, he liked automatic writing; and when he went "on record" in his 1909 essay "The Confidences of a 'Psychical Researcher'" for "the commonness" of such phenomena as automatic writing, he explained that

> there is a hazy penumbra in us all where lying and delusion meet, where passion rules beliefs as well as conduct, and where the term "scoundrel" does not clear up everything to the depths as it did for our forefathers. . . . Whoever encourages it in himself finds himself personating someone else, either signing what he writes by a fictitious name or spelling out, by ouija-board or table-tips, messages from the departed. Our subconscious region seems, as a rule, to be dominated either by a crazy "will to make-believe," or by some curious external force impelling us to personation. The first difference between the psychical researcher and the inexpert person is that the former realizes the commonness

and typicality of the phenomenon here, while the latter, less informed, thinks it so rare as to be unworthy of attention. (EPR, p. 372)[30]

The automatic writing that Stein and Solomons were looking for in their experiments was writing that had nothing behind it, neither the person whose hand wrote it nor the "secondary consciousness" in hysterics that, as James noted, was "susceptible of being tapped" and thereby "made to testify to its existence." No such writing was found; there really was no writing without consciousness. The automatic writing that James examined as a psychical researcher was something entirely different, concatenations of words produced by mediums—human agents—writing for, or in the name of, other persons. By definition, there was always someone or something behind the writer, whether "a crazy will to make-believe" or "some curious external force impelling us to personation."

Not so curiously, this *external* force matches up with the "initiative from *within*" to which Stein (in the celebrated notebook jotting written about the same time as James's essay) credited her first literary innovations and which she characterized as "a propulsion" that she neither "controlled" nor "created." The middle figure, or medium, in which James and Stein come together is of course the Emerson who counseled his reader to "place yourself in the middle of the stream of power and wisdom which animates all whom it floats, and you are without effort impelled to truth, to right, and a perfect contentment" (EL, p. 309). Stein in fact recognized a movement in her career from an early excessive concentration on "the inside," still operative at the time of the notebook entry, to some middle ground, as in the observation already cited that during the summer of 1912 her "style gradually changed": "Hitherto she had been interested only in the insides of people, their character and what went on inside them, it was during that summer that she first felt a desire to express the rhythm of the visible world" (ABT, p. 119). This shift is elaborated some pages later. The manuscripts written in Spain, among them a substantial part of *Tender Buttons*, "were the beginning, as Gertrude Stein would say, of mixing the outside with the inside. Hitherto she had been concerned with seriousness and the inside of things. In these studies she began to describe the inside as seen from the outside" (p. 156). In so doing, she heeded the call to place herself "in the middle." Although Emerson was careful not to delineate the impediments to actually getting into the middle, reading him made these clear enough (as would the effort, in acts of one's own composition, of seeing how and if the thing could be done). The difficulty lay in convincing oneself that one actually was in the middle or even knew exactly where the middle was. At the same time one could not just say, could not say just what the difficulty was or if there really was any. "It was a long tormenting process," Stein recalled, "she always was, she always is, tormented by the problem of the external and the internal" (ABT, p. 119).

In describing herself and her work thus, Stein added that among contemporary painters it was Picabia who had most deliberately confronted the same insoluble problem of inside and outside. In his case, it took the form of the paradox, for a painter, that "the human being essentially is not paintable"—is, in James's terms, composed of *consciousness* as well as *content* (p. 119). This was the context for the remark, already cited with respect to Whitehead's notion of "vibratory organic deformation," that Picabia

> had conceived and is still struggling with the problem that a line should have the vibration of a musical sound and that this vibration should be the result of conceiving the human form and the human face in so tenuous a fashion that it would induce such vibration in the line forming it. It is his way of achieving the disembodied. (p. 210)

The tenuous "vibrant line" echoes, even vibrates with, the "hazy penumbra" that James perceived "in us all," as he imagined the disembodied speaking through us. Nevertheless, Stein immediately distinguished her work, and Picabia's, from any kind of mysticism. She did this by invoking the passion for exactitude she shared with Juan Gris—the only painter, she claimed, whom Picasso ever felt threatened by and consequently "wished away." Hers was an "intellectual passion," she proposed, whereas in Gris "exactitude had a mystical basis." "As a mystic it was necessary for him to be exact. In Gertrude Stein the necessity was intellectual, a pure passion for exactitude" (pp. 210–11).

This distinction was vital for Stein; clearly, William James set less stock by it. He was willing to "go on record" for some kind of "cosmic consciousness," and to identify himself with "psychical research" (EPR, p. 374).[31] For Stein, the crucial thing about James's position was that he still found it necessary to characterize the "larger psycho-physical world" in terms of writing (p. 375). He might use as an example automatic writing or, as often happened, have recourse to the figuration of writing in such details as his twice-repeated gesture of "going on record," but it seemed that the only thing he could say with any certainty about the cosmic consciousness was that it took the form of written language. Actually, whenever James talked of consciousness, large or small, he framed it in similar "graphic" terms. He is often criticized, for example, for the apparent naïveté of his introspection, the way he talked about his own motives and feelings.[32] Yet it only appears naïve in light of the most schematic Freudian analysis. Instead of dwelling solipsistically on what was going on inside him, abstracting feelings and thoughts from their immediate context, James preferred to locate himself neuraesthetically on the interface of inside and outside, in the perceptual and grammatical realm of the stream of consciousness. John Dewey, in his celebrated essay on "The Development of American Pragmatism," called attention to the "reinterpretation of introspective psychology" that James accomplished in *The Principles of Psychology*: "James denies that sensations, images and ideas are discrete," and "replaces them by a continuous stream which he calls 'the stream of consciousness'" (p. 15). The key element in the reinterpretation was the continuity, that is to say, the continuous movement, of the stream; and although James certainly used the empiricist terminology Dewey invoked, often and with much greater originality he described such continuity in grammatical terms.

The transitions we feel between thoughts, he insisted, in accordance with his radical empiricism, are quite as much states of consciousness as those elements we choose to consider substantive. (Actually, James preferred to speak of thoughts or feelings rather than "states of consciousness," because with his emphasis on action he wanted nouns with cognate verbs.) Such "bare images of logical movement" both designate mental states and call them forth (PR, p. 244). "There is not a conjunction or a preposition," he noted in one oft-cited passage,

> and hardly an adverbial phrase, syntactic form, or inflection of voice, in human speech, that does not express some shading or other of relation which we at some moment actually feel to exist between the larger objects of our thought. . . . We ought to say a feeling of *and*, a feeling of *if*, a feeling of *but*, and a feeling of *by*, quite as readily as we say a feeling of *blue* or a feeling of *cold*. Yet we do not: so inveterate has our habit become of recognizing the existence of substantive parts alone, that language almost refuses to lend itself to any other use. (p. 238 [BC, pp. 161–62])

So inveterate is the habit that James, in alerting us to it, falls into it himself—turning conjunctions and prepositions (*and*, *if*, *but*, *by*) into substantive parts of speech ("a feeling of *and*," and so on). It was precisely this habit that Stein set out to break in her writing after 1903, first by simplifying "speech" and then after *The Making of Americans* by mixing it up and in the process mixing inside with outside. Her preference for the relational parts of speech—she especially liked, as she said in her 1934 lecture "Poetry and Grammar," to write "with prepositions and conjunctions and articles and verbs and adverbs but not with nouns and adjectives"—was a literary

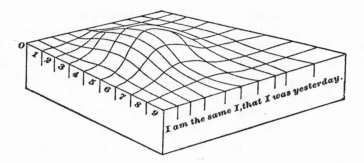

Figure 12. "I am the same I that I was yesterday." (From William James, *The Principles of Psychology*, vol. 1, p. 283.)

prejudice that James, framing his psychological hypotheses in grammatical terms, had confirmed her in (LIA, p. 213). "It is this," she insisted in another lecture, "that makes the English language such a vital language that the grammar of it is so simple and that one does make a fuss about it" (p. 147).

James also made the following observation, equally fundamental to Stein, in his famous discussion of "the stream of thought." Suppose one were formulating a sentence. If the stream could be frozen at a particular moment and that slice of time examined, one would discover that the thought thus isolated contained both the word being uttered and the whole sentence of which the word was a part. Over time the emphasis would change, moving from word to word, and the state of consciousness with it, but the same sentence—"I am the same I, that I was yesterday," in James's example—will have remained present to consciousness all along. James then asked his reader to imagine "a solid wooden frame with the sentence written on its front, and the time-scale on one of its sides," illustrating the "pulsation of consciousness . . . with *same* most prominent" (see Figure 12). "If we spread flatly a sheet of India rubber over its top, on which rectangular co-ordinates are painted, and slide a smooth ball under the rubber in the direction from 0 to 'yesterday,' the bulging of the membrane along this diagonal at successive moments will symbolize the changing of the thought's content." "In cerebral terms," he added, "it will show the relative intensities, at successive moments, of the several nerve-processes to which the various parts of the thought-object correspond" (PR, pp. 272–73).

James is *not* claiming that the echoes in a moment of consciousness are restricted to the surrounding words, any more than that consciousness has to take the form of sentences. One may feel thunder, even if one is deaf; and as one feels it, one will feel a thousand other things as well, including the sudden absence of silence. But if one is expressing in words what one feels and thinks, the bare minimum present at any moment is the sentence.

This is, to be sure, inadequate as anything more than a bare-bones description of either a reader's or writer's actual state of mind. In the first place, the sentence is likely to change in the course of its being written, as the writer's sense of the completed sentence, the sentence to be completed, changes—as it is, in effect, rewritten. Even so, the writer will have some sentence in mind at any given moment. Nor can one know, as a reader, how a written sentence will end until the full sentence has been registered. Yet if one is to make sense of the part that one has read, one must have some idea of the whole sentence. So there will be a sentence in the reader's mind even if it differs from the sentence on the page. No doubt one may read with a limited sense of the "sense" as well. James discusses, for instance, how a "foreboding of the coming grammatical scheme combined with each successive uttered word" may enable "a reader incapable of understanding four ideas in the book he is reading aloud [to] read it with the most delicately modulated expression of intelligence" (PR, p. 245 [BC, p. 164]). This is the kind of reading Stein's writing demands, at least on a first encounter, whether of *The Making of Americans* or *Tender Buttons* or what she termed her "real achievement of the commonplace," *Stanzas in Meditation* (ABT, p. 225).

Stein may be understood as refining this picture of the sentence swimming in the stream of thought, first in *The Making of Americans* and then, very differently, from 1912 on. She kept the sentence, whatever sentence, in front of her when she was writing and deliberately dulled the echoes, the associations that would naturally come with the sentence and distract one from it. Here, for example, is a paragraph already cited from *The Making of Americans*, which illustrates a relatively early, and straightforward, mode of such refinement. Rather than making changes in the sentence by varying the syntax, Stein substitutes one similarly functioning phrase for another:

> Some have virtuous feeling in them from having in them concrete and generalised virtue *always* really in them. Some have virtuous feeling in them from having in them concrete and generalised virtue *almost always* really in them. Some have virtuous feeling in them from having in them concrete and generalised virtue *very often* really in them. Some have virtuous feeling in them from having in them concrete and generalised virtue *sometimes* really in them. Some have virtuous feeling in them from having in them concrete and generalised virtue *sometime* really in them. (p. 504, emphasis added)[33]

The sentence on which Stein works her variations has as its basis the near-tautological proposition that persons feel virtuous because they are virtuous. Feeling and being are thus intimately connected, and it is this intimacy that the sentence details. A person's feelings, for instance, do not just happen to exist but are the result of something that causes one to feel a certain way. This is something that exists inside one, not outside. It is, Stein writes, both concrete and generalized. Does she mean, then, that it feels both concrete and generalized? Or has she simply chosen not to determine its exact nature? Perhaps the virtue of this "virtue" is its indeterminacy? Although the etymon of "virtue" is *vir*—Latin for "man"—here the gender, and much else, is left unspecified.

Instead of explaining how particular feelings (in this case, one's feeling of being virtuous) actually get produced, Stein describes how different people define virtue (namely, their own virtues) differently. What they all share is an emphasis on the virtue's existence *in them*, an emphasis that Stein's sentence literally repeats: *Some have virtuous feeling **in them**; they have **in them** concrete and generalised virtue; it is really **in them**.* If there is no special emphasis on the phrase in its first appearance, in the second it is notably wrenched out of place—squeezed between the verb and the all-encompassing object—and by the end it has become the focus of one's attention. This is a sentence, and paragraph, designed to convey "the insides of people, their character and what went on inside them," and nothing else. The analysis of character takes the form of an equation with one variable, which hinges entirely on the relative frequency, ranging from always to rarely, that different persons feel "concrete and generalised virtue" to be "in them." The result is a "vibration" not unlike that which Stein described Picabia as aiming for, only in reverse. Instead of "conceiving the human form and the human face . . . tenuous[ly]," she conceives human "insides" with the utter specificity of her substitutions. There is nothing at all tenuous about the manner in which her vibrating sentence, at once concrete and generalized, expresses a range of disembodied "characters" and "insides."

Although James limited his own analysis of thought to the sentence removed from its "original halo of obscure relations," he still insisted that to "feel" the full "idiosyncracy" of any sentence, the entire "horizon" that "bathed" the sentence would have to be reproduced (PR, p. 266). Joyce and Proust, for instance, among Stein's contemporaries, might be said to have worked in different ways for this more idiosyncratic, comprehensive horizon, but Stein took the alternative route of removing every association from the sentence and thereby limiting the range of likely echoes. The less "obscured" the sentence was, the more idiosyncratic it became, as it ceased to resemble its less self-enclosed, and more typical, cousin. Stein did not want an idiosyncratic horizon, she wanted idiosyncratic words and sentences and paragraphs: words without echoes that functioned as their own echoes.

For portraying, among other things, the "innumerable consciousnesses of emptiness"—"no one of which," as James observed, "taken in itself has a name but all different from each other"—Stein developed two distinct sets of techniques (PR, p. 243).[34] Both did away with acquired associations. The first method, partly achieved in "Melanctha" (which depends for many of its effects, however, on local details of the invented speech) and then more thoroughly in *The Making of Americans* and the first set of portraits of 1910–11, consisted in repeating sentences that resembled one another but which were, in some important respect, not repetitions. Stein would try to catch or portray the process of someone working something through. Thus in the paragraph above on "virtuous feeling"—which, all the same, is less a portrait than an abstraction of one, as Stein was only just beginning to substitute the portrait of a person for the description—the logical and diminishing movement from sentence to sentence of the adverb of frequency ("always," "almost always," etc.) was both the point and carried the point across.

The opening paragraph of Stein's 1911 portrait of Picasso, to cite another example, consists of four strikingly similar sentences:

> One whom some were certainly following was one who was completely charming. One whom some were certainly following was one who was charming. One whom some were following was one who was completely charming. One whom some were following was one who was certainly completely charming. (PP, p. 17)

The only elements that vary in these sentences are the adverbs *certainly* and *completely*. The second and third sentences are identical to the first except that in the second *completely*, and in the third *certainly*, has been removed; both terms are then joined in a single phrase in the fourth. In effect, the initial sentence is a composite of the two that follow it: *One [whom some were certainly following was one who was charming]* plus *One [whom some were following was one who was completely charming]* equals *One [whom some were certainly following was one who was completely charming]*. The "sum" of one and one is still one.

Moreover, just as the first sentence is broken down analytically into the second and third, the terms *certainly* and *charming* themselves function as composites. *Certainly* can be taken either as an editorial comment on the part of the person making these observations—it is all quite certain to this observer—or as characterizing the actors themselves, who, certain that they are following someone "completely charming," follow with certainty. Similarly, the adjectival use of *charming* is combined with its participial use ("one" is not only a charming individual but is also in the process of charming "some"), with the result that the reader—here "following" the writer—may, with some justice, feel "completely" certain that the term is "certainly completely" in play. While holding in each of these sentences to the strict formal constraints of the stripped-down *One whom some were following was one who was charming*, Stein uses the adverbial forms of *completeness* and *certainty* to convey the partiality and uncertainty of any particular assertion one might make. If the combined followers-and-charm of Picasso is the first thing that strikes one about him, it is not enough just to assert the existence of this interesting combination. Like Picasso in his own work, one is furthermore obliged to break one's impression into its elements; and those that Stein has chosen to focus on in this paragraph are the apparent certainty and completeness themselves. Surely, Picasso's charm is the principal imponderable here, but his is not the only one as Stein weaves her sentences—each "following" from the others—into a charm of her own.[35]

The vocabulary of these sentences and paragraphs is of the simplest kind, rather like the Basic English of Ogden and Richards: words meant to be used and not weighed, calling minimal attention to themselves and maximally free of personal association.[36] The vocabulary is as unpoetic, as anonymous, as possible. Conversely, the second technique that Stein developed carried association to the point where even the most elementary associations were almost impossible to follow.[37] Beginning in 1912, the words called maximum attention to themselves, and a line such as "Dirty is yellow" (from "A Piece of Coffee" in *Tender Buttons*) might, as late as 1946, be criticized by Stein for the unseemly dirt it brought with it. "Dirty has an association and is a word that I would not use now. I would not use words that have definite associations" (TI, p. 26).[38] This is not prudish posturing on Stein's part. She rejected all "definite associations" on principle, and those of *dirty*—whether in the common expansion of *dirt* to cover all manner of uncleanliness (as in "soiled") as well as in the application of the term to erotic matters—happened to be especially difficult to remove. That her own phrasing merely inverted, however parodically, the heavily freighted "yellow is dirty" only made things worse. In fact, she had stopped writing this rigorously almost fifteen years earlier, and here was just trying to sanitize herself for public consumption. But the principle still held.

Stein objected to association, whether lexical or syntactical, on two counts. First, it distracted from the writing by removing one's attention from the object on the page and so breaking one's concentration. Second, and still more damning, it was entirely habitual. One had no control over one's associations—it was hardly possible to stop them—and as such they were a sign of one's dependence on habit. By contrast, the writing in her experiments with Solomons could not have been less automatic. It showed her how one might, with training, overcome the habit-forming habit. Beginning with those first experiments, and through the writing of *The Autobiography of Alice B. Toklas*, she was continually in training—training herself to break with her training.

Consequently, in more than thirty years of radically experimental work, Stein continued the line of anti-associationism that extended from Coleridge, with his numerous refutations of David Hartley's psychological doctrine of the association of ideas, through James, who proposed "purely *physiological* principles of association" in place of associations of ideas (Myers, p. 247).[39] Instead of limiting her investigations to Coleridge's "organic imagination," or James's physiological scheme, or Freud's materialistic one (in which the dynamic machinery of "concealed purposive ideas" supplanted the surface mechanism of Hartleian association), however, Stein conducted experiments that were designed to test the organic nature of writing itself—as the medium, or middle ground, of body and idea.[40] No doubt much writing is mechanical, little more than a vehicle for communicating information. Yet—to invoke Whitehead's distinction—might not some compositions function as "organic mechanisms" rather than as "mechanisms of matter," obliging one to recognize that they operate along neuraesthetic lines in order for them to work at all (SMW, pp. 80, 75)? As I have argued here, Stein's *self-consciously* radical empiricist word portraits and "meditations in stanzas" demonstrate that writing can serve as a legitimate medium for scientific experimentation.[41] Perhaps literary composition may prove a fit subject for a more truly self-conscious organic science as well.[42]

CHAPTER SIX

Every Field Incomplete:
Mapping "The Very Abysses of Our Nature"

"The man," Emerson wrote, "is only half himself, the other half is his expression" (EL, p. 448).[1] James, neglecting the duo of *self* and *expression*, accounted instead for the dualism of *consciousness* and *content*. In effect, as I have suggested, his explanation of the "separation" of experience "into consciousness and content"—by the addition, as he said, of "sets of experiences . . . to a given concrete piece"—was modeled after acts of reading for which an original experience of writing was irretrievable and hence irrelevant.[2] It was as if one were to understand writing exclusively in terms of the consciousness of the reader, on the one hand, and the content or subject matter on the other. James may have aimed to discredit this division; nevertheless, it determined the form of his thought, thereby limiting the range of his radical empiricism. Is consciousness something, then, that only readers possess, even supposing that *reader* is defined broadly enough to include anyone trying to make sense of the world as composed of collections of signs, any semiotician whatsoever? What of the writer's own consciousness of the writing? Is this quite the same as that of a reader? Is the writer just another reader? And what of the consciousness that readers posit in trying to understand the "content" of a piece of writing? Must every expression of self be an expression of knowledge (or self-knowledge) articulable in the form of a description? Whatever happened to *knowledge of acquaintance* in this hermeneut's paradise?

EXCEPTIONAL MENTAL STATES

Midway through *The Principles of Psychology* James suggested that the "various confused and scattered mysteries" to be encountered in explanations of memory and the other major topics in psychology might be pooled "into one great mystery, the mystery that brain-processes occasion knowledge at all."[3] What then of the mystery of expression, whether descriptive or not? "It is surely no different mystery," he continued, "to *feel* myself by means of one brain-process writing at this table now, and by means of a different brain-process a year hence to *remember* myself writing. All that psychology can do is to seek to determine *what* the several brain-processes are" (PR, p. 649).[4] From this thoroughly psychological perspective, writing was no different from any other activity in which the writer of these lines might have engaged. Differences between writing and the recollection of writing had to be regarded as insignificant in light of the greater unknown that applied equally to both, namely, the precise nature of the mechanism that enabled any brain-process to "occasion" knowledge, or mental states, "at all."[5]

For Stein, however, the difference between feeling herself "writing at this table now" and the feeling she experienced halfway through *The Making of Americans* as she transcribed "Fernhurst," or "The History of Philip Redfern / A Student of the Nature of Woman" into the longer work—reading a tale she had composed four or five years earlier and trying to remember herself writing it—comprised a separate mystery. About "so complete a changing of experiencing in feeling and thinking, or in time or in something," her alter ego in *The Making of Americans* first comments that "this is very true," and then carefully and precisely spells out what it is true "of" and just what it is that is true:

> This is very true then of the feeling and the thinking that makes the meaning in the words one is using, this is very true then that to many of them having in them strongly a sense of realising the meaning of the words they are using that some words they once were using, later have not any meaning and some of them have a little shame in them when they are copying an old piece of writing where they were using words that sometime had real meaning for them and now have not any real meaning in them to the feeling and the thinking and the imagining of such a one. (p. 441)

In the change of feeling described here, an absence of "real meaning" replaces the "sense of realising the meaning of the words," and "a little shame" gets mixed in as well, owing to an excessive consciousness of the change, or self-consciousness. No doubt, any such change might readily be attributed to the operations of various brain-processes. Yet so long as Stein limited herself to the terms of James's psychology, she would not be able to do justice to her narrator's sense that "every word I am ever using in writing has for me very existing being"—not just that it *is*, like every other word, but that it *is there* and as such possesses "*very* existing being" (MA, p. 539). She would remain unable to articulate what it was about the experience of writing that made all this so "very true" to her narrator and to herself.

Moreover, in a passage like this one, the liveliness or tangibility of the language—assuming that its tactile qualities are successsfully conveyed to the reader—is due more to manipulation of the punctuation, as in Laurence Sterne, than to any creative juxtaposition of the words. Although the second comma, which quite literally punctuates the observation that "some words they once were *using, later* have not any meaning," makes no strictly grammatical sense, it appears in both the typescript and the manuscript. In fact, the term *using*, which precedes the comma, completes a manuscript page, where the comma is marked twice as if for emphasis. It is possible, of course, that Stein simply made a mistake here, either misreading the passage when she transcribed it from an earlier draft or at some later date. Whether the placement is mistaken or not, deliberate or not, she presumably added the comma to clarify the interpolative status of the material between it and the previous comma: "the words one is using, *this is very true . . .*" The problem is to determine exactly where the interpolation should have ended. A more logical place would be several words back, following the same term: "this is very true then of the feeling and the thinking that makes the meaning in the words one is using, // this is very true then that to many of them having in them strongly a sense of realising the meaning of the words they are *using*[,] // that some words they once were *using*[ ] later have not any meaning . . ." The misalignment of subjects that ensues—"the words *one* is using," "the words *they* were using"—is hardly unusual for this author. Moreover, since the passage is itself about words being "used" and ceasing to make sense, Stein might well have chosen to add the comma where she did both to illustrate her point and to convey the feeling one gets "when the words one is using . . . have not any meaning." It was, after all, with *The Making of Americans* in mind that she had Toklas comment that typing or proofreading a book "does something to you that only reading never can do" (ABT, p. 113). Whatever this *thing* is that reading cannot do by itself, it marks the difference between reading and writing; and it was the recognition of this difference, and of just how "complete a changing" was involved, that particularly distinguished Stein and her model reader, Toklas, from James.

Having generally refrained from addressing metaphysical (and grammatical) questions like these in the strictly scientific psychology of 1890, James dedicated much of his work of the next two decades to understanding consciousness in terms of the radical empiricism he located in the hazy area between a science and a philosophy of mind.[6] In particular, manifestations of apparent subconscious activity were of central concern to him over the years; and his "mistrust" of " 'consciousness' as an entity" was linked to a conviction that secondary "extra-marginal" consciousness entered into the composition of what he called, in a series of lectures delivered at Boston's Lowell Institute in 1896, "exceptional mental states."[7] An impressive range of experiences—dreams, hypnotism, automatisms, hysteria, multiple personality, demoniacal possession, witchcraft, manias, and genius alike—seemed to testify to the existence of states of mind that were exceptions to the general rule that a mental state, in order to exist, had to be conscious. Common to them all was the subject's apparent loss of control over his or her own actions and the failure to know why or how something was being done or even that it was happening at all.

Feelings, James had said in *The Principles of Psychology*, "may be faint and weak; they may be very vague cognizers of the same realities which other conscious states cognize and name exactly . . . but that does not make them *in themselves* a whit dim or vague or unconscious." "They *are* eternally as they feel when they exist," he continued, nailing his point down, "and can, neither actually nor potentially, be identified with anything else than their own faint selves." Several lines later, he reaffirmed that "it is the destiny of thought that, on the whole, our early ideas are superseded by later ones, giving fuller accounts of the same realities. But none the less do the earlier and the later ideas preserve their own several substantive identities as so many several successive states of mind" (p. 175). The only way to reconcile this psychological principle with the mental states that concerned him in the Lowell Lectures was to broaden the domain of consciousness. Such, then, was the task that he set himself.

"Of late years, or rather, one may say, of late months," he had already informed the reader of *The Principles of Psychology*, "the classical reasons for admitting that the mind is active even when the person afterwards ignores the fact . . . have been reinforced by a lot of curious observations made on hysterical and hypnotic subjects, which prove the existence of a highly developed consciousness in places where it has hitherto not been suspected at all" (pp. 199–200). Several recently published studies of " 'Unconsciousness' in Hysterics" were then summarized, and James prophesied that

all these facts, taken together, form unquestionably the beginning of an inquiry which is destined to throw a new light into the very abysses of our nature. . . . They prove one thing conclusively, namely, that we must never take a person's testimony, however sincere, that he has felt nothing, as proof positive that no feeling has been there. It may have been there as part of the consciousness of a "secondary personage," of whose experiences the primary one whom we are consulting can naturally give no account. (pp. 200, 208)[8]

At this early date James saw no reason to distance himself from talk of the "existence" of "a highly developed consciousness," even if it took the questionable form of the "consciousness of a 'secondary personage.'" Whatever mistrust he meant his inverted commas to suggest was directed at the notion of a "secondary personage," not at consciousness per se; thus over several pages he might refer to the newly discovered form of consciousness as alternately a "submerged consciousness," a "sub-conscious self," an "under self," a "secondary self," a "buried self," a self that was "split-off" (pp. 203–4, 206).The idea of its being an entity of any kind clearly made him uneasy, but he kept his suspicions largely to himself.

Unconsciousness was another matter. "Sleep, fainting, coma, epilepsy, and other 'unconscious' conditions," he observed at the beginning of the same chapter ("The Relations of Minds to Other Things"), "are apt to break in upon and occupy large durations of what we nevertheless consider the mental history of a single man" (p. 197). Other researchers may have uncritically posited unconsciousness in hysterics, but for James it only existed within quotation marks. The distinction "between the unconscious and the conscious being of the mental state," he said in no uncertain terms, "is the sovereign means for believing what one likes in psychology, and of turning what might become a science into a tumbling-ground for whimsies" (p. 166). In an earlier chapter James had refuted ten "so-called proofs" of the proposition that unconscious mental states really did exist, and argued that the proofs either involved mislabeling a brain-process as a mental one or, as in the tenth proof, required the attribution of subsequent knowledge to an earlier state. He characterized this final confusion in explicitly literary terms: "Two states of mind which refer to the same external reality, or two states of mind the later one of which refers to the earlier, are described as the same state of mind, or 'idea,' *published as it were in two editions*; and then whatever qualities of *the second edition* are found openly lacking in *the first* are explained as having really been there, only in an 'unconscious' way" (p. 173, emphasis added). The unconscious was the last refuge of the "*great* snare of the psychologist": "the confusion of his own standpoint with that of the mental fact," often by uncritically assuming "that the mental state studied must be conscious of itself as the psychologist is conscious of it" (p. 195).[9]

When, in the summer of 1922, Stein's close friend Kate Buss announced in a letter that she had discovered that Stein wrote "from [the] subconscious mind" and seemed "able to express the subconscious[,] . . . to control or be controled [sic] by it," Stein's response was right out of *The Principles of*

Psychology: "Yes but Kitty don't you see there is no demarcation between my conscious and my unconscious self. I am as conscious of my unconscious self as I am of my conscious self in other words there ain't no such animal."[10] On this point she and James agreed, but beyond it they parted company, with James trying to account for automatic writing and the like in terms of "extra-marginal consciousness," and Stein aiming for "xtra consciousness, excess," in order to write as non-automatically as possible. The difference between them was no greater than that between "xtra" and "extra-marginal," but defining the "margin"—literally splitting the difference—gave James such trouble that he was never able to resolve the matter to his satisfaction.

THE MARGINS OF CONSCIOUSNESS

James's work after 1890 on exceptional mental states offers an exact parallel, in psychological terms, to the deliberately less scientific conceptual framework of Stein's literary experiments of 1911 and 1912. Stein, in her experimental writing, rid herself of James's concentration on the psychological and replaced it with the extraordinary concentration on writing that the years spent composing the "Beethovian passages" of *The Making of Americans* made possible (TI, p. 17). In order to understand the appropriateness—even the inevitability—of her substitution of writing for psychology, it is necessary to follow James to the impasse he reached through his continuing involvement in psychical research. By 1901 he had begun to question publicly the notion of a subconscious or "under self," whatever the superiorities that the "vaguer terms 'subconscious' or 'subliminal'" possessed over "the adjective 'unconscious'" (VAR, p. 207). In his memorial that year for Frederic W. H. Myers, the British psychical researcher who had posited the existence of a "subliminal consciousness," he felt obliged to register a mild protest: "I think the words subliminal and supraliminal [the latter referring to "the classic-academic consciousness . . . teleologically evolved for adaptation to our natural environment"] unfortunate, but they were probably unavoidable" (EPR, p. 196).[11] His earlier characterization in the Lowell Lectures of the "phenomena" that a "subliminal" consciousness was supposed to explain suggests why James might have thought the new terminology misleading. These mental states, he had said, looked more "like consciousness *beyond the margin*": *extra*marginal and not *sub*liminal, or beneath the margin (ML, p. 70).

In the draft of a lecture, possibly one of those delivered at the Lowell Institute, he elaborated further on the "difficulties" of the margin.[12] In relatively simple cases, such as when a "good hypnotic subject" experienced "*negative* hallucinations" (causing the subject *not* to "see a certain mark, a certain word in a printed sentence, a certain object in the room," *not* to "hear a certain person's words"), some doubt still remained as to whether the "discriminat[ion of] the object" that was required to make it invisible or otherwise intangible was better characterized as being inside or outside the margin of everyday consciousness. "But in other cases," James continued, "it is surely extra marginal altogether," as when "an order [is] given, during [hypnotically] induced sleep, to do something at a designated moment after waking," and it is "punctually obeyed, even altho on being waked the subject's mind will preserve no recollection of the matter." The mind "loses its quality of unity, and lapses into a polypsychism of fields that genuinely coexist and yet are outside of each other['s] ken and dissociated functionally" (ML, pp. 61–62).

James's objection to the terms *subliminal* and *subconscious* (as well as to the related term *supraliminal*) was less to the implied hierarchy of "under" and "above" than to the degree that the terms made the margin between fields appear more definite than it was. In *The Varieties of Religious Experience*—in which he was concerned with showing how the "discovery of a consciousness existing beyond the field, or subliminally as Mr. Myers terms it, casts light on many phenomena of religious biography"—James stressed that the critical fact about such consciousness, almost the only thing one could be sure of, was its vagueness (p. 233). "Until quite lately," he explained,

> the unit of mental life which figured most was the single "idea," supposed to be a definitely outlined thing. But at present psychologists are tending, first, to admit that the actual unit is more probably the total mental state, the entire wave of consciousness or field of objects present to the thought at any time; and, second, to see that it is impossible to outline this wave, this field, with any definiteness. (p. 231)[13]

"The important fact," he reiterated, "is the indetermination of the margin," which the "'field' formula commemorates" (p. 232).

James's acknowledgment of "extra-marginal" consciousness (which in *The Varieties of Religious Experience* is said to comprise, alternately, an "ultra-marginal life," "the transmarginal region," "the transmarginal field," "our transmarginal consciousness," as well as the inadequate but more customary "subconscious self" and "subliminal region") was consequently of a piece with his denial in "Does 'Consciousness' Exist?" of any "inner duplicity" between what he called here the "wave of consciousness" and the "field of objects."[14] As he had already observed in notes for a seminar on "the Feelings" that Stein attended in the fall of 1895: "There *is* no stuff any-where but data. The entire world (obj. & subjective) at any actual time is a datum. Only within that datum there are two parts, the ob. & the subjective parts, seen retrospectively" (ML, p. 219). The last phrase is the key one. All that exists at any "actual" time, as distinct from whatever may be "seen ret-rospectively," is the "given undivided portion of experience," the "datum." Everything else, whether the mind or the "natural environment," the "ordi-nary" consciousness or the subliminal one, only exists after the fact (VAR, pp. 234–35).

This was the same point James would make "seven or eight" years later in "Does 'Consciousness' Exist?" when he proposed, first, that "pure expe-rience" is separated into objective and subjective parts by "the addition, to a given concrete piece of it, of other sets of experience"; second, that an "undivided portion of experience, taken in one context of associates, play[s] the part of a knower, of a state of mind, of 'consciousness'; while in a different context the same undivided bit of experience plays the part of a thing known, of an objective 'content'"; and, third, that dualism "is still preserved on this account," but, as "an affair of relations, it falls outside, not inside, the single experience considered, and can always be particular-ized and defined." Just as "within the datum"—James's notes for the 1895 seminar continue—"the one part is to the other, so will the datum itself in its entirety appear as the subjective part in the next datum which will con-trast it with the objective part of its own content" (ML, p. 219). Or, as he also put it:

> We admit a duality, indeed, in admitting the transition of the one datum to another. The datum itself, as immediate, seems to be an abstraction, something incomplete. But the duality is not immediate, as in the common theory, it is a relation outwards. Only in the system of related data do known & knower appear as such. (p. 226)

Earlier in the same set of notes he had equated "the phenomenon," "the da-tum," and "'pure' experience," and at one point he reminded himself to "use the word 'field' here for 'datum'—it is conveniently ambiguous." An-other synonym was "point of view," so his "whole system" came down to "a pluralism of 'points of view,'" with "every field incomplete" (pp. 213, 220, 228–30).

Consequently, the foundations of radical empiricism were already in place, and making themselves felt, by Stein's junior year at Radcliffe. That year she took two courses with James: Philosophy 20a ("Laboratory exer-cises and special investigation for advanced students"), which she also attended her sophomore and senior years, and Philosophy 20b ("First half-year: the Feelings.—Second half-year: Discussion of certain theoretic problems, as Consciousness, Knowledge, the Self, the relation of Mind and Body, etc."). She received grades for one semester of laboratory work (an A) and both semesters of the seminar (an A for the first half, a C for the second), and is even referred to in James's own notes for the seminar on the feelings. He regularly included lists of the publications that he wanted to discuss and on one occasion penciled in the names of the students responsible for particular works. Stein, the first mentioned, was to report on a pair of articles by Dickinson Sergeant Miller on "the meaning of truth and error" and "the confusion of content and function in mental analysis" (ML, pp. 217, 499).[15]

Of course, the dualism of consciousness and content posited by James in "Does 'Consciousness' Exist?" differs markedly from the "polypsychism of fields" of the 1896 lecture. The former, as James wrote, "is an affair of relations, it falls outside, not inside, the single experience considered, and can always be particularized and defined," whereas the latter consists of "fields that genuinely coexist and yet are outside of each other[']s ken and dissociated functionally." The dualism proper falls outside the single experience; the polypsychism consists of fields that fall outside each other. This means that although in any particular case the relation of consciousness and content "can always" be defined in terms of James's radical empiricism (from the outside, as it were), the mapping of dissociated fields of consciousness remains troublesome. They are described at one and the same time as existing outside each other—hence as "definitely outlined thing[s]"—and as possessing an "indeterminate" margin, which is what makes them fields in the first place.

It was at this impasse that Frederic Myers's notion of "sensory and motor automatism" quite literally filled the breach. These are the hallucinations and body movements which, as James said, were "broadly" conceived by Myers "as a message of any kind from the Subliminal to the Supraliminal." They provided the evidence for the existence of a "subliminal region," in the form of the "discontinuous series of phenomena" that James examined in his lectures on exceptional mental states (EPR, pp. 197–98). They also made it impossible, given their variety, to set definite margins for either ordinary consciousness or the "subconscious self." The trick was how to determine from the messages themselves "the precise constitution" of the region they "burst" from and thereby to map its "extent" (p. 196; VAR, p. 236). Because Myers had offered "the only scientifically serious investigation" to date of the phenomenon, James proposed that it "deserve[d] to figure in our Science hereafter as the problem of Myers" (EPR, pp. 215, 196).

"Myers's map" really did create a problem for his fellow-researcher, and not just concerning the bafflement that James admitted feeling "as to spirit-return" (pp. 215, 196). By James's reckoning, the subliminal arena that Myers had mapped consisted of three "strata or levels," really three regions within the larger one. "Much of the content," he noted in 1901, "is certainly rubbish, matter that Myers calls dissolutive, stuff that dreams are made of, fragments of lapsed memory, mechanical effects of habit and ordinary suggestion; some belongs to a middle region where a strange manufacture of inner romances perpetually goes on [involving a "curious subconscious mania for personation and deception"]; finally, some of the content appears superiorly and subtly perceptive" (pp. 196, 199). Several years later, in a review of Myers's *Human Personality and Its Survival of Bodily Death* (a text that was itself published posthumously), James combined the first two regions into a single "zone," thereby marking "the parasitic ideas of psycho-neurosis, and the fictitious personations of planchette-writing and mediumship" as thoroughly dissolutive if not exactly rubbish (p. 213). At the same time he added a "supreme" zone, possibly out of respect for the subject matter of Myers's book but also as a result of his own intervening lectures on "the varieties of religious experience," in which he spoke, for example, of "the God with whom, starting from the hither side of our own extra-marginal self, we come at its remoter margin into commerce" (VAR, p. 518).

Were there consequently "three zones of subliminal life," James asked,

> of which the innermost is dissolutive, the middle one superior (the zone of genius, telepathy, etc.), and the outermost supreme and receptive directly of the impact of the spirit-world? And can the two latter zones reach the supraliminal consciousness only by passing through the interior and inferior zone, and consequently using its channels and mixing its morbid effects with their own? Or is the subliminal superior throughout when considered in itself, and are the curious parasitisms of hysteria and alternate personality, and the curious uncritical passivity to the absurdist suggestions which we observe in hypnosis to be explained by defective brain-action exclusively, without bringing in the subliminal mind? Is it the brain, in short, which vitiates and mixes results, or is it the interior zone of the subliminal mind?

"I make no attempt to solve the question," James commented; yet just in posing it he exhibited how far his inquiry into the existence of extramarginal consciousness had taken him from the psychology of 1890 (EPR, p. 214). He was on the verge of asking (as the logical extension of Myers's proposal that such phenomena were "manifest[ed] by physiological means") what the "preformed avenues of expression" were between exceptional mental states and the experiences of sensory and motor automatisms for which some form of extramarginal consciousness seemed to make up for the absence of the ordinary kind (pp. 213, 198).

Nonetheless, even in this passage James was careful not to hypothesize channels or avenues linking mind and brain. Was it the brain, he asked— and "defective brain-action exclusively"—or was it the "interior zone" of the subliminal mind that accounted for the vitiated and mixed results? To have incorporated the "mystery that brain-processes might occasion knowledge" into the fabric of his psychology (even in the inverse form of how knowledge or consciousness caused brain-processes to function) would have obliged him either to try his hand at solving the mystery or to confess that until a solution was found his expanded psychology was little better than sleight of hand. As science, the channels between mental state and "brain-action" had to be included on any adequate map of extramarginal consciousness, and James did not see how this was possible. It is this task that contemporary neuroscience, perhaps most thoroughly in the work of Gerald Edelman and his colleagues, has begun to address in terms of the development, or "gradual making," of the brain's organic mechanisms of mapping.

As long as James viewed the process by which extramarginal consciousness expressed itself purely in terms of content—that is, "as a message of any kind from the Subliminal to the Supraliminal," a burst from one form of consciousness into another—he was able to accommodate the experience within his interpretative framework of *consciousness* and *content*. But to the degree that it involved consciousness actually expressing itself in motor and sensory form, he was left at a loss—of a very familiar kind, to be sure. It was merely a particular form of the more general mind-brain conundrum. He could no better account for the process whereby he wrote out his own thoughts than for how pieces of automatic writing were dictated by apparently extramarginal consciousnesses. In either case the mystery was precisely the "avenues of expression" and he had nothing to say about these, at least not in scientific terms. The vagueness at the margins that he made definitive of ordinary, no less than of extramarginal, consciousness held only for the relation between fields of consciousness. Between mental and both motor and sensory phenomena the margin opened up like an abyss. In this respect, the "new light" that inquiry into exceptional mental states was supposed to throw on "the very abysses of our nature" had yet to shine forth, and Myers's map only added to the confusion, with its unfortunate vagueness about the difference in kind between mind and brain coupled with the too definite margins with which it burdened consciousness.

THE CONSCIOUSNESS OF WRITING

Without definite margins, Myers's map lost whatever topographical coherence it may have seemed to possess; yet as far as James was concerned the region being mapped was defined precisely by such vagueness. Stein, by substituting writing processes (and more generally procedures of expression) for brain processes understood on the model of the reductionist physiology of the day, was able to resolve this impasse, although not, to be sure, exactly on her mentor's terms. The ghost in James's mechanics, the link between brain and mind that escaped him, was essentially a creation of his reader-based theory of consciousness. The problem disappeared if one concentrated instead on what it was that made any act of writing significantly different from all subsequent acts of reading. This was precisely the form of concentration that Stein prepared herself for, first in rewriting *Quod Erat Demonstrandum* as "Melanctha," and then when she learned, in composing *The Making of Americans*, how to write all over again—learned, that is, to train her attention more and more on the writing and less on the information that was to be processed and so conveyed to the reader.[16]

By the time she returned to *The Making of Americans* in 1906, three years after having composed a first draft of roughly forty pages, the neuro-anatomical work at Johns Hopkins was far behind her and her explicitly scientific concerns were once again primarily psychological. Over the course of the next half dozen years the project of delineating, or "diagramming," the "bottom natures" of all persons gradually lost its edge as she determined that it was actually possible to describe human nature according to exact ratios of "resisting" and "attacking." The genuine challenge, she began to feel, would be to produce writing that no longer aimed at the twin goals of description: the invisibility of the researcher and the objectivity, the perfect visibility, of what was described. In this new writing nothing would be hidden because there would be no intention of making anything clear. Of the compositions she then started to produce, first transitional works like "Two" and "Matisse Picasso and Gertrude Stein," then *Tender Buttons* and the steady stream of fragmented writing of the next twenty years—literally *pieces* of writing, as she often suggested—the observation in the 1932 anthology *Americans Abroad* that it "means exactly what it says" was exactly right.[17] Nothing more needed saying, for the writing said all there was to say; nothing counted but how it was written, that is, how the words were arranged on the page and what the act of writing involved. The descriptive *content* no more dictated the significance of the writing than the associations of the writer's *consciousness* did. Instead of the writing being beside the point, as it was in James's psychology, Stein now aimed to make the subconscious and the unconscious, the interpreter's appeals of last resort, quite irrelevant.

Sidestepping the abyss between mind and brain, she proposed to map the act of writing in terms of her own "excess" consciousness, namely, her consciousness of the writing. She would map her writing processes, or procedures, in relation to the consciousness that was both their cause and effect, and she would do so in the writing itself. It was the summer of 1912 when, as she said, she began the "long tormenting process" of "mixing the outside with the inside," of "describ[ing] the inside as seen from the outside," essentially a matter of portraying the world not only as if it were writing but as if it were composed of her writing. Hence, in mapping the "astronomical interspaces" between the words she used, she would also be rewriting the world in the image of her own compositions. Instead of sketching Evelyn Whitehead, for instance, in terms of local or even personal history—with reference, that is, to a world existing outside the writing—Stein portrayed her host in relation to her own act of writing. The procedures used in recreating the words would "incidentally" recreate subject and writer as well, with the margin between *these* "fields of consciousness" being made "indeterminate" as a result. James's model of a mind that "loses its quality of unity and lapses into a polypsychism of fields" would thus be realized by Stein in her chosen medium of writing. Moreover, with the substitution of "philosophy" for "science" in her new work, both mind and brain (as synecdoches for the broadest spiritual and corporeal realms, or media, respectively) would be refigured in terms of writing, and the apparent abyss that had threatened to make nonsense of James's science would itself be swallowed up (LIA, p. 157).

For example, take the mental processes of James's "good hypnotic subject," someone who displays striking success as a medium for communication from "beyond the margin" and therefore seems to possess unusual access to the "transmarginal" realm. These correspond quite precisely to the unconventional compositional techniques introduced by Stein in early and mid-1912, especially the riddling form of negation that appears so often in works of the period. Of hypnotically induced "negative hallucinations," James had observed (in remarks Stein may well have heard) that

> the state of mind is here very peculiar. There is no real sensorial insensibility produced, and no mere failure to notice through ordinary inattention, but a mental deafness and blindness which is more complex, something like an active

dissociation or shutting out of certain feelings and objects from the field of consciousness that counts as thought and governs conduct. It is as when one cuts an acquaintance, ignores a claim, or refuses to be influenced by a consideration of which nevertheless one remains "marginally" and ineffectively aware. I say marginally, but the difficult question to answer, even in these cases, is whether the idea excluded from influence is really inside the margin of the conscious field or outside of it altogether, forming a separate coexistent bit of consciousness flocking all alone by itself.

In relatively "simple" cases of hysterical anaesthesia and hypnosis, James noted, the excluded feeling or object "would seem to quiver directly *on* the limit . . . sometimes being in and sometimes out, and at all times ready to make connection" (ML, pp. 61–62).

In the opening paragraph of her 1934 lecture "Plays," Stein revised James's paradigm of the sentence swimming in the stream of thought in a manner that expressly linked his focus on states of mind and hers on writing. "In a book I wrote called How To Write," she began,

> I made a discovery which I considered fundamental, that sentences are not emotional and that paragraphs are. I found out about language that paragraphs are emotional and sentences are not and I found out something else about it. I found out that this difference was not a contradiction but a combination and that this combination causes one to think endlessly about sentences and paragraphs because the emotional paragraphs are made up of unemotional sentences. (LIA, p. 93)

Three sentences, three ways of saying the same thing—*sentences are not emotional and paragraphs are, paragraphs are emotional and sentences are not, emotional paragraphs are made up of unemotional sentences*—a single paragraph, the beginning of *endless* thought. Individual sentences prove to be the verbal equivalent of "idea[s] . . . quivering directly on the limit" between fields of consciousness, while paragraphs are the equivalent of states of mind or feelings and thus might be said to be emotional. In Whitehead's terms, individual sentences are patterns or eternal objects whereas paragraphs are rhythms or vibratory organisms; in Gerald Edelman's more physiological terms, they might even be said to correspond respectively to protein molecules (and the genetic blueprints that determine the configurations of these molecules) and to the neurons that activate, or inhibit, the production of molecules in the outer membranes of cells, regulating cellular adhesion and mobility.

Stein's creative paragraphs differ from those of ordinary discursive prose (which is composed, after all, for purposes of communication, for getting ideas *across*) in that the noncontradictory "combination" is itself twofold. In addition to the usual unemotional sentences coexisting in her paragraphs, multiple states of mind (and typically states of *different* minds) coexist in them as well. In other words, instead of a paragraph expressing a single state of mind or feeling, as is the norm, Stein's paragraphs are quite literally of two minds; yet, like the more "fundamental" relation between sentences and paragraphs, the relation between the coexisting personalities is "not a contradiction but a combination."[18] If any sentence, taken by itself, is ambiguous and so requires a context to acquire determinate meaning, in prose that minimum context is the paragraph. In Stein's paragraphs, however, the context was always double and consisted both of herself writing and of the separate state of mind she was portraying, such as that of Mrs. Whitehead. The difference between her writing and that of other "creative" writers was principally a function of the extent to which she remained conscious of this doubleness, deliberately attending to her own writing even as she distanced herself from matters "outside" the writing. As she wrote, her consciousness did not exist apart from the writing, merely taking the words and sentences as its object, but was itself composed of the words on the page—as was the individual state of mind and being and feeling she aimed to reproduce verbally.

Of course, however extensively her writing functioned simultaneously as subject and object, Stein wasn't entirely its creation, or her own. She existed in relation to any number of other people and in any number of capacities: for example, as Gertrude Stein lecturing to an audience on the topic of her plays. Still, as a lecturer, her consciousness *of* the writing was no different in kind than that of her auditors. She was obliged to suppress her awareness of the writing as such in order to make room for conversation, argument, description, explanation. As a result, the more fully she described her "discovery" concerning paragraphs and sentences, the less adequately she would be able to convey it. Even so, she was able to help her audience by framing her account in a paragraph that echoed the repetitions of paragraphs composed in her "first manner." It was repetition of this kind that had initially given her enough distance from the content of her writing to become conscious of the writing as writing. Only then had she been able to focus on the ways that the mechanisms of writing might also function in the production of consciousness. Still, the "discovery" was something that she had practiced for years before she actually made it; or to put it another way, it was something she knew in her writing, as knowledge of acquaintance, long before she knew it apart from the writing, as knowledge-about. More recently, she had merely discovered a way of *describing* the earlier discovery.

"EXCESS" MARKS THE SPOT

"Settled is it . . ."

In pieces ranging from "In Between," "Orange In" (a hybrid title that combines *origin*, *arranging*, and the prelapsarian *orange* or golden apple), and
"A Centre in a Table"—all in *Tender Buttons*—to "In" of 1913, "In One"
of 1914, and "A Circular Play" (subtitled "A Play in Circles") of 1920,
through "Wherein the South Differs from the North," "Wherein Iowa Differs from Kansas and Indiana," and "Mildred Aldrich Saturday" of 1924,
and on to the 1932 *Stanzas in Meditation* (the punning title of which moves
directly from *Stein's* to *in medias res*), Stein returned repeatedly to the space
she was simultaneously clearing, creating, and filling in her writing, and
meditated on the words that served to describe it as well as on her own relation to it. "Next. / Not next. / Not next to north. / Not annexed. / Not
next to it. / And not next to it. / Next to it" runs one sequence of lines from
"Wherein the South Differs from the North" (UK, p. 28). The combination
of "next" and "annexed," which perfectly describes the "polypsychism" of
James's fields of consciousness, is realized here quite literally in the terms
not and *north*. Not only does *not* fall next to *north* alphabetically ("'Not'
next to it ['north']. / And not next to 'it'"), it is also annexed, in so many
letters, by *[no]r[t]h*.

Several terms referring to spatial arrangements, specifically spatial proximity, are used in these lines to describe relations among words that arise,
first, from the fact that the words are written and, second, from how they
are written. *Not*, for instance, would be nowhere near *north* if it were
spelled *k-n-o-t*. At the same time, Stein's immediate concerns are signaled by
the words she chose to compare. Negation thus plays a crucial role in both
her use of language and her meditation on how language works, while
"north," like "next" and "annexed," itself signifies a form of spatial relat-
edness. Still, it is not exactly clear how words can be more or less *north* in
writing (or more or less *south*, for that matter) nor what difference it makes
to say that they are. The piece of writing in which these lines occur aims to
elucidate this difference.

This is not to say that Stein is concerned here only with *writing*; the
mapping covers a good deal of ground that would not normally be thought
of as written. On the same page, for example, another sequence of lines
traces a movement from "attention" to "intention" which takes the form of
the syntactic and morphemic movement of *in* across the length of a given
line:

She was not deceived any more in the north she was not deceived
any more as to the south.
Any more as to the South.
In the middle of attention.
Any more as to the north.
In the middle of inattention.
Any more as to the north.
Any more as to the north.
In the middle as an attention.
Any more as to the north.
In the middle as in attention.
Any more as to the north.
In the middle of an intention.
Any more as to the north.
And any more as to the north.

(p. 28)

In the initial sentence, deception—or more precisely its absence—is both
located ("in the north") and characterized ("as to," or concerning, "the
south"). Having thereby provided a significant psychological-cum-episte-
mological state with both context and content, Stein then gets down to the
business of translating psychology into writing. To begin with, the content
is made unmistakably verbal by replacing *south* with *South*. Yet, at the
same time that the lower-case / upper-case distinction designates the act of
writing, the capitalized term itself alludes to the American South, and in
particular the former Confederate States of America. Stein described the
volume in which the piece appeared, *Useful Knowledge*, as "a collection of
. . . all the short things she had written about America"; and "Wherein the
South Differs from the North" is, among other things, a study of the difference that it made in the Civil War for the South not only to *be*, but also to
be *called*, "the South," and the North "the North" (ABT, p. 241).

Substituting "as for the south" for "in the north" at the outset of this
sonnet's worth of lines prepares the way for a complicated series of alternating phrases. The second, fourth, sixth, seventh, ninth, eleventh, thir-
teenth, and fourteenth lines—eight in all—echo, refrainlike, the close of the
first. Yet, although "the south" may dictate the terms of the opening cou-
plet ("as to the south . . . as to the South"), it is itself quickly removed, replaced by "the north" in the seven other lines, and these alternate, in turn,
with the sequence formed by the remaining lines. The north wins this war of
words rather more decisively than the North did the war between the states.

Taking its cue from the initially displaced prepositional phrase *in the north*, the second sequence serves as commentary on its own writing as well as on that of the surrounding lines. The commentary operates on at least two different levels. In the first place, the third through fourteenth lines can be viewed as a set of variations on the phrase *in the north*. Five times the phrase is opened up, and the excluded "middle"—the area of overlap between north and south, which allows the north, again like one of James's fields of consciousness or "attention," to substitute for, and occupy, the south—is made the subject of Stein's, and her reader's, attention:

> *In* [the middle of attention.
> Any more as to] *the north.*
>
> *In* [the middle of inattention.
> Any more as to the north.
> Any more as to] *the north.*
>
> *In* [the middle as an attention.
> Any more as to] *the north.*
>
> *In* [the middle as in attention.
> Any more as to] *the north.*
>
> *In* [the middle of an intention.
> Any more as to the north.
> And any more as to] *the north.*

As if this were not enough, Stein has also rewritten the phrase *in the middle of attention* four times, paying particular attention to the place of *in* in each line. The first of the four variations is morphemic ("attention" to "*in*attention"), the second morphemic and syntactic ("of inattention" to "*as an* attention"), the third syntactic ("as an attention" to "as *in* attention"), and the last again combines both modes ("as in attention" to "*of an in*tention"). The psychological states of attention, inattention, and intention (each of which necessarily enters into the act of writing as Stein understood and practiced it) are shown, when subjected to her literal-minded "attention," her attention to the letters, to exist in the construction and relation of the terms themselves. This is writing "which has in it all the history of its intellectual recreation," as Stein characterized "language as a real thing" (LIA, p. 238). Which came first, one may then wish to know—the writing or the psychology, north or south?

"Settled is it," Stein inquires in the next line, and continues:

Is it settled.
Settled is it.
In attention as to the south.
Settled is it.
In attention as to the north.
It is settled is.
In attention as to the south.
In attention in intention.
It is settled.
As to the south.

(p. 28)

Having lined up her troops (*In attention in intention*), and having asserted that the matter is thereby settled, the writer proceeds, by way of conclusion, to unsettle the whole matter. It is settled, in other words, only so long as one limits oneself to the "southern" half of the equation: *As to the south*. For a settlement to be final (instead of being temporary, transitional, *always* prepared to be unsettled), it must be imposed by one party on the other, in the form of capitulation. The loser, in this case the south, can then be settled, made habitable by (and for) the winner—here the north. Nevertheless, in reorganizing the world along such lines, dictating unidirectional terms of settlement, "the winner loses," as Stein titled the concluding section of the third volume of her autobiography, *Wars I Have Seen*. This is not just a matter of politics or psychology but is itself dictated by the operations, the "astronomical interspaces," of the words themselves that are used to describe and settle all such disputes of public and personal policy. It is this linguistic aspect of apparently extralinguistic occasions that Ludwig Wittgenstein addressed in his influential account of "philosophical grammar"; and in the next chapter, in the course of examining the Jamesian heritage Wittgenstein shared with Stein, I shall consider how they each extended the range of grammatical and syntactical analysis in their contemporaneous investigations of the pragmatics of language use.

"Not only but also . . ."

Repeatedly in her radically experimental writing Stein demonstrated that the medium's elasticity—its "elastic steel," in Emerson's terms—depended on the multiple ways that heterogeneous elements, such as nouns and verbs, or sentences and paragraphs, or one person and another, or the same person as an adult and as a child, had of "being present in [one] another," as Whitehead characterized the trophic phenomena he was principally concerned to elucidate in his philosophy of organism (EL, p. 696; PRO, p. 50). James's image of a "cosmic environment of other consciousness" (an environment composed of "a lot of diffuse soul-stuff, unable of itself to get into consistent personal form or to take permanent possession of an organism, yet always craving to do so") might seem to refer to a flux similar to the one Stein envisioned when she observed, in the first of her lectures on narration, that "if you arranged and concentrated and took away all excrescences[,] you could make [words] do what you needed to do with them" (EPR, p. 373; N, p. 13). "The pressure being brought to bear on them," she added, would make the words *"move in every and in any direction"* (N, p. 14, emphasis added). Yet, despite his further characterization of the flux as a "common reservoir," James's universe was fated to move in only one direction; the *soul-stuff*, possessed as it was by the "craving" to take possession, was always threatening to take the high ground. For James, the "dingy little mediumistic facts" investigated by the psychical researcher alone offered any hope of science ever coming to terms with the brute fact of "this bank upon which we all draw"—any prospect, that is to say, of the stream of consciousness actually turning back on itself, *diverting* itself, *understanding itself* (EPR, pp. 374–75). Significantly, from the perspective of psychical research the "individual force [of] actual creation," in Stein's phrasing, comes down to mere accident (ABT, p. 228). "There is," James suggested, "a continuum of cosmic consciousness against which our individuality builds but *accidental* fences" (EPR, p. 374, emphasis added). Perhaps any non-idealizing account of individual creativity has to start from chance or chance mistakes, but James did not see how he might move beyond his vague notion of "accident" in supporting the creation (and creations) of individuals out of the vast "continuum of . . . consciousness."

If James came close to making consciousness a universal principle (and thereby endorsing a " 'panpsychic' view of the universe"), Stein deliberately limited the experience of "cosmic consciousness" to the vigilant *self-consciousness* she displayed toward the act of writing (EPR, p. 374).[19] It was such awareness that distinguished her work from any kind of automatic writing. In effect, by replacing considerations of the universe with autopoietic acts of writing, and "diffuse soul-stuff" with arrangements of words on the page, she rewrote James's theory of consciousness as a theory of writing. In so doing, she repeatedly demonstrated the inadequacy of any reduction, such as his, of writing to forms of consciousness that are not themselves forms of writing. Automatic writing had been so convenient for James's science because it served both to distinguish writing definitively from consciousness and to show that writing required consciousness all the same. Consciousness of writing seemed to play no essential role in the consciousness of a person actually writing, yet some consciousness, even if it only took the form of "a crazy will to make-believe," still had to be understood as dictating the writing.

Especially in the works she composed between 1912 and 1932, Stein conducted a sustained assault on this premise that consciousness dictates writing but writing does not dictate consciousness. "Using every form that she [could] invent," she portrayed the inevitable mingling of writing with consciousness—inevitable, that is, for creatures who write or, at the very least, possess a common history of writing.[20] The extreme methodological self-consciousness that she brought to the task of mapping what James called the "topography" of the "larger psycho-physical world" differed from his own feeling-centered science of psychology essentially in her aim to record, and *thereby* to understand, the broader relations between consciousness and writing, instead of focusing on the more narrow mechanisms of consciousness per se (EPR, pp. 374–75).

The methodology Stein embraced in writing *The Making of Americans* was essentially the same as that which James evoked in his eulogy of Frederic Myers. Myers, James predicted, "would always be remembered in psychology as the pioneer who staked out a vast tract of mental wilderness and planted the flag of genuine science upon it. He was an enormous collector. He introduced for the first time comparison, classification, and serial order into the peculiar kind of fact which he collected. He was a genius at perceiving analogies; he was fertile in hypotheses; and as far as conditions allowed in this meteoric region, he relied on verification" ("Service," p. 202).[21] Stein too was a scientifically trained collector and classifier, a genius at perceiving analogies; nonetheless, in rewriting James's science, first in *The Making of Americans* and then quite differently in the later works, as something more self-conscious, more rigorous in certain respects than his had been, she transcended as well as deconstructed it. Not only did she bring out the contradictions and, as a critic, make something of them, but as an artist she also brought them under control and made something with them.

"Not only but also," as she explained in the delightful self-parody written in the style of an instruction manual (a "know how to" book), two-thirds of the way into "Wherein the South Differs from the North":

> Not only but also the explorer should be able to know how to and also to recognise the spots he has seen before and which he will recognise again as he occupies as he occupies successively the places he recognises and not only that he occupies them successively but also that he will later be able to make maps of

the region which he has traversed. Such is the duty of an explorer. In short it depends upon him in short he is to realise that he is to acquire knowledge of the directions of the direction of a direction of previous visits and successive visits. It becomes necessary therefor that he indulges in active plans and map drawing and also in constant observation and relative comparisons. In this way he easily finds his way. (UK, p. 32)

In one of her American lectures, Stein observed that the difference between paragraphs and sentences "was not a contradiction but a combination"; in another, she observed that "if you are to be really and truly alive it is necessary to be at once talking and listening, doing both things, both as if there were one thing, not as if they were two things, but doing them [as] part of the same thing" (LIA, pp. 93, 170). In each case the logic is identical: *not only* emotional paragraphs *but also* unemotional sentences, *not only* talking *but also* listening.

Yet the logic is not asserted as such in the paragraph from "Wherein the South Differs from the North." Instead, observations that might have served to describe the role of mapping in the work of Myers and other nineteenth-century explorer-cartographers are rewritten as a simultaneous portrait and example of the work of their twentieth-century equivalents, such as Stein herself, or Whitehead in philosophy, or Edelman, Varela, and Haraway in the life sciences. Myers's map, in other words, was redrawn by Stein, largely due to her recognition that the double logic or "postlogic" of *not only but also* was premised on a heterogeneous dialectic—and not, as Myers seems to have assumed, on a homogeneous one.[22] For Myers, as for James, this *written* phrase (which sums up all that was really known about the "poly-psychism of fields" of consciousness, namely, that they were "dissociated functionally" yet "co-existed") might readily be characterized as a message from, and consequently a sign of, some such field. For Stein, on the contrary, the phrase's existence as a piece of writing complicated this picture by calling into question the assumption that a piece of writing, even the single word *in*, let alone the juxtaposition of *not*, *only*, *but*, and *also*, could always be represented accurately *as* a representation. Mapping, in Stein's hands, did not look anything like the mapping of the previous century, or even the previous generation, because she was even more determined, as the cliché has it, to go where no man had gone before. To the degree that a map looked like something recognizable, it was an imitation of some other map rather than the product of actual exploration—which, to an Emersonian way of thinking, was always a matter of self-exploration, of "mixing the outside with the inside," whatever else was ostensibly being mapped. If Myers's and James's maps were chiefly imitations, however critical, of other maps and others' maps, this was because from Stein's viewpoint neither man was adequately *self-conscious* in his pursuit of truth. They did not see fit to include their own mapping in the maps they produced.

Mapping begins to sound suspiciously like writing at this point, and in the broadest sense, as in Edelman's notion of "reentrant signaling" between neuronal maps, the two activities are genuinely isomorphic.[23] In a paragraph concerning an *explorer who should be able to know how to* Stein maps her own act of rewriting, an act really no different from that of any writer except for the "xtra consciousness" she brings to it. Not only is she conscious of the rewriting, as any genuinely creative writer must be, but she is also deliberately, consciously mapping herself "in the act," so to speak— beginning with the phrase *Not only but also*, which immediately situates her explorer in a universe in which consciousness is necessarily doubled. It isn't that there are two minds here but that a single mind is being made up. "Which way to go?" "Have 'I' been here before?" This combined decision-making and self-invention is not achieved merely through an act of consciousness, however clear or indeterminate, nor through writing per se, but through the concentrated, and concentrating, act of rewriting. Both consciousness and writing—*not only* one's own *but also* others'—are revised in the process.

Some of the paragraph's self-mapping might be unpacked as follows, in the sort of running commentary Stein herself provides as she passes from phrase to phrase, from state of mind to state of mind, and between phrases and states of mind:

> ### *"Not only but also . . ."*

This starts us off on the proper footing, in an appropriate state of mind, in the middle of things—especially as there is no prior referent for *not only*, which looks forward, not back, toward unknown, if not entirely unfamiliar, territory. We have not been here before; yet we might have been. *Not*, of course, is something like *North*, and *also* has something of the *south* in it.

> ### *". . . the explorer should be able to know how to . . ."*

"The explorer should be able to—perhaps *should know how to* is preferable—should know how to, then."
Know how to *what*?

> ### *". . . and also . . ."*

Knowing how to isn't just a state of mind; it is also a phrase. Yet we normally choose to forget this and just see, or imagine we see, the expertise stored up somewhere. Perhaps in the back of the mind; or in the athlete's hands or legs; or in the coordination of hands and eyes. *And* not only is *to know how to* a phrase but *so* is its object, which may or may not follow from it but in any case follows:

> *". . . to recognise the spots he has seen before . . ."*

First, the statement, *the explorer should know how to*—which might also be the first half of a sentence. Then, the fragment, *to recognise the spots he has seen before.* Put them together and you get *The explorer should know how to recognise the spots he has seen before.* These are the verbal operations. Have we ever seen this exact sentence before? Certainly not. Something like it?

> *". . . and which he will recognise again . . ."*

These *spots which he has seen before* are also spots *he will recognise again.* Indeed, he will only know that he has *seen them before* if he has *recognised them again.*

The term *recognise* has already been used twice in this sentence. Not only that, but its very construction (*re-cognise*) implies such doubling as well.

> *". . . as he occupies . . ."*

It is not a matter, however, of *recognising spots* without actually being in those spots—as if he were looking at them from some distance. Rather, he *recognises* them *again* only *as he occupies* them.

> *". . . as he occupies successively the places he recognises . . ."*

As he occupies them: again.

Here the experience in question is spelled out. *Recognises* is a place—a word—that has now been occupied, or used, for the third time.

The phrase *as he occupies* is itself occupied *successively.*

And *recognition* occurs, one recognizes, when a place has been *occupied successively*—along the lines, that is, of what occurs here. It is all of a piece.

> *". . . and not only that he occupies them successively . . ."*

The Cheshire Cat-like phrase with which the paragraph began begins to reappear, Cheshire Cat-like. Not only once but twice. It too is in the process of being re-cognized, occupied again. First, *recognise* was repeated three times; now it is the turn of *occupies* to be re-reoccupied.

And not only that: There is also the suggestion that besides occupying *the places* successively—being so occupied—the explorer also occupies *them* successively. In other words, different names for the same thing make a difference worth registering.

". . . but also that he will later be able to . . ."

Here the full force of the opening phrase is felt. *Not only but also*, one more time around.

If earlier it was proposed that the *explorer should be able to recognise the spots he has seen before*, now the other shoe has dropped. From *before* to *later*. *Later able to . . .* able to *what*?

Also: Have we noticed the heavy alliteration, all those *b*'s, *l*'s and *t*'s, in the passage from *but also* to *able to*?

". . . makes maps of the region which he has traversed . . ."

One does not merely explore for the sake of exploring—just as Stein is not putting herself through this merely for the thrill of discovery—but in order to *make* (i) *maps*, (ii) *maps of*, (iii) *maps of the*, (iv) *maps of the region*, (v) *maps of the region which*, etc. Not only for the thrill but also for what comes after, beginning with the . . .

end of the sentence.

New sentence:

"Such is the duty of an explorer."

Explorers, one is obliged to acknowledge, are not freed of all responsibilities. Even so, it remains unclear whether these are owed principally to themselves or to society, directed inwardly or outwardly.

What is clear is—Ready? Here goes—that it is the duty of an explorer such as the writer of this sentence to write sentences like these.

"In short it depends on him . . ."

This is just another way of saying that the explorer has some duty or other.

In short, something hangs in the balance. The balance of what? Of the sentence? Sentences? Paragraph?

Just how short?

". . . in short . . ."

In short again. *Successive occupation* again. The second sentence, we now notice—already well into the third—the second, so much shorter than the first, was probably too short, requiring elaboration. If it wasn't clear what the duty was, it did seem perfectly clear that there was one: possibly too clear. The second *in short* draws things out, in short.

"... he is to realise that he is to acquire knowledge of ..."

Whatever it may be that *depends upon him* seems to depend on his *acquiring knowledge* of a certain kind. Earlier, there had been the doubling of *be able to / know how to*. Now, there is the comparable doubling: *he is to realise that / he is to acquire knowledge of*. Four phrases in all, each requiring an object, and on each occasion the object is initially postponed by substituting the second of the paired phrases: making *knowing how* the object of *being able to* and *acquiring knowledge* that of *realising*. Each time we have already been here before, especially the second time.

Yet it's not quite the same, this second time. Two different forms of knowledge are concerned. First, *know how*—You know, our old friend *knowledge of acquaintance*—and now just plain old *knowledge of*. Knowing how to do things and knowing things *about* other things.

What sort of knowledge, then, is to be acquired? Of what kinds of things?

"... the directions of the direction of a direction ..."

One is given no direction whatsoever here. Instead, one is presented with a choice, which enables one to choose one's own direction, go one's own way, clear one's own path. Is this not so?

Or does it go like this: Although the general form of the direction that one may take is thoroughly determined, the particulars are still of one's own making. Hence the indefinite *a direction* has a specific direction (*the direction of a direction*), which in turn has a set of very definite coordinates (*the directions of the direction*). Not unlike the contours of Stein's own paragraph.

"... of previous visits and successive visits."

In the end, then, is our beginning: one more time. If it all comes down to a matter of *previous visits and successive visits*, we would seem to have returned precisely to where we began: to the previous visits and *the spots he has seen before*, the successive visits and the spots *which he will recognise again*. Two time-frames meeting: When? In what manner of *in between*?

Nor does the paragraph end here. The fourth and fifth sentences may impress one as much more straightforward than the earlier ones—as indeed they would be, were it not for the awkward fact that they follow them. *Succession* is not something one can just take for granted in a paragraph like this. Rather, it is the sort of *fact* that Stein invoked in *Tender Buttons*: "A fact is that which when the place was replaced all was left that was stored and all was retained that would not satisfy more than another" (p.65). The *active plans*, the *map drawing*, the *constant observation*, the *relative comparisons* are all parodic: automatic phrases with nearly identical syntactical forms, generalities that require no more active planning, map drawing, constant observation, and the like, than the "general ideas and art values and musical development and surgical operations and Heaven knows what all" which, in *Q.E.D.*, Adele complains pass for thinking in her lover Helen's conversation (TL, p. 221). Yet at the same time Stein is being entirely serious, for her writing requires exactly these activities, both of herself and of her readers. *Not only but also.* "In this way," she concludes, "he easily finds his way." Sentence and sentiment point to the model for her explorer, none other than the essayist whose advice she takes even as she revises it. "Place yourself," Emerson directed his reader, "in the middle of the stream of power and wisdom which animates all whom it floats, and you are without effort impelled to truth, to right, and a perfect contentment" (EL, p. 309). If, in the process of rewriting Emerson's line, Stein easily finds *his way* in *t[his way]*, that is just her way, both in manner and direction.

"The Physiognomy of the Thing": Sentences and Paragraphs in Stein and Wittgenstein

This very desk which I strike with my hand strikes in turn your eyes.

—WILLIAM JAMES, *A Pluralistic Universe*

In his 1909 overview of "the present situation in philosophy," *A Pluralistic Universe*, James offered the pithy formulation of the radical empiricist perspective cited here, with the same entity functioning "at once as a physical object in the outer world and as a mental object in our sundry mental worlds" (p. 269). Nevertheless, his language betrayed him, for the dual-function entity he had in mind was not the entity the reader probably conceives him to be talking about, some physical desk in the external world. *That* is merely one aspect of the entity in question. Instead, James was addressing *this very desk*, or more exactly *this-very-desk-which-I-strike-with-my-hand*. In a remark already cited in Chapter 1, Susanne Langer suggests that "*the very existence* of 'things' is modeled on [one's own] inward expectation of strains, directions, and limitations of [one's] felt actions." No less than James's sense of the desk as *this very desk*, the viewer's (and even the reader's) sense of it involves the projection of bodily feelings onto something that, in Langer's phrasing, can be "objectified as a material body" only as a result of such projection (M, p. 321, emphasis added). James's desk strikes him no less than he does it; and in order for him to be so taken by it as to select this very object from his, and its, immediate surroundings as an item suitable for striking (if only to make a point, and even if he never actually bruises the desk but only makes his point verbally), he has to experience it as in some sense capable of physiological experience—hence not just as a material desk but as *a living, moving desk*. The physical object may not be alive, but the entity James confronts (or the one you or I might imagine confronting) certainly is. For that is what it means for him to experience it as something that *really* exists, whether he should come into contact with it through the medium of his hand or in his head or on the page. "What really *exists*," as he remarked in *A Pluralistic Universe*, "is not things made but things in the making" (p. 263).[1]

All varieties of "corporeal feelings," Langer explained half a century later, are " 'seen' in the shapes that meet our eyes." In fact, the projection of such feelings ("kinesthetic, thermal, tactual") is responsible for the significance that shapes acquire as "potential opportunities for action if not actual ones at the moment" (M, p. 322). Although objectification ordinarily operates implicitly, at the level of well-practiced habit, it becomes explicit in *physiognomic seeing*, which, according to Langer, involves "a perception of *expressiveness*" that "may not only accompany, but [can] even precede any clear comprehension of the physical shape and properties of a confronting object" (p. 323, emphasis added). "Inward feeling [is reflected] in the most typically outward, objective data of sensation," with the result that *any* "individuated form of nature [may] appear as [a] potential agent"—including the whole of nature (pp. 76–77, 323). The viewer experiences "expressive value in visual forms" (such as "an inviting or forbidding look, or some other air of non-pragmatic value"), regardless of the actual presence of "true or [even] suggested faces" (pp. 266, 270). When Stein's narrator, for instance, confesses in *The Making of Americans* that "every word I am ever using in writing has for me *very existing being*," she is acknowledging a sense of *this very word* that corresponds to James's *this very desk* (p. 539, emphasis added). Although neither word nor desk is experienced as literally wearing an inviting look, as would occur with physiognomic seeing proper, each nonetheless invites the viewer to regard it as a physiological being, possessor of "very existing being."

Of course, it is not always possible to regard words in this manner, perhaps least of all while listening to a lecture or delivering one. (Recall Stein's caveats from Chapter 2.) James initially prepared *A Pluralistic Universe* for delivery as a series of lectures at Oxford, and pointedly complained of the inadequacies of lecturing for addressing "things in the making." Aside from the reference to Bergson, he sounds remarkably like Wittgenstein:

> As long as one continues talking, intellectualism remains in undisturbed possession of the field. The return to life can't come about by talking. It is an *act*; to make you return to life, I must set an example for your imitation, I must deafen you to talk, or to the importance of talk, by showing you, as Bergson does, that the concepts we talk with are made for purposes of practice and not for purposes of insight. (p. 290)

As a description of the unenviable position occupied by a lecturer critical of his own tendencies toward intellectualism (which is not the same thing as an anti-intellectual lecturer), Stein would doubtless have acquiesced to this statement. Like James, she was concerned to return herself and her readers *to life* from the condition of relative nonlife that prevailed in discourse. Yet James premised his criticism of *talk* on a highly questionable distinction between "logos or discursive thought" and "raw unverbalized life" (p. 272). This was unacceptable for someone who, like Stein, regarded the thoroughly "verbalized" phenomenon of writing as both irreducible to the logic of discourse and exemplary of what James characterized as "reality, life, experience, concreteness, immediacy, use what word you will" (p. 212).

Because the expressive features of a sentence like *This very desk which I strike with my hand strikes in turn your eyes* ordinarily remain so indeterminate, hiding behind the "very desk," as it were, the string of fourteen words isn't likely to strike one *as a sentence* beyond the intellectual contribution it makes to James's argument. (In this respect, it is irrelevant whether one views the double use of "strike" as awkwardly obscuring the argument or as bringing it home more effectively.) By contrast, Stein's increasingly visible sentences dominate one's experience of her compositions; and, beginning with the transitional works of 1911–12, the reader is obliged to attend to them much as she did: painstakingly, word by word, as children do in mastering the first and second of the three R's until the procedures necessary for fluency finally, *finally*, become habitual. Yet, in Stein's case, the object was neither fluency nor ever-improving habits. For her, lasting accomplishment, at once scientific and literary, resided in the singular success she exhibited in rendering the organic mechanisms that operate in all sentence composition and comprehension—that is to say, in rendering them *visible*.

Throughout the two decades of experimental writing framed by *Tender Buttons* and *Stanzas in Meditation* runs the implicit question—several studies of the late 1920s address it explicitly—as to whether the physiognomic writing and reading demanded by sentences that strike the reader as alive (at least in the sense that it is impossible to predict what will follow from what) is chiefly a matter of attending to individual words or to the expressive relations among them; and if the latter, whether such relations are limited to those ordinarily occurring within individual sentences or whether they extend *beyond* the sentence. The same concerns also preoccupied Wittgenstein, although he addressed them in terms of philosophical and psychological propositions that, like those of James, raised the question of *how anyone might ever have come to make such a strange claim* rather than in terms of sentences like Stein's, which elicited the complementary question: *How ever did she come to put these words together?*

FORMING, CREATING, AND LIMITING EMOTIONS

"Why," Wittgenstein asked himself early in Part Two of *Philosophical Investigations*, "does it sound queer to say: 'For a second he felt deep grief'?" The tentative response which follows—"Only because it so seldom happens?"—seems to posit an empirical basis for the impression. Yet the full "remark," or *Bemerkung*, suggests that the oddity is due not to empirical limitations but to logical and grammatical ones: " 'For a second he felt violent pain.'—Why does it sound queer to say: 'For a second he felt deep grief'? Only because it so seldom happens?" The syntactic similarity of the pair of utterances juxtaposed here (*For a second he felt violent pain*, *For a second he felt deep grief*) turns out to be misleading, because "the concept of grief" is used differently, and therefore differs grammatically, from "the concept of a sensation" like pain. Wittgenstein explains:

> "Grief" describes a pattern which recurs, with different variations, in the weave of our life. If a man's bodily expression of sorrow and of joy alternated, say, with the ticking of a clock, here we should not have the characteristic formation of the pattern of sorrow or of the pattern of joy. (PI, p. 174e)

Grief just isn't the sort of thing that possesses the regularity of the ticking of a clock and can therefore be timed to the nearest second, as a sensation may be measured. Moreover, as Langer would subsequently observe, emotions invariably last longer than a second or two, since they serve as "reactions . . . to our own [felt] impulses in situations which do not immediately let them pass into action, that is, obstructions, long or briefly unmet needs, and especially conflicting motivations" (M, p. 262). This account certainly does get at some of the queerness of "For a second he felt deep grief"; still, the complementary explanation proposed decades earlier by Stein was even more radically grammatical and hence, in the end, more Wittgensteinian.

"A sentence is not emotional a paragraph is," she famously wrote, arriving at this gnomic conclusion in the course of meditating on sentences that sound queerly like Wittgenstein's:

He looks like a young man grown old.

It looks like a garden but he had hurt himself by accident.

A dog which you have never had before has sighed.

Once when they were nearly ready they had ordered it to close. (HTW, pp. 25–29; cited in LIA, p. 226)

For a second he felt deep grief. Marjorie Perloff, writing about Stein in her recent study of Wittgenstein as literary modernist, demonstrates how a narrative context may be devised for each of these sentences in which it would make sense for someone to utter so extraordinary a remark (*Ladder*, p. 91). To be sure, one would have to wait a long time for the appropriate situation to arise. As Wittgenstein remarked, "it so seldom happens" that one finds the occasion to say, for instance, "He looks like a young man grown old," and does not turn out to be misspeaking, or speaking inexactly. In composing sentences like these, however, Stein was no more interested in narrative completion than was Wittgenstein. Rather, she was interested in how the grammar of such sentences enabled them to form emotionally resonant wholes (as sentences in ordinary prose cannot), even as her well-wrought compositions-in-minimum remained unmoored and open-ended—so obviously, deliberately, incomplete.

In *The Autobiography of Alice B. Toklas* Stein provided a charming account of her "discovery" of the precise manner in which sentences and paragraphs differ. Speaking of the spring of 1929, she recalled,

> We now had our country house, the one we had only seen across the valley and just before leaving we found the white poodle, Basket. He was a little puppy in a little neighborhood dog-show and he had blue eyes, a pink nose and white hair and he jumped up into Gertrude Stein's arms. A new puppy and a new ford we went off to our new house and we were thoroughly pleased with all three. Basket although now [that is to say, in the summer or fall of 1932, when Stein was composing the *Autobiography*] he is a large unwieldy poodle, still will get up on Gertrude Stein's lap and stay there. She says that listening to the rhythm of his water drinking made her recognise the difference between sentences and paragraphs, that paragraphs are emotional that sentences are not. (pp. 247–48)

In February of 1929 Stein had already announced to Sherwood Anderson that she was "making a desperate effort to find out what is and isn't a sentence, having been brought up in a good old public school grammar and sentences are a fascinating subject to me" (White, p. 68). The same month she informed Virgil Thomson: "I do want to know if there is a sentence, I thought perhaps there wasn't but I am almost beginning to be able to explain that there is."[2] Having completed "Sentences," with its hundred pages of "sentences about the sentence," shortly after taking up residence at the new house, she continued her "intensive study . . . of the sentence" over the course of the next year, in Paris as well as in the countryside.³ From "Saving the Sentence" she graduated to "Sentences and Paragraphs," and then on to "More Grammar for a Sentence."

The first of these works expressly concerns the "caniche" Basket. Not only does it start with the French phrase, "Qu'est-ce que c'est cette comedie d'un chien," but it includes grammatical observations such as "When a dog is no longer a lap dog there is a temporary inattention" and "Hers and his the houses are hers and his the valley is hers and his the dog named Basket is hers and his also the respect of the populace is hers and his" (HTW, pp. 13, 20). In this work, the sentence requiring "saving" was still the locus of Stein's attention. By contrast, "Sentences and Paragraphs," as the title suggests, is an intermediate work in which Stein sought to determine, as she put it in 1934, "exactly what the balance the unemotional balance of a sentence is and what the emotional balance of a paragraph is and if it were possible to make even in a short sentence the two things come to be one" (LIA, pp. 225–26). The result was the "series" of attempts "to save a sentence" cited above, such portmanteau sentences as *He looks like a young man grown old* and *A dog which you have never had before has sighed*—so like, and unlike, Wittgenstein's *For a second he felt deep grief*, in that what Stein takes to be an unambiguous expression of a manner of being (or more exactly, a manner of being *there*, the expression of a particular experience, of being somewhere in particular), Wittgenstein perceives simply as an error of judgment (HTW, pp. 29, 33). Finally, in "More Grammar for a Sentence" (as the original title, "Paragraphs," confirms) the emphasis is less on the sentence and more on the *More* and just what it is that distinguishes paragraphs from sentences. It is here, in the sequence of passages I have excerpted and italicized below, in the midst of more general remarks about sentences and paragraphs, that Stein expressly portrays the connection between the rhythm of Basket's drinking and the emotional nature of paragraphs (even if she uses the term *emotional* only once in the composition). "*To think well of any paragraph*," she writes, "*they must have affection*":

> *Did he drink out of his water because of well well;*
>
> Sentences are not natural paragraphs are natural and I am desperately trying to find out why;
>
> *What is a paragraph, no place in which to settle. Because they have been moved;*
>
> *A paragraph is different that is it affects me. That is it it is why they are relished. As for a sentence in what way do they stop;*

A sentence is a hope of a paragraph;

What is a paragraph. Right off. Write often. What is a paragraph. He drinks as if in wishing. He drinks of if in washing;

A paragraph always lets it fall or lets it be well and happy or feels it to be so which they never were themselves as worried;

A paragraph has to do with the growth of a dog;

A paragraph is never finished therefore a paragraph is not natural;

There is a difference between natural and emotional;

A paragraph is natural because they feel like it;

A sentence it is so easy to lose what a sentence is. Not so easy with a paragraph it is not so easy to lose what is a paragraph;

A sentence can not exist if it does not come back no not if it does not come back. A paragraph finishes.
    This is it.

(SR, pp. 551–63, emphasis added)

With the last three sentences, and the closing three-word paragraph, this sequence of grammatical investigations into the gray area lying just outside the confines of the sentence comes to a ringingly ostensive conclusion.

Even so, Stein's thinking about sentences and paragraphs didn't end here. In 1935 she summed up the current state of her investigations in the second of her lectures on narration: "Think," she instructed, "how a sentence is made by its parts of speech and you will see that it is not dependent upon a beginning a middle and an ending but by each part needing its own place to make its own balancing, and because of this there is no emotion, a sentence does not give off emotion" (N, pp. 22–23). Despite the fact that anything "balanced within itself does not give out nor have within any emotion," when sentences are arranged "in succession one after the other and make a paragraph," they turn out to "have the emotion that any succession can give to anything" (p. 22). Whereas each sentence "exists within by the balance within . . . the paragraph exists not by a balance within but by a succession. Anybody really anybody can realize this thing," just as "anybody listening to any dog's drinking will see what I mean" (p. 22; LIA, p. 223). *He drinks as if in wishing. He drinks of if in washing. . . . A paragraph always lets it fall or lets it be well and happy or feels it to be so which they never were themselves as worried.* The rhythm of canine drinking does not emerge because an inner balance has been reached (like that which occurs among the "parts" of speech in a sentence) but through a process of succession (like a paragraph, with its beginning, middle, and end). "One sentence coming after another sentence makes a succession and the succession if it has a beginning a middle and an ending as a paragraph has does form create and limit an emotion" (N, p. 23).

Having demonstrated that sentences and paragraphs are logically or grammatically distinct, Stein proceeded to speculate on the possibility of deconstructing the traditional, empirical form of the distinction. She did this by calling into question the apparent inevitability of widely accepted norms of prose composition: the *language game* of prose composition, to use Wittgenstein's phrase. As she put it, "for a long time [prose had] been made of sentences and paragraphs" (p. 22). "Perhaps now there is no longer any need for a sentence to be existing," no reason for a paragraph to require the "internal balancing" of individual sentences (p. 18). Moreover, she cautioned, "do not forget that . . . succeeding one thing succeeding another thing is succeeding and having a beginning a middle and an ending is entirely another thing." Because "these are two things" and "not one thing," paragraphing might avoid the rather limited progressive form which it had traditionally taken, so long as it continued to "make a succession" and therefore conveyed the impression of movement and emotion (p. 23). Indeed, sentences like *He looks like a young man grown old* and *Once when they were nearly ready they had ordered it to close* were certainly not sentences in the traditional sense *nor* did they "depend upon a beginning a middle and an ending" (pp. 22–23). In addition to being internally *unbalanced*, if not exactly unhinged, they utilized nonprogressive succession to "form create and limit an emotion." Sentences like these—and like *There can be natural sentences if they are halting which whichever that is with renown that without that waving that if they or through. This is a sentence*, in "More Grammar for a Sentence"—"save the sentence," although at the expense of the traditional rationale for sentences (and the rationale for traditional sentences), which so long as it *required* "internal balancing" couldn't be saved (SR, p. 556). As the often brutal language games of the twentieth century all too convincingly reveal (with *language game* understood as applying broadly to all forms of organized human behavior as well as, more narrowly, to writing like Stein's and Wittgenstein's), such internal balancing is and has always been an empirical rather than a logical necessity, hence not a necessity at all.

In her 1934 lecture "Plays," Stein offered the account cited in the last chapter of her "discovery" of the fundamentally combinatory nature of language games. The three-sentence paragraph itself partakes of the combinatory logic it describes. At the level of relatively abstract *thought*, Stein proposes a disjunction between unemotional sentences and emotional paragraphs (a disjunction that "causes one to think endlessly" about them); yet at the considerably more concrete level of *experience*, she posits a conjunction of the same ("emotional paragraphs are *made up* of unemotional sentences"). This, in a sentence, is Stein's argument. It is also the mechanism by which her argument is realized: three sentences and a paragraph combined in a heterogeneous dialectic. A homogeneous dialectic would have left one empty-handed or worse, with some unresolvable paradox of self-reflexivity to resolve. Moreover, the picture revisited here, of the sentence swimming in the stream of thought so vividly sketched by James in *The Principles of Psychology*, is the very picture Wittgenstein sought to emend in his grammatical investigations. For Stein's beloved mentor played an equally significant role in the development of Wittgenstein's philosophy; and it is largely due to James that the relation between these two lifelong students of grammar isn't merely analogical.

"THE SENSATIONS AROUND MY EYES"

In mid-June of 1912, at the end of his first year in Cambridge and shortly after turning twenty-three, Wittgenstein wrote to Bertrand Russell:

> Whenever I have time I now read James's "Varieties of religious experience."
> This book does me a lot of good. I don't mean to say that I will be a saint soon,
> but I am not sure that it does not improve me a little in a way in which I would
> like to improve *very much*: namely I think that it helps me to get rid of the
> *Sorge* (in the sense in which Goethe used the word in the Second Part of *Faust*).
> (McGuinness and von Wright, p. 14)

Brian McGuinness, in his biography of Wittgenstein, alludes to this letter when he comments that a year later Wittgenstein still "felt that his life had no meaning." "He was afflicted with the sense of futility, the *Sorge*, he mentioned to Russell in the previous summer. He could recognize his own condition in William James's chapter on 'The Sick Soul,'" which included extensive material cited from Tolstoy's *My Confession*—"A wonderful account," James commented, "of the attack of melancholy which led [Tolstoy] to his own religious conclusions" (*A Life*, pp. 156–57; VAR, p. 149). In a letter to Ottoline Morrell in late 1919, reporting on his first meeting with Wittgenstein in six years, Russell recalled the early influence of James and filled in some of the details of Tolstoy's subsequent importance for the young logician:

I had felt in [Wittgenstein's early work, the *Tractatus Logico-Philosophicus*] a flavour of mysticism, but was astonished when I found that he has become a complete mystic. He reads people like Kierkegaard and Angelus Silesius, and he seriously contemplates becoming a monk. It all started from William James's *Varieties of Religious Experience*, and grew (not unnaturally) during the winter he spent alone in Norway before the war, when he was nearly mad. Then during the war a curious thing happened. He went on duty to the town of Tarnov in Galicia, and happened to come upon a bookshop which however seemed to contain nothing but picture postcards. However he went inside and found that it contained just one book: Tolstoy on the Gospels. He bought it merely because there was no other. He read it and re-read it, and henceforth had it always with him under fire and at all times. But on the whole he likes Tolstoy less than Dosteoewski (especially Karamazov). He has penetrated deep into mystical ways of thought and feeling, but I think (though he wouldn't agree) that what he likes in mysticism is its power to make him stop thinking. (McGuinness and von Wright, p. 140)

Traces of James's Gifford Lectures can readily be discerned in the mystical features of the *Tractatus*—Russell dismissed these as his former student's "syntactical mysticism"—and Wittgenstein continued to have, as one of his own students reported, "a great admiration for James," with *The Varieties of Religious Experience* being "one of the few books he insisted I must read" ("Logical Positivism," p. 370; Drury, "A Symposium," p. 68).

It has also been suggested, quite plausibly, that Wittgenstein's signature notion of "family resemblance" itself bears more than a passing resemblance to James's account of the "varieties" of the subject under study. Drury remarks that "if I am not mistaken the category of *Varieties* continued to play an important part in his thinking" ("Some Notes," p. 108). Fann notes:

At the beginning of his second lecture on *The Varieties of Religious Experience*, James writes that "Most books on the philosophy of religion try to begin with a precise definition of what its essence consists of"; and a little later says: "The theorizing mind always tends to the oversimplification of its materials. This is the root of all that absolutism and one-sided dogmatism by which both philosophy and religion have been infested. Let us not fall immediately into a one-sided view of our subject but let us rather admit freely at the outset that we may very likely find *no one essence but many characters which may alternately be equally important to religion*." (*Wittgenstein's Conception*, p. 47, emphasis added)[4]

Nevertheless, it was principally Russell, not James, whom Wittgenstein sought to build on and correct in the *Tractatus*. Russell had long ceased to provoke the former syntactical mystic into thought when he returned to

Cambridge a decade later; and over the next dozen years James came to assume a role in Wittgenstein's meditations comparable to that formerly occupied by Russell—not, however, as the author of *The Varieties of Religious Experience* but of the earlier masterpiece, *The Principles of Psychology*.

Before World War I, experimental psychology had provided Wittgenstein with much-needed diversion from his work in logic, and after he resumed his philosophical studies in the late 1920s he often quarried psychology for examples of grammatical or "philosophical mistakes."[5] These were due, as he argued, to the virulent combination of "experimental methods and conceptual confusion" that characterized experimental psychology and cast doubt on the discipline's legitimacy as an empirical science (PI, p. 232e). Instead of leading to valid empirical propositions, the experimental methods of psychology compounded the conceptual confusion endemic to the discipline. "The existence of the experimental method," Wittgenstein proposed in wrapping up Part Two of the *Investigations*, "makes us think we have the means of solving the problems which trouble us; though problem and method pass one another by" (p. 232e). Or, as he observed in *Remarks on Colour*, where he linked "James's psychology," and in particular his theory of emotion, with Goethe's *Farbenlehre*:

> Goethe's theory of the origin of the spectrum isn't a theory of its origin that has proved unsatisfactory; it is really not a theory at all. *Nothing* can be predicted with it. It is, rather, a vague schematic outline, of the sort we find in James's psychology. There is no *experimentum crucis* for Goethe's theory of colour. (p. 32e)

Ever careful to distinguish his own "remarks on the philosophy of psychology" from the empirical study of psychology (which he regarded as based on sleight of hand, or sleight of mind, since psychology was neither empirical nor theoretical in the way that physics was), Wittgenstein typically used statements from *The Principles of Psychology* as starting points for the psychological investigations that preoccupied him in the mid- and late 1940s, and which were already central to Part One of *Philosophical Investigations*.[6] The 1970 *Wittgenstein Workbook*, for instance, lists nearly a fifth of the remarks in Part One (which Wittgenstein composed between 1936 and 1945), and fully a quarter of those in *Zettel* (dating for the most part from 1945 to 1948), as directly paralleling passages in James's textbook on matters ranging from "feelings of *if*, *but*, etc." to "feelings of tendency," " 'fringe' experiences," "producing and understanding sentences," "thought without language (the Ballard case)," "the Self of selves" and "emotions and bodily feelings" (Cope et al., p. 48). In investigating how we talk about psychology, Wittgenstein was in fact investigating how *James* talked about psychology. One student recalled how he "frequently referred to James in his lectures, even making on one occasion—to everybody's astonishment—a precise reference to a page-number" (cited in Passmore, p. 434). Another student reported that "when he was lecturing on belief," Wittgenstein highly uncharacteristically "read extracts from James's *Principles of Psychology*, and discussed them critically" (Mays, p. 83). The grammatical investigations of psychology of this most independent-minded of philosophers turn out to have largely been grammatical investigations of *The Principles of Psychology*.

Of particular interest, in the context of Stein's claims for the emotional character of paragraphs and the unemotional nature of sentences, are several remarks of Wittgenstein's in which he revisits James's theory of emotion. The first of these dates from 1934 or 1935, making it exactly contemporaneous with Stein's six-month lecture tour of the United States. "You will find," Wittgenstein observes,

> that the justifications for calling something an expression of doubt, conviction, etc., largely, though of course not wholly, consist in descriptions of gestures, the play of facial expressions, and even the tone of voice. Remember at this point that the personal experiences of an emotion must in part be strictly localized experiences; for if I frown in anger I feel the muscular tension of the frown in my forehead, and if I weep, the sensations around my eyes are obviously part, and an important part of what I feel. This is, I think, what William James meant when he said that a man doesn't cry because he is sad but that he is sad because he cries. The reason why this point is often not understood, is that we think of the utterance of an emotion as though it were some artificial device to let others know that we have it. ("The Brown Book," p. 103)

As the reader will recall, emotional consciousness was not, according to James, "a primary feeling, directly aroused by the exciting object or thought," but "a secondary feeling indirectly aroused [by] the organic changes, muscular and visceral, of which the so-called 'expression' of the emotion consists" (PBE, p. 346). It was this auto-sensation, the body feeling itself move in response to an initial sensation, which one experienced as emotion. This, in a nutshell, was James's theory of emotion, although it was not the theory Wittgenstein attributed to him.

Consider, for example, the following remarks, which date from 1946 or 1947:

> 451. And how does it come about that—as James says—I have a feeling of joy if I merely make a joyful face; a feeling of sadness, if I make a sad one?

That, therefore, I can produce these feelings by imitating their expression? Does that shew that muscular sensations are sadness, or part of sadness?

452. Suppose someone were to say: "Raise your arm, and you will feel that you are raising your arm." Is that an empirical proposition? And is it one if it is said: "Make a sad face, and you will feel sad"? . . .

456. Now granted—although it is extremely doubtful—that the muscular feeling of a smile is a constituent part of feeling glad;—where are the other components? Well, in the breast and belly etc.!—But do you really feel them, or do you merely conclude that they *must* be there? Are you really conscious of these localized feelings?—And if not—why are they supposed to be there at all? Why are you supposed to mean *them*, when you say you feel happy?

457. Something that could only be established through an act of looking— that's at any rate not what you meant.

For "sorrow," "joy" etc. just are not used like that. (RPP, I, pp. 88e–89e)

A decade earlier Wittgenstein had quite correctly suggested that James's theory of emotion differed from ordinary accounts in that James held the "expression" of the emotion to be "a constituent part" of the emotion's *internal composition*—contributing to the way the emotion feels to the person feeling it—and only secondarily a symptom, or sign, permitting *an external viewer* to infer the emotion from "gestures, the play of facial expressions, and even the tone of voice." "If I weep," Wittgenstein had observed, "the sensations around my eyes are obviously part, and an important part of what I feel. This is, I think, what William James meant when he said that a man doesn't cry because he is sad but that he is sad because he cries." Had this been the full extent of James's theory, then he was guilty only of expressing a noncontroversial thesis in an exaggerated manner. In his subsequent criticism, however, Wittgenstein took James's manner much more seriously. The neat inversion of "a man doesn't cry because he is sad but . . . is sad because he cries" turned out to involve considerable cognitive distortion, in particular the supposed reduction of emotions to sensations no different in kind from those one feels "around [one's] eyes when one is crying."

Wittgenstein insisted that, misled by the grammar of his theory, James imposed a third-person perspective on an inherently first-person experience. It was as if an emotion were "something that could only be established through an act of looking," whether by inspecting one's own face in order to determine "the muscular feeling of a smile" or by introspecting "localized feelings . . . in the breast and belly etc." Now, it is quite true that James alluded to feelings that were "localized" internally, as in his comment in "The Physical Basis of Emotion" that, however "hard" it proved "to describe" them, the sensations of internal bodily activity that accompanied externally observable bodily movement were undoubtedly "localized in divers parts of my organism" (p. 359). Yet James distinguished *these* sensations from the "sensible quality" that initiated the bodily movement in the first place. The experience of an emotion wasn't simply the summation, in no particular order, of a set of sensory "components" (such as "the perception of the exciting fact" plus "the muscular feeling of a smile" plus several localized feelings "in the breast and belly etc.") but the experience of a particular "succession" of sensations—sensations that, in Stein's phrasing, "make a succession" together.

James did not wish to "shew that muscular sensations *are* sadness," nor that such sensations are "part of sadness" in the sense that there is something *prima facie* emotional about them. As Wittgenstein himself observed a year later, even as he was taking James to task yet again for supposedly equating a "bodily sensation," in this case an imagined one, with an emotion or "something like it":

> Is it clear a priori that whoever imitates joy will feel it? Couldn't the mere attempt to laugh while one was feeling grief bring about an enormous sharpening of the grief? (RPP, II, p. 61e)

The only problem with this remark is that, far from demonstrating the inadequacies of James's theory, it actually proves quite consistent with it. Despite Wittgenstein's contention that James relied on a misleading analogy between sensation and emotion, the formulator of radical empiricism no more identified sensation and emotion than Stein equated sentences and paragraphs. Just as "emotional paragraphs" were "made up of unemotional sentences," emotions were composed of unemotional sensations.[7] What Stein recognized as she watched her poodle drinking water was that sentences and paragraphs were related in exactly the same way that sensations and emotions were; indeed, her thesis concerning the emotional nature of paragraphs was itself a variation on James's theory of emotion, only extended to writing.

A MORE COMPREHENSIVE SYNTAX

Wittgenstein's own mistake in the *Tractatus*, he explained to Friedrich Waismann and Moritz Schlick late in 1929, a year after his return to Cambridge, was in having relied on too circumscribed a notion of syntax. As a result, he had failed to attend to "the inner connection of propositions," that is, the grammatical connections between propositions, which formed a "more comprehensive syntax about which I did not yet know anything at the time" (Waismann, p. 74). His present "philosophical task," as Ray Monk observes in *Ludwig Wittgenstein: The Duty of Genius*, "lay in describing this more complicated syntax, and in making clear the role of 'internal connections' in inference" (p. 285). Ironically, the same year that Wittgenstein began to investigate the new syntax, Stein was demonstrating in her own studies that even as he extended the parameters of *syntax*, his conception of *grammar* remained overly circumscribed. If the model he proposed, of a sentence operating in the context of a language game rather than in the stream of consciousness, succeeded in emending both James's scheme and his own former conception of sentences or propositions removed from the stream, it also failed correspondingly to accommodate the paragraph. Despite the conception of a "more comprehensive syntax," and perhaps even due to it, the individual sentence remained the most comprehensive grammatical unit short of an entire language game. Yet, as anyone familiar with Wittgenstein's later work will know, the basic compositional unit of his writing shifted from the sentence, as in the *Tractatus*, to the paragraph, in the form of "remarks" (*Bermerkungen*) or "cuttings" (*Zettel*). This renders all the more striking the neglect in his "philosophical grammar" of the intermediate unit whose grammatical significance Stein was investigating in compositions like "More Grammar for a Sentence."

Stein's differences with Wittgenstein on the topic of grammar emerge particularly clearly in their respective phrases for the gray area that lies just outside the confines of the sentence and provides the minimal basis for judging a proposition's import: namely, *more grammar for a sentence* and *a more comprehensive syntax*. The difference in wording corresponds exactly to the *xtra* and *extra-marginal* that distinguished Stein from James. Whereas Wittgenstein proposed an expanded notion of syntax that remained continuous with the ordinary notion, Stein speculated on the possibility of a grammar that conjoined syntactically discrete units so as to provide "more grammar [more *breathing room*, more *life*, more *time* even] for a sentence" than that permitted by strictly syntactical, hence completely rational, systems. The "syntax" of a paragraph wasn't anything like the syntax of a sentence, and consequently Wittgenstein's expansion of the notion from sentence to language game skipped over a crucial stage in the production of meaning. Sentences in the Wittgensteinian universe only made sense in the context of use determined by particular language games; for Stein, by contrast, the minimal context in which a written sentence made sense was the paragraph. Although a given language game provided a more or less stable background, the sentence made unambiguous sense only with respect to the manner of "succession" that determined the "emotional balance" of the paragraph containing it. Therefore the meaning of any particular sentence proved, willy-nilly, a function of emotion and ultimately of physiology. Wittgenstein, however, eschewed both emotion and physiology in seeming to bridge sentence and language game without a hitch.

Needless to say, emotion returned through the back door. For what Wittgenstein didn't say, he showed—not because the matter at hand was logically impossible to state, as he suggested in the *Tractatus*, but because it was inconsistent with his theory. Wittgenstein once observed that Russell's failure (and his own) to provide specific examples of the elementary propositions posited by logical atomism should have indicated to them that there was something wrong with the theory. The equivalent problem with "practical holism," as David Stern has labeled the perspective expressed in Wittgenstein's later philosophy, is not the inadequate number of examples— there's no shortage of these—but the difficulty one encounters in trying to determine just what they are examples *of* (p. 120). Does the imagined utterance *For a second he felt deep grief* acquire its significance (or lack thereof, as an example of the sort of senseless non sequitur Wittgenstein sought to expose throughout his career) within the broader language games of English and German syntax, for instance, or only in the context of his immediate remarks, remarks that so often took the form, in his later writing, of discrete paragraphs?

Despite the apparent idiosyncrasy of his manner of composition, Wittgenstein in fact extended a long tradition of aphoristic, paragraph-length meditations in German- and French-language philosophical prose; unsurprisingly, he tended to narrate the development of his style within the framework of his own career. In the most celebrated of these accounts, the 1945 preface to *Philosophical Investigations*, he confessed that "after several unsuccessful attempts to weld my results together into . . . a whole," in which "the thoughts should proceed from one subject to another in a natural order and without breaks," he

> realized that I should never succeed. The best I could write would never be more than philosophical remarks; my thoughts were soon crippled if I tried to force them on in any single direction against their natural inclination.—And this was, of course, connected with the very nature of the investigation. For this compels us to travel over a wide field of thought criss-cross in every direction.—The philosophical remarks in this book are, as it were, a number of sketches of landscapes which were made in the course of these long and involved journeyings.

In other words, because his "natural inclination" was to presume that everything was connected, and yet, on the basis of his own argument in the *Tractatus*, he was obliged to reject the idea that a part was capable of synecdochically serving as a key to the whole, the only viable option was to "travel . . . criss-cross in every direction." Nevertheless, in characterizing the resulting "album" as "the *precipitate* of philosophical investigations" which had "occupied" him, as of 1945, "for the last sixteen years," Wittgenstein confirms the impression suggested by his reference to the "short paragraphs" in which he had "written down [his] thoughts," as comprising "a number of sketches of landscapes . . . made in the course of . . . long and involved journeyings" (PI, p. v). Clearly, he conceived of grammatical phenomena as features of an external rather than an internal landscape, in which meaning was a function of precipitation (on the model of chemical processes) rather than of emotion (on the model of physiology). This is not to say, of course, that he understood philosophy to be a sort of chemistry or physics, but rather that the increasingly comprehensive syntax he outlined was consistent with the external perspective of physics rather than with the internal or physiological perspective of James's radical empiricism.

Another account of Wittgenstein's compositional practice, dictated to a student a dozen years earlier, took its lead from "Schopenhauer's view that philosophy is an organism, and that a book on philosophy, with a beginning and end, is a sort of contradiction." "One difficulty with philosophy," Wittgenstein continued, "is that we lack a synoptic view. We encounter the kind of difficulty we should have with the geography of a country for which we had no map, or else a map of isolated bits. The country we are talking about is language, and the geography its grammar." Observing that each philosophical problem might be likened to a road on a map of this country, he added, "In philosophy matters are not simple enough for us to say 'Let's get a rough idea,' for we do not know the country except by knowing the connections between the roads." "So I suggest repetition," he concluded, "as a means of surveying the connections" (Nedo, p. 53, cited from Ambrose). In *Philosophical Investigations* he elaborated:

> The same or almost the same points were always being approached afresh from different directions, and new sketches made. Very many of these were badly drawn or uncharacteristic, marked by all the defects of a weak draughtsman. And when they were rejected a number of tolerable ones were left, which now had to be arranged and sometimes cut down, so that if you looked at them you could get a picture of the landscape. (p. v)

This is the closest Wittgenstein gets to discussing his compositional practice of "remarks" and "cuttings," but it is enough to demonstrate that although he denied the possibility of a "synoptic view" of the geography of language, he still conceived of grammar as "something that could only be established through an act of looking" and hence from the third-person perspective of traditional science (as he quite rightly suggested emotion could not be). Although Stein also stressed the centrality of looking in her compositional practice—"it is her eyes and mind that are active and important and concerned in choosing," she observed of herself—there was one crucial difference (ABT, p. 75). Stein conceived of such "active" looking along physiological lines rather than, like Wittgenstein, exclusively as a function of physical optics. "You see," she might thus explain to Toklas in the *Autobiography*, concerning the "surpris[ing]" absence of anything written in French among her reading matter: "I feel with my eyes and it does not make any difference to me what language I hear, I don't hear a language, I hear tones of voice and rhythms, but with my eyes I see words and sentences" (and, one might add, paragraphs). "There is for me only one language and that is english" (p. 70). *Feeling with one's eyes* is not exactly what Wittgenstein had in mind in composing *Philosophical Investigations* as he did, yet his writing inevitably calls forth some such experience in the reader determined to make sense of this most Emersonian of twentieth-century photo albums.

"The actual key to understanding" Wittgenstein's philosophy, Michael Nedo has suggested, "is the study of the connections between remarks: the complex trains of thought which run from one to the other" (p. 53). This is undoubtedly true, and it is what Wittgenstein himself implies, yet it also raises two questions. First, why should the remarks so consistently take the form of paragraphs; and second, what is such blatantly psychological phrasing ("complex trains of thought") doing here, when Wittgenstein expressly sought to substitute a logical and syntactical account of meaning for the traditional psychological account? The answer to both questions is not, it seems to me, that Nedo has made an embarrassing slip. Rather, Wittgenstein's paragraphing does the work, in his adamantly nonpsychological account, of the emotional or physiological mechanisms of psychology, without which neither he, nor his readers, would be able to get on with the masterful job of "surveying the connections." Such surveying requires the projection of "body feelings" whereby, as Langer argues, one models the "wholeness and simplicity of molar objects on that of [one's own] soma" (M, p. 321). To acknowledge this is certainly not to deny the great value of Wittgenstein's account of grammar, and the even greater value of his grammatical investigations. Yet it does require that one reject the residual appeal of a logic capable of producing the sort of self-contradiction that exists between his admittedly elegant, homogeneous model of *grammar as syntax* and the actually heterogeneous grammar of his investigations, composed of differences that, in Stein's terms, function not as contradictions but as combinations. The self-contradiction, it might be noted, sharply contrasts with the phoenixlike self-immolation that concludes the *Tractatus Logico-Philosophicus*.

FALSE ANALOGIES

Late in Part One of the *Investigations*, Wittgenstein rounded off a brief remark with the obscure observation, "Meaning is a physiognomy" (p. 151e). He was alluding here to a line of reasoning that stretched back at least a dozen years, to the "Big Typescript" of 1933, where he characterized the procedure of grammatical investigations such as his, in gradually mapping out a "more comprehensive syntax," as "mak[ing] a tracing of the physiognomy of every error" in order to make sense of its lack of sense. "The point is to hit upon the physiognomy of the thing" ("Philosophy," p. 165). By contrast, for Stein, as she put it in *The Autobiography of Alice B. Toklas*, "the human being essentially is not paintable," due to the inherently flat surface of painting (p. 119). Hence, from her perspective, Wittgenstein's likening of meaning to a traceable physiognomy was an error of precisely the kind he was using the analogy to specify. "If I correct a philosophical mistake," he had proposed,

> and say that this is the way it has always been conceived, but this is not the way it is, I always point to an analogy . . . that was followed, and show that this analogy is incorrect. . . . The effect of a false analogy . . . is as if a thing seemed to be a human being from a distance, because we don't perceive anything definite, but from close up we see that it is a tree stump. ("Philosophy," p. 163)

Drawing an analogy between meaning and a physiognomy that one might trace had the consequence, from Stein's perspective, of removing the emotional or physiological dimension from human beings and, in effect, reducing "the human form and the human face" to something compositionally indistinguishable from a tree stump (PCW, p. 40).[8]

"The philosopher strives," Wittgenstein continued in his remarks in the "Big Typescript," "to find" the word, or correct choice of words, that "finally permits us to grasp what up until now has intangibly weighed down our consciousness," and so "make a tracing of the physiognomy" of this "grammatical unclarity," this false analogy or "false thought process"

("Philosophy," p. 165). For in grasping the error *as* an error, in "hit[ting] upon the physiognomy of the thing," one rids oneself of something whose effect has been "a constant battle and uneasiness" (pp. 165, 163). Wittgenstein further likens this irritability to the experience of having "a hair on one's tongue: one feels it, but cannot grasp it, and therefore cannot get rid of it." When "the *irritating* character of grammatical unclarity" is removed, one is able to move forward unimpeded: "The car [now] placed on the tracks precisely so . . . can keep rolling correctly" (p. 165, emphasis added). "Philo-sophical problems arise when language goes on holiday," Wittgenstein fa-mously remarked in the *Investigations* (p. 19e). They arise, that is, "when language is like an engine idling, not when it is doing work"; and the idling is experienced as quasi-neurasthenic irritability (p. 51e).

In hitting upon the physiognomy of the thing, then, one sees its true face and true character. One sees what it means ("meaning is a physiognomy"), and in the case of error, or false analogy, one sees that it is actually a non sequitur, and therefore without meaning. Within this framework, meaning is understood to be a function of "a more comprehensive syntax," which operates on an exclusively analogical basis. Hence "tracing the outline of [a] thing's nature" involves tracing the network of analogies that constitutes it. Yet one may still inquire whether this physiognomic frame is itself im-mune from the criticism directed by Wittgenstein at "philosophical prob-lems" in general, and at those that had concerned him in the *Tractatus* in particular.

In philosophy, he observed, "naming appears as a *queer* connexion of a word with an object":

—And you really get such a *queer* connexion when the philosopher tries to bring out *the* relation between name and thing by staring at an object in front of him and repeating a name or even the word "this" innumerable times. For philosophical problems arise when language *goes on holiday*. And *here* we may indeed fancy naming to be some remarkable act of mind, as it were a baptism of an object. And we can also say the word "this" *to* the object, as it were *address* the object as "this"—a queer use of the word, which doubtless only occurs in doing philosophy. (PI, p. 19e)

Similarly, he remarked of proposition 4.5 of the *Tractatus* ("The general form of propositions is: This is how things are"):

That is the kind of proposition that one repeats to oneself countless times. One thinks that one is tracing the outline of the thing's nature over and over again, and one is merely tracing round the frame through which we look at it.

In the *Tractatus* a *"picture* held us captive," Wittgenstein concluded. "And we could not get outside it, for it lay in our language and language seemed to repeat it to us inexorably" (PI, p. 48e). This idling, the compulsive repetition of the same mystifying (and mystified) picture of propositional syntax, was due to "grammatical unclarity," and could only be resolved by exactly tracing the physiognomy of the false analogy in terms of which it was framed.

Yet a picture held Wittgenstein captive in the *Investigations* as well. This was the picture of *looking* (understood exclusively as a form of analysis, the tracing of syntactical relations) that he carried over to philosophy, analogically, from physics. Hence, according to Wittgenstein, when "William James got the idea" through a process of introspection "that the 'self' consisted mainly of 'peculiar motions in the head and between the head and throat,'" what this actually "shewed" was

> not the meaning of the word "self" (so far as it means something like "person," "human being," "he himself," "I myself"), nor any analysis of such a thing, but the state of a philosopher's attention when he says the word "self" to himself and tries to analyse its meaning. (pp. 124e–125e)

Needless to say, Wittgenstein was mistaken here. James's state of attention was *not* the ordinary "state of a philosopher's attention," not at least of the sort of philosopher who compulsively repeats "this" or "this is how things are" or even "this is how things look, analogically speaking." Jamesian introspection didn't actually show a "state" of attention at all, but a physiological *process* of attending; and Wittgenstein's description of James may usefully be contrasted with Stein's description of Picasso's manner of looking, in her 1938 account of his career—a very different form of physiognomic attention, indeed.

"The souls of people do not interest him," she observed. "That is to say for him the reality of life is in the head, the face and the body and this is for him so important, so pertinent, so complete that it is not at all necessary to think of any other thing and the soul is another thing." "A child," she explained,

> sees the face of its mother, it sees it in a completely different way than other people see it, I am not speaking of the spirit of the mother, but of the features and the whole face, the child sees it from very near, it is a large face for the eyes of a small one, it is certain the child for a little while only sees a part of the face of its mother, it knows one feature and not another, one side and not the other, and in his way Picasso knows faces as a child knows them and the head and the body.

In Wittgenstein's terms, the child does not see the parts of its mother's face as being each in an *analogous* relation to a whole; and consequently the child cannot trace its mother's physiognomy, "trace the outline of [her] nature." It isn't that there is something *there* which the child fails to see; rather, as Stein said of Picasso, it is a matter of "things [being] seen not as one knows them," not as a function, that is, of one's prior "convictions about what people are" and what "the human form and the human face" are, but of things seen "as they are when one sees them without remembering having looked at them," the way an infant may be supposed to see (PCW, pp. 40–41). In this way one actively "feels with [one's] eyes," as Stein suggested she did in her writing, and as Picasso did in painting and James in introspecting, rather than passively "tracing round the frame" through which "the physignomy of the thing" is registered *as* a physiognomy—as Wittgenstein continued to do in conceiving of meaning physiognomically.[9]

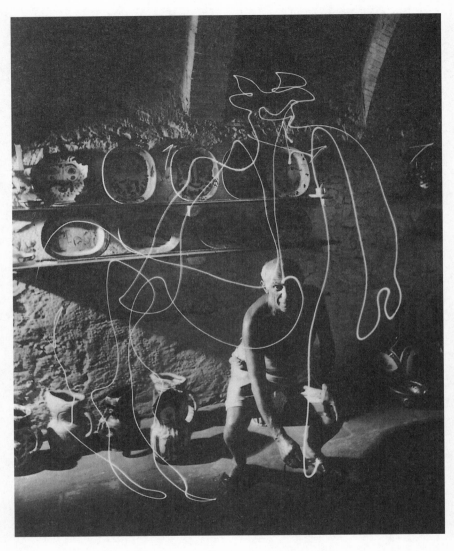

Figure 13.   A passionate line. (Gjon Mili / *Life Magazine*, January 30, 1950. © Time Inc.)

CHAPTER EIGHT

Conclusion: "Sentences Singing Themselves"

Consider an especially famous "passionate line" (Figure 13). At once un-broken in extension and incomplete in outline, this sketch of a centaur was recorded by the photographer Gjon Mili and published in 1950 in *Life*, aptly named crucible of twentieth-century photojournalism.[1] Now, on ex-actly what basis would a viewer refer to Picasso's drawing as *a passionate line*, forcibly yoking linear and nonlinear registers? The oxymoronic char-acterization occurs near the close of an important recent account of the neu-rophysiology of consciousness by J. Allan Hobson, in which human experi-ence is mapped in terms of the interrelations among three conscious states: waking, dreaming (or REM sleep), and deep NREM (non-rapid eye move-ment) sleep. Director of the Neurophysiology Laboratory at Harvard Med-ical School and professor of psychiatry there, Hobson describes Picasso as composing the sketch, magicianlike, "on *thin air* in the dark, with a light instead of a pencil" (p. 219, emphasis added).[2] "Hopped up on wild cre-ative and sexual energy, [he] turned himself loose on his canvas to create records of dynamic passion." Hobson clearly views Picasso as something of a centaur, half-animal, half-human; and no doubt this is how Picasso sought to portray himself in the photograph, with the centaur an extension of the protean artist and the two figures joined by the barely legible flashlight in the lower right-hand corner. Several pages later Hobson notes that, in pre-paring lectures (and, by implication, in assembling his profusely illustrated study), he tends to use "visual images" to "convey [his] points" (p. 222). What point does the Mili photograph convey? Presumably, if Picasso is "*hopped up* on wild creative and sexual energy"—hence subject to "power-ful automatic forces"—yet he also "personifies the plastic potential of hu-man consciousness," as Hobson states, then he perfectly illustrates the "paradoxical dynamic" that, according to Hobson, distinguishes the behav-ior of "the brain-mind" from that of other complex systems (pp. 218–19). In other words, Picasso offers an exemplary conjunction of the two varieties of irresistible dictation jointly responsible for the all-too-human predicament of being (and feeling oneself to be) simultaneously passive and active, stimulated and self-motivated.

Echoing Whitehead's three-quarter-century-old coinage *organic mechanism*, Hobson uses the phrase *creative automaton* to sum up this heterogeneous dialectic: "Without automatism we could not survive. Without creativity we could not embellish and refine our survival" (p. 219). More immediately, as he acknowledges in jumping straight from the Picasso self-portrait to a brief verbal sketch of B. F. Skinner, he seeks with his "paradoxical" phrasing to correct Skinner's overemphasis on the role of reflex conditioning in human behavior. "It is a little-known fact," he observes, "that Skinner participated in some of the earliest experiments on the brain basis of consciousness." Apparently, "Skinner's friend and colleague Hallowell Davis . . . hooked [him] up to his EEG machine in the physiology department at Harvard Medical School one day in 1937":

> [Aiming] to demonstrate the dependence of conscious state upon brain (and vice versa), Davis asked Skinner to close and open his eyes, whereupon the alpha rhythm in Skinner's EEG waxed and waned. Then, to show the effect of intense mental effort on the EEG, Davis asked Skinner to solve some difficult math problems in his head. Amusingly, the most impressive EEG activation occurred when Skinner was told that one of his calculations was incorrect. Davis and Skinner were studying not only activation and alertness but the contribution of emotion to conscious state as well.

"To Skinner's great credit," Hobson adds, "he carefully kept these precious historical artifacts and generously shared them with me. But I don't think he ever imagined that these very records would provide a link between his behaviorism and today's cognitive science, a field whose validity and promise he so steadfastly denied" (p. 220).

Hobson's decision to express Skinner's empiricist preference for discrete objects in his own phrasing (creative *automaton*) in lieu of the Whiteheadian emphasis on process (organic *mechanism*) is entirely consistent with the desire to retain the link with Skinner, and so establish a prestigious, if unlikely, pedigree for cognitive science. Yet within its natively empiricist framework *creative automaton* is truly paradoxical, or self-contradictory, and only serves to confuse the picture—unlike *organic mechanism* in a radical empiricist framework. All oxymorons, it seems, are not equally viable; what, then, of *a passionate line*? In the first place, a line makes for a rather peculiar object. Typically, it functions as a means of distinguishing a given object from its surroundings, or two objects against a common background.

(Here one might recall the discussion, in Chapter 5, of the dynamic unconscious as *a dividing line*.) It is also, of course, an abstraction as well as the building block for ever higher levels of abstraction. A passionate line, by contrast, has ceased to function geometrically—and, in failing to delineate the requisite borders, can no longer be classed as an exclusively abstract phenomenon. The question that then presents itself is whether a line that possesses "the vibration of a musical sound," as Stein characterized the equivalent "problem" confronted by Picabia, is exclusively a function of *physical* vibrations or whether it ought to be construed as an inherently *physiological* matter, and more radically as an *emotional* experience, so that one can't be accused of speaking metaphorically in calling it "passionate" (ABT, p. 210). By the same token, one must ask whether Hobson, in alluding to Picasso's sketch as he does, is speaking from the vantage point of an empiricist, hence metaphorically, or whether he means exactly what he says, in proper radical empiricist fashion.

I take it that the sense of fit, or propriety, which accompanies the allusion is due to the fact that no strict dividing line exists between the drawing and the artist, as Mili's photograph so clearly demonstrates. (The clarity does not take the form of a clear and distinct idea, however; as an emergent property of the process Stein labeled *composition as explanation*, it is experienced as knowledge of acquaintance rather than as knowledge-about.) Any drawing consists, quite literally, of traces left behind by the artist; what sets the joint Picasso-Mili venture apart is that here this is *patently* the case. Yet the compositional tour de force does not suffice to explain the attribution of passion to the line. Instead, the work's suggestiveness, its resonance, derives from the multiple correlations among its features, starting with the parallel that Hobson draws between Picasso and the centaur. Corresponding to this hybrid creature (Picasso-centaur), there is both the inner hybridity of the centaur itself (animal-man) and the hybrid form of the artistic medium (drawing-photograph). Moreover, coincident with Picasso fashioning flesh and bones for some purely imaginary thing, Mili improbably captures the quasi-divine act on film; and while Picasso grasps the mythological creature's lineaments in his mind's eye—*actively feeling with his eyes*, as I termed the process in Chapter 7—Mili records Picasso's internal experience in the external medium of the photographic image. Finally, in connecting Picasso's hand (poised to begin sketching) to his eyes (already establishing parameters for the sketch), the illuminated drawing suggests a coordination that preexists the organs' synchronized movements. Frozen without exactly being quieted, situated directly at the centaur's navel, the artist's eyes inhabit a state of mind where pure potential proves indistinguishable from impure thoughts. The vibrating line, the experience of passion, even Mili's photograph, are all *Picasso's*—that is, they are his because they are compositions of his as well as autopoietic renderings of himself.

The point I want to emphasize, as the present cross-disciplinary study draws to a close, is that multiple correlations among diverse modalities are not only responsible for the viewer's sense of Picasso's sketch as intrinsically passionate; they also serve as the basis for Hobson's explanation of "the unity of consciousness in the face of the modularity of the brain" and for the mechanisms whereby Stein's own dissociative sentences function as *vibrating lines* (p. 72). Hypothesizing that "the brain creates the unity of conscious experience via the synchronization of its elements," Hobson further speculates that such synchrony occurs concurrently not just at one level but at two (p. 57). In the first place, neurons apparently oscillate in unison at greater and lesser frequencies, resulting in "electrical synchrony" throughout the brain, or "global binding" (pp. 73, 72).[3] Such "brain cell rhythmicity" is complemented by metabolic modulation, which "alter[s] the chemical microclimate in which the neurons of various modular components of the brain" operate according to "guidelines" set by the reticular formation. (The formation is an "intricate network [of] cellular interconnections," which, looking something "like a pair of sausages, occupies the central core on each side of the brainstem as it ascends from the medulla upward through the pons and the midbrain to the hypothalamus.") "Our experience of consciousness," Hobson explains, "is determined by the neurochemical modulatory systems of the brainstem core," among them "the locus coeruleus-based noradrenergic system[,] the raphe nucleus-based serotonergic system[,] the midbrain-based dopaminergic system[,] and the hypothalamus-based histaminergic system," which are variously implicated in conscious functions such as alertness, "restraining motor action," and "facilitating . . . positive emotion" (pp. 72–73, 68–69, 73–74).

To illustrate how the reticular formation serves to integrate consciousness, Hobson instructs the reader to "let [the] reticular nucleus [of the thalamus] relax a bit." "You will feel drowsy. Let go a bit more and your eyes will glaze, then close, as you drift off to sleep. For this to occur, the level of firing of the cells in the midbrain and pontine reticular formation must fall enough to allow the thalamic reticular cells [to begin] beating to an intrinsic rhythm that is a function of their own excitatory and inhibitory features." With the activation of "this intrinsic oscillation[,] the thalamic relay cells [cease to be] available to transmit data from the body and the world to the cortex and back again in an organized way." Consciousness is thereby "impaired," permitting the onset of sleep (p. 71). In Chapter 2, I proposed that

Stein's compositional procedures in the dissociative writing she produced between 1912 and 1932 *involved a form of meditation which, although it certainly did not result in sleep, and was voluntary rather than involuntary, did induce a form of rest or withdrawal from the anxieties of daily living that might readily be confused with the neurasthenic symptoms of encephalitis.* I can now add, availing myself of Hobson's terms, that in the writing of the previous decade, between 1903 and 1912, she methodically trained herself to accommodate "the oscillations of the thalamocortical circuits" in such a manner that the metabolic synchrony did not lead directly to sleep but instead served to increase her neuraesthetic awareness, although at an apparent cost to "organized . . . consciousness" (p. 71).[4]

In that decade Stein had progressed from a fairly traditional conception of writing as a tool for thinking about matters that intimately concern one to an understanding of it as a medium that, through better acquaintance, permits one to become increasingly attuned to the complex interrelations that actually compose the objects of one's thought (as well as one's sense of oneself). This shift involved, first, replacing the generally derivative style and narrative frame of *Q.E.D.* with the uncanny juxtaposition in "Melanctha" of a prose style that seems to break free of all available templates and a narrative organized around the brute fact of Melanctha's death. Then, between 1906 and 1911, Stein brought her considerable analytic resources to bear on conjoined studies of the elementary rhythms of prose and the full range of personality types. Finally, after 1910 these general investigations were supplemented by equally ambitious studies of individual rhythms of speech and self-expression in portraits of acquaintances as well as in literally unclassifiable works like "G.M.P." and "Two." Consequently, it was only with close to a decade's worth of disciplined attention to intonational patterns already behind her that Stein set out to investigate the aperiodic rhythms, "correlating sight, sound and sense," which functioned as the warp (to the intonational woof) of her compositional practices over the next two decades.

The compositionally heterogeneous works of 1911–13 show Stein gradually substituting one variety of vibratory line for another. Strings of words in which individual phrases acquire resonance against a backdrop of similarly constructed sentences make way for others that contain traces of their compositional landscapes within themselves, in "interspaces" that function synaptically as well as syntactically. These works also suggest a basic complementarity among the two sorts of sentence construction, for even in patently dissociative writing Stein sought to recreate the resonance carried by vocal intonation, albeit in an expressly *visual* medium. Typically, in reading sentences composed in the second manner one finds oneself, sooner or later, at an utter loss as to how to proceed. The hesitancy continues until one shifts one's attention from the absent intonational cues (so crucial for following *The Making of Americans* and the earliest portraits) to visual cues designed by Stein to communicate the requisite eye movements, which, in conjunction with patterns of sound and word meaning, permit one to enjoy, and so begin to understand, otherwise impenetrable sentences. Sentences such as these: "Way mouth, soph, chive, bee, so, it, any, muse, in, lee, vie"— see Chapter 2—or "The regular way of instituting clerical resemblances and neglecting hazards and bespeaking combinations and heroically and heroically celebrating instances, the regular way of suffering extra challenges, the regular way of suffering extra changes, the regular way of suffering extra changes the regular way of submitting to examples in changes, the regular way of submitting to extraordinary celebrations, the certainty, because keep centre well half full whether it has that to close when in use, no not repeatedly, he has forgotten" (Chapter 4), or "Next. / Not next. / Not next to north. / Not annexed. / Not next to it. / And not next to it. / Next to it" (Chapter 6), or "He looks like a young man grown old" (Chapter 7). Of course, from sentence to sentence the cues vary; for example, in the portmanteau sentence just cited from "Sentences and Paragraphs," one finds oneself hesitating only *after* having completed it. Everything seemed to follow, yet somehow it doesn't add up. To be sure, in sentences like this one Stein no longer sought to "correlat[e] sight, sound and sense"; on the contrary, she was now "eliminating sight and sound" as compositional variables in order to investigate a host of *grammatical* features instead. Still, in deliberately eliminating (that is to say, repressing) the two sensory modalities, she guaranteed their indirect participation in the composition of her most recent sentences. *He looks like a young man grown old* is, after all, a highly recursive piece of writing, however straightforward and unadorned it may appear at first glance. The reader keeps returning to it to see if something has been overlooked, and this inability to let go, to move on, creates the conditions for the line's emotional resonance. It also provides a physiological basis for recreating what Stein variously termed "real thinking" and "real conversation."[5]

THE WAY PEOPLE REALLY TALK

In Chapter 5, I cited James's observation in *The Principles of Psychology* that "a reader incapable of understanding four ideas in the book he is reading aloud [may] nevertheless read it with the most delicately modulated expression of intelligence." James accounted for this discrepancy between "expression" and "understanding" by positing a "foreboding of the coming grammatical scheme combined with each successive word." "How comes it about," he asked,

> that a man reading something aloud for the first time is able immediately to emphasize all his words aright, unless from the very first he have a sense of at least the form of the sentence yet to come, which sense is fused with his consciousness of the present word, and modifies its emphasis in his mind so as to make him give it the proper accent as he utters it?

"Emphasis of this kind," he added, "is almost altogether a matter of grammatical construction" (p. 245 [BC, p. 164]). Yet is intonation so readily reducible to grammar, at least grammar understood, as James understands it here, as an exclusively formal consideration? What of his own sentence, which even as it takes the form of a question supplies an answer to the question being asked? Can someone articulate James's words "aright" without recognizing that they serve simultaneously as question and as answer? The words exist in both a grammatical and an extra-grammatical register, and a "proper accent" testifies to the recognition, however vague, that the meaning of the sentence hinges on the way it answers itself. In thus turning in or turning back on itself, the sentence adds resonance to the more mechanical grammatical construction.

It is important to note that when James speaks of the "proper accent," he is characterizing the accent proper to the sentence—the pattern of accentuation that elicits its general meaning, that renders it intelligible—rather than a set of habituated speech patterns that the reader might be expected to bring to the sentence. The proper accent is not Boston Brahmin or late nineteenth-century International American. Nonetheless, James's "man reading something aloud for the first time" is clearly not reading for the first time; nor is he reading something like *this* for the first time. Had the sentence turned out to possess an entirely unfamiliar shape—had it been, for instance, one of the "delicately modulated" long sentences of the late novels of William's brother Henry—and had the reader been exposed hitherto only to the sentence constructions of the daily press, then the grammar would presumably have served to *prevent* a properly accented first reading. Stein routinely encountered some such discrepancy between present and prior experience when she tried to get her compositions published, and Georgiana Goddard King confronted it as well when she sought to place an article on Stein in mid-1913. A specialist in Spanish art and culture, King taught at Bryn Mawr from 1906 through the 1930s, first in the English department, where Marianne Moore studied "Imitative Prose" with her, and after 1912 in the newly formed Art History department. As early as the winter of 1907, Stein was making arrangements for King to read the tales later published as *Three Lives*, and until well into the next decade she regularly sent copies of manuscripts to King to read. In a letter dated July 13, 1913, King described her unsuccessful attempts to find a publisher for her own essay: "I wrote a piece about you for Harper's Weekly that I am not sure you would have approved—it was a sort of easy introduction to the real thing—but Mr. Martin took fright & would not have it as an editorial & Lawrence Gilman is no friend of mine & would not have it elsewhere. Mrs. Dodge [Mabel Dodge] talked of Collier's but they would not either—& I tried the Newark Sunday Call, which has a big circulation, & which took my piece about the pictures [in the recent Armory Show]—but even that balked."

In the still-unpublished essay, King alludes to the verisimilitude of the dialogue in Henry James's more recent fiction and notes that instead of crafting "carefully dovetailed" utterances, with "each speaker answering the foregoing and leading up to the next," James writes "the way people really talk."[6] As in actual conversation, "nobody answers the last sentence uttered" but rather "answers something away back, or just about to be said." In addition to constructing dialogue this way, James "let[s] his sentences sprout and ramify and flow in the direction that actual talk goes" as well. When King spells out the consequences that such fecund prose may have on the experience of reading it, her characterization strikingly echoes William James's more general claims for reading aloud. "Who ever has read aloud one of the later novels," she observes, "knows how the long, beautiful sentences unroll themselves with the voice, and how it is simply impossible to read them wrong or to miss the point."[7] Against William James's suggestion that proper accentuation may be dissociated from understanding—that it is possible to read aright *and* miss the point—King proposes that at least in the case of his brother's fluent sentences it cannot be done. With respect to these long, beautiful sentences, "reading right" and "getting the point" are necessarily correlated, and as a result the writing of the younger James serves as a counterexample to the elder's claims for the "expression of intelligence."[8] It may appear that King extends the parameters of her own observation quite improbably to *anyone* "reading aloud one of the later novels," but this is not so. She does not suppose that every reader will share the experience she describes. Her reader must have chosen to read Henry James aloud (the better, presumably, to catch the "delicate modulations" of his sentences); this does not include readers who, having found the sentences too long and the studied intricacies ever so meaningless, never reach this stage.

The correlation of intonation and meaning that operates in James's sentences is a particular instance of what the novelist Hugh Vereker, in James's 1896 novella "The Figure in the Carpet," refers to as his "little point": "It's stuck into every volume as your foot is stuck into your shoe. It governs every line, it chooses every word, it dots every i, it places every comma." This is the writing's "organ of life"; and when the narrator suggests that it is "something like a complex figure in a Persian carpet," Vereker replies: "It's the very string . . . that my pearls are strung on!" (pp. 206, 210, 217). Quite appropriately, Dwight Bolinger makes use of the same figure in his magisterial study, *Intonation and Its Parts: Melody in Spoken English*:

> Running through [the] fabric of organized sound there is a master thread that
> holds it all together and by its weavings up and down and in and out shows the
> design of the whole—the motifs from phrase and sentence to paragraph and
> discourse.

"These points of emphasis," Bolinger continues, "that are made so naturally by the human voice can only be suggested in writing" (p. 3). Yet surely King's point is that James does more than *only* suggest (supposing, for the moment, that suggestion in writing actually is less "naturally" emphatic than is speech). It is the writing's correspondence with "actual talk," the way the sentences, "unrolling themselves with the voice," display something like perfect pitch, that best describes his achievement.

If James recreates the rhythms of speech in writing, Stein takes the next step in "catching that fugitive essence, thought, and reweaving the many colored web with all its evernescent [sic] shades and shifting tones." For King (and, as she argues, for Stein), the "stuff of consciousness" is largely composed of ever nascent, ever fugitive shades and tones, like those rendered in the "very curious" style of "Melanctha." These are "intricate and yet simple, colorless and yet surcharged with personality, full of repetitions and insistences and recurrent formulas falling into a kind of rhythm like nursery crooning." With "Melanctha," King goes on to observe, "it seemed as if simplification could no further go to the conscious naiveté that deliberately makes itself as a little child, throws over all the formulas of style so painfully learned, and resolutely sets down the things that happen inside one, actually as they happen."

Yet, according to King, Stein's subsequent portraits of Matisse and Picasso did not merely conserve this neuraesthetic "chanting tune." In them, the tunefulness "was much more marked" than it had previously been, with "the sentences [singing] themselves like an air on a shepherd's pipe":

The odd colorless fidelity to intellectual processes was preserved, and now there was a kind of further abstractness of form, a deliberate neglect of those grammatical constructions which are too sharp and too rigid to express the incessant flux, the perpetual becoming of consciousness.

By reducing "formal logic" and "formal grammar" to their simplest terms (and therefore preserving a "colorless fidelity to intellectual processes" even as she "supplants the relative clause . . . by the participle, the noun by the pronoun, the active verb by the auxiliary"), "the author," as King puts it, "wonderfully emancipat[es] thought."[9] Such liberation would not have passed muster, however, had Stein not also recreated the stream of consciousness in terms of "the stream of sound," in Bolinger's happy formulation (p. 3).[10]

Bolinger argues in *Intonation and Its Parts* that patterns of accentuation, which express the speaker's feelings about what is being said, always have some bearing on an utterance's discursive meaning. As he remarks in the companion volume, *Intonation and Its Uses*, "how we feel about what we say" is never simply a matter of "how we feel *when* we say," for in shaping what we say, the feeling becomes part of what we have to say (p. 1). This is presumably why he speaks of "the fundamental iconic nature of intonation"; and, as such, intonation represents a particular form of the more general phenomenon that Stein labeled *composition as explanation* (p. viii). "Accent configurations" or "profiles" occur in three distinct varieties, depending on "how the pitch jump cueing the accent is realized" (INT, p. 139). In Profile A an "accent at a relatively high pitch" is "followed by a jump down" (p. 142). In Profile B "the accent is jumped up to" (p. 152). In Profile C it is jumped down to.[11] Bolinger also distinguishes between the "composition" of an intonation, whereby "'ideas' are communicated metaphorically through the feelings that express them," and the "organization" of a sentence (its diction, grammar, and phonemics), which is "largely a computational skill." If, as Bolinger argues, "the choice of the words . . . from more or less arbitrary sets of words," their combination according to "the fairly exact rules of grammar," and their coding "using a precise and limited set of sounds that combine not freely but in ways differently determined" are all largely computational rather than compositional tasks, the wordplay introduced by Stein into her writing in 1911 and 1912 was clearly intended to transform such computational procedures into more compositional ones (pp. vii–viii).

According to Bolinger, profiles make up a "domain of ups and downs that are significant as ups and downs and not merely as obtrusions from a

reference line." The meanings associated with change in pitch "ultimately
. . . derive (whether historically or ontogenetically or both) from metaphors
associated with rising and falling, which are shared with facial expressions
and bodily gestures." Thus Profile A "conveys notions related to termination," because its terminal fall is "a coming-to-rest" (p. 341). It is "the assertive profile par excellence" (p. 164). By contrast, the meaning of B, "the
opposite of A on the 'finality' axis," is " 'upness' carried through various
metaphorical transformations, two especially: 'up-in-the-airness' or 'incom-
pletion,' and 'keyed-upness' or high emotivity, which may be excitement,
anger, surprise, or merely the curiosity that goes with having a question to
ask" (p. 341). Finally, C, which "is typified by a holding down of the accented syllable but with no downward jump from that syllable," has "metaphorical associations related to reining in, checking, restraint" (p. 342).
"Where A singles things out," Bolinger remarks, "B ties them in"; "where A
tends to play up, to emphasize, to suggest contrast or newness, C plays down,
deemphasizes, and often implies foreknowledge" (pp. 166, 178).

Intonation serves as a primary compositional principle in Stein's writing—sometimes dominant, sometimes less so, sometimes almost wholly absent. It is probably most decisive in large portions of *The Making of Americans*, where what Stein calls "rhythm" (King's "chanting tune") sets the
tone and, consequently, the meaning. Because the sentences repeat one another, with only slight shifts of emphasis, and are often inwardly patterned
as well, their shapes can be anticipated, if not entirely predicted, on the basis of how they begin. Wordplay involving single words, and wordplay between words, is kept at a minimum. In a composition like the 1911 "Matisse," intonation still dominates wordplay, whereas in "If I Told Him. A
Completed Portrait of Picasso," dating from 1923, the two are more
equably balanced. By contrast, the pieces collected in *Tender Buttons* are
carefully composed *against* the establishment of intonational norms, especially those repeated sentence to sentence. Sound continues to play a central
role—correlated, as Stein suggested, with "sight . . . and sense"—but it is
dissociated from "rhythm" (TBr, p. 13). The foreboding of the coming intonational scheme (to slightly revise James's phrasing) is deliberately dis-
rupted: "A kind in glass and a cousin, a spectacle and nothing strange a single hurt color and an arrangement in a system to pointing. All this and not
ordinary, not unordered in not resembling. The difference is spreading"
(TB, p. 9). Insisting on *difference* creates its own system of ordering; nevertheless, as a principle of composition, *spreading* sets itself directly against
the ups and downs of more accentually based procedures.

"Now I am trying grammar and eliminating . . . sound," Stein observed in distinguishing her present experimental parameters from the equivalent "problem" she had tackled sixteen years earlier. The works that emerged from the more recent program contain sentences constructed very differently from those in *Tender Buttons*, yet an accurate "foreboding" of their contours proves equally impossible. In "Arthur A Grammar," presumably the work she was directly contrasting with *Tender Buttons*, Stein asserts that "there can be no confusion between a sun behind a cloud or behind a mountain. / Landscape is not grammar" (HTW, p. 98).[12] As grammatical constructions, *behind a cloud* and *behind a mountain* are formally identical, but situating them in a landscape removes any possible confusion. Bolinger makes a similar claim for intonation when he observes that "though strictly speaking the term INTONATION includes the mere fact of there *being* one or more accents, it is generally used to refer to the overall landscape, the wider ups and downs that show greater or lesser degrees of excitement, boredom, curiosity, positiveness, etc." (INT, p. 11). Intonation is not grammar; rather, it provides a compositional landscape for grammar, and thereby provides grammatical constructions with determinate significance. It is certainly not the only "landscape" that can do so, nor is it the only one that Stein made use of in her compositions. Other comparable landscapes include the paragraph, the manuscript page, and the manuscript notebook. In addition, more obviously poetic devices such as stanzas and other verse or metrical forms serve a similar function, although these are typically less central to Stein's writing; and, of course, she used portmanteau sentences and an astonishingly wide range of grammatical wordplay to put the very conception of grammar as a strictly formal, rule-bound phenomenon to the test. Even so, attending to the intonational contours of her sentences generally enables one to recite them with the sort of "delicately modulated expression of intelligence" that William James mistakenly believed did not entail genuine understanding.

It is this impression of intelligibility—of meaning carried by intonation—that Stein herself supplied in reading her work aloud, as the American sculptor Jo Davidson noted in his autobiography *Between Sittings*:

> While I was doing her portrait [in 1922], she would come around to my studio with a manuscript and read it aloud. The extraordinary part of it was that, as she read, I never felt any sense of mystification. "A rose is a rose is a rose," took on a different meaning with each inflection. When she read aloud, I got the humor of it.

Similarly, on hearing Stein read aloud a portrait that she had composed of him, Davidson thought it "wonderful"; and Lincoln Steffens testified in his

Autobiography that, having witnessed Stein recite the portrait but "unable to hear distinctly all the words, the reading sounded like the sculptor mono-loguing at his work—but exactly" (Simon, *A Composite Portrait*, p. 96; Mellow, p. 304). Yet Davidson adds that when the portrait was published soon after in *Vanity Fair*, and he "tried to read it out loud to some friends, or for that matter to myself, it didn't make much sense." The sentences did not unroll themselves with his voice. This failure to read with sufficient ex-pression of intelligence was due not to any inadequacy of voice or text but to the sculptor's relatively undeveloped sense of the mechanisms, the *or-ganic* mechanisms, that enabled "proper accentuation" to create a setting for Stein's writing—a landscape, as he noted, within which "each inflec-tion" might take on "a different meaning."[13]

INTONATIONAL CONTOURS

"That is what makes life," Stein explained in a passage already cited in Chapter 4, and then again in "The Will to Live": "that the insistence is dif-ferent, no matter how often you tell the same story if there is anything alive in the telling the emphasis is different." According to Stein, she herself "first really realized" the significance of this principle, and so became "really con-scious of it," only after she returned to Baltimore at the age of seventeen to live "with a lot of my relations and principally with a whole group of very lively little aunts who had to know anything":

> That inevitably made everything said often. I began then to consciously listen to what anybody was saying and what they did say while they were saying what they were saying. This was not yet the beginning of writing but it was the begin-ning of knowing what there was that made there be no repetition. (LIA, pp. 167–69)

It was this finely honed sense of intonation's import—of what gets said *while* something is being said—that Stein brought to her writing, both in composing it and in reading it aloud. Listening to her aunts "was *not yet* the beginning of writing," however, since "the same person [was not doing] the talking and the listening." Stein was listening but not to herself. Conse-quently, she couldn't yet be said to have acquired an adequate sense of *writ-ing*, of what it felt like, as she proposed forty years later, to be "most in-tensely alive, that is being one who is at the same time talking and listening, . . . doing both things, not as if there were one thing, not as if they were two things, but [as] part of the same thing" (p. 170).

Several months into the triumphant 1934–35 lecture tour, which was itself structured around a similar division of labor, Stein made the audio recording at Columbia. Like *Geography and Plays* a decade earlier, it contained examples of a wide range of her experimental work; yet unlike that collection, or *Portraits and Prayers*, published to coincide with the start of the tour, or for that matter any of her published texts, it also demonstrates the extent to which careful articulation of the intonational patterns woven into her compositions permits one to make sense of them.[14] Hence as a final approach to the *irresistible dictation* that Stein devoted so much of her writing life to investigating, I have elected to diagram the intonational contours of several excerpts from the recording—limiting myself to two brief paragraphs from *The Making of Americans*, the opening paragraph of "Matisse," and the first third or so of "If I Told Him. A Completed Portrait of Picasso." These diagrams should not be confused, however, with the *self-diagramming* of sentences, "the one thing," Stein admitted, that she found "completely exciting and completely completing" (LIA, p. 211). No doubt, as she patiently explained to audience after audience from the New School for Social Research in New York to Mills College in Oakland, her sense of sentences putting themselves together as they went along could be traced back to the grammar-school experience of analyzing already completed sentences in terms of their formal constituents. Still, the sentence diagramming that so excited her differed from that taught "at school" in two crucial respects. First, she extended the practice to all sorts of compositional elements, not just grammatical ones; and second, she credited the sentences with having a hand in their own diagramming.[15] From her perspective, the "everlasting[ness]" that adheres to the "feeling of sentences diagramming themselves" does so not because grammatical structure exists in an abstract, timeless realm, but because it exists concretely, in recursive, self-diagramming acts of composition.[16] Hers is an understanding of grammar, and of the role that grammar plays in understanding, designed to appeal to the sort of person for whom, as Whitehead said of James, "abstract generalization" and "detailed facts" possess interest, and are therefore felt to exist, only in *relation* to each other (SMW, p. 3).

The intonational diagrams constructed below are variants of the sentence diagrams taught (or once taught) in grammar schools, applied to Stein's own self-diagramming sentences. For these diagrams I have adopted the framework developed by Bolinger in *Intonation and Its Parts*, in which the contour of an utterance is built up from profiles detailing "how much intonational ornamentation, so to speak, can surround one accent" (p. 141). An accentual profile comprises the "minimal morphological unit of intonation," while a contour, as "the shape of a complete intonation," functions as the "syntactic unit" and takes the form of one or more profiles (pp. 140, 254). I have also heeded Bolinger's observation that "probably the majority of well-executed longer utterances have a shape and an organizational base that corresponds to [a] question-answer pair," with "the second half 'answer[ing]' the question" implicit in the first half (p. 46). ("'Well-executed' represents an ideal," Bolinger admits: "The speaker plans ahead and is not interrupted." Obviously, in Stein's case, as in *real* conversation, the plan typically involves leaving room for interruption.) James's self-answering question turns out to be the rule rather than the exception, even if B + A contours, which Bolinger also calls "hat-patterned" utterances because a jump *up* to an accent is brought to a close with a jump *down* from a subsequent accent, rarely take so grandly rhetorical a form.

The diagrams should be self-explanatory. I've tried to limit the representation of pitch to three basic levels, with a horizontal line marking the middle level, and with each level supporting three very approximate registers (slightly higher, slightly lower, and median). Repeated consonants or vowels indicate that the sound in question has been lengthened or otherwise made to stand out. Contours of completed utterances that don't coincide with the end of a sentence are distinguished with a double line (//). (I have also used this symbol to frame contours that consist of a single profile.) At the end of each excerpt I comment briefly on some of the ways the intonational scheme contributes to the "point" of the writing. These remarks are intended merely to suggest directions that a more complete intonational analysis of Stein's writing might take.

The Making of Americans *(selection)*

Repeating then is in every one, in every one their being and their feeling and their way of realising everything and every one comes out of them in repeating. More and more then every one comes to be clear to some one.

Slowly every one in continuous repeating, to their minutest variation, comes to be clearer to some one. Every one who ever was or is or will be living sometimes will be clearly realised by some one. Sometime there will be an ordered history of every one. Slowly every kind of one comes into ordered recognition. More and more then it is wonderful in living the subtle variations coming clear into ordered recognition, coming to make every one a part of some kind of them, some kind of men and women. Repeating then is in every one, every one then comes sometime to be clearer to some one, sometime there will be then an orderly history of every one who ever was or is or will be living. (p. 284)

1. *Repeating then is in every one, in every one their being and their feeling and their way of realising everything and every one comes out of them in repeating.*

Repeating then   ev   be   feel

_____ / is in   ery   // in   ery on-n-ne / their ___ing /_____ing /
            ev   one   and their

                                            ev

andtheir way of_____ / _erything /_____ eryon-ne /
                     realising   ev   and

comes out of

_____ them / in re _____ .
                 peating

2. *More and more then every one comes to be clear to some one.*

More and more then   ev   one   clear

_____ / _ery_ / comes to be   / to _____ .
                                     someone

3. *Slowly every one in continuous repeating, to their minutest varia-*
tion, comes to be clearer to some one.

Slow   peat   ut

_____ ly / every one / in continuous re   ing / to their min   est /   i   tion /
                                                   var a

comes   clear

_____ to be /   er / to _____ .
                 some one

4. *Every one who ever was or is or will be living sometimes will be*
clearly realised by some one.

Ev   ev   wa-a-s   i-i-s   some

_____ ery on-ne / who   er   / or   / or will be living /_____times /
      clearly   realised

will be   /   / by _____ .
                           some one

5. *Sometime there will be an ordered history of every one.*

Some   ordered   his

_____ time / there will be an   /   tory / of   ery   .
                                        ev   one

6. *Slowly every kind of one comes into ordered recognition.*

Slow_{ly}   kínd   órd
_____/ every_____of one / comes into /_____ered / recog_____.
                                                    ni tion

7. *More and more then it is wonderful in living the subtle variations coming clear into ordered recognition, coming to make every one a part of some kind of them, some kind of men and women.*

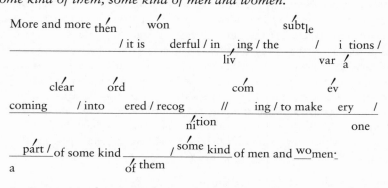

More and more th́en   wón   súbt_{le}
_____/ it is_____derful / in__,__ing / the_____/___i tions /
                                  liv   var á
                                                          a

      cléar   órd   cóm   év
coming   / into_____ered / recog_____//_____ing / to make   ery   /
                          ni tion
                                                                one

___párt /__of some kind_____/ sóme kind_of men and wo men·
a   of them

8. *Repeating then is in every one, every one then comes sometime to be clearer to some one, sometime there will be then an orderly history of every one who ever was or is or will be living.*

Re peat ing   i-ís   ́ev   sóme
_____then /_____in / ́ev_____//_____ery one / th́en comes_____time /
                                    eryone

      cléar   sóme   th́en   ́or derly
to be   er to_____//_____time / there will be_____/ an_____/
            some one

hís   ev wa-a-s   ́
                                    i-i-s
_____tory of ́ev ery_____/ who er_____/ or_____/ or will be_____.
            one   líving

These paragraphs immediately precede the familiar meditation on "writing for myself and strangers" and "loving repetition" that opens the fifth section of *The Making of Americans*. With them, Stein returns to a subject she had briefly introduced a hundred pages earlier, when she explicitly characterized repetition from the perspective of *listening*: "Many things then come out in the repeating that make a history of each one for any one who always listens to them. Many things come out of each one and as one listens to them listens to all the repeating in them, always this comes to be clear about them, the history of them of the bottom nature in them, the nature or natures mixed up in them to make the whole of them in anyway it mixes up in them. Sometime then there will be a history of every one" (p. 183). The exact relation between "bottom nature" and repetition, as well as the nature of their mutual relation to *individuality*, is clarified several pages later:

> There are then many things every one has in them that come out of them in the repeating everything living have always in them, repeating with a little changing just enough to make of each one an individual being, to make of each repeating an individual thing that gives to such a one a feeling of themselves inside them. I said each repeating in each one has each time in it a little changing, this some-times comes nearly not to happening. Some keep on copying their repeating in their talking in the moving of their hands and shoulders and bodies in living, some keep on copying others around them, some have almost nothing in them of themselves inside them, every one has though always in them their own bottom nature their own kind of being, that is always in them repeating, that is always in them a real being. (pp. 191–92)

Whereas in the passage cited above from "Portraits and Repetition" Stein describes her early interest in what it is "that ma[kes] there be no rep-etition," here she characterizes herself as "some one" whose aim it is to "clearly realise" how even the "minutest variation" serves as a form of "con-tinuous repeating." "Subtle variations" are still variations *on* something, and the challenge she faces is to demonstrate how apparent difference testi-fies to actual sameness, how "every one" is at bottom "a part of some kind . . . of men and women." What makes living "wonderful" for this writer is the way these variations "more and more . . . com[e] clear into ordered recognition."[17] Although Stein may well have endorsed some such rage for order when she wrote these lines, they are followed in the Columbia record-ing by the brief parable of the father and son making "a collection of but-terflies and beetles," which is expressly concerned with how the pursuit of knowledge may require one to kill that which one wishes to know (MA, pp. 489–90). The "wonder" of Stein's sentences actually lies in the subtlety of the variations she introduces in their composition rather than in the clarity promised at the discursive level. The recognition that the variations are in-deed ordered does not detract from their liveliness, since, regardless of the similarities, "the emphasis [in each] is different"; consequently, the story they tell is very different from what Stein's narrator is saying with them.

To find meaning *in* Stein's writing (as distinct from imposing meaning on it) the reader need only assume that she never repeats herself, even when, as in this passage, her subject is the way that "repeating . . . is in every one." Words, phrases, sounds *are* repeated but, as in the similar endings of the second, third, and fourth sentences here, always with a significant difference. The opening sentence provides a particularly graphic example of this. It consists of two contours—that is, two complete utterances—which Stein has combined. The first (B + CA) contains two profiles; the second, eight (B + . . . + A + C); and the pair of phrases that make up the first contour ("repeating then" and "is in every one") are nearly identical to the phrases framing the second ("in every one" and "[comes out of them] in repeating"). The difference, of course, is that the order is reversed. Less clear is the significance due to this reshuffling; and it is here that the intonational scheme plays a decisive role. The initial contour is a variant on a hat pattern (B + CA instead of B + A) in which the question of "repetition" is *raised*— hence the questioning profile, B, its accent jumped *up* to—and the assertion follows that it "is in every one" (CA). "Typically," Bolinger observes of CA profiles, "the accented syllable is at a low pitch, and the peak is then taken by the immediately following syllable, after which there is the drop characteristic of A" (INT, p. 156). The result is "a sort of intensification of A, common in emphatic discourse" (p. 181). The second contour begins by re-opening the question of "every one" (B), with the subsequent profiles serving to characterize this generalized individual (in terms of "being," "feeling," and "way[s] of realizing"). The next-to-last profile brings the utterance to an assertive close with an A profile, which gives the second contour, like the first, the general shape of a hat pattern (B + A). Finally, with the concluding C profile, the assertion is explicitly linked to the question of repetition—but *sotto voce*, since "repetition" isn't being reopened as a subject and is introduced merely to remind one that it has been the concern of the utterance (and of this speaker) all along.[18]

The concluding sentence provides an excellent example as well of how Stein's sentences build on one another. Here the speaker combines elements of the first, second (and third), fifth, and fourth sentences—thereby approaching the universalist ideal that she articulates. (*One sentence fits all.*) Instead of a single "orderly history," however, in which heterogeneous experience is made more manageable through a narrative of homogeneous "kinds," a self-regarding, autopoietic sentence is composed which, rather than superseding its components, enters into dialogue with them. It is more than the sum of its parts, more than the parts it summarizes, yet the parts are more than that as well.

"Matisse" (first paragraph)

One was quite certain that for a long part of his being one being living he had been trying to be certain that he was wrong in doing what he was doing and then when he could not come to be certain that he had been wrong in doing what he had been doing, when he had completely convinced himself that he would not come to be certain that he had been wrong in doing what he had been doing he was really certain then that he was a great one and he certainly was a great one. Certainly every one could be certain of this thing that this one is a great one. (PP, p. 12)

1. *One was quite certain that for a long part of his being one being living he had been trying to be certain that he was wrong in doing what he was doing and then when he could not come to be certain that he had been wrong in doing what he had been doing, when he had completely convinced himself that he would not come to be certain that he had been wrong in doing what he had been doing he was really certain then that he was a great one and he certainly was a great one.*

One was quite ⟋ tain-n
    cér / that for a ⟋ part / of his ⟋ing one /   /
       long   be   being li⟋ing

    trý
he had been ing / to be cér-tain / that he was / in dóing / what he was dóing /
              wróng

  thén
and / when he could not cóme / to be ⟋ tain / that he had been ⟋ /
            cér   wróng

            pléte ly con
     hád   / when he had / vínced him /
in doing what he been doing   com   self

    nót come
that he would / to be ⟋ tain / that he had been ⟋ /
      cér   wróng

        he was réal cér then
     hád   / ly / tain /
in doing what he been doing

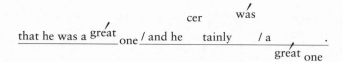

2. *Certainly every one could be certain of this thing that this one is a great one.*

Cér   év   cér

tainly /   ery one could be /   tain / of this   /

                                           thing

that this one / is a _____.
                great one

If "the way of realising everything" described in the excerpt from *The Making of Americans* takes the form of "coming into ordered recognition," in these lines Stein characterizes Matisse's "way of realising everything" as a form of "coming to be certain." The two stories being told concurrently in *The Making of Americans*, the one Stein's narrator tells about herself and the one her intonation tells about itself and hence about her, may be at odds, but here there's just a single story, a narrative of certainty achieved, confirmed by the intonation. The first sentence moves from a series of C profiles constructed around the word *certain*, in each of which the certainty is characterized as less-than-certain ("quite certain," "trying to be certain," "could not come to be certain," "would not come to be certain"), to an A profile where certainty is fully *realized* ("He certainly was a great one"). This is preceded by another A profile, making it *really* certain.

As for the contour of the second sentence, in which "certainty" is again achieved in full, that can be represented as $A + A + A + C + A + C$. Although the assertion concerns Matisse's "greatness," its force falls primarily on the fact of certainty. "This thing," that Matisse "is a great one," only stands out through deaccentuation (with a C profile); consequently, priority is ceded to the quest for certainty—which, on this account, is what makes Matisse who he is and only secondarily makes him great.

"If I Told Him. A Completed Portrait of Picasso" (first third)

If I told him would he like it. Would he like it if I told him.

Would he like it would Napoleon would Napoleon would would he like it.

If Napoleon if I told him if I told him if Napoleon. Would he like it if I told him if I told him if Napoleon. Would he like it if Napoleon if Napoleon if I told him. If I told him if Napoleon if Napoleon if I told him. If I told him would he like it would he like it if I told him.

Now.

Not now.

And now.

Now.

Exactly as as kings.

Feeling full for it.

Exactitude as kings.

So to beseech you as full as for it.

Exactly or as kings.

Shutters shut and open so do queens. Shutters shut and shutters and so shutters shut and shutters and so and so shutters and so shutters shut and so shutters shut and shutters and so. And so shutters shut and so and also. And also and so and so and also.

Exact resemblance. To exact resemblance the exact resemblance as exact as a resemblance, exactly as resembling, exactly resembling, exactly in resemblance exactly a resemblance, exactly and resemblance. For this is so. Because.

Now actively repeat at all, now actively repeat at all, now actively repeat at all.

Have hold and hear, actively repeat at all.

I judge judge.

As a resemblance to him. (SR, p. 464)

1. "If I Told Him. A Completed Portrait of Picasso"

If I   plét   p₁cás

"   // a   ed portrait of /   "

told him   com   so

2. If I told him would he like it. Would he like it if I told him.

If I told him   would he like it   Would he like it   if I told him

/   .//   /   .

3. Would he like it would Napoleon would Napoleon would would he like it.

Would he like it   would NaPóleon   would NaPóleon   wo-would   would he like it

/   /   /   /   .

4. If Napoleon if I told him if I told him if Napoleon. Would he like it if I told him if I told him if Napoleon. Would he like it if Napoleon if

Napoleon if I told him. If I told him if Napoleon if Napoleon if I told him.
If I told him would he like it would he like it if I told him.

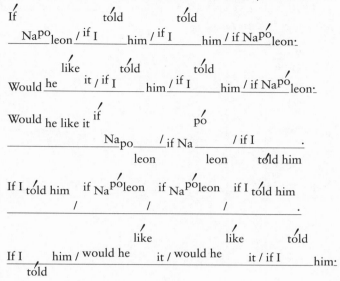

5. *Now.*
Not now.
And now.
Now.
Exactly as as kings.
Feeling full for it.
Exactitude as kings.
So to beseech you as full as for it.
Exactly or as kings.

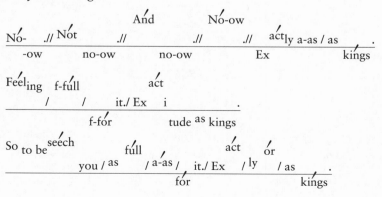

6. *Shutters shut and open so do queens. Shutters shut and shutters and so shutters shut and shutters and so and so shutters and so shutters shut and so shutters shut and shutters and so. And so shutters shut and so and also. And also and so and so and also.*

Shut   shút   o-o
   ters   and   pen-n / so

do queéns

Shut   shút   ers   so shut   shút ańd   só
  ters   and shut[ter] / and   ters   /   shutters / and   /

  so shút   so shut   shút   so shut   shút
and   ters / and   ters   / and   ters   / and shutters and   .
                                 so

    shut   shút   ál
And   ters   / and   and   .
 so   so   so

 ál   ál
And   so and   / and so and   .
 so   so

7. *Exact resemblance. To exact resemblance the exact resemblance as exact as a resemblance, exactly as resembling, exactly resembling, exactly in resemblance exactly a resemblance, exactly and resemblance. For this is so. Because.*

 áct   to   áct   thé-e   act
Ex___ re   blance /___ex___ re   blance //___ex___ re   blance //
   sem   sem   sem

ás   act   áctly   áctly
___ex___ / as   re   blance //___ex___ as resem   //___ex___ resem   //
   a-á   sem   bling   bling

act   ín   act   a-á   act
ex___ ly   re   blance //___ex___ ly   re   blance //___ex___ ly   re   blance.
   sem   sem   ańd   sem

For ^{this} is

so͞-o.// Be ___ .

cause

8. *Now actively repeat at all, now actively repeat at all, now actively repeat at all.*

Have hold and hear, actively repeat at all.

I judge judge.

As a resemblance to him.

Now ^{act}ively   péat   act   peat at a-all

/ re   at a-all // now   ively / re   //

actively

now /   repeat at a-all.

Hav-ve   hold-d   hear-r   actively

/   / and   /   repeat at a-all.

I

judge   .// As a re   blance / to   .

judge   sem   him

In *The Autobiography of Alice B. Toklas* Stein attributes the increased attention to rhythm in "If I Told Him," as well as in other works written during the summer of 1923, to her "delight" in "the movement of the tiny waves on the Antibes shore" (p. 222). This heightened attention carries over to the movement of the shutters, opening and closing in the breeze, which Stein presumably heard at night while she was composing this portrait of the intense little Iberian who, in the course of their acquaintance, had emerged—it is no exaggeration to say—as the emperor of modern painting.

Of the two contours that comprise the work's title, the first takes the form of a single C profile. As such, it suggests neither a question nor an assertion; one's attention has been caught but nothing definitive is made of it. In the ensuing portrait, however, Stein proceeds to make a great deal out of this nothing. If she never says outright what she is contemplating "telling" Picasso, her manner of telling—her intonation—says a great deal, and by the end it will have provided one with something definite. Indeed, the second contour, a hat pattern (B + A), promises just this kind of resolution—suggesting, moreover, that she may *tell Picasso*, where "Picasso" is *what* she will tell (in composing his portrait), and not just *whom* she might tell it to.

The portrait's first line consists of two identical contours (B + C, B + C), with the phrases in each reversed. In the third paragraph, the last line consists of the same words, in the same order, but the contours have changed (C + B, B + B), dramatically revising the meaning. Whereas B + C is experienced as a variation on a hat pattern (B + A), which suggests resolution even if it doesn't "realise" it, C + B and B + B leave one hanging. They articulate real, not rhetorical, questions.

In pairing the phrase "Would he like it" with her title "If I Told Him," Stein echoes the title of the Shakespeare play that was most important to her, *As You Like It*. The portrait of Picasso in fact offers an extended meditation on the nature of *as*, that is, of *likening*, and more specifically on the likeness that a person (in this case, Picasso, master portraitist) bears to his own proper name. Hence the portrait is riddled with plays on Picasso's name, beginning with the inquiry concerning the extent to which his name and person can be compared with Napoleon's. Later, when Stein concludes her analysis of "exact resemblance," she observes, "For this is so. Because." The joke, which the intonation carries (in the form of two C contours) is that these are explanations purely for form's sake; they are not answers. But there is additional wordplay as well, since the line contains Picasso's name rearranged: *so. Because: Because. so: Picasso*. Although this likening is principally visual and aural rather than intonational, there are accentual cues as well. Both "so" and "-so" are uttered with low pitch, even if one is accented and the other is not, and "-cause" and "-cas" are each stressed, although one is low and the other high. Similarly, later in the portrait the reader is treated to a single-line portrait of Picasso: "As a so" (SR, p. 466).

The last lines of the section I have diagrammed are all concerned with "active repetition," that is, repetition that doesn't just repeat itself. For instance, the three contours that repeat the words *now actively repeat at all* are all differently shaped: B + A (a hat pattern), A + B, and C + A. The next contour concludes with a hat pattern, giving it in turn a closing profile nearly identical to the previous contour. Each of the intermediate verbs ("have hold and hear") takes the form of a command; and, combined, the three verbs of possession assert that the listener, as an *active* listener "at the same time talking and listening"—in the first instance Stein herself—has taken full possession of what he or she has heard. This is to be understood.

For a portrait so concerned with "exactitude," there are two notable inexactnesses in the recording. In the first place, Stein repeats one syllable one time too many when she recites the litany of shutters—the word *shutters* remains open when it should be an "open and shut" matter. (I have indicated this addition with a bracketed [ter].) More important, there is a significant discrepancy between the recital and the text I have provided. Whereas Stein reads "Exact resemblance to exact resemblance" as a single contour, which is exactly how the words appeared in the just-published *Portraits and Prayers*, what she had actually written a dozen years earlier, as Ulla Dydo discovered in establishing a copy-text for the *Stein Reader*, was "Exact re-semblance. To exact resemblance" (pp. 453–54). In the printed version, the verb *to exact* became a simple repetition of the adjective *exact*. Although both verb and adjective can be *seen* in either version, each text clearly emphasizes one or the other. In the manuscript version, the explicitly verbal form of *exact* retrospectively clarifies an initially ambiguous use of the term; in *Portraits and Prayers*, by contrast, the adjective takes primacy over the verb. Here one encounters the limits of intonation as a compositional principle, for it is impossible to enunciate both forms of *exact* simultaneously. At this point other compositional principles come into play.

CORRELATIONS OF WRITING AND SCIENCE

In his 1962 volume *Understanding Whitehead*, Victor Lowe remarks on the "startl[ing] likeness" that Whitehead's 1931 presidential address to the eastern division of the American Philosophical Association, "probably the classical exposition of his experientialism," bears to "James's classical de-scription of the 'Stream of Thought'" in *The Principles of Psychology*. "The two sets of words tell the same story, and the same conclusion—that we are directly acquainted with the efficacy of our own immediate past—is drawn." "This is enforced," Lowe adds, "by the same main illustration—*a speaker uttering a phrase*" (pp. 342–43, emphasis added). James's "analysis of what passes through the mind as we utter the phrase *the pack of cards is on the table*" is matched by Whitehead's invocation in "Objects and Sub-jects" of "a reasonably rapid speaker enunciating the proper name 'United States'" (PR, p. 269; AI, p. 181). How is it, Whitehead inquires, that, de-spite its fully documented passing, the immediate past ("roughly speaking, . . . that portion of our past lying between a tenth of a second and half a sec-ond ago," so that, for instance, when "the third syllable [of 'United States'] is reached, probably the first is in the immediate past") "surviv[es] to be again lived through in the present"? By exactly what mechanism is "the speaker . . . carried from 'United' to 'States,' and the two [words] conjointly live in the present," if not "by the *energizing* of the past occasion as it claims its self-identical existence as *a living tissue* in the present" (pp. 181–

82, emphasis added)? Whitehead's and James's shared recourse to the spoken phrase in order to exemplify "the practically cognized present" proved at once an inspired choice and the source of considerable confusion (PR, p. 574). The inspiration—the genius, as it were—lay in the apparent immediacy of the gesture; here were Whitehead and James each *speaking* about *speech*, practicing what they were preaching. The confusion stemmed from the fact that not only were they actually doing no such thing—neither "The Stream of Thought" nor "Objects and Subjects" remotely resembles "the way people really talk"—but the representations of speech in their powerfully worded arguments were nothing like "real conversation" either. Where both speech and writing were concerned, the two radical empiricists remained subject to the very fallacies of thought they so aggressively sought to expose in their own and others' reasoning—most notably, in James's case, in denying that the word *consciousness* "stands for an entity," and, in Whitehead's, that *matter* does.

Whitehead's insistence on "taking time seriously" certainly distinguished him from most of the systematic thinkers who preceded him, if not from James; yet, again like James, he failed in his philosophy of organism to take writing seriously enough—in particular, to appreciate its capacity, no less than that of speech, to communicate emotion as well as information, to suggest as well as to state.[19] In this respect, Stein's radical empiricism serves to correct, not just complement, theirs; by the same token, the extreme alertness she displayed to the organic mechanisms operating in writing should prove exemplary for the various approaches to the biological sciences that, at the juncture of the twentieth and twenty-first centuries, offer an increasingly nuanced radical empiricist account of the world and how we live in it. The convergence of radical empiricism and the life sciences is hardly due to chance, given that radical empiricists have always tended to frame their intuitions in biological terms. For the radical empiricist, physical concepts such as *energy* exist most immediately within a biological context of *living tissue*, rather than the reverse, and *meta*physics turns out all along to have been just another way, albeit a fairly abstract one, of talking about biological processes.

To be sure, none of the principal figures I discuss would have been prepared to make so reductive-sounding a claim. Whatever the extent that the biology, and especially the physiology, of their days informed their perspectives, it remained a paltry thing compared to the perspectives thus formed. Whitehead, for instance, criticized the fallacies committed by physiologists who insisted that "in the transformations of matter and energy which constitute the activities of an animal body no principles can be discerned other than those which govern the activities of inorganic matter." No more tolerant was Stein, in faulting Henry Knower for having failed to distinguish between the brain stem viewed *concretely*, as a region, and *abstractly* as a clearly articulated set of interlocking structures (*Function*, pp. 8–9). Nevertheless, building on the appeal that the philosophy of organism possessed among developmental biologists in the 1930s, as well as on the model James constructed of the physiological correlates of the self, the life sciences today contain many more currents suited to the radical empiricist temperament than were available a hundred and fifty or even seventy-five years ago. These include nonreductive approaches to the neurophysiological composition of consciousness (such as Edelman's theory of neuronal group selection, Hobson on the mechanisms of sleep and waking, Antonio Damasio on emotion, and Israel Rosenfield on the mechanisms of memory and speech, all of whom explicitly locate themselves within a Jamesian heritage). Accounts focusing on the interpenetration of organism and ambient (ranging from Lynn Margulis's "physiological autopoiesis" to Andy Clark on "wideware" and the ecological psychology of James J. Gibson) are also plentiful, as are evolutionary claims such as Stephen Jay Gould's concerning "spandrels" and "punctuated equilibria" (which he first advanced in the 1970s in papers jointly authored with Richard Lewontin and Niles Eldredge), Terrence Deacon's speculations on "the co-evolution of language and the brain," and the "resynthesis" of evolutionary and developmental biology recently outlined by Scott F. Gilbert, John M. Opitz, and Rudolf A. Raff. Not only do Gilbert and his coauthors "emphasize . . . areas of biology that had been marginalized by the Modern Synthesis of genetics and evolution," thereby calling into question the dominant disciplinary consolidation in twentieth-century biology, but they do so in terms of neo-Whiteheadian notions resistant to "the physiologist's premise," as William Calvin has called it, that "everything that happens in man's body is as mechanical as what happens in a watch" (p. 357; Calvin, p. 29).[20]

By now it should be clear that when I speak of *the correlations of writing and science*, I am not simply alluding to the fact that in her writing Stein exhibits a perspective similar to that articulated by this cohort of late-twentieth-century speculative biologists, nor even that she shares with James, as with Emerson and Whitehead, "the rather cold metaphysical picture" of *Essays in Radical Empiricism*. (As Hilary Putnam has remarked, James's position comes down to a sense that although the Kantian "problem" of "show[ing] that the unity of the world is correlative with the unity of the self" turns out to have been sadly misconceived, it nevertheless remains possible to demonstrate "that the *disunity* of the world is correlative with the *disunity* of the self" [pp. 233–34, emphasis added]). Writing and the biological sciences are not *merely* correlated. Viewed from one direction, biological investigation (like all scientific investigation) involves ever more complex extensions of writing practices, ever more broadly distributed technologies of writing; viewed from the other direction, writing is itself an extension or externalization of the human central nervous system. Writing, then, is a function of neurology; the life sciences are a function of writing; and investigations such as Stein's of the organic mechanisms involved in writing ought to prove no less suggestive for biological research than Stein found James's biocentrism to be for achieving her own experimental objective of an ever "fuller" understanding of her "self-understanding" compositions.[21]

In closing, I should like to consider two final correlations between Stein's decades-long series of "studies in description" and late-twentieth-century neuroscience. Michael I. Posner and Marcus E. Raichle thus open *Images of Mind*, the 1994 account they coauthored of their own pioneering applications of positron emission tomography (PET) for investigating the mind-brain relation, by commenting that "when you scan the words of a novel, you create in your mind a sense of what is being described. You [may] even create a [vivid] mental image of a character" (p. 1). What, they ask, "is taking place in your brain as the visual information enters from the page and is transformed into meaningful pictures?" Applying neuroimaging techniques that allow them "to picture the neural systems actually involved as mental operations are performed," Posner and Raichle concentrate on visual spatial attention, "the act of attending to a location in the spatial field." Although not all shifts in visual attention involve actual eye movement, it still "seems likely," they remark, that "the midbrain plays a role in moving covert attention from one location to another in much the same way as it does for eye movements" (pp. 47, 164). They point to "an area in the midbrain called the superior colliculus" as possessing "cells involved in selective attention," and observe that "patients with lesions in this area show a disruption of both eye movements and covert shifts in attention" (p. 50). True to form, the superior colliculus directly connects to the neighboring nucleus of Darkschewitsch; it turns out that in her neuroanatomical investigations Stein was examining several of the structures implicated in the innermost mechanisms of close reading, or "reading in slow motion."[22]

"Most people in our society," Posner and Raichle assert, "become experts in reading English words" (p. 238). In their inaugural 1988 study using "PET scans . . . to learn more about language organization in the human brain," Posner and Raichle (with their colleagues Steven Petersen, Peter Fox, and Mark Mintun) designed the following experiment to establish "the brain processes underlying . . . the seemingly simple task of giving an appropriate use in response to a visually or auditorily presented common English noun." The experiment's "hierarchical design" has subsequently "become standard in laboratories doing this type of research":

> In the first [of four] level[s], subjects, all undergraduates and graduate students at Washington University, were asked to fix their gazes on a small crosshair—it looks like a small plus sign—in the middle of a television monitor. While they gazed at the crosshair, an image of brain activity was obtained by measuring blood flow with PET. In the second level, the subjects continued to gaze at the crosshair while blood flow was measured, but during this scan common English nouns appeared below the crosshair on the television monitor, or, in a separate scan, the same nouns were spoken to the subjects over earphones. In both the visual and auditory cases, the nouns were presented to the subjects at the rate of 40 words per minute, and the subjects looked or listened passively. In the third level, subjects were asked to speak the word they either viewed or heard. Finally, in the fourth level, the subjects were asked to say aloud a use appropriate for the noun they either viewed or heard. In all cases, separate scans were performed for auditory and visual presentations.

By "subtracting the first level from the second," the experimenters were able to "isolate the brain areas concerned with visual and auditory word perception. Subtracting the second level from the third isolated those areas of the brain concerned with speech production. And, finally, subtracting the third level from the fourth level isolated those areas concerned with selecting the appropriate use" (pp. 112–14). (See Figure 14.)

The faulty assumption that vitiates this elegant design is, of course, the implicit claim that, at its most elementary, reading comes down to the reading of individual words. Posner and Raichle believe that by showing how "the component operations of auditory and visual word processing are localized," they have provided evidence for the general principle that "elementary operations are localized in discrete neural areas"; in fact, they have done nothing of the kind (pp. 242, 241). Their error, or more exactly, the disjunction between what they claim to have shown and what they actually demonstrate, takes the form of the variant of the fallacy of misplaced concreteness to which empiricists seem congenitally prone: insufficient attention to context. The "elementary" operations in this instance—listening to, or looking at, a stream of nouns; generating appropriate verbs for given nouns—are actually *abstractions* from the ordinary operations of auditory and visual word processing. As Stein so compellingly demonstrates, actual reading is never *either* auditory or visual but is always to some extent cross-

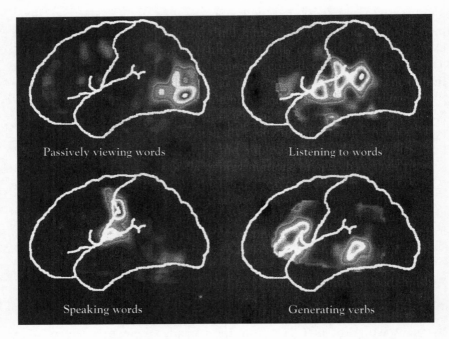

Figure 14. Distinct sets of brain areas for distinct tasks. (From Michael I. Posner and Marcus E. Raichle, *Images of Mind*, p. 115. © 1994 Scientific American Library. Used by permission of W. H. Freeman and Company.)

modal. Hence, by subtracting the first level (brain activity due to fixing one's gaze on a crosshair in the middle of a television screen) from the second (activity due to fixing one's gaze on nouns that appear below the crosshair, or listening to nouns while fixing one's gaze on the crosshair), Posner and Raichle cannot have isolated the brain areas devoted to seeing or listening to words. To the extent that one is actually seeing *a particular word* and not just a bunch of squiggly lines, or that one is still focusing on the crosshair while listening to the word, one's experience is not going to be exclusively auditory or exclusively visual. More important, Posner and Raichle have certainly not localized the ordinary experience of *passively viewing words* (namely, reading understood as information processing, as distinct from writing or even "reading in slow motion") nor the typical experience of *listening to words* (listening to someone speak, possibly one-self). At best, the scans localize the process of *abstraction*. These experimental subjects have been instructed either to listen to, or to look at, a set of discontinuous words streaming by at the rate of forty a minute, with no re-reading or repeating permitted. By implication, they are to ignore any possible relations among the words. This is bound to take a good deal of work and is hardly a passive process. Whether it has much to do with ordinary reading and listening, that is to say, with sentence comprehension, remains an open question. What is clear is that we have been here before; just take another look at Chapter 5.

In raising these objections to Posner and Raichle's analysis of their 1988 experiment, I am hardly seeking to discredit the use of PET scans and other noninvasive imaging techniques for picturing the mechanisms of consciousness generally and of writing and reading in particular. Rather, I am arguing for the usefulness of keeping Stein's own experiments in mind for what Andy Clark has called "ecologically realistic study" (p. 275).[23] In particular, empiricist claims for "brain localization"—the hypothesis, as Posner and Raichle characterize it in their preface, that "mental operations as studied in cognitive science [are] localized in separate brain areas"—set bells aflashing and lights awhistling from a radical empiricist perspective (p. viii). The gap between empiricism and radical empiricism is perhaps best measured in these terms, and Posner and Raichle provide a signal opportunity for such measurement when, in the final chapter of their study (titled "Future Images"), they seem to find common ground with a figure I have been representing as an exemplary radical empiricist, Gerald Edelman. Posner and Raichle approvingly cite Edelman on his "theory of neuronal group selection" as well as on the notion of "reentrant signaling" that he has advanced as the principal mechanism for such selection. "It has been clear for many years," they write, "that the front and the back of the brain are linked by anatomical connections leading in both directions. However, we are just beginning to understand the functions of the connections that *feed back* information from frontal areas to posterior ones." For instance, when a "voluntary [visual] search" occurs, "a particular posterior area sensitive to visual features is active shortly after visual input and then becomes active again later as the mind searches for the visual feature" in question. "The search can only take place" if information from other areas is "*fed back* to *reenter* the critical area" (pp. 242–43, emphasis added). Earlier, Posner and Raichle explain that the "information *fed back* to sensory-specific areas" is sometimes called *reentrant processing* because "a brain area that has already performed a function now receives a new signal fed from some higher level. In other words, a signal *reenters* the cortex that had handled the signal previously"—or more exactly, that had already handled another, related, signal (p. 144, emphasis added).

The interesting thing about this account of reentry is that it bears only the most cursory resemblance to the "large-scale recursive interaction of ongoing neural activity," which, according to Edelman, serves as "the most prominent dynamic principle underlying . . . the temporal correlations of neuronal firing across [the very] large networks" that are responsible for providing "functionally segregated . . . circuits" with whatever significance they possess ("Building a Picture of the Brain," p. 65). As a final instance of the correlations linking Stein's investigations of writing with investigations in contemporary neuroscience, consider the process Edelman terms *reentry*, which involves the formation and strengthening (or weakening) of connections between neuronal maps through experiential selection. The units of selection are not individual neurons but neuronal *groups*, ranging "from perhaps 50 to 10,000 neurons" in size, and Edelman speculates that each brain contains as many as one hundred million of these (BABF, p. 89). Moreover, the brain maps in question are not "representation[s] in the ordinary sense," as Oliver Sacks succinctly put the matter a half-dozen years ago in an article in the *New York Review of Books*, but in each case form "an interconnected series of [hundreds of] neuronal groups that respond selectively to certain elemental categories," such as "movements or colors in the visual world." Similarly, Sacks suggests, the "synchronization" of "scattered mappings" (in effect, the synchronization of prior synchronizations, which permits one to recognize a chair *as an object*, let alone as a chair) is more accurately thought of as "a giant and continually modulating equation of the outputs of innumerable maps, connected by reentry," than as "a single image or representation." Instead of being representations, these maps—and "maps of maps"—are the processes that make the experience of representation possible ("A New Vision of the Mind," pp. 106–8).[24]

Sacks credits Edelman with "achiev[ing], or aspir[ing] to achieve, what no other theorist has even tried to do, a biologically plausible model of how consciousness could have emerged"; at the same time, he acknowledges that none of Edelman's speculations about the mechanisms of neuronal group selection "can yet be proved: we have no way of seeing neuronal groups or maps or their interactions; no way of listening in to the reentrant orchestra of the brain. Our capacity to analyze the living brain is still far too crude" ("Making Up the Mind," p. 46; "A New Vision," p. 116). For this reason, much of Edelman's recent work involves simulations of the brain through the construction of "synthetic animals" designed to test his theory. "Although these 'creatures' make use of supercomputers," Sacks notes, "their behavior (if one may use the word) is not programmed, not robotic" (p. 117). Edelman's goal with these hybrid creatures is "nothing less than 'to do what seems impossible,' " as one journalist observed a dozen years ago in *The New York Times*, "to make a nervous system inside a creature inside a world, and then let it run in the world" (Hellerstein, p. 27). Seventy-five years earlier, Stein too sought to generate "intellectual recreations" that were not just representations of her subjects but "highly connected, layered local structures with massively reentrant connections," composed, in her case, of words and their interactions (BABF, p. 117). When Edelman asks "Is it possible to construct a conscious artifact?" and answers in the affirmative, one may perhaps be excused for wondering whether Stein beat him to the punch, providing an alternative manner of visualizing the brain's reentrant signaling with the vibrating lines and portmanteau sentences of her equally "impossible" project (p. 188).[25]

The crucial thing to recognize in this context is that the visualization involved is not limited to the objectifications of *sight* but includes necessarily proprioceptive and neuraesthetic aspects as well. Here, there really is a *there* there, by contrast with Rodney Brooks's self-programming robot, Cog. In remarking, in a passage already cited in each of the first five chapters of the present study, that sometime in 1912 "a desire to express the rhythm of the visible world" replaced Stein's former "interest" in "the insides of people . . . and what went on inside them," Toklas (Stein) suggests that the visible world itself possesses *an inside* (ABT, p. 119). It is at once external (it is the visible world, after all) and internal (it is experienced rhythmically). Consequently, it "behaves physiologically and not mechanically," as Lynn Margulis has described the Earth's own characteristically autopoietic mode of activity ("Big Trouble," p. 278). Wherever there is a *there*, in other words, there is bound to be an *in*—which is not equivalent to saying, however, that something "existent *in* itself" exists *by* itself (ABT, p. 224, emphasis added). Had Picabia succeeded, for instance, in actually creating his vibrant line, even it would not have "existed by itself." On the contrary, it would have remained, in Stein's careful phrasing in the *Autobiography*, "dependent upon the emotion of the object which compels the vibration" (pp. 210–11). Just a year earlier, Whitehead supplied the following gloss in disentangling the "subject-object" relation from the "knower-known" relation: "The occasion as subject has a 'concern' for the object. And the 'concern' at once places the object as a component in the experience of the subject [that is, in the relevant occasion of experience—in Picabia's case, an occasion of painting; in Stein's, of writing], with an affective tone drawn from this object and directed toward it" (AI, pp. 175–76).[26]

Returning, shortly before the close of *Everybody's Autobiography*, to the "problem of space" she associated with Picabia, and still presenting herself as entirely willing to suspend disbelief as to the likelihood of a solution ("technique can do it he says and I am not certain that he is not right"), Stein commented, "Ever since Cezanne everybody who has painted has wanted to have a feeling of movement inside the painting not a painting of a thing moving but the thing painted having inside it the existence of moving." "I am always hoping," she added,

> to have it the picture be alive inside in it, in that sense not to live in its frame, pictures have been imprisoned in frames, quite naturally and now when people are all all peoples are asking to be imprisoned in organisation it is quite natural that pictures are trying to escape from the prison the prison of framing. For many years I have taken all pictures out of their frames, I never keep them in them, and now that I have let them out for so many years they want to get out by themselves, it is very interesting. (EA, p. 321–22)

For Stein, as she had sought to demonstrate all this time in her own experimental compositions, neither writing nor speech exists in such a confined, and confining, space, in the sort of prisonlike environment one might wish to escape from or even into. Instead, a far more fluid sense of spatial orientation operates in the linguistic domain than is realizable, in the end, in painting.

Typically, however, human beings remain only vaguely aware of the language-inflected vortices they are continually setting in motion, despite passing much of their waking lives in the midst of verbal flux. By contrast, Stein "found [her]self plunged," as she put it, "into a water of words" (ALL, p. 231). Not only did she seek to recreate the experience in hundreds of ways and hundreds of compositions, but she also found that writing functioned readily as a medium for investigating how "organisation" might be reconceived, as something other than a "prison of framing." The ensuing *reorganization* proved consistent with the core intuition of the philosophy of organism, as Russell recalled Whitehead formulating it early in their acquaintance. "You think the world is what it looks like in fine weather at noon day," Whitehead announced to Russell; "I think it is what it seems like in the early morning when one first wakes from deep sleep" (*Portraits from Memory*, p. 39). In keeping with Emerson's description of himself in "Circles" as "an experimenter . . . unsettl[ing] all things," and James's insistence on "reinstat[ing] the vague"—no less than with Stein's own determination to "make confusion clear," as she described the object of her neuroanatomical investigations to Lewellys Barker—Whitehead's unmistakably neuraesthetic vision befits the "strange quality of an earth," which, from the vantage of the airplanes Stein traveled in "pretty much all the time" during her tour of the United States, so closely echoed "the mingling lines of Picasso" as well as Braque's "simple solutions" and Masson's "wandering lines" (EL, p. 412; PCW, pp. 88, 91).[27]

Like the work of these painters, and like the twentieth century as Stein conceived it, the vision owed its "splendor" to the recognition that "everything destroys itself" and "nothing continues" (PCW, p. 91). At the same time, it set itself directly against the characteristically *evolutionary* perspective of the previous century. Instead of seeing things "evolve as people saw them evolve in the nineteenth century"—here Stein could just as well have been speaking of her own or of Whitehead's "genius" as of Picasso's—the painter of modern life "saw things evolve as they did not evolve," as natural "phenomena," not just "daily events" (pp. 80, 87). Thirty years earlier, Stein was already expressing the same unabashedly radical empiricist perspective when she acknowledged, in her notes for *The Making of Americans*, that the "aesthetic has become the whole of me." This claim may not have been "reasonable . . . in the scientific sense," as she remarked in contrasting nineteenth-century "reasonableness" with the self-isolating, self-destroying splendor of the twentieth century in her 1938 account of Picasso's exemplary career, yet it was all the more splendid, and, as I have tried to demonstrate, all the more scientific for that.

Coda in Three Voices

In his notes to the Library of America edition of Emerson's *Essays and Lectures*, Joel Porte comments, "Facing ecclesiastical persecution, Galileo denied his observation that the earth turns round the sun, but then added: And yet it does move" (p. 1144). Emerson, Whitehead, and Stein all composed variations on Galileo's turn on himself.

* * *

Gladly we would anchor, but the anchorage is quicksand. This onward trick of nature is too strong for us: *Pero si muove*. When, at night, I look at the moon and stars, I seem stationary, and they to hurry. Our love of the real draws us to permanence, but health of body consists in circulation, and sanity of mind in variety or facility of association. (EL, p. 476)

* * *

The ultimate freedom of things, lying beyond all determinations, was whispered by Galileo—*E pur si muove*—freedom for the inquisitors to think wrongly, for Galileo to think rightly, and for the world to move in despite of Galileo and inquisitors. (PR, p. 47)

* * *

As I say what one repeats is the scene in which one is acting, the days in which one is living, the coming and going which one is doing, anything one is remembering is a repetition, but existing as a human being, that is being listening and hearing is never repetition. It is not repetition if it is that which you are actually doing because naturally each time the emphasis is different just as the cinema has each time a slightly different thing to make it all be moving. And each one of us has to do that, otherwise there is no existing. As Galileo remarked, it does move. (LIA, p. 179)

Reference Matter

The abbreviation YCAL used below refers to the Gertrude Stein and Alice B. Toklas Papers, Yale Collection of American Literature, Beinecke Rare Book and Manuscript Library.

Chapter 1

1. For studies of these poets that emphasize their connections to science, see Bell, Kayman, Albright, Crawford, and Kadlec. Williams's most extensive discussion of the relation between writing and science may be found in his collection *The Embodiment of Knowledge*; as for Pound, Maria Luisa Ardizzone's recent selection of hitherto unpublished material from the middle years in Italy is particularly helpful.

2. Weissmann, in particular, argues that Stein's "revolution in words is based on [Loeb's] mechanistic conception of life" (p. 88). "Leader of the new, mechanistic school of American biology, the adherents of which tried to explain the phenomena of biology by the equations of physics," Loeb served as the model for Max Gottlieb in Sinclair Lewis's Pulitzer Prize-winning novel *Arrowsmith* and spelled out his "physico-chemical viewpoint" in such works as *The Mechanistic Conception of Life* and *The Organism as a Whole* (Weissmann, p. 86; also see Pauly).

3. Interestingly, the use of the term *deconstruction* in relation to Stein's practice is less anachronistic than one might imagine. Mina Loy, in an essay on Joseph Cornell dating from 1950, recalled that Stein had "explained the aim of Cubism to me as 'deconstruction preparatory to complete reconstruction of the objective'" ("Phenomenon," p. 300). *Deconstruction* was a term with considerable currency in the early 1950s. Robert Duncan, for example, used it in two works of 1953, "For a muse meant" as well as the charmingly titled "Deconstruction a Discussion" (the discussion in fact centers on Stein's writing).

4. Stein used the phrase "first manner" twice in her 1921 composition, "A Sonatina Followed by Another"—both in the first and the second persons. Several

sentences into the work she wrote: "Not in the form of games not in the way of repetitions. Repetitions are in your first manner and now we are in the South and the South is not in the North." The subsequent reference is similarly, if more appreciatively, dismissive: "I approach the wonder. I wonder why I have so many wishes. I wish to please and to be repeated. This is in my first manner. Thank you so much for your first manner. That is most kind of you" (BTV, pp. 4, 15).

5. Largely due to Stein's own compelling analysis in her lecture "Portraits and Repetition," the category of the literary portrait has remained central to considerations of her writing. The fullest discussion is still Steiner's; more recent studies include those of Sayre, Bowers, and Cope.

6. Because *Psychology: Briefer Course*, an abridgment of PR, was an assigned text in courses at Harvard, I have included page references to both works, when there are equivalent passages. Often, as here, there is none—although James does stress the distinction in question early on in BC.

7. This is the title of a work of Stein's that Laura Riding and Robert Graves published in 1929, at the Seizin Press.

8. Many critics have discussed James's influence on Stein's writing, but those who argue for an ultimately nonmechanistic interpretation of her practice tend to do so in a manner that removes the writing from the realm of science. Donald Sutherland, author of the first extended study of Stein, demonstrates this process of abstraction in exemplary fashion. Stein's conviction that "present thinking is the final reality," he writes, "is neither validated nor invalidated by what happens . . . in philosophy or psychology. . . . As with the theory of humors to the Elizabethans, any philosophical or scientific theory is to an artist a working articulation of the universe, a language or an alphabet, with which to express experience. Everything depends on the eloquence, completeness, and exactitude with which the living experience is expressed by the language used" (p. 7). Insofar as Stein produces works of art, the truth-value of whatever "philosophical or scientific theory" she may be investigating is held to be irrelevant; that the writing continues to function as science after she moves beyond her "deterministic theories of personality" is hardly conceivable (Hoffman, *Development*, p. 207).

9. For additional discussions of Cog, see Dennett ("When HAL Kills") as well as Freedman and Hayles.

10. Because the line cited is from *Mother Goose* does not mean, of course, that Stein first read or heard it as a child. Richard Bridgman, who notes its first appearance in Stein's writing in her 1929 composition "Saving the Sentence," has observed that she "would have encountered [it] in one of her assigned texts at Radcliffe, Josiah Royce's *The Spirit of Modern Philosophy*. Royce used the verse to illustrate Kant's contention that the phenomena of the sense-world 'recognize the authority of my thought-forms, or categories'" (p. 242). Royce, citing a variant formulation, writes: "*If I be I, as I think I be*, says the little old woman of the song, *then will my little dog know me*. The poor woman is striving, you remember, to recover the unity of her apperception, of which a sad and recent incident has

deprived her. She seeks it, and how? By striving to link fact to fact in her sleepy experience. Well, even so, Kant holds, that if I be I, as I think I be, then will the phenomena of my sense-world in a certain deeper just sense know me, that is, recognize the authority of my thought-forms, or categories. The little woman, then, had, in her way, grasped the idea of that most puzzling part of Kant's 'Critique,' the so-called transcendental deduction of the categories" (p. 128).

11. As Stein put it in EA: "The laws of science are like all laws they are paper laws, as the Chinese call them, they make believe that they do something so as to keep everyone from knowing that they are not going on living" (p. 251).

12. "What is knowledge," Stein asks in "Plays." "Of course knowledge is what you know and what you know is what you do know" (LIA, p. 94). "As I have said," she reiterates several pages later, "knowledge is what you know and I naturally tell you what I know, as I do so very essentially believe in knowledge" (p. 101). The second of her four lectures on narration begins likewise: "I have said and anybody can say anybody might say that knowledge is what you know. Knowledge is what you know and there is nothing more difficult to say than that that knowledge is what you know" (N, p. 16).

13. As Gerald Myers observes in his notes for BC, James derived the distinction from the first volume of John Grote's 1865 *Exploratio Philosophica* (p. 1178). "Our knowledge may be contemplated in either of two ways," Grote remarked, "or, to use other words, we may speak in a double manner of the 'object' of knowledge. That is, we may either use language thus, we *know* a thing, a man, &c.: or we may use it thus: we know such and such things *about* the thing, the man, &c." "Following its true logical instinct," Grote added, "language in general . . . distinguishes between these two applications of the notion of knowledge, the one being γνῶναι, *noscere, kennen, connaître*, the other being εἰδέναι, *scire, wissen, savoir*" (p. 60).

14. Despite his sensitivity to the difference between the feeling of such pain and the kind of "mental work" ordinarily associated with knowledge-about, Humphreys refers to sensation, as he does to perception, exclusively in terms of knowledge-about. The two experiential modes differ in degree and in object but not in composition; thus "while sensation provides relatively direct and certain *knowledge about* 'what is happening to me,' perception can provide only relatively indirect and conditional *knowledge about* 'what is happening out there'" (p. 102, emphasis added). Humphreys leaves no room for knowledge of acquaintance, understood as a distinct category, although he does leave plenty of wiggle room for himself with his qualifications, "*relatively* direct" and "*relatively* indirect."

15. Completing his doctorate at Oxford at the time, Church subsequently taught at Cornell and Santa Barbara, and wrote works on Malebranche, Hume, and Bradley as well as studies of "critical appreciation" and the nature of resemblance. Stein expressed her satisfaction with his article (which she had encouraged him to publish) in a letter dated October 28, 1928: "I knew you were going to be good but I did not know you were going to have so much power in

your words, your last sentence is one of the big [?] sentences and the paragraph beginning from the bottom of page 166 is remarkable" (YCAL). Stein refers here to Church's concluding sentence—"Nothing need nor can substitute for what in words is wholly given"—as well as to the following paragraph: "Yet [the] dogma [that writing must be about something] insists that all writing must in the end somehow achieve some given effect, which plainly cannot be merely the presence of meanings in the conventional sense. All that process of thinking meanings which conventional writing and reading is, must at least evoke something final; for its avowed purpose is that. Usually what discourse manages to evoke remains vague. Otherwise the writer is called great. And that is because what he realizes and presents is the apprehension of an essence sometimes complicated, as often in the poetry of Coleridge. Never, as with Pope, is this writing dubbed great in any way didactic or in any sense descriptive. It is about nothing, and necessarily so, since its entire meaning comes out of what is read. The essence or reality then present cannot be illustrated by something else. But if such writing can be said to be without meaning, or abstract, that is saying only that what it presents is intrinsically individuated without external reference, and ultimate. No writing that is final can be discursive—as the taste for literature would have it. Discourse cannot be final simply because the meaning of discourse is essentially derivative and altogether transitive. To afford an apprehension unmediated by references to it of some esssence, writing must transcend common sense and its meanings." "So with Miss Stein's writing," Church concludes. For an excerpt from an otherwise unpublished memoir by Church, partly concerning Stein, see Samsell.

16. In YCAL, there are three drafts (one manuscript, two typescript) of the composition that contains these lines. The manuscript, as well as one of the typescripts, is labeled "Pathé," and the New York files of the Pathé News Library (which is now part of the Sherman Grinberg Film Libraries) record a 1934 News Flash on Stein's arrival in America: "Gertrude Stein, Writer, Returns / Close-up of Gertrude Stein reading some / of her so-called famous descriptions." The two-page "Pathé" would presumably have been written for this occasion. A transcription of one typescript draft may be found in Burns and Dydo.

17. Early in the first lecture of *Our Knowledge of the External World* Russell distinguishes " 'logical atomism,' for want of a better name," from two other "types . . . among present-day philosophies." "The first of these, . . . the classical tradition, descends in the main from Kant and Hegel; it represents the attempt to adapt to present needs the methods and results of the great constructive philosophers from Plato downwards. The second type, which may be called evolutionism, derived its predominance from Darwin." Among the principal proponents of evolutionism Russell lists James. As for logical atomism, the "type of philosophy . . . that I wish to advocate," it "represents the same kind of advance as was introduced into physics by Galileo: the substitution of piecemeal, detailed, and verifiable results for large untested generalities recommended only by a certain appeal to imagination" (pp. 13–14).

18. See Putnam, however, for a critique of the received notion that logical positivism had achieved hegemonic status in American academic philosophy in the 1950s.

19. Marsh would have been directly acquainted with Whitehead's waning influence at Harvard, as he received his doctorate there for a 1951 dissertation on Russell.

20. Zeki's generally dismissive attitude toward philosophers may be gleaned from the following statement: "It is . . . fortunate that neurobiologists are not philosophers, for they might otherwise find themselves immersed, like the philosophers, in an endless and ultimately fruitless discussion on the meaning of words such as 'unconscious' or 'inference' or 'knowledge' and 'information' instead of trying to unravel important facts about the brain. They would, in brief, end up contributing as meagerly to an understanding of the brain and of the mind as philosophers have" (p. 7).

21. Zeki uses the expression "our knowledge of the external world" on the first page of his "Prologue" and the penultimate page of the "Epilogue," although he doesn't mention Russell by name anywhere in the study.

22. Goethe's *Farbenlehre*, or *Theory of Colors*, proves an exception of sorts to this rule of poetic radical empiricism predating the more straightforwardly scientific form. The science of a poet, the *Farbenlehre* nonetheless contrasts sharply with the transcendental tenor of Goethe's other biological studies, whether in prose or verse. Although the great nineteenth-century physiologist Hermann von Helmholtz criticized the color theory every bit as thoroughly as he praised the morphological studies, recent experiments by Zeki, and earlier ones by Edwin Land, have confirmed Goethe's insistence that, as Oliver Sacks puts it, "color was not a simple sensation [corresponding to a given wavelength] but an 'inference' or 'act of judgment'" ("Scotoma," p. 157). For diverse considerations of Goethe's poetic science, see Helmholtz, Zeki, Zajonc, Seamon and Zajonc, and Sacks ("The Colorblind Painter" as well as "Scotoma").

23. The suggestion that Shelley's verse is generally radical empiricist in motivation rather than idealist may strike many readers as counterintuitive; yet this is exactly what Whitehead proposed in SMW when he declared, "What the hills were to the youth of Wordsworth, a chemical laboratory was to Shelley," adding, "If Shelley had been born a hundred years later, the twentieth century would have seen a Newton among chemists." This "poet, so sympathetic with science, so absorbed in its ideas, can simply make nothing of the doctrine of secondary qualities which is fundamental to its concepts. For Shelley nature retains its beauty and its colour. Shelley's nature is in its essence a nature of organisms, functioning with the full content of our perceptual experience" (pp. 84–85).

24. Phoebe Ellsworth has recently observed, "For the last hundred years, the scientific influence of James's writings on emotion has been predominantly the influence of [the single] paragraph" in "What Is an Emotion?" that contains both this sentence and the memorable observation that, in the seemingly unexceptional

"common-sense" proposition "we meet a bear, are frightened and run," the "order of sequence is incorrect" (p. 222). Ellsworth rightly argues that ambiguities in James's phrasing, ambiguities he sought to clear up a decade later in "The Physical Basis of Emotion," caused him to be "misread" not only as "saying 'Emotion is (nothing but) bodily sensations' but further [that] 'Emotion is (nothing but) autonomic [i.e., visceral] sensations'" (p. 225). Nevertheless, Ellsworth is herself mistaken when she claims that although James "used the phrase 'the feeling of [the bodily] . . . changes as they occur *is* the emotion,' the context makes it clear that he meant that the sense of the bodily changes provides the *emotionality* to what would otherwise be a neutral perception or interpretation of the situation" (p. 223). As I suggest below, the "perception" or "interpretation" of a situation is rarely, if ever, "neutral" for James, and "emotionality" is certainly not something added to an "otherwise" value-free substrate.

25. This phrase, which Moore once attributed to Yeats, has never been traced and is likely to have been her own invention. Moore was unquestionably a close reader of James. On one occasion, responding to the portentous query "What Books Did Most to Shape Your Vocational Attitude and Your Philosophy of Life?" she listed PR among works ranging from Jacob Abbott's *Beechnut, Grimkie, Florence and John* to Martin Buber's *I and Thou* (*Complete Prose*, p. 671).

26. Langer dedicated her classic study *Philosophy in a New Key* "to Alfred North Whitehead, my great Teacher and Friend." Moore's choice of the title *Observations* for her 1924 collection of poetry pointedly exemplifies this revaluation of perception along radical empiricist lines. These are certainly not observations in the "naive empiricist" sense.

27. To summarize: James's account of emotion emphasizes the heterogeneous nature of the mechanism of appreciation, as involving bodily movement as well as bodily sensation. It is precisely this heterogeneity in the composition of emotion that writers like Wordsworth, Shelley, and Emerson investigated in their poetic science, a heterogeneity that may account for James's striking use of the term *appreciation* as a general category for emotional and aesthetic experience, echoing the title of Walter Pater's 1889 volume, *Appreciations*. Emotional experience, compositionally hybrid, cannot be measured accurately by fixed, standardized ratios; it compels an emotional response, involving a degree of appreciation or depreciation but admitting no zero degree of neutrality. The contrary insistence, that science requires a neutral perspective, leads Daniel Dennett astray, for instance, in his vigorously empiricist "explanation" of consciousness. "Serious phenomenology," Dennett proposes, is in great need of "a clear, neutral method of description," a "heterophenomenological method" that "neither challenges nor accepts as entirely true the assertions of subjects, but rather maintains a constructive and sympathetic neutrality, in the hopes of compiling a definitive description of the world according to the subjects" (*Consciousness Explained*, pp. 66, 83; also see Radner). "This tactic of neutrality," he adds, "is only a temporary way station on the path to devising and confirming an empirical theory that could in principle

vindicate the subjects" (p. 83). In fact, the "tactic" is central to Dennett's empiricism; for the only strictly empiricist theory of consciousness that can be confirmed
is the one he comes up with, that so-called subjects are *not* justified in viewing
themselves as subjects. This theory only makes sense if neutrality makes sense to
begin with, and it is precisely this stance that radical empiricism disputes. No
empiricist theory (which is what Dennett has in mind when he speaks of an
"empirical" theory) can "*in principle* vindicate the subjects" and their "beliefs in
their own phenomenology"—beliefs in "the fauna and flora . . . that inhabit *our*
conscious experience, . . . the things that swim in the stream of consciousness," as
he charmingly and misleadingly puts it (pp. 44, 84). One might fruitfully contrast
Dennett's "constructive and sympathetic neutrality" with Louis Marin's strictures
concerning "the neutral": "Neither yes nor no, true nor false, one nor the other,
this is the neutral. Of course this is not the neutral as neutrality, the ideological
trick played by institutions propped up by class rule. Neither is this the neutral as
the utopic figure that seems to be freed from society as it is historically and
geographically positioned but all the while constructing its perfect representation.
Rather, this neutral is the span between true and false, opening within discourse a
space discourse cannot receive. It is a third term, but a supplementary third term,
not synthetic"—that is to say, it is an instance of Whiteheadian rather than
Hegelian dialectic, heterogeneous, not homogeneous (*Utopics*, p. 7; also see
Marin's "Frontiers of Utopia").

28. See CBM for a compelling account of the polemical basis of Edward
Boring's much-cited argument that, despite James's prior claim, Wundt's experimental laboratory was "the first real laboratory of experimental psychology to be
founded in the world" (pp. 9–10).

29. For another, equally striking example of the diagnostic value of the "fallacy
of misplaced concreteness," see Haraway on the correspondence between Whitehead's analysis of "objectifications" and her own account of "gene fetishism"
(*Modest_Witness*, pp. 146–47).

30. Notebook 14 (NB-14), p. 3, among the unpublished notebooks and
working notes for MA in YCAL. (Subsequent references to these notebooks will
take the abbreviated form NB-, as in NB-14 or NB-M.) According to Walker in her
summary of Katz, NB-14 dates from the second half of 1908, when Stein was still
working on the first 150 pages of her 925-page novel (p. 152).

31. Walker cites this passage as "a vortex of words, burning words, cleansing
words, liberating words, feeling words" (p. 149). The significantly different
phrasing is presumably due to the fact that until 1988 the essay remained unpublished and was only available in a handwritten draft. Often difficult to decipher,
Stein's handwriting can, as here, serve to liberate the words, not just from their
mooring but even from themselves.

32. Stein tended to drop the *e* in words that begin with *ex-*.

33. See Walker for an especially illuminating discussion of this work.

34. I cite this passage from Leon Katz's transcription of Stein's notes for MA;

see folder 8, p. lxxviii, where the reverse side of note-sheet #18 is transcribed (YCAL). According to Katz, Stein misspells the first "too" (as "to") and "effect" as "affect." The sheet almost certainly dates from late 1911, since it includes a mock title page, listing "A Man," "Five or Six Men," "Two Women," and "Italians," which at the time Stein was trying to persuade the English publisher Grant Richards to collect in a single volume. The correspondence between Stein and Richards in YCAL indicates that she proposed the collection no earlier than mid-October and that he had declined it by mid-December.

35. Although Stein describes the thoughts of Leo and Sally in "Two," she does so only on the basis of what they say, as the following passages make explicit: "He was thinking in being one having sound coming out of him. He was thinking in this thing. He was thinking about this thing about being one having sound come out of him" (p. 4). "She was different from him in having sound come out of her. She was thinking this thing. She was thinking in this thing. She had sound coming out of her. She was thinking in this thing" (p. 5).

36. In the manuscript of "Two," as in other manuscripts of the period, Stein composed brief notes to herself characterizing the theme or subject she expected to pick up when she resumed writing. In one particularly fascinating instance, the words "Go on with her" are crossed out so as to distinguish them from the paragraph which directly follows in the text: "Going on within her, going on in her, going on and not gaining going, going on and indicating, going on and one staying where talking is not receiving undertaking existing, she was the one believe her, she was that one. She said believe her she was the one, going on within her, going on in her, believe her, she said believe her, she said she, believe her, she was one" (T, p. 110).

37. The exact dating of the composition of "Two" has been the source of some confusion, as a result of a postcard dated June 17, 1912, which Georgiana Goddard King sent to Stein. "I have sent your MS reluctantly without finishing the Two because I am afraid you will want it," King wrote. "Give me another chance later" (YCAL). On the basis of this remark, Walker has proposed that "Two" must have been finished by June 17, and Brenda Wineapple in her recent double biography of Stein and her brother suggests that Stein "had finished much" of the work by that date. Wineapple herself supplies the necessary clue for determining just how *much* this was when she observes that, in one of the notes in the manuscript of "Two," Stein was responding to a letter from Leo dated June 6, 1912. In that letter Leo had "mocked [the] 'good middle class' opposition" displayed by Stein's former lover May Knoblauch "to Teddy Roosevelt's presidential bid" (Wineapple, p. 349). The note in "Two" which mentions "His strikes about [indecipherable] & May about Roosevelt" precedes the paragraph on page 95 of the printed text, which begins, "If saying that a thing that will happen means that feeling is dying. . . ." Therefore, Stein could not have gotten very far into volume 5 (which starts on page 87) before giving King the incomplete manuscript to read. The unexpected urgency with which she recalled the manuscript from King may well have been due to the

arrival of Leo's letter. Three paragraphs into volume 5 the topic of "religion" is introduced, with a line drawn between the previous paragraph and the new paragraph, "If he were hoping what he would be hoping if he were eating what he would be eating . . ." (p. 87). I take it that the line indicates the point where Stein stopped work on "Two" before leaving Paris; and that when she and King met up in Madrid early in June, she probably gave King the first four notebook volumes to look over. The introduction of religion and spirituality at this point in the text— Stein had intended all along to address the topic—may have been triggered by the stay in Avila. "I immediately lost my heart to Avila," she had Toklas say in ABT. "I must stay in Avila forever I insisted. Gertrude Stein was very upset, Avila was alright but, she insisted, she needed Paris. I felt that I needed nothing but Avila. We were both very violent about it. We did however stay there for ten days and as Saint Theresa was a heroine of Gertrude Stein's youth we thoroughly enjoyed it. In the opera Four Saints written a few years ago she describes the landscape that so profoundly moved me" (pp. 115–16).

38. Three separate notes allude to Sally's "impermeability." The first of these ("Go on discuss [?] impermeability, memory") precedes the paragraph on page 73 which begins, "If she discovered that discovering being existing feeling has meaning, she did discover that she was feeling . . ." The other two notes introduce paragraphs on pages 74 and 75.

39. In a manuscript note Stein characterized the subject of the paragraphs that contain these lines as her sister-in-law's "painting then failure and C.S. [Christian Science]."

40. This sentence is transcribed from NB-M, p. 30, as Walker observes in citing it (p. 159).

41. For a series of extraordinary meditations on Donne's engagement with the cutting-edge science of his day, see Empson (*Donne and the New Philosophy*).

42. In this light, see Sherrington on Goethe, and Needham on Coleridge.

43. Besides coining the term *biology*, Treviranus preceded Broca by fifty years in associating the hippocampal gyrus of the so-called limbic lobe with the olfactory nerve and also "corrected the error of earlier microscopists who saw only globules" in the retina by substituting rods or "papillae" for the globules (Finger, pp. 79, 286). Mayr, in his magisterial study of "the growth of biological thought," notes that *biology* was "independently proposed also by [Karl Friedrich] Burdach in 1800" (p. 108).

44. According to Gifford, Coleridge "report[ed] that it took [the Wordsworths and him] several months in 1797–98 to learn to take field notes 'with the object and imagery immediately before my sense'" (p. 11). Gifford cites this remark from Coleridge's description in *Biographia Literaria* of his preparations for "The Brook," a long poem that he failed to complete (I, p. 196).

45. Historians of science often distinguish biology from natural history on the basis of the methodological shift from an observational to an experimental science that occurred gradually over the course of the nineteenth century, and which on

some accounts didn't really get under way until the end of the century, when controlled experimentation became dominant in biological research. Nonetheless, the emphasis on experimentation already pervades Goethe's investigations, particularly his studies of color vision, where his critique of Newtonian optics prefigures more recent work on visual perception as a function of the nervous system and not just of the abstracted ocular apparatus. Interestingly, Wordsworth composed the first part of "The Two-Part Prelude" during the winter of 1798–99 when he and his sister were living in Goslar, near Goethe in Weimar, although there was certainly no communication between the two poet-scientists.

46. On one occasion, commenting on the extent of her reading, Stein asserted that she was "one of the few people of her generation that has read every line of Carlyle's Frederick the Great and Lecky's Constitutional History of England besides [Richardson's] Charles Grandison and Wordsworth's longer poems" (ABT, p. 74). Elsewhere, in a letter to Lindley Hubbell postmarked May 23, 1931, she recalled the "passion" she had felt "in [her] youth for the long dull poems of Wordsworth and Crabbe," adding that "at present" she was "trying a long narrative poem" (presumably a reference to "Winning His Way") as she had always "want[ed] to do a long dull poem too" (YCAL). One acquaintance even recalled her reciting Wordsworth during the years at Johns Hopkins (Wineapple, p. 128).

47. Striking examples of such investigations by Wordsworth include the passage in "The Two-Part Prelude" which concerns the child's "chastisement" upon his father's death (and the subsequent "correction" of his excessive reliance on the sense of sight with a mix of "spectacles and sounds" [I, ll. 327–74]) as well as the astonishing poem that closes the last of Wordsworth's "Essays on Epitaphs," describing the deaf-and-dumb Dalesman whose deafness is remedied by the "familiar voice" of his reading (p. 164).

48. Obviously, Wordsworth links his naturalism with some sort of super-naturalism, as is evident in the reference to "immortality" and even to the imagination's "celestial soil." Whether such supernaturalism is real or only apparent—at just what points it shifts from figuration to literal belief—is a highly vexed issue for any account of the poet's career. Here I am concerned only with the few years at the turn of the century when he was a thoroughgoing naturalist, if no more willing than Emerson or James or Stein to remove ecstatic experience from his ken, whether by excessive reduction or excessive elevation. When, in this passage, he suggests that he was "guided" by one of his "own primary consciousnesses," he appears to mean something like the following experience, recalled by Thomas De Quincey. Having "appl[ied] his ear to the ground, so as to catch any sound" of the wheels of a mailcoach bringing news from London, and then "slowly rising from this effort," Wordsworth caught sight of "a bright star . . . glittering" between two mountains. After he had "gazed upon it for a minute or so," he explained his behavior: " 'I have remarked, from my earliest days, that if, under any circumstances, the attention is energetically braced up to an act of steady observation, or of steady expectation, then, *if this intense condition of*

vigilance should suddenly relax, at that moment any beautiful, any impressive
visual object, or collection of objects, falling upon the eye, is carried to the heart
with a power not known under other circumstances. Just now . . . at the very
instant when the organs of attention were all at once relaxing from their tension,
the bright star hanging in the air above those outlines of massy blackness, fell
suddenly upon my eye, and penetrated my capacity of apprehension with a pathos
and a sense of the Infinite, that would not have arrested me under other circumstances' " (cited in Wordsworth, *Selected Poems*, p. 551).

49. Although James cites the phrase "the specious present" from Clay's 1882
study *The Alternative*, it was his own adoption of the phrase that led to its popu-
larity, perhaps most immediately in the dissertation of his graduate student Alfred
Hodder, published in 1901 with the ambitious title, *The Adversaries of the Sceptic;*
or, The Specious Present: A New Inquiry into Human Knowledge. Hodder's
experience on the job market prompted James to write his famous diatribe against
academic specialization, "The Ph.D Octopus," and he also served as Stein's model
for Philip Redfern in her early novella "Fernhurst," later incorporated into MA.
For more on Stein and Hodder, see Wineapple.

50. The term *ecstasis* derives etymologically from "the Greek *existanai*, to drive
out of one's senses: *ek-*, out + *histanai*, to place"—in effect, the experience of
"be[ing] beside oneself" (*American Heritage Dictionary*, p. 438; Weekley, I, p.
494). For important discussions of Wordsworth's figuration of "hanging," see de
Man ("Wordsworth and the Victorians") and Hertz ("Lurid Figures").

51. See Quartermain for documentation of Zukofsky's silent collaboration with
Williams.

52. It doesn't seem much of a stretch to argue that Stein is responding directly
to Williams here, since "The Work of Gertrude Stein" appeared in the January–
March 1930 issue of *Pagany* and HTW wasn't published until November 1931.
An alternative account of the volume's format is offered in ABT, where Toklas
reports that, having been "[dis]satisfied with the get up" of *Lucy Church Amiably*,
she "decided," in her capacity as publisher of the Plain Edition, "to have the next
book [HTW] printed at Dijon and in the form of an Elzevir" (p. 243). The *Oxford*
English Dictionary notes that the term *elzevir* was "formerly applied to editions
printed in the small neat form and with the kind of type adopted by" the Elzeviers,
a family of Dutch printers, "famous chiefly for their editions of the classics" (I, p.
847).

53. This use of the expression *thought experiment* may itself seem "strangely
whimsical" in the context of the thought experiments that dominate contemporary
speculative physics, such as the quantum analysis of Schrödinger's cat. Yet Sterne's
thought experiments, like those of Wordsworth and James and Stein, are often
considerably *less* whimsical than those of theoretical physics, since they are
designed to test the neurophysiological parameters of thought as an expression of
feeling. Hence they are significantly less abstracted from actual experience. More
immediately concerned with the nature of *thought*, they also presuppose their own

embodiment (as *experienced* thought) in ways that remain unavailable to the more abstract, and ultimately less self-reflective, experiments of speculative physics. This must remain the case so long as physics continues to mix empiricism and rationalism while falling short of the conjunctions of radical empiricism—so long, that is, as it abstracts itself from the physicist's own physiological, and not merely physical, matrix. Whitehead's distinctive brand of speculative physics may be regarded as at least a partial correction of this state of affairs.

54. Noam Chomsky's linguistic formalism provides an especially influential example of this misleading species of abstraction.

55. See the last four books of *Tristram Shandy* for an extended meditation on the military metaphor implicit in "verbs auxiliary."

56. Although there is no direct evidence that Stein coined the phrase "tender buttons" with Tristram's account in mind, there is plenty of evidence concerning her intimate knowledge of eighteenth-century British literature. Not only did she copy out extended passages from Swift's *A Tale of a Tub* in a manuscript notebook for "Melanctha," but soon after completing *Three Lives* she commented to Mabel Foote Weeks that the volume was "a noble combination of Swift and Matisse" (YCAL, undated). Decades later, she likened ABT to Boswell's *Life of Johnson* as well as Defoe's *Robinson Crusoe*; and in a 1939 essay she remarked that she considered Richardson's *Clarissa Harlow* "the greatest of all novels" (ABT, p. 252; N, pp. 45, 60; "Debt," p. 113). Moreover, according to Burns and Dydo, the code Stein and Toklas used in "intimate love exchanges" on the margins of manuscripts derived from Swift's *Journal to Stella* (in which letters to Esther Johnson and her chaperone Rebecca Dingley were addressed to MD [My Dears] and DD [Dearest Dingley]). In the hands of Stein and Toklas, this was tranformed into DD and Y[our] D[ear] (p. 86).

57. Some 35 pages after Stein has Toklas observe in ABT that "hitherto [Stein] had been interested only in the insides of people, their character and what went on inside them," Toklas repeats the observation: "Hitherto she had been concerned with seriousness and the inside of things, in these studies she began to describe the inside as seen from the outside" (p. 156). The prior seriousness contrasts sharply with the joy and amusement experienced in Granada. As so often occurs with Stein, the adjectives in question are set in motion, enabling them to operate at several levels at once. Here they bridge the concerns of her compositional practices in 1912 and her social interactions in Spain during the same period.

58. Stein used the phrases "phenomena of nature" and "natural phenomena" interchangeably—referring, for instance, to the mid-1920s composition "Natural Phenomena" as "the Phenomena of Nature" (ABT, p. 224).

59. Wordsworth typically juxtaposes heterogeneous sensory modalities in order to conjure up an "*eternal* beauty" with which the "beating mind" engages in "unconscious discourse" (PRE, pp. 14, 11). Hence in the opening verse-paragraph of "Tintern Abbey" he joins the mountain-springs' "sweet inland murmur" to the sight of "steep and lofty cliffs[,] connect[ing] / The landscape with the quiet of the

sky" (LB, p. 113). The notion of a *heterogeneous dialectic* was introduced by Gregory Vlastos in distinguishing Whitehead's logic from that of Hegel.

60. I cite the term *quasi-object* from Michel Serres by way of Latour.

Chapter 2

1. A dozen years earlier Fishbein played a much more constructive role in the genesis of Sinclair Lewis's Pulitzer Prize–winning novel *Arrowsmith*; the circumstances are described in Mark Schorer's "Afterword" to the novel. Interestingly, the bulk of the *Newsweek* article cites Fishbein paraphrasing an account of Stein's writing by the behaviorist B. F. Skinner. This had appeared the previous month in the *Atlantic Monthly* and concerned several experiments that Stein had conducted four decades earlier at the Harvard Psychological Laboratory. Fishbein's diagnosis is replaced by that of Skinner, and in the process psychology subsumes physiology. See Chapter 5 for a more detailed discussion of Skinner's argument.

2. "It is impossible to overstate the influence of Aristotle's use of the term *organon* to designate a functional part (*morion*) of an animal or vegetal body such as a hand, beak, wing, root, or what have you," Canguilhem observes. "Until at least the end of the eighteenth century anatomy and physiology preserved, with all its ambiguities, a term that Aristotle borrowed from the lexicon of artisans and musicians, whose use indicates implicit or explicit acceptance of some sort of analogy between nature and art, life and technics" ("Normality," pp. 128–29). For Canguilhem, biology becomes increasingly scientific only to the extent that the "analogy between nature and art" is rejected, and life is "studied as far as possible as though it were nonlife" ("History of the Life Sciences," p. 118).

3. B. C. Southam makes the somewhat far-fetched suggestion that Eliot may have derived his image from an illustration that accompanied a January 1897 article on "Seeing the Brain" in the *St. Louis Globe-Democrat*. The illustration "show[s] a man seated in front of a powerful light," which projects "a patterned X-ray of his brain on to a screen" (Southam, p. 41). Eliot would have been only eight years old when the article appeared.

4. For a fascinating account of victims of this epidemic, see Sacks (*Awakenings*).

5. I discuss Stein's articles in Chapter 5 below. Leon Solomons, who co-authored the first of these with her, remarks in an article on "the intensity of coloration" that "owing to the training required the experiments were made only by Miss Stein and the writer" ("The Saturation of Colors," p. 51). In the same issue of the *Psychological Review*, Stein is also mentioned as a subject in an experiment on "the oscillation of feeble impressions," using "optical, tactual and thermal stimuli" (Hylan, pp. 56–57). The *Psychological Review* served as a frequent forum for James as well. In 1894 and 1895 he published important articles there on "The Physical Basis of Emotion" and "The Knowing of Things Together," and subsequent writing of his that appeared in the journal includes

articles on "Psychical Research" (in 1896) and "Consciousness under Nitrous Oxide" (in 1898) as well as many brief notices.

6. Course descriptions are cited from the Harvard Course Catalogue for 1896–97.

7. The lumbar ganglion is the dorsal (sensory) root of the nerves found in the spinal cord between the lowest ribs and the pelvis; it serves the external genitalia as well as parts of the abdomen and of the lower extremities.

8. For an admittedly "dys-lexic" juxtaposition of Stein and Bergson, see Riddel (p. 91).

9. See Froula for a provocative study that "take[s] Stephen's self-described 'vivisective' modernity as a master metaphor for Joyce's autobiographical art" (p. 2).

10. In the late nineteenth and early twentieth centuries, George Beard popularized the term *neurasthenia* (which he used to designate "functional nervous weakness" and "nervous disability") in such works as *The Nature and Diagnosis of Neurasthenia* and *American Nervousness*. See Lutz for a fascinating account of neurasthenia in its American, and self-consciously "modern," context, and Rabinbach for its European context. I prefer to use the term *neuraesthesis*, rather than related terms such as *proprioception, kinesthetics, muscle sense, vestibular sense, somatics, somaesthesis,* and *somaesthetics,* in order to highlight the central role that the nervous system plays in all body awareness. For discussions of these terms and their interrelations, see Gibson ("The Uses of Proprioception"), Boring, Reed (*From Soul to Mind*), and Shusterman (*Practicing Philosophy*).

11. See Risse and Canguilhem on the late-eighteenth-century Brownian system, with its principle of "excitability" and two different states of "disease predisposition": *sthenic* ("produced by excessive stimulation") and *asthenic* ("due to deficient stimulants").

12. This composition is dated February 26, 1895, hence about seven months after Pater's death. The principal instructor in the course was William Vaughn Moody. Only five years older than Stein, he moved to the University of Chicago the next year and continued to teach there until 1907. In addition to well-regarded poetry and plays, he co-authored the textbook *A First View of English Literature* with Robert Morss Lovett; see Hollander for a selection of his poems and a biographical sketch.

13. As defined in the *American Heritage Dictionary*, a sounding board is "a thin board forming the upper portion of the resonant chamber in a musical instrument, such as a violin or piano, and serving to increase resonance."

14. A sense of Stein's compositional procedure in a work like "Mildred's Thoughts" may be caught from the reverberations of the title, which functions as a "tuning fork" or "metronome" throughout the work. To be sure, this is only one strand in a very complex composition, and as such it provides no more than a rhythmic frame for her meditations, in all their "complicated simplicity" (TI, p. 34). The meditations don't just concern Aldrich's thoughts but also "Mildred's

Thoughts," the work Stein was in the process of composing, and her own thoughts of Aldrich as well:

1. I think, I think, I think it is a victory a victory of force over intelligence and I I do not agree, I think it is a victory a victory (p. 648);

2. Give a thought to them, and give them my thoughts (p. 648);

3. I have thought very much about heat. . . . We know what we think (pp. 648–49);

4. Mildred's thoughts are where. There with pear, with the pears and the stairs Mildred's thoughts are there with the pears with the stairs and the pears (p. 649);

5. Can you think. Of me (p. 649);

6. Let us think Mildred thinks. What do you think. Read me read for me read in me, read my notes (p. 650);

7. Now we will credit Mildred with this thought (p. 650);

8. Mildred has thought a great deal. She thinks once at a time and without difficulty. She thinks twice (p. 650);

9. And now to introduce a play. / Mildred's Thoughts (p. 650);

10. And may I go on with Mildred's thoughts (p. 656);

11. I think the silver ones are prettier than the gold ones . . . I think the silver ones are far prettier than the gold ones (p. 659);

12. And now think. / Think all together. / How can we think such thoughts (p. 662);

13. And I have enjoyed meeting Merry thoughts (p. 663);

14. Thoughts. / I think very well of my mother. / Mildred's thoughts. How well we finish the water (p. 664);

15. I wonder how they happened to think that I knew them when they came again (p. 665);

16. Mildred's thoughts. I think strongly. And riches how often are there different ways of re-editing worlds (p. 665);

17. Mildred I think. Mildred I do think that you have been rich that is to say wealthy. / She never thinks about them. / Mildred never thinks about Marsden Hartley or Marcel Duchamp or Martin Dehmuth. Mildred never thinks about Marsden Hartley or Marcel Duchamp or Martin Demuth presently (p. 666);

18. Mildred thinks of them. She thinks of George, Marsden, Marcel, Martin and Lee Master. She thinks of busy ways and mistakes. She thinks of relief (p. 666);

19. Mildred's thoughts when Susan has deserted her and when Alfred has sent her his book (p. 668);

20. Give a thought to Cuba (p. 669);

21. Mildred thinks that chicken made of glass a horseshoe made of glass, a king's messenger made of glass, she feels that we have taught the workingman

to feel what he feels. And I, I please myself. I teach myself to feel what I feel. I beg your pardon. I did not mean. I meant that I am taught to feel what I feel and I feel what I feel when I am taught to feel what I feel. I feel for them. They feel for me. Frank feels very well. And Katherine Buss (p. 669);

22. Mildred thinks that the world has accepted its manhood its womanhood and its age and its childhood. She thinks that she herself so feels no effort is necessary. Please buy a clock. Mildred is still thinking (p. 669).

"Mildred's Thoughts" was first published in 1927 in the inaugural *American Caravan*, "a yearbook," as the collection was subtitled, "of American literature." Unaccountably, when the piece was finally reprinted in a collection of Stein's writings, in 1973, only a small portion of the text was included (although a subsequent reissue apparently contains the full text).

15. Recently Kay Turner has argued, on the basis of incontrovertible evidence in a sequence of notes between Stein and Toklas, that Stein's frequent references to "having a cow" in association with Toklas (here "baby mine") concern apparent difficulties that Toklas had defecating. *Having a cow* does not refer, as has often been assumed, to *having an orgasm*. Nevertheless, the experience portrayed (like that of "Pig Cupid . . . Rooting erotic garbage") remains intimately involved in the "variations of cycles, and of cycles of cycles," of life. (See Chapter 4 for a fuller discussion of this last phrase, cited from Whitehead's *Function of Reason*.)

16. Among the books from Stein's library shipped to Yale University after her death were eleven volumes of the 12-volume Sterling edition of George Eliot's works, published in Boston in 1887. These included *The Mill on the Floss* (volume 2), *Middlemarch* (volumes 7 and 8), and the *Complete Poems* (volume 9).

17. Rothfield observes of Eliot's allusion to "oxy-hydrogen" that it is, "as usual in Eliot, historically precise: oxyhydrogen, introduced as a light source for microscopes in the late 1820s, . . . improved microscopic resolution of details" (p. 96).

18. I have followed Stein's manuscript rather than the printed text in the layout of this passage.

19. See Schoenberg for the fullest, most evenhanded account to date of Stein's medical career at Johns Hopkins.

20. "For the first time in an American medical school," W. Bruce Fye observes, "all of the basic science teachers devoted their whole time to teaching and research." In addition, the school's scientific chairs went to individuals who were all "deeply committed to physiology as the basis for modern scientific medicine" (pp. 206–7). As Sherwin Nuland notes, "the fifteen men and three women who made up the entering class of the medical school fulfilled the most rigorous requirements that had ever been asked of any entering medical students anywhere," including the "first complete medical laboratory courses" in the United States. "The thirty Hopkins years surrounding the turn of the twentieth century," Nuland adds, "surely rank with even the glorious decades of the Paris and Vienna Schools as the most fertile periods for progress that medical history has yet seen"

(pp. 403–4). Interestingly, two of the four Baltimore women who formed the Women's Fund Committee, M. Carey Thomas and Mary Gwinn, were later to feature in Stein's early story "Fernhurst," which she incorporated into MA. "Fernhurst" offers a thinly disguised account of the triangle between Thomas, Gwinn, and Alfred Hodder, who in 1895 was hired to teach English literature at Bryn Mawr, where Thomas was president and Gwinn, her companion, taught English. By 1904, Hodder had separated from his wife, and he and Gwinn had married. The story's title is derived from the English village, Greenhill-Fernhurst, where in 1902 Stein and her brother Leo spent the better part of a month near Bernard and Mary Berenson, acquaintances from Florence. Like the Steins, Bernard Berenson had known Hodder at Harvard, and his wife was a cousin of Carey Thomas. Consequently, there was much discussion of the affair, and Stein wrote "Fernhurst" soon after. For a comprehensive account of the relations between Thomas, Gwinn, and Hodder, see Horowitz, as well as Wineapple's recent double biography of the Stein siblings, which includes fascinating new material concerning their connections to this Bryn Mawr circle.

21. Leo Stein, in a letter to Albert Barnes dated October 20, 1934, recalled that his sister "made fun" of "her 'research' work at medical school[,] saying that the women who were at Johns Hopkins for the first time fell in with Mall's hobby for making models of the brain tracts, to show how interested they were; that the men wouldn't waste their time on it." "She told me," he added, "that she didn't mind doing it, as it was purely mechanical work and rather restful" (*Journey Into the Self*, p. 148).

22. Shepherd devotes several pages in *Foundations of the Neuron Doctrine* to Barker's study, as "important" in "spreading the word" in "the English-speaking world, particularly [among] Americans" (p. 256).

23. Nauta and Feirtag characterize "the nucleus of the posterior commissure, the interstitial nucleus of Cajal, and the nucleus of Darkschewitsch" as "the so-called accessory oculomotor nuclei, high in the midbrain" (p. 214). However, Barker did not distinguish the nucleus of Darkschewitsch from the nucleus of the posterior commissure, nor does it appear that the interstitial nucleus of Cajal had yet been expressly identified. Only the nucleus of Darkschewitsch is discussed in his text, although several illustrations identify the "*Nu.f.l.m.*" as the "nucleus fasciculi longitudinalis medialis, or nucleus commissurae posterioris (*oberer Oculomotoriuskern* of Darkschewitsch)" (p. 722–23). (See Figure 3 above.) The authors of a 1962 anatomy of the nervous system observe that "the nucleus of Darkschewitsch is sometimes termed the ventral nucleus of the posterior commissure"—not to be confused with the nuclei of the posterior commissure, a small strand of fibers connecting the superior colliculi and hence also involved in the coordination of vision-related reflexes. To complicate matters further, they add that the "inconspicuous nuclear mass . . . to which the name 'nucleus of Darkschewitsch' is applied . . . is probably not the nucleus described by that author" (Crosby et al., pp. 267–68, 245). Barker supplies the relevant reference:

"Cf. Darkschewitsch, L. Einige Bemerkungen ueber den Faserverlauf in der hinteren Commissur des Gehirns. Neurol. Centralbl., Leipz., Bd. v (1886), S. 99–103" (p. 721). According to Nauta and Feirtag, L. O. Darkschewitsch was a Russian neurologist (p. 218). In a recent overview of "the first moderns," Everdell suggests that Freud "studied neighboring parts of the brain with Darkschewitsch himself back in 1885," but I have not been able to confirm this (p. 131).

24. The medial longitudinal fasciculus is "a tract within the brain stem and upper spinal cord that links the visual world and vestibular events with the movements of the eyes and the neck, in addition to linking up the nuclei that are responsible for eye movements" (Hendelman, p. 124).

25. It is quite probable that Stein's description here of the nucleus of Dark-schewitsch actually applies (like Darkschewitsch's own) to the nucleus of the posterior commissure rather than to the structure that has subsequently been labeled the nucleus of Darkschewitsch. Florence Sabin, in her *Atlas of the Medulla and Midbrain*—see below—would seem to confirm this: "Just at the junction of the pillars of the [posterior] commissure with the fasciculus longitudinalis medialis and the proximal capsule of the nucleus ruber [the red nucleus] is the groove for the nucleus of Darkschewitsch." She also notes that certain "fibres [which] slant into the posterior commissure from the superior colliculus . . . decussate [intersect] in the arch and pass down in the pillars to the nucleus of Darkschewitsch." Like Barker, Sabin identifies the nucleus of Darkschewitsch as "Nucleus fasciculi longi-tudinalis medialis or nucleus commissurae posterioris (*oberer Oculomotoriuskern* or [sic] Darkschewitsch)"; however, she labels the "Nucleus commissurae posterior, or nucleus fasciculi longitudinalis medialis" separately as well, identifying it as a "posterior longitudinal bundle" (pp. 101–102, 117).

26. "By his own accounts," Eugene Taylor observes, James "ceased to keep up with developments in the most recent literature on brain neurophysiology" in the 1890s. Nevertheless, Taylor cautions, "This is not altogether true, since we know that after 1890 James had read and annotated books on the structure and function of the nervous system, underlining sections, for instance, that described new find-ings on the autonomic nervous system and the antigen-antibody response" (CBM, pp. 57, 164). Also, in the first of his Ingersoll lectures on "Human Immortality," which he delivered in the fall of 1897, James discussed recent findings concerning the "association-centres" in the hemispheres (*Writings 1878–1899*, p. 1103).

27. By 1909 James was partly reconciled with Hegel. Against the "incorrup-tible logic of self-identity" (which "teach[es] us that to call a thing and its other the same is to commit the crime of self-contradiction"), James found himself embracing the Hegelian "logic" that "things are their own others" (*Pluralistic Universe*, pp. 722, 629). "The full truth about anything involves more than that thing." "Everything is in an environment, a surrounding world of other things, and . . . if you leave it to work there, [its] rivals and enemies will destroy it unless it can buy them off by compromising some part of its original pretentions." Hegel, regrettably, "saw this undeniable characteristic of the world we live in *in a non-*

empirical light"; for, despite his "vision of a really living world, . . . he clung fast to the old rationalist contempt for the immediately given world of sense and all its squalid particulars" (pp. 670–71, emphasis added). Illogically, Hegel chose to call his new method by the name of precisely what it was not, *logic*. Yet if "life is logically irrational," as James concluded, then it was only "*livingly*" that "things [were] their own others"—and *not* logically, as Hegel had insisted (pp. 724, 629, emphasis added).

28. The earlier of these comments was actually made by Toklas in a letter dated April 11, 1924, to Ellery Sedgwick, the editor of *The Atlantic Monthly*. Writing on behalf of Stein—the letter is signed "A.B.T. / for Miss Gertrude Stein"—Toklas outlined Stein's "theory of her literary art": "Miss Stein feels that the development of her work in the last fifteen years can be traced in her books— Three Lives, Tender Buttons, Geography and Plays. Her original effort was for concentrated rhythms, then through the study of the relation of words in meaning sound and volume she attempted to give completed composition." This was clearly Stein's own manner of formulating her literary theory (Gallup, "Gertrude Stein and the *Atlantic*," pp. 115–16).

29. Wineapple remarks, "At Hopkins, fourth-year medical students devoted themselves—as they still do today—almost entirely to clinical experience and exposure. In addition to witnessing and assisting surgery, these students, divided into four groups, served two months in rotation in the surgical, gynecological, and obstetrical departments of the hospital, each morning visiting the well-scrubbed wards to familiarize themselves with various cases and presumably develop a rapport with the patients. They prepared surgical dressings and performed minor operations, and for obstetrical duty visited patients throughout the city and assisted in childbirth" (p. 140).

30. See Farnes for a consideration of Mendenhall's accomplishments in medical science, perhaps most notably her description in 1902 of "the characteristic cell of Hodgkin's disease," which was subsequently "co-named" for her as "the Reed-Sternberg cell" (pp. 275–76).

31. This account matches the one Mendenhall gave to Wilson: "Florence worked over it for several nights and came back to Dr. Mall with the answer that Miss Stein must have embedded the cord turned back under the embryo brain, instead of extended from it, and the centers of the outborne cells of the cord she had located in the brain, and other mysterious features of the reconstruction, could be explained only in this way" (*Upstate*, p. 63).

32. After publishing *An Atlas of the Medulla and Midbrain: A Laboratory Manual* in 1901, Sabin stayed on at Johns Hopkins, specializing in the lymphatic system. In 1917 she was appointed Professor of Histology, the first woman to become a full professor at the Medical School. Although Mall died that year, "the position of Professor of Anatomy and Head of the Department [was not] offered to her"; instead, as Philip McMaster and Michael Heidelberger delicately phrase the matter, "it was occupied by one of her former students" (p. 288). After serving

as president of the American Association of Anatomists in 1924, Sabin was elected the following year to the National Academy of Sciences. She also moved in 1925 to the Rockefeller Institute for Medical Research—again, as at the Johns Hopkins Medical School and the National Academy of Sciences, "the first woman to become a full Member of that institution"—and continued to conduct research on bodily defenses against infectious diseases for another thirteen years (p. 289). Shortly after retiring to Colorado in the late 1930s, she was asked to chair the government committee on public health, and successfully campaigned for the modernization of the state's health laws—in 1951 receiving the Lasker Award from the American Public Health Association for "outstanding achievement in the field of public health administration" (p. 295). The same year, the Florence R. Sabin Building for Research in Cellular Biology was dedicated at the University of Colorado Medical Center.

33. Volume 9 of the *Johns Hopkins Hospital Reports*, subtitled *Contributions to the Science of Medicine*, was "dedicated by his pupils" to William Henry Welch—Professor of Pathology at Johns Hopkins—"on the Twenty-Fifth Anniversary of his Doctorate." The volume includes articles by Stein's close friend, Claribel Cone, as well as by Mall, Barker, Reed, and Williams. See H. Damasio for a late-twentieth-century equivalent of Sabin's *Atlas*.

34. Under Mall's supervision, Sabin extended "the method of [Gustav] Born for making wax models from serial sections," and thereby replaced an exclusive focus on "the *external* form of the neural tube"—the early embryonic structure which in the course of development turns into the brain and the spinal cord—with careful attention to "the form of the *internal* structures" of the CNS, or central nervous system. According to Sabin, Born's method involved the following set of procedures: "It is necessary (1) to have an accurate drawing of each section magnified to a certain degree, (2) to transfer the drawing to a wax plate (care being taken to magnify the thickness of the section in the same proportion as the length and breadth), (3) to cut each structure from the plates, (4) to pile each so as to show its own form and its relations to all other structures and (5) to fuse the pieces of each structure into a unit" (*Atlas*, pp. 13–14, emphasis added).

35. I am grateful to the Alan Mason Chesney Medical Archives at the Johns Hopkins Medical Institutions for permission to cite from the correspondence between Barker and Knower as well as from the letters between Stein, Barker, and Mall cited below.

36. I want to thank the audience at Washington University, where I first delivered this section of Chapter 2, for their lively discussion of the "look" of Stein's letter, and in particular Sarah Kelen for her suggestion concerning the two levels of correction that the letter displays.

37. In several instances, as here, I have added virgules to Stein's prose for the sake of expediency, since in removing punctuation and thereby providing breathing room for her words, she often requires her reader to slow down, if only to extricate oneself from the words' unanticipated diffractedness.

38. See Ashton for a compelling discussion of this passage in the context of a more general consideration of Stein's "project of rendering movement in prose" through the "mistakes one can make with parts of speech" (p. 322).

39. Abrams suggests that "the basic nature of the shift from psychological criticism in the tradition of Hobbes and Hume to that of Coleridge can, I think, be clarified if we treat it as the result of an analogical substitution—the replacement, that is to say, of a mechanical process by a living plant as the implicit paradigm governing the description of the process and the product of literary invention" (p. 158).

40. At the same time, Coleridge's notion of organic form is perfectly consistent with the organicism associated, in the United States at least, with the New Criticism, the explanatory limits of which are often taken to demonstrate the common failings of all forms of organicism. Cleanth Brooks, for instance, used the "figure" of a growing plant in his 1948 essay on "Irony and 'Ironic' Poetry" to characterize the "organic relation" which "the parts of a poem have . . . to each other." The parts, he suggested, "have a closer relation to each other than do the blossoms juxtaposed in a bouquet. The parts of a poem are related as are the parts of a growing plant. The beauty of the poem is the flowering of the whole plant and needs the stalk, the leaf, and even the hidden roots." In the event that this figure might strike the reader as "high-flown," Brooks immediately substitutes a "more obvious" figure, that of the poem as "a little drama" with "no waste motion" and "no superfluous parts" (p. 232). Needless to say, this supplementary figure, rather than replacing the plant metaphor, merely renders all the more obvious several features of plants that distinguish them from other organisms as especially appropriate figures of organic unity. Moreover, in characterizing the "organic relation[s]" of a poem in terms of ideals drawn directly from the domain of mechanics ("no waste motion," "no superfluous parts"), Brooks inadvertently illustrates the contradiction at the heart of Coleridgean organicism. Also see Brooks's essays, "The Poem as Organism" and "Implications of an Organic Theory."

41. Stein returns to the subject of "lively words" at the beginning of "Poetry and Grammar," where she writes: "I have said that the words in plays written in poetry are more lively than the same words written by the same poet in other kinds of poetry. It undoubtedly was true of Shakespeare, is it inevitably true of everybody. That is one thing to think about. I said that the words in a play written in prose are not as lively words as the words written in other prose by the same writer. This is true of Goldsmith and I imagine it is true of almost any writer" (LIA, p. 209).

42. Krieger cites this passage in *A Reopening of Closure*, his study of the origins of the "organicist theory of metaphor" in Renaissance poetry and its survival in contemporary literary theory. "Far from being an antagonistic intrusion," he argues, "the *variety* side of the *unity-in-variety* motto is built into organicism's sense of itself and requires a fuller reading" than that offered by contemporary critiques of organicism (pp. xiii, 50). De Man's insistence on a radical break between "the natural world" and some sort of "discontinuous world

of reflective irony and ambiguity" is ubiquitous in his writing; see, for instance, the discussion of "ideology," in "The Resistance to Theory," as "the confusion of linguistic with natural reality, of reference with phenomenalism." "It is not *a priori* certain," he states, "that language functions according to principles which are those, or which are *like* those, of the phenomenal world" (p. 11). For a related critique of de Man, see Shusterman (*Pragmatist Aesthetics*).

43. James's criticism of Meynert's scheme has recently been reaffirmed by Antonio Damasio. Against the "seemingly sensible view" that "the old brain core handles basic biological regulation down in the basement, while up above the neocortex deliberates with wisdom and subtlety," Damasio proposes that "the apparatus of rationality, traditionally presumed to be *neo*cortical, does not seem to work without that of biological regulation, traditionally assumed to be *sub*cortical. Nature appears to have built the apparatus of rationality not just on top of the apparatus of biological regulation, but also *from* it and *with* it. The mechanisms for behavior beyond drives and instincts use, I believe, both the upstairs and the downstairs: the neocortex becomes engaged *along with* the older brain core, and rationality results from their concerted activity" (*Descartes' Error*, p. 128). Along similar lines, Lieberman observes, "It has become clear that most complex aspects of human behavior, including language, are not regulated in a single localized region of the brain." "The comprehension of a sentence," for instance, "involves circuits that link many cortical and subcortical neural structures" (p. 103).

44. See Sulloway and Greenberg, as well as the recent volume on "Freud and the neurosciences" edited by Guttmann and Scholz-Strasser, for extended considerations of Freud's invention of psychoanalysis in relation to his work on neuroanatomy.

45. The "fasciculus retroflexus of Meynert," or "Meynert's bundle," is also known as the *habenulopeduncular tract*, because it contains fibers that run "from [the] habenular nuclei," in the epithalamus, "through the red nucleus to gain the interpeduncular nucleus" in the midbrain (Peele, p. 547).

46. I take these definitions from several of the examples of the term's use cited in the *Oxford English Dictionary*: "1825 Hamilton *Dict. Terms Art, Perule*, in *Botany*, the cover of a seed. 1856 Henslow *Bot. Dict.*, 133 *Perule* (a little pouch), a sac formed in some Orchideae by the prolonged and united bases of two of the segments of their perianth. The cap-like covering of buds, formed by the abortion of their outer leaves. 1866 *Treas. Bot., Perule*, the covering of a leaf-bud formed by scales; also a projection in the flower of the orchids formed by the enlargement of two lateral sepals" (II, p. 2144).

47. The inner or intrinsic movement contrasts sharply with the deterministic notion, in MA, of "bottom nature." Rather than *enabling* one to move, this *makes* one move.

48. See Keller (*A Feeling for the Organism*) for a fascinating account of McClintock's investigations of genetic transposition, and Margulis and Sagan for a complementary account of the *earth* as an organism, "complete and fructifying."

Introduction to Part II

1. As early as March 1851, Emerson presented a set of lectures in Pittsburgh on "the conduct of life," although he didn't publish the volume derived from them, introduced by "Fate," until 1860. "Because he had not finished writing the opening remarks," one biographer observes of the Pittsburgh series, "Emerson gave first an old lecture on 'England,' then on subsequent days he presented his new talks, 'The Laws of Success,' 'Wealth,' 'Economy,' 'Culture,' and 'Worship.' The subjects and even the order in which they were treated are very much the same as they would appear about ten years later" (Richardson, p. 490). According to Gay Wilson Allen, Emerson "managed to finish writing his lecture on 'Fate' . . . in time to read it" that December in Cincinnati, during "the most extensive tour in the West he had yet undertaken" (*Waldo Emerson*, pp. 565–66). The next month, in Boston, he opened the "Conduct of Life" series with it, as he did a month later in New York (Richardson, p. 500). Presumably, the opening lines of the published version hark back to that winter, when Emerson was indeed "reading a discourse to the citizens of Boston or New York" on the "practical question of the conduct of life": "It chanced during one winter, a few years ago, that our cities were bent on discussing the theory of the Age. By an odd coincidence, four or five noted men were each reading a discourse to the citizens of Boston or New York, on the Spirit of the Times. . . . To me, however, the question of the times resolved itself into a practical question of the conduct of life. How shall I live? We are incompetent to solve the times."

By late 1860, when the essay was finally published, this assertion of incompetency reverberated not just with the prospect of civil war but also with Lincoln's recent election. The practical question of the conduct of life was "resolving" itself back into "the question of the times," only this time—in the face of fierce public debate over the conduct entailed by citizenship in a polity composed of states and not just cities—it took the form of doubts concerning the competency of this *we*, a matter not just of "how I shall live" but of *how we are going to continue living together*.

2. In the earlier of two extended readings of "Fate," Stanley Cavell discusses the linguistic conditions of such dictation as well as the way it conditions the operations of language in turn in the composition of a work such as "Fate"; see "Emerson, Coleridge, Kant" and "Emerson's Constitutional Amending."

3. Vlastos's characterization of a *heterogeneous* dialectic might usefully be compared to Louis Marin's description of the deconstructive logic whereby a "complex" relation between *contraries* is reconfigured as a "neutral" (utopic) relation between the *contradictions* of each of the contrary terms. "In [A.-J.] Greimas's terms for the elementary structure of signification," Marin writes in "Frontiers of Utopia," "the neutral relationship is the one that connects two 'contradictory' terms—non-A/non-B—and the 'complex' relationship articulates two 'contrary' terms—A/B. . . . My theoretical (and experimental) move consists in

deconstructing the complex relationships through which the subject of Utopia, constituted as an imaginary one, would be the autonomous Kantian or Rousseauist subject, simultaneously political and ethical sovereign law-giver and law-given subject. Our deconstructing gesture operates (1) by negating the 'contrary' terms of the relation, making them 'indefinite,' 'undetermined' terms without any logical limit, except that they are neither A nor B and (2) by relating them as 'contradictory' terms by the neutral relationships. To take an example, [Sir Thomas] More's *Utopia* is simultaneously a representation of both England and America, but its creative energy, its performative force, springs from the fact that Utopia is neither America nor England (it is at the same time non-Europe and non-America). In other words, it is the name and the figure of their indefinite interval" (pp. 404–5). It is in this interval that Emerson, to take another example, locates human "bravery," and by implication the will to act: in the belief that one "cannot shun a danger that is appointed, nor incur one that is not." For a surprisingly sympathetic account of "what [Hegel] did with the category of negation," understood as "his most original stroke," see James (*Pluralistic Universe*, p. 672). Also see Lenoir for an historicist critique of the Greimas-inflected "semiotic turn" in recent science studies.

4. "The best practical knowers of the human soul," James observed in a 1907 article on "The Energies of Men," "have invented the thing known as methodical ascetic discipline to keep the deeper levels [of vital energy] constantly in reach." After alluding to "Ignatius Loyola's spiritual exercises" as an example of such discipline, he noted that "the most venerable ascetic system, and the one whose results have the most voluminous experimental corroboration is undoubtedly the Yoga system in Hindustan" (pp. 251–52). See Taylor (CBM) and Kalupahana for a wealth of information concerning the extensive correlations between Jamesian psychology and various forms of Asian psychology. Stein was almost surely familiar with the article in question, since in late 1907 she was already inquiring about it. Among the notebooks and working notes for MA in YCAL is the draft of a letter to an unnamed correspondent in which she writes: "Send November number of American with article of James in it. If anything by James or anything of importance in the field of Pragmatic literature comes out to let me know." James only published two articles in the *American Magazine*: "The Powers of Men" in October 1907 (subsequently retitled "The Energies of Men") and "Confidences of a 'Psychical Researcher'" in October 1909. Stein's reference can only be to the former, since she drafted the letter on the last page of a notebook that also contains drafts of passages that appear between pages 92 and 115 in the published version of MA. This material was probably finished by the winter of 1907–8 and certainly by the summer of 1908. The notebook (labeled #19 by Katz) is in Folder 285, Box 17, of the Stein papers.

5. A small notebook, or *carnet*, contains the page reproduced here as well as several notes for LCA, referred to as "A Novel No.2 / Geographical" in the notebook (YCAL, Box 35, Folder 727). The inaugural *A Novel* was subsequently

retitled *A Novel of Thank You*. In addition to a draft of a letter to Jean Cocteau as well as a sketch of Toklas by Stein, the *carnet* also includes, among Stein's preliminary notes for her new novel, the work's opening lines, "Begins the middle of May. / There were as many chairs there and there were two . . ." This suggests that the notebook dates from May 1927. By August of that year, Stein was reporting to Carl Van Vechten that she had "gotten awfully interested in narrative" and was hard at work "telling the pleasant events in the life of Lucy Church" (SVV, I, p. 152). The five syllables trailing down the page form a discrete composition, and on the basis of their close proximity to the drawing of Toklas, it seems reasonable to identify Toklas as the "Belle" of the portrait. One might conjecture as well that "Belle" echoes "syllable"—or, more precisely, that Stein has recast *irresistible* into syllables because of the suggestion of sylla*ble* in irresisti*ble*. What, then, of the phrase *Begins the middle of May*, which in the notebook directly follows the sketch of Toklas? The middle of *irresistible* is *sis*, or *Sis*, but *May* lacks a middle syllable (although not a middle letter), since it contains just one syllable, isomorphic with the word taken as a whole. In effect, the term *irresistible* has been reorganized so that each syllable possesses the heft of a one-syllable word like "May." That *May* is also the name of Stein's former lover May Bookstaver may not be inconsequential; in any case, the following remark from EA is certainly pertinent. There, Stein writes of Isabel Lathrop, the former director of the American Fund for French Wounded—under whose aegis she and Toklas had distributed supplies to French hospitals during World War I—that "we used to be pleased when Mrs. Lathrop said organization, she made each syllable in it a separate thing to be organized into one" (p. 66).

Chapter 3

1. According to James Elliot Cabot, editor of Emerson's posthumously published *Natural History of Intellect and Other Papers*, the title essay derived from the 1870–71 course at Harvard. See Simmons on the pivotal role Cabot played in his capacity as Emerson's first editor.

2. Emerson's interest in science has received considerable attention lately; see especially Brown, Robinson, Dant, and J. Richardson as well as earlier works by Clark, Strauch, and Allen.

3. Emerson cites Owen's 1860 volume *Paleontology*, subtitled "a systematic summary of extinct animals and their geological relations." For a superb biography of Owen, see Rupke.

4. As it turns out, Emerson's phrasing ("the Chaldean *Zoroaster, who wrote it thus*") was the immediate source of Nietzsche's title *Thus Spake Zarathustra*. Nietzsche also derived the title of his companion text *Fröhliche Wissenschaft* [*The Gay Science*] from a remark in the same essay: "Poetry is the gai science" (p. 455). *Letters and Social Aims*, which included "Poetry and Imagination," was published

in German as *Neue Essays* in 1876, the same year it came out in the United States and a year before the British edition (Myerson, p. 342). Nietzsche published *The Gay Science* in 1882 and *Thus Spake Zarathustra* between 1883 and 1885.

5. With the exception of Strauch's article (and to a more limited degree Richardson and Robinson), the articles cited above dealing with Emerson's interest in science focus almost exclusively on the earlier stages of his career. Here, as elsewhere in the present study, I concentrate instead on the radical empiricist of the middle period (1843–60).

6. In "Self-Reliance," Emerson had written in a quasi-Lamarckian vein: "Perception is not whimsical, but fatal. If I see a trait, my children will see it after me, and in course of time, all mankind,—although it may chance that no one has seen it before me. For my perception of it is as much a fact as the sun" (EL, p. 269).

7. "Many years ago," Susanne Langer notes in her own account of the relation between organism and ambient, "Jakob von Uexküll (1909) called attention to the fact that two different organisms in the same environment were likely to exist in widely differing environmental situations, or, as he called them, different 'ambient worlds' ('*Umwelten*'), due to the selective powers with which their respective peripheral organs (their integuments, as well as specialized sense organs) could filter out noxious or even merely useless influences. Besides these differences in the reception of outside influences, there is an immense variation in the value an influence, once received, has for various creatures." The ambient, Langer adds, "defines itself and changes with the creature" (M, pp. 110–11, 129).

8. For further consideration of this exchange, in particular Stein's description of "american character," see my introduction to MA.

9. "The twentieth century," Stein noted, "did not invent but it made a great fuss about *series production*, *series production* really began in the nineteenth century, that is natural enough, machines are bound to make *series production*" (PF, p. 23, emphasis added). The repeated use of the phrase itself exemplifies such mechanical "production in a series"—namely, the idea that "one thing should be like every other thing, and that it should all be made alike and quantities of them" (p. 61).

10. In the essay "Nominalist and Realist" Emerson made use of the term *lustres* in a similar context: "I read for the lustres," he wrote, "as if one should use a fine picture in a chromatic experiment, for its rich colors" (EL, p. 579).

11. For an extended consideration of Stein and Henry James, see Caramello.

12. William James used the phrase *lords of life* in his chapter on "Will" in PR, writing that "The world finds in the heroic man its worthy match and mate; and the effort which he is able to put forth to hold himself erect and keep his heart unshaken is the direct measure of his worth and function in the game of human life. He can *stand* this universe. He can meet it and keep up his faith in it in presence of those same features which lay his weaker brethren low. He can still find a zest in it, not by 'ostrich-like forgetfulness,' but by pure inward willingness

to take the world with those deterrent objects there. And hereby he becomes one of the masters and the lords of life" (p. 1181 [BC, p. 425]). "O ostrich-like forgetfulness! / O loss of larger in the less," Emerson famously wrote in "Threnody," composed after the devastating loss of his five-year-old son (*Collected Poems*, p. 120). In identifying "the heroic man" as at least potentially a lord of life, James removes the sting from Emerson's remarks, where the "lords of life" lord it over every individual, and heroism consists of facing one's own fragmentation head on.

13. Cited from "The Watchers" (*Collected Poems*, p. 63). The contemporary British poet Geoffrey Hill has employed Auden's phrase as the title for an important collection of essays "on literature and ideas."

14. See Edmundson for a compelling discussion of Freud and Emerson.

15. Cited from the epilogue to Beaumont and Fletcher's play *Honest Man's Fortune*.

16. An enormous literature concerning what Myra Jehlen has called "American incarnation" has developed since the publication of Henry Nash Smith's *Virgin Land* in 1950; for a useful overview, see Bercovitch and Jehlen. More recently still, this concern has been filtered through the burgeoning field of eco-criticism, as in Lawrence Buell's magisterial *The Environmental Imagination*.

17. More fully, Emerson writes (in lines he attributes to "a certain poet"): "So when the soul of the poet has come to ripeness of thought," nature "detaches and sends away from it its poems or songs,—a fearless, sleepless, deathless progeny, which is not exposed to the accidents of the weary kingdom of time: a fearless, vivacious offspring, clad with wings (such was the virtue of the soul out of which they came), which carry them fast and far, and infix them irrecoverably into the hearts of men." The analogy here is, rather surprisingly, to a "poor fungus": "Nature, through all her kingdoms, insures herself. Nobody cares for planting the poor fungus: so she shakes down from the gills of one agaric countless spores, any one of which, being preserved, transmits new billions of spores to-morrow or next day. The new agaric of this hour has a chance which the old one had not. This atom of seed is thrown into a new place, not subject to the accidents which destroyed its parent two rods off. *So when the soul of the poet . . .*" (pp. 457–58, emphasis added). Emerson is caught here, as in a double exposure, joining a Transcendentalist tenor and a radical empiricist vehicle. The disjunction between an idealizing account of the poet's soul and a description of nature operating by *chance* as well as by *accident* (that is to say, by creating opportunities, not just dictating conditions) is matched by the transcendence of time in one setting ("not exposed to . . . the weary kingdom of time") and the respect accorded it in the other ("the new agaric of *this hour*").

18. See R. Richardson for a superb response to this biographical challenge.

19. "So loose a method had this advantage," Emerson commented with respect to Bacon, "it allowed of perpetual ammendment and addition." From the "many fragments [which] remain to us among [Bacon's] works, . . . we may see the

manner in which all his works were written. Works of this sort which consist of detached observations and to which the mind has not imparted a system of its own, are never ended" ("Lord Bacon," p. 335).

20. "We are far from having exhausted the significance of the few symbols we use," Emerson wrote: "We can come to use them yet with a terrible simplicity" (EL, p. 455).

21. In this respect, Stein likened a painting to a face: "You may find something new in a new face you may be surprised by a different kind of face you may like or not like a new kind of face but you cannot refuse a new face. You must accept a face as a face. And so with an oil painting" (LIA, p. 80).

22. If anything, the influence went the other way. For a particularly helpful discussion of Sitwell's relation to Stein, both in her own writing and as a propagandist for Stein, see Pondrom. It was Sitwell, for instance, who persuaded Stein to accept the invitation to lecture at Cambridge which resulted in CE; and an argument can certainly be made for Stein's influence on the lecture's publisher, Virginia Woolf, particularly in *The Waves*. According to Margaret Drabble, Woolf's "starting-point" for the novel was an entry in her diary dated September 30, 1926: "One sees a fin passing far out" (p. 1050). That November, the Hogarth Press issued CE, which contained a sampling of Stein's writing in addition to the lecture.

23. This would include "every possible kind of pairs of human beings and every possible threes and fours and fives of human beings and every possible kind of crowds of human beings" (LIA, p. 148).

24. Although "A Long Gay Book" and "Many Many Women" are both longer than "Matisse Picasso and Gertrude Stein," each is actually much shorter than Stein had initially imagined it would be—cut short, quite literally, by the changes in her writing.

25. Emerson famously wrote in "Self-Reliance," "I shun father and mother and wife and brother, when my genius calls me. I would write on the lintels of the doorpost, *Whim*. I hope it is somewhat better than whim at last, but we cannot spend the day in explanation" (EL, p. 262).

26. See Suleiman for an account of the experience of women in French Surrealist circles.

27. "The Architect's Table" is one of several paintings that Picasso executed during this period with the "Ma Jolie" motif. For a discussion of "Woman with Guitar"—also called "Ma Jolie"—in relation to Stein's short piece "Susie Asado," see Perloff (*Poetics of Indeterminacy*). Also see T. J. Clark's discussion of "The Architect's Table" and of "Ma Jolie" in the context of what Clark calls "the pretense," indispensable to Cubist works of this period, that "what is being done to the world in the oval is done not by 'painting' alone but by painting-in-the-service-of-epistemology" (p. 185).

28. On the basis of autoradiographs and X-radiographs of the portrait, Lucy Belloli argues that Picasso appears to have "painted out the *face*," not the head,

before he left Paris—and only moved the head, and redid the face in a manner
"more suited to the near frontal head position [he] finally chose," upon his return
(p. 17, emphasis added). Of course, Stein would have seen a new face and a new
head when she viewed the completed portrait that fall.

29. Insofar as it enables Stein to create a ghostlike persona, such positive
negation may usefully be compared to Angus Fletcher's analysis of Coleridge's
effort, in his poem "Limbo," to "*posit* negation as the ultimate daemon," hence
creating a "personified 'positive negation'" (*Colors of the Mind*, p. 186; also see
Fletcher's earlier article on positive negation).

30. Among the unpublished notebooks and working notes for MA is a sheet of
hotel stationery, note #167, with "Gran Hotel de Rusia . . . Madrid" printed on
the front along with the date "191_" (YCAL). On the reverse, Stein has jotted
down the lines cited here: "Now I have it. Now I see. this is the way. not that way.
the other way is not the way."

31. For extended discussions of Emerson's observation in relation to Stein, and
in particular to the oft-repeated line, "Rose is a rose is a rose is a rose," see Poirier
(*A World Elsewhere*) and Sitney.

Chapter 4

1. It should also be read against the backdrop of juxtapositions of Stein and
Whitehead by their contemporaries—whether in a negative vein, as in Wyndham
Lewis's 1927 jeremiad *Time and Western Man*, or striking a more positive note,
as Edmund Wilson did in his 1931 study of "the imaginative literature of 1870–
1930," *Axel's Castle*. In this work, Wilson suggested that "the language of
Symbolism" exemplified in Stein's writing "may actually have the effect of
revolutionizing our ideas of syntax, as modern philosophy seems to be tending to
discard the notion of cause and effect." "This new language," he concluded, "is
evidently working, like modern scientific theory, toward a totally new conception
of reality" (pp. 296–97). Several early essays of Wilson's on Whitehead, reprinted
in Groth and Castronovo, demonstrate that *Axel's Castle* emerged directly out of a
reading of SMW.

2. "The exact nature of these processes," Pearsall Smith added, "is still a
matter of dispute, yet the notion of subconscious thought, taken simply as an
unexplained fact of experience, has helped in some degree to make more definite
the meanings of the terms we have been discussing" (p. 118). I address Stein's
broad criticisms of "the modern conception of the unconscious self" below,
especially in Chapter 5. For an extended study of the fortunes of "self-proclaimed
genius" in twentieth-century experimental writing, see Perelman.

3. The only work of any length written by Stein in French, *Picasso* was
promptly translated into English by Toklas. If Stein sought in ABT to recreate
Toklas's person or voice, here Toklas had the opportunity to recreate Stein's own

voice (at least the public voice of the lectures and EA). At the same time, in composing the study in her fluent but imperfect French, Stein acknowledged both the intimacy of her relation with Picasso and the element of self-alienation that entered into the relation. French was their common language, a language to which they were equally foreign and which was nonetheless the language of daily life in their adopted home.

4. The naturalistic understanding of *genius* articulated by Stein should not be confused with more typically idealizing accounts, whether of genius or the unconscious, such as Otto Weininger's in *Sex and Character*. See Katz on Weininger's importance for Stein when she was composing the middle chapters of MA; and for more general discussions of Weininger, see Battersby, Kerr, and Žižek.

5. When Emerson characterizes genius as *secular*, he is not distinguishing it from religious experience but merely emphasizing its solitary nature. A secular clergyman belongs to no religious order. For a carefully nuanced analysis of Emerson's understanding of genius, see Poirier ("The Question of Genius").

6. In 1931, Kurt Gödel demonstrated with respect to "*Principia Mathematica* and related systems" that, as Whitehead later put it, "every finite set of premises must indicate notions which are excluded from direct purview" (MT, p. 2). This meant that mathematics could not be completely described in terms of logic. Although the argument was first "embodied in a formal proof" by Gödel, Whitehead observed in 1938 that "the foundation of logic upon the notion of inconsistency was first discovered and developed by Professor Henry Sheffer of Harvard, about twenty years ago"—on the heels of the publication of the *Principia* between 1910 and 1913 (MT, pp. 2, 52). One might also note that Gödel in effect offers a logically compelling account of the distinction between *knowledge of acquaintance* and *knowledge-about*. The notions that are "excluded from direct purview," and hence excluded from any particular logical system regarded exclusively in terms of knowledge-about (that is, as a "finite set of premises") are nevertheless "*indicated*" by the same premises. Consequently, insofar as the notions remain excluded, they are only known in the form of knowledge of acquaintance—as a function of indication or suggestion and not of direct statement. For an illuminating discussion of Gödel in the context of recent literary theory, see Thomas.

7. First published in a slim volume in February 1934, the lectures were reprinted four years later in MT, together with a set of lectures on "creative impulse" and "activity" delivered by Whitehead at Wellesley College in 1937–38.

8. See Cavell ("Finding as Founding") and Poirier (*Poetry and Pragmatism*) for illuminating readings of the concluding lines of "Experience."

9. For a provocative reading of this line, see Cavell ("Finding as Founding").

10. Like the photographer, Stein listens to what she hears. In this instance, her listening found expression in a series of meditations on the invitation from heaven that the photographer's response provided. "I found [his remark] very interesting," she observed in EA, "and of course it is so, of course nobody can listen if they have

to remember what they are hearing and that is the trouble with newspapers and teaching with government and history. The lecture I wrote for the Chicago University [the third of her four lectures on narration] has to do with this thing and the difference between original writing and anything which is a remembered thing and a great deal that I wrote in the Geographical History of America which is about identity and the lecture I wrote for Oxford and Cambridge about What Are Masterpieces And Why Are There So Few Of Them all have something to do with this and so thank you the photographer who said this thing" (p. 225). Nearly a dozen years after the exchange, Stein returned to it at the conclusion of TI, recalling that when she was "in America one day there were three young newspapermen and a photographer, and they had just come out of college and took themselves very seriously, but eventually we got talking about things in general. The only one of the four of them who understood my writing was the photographer. He said, 'I don't have to remember what you say, I am not involved with the mechanics of remembering it, and so I can understand it. They are too busy trying to remember what you say'" (p. 34).

11. The famous deathbed exchange between Stein and Toklas, whether apocryphal or not, remains consistent with this deeply held conviction. According to Toklas, one of several surgeons at the American Hospital in Paris who had decided *not* to operate on Stein's cancer (because "she was not in a fit condition any more") nevertheless proposed to go ahead with the operation, as he had given his "word of honor" to do so. "In a sad state of indecision and worry," Toklas recalled of Stein, "she said to me early in the afternoon, What is the answer? I was silent. In that case, she said, what is the question?" (WIM, p. 173). Stein is hardly being insouciant; yet Toklas doesn't fully account for her irresolution in asserting that, due to the bleakness of the options, "the whole afternoon was troubled, confused and very uncertain" (p. 173). As she had so often done in her writing, Stein was *embracing* uncertainty instead of settling for a false certainty. Faced with death, she opted for the splendid illogic of life, if only (as ever) in passing.

12. See Riddel for a contrary view of Stein as a poet of the future anterior, "a time conditioned and even strangely determined by the future" (p. 91).

13. Stein's phrasing here (*unless / not even then / when*) offers a particularly clear example of her rationale for refusing to erase the traces of present thinking, of hesitation and midsentence correction, in her writing. She wasn't just being perverse, or sloppy. In registering the change in direction of her thoughts, her *change in mind*, she was demonstrating the difference asking another question makes with respect to one's sense of time, by contrast with merely passively "listening to an answer." *Unless not even then when you are very little* casts doubt as to the straightforward linearity, and hence the very existence, of time's proverbial arrow, in a way that neither of the alternatives—*unless you are very little* joined at the hip, as it were, with *not even when you are very little*—does in itself.

14. I take the term *gnomic utterance* from Angus Fletcher, who defines "gnomics," or "gnomic utterances," as "the fundamental units of discourse

whenever there is ontological difficulty and simple obscurity" (*Colors*, p. 102). "Every true gnome (another classical name for gnomic utterance) will be opaque in some ultimate sense, hence nondecodable" (p. 103). The question Whitehead poses is whether Emerson's paradoxes are indeed "true gnomes." Proposing, in an essay on "Philosophic Method," that "*the very purpose of philosophy is to delve below the apparent clarity of common speech*," Whitehead turns to his own favorite Platonic paradox, the assertion "in the *Sophist* . . . that 'not-being' is a form of 'being'"—of which Emerson's third "absurdity" is a variant. "At once an extreme instance of the breakdown of language, and the enunciation of a profound meta-physical truth," its profundity can readily be retrieved from the broken-down language. "To speak of anything," Whitehead explains, "is to speak of something which, by reason of that very speech, is in some way a component in that act of experience. In some sense or other, it is thereby known to exist." This is what makes "Not-being . . . itself a sort of being" (AI, pp. 222–23). Plato, Whitehead adds, "applied this doctrine to his eternal forms. He should have applied the same doctrine to the things that perish. . . . Thus we should balance Aristotle's—or more rightly, Plato's—doctrine of becoming by a doctrine of perishing. When they perish, occasions pass from the immediacy of being into the not-being of imme-diacy. But that does not mean that they are nothing. They remain 'stubborn fact'" (p. 237). Whitehead referred to the same Platonic riddle at a symposium held on the occasion of his seventieth birthday, and again in MT seven years later; see "Process and Reality," p. 117, and MT, p. 53.

15. By *objectivism*, Whitehead meant the "creed . . . that the actual elements perceived by our senses are in themselves the elements of a common world[,] and that this world is a complex of things, including indeed our acts of cognition, but transcending them." By *subjectivism*, he meant "the belief that the nature of our immediate experience is the outcome of the perceptive peculiarities of the subject enjoying the experience," and that "what is perceived is not a partial vision of a complex of things generally independent of that act of cognition; but that it merely is the expression of the individual peculiarities of the cognitive act" (SMW, p. 88).

16. According to *absolute idealism*, "the world of nature is just one of the ideas, somehow differentiating the unity of the Absolute"; for *pluralistic idealism*, by contrast, which involves "*monadic* mentalities," the natural "world is the greatest common measure of the various ideas which differentiate the various mental unities of the various monads" (SMW, p. 64, emphasis added). Whitehead summarizes the scientific scheme in question, "the famous mechanistic theory of nature, which has reigned supreme ever since the seventeenth century"—"classical scientific materialism, with its doctrine of simple location"—as follows: "To say that a bit of matter has *simple location* means that, in expressing its spatio-temporal relations, it is adequate to state that it is where it is, in a definite finite region of space, and throughout a definite finite duration of time, apart from any essential reference [to] the relations of that bit of matter to other regions of space and to other durations of time. . . . This idea is the very foundation of the

seventeenth century scheme of nature. Apart from it, the scheme is incapable of expression" (pp. 50, 91, 58). In line with his own radical empiricism, Whitehead goes on to assert that "among the primary elements of nature as apprehended in our immediate experience, *there is no element whatever which possesses this character of simple location*," adding that "it does not follow, however, that the science of the seventeenth century was simply wrong." Instead, he "hold[s] that by a process of constructive abstraction we can arrive at abstractions which are the simply-located bits of material, and at other abstractions which are the minds included in the scientific scheme. Accordingly, the real error is an example of what I have termed: The Fallacy of Misplaced Concreteness" (p. 58, emphasis added).

17. Whitehead's imagery of molecules and the human body "blindly running" derives from Tennyson's *In Memoriam*, which he regarded as one of the "great serious poems in English literature" (SMW, p. 77).

18. "Cartesian philosophers had to work fairly hard," Rorty comments in a recent article, "to create 'consciousness' as a refuge for Aristotelian notions of substance, essence, and intrinsicality. . . . Thanks to their efforts, even after the colorfully diverse contents of Aristotelian nature were smeared together into one big swirl of corpuscles—one big substance called 'matter'—there remained, here below, one other substance: the mind" ("Holism," p. 193). In his early article "The Subjectivist Principle and the Linguistic Turn," Rorty carefully analyzed Whitehead's criticism of Descartes in terms of what Whitehead called *the subjectivist principle* ("the principle that 'the whole universe consists of elements disclosed in the analysis of the experience of subjects'") and then went on to criticize Whitehead's non-Cartesian account in terms of *the linguistic turn* (p. 135). This was "the view that philosophical problems are problems which may be solved (or dissolved) either by reforming language, or by understanding more about the language we presently use" (Rorty, "Introduction," p. 3). In "Matter and Event," which like "The Subjectivist Principle" dates from 1963, Rorty examined Whitehead's relation to Aristotle, especially in terms of Aristotle's substance/property and form/matter distinctions. See Modrak for a fascinating study of the *hylomorphic* basis of Aristotelian "psychophysical analysis" (that is, as positing some *composite* of form and matter).

19. Rorty uses this phrase in a recent discussion of "the Darwinian suggestion that we think of human beings as more complex animals, rather than as animals with an extra added ingredient, called 'intellect' or 'the rational soul'" ("Philosophy and the Future," p. 199). Concerning what Whitehead called "the realm of possibility" or "realm of eternal objects" (that is, the domain of intellect), Rorty observed in "Matter and Event" that Whitehead protests against "the assumption that there are two equally atomic sorts of things: actual X's and potential X's" (SMW, pp. 165, 161; "Matter and Event," p. 508). Instead of searching for that "'extra something' which transforms a potential X into an actual one . . . Whitehead tells us that if we are going to keep and use [the] distinction" between potentiality and actuality, "we must start all over again. We must get rid of the

notion of potential X's, substitute the notion of 'potentialities *for* X,' and abandon the assumption that 'the only possible entities are actual ones.' A possible entity, for Whitehead, is not a half-baked version of an actual entity" ("Matter and Event," pp. 508–9). Cognitive experience consequently should not require an "extra something" in the sense of an added ingredient. In order to grasp just what kind of entity these intellectual, or potential, entities are, however, one needs to reconceive the notion of an entity altogether. A "true object," that is, an object as we normally conceive of it (a solid independent substance, existing in itself and hence abstracted from the events or processes in which objects actually occur) turns out to be "a mere pattern" or intellectual construction (ENQ, p. 198).

20. I examine this gradual evolution in the narrator's perspective in considerably greater detail in my introduction to MA.

21. See Chapter 1 above, for further consideration of Russell's work. Interestingly, the bulk of SMW consisted of Whitehead's own "set of eight Lowell Lectures delivered in the February of 1925" (p. viii). A year later, he delivered a second set of four Lowell Lectures, subsequently published as *Religion in the Making*.

22. Whitehead delivered the paper "on the morning of April 8, 1914" at the First Congress of Mathematical Philosophy, "convened in Paris under the combined sponsorship of the Société Française de Philosophie and the editors of the *Encyclopédie des Sciences Mathématiques*" ("Whitehead's *Relational Theory*," p. 743). Part III of the *Enquiry*, roughly a third of the whole, is devoted to an elucidation of "The Method of Extensive Abstraction."

23. Hurley refers here to a remark of Russell's in *My Philosophical Development* (p. 103).

24. This characterization of the contents of GP appears on the work's dust jacket. Stein's publisher, Edmund Brown, explained in a letter dated September 23, 1922, that he had "arranged a paper jacket very much in accordance with your suggestions. I have nothing on the front except the title, author, and a reference to the preface by Mr. [Sherwood] Anderson, which I think is a good selling point—and your own suggestion for the back of the jacket" (YCAL). For further discussion of the correspondence between Stein and Brown, see my essay "Gertrude Stein."

25. Whitehead defines " 'uniform' objects" as "objects with a certain smoothness in their temporal relations, so that they require no minimum quantum of time-lapse in the events which are their situations. These are objects which can be said to exist 'at a given moment.' For example, a tune is not an uniform object; but a chair, as ordinarily recognised, is such an object" (ENQ, p. 167).

26. I take the example of waves from a description in ENQ of the same minimally rhythmic quality. There Whitehead observes that the "atomic character" that a pattern "impresses . . . on a certain whole event . . . does not imply a discontinuous existence for a rhythm; thus a wave-length as marked out in various positions along a train of waves exhibits the whole rhythm of the train at each position of its continuous travel" (pp. 198–99).

27. "How Writing Is Written" was delivered at the Choate School in Walling-ford, Connecticut, in January 1935, and published the next month in the school's literary magazine. It is not clear whether the entire talk was extemporaneous, although parts of it no doubt were, including the lines cited here. The sole manuscript version in YCAL is a typewritten copy of a "stenographic report" of the lecture, which is identical with the published version. For additional details of the circumstances of the lecture's delivery, see my "Gertrude Stein."

28. Whitehead makes a similar claim with respect to Plato. Substituting *transition* for *process*, he observes that Plato understood mathematics as "the science of a static universe," with any "transition conceived as *a transition of static forms.*" "Today," by contrast, "we conceive of *forms of transition*"—such as "the modern concept of an infinite series," where "the character of the series as a whole is such a form" (MT, p. 82).

29. Laura Riding thus remarked that Stein's "words are primitive in the sense that they are bare, immobile, *mathematically placed*, abstract," and Robert Coates suggested that she introduced "an almost *mathematical* lucidity . . . into the treat-ment of the English language" (*Survey*, p. 274; *View*, p. 213, emphasis added). Devlin's phrase *the science of patterns* usefully summarizes Whitehead's observa-tion that "the general science of mathematics is concerned with the investigation of *patterns of connectedness*, in abstraction from the particular relata and the particular modes of connection" (AI, p. 153, emphasis added).

30. These are the titles Whitehead gave to the two Chicago lectures on "Nature and Life" when he reprinted them in MT in 1938.

31. Part I of the "Two-Part Prelude" of 1798–99 is roughly equivalent to the first book of the fourteen-book 1850 version, which remained the only version in print until Ernest de Selincourt brought out his edition of the thirteen-book 1805 *Prelude*, the year after Whitehead lectured in Boston on "science and the modern world." The "Two-Part Prelude" was not published until 1974.

32. The sentence in SMW follows directly from Whitehead's remark on physiology "put[ting] mind back into nature": "The neurologist traces first the effect of stimuli along the bodily nerves, then integration at nerve centers, and finally the rise of a projective reference beyond the body with a resulting motor efficacy in renewed nervous excitement" (pp. 147–48). As for the sentence in PRO, it is suggested by an allusion to the modern physical theory that energy is "trans-ferred in definite quanta": "This quantum theory also has analogues in recent neurology" (p. 239). Rorty's unfortunate pairing of Whitehead with Russell (in an essay that appeared in a 1982 volume entitled *Mind in Nature*) on the basis of a shared acceptance of "the original Cartesian notion of the mind as the immediately knowable, the given," whether in the form of "Russell's 'views' or Whitehead's 'prehensions,'" is due in no small part to Whitehead's own near silence concerning this crucial aspect of his thought ("Mind as Ineffable," pp. 68, 67).

33. Although Langer occasionally uses Whitehead's terminology (as in "a sim-pler *organic mechanism* for . . . covert acts of cerebration" or "the '*presentational*

immediacy' of the momentary experience itself"), she doesn't expressly identify her project with his (M, pp. 258, 293, emphasis added). Nor is she the only thinker who has extended the philosophy of organism into the biological domain of "the larger organisms" (SMW, p. 103). Already in 1936, A. D. Ritchie acknowledged in his *Natural History of Mind* that "the discerning reader will not fail to notice the influence of Whitehead," even as he professed uncertainty as to whether his was "the true Whiteheadian faith" (p. v). More recently, Haraway has suggested that "this philosopher-mathematician lurks in the tissues of many a resister to gene fetishism in feminist science studies and elsewhere" (*Modest_Witness*, p. 297). See also Needham, Gilbert ("Origins of Developmental Genetics"), and Latour ("Scientific Objects").

34. For recent considerations of Whitehead's contribution to speculative physics, see Shimony, Griffin, Cobb and Griffin, Malin, and Stapp.

35. To take just one example: Langer set great store on the distinction between an *image* and a *model*, with the former "show[ing] how something appears" and the latter "how [it] works" (M, p. xiii). Because "the direct perception of artistic import [is] intuitive, immediate," she concluded that "no amount of artistic perceptiveness ever leads to scientific knowledge of the reality expressed, which is the life of feeling" (p. 29). Instead, in "the arts, and especially in their technical triumphs, lies the store of prescientific knowledge from which a science of psychology," for instance, "may draw its first inspiration" (p. 31). The artist creates images; the scientist creates models; and there is no overlap. Obviously, the premise of the present study is that a middle ground does exist, along the lines of Stein bridging Picasso and Whitehead, and that in some works, such as the experimental writing Stein composed between 1912 and 1932, the distinction between portraying "how something appears" and investigating "how [it] works" can't be made so readily. Because knowledge-about (the lingua franca of scientific modeling) is an essentially discursive phenomenon, this conjoining of image and model may be unique to the language arts among expressly aesthetic modes of inquiry. For a recent study of the conjunction of "image and logic" at the other end of the spectrum, in mid-twentieth-century microphysics, see Galison.

36. Of course, in order for the state of mind to become an issue, one must acknowledge that there is some point in distinguishing between *motivation* and *causation*. See Langer for a compelling argument on behalf of this anti-behaviorist distinction. When Stein returned to a consideration of these sentences at the outset of "Sentences and Paragraphs," composed later that spring, she included the commentary about their relative usefulness in her text. For additional discussion of *He looks like a young man grown old*, see Chapter 7.

37. See Donald et al. for a recent anthology that collects a wide range of articles from *Close Up*.

38. Correspondence from Macpherson to Stein, dated July 20 and July 28, 1927, indicates that she was unable to proofread "Mrs. Emerson" because she didn't have a copy of the manuscript with her in the countryside (YCAL). In the

second letter Macpherson apologizes "for the inconvenience you must have been caused by not having had your manuscript in order to correct proof." "It was finally sent to me," he adds, "despite the fact that I had given full instructions that it should go to you, and though I sent it on at once I am afraid it reached you too late." As a result, occasional errors in vocabulary crop up in the published text, which remained uncorrected in the 1973 reprint. The first of these occurs in the opening paragraph, where "exemplars" was substituted for "examples." I have silently corrected this mistake here.

39. Stein also makes the rather more obvious play on *white* when she writes: "They expect all *the blues* to take of all the other *families, the whites* are extra they are beside all that, they make a little house and through and beside that they live in Paris" (p. 155, emphasis added). The Whiteheads' *little house* was *not* in Paris, yet for Stein it was the next best thing to being at home in Paris, and served as a greatly appreciated refuge in (and from) the British Isles. I should perhaps add that although "Mrs. Whitehead" is divided into three parts in GP, it would take an awfully attentive reader to notice this, as the two subheadings ("Corrections" and "Next stretching") are only indented one more stop than is the paragraphing. In a layout of mostly single-sentence paragraphs, often only three or four words long, the headings are not distinctly set off from the text. They are much clearer, how- ever, in the manuscript notebook; Stein wrote each one (including the title) on the verso side of a sheet and then began the text proper on the facing recto or right- hand side, continuing to compose only on the recto sides.

40. In a letter that he sent to Mabel Weeks in the late summer of 1902, when the Steins were living near Russell's in-laws, in Greenhill-Fernhurst, Leo Stein reported that his sister "was the other day trying to hold up the American end of a general discussion against Russell, Berenson and a young journalist, Dill" (cited in Mellow, p. 66).

41. Despite her family's Anglo-Irish roots, Evelyn Whitehead wasn't exactly *English*, having been born and raised across the Channel in Normandy. When A. N. Whitehead met Evelyn Wade in 1890—she was then twenty-four and earned her living by teaching French—the future Mrs. Whitehead's "English was not yet good enough for him to understand just what she was saying; his French was much worse; so they took to looking at pictures" (Lowe, I, p. 175).

42. I say *unacknowledged*, because at the outset of what proved to be thirteen years of conversations recorded by Lucien Price between 1934 and 1947, White- head admitted reading Emerson "a good deal when . . . younger," but hastened to add that "if my good neighbors, the Forbeses, will pardon me for saying so"— these were grandsons of Emerson—"he was not so original" as to merit being designated "a lasting contribution to the world." Whitman, by contrast, "brought something into poetry which was never there before" (p. 22).

43. For several years, following a frank discussion with Evelyn Whitehead about the Whiteheads' financial difficulties, Russell had "found himself 'in an alliance with her to keep [Whitehead] sane.'" "His part," Lowe remarks, "was to

give her money secretly," and the addition to the Whiteheads' house outside Cambridge was one of the first products of this generosity (I, p. 244).

44. Evelyn Whitehead "continued to have 'heart trouble' . . . until she died— sixty years later" (Lowe, I, p. 240). On the authority of Norah Schuster—"who lived with the Whiteheads in London for fourteen months in 1920–22, when she was Assistant Pathologist at St. George's Hospital," and administered "a general physical examination" in the wake of one such attack—Whitehead's biographer diagnoses the angina pectoris as pseudoangina, "strictly functional, with no organic lesions but with a neurotic and hysterical factor present." Lowe further conjectures that, "conscious only of real pain," Mrs. Whitehead "unconsciously . . . used [the] illness to get what she wanted," without letting it serve "as an excuse for inactivity," as "the Victorian type" would have done (pp. 240–41).

45. I take it that Russell visited more than once during the stay at Lockeridge, since, according to ABT, he was present when North Whitehead "left for the front" three weeks into August, yet internal evidence suggests that Stein composed "Mrs. Whitehead" in *mid-September*, with Russell's arrival imminent. Twice in the portrait's middle section, the reader is informed, "It is eleven weeks from the middle of September"; and, as of mid-September, eleven weeks had indeed passed since July fifth, when she and Toklas had embarked for England (GP, p. 155; ABT, p. 144). No doubt, Stein may have conflated Russell's September visit with North Whitehead's earlier departure when, two decades later, she recorded these events. As for Evelyn Whitehead's appreciation of *creative irregularities* in matters of the heart, as well as in the organization of daily life, this is readily gleaned from the following letter. One of fourteen missives that she sent Stein and Toklas over a span of four months, in the fall and winter of 1914, it conveys a fairly good sense of her "spoken personality." She had just arrived back from Paris, where she had accompanied Stein and Toklas on *their* return. "Dearest Gertrude," she wrote: "I am still in bed (11.30) & so are you, & Alice is doing much all the time, we are missing, missing, missing you both—I returned to a mute Jessie [the Whiteheads' daughter], stammering as never before, the Dr. came & said 'give her a severe talking to. I tried while you were away but it was no use.' I have just finished making her life a misery & she is quite bright and voluble! Here the minutest fraction of news only[,] I long for the Paris edition of the D.W. H[arry] G[ibbs] [the English painter and longtime acquaintance of Stein, whom she had introduced to the Whiteheads] is brighter, R.A. has rather messed up his affair with Miss A. 'It is a very special friendship' he said 'but she is afraid of her brothers.' I looked blank & let him run on but at the same time I gave him wholesome advice of giving the brothers a wide berth as the 'peculiar quality of their friendship might be spoilt'—thrilling is it not. Confine this intelligence to you & Alice only—Bridget turned up at Fontainbleau & sat for four hours watching Miss A's door, then R.A. took fright for her sister—H.G. thinks Bridget is in London & is very frightened of seeing her, he believes that the man will marry her if he has not already done so. & such a big raid we have, Altie [as she called her husband] is writing. Dearest love, EW" (YCAL). The letter is dated October 27.

46. See Sitney for an extended consideration of this encounter. In her lecture "Plays," Stein alluded to a middle stage between theater and cinema, observing that the turn-of-the-century American actor and dramatist William Gillette "had conceived a new technique" of "silence stillness and quick movement," which he applied to "the whole stage the whole play." He thereby "created what the cinema later repeated by mixing up the short story and the stage" (LIA, pp. 116–17).

47. See Gibson for a compelling analysis of the non-illusory nature of experiences of depth and movement, as well as Reed's intellectual biography of the founder of ecological psychology. Gibson's "ecological approach to visual perception" grew in large part out of his pioneering use of film in psychological inquiry.

48. The concluding paragraph of Stein's first play, "What Happened," offers a glimpse into her thinking at the time she composed it—early in 1913—regarding the relation between her new manner of writing and the "trouble" with photographs. "What is a photograph," she wrote, "a photograph is a sight and a sight is always a sight of something. Very likely there is a photograph that gives color if there is then there is that color that does not change any more than it did when there was much more use for photography" (GP, p. 209). One might say that in her plays, as in her portraits, Stein put photographs or their equivalents in motion, figuring organic mechanisms of "change" in a way that struck her as beyond the capacity of the cinematic medium. For further consideration on her part of the medium's limitations in the wake of the publication of "Mrs. Emerson" and "Three Sitting There" in *Close Up*, see her 1929 scenario "Film" (subtitled "Deux Soeurs Qui Ne Sont Pas Soeurs") in which the starring role is given to a photograph of two white poodles. The photo is quite literally a *moving picture*, as it passes from hand to hand, and figuratively one as well, in eliciting a full spectrum of emotions from its viewers. The scenario concludes with the facsimile exchanged for "un vrai caniche," a real poodle sitting in a car that drives past with two women in it—no doubt, Stein and Toklas, who had just acquired Basket, the *caniche* immortalized in Stein's writing of the next decade (OP, p. 400).

49. See Brakhage for the perspective of a filmmaker who has taken up Stein's challenge.

50. In TI Stein alludes to a "background of word-system," with reference to "the idea that in composition one thing was as important as another thing" and "each part . . . as important as the whole" (p. 15). See Perloff for further consideration of "poetry as word-system."

Introduction to Part III

1. See CBM on James's general dislike of laboratory-based psychological experimentation, as well as on the differences between his psychological laboratory at Harvard and that of Wilhelm Wundt in Leipzig. For broad-ranging accounts of nineteenth-century psychophysics, especially in Germany, see Danziger and Lenoir.

2. See Bush for an appreciative gloss of these lines. An invaluable contemporary account of the enlarged Harvard psychological laboratory appeared in *McClure's Magazine* just before Stein arrived in Cambridge in 1893. Its author was Herbert Nichols, who, according to James, was hired in 1891 to assist him in the "laboratory exercises" that became "a regular part of the undergraduate psychology course" that year. See CBM for careful consideration of the claims and counterclaims that have been made concerning the founding of the first psychological laboratory in the United States, including the full text of James's important letter to the editor of *Science* dated October 19, 1895, which I cite here.

3. Edward Reed has observed of contemporary cognitive science, "Currently, the cutting edge . . . involves strapping subjects into a PETscan or similar device (a machine for reading and mapping brain activity) . . . One cannot do much of anything when strapped into these scanning machines. Thus through the magic of information technology, studying how people think when they are not doing anything becomes elevated into 'cognitive neuroscience'" (*The Necessity of Experience*, p. 46). Little seems to have changed, at least in this respect, in the last hundred years. See Gazzaniga et al. for an account of the origin of the phrase *cognitive neuroscience* "in the back seat of a New York City taxi" (p. 1).

4. The equivalent statement in "The Will to Believe" runs: "The thesis I defend is, briefly stated, this: *Our passional nature not only lawfully may, but must, decide an option between propositions, when ever it is a genuine option that cannot by its nature be decided on intellectual grounds; for to say, under such circumstances, 'Do not decide, but leave the question open,' is itself a passional decision,—just like deciding yes or no,—and is attended with the same risk of losing the truth*" (*Writings 1878–1899*, p. 464).

5. I take this distinction from James's great essay on human immortality, delivered as the Ingersoll Lecture at Harvard in the fall of 1897. James's thesis was that "when we think of *the law that thought is a function of the brain*, we are not required to think of productive function only; we are entitled also to consider permissive or transmissive function" (p. 1110, emphasis added). By *productive* function, James meant the process of "inwardly creating or engendering [an] effect," as when one says that "Steam is a function of the tea-kettle" or "Light is a function of the electric-circuit" (p. 1107). By contrast, the trigger of a crossbow, in "remov[ing] the obstacle that holds the string, and letting the bow fly back to its natural shape," has a "*releasing* [or *permissive*] function." Finally, "in the case of a colored glass, a prism, or a refracting lens, we have a *transmissive* function. The energy of light, no matter how produced, is by the glass sifted and limited in color, and by the lens or prism determined to a certain path and shape" (pp. 1109–10). James went on to suggest in a footnote that "the transmission theory connects itself very naturally with that whole tendency of thought known as transcendentalism," even if "it is not necessary to identify the consciousness postulated in the lecture, as pre-existing behind the scenes, with the Absolute Mind of transcendental Idealism." "For the purposes of my lecture," he added, "there might be

many minds behind the scenes as well as one" (pp. 1113–14). These statements are unobjectionable on their own terms; the same cannot be said, however, of James's decision to cite, as an example of the transcendentalist bent, the lines from Emerson's "Self-Reliance" already quoted in Chapter 3: "We lie in the lap of immense intelligence. . . ." This passage can be read either way, perhaps more obviously as delineating a transmissive function (as James chose to read it) yet also as the projection of a productive function. Emerson was obliged to resort to such projection due to the reductiveness of contemporary neurophysiological accounts when set alongside his own concrete neuraesthetic experience. What appears *transmissive*, from a perspective that abstracts a *passive* organism from an *active* ambient, turns out to be *productive* once one recognizes that the relevant unit or unity consists of the organism *plus* the ambient. This heterogeneous unit is the new organism.

Chapter 5

1. For a related critique of "naïve" empiricism, see "Two Dogmas of Empiricism," the landmark article by another of Whitehead's students at Harvard, W. V. O. Quine. "Modern empiricism," Quine writes, "has been conditioned in large part by two dogmas. One is a belief in some fundamental cleavage between truths which are *analytic*, or grounded in meanings independently of matters of fact, and truths which are *synthetic*, or grounded in fact. The other dogma is *reductionism*: the belief that each meaningful statement is equivalent to some logical construct upon terms which refer to immediate experience," where immediate experience is understood as a function of sense-data (p. 20).

2. See Goodwin for a measured discussion of "claims that understanding genes and their activities is enough to explain the properties of organisms," and Pollack for a compelling analysis of the limits of the empiricist blueprint in molecular biology (p. 3). As for the general problem of "realism in relation to science, literature, and culture," see the collection edited by Levine on this subject.

3. Compare Whitehead's remark in SMW: "I hold that by a process of constructive abstraction we can arrive at abstractions which are the simply-located bits of material and at other abstractions which are the minds included in the scientific scheme" (p. 58). One might also compare the "verifiable and concrete" dualism James attributed, generally, to viewing a painting with Stein's 1934 description of Cézanne's "pictures": "The apples looked like apples . . . and it all had nothing to do with anything because if they [the apples] did not look like apples . . . they were [still] apples. . . . They [the apples] were so entirely these things that they [the apples] were not an oil painting and yet that is what the Cezannes were they [the paintings] were an oil painting. They [the paintings] were so entirely an oil painting that it was all there whether they were finished, the paintings, or whether they were not finished" (LIA, pp. 76–77).

4. DCE serves as the lead essay in James's posthumously published *Essays in Radical Empiricism*. Particularly in light of the parallels discussed below between his psychical research and Stein's writing practice, it may be noted that James first used the phrase *radical empiricism* in the preface to *The Will to Believe*, which concluded with his 1896 Presidential Address to the British Psychical Research Society, "What Psychical Research Has Accomplished."

5. James's 1908 Hibbert Lectures on "the present situation in philosophy" were published the following year as *A Pluralistic Universe*.

6. Two pages after this description of his imagined reader, James cited a comparable passage from the *Grundzüge der Psychologie* of his colleague Hugo Münsterberg: " 'I may only think of my objects,' says Professor Münsterberg, 'yet, in my living thought they stand before me exactly as perceived objects would do, no matter how different the two ways of apprehending them may be in their genesis. The book here lying on the table before me, and the book in the next room of which I think and which I mean to get, are both in the same sense given realities for me, realities which I acknowledge and of which I take account. If you agree that the perceptual object is not an idea within me, but that percept and thing, as indistinguishably one, are really experienced *there, outside*, you ought not to believe that the merely thought-of object is hid away inside of the thinking subject' " (DCE, p. 1149; cited from Münsterberg, I, p. 48).

7. For self-styled pragmatic accounts of literary interpretation that follow James here, see Knapp and Michaels as well as Fish and, in a less obviously literary context, Rorty (for instance, "Inquiry on Recontextualization"). For a quite different, and considerably more Emersonian, account of "pragmatism as a form of literary skepticism," see Poirier in *Poetry and Pragmatism* as well as Posnock's review of that volume.

8. On Emerson's literary passion, see Firkins, Packer, Ellison, Poirier (*The Renewal of Literature*), and especially Cavell in the ongoing sequence of studies that includes *In Quest of the Ordinary*, *This New Yet Unapproachable America*, *Conditions Handsome and Unhandsome*, and "What Is the Emersonian Event?" As Cavell observes in his most recent return to Emerson's "self-aversive sentences": "What is at once the most obvious and the most obscure fact about Emerson, that he writes[,] this is his vocation, what he does and what he suffers" ("Event," p. 958). In other words, the act of writing is at once an expression of abiding *patience* for Emerson and of *passion* realized.

9. For instances of Stein's self-conscious concentration on *concentration*, see LIA (pp. 170, 197) and N (pp. 13, 56). As for Emerson, see his lecture "Circles" in *Essays: Second Series* (in EL). Although such second-order concentration serves to distinguish Stein and Emerson from James, it is certainly not unique to them. The late novels of William's brother Henry, for example, possess it in abundance, and, from another angle, it forms the basis for I. A. Richards's conjectures concerning Coleridge's literal imagination and, more generally, on what Richards termed "the interinanimation of words" (*The Philosophy of Rhetoric*, p. 47).

10. Empson's distinction between the word as "solid tool" and as "a member of the language" clearly parallels, even if it doesn't exactly correspond to, Saussure's structuralist distinction between *parole* (in the sense of "speech") and *langue* ("the language" or "linguistic system"). For helpful analysis of the *parole/langue* distinction, see Roy Harris's translation of Saussure's *Course in General Linguistics* as well as *Reading Saussure* and *Language, Saussure and Wittgenstein*, both also by Harris.

11. Although Hugo Münsterberg actually directed Stein's first experiments with automatic writing, it was James, according to Stein, who originally suggested that a planchette be used. I cite the passage in question, from EA, later in this chapter.

12. Now in YCAL, the letter is postmarked December 17, 1932. Its addressee was Lindley Hubbell, whose verse tribute "A Letter to Gertrude Stein" had appeared two years earlier in *Pagany*. See CBM for an account of the establishment of *The Psychological Review* several years before the Solomons-Stein article appeared.

13. *Verbal Behavior* is, of course, the text that launched Noam Chomsky when he reviewed it in 1959 in the then "obscure" journal *Language*, "subject[ing] nearly every facet . . . to criticism and much of it to ridicule . . . [i]n thirty tightly reasoned and scathing pages" (Gardner, p. 32). Skinner's empiricism more than met its match in "the rationalist Cartesian aspects of Chomsky's work" (p. 33). Missing from this fight to the death was any sense of the *radical* empiricism propounded by Whitehead—hence the hard-and-fast binary opposition. "We now know," Howard Gardner recently concluded an omnibus review of several works (among them *The Language Instinct* by Steven Pinker, a colleague of Chomsky at MIT), "that Skinner's effort was flawed. What remains to be seen is whether Chomsky [and his] associates, individually or collectively, can shed more light on the question" than Skinner did. "Perhaps an entirely different perspective will be required" (p. 38). Or perhaps what's called for is another look at Whitehead's perspective on such matters—leavened with a healthy dollop of Stein.

14. The insufficiently radical nature of Skinner's empiricism, his impoverished sense of the complex play of interrelatedness operating in linguistic activity, is pithily demonstrated in the first epilogue to *Verbal Behavior*, which addresses the "verbal behavior" involved in composing the book. Astonishingly, Skinner had nothing to say concerning his decision to situate this self-reflexive gesture (along with the discussion of the immediate origins of his behaviorist investigation of language) in a pair of epilogues. It is as if he imagined the subject to lie outside the frame of his study, as if he didn't have to say anything *about* the epilogue when he discussed the composition of the book as a whole *in* the epilogue. Nor, aside from alluding to it, did he apparently feel any obligation to address the fact that the first public version of the work, concluding with the material in the epilogues, took the form of the William James Lectures delivered at Harvard in 1947. Were these lacunae merely whimsical or were they integral to his argument? Either way, in banishing Emersonian *whim* both stylistically and intellectually from the behaviorist

account of language, Skinner left no room in his "lawfully determined system" for "the sources of human distinctiveness, imagination, and playfulness"—the very concerns, according to Howard Gardner, which prompted Whitehead to pose his challenge to Skinner in the first place, and whose absence distinguishes a Skinnerian functionalism from the Jamesian variety (p. 38).

15. For additional considerations of Skinner's article, see Hoffman, Weissmann, Koutstaal, and Armstrong; also see Levinson for a telling rebuttal of Skinner, which appeared in the January 1941 issue of *The American Journal of Psychology*. Claims such as Claudia Roth Pierpont's in a recent issue of *The New Yorker*, that Stein's writing was "marked" by "emotional anesthesia," ultimately derive from Skinner's attribution of "emotional coldness" to this "hypothetical author," and are similarly flawed (p. 84).

16. Skinner's concept of the "inferential author" clearly links up with the notion Wayne Booth would develop thirty years later of the "implied author," who "chooses, consciously or unconsciously, what we read; we infer him as an ideal, literary, created version of the real man; he is the sum of his own choices" (pp. 74–75). The connections between scientific psychology and literary theory, which I am examining here in the particular cases of Skinner and Stein as well as of Stein and James, constitute an important pathway of twentieth-century thought; and they certainly don't travel in just one direction. See Elms for a consideration of Skinner's literary aspirations, and an analysis of their role in his life and work. Although Skinner criticizes Stein on the basis that her "inferential author" falls so far short of the "ideal," behind this critique lies a more substantial one, expressed by many readers. The implied author may be immature, but "the implied reader," to use Wolfgang Iser's term, seems to have been forcibly removed from the picture. For considerations, *pace* Skinner, of the very real place and active role of the reader in Stein's texts, see Schmitz, Dydo (*"Stanzas in Meditation"*), and Chessman.

17. Stein studied with Hugo Münsterberg in her freshman and sophomore years. Writing from shipboard after the 1894–95 school year was over, Münsterberg praised her for having been an "ideal" student: "I thank you above all for that model-work you have done in the laboratory and the other courses wherever I met you. My contact with Radcliffe was in every way a most charming part of my Cambridge experience. But while I met there all types and kinds of students, you were to me the ideal student, just as a female student ought to be, and if in later years you look into printed discussions which I have in mind to publish about students in America, I hope you will then pardon me if you recognize some features of my ideal student picture as your own" (FF, p. 4). Münsterberg didn't return to Harvard until shortly after Stein left for Baltimore, when James handed the Psychology Laboratory over to him and arranged to have his own title changed from Professor of Psychology to Professor of Philosophy. Over the next few years Münsterberg's relation with his American sponsor became increasingly vexed; see CBM and the Spillmanns on Münsterberg's career, as well as Bush's consideration

of the subsequent development of his quasi-scientific social psychology in relation to Stein.

18. Recent neurophysiological accounts of these phenomena and related ones may be found in Rosenfield (*Anatomy*), Ramachandran and Blakeslee, A. Damasio, and Dennett (*Consciousness Explained*).

19. The "decidedly rhythmic character" of circles or double circles ("figure eights")—and of long curves or double curves ("m-figures")—is decidedly *periodic* in nature, by contrast with the *aperiodic* rhythms implicit in all writing and explicit in Stein's more experimental compositions. For further considerations of the *Psychology Review* articles, see Sutherland, Hoffman, Bush, Weissmann, and Armstrong. Although she barely addresses Stein's 1898 article, Koutstaal carefully situates the Solomons-Stein piece in relation to contemporaneous and subsequent research on automatic writing—including papers that attempt, as recently as 1980, "to extend the work of Solomons and Stein" (p. 18).

20. Against "Mr. Skinner's view" that "the true and only begetter of these verbal patterns is Miss Stein's right arm," since "nothing rising to the dignity of a purpose is involved in these esoteric utterances," Levinson may already be found in 1941 attributing "a definite purpose" to Stein's "radical breach with the grammar of her native tongue": namely, "a program of linguistic usage" based on conceptions similar to James's, and "in all probability derived from the distinguished teacher of her Radcliffe days" (pp. 125, 127). Weissmann, by contrast, follows Skinner's lead in most of the details of his account, although he is careful to distinguish Stein's "automatic writing" from her later experimental writing.

21. The linkage, especially in the second half of the nineteenth century, of women and hysteria—etymologically, "hysteria" derives from Greek *hustera*, or "womb"—has been the subject of much recent academic study; see, for example, Smith-Rosenberg, Bernheimer and Kahane, Evans, Beizer, Baer, and Micale (*Approaching Hysteria*).

22. The letter, tentatively dated February 1934, is now in YCAL. Although, as noted above, Stein customarily dropped the *e* in words beginning *ex-*, it appears from the manuscript that in this case she originally spelled "excess" without the initial "e" and then added it as an afterthought—perhaps as an immediate example of the sort of "[e]xcess" consciousness she had in mind.

23. The distinction "between the unconscious and the conscious being of the mental state," James argued in *The Principles of Psychology*, was not required to explain the "great class of experiences in our mental life which may be described as discoveries that a subjective condition which we have been having is really something different from what we had supposed" (pp. 166, 172). One might note with respect to the strikingly different conclusion reached by Freud in *The Psychopathology of Everyday Life*, his central text on the role of the unconscious in this common experience, that he does not make an especially convincing case for the claim that the unconscious is the determining factor in the parapraxes he marshals

forth. To be sure, as Freud observed in a 1924 footnote, the book was "of an entirely popular character; it merely aims, by an accumulation of examples, at paving the way for the necessary assumption of *unconscious yet operative* mental processes, and it avoids all theoretical considerations on the nature of this unconscious" (p. 346). Not only is Freud's tendentiousness suspect, however—his success in providing explanations for every parapraxis he meets only shows that he could reduce them all to equations with one unknown, the unconscious—but he was puzzlingly untroubled by the existence of alternative explanations. "It remains an open question," he wrote, "whether there are, within the range of normality, yet other factors that can—like the unconscious motive, and in place of it—create parapraxes and symptomatic acts along the lines of these [physiological and psychophysical] relations. It is not my task to answer this question" (p. 345). Yet it is this very question that challenges the strict determinism of his "psychology of the unconscious" (p. 330). The possibility that the experiences of "everyday life" are overdetermined has as its corollary the underdetermined state of his own determinism. This is a matter that Stein, following James, deliberately kept open.

24. In an important series of essays that chart a linked "defiance and acceptance" on Stein's part of "bourgeois heterosexual ideology," Catharine Stimpson demonstrates the ways that Stein "juxtapose[d] a reconstitution of patriarchal ideals about gender against the repudiation of those ideals" in her writing ("Humanism," p. 316; "Transposition," p. 10).

25. The earliest example cited by the *O.E.D.* for the use of *hysteria* in the "transferred" or "figurative" sense of "morbidly excited condition; unhealthy emotion or excitement" is in fact a line of Poe: "An evidently restrained *hysteria* in his whole demeanor." Women are "much more liable than men to this disorder," the compilers of the dictionary observe of the term in its principal, pathological sense, and the example's masculine pronoun (*"his* whole demeanor") may well have signaled for them the figurativeness that they attributed to Poe's usage. For recent considerations of male hysteria, see Hertz (with the responses by Gallagher and Fineman), Micale ("Charcot," "Hysteria Male"), and Goldstein.

26. See Ruddick for a very different account of Stein's understanding of the unconscious, and of the relation that her *analysis of the psyche* bears to Freudian *psychoanalysis*. As Ruddick notes, Stein's narrator in MA explicitly invokes a dynamic unconscious on several occasions; no doubt, at this stage in her career Stein could well have taken the Freudian route. The question, then, is why she ended up going the way she did, why her later statements critical of the unconscious are *not* repressions, why it is in fact misleading to view them as misleading—as well as just what the exact circumstances were that permitted her to move beyond the unconscious as an explanatory principle. Ultimately, I am suggesting that Freud's model of the unconscious may turn out to have been subject to the same vicious circle afflicting Skinner's postulate of a secondary consciousness—the same flaw that dogs any insufficiently radical empiricism. In this context see Miller on Chomsky's "epoch-making criticism of Behaviorism," as

rooted in his invocation of "a linguistic Unconscious" to "account for the distinctive creativity of language," and thereby to explain "our ability to utter and understand sentences that had never previously been spoken or heard" (p. 31). Also see DeKoven for a discussion of Stein's writing in light of Chomskian linguistics.

27. "Sidis" is Boris Sidis, who went on to become "the leading American exponent of the 'subpersonal self,'" publishing classic studies on "the psychology of suggestion" and "multiple personality" (Armstrong, p. 214). See CBM on Sidis's relations with James and Münsterberg.

28. For an extended reading of "My Life had stood—a Loaded Gun—" (#754), see Howe, whose study begins: "In the college library I use [as it happens, the library at Yale University, where Stein's papers are housed] there are two writers whose work refuses to conform to the Anglo-American literary traditions these institutions perpetuate. Emily Dickinson and Gertrude Stein . . ." (p. 11).

29. Taylor offers the following definition of a planchette: "an automatic writing device consisting of a heart-shaped disc with three legs, one of which is a pencil; one or both hands resting on the disc will record, on a piece of paper, involuntary muscle movements as well as unconscious writing" (*Exceptional Mental States*, p. 43).

30. One might compare James's description of this "subconscious region" with Bruno Latour's characterization of the "new actor[s]" who "intervene" in Robert Boyle's mid-seventeenth-century account of his experiments with the air pump: "inert bodies, incapable of will and bias but capable of *showing, signing, writing, and scribbling on laboratory instruments* before trustworthy witnesses." "Endowed with their new semiotic powers," these nonhumans "contribute to a new form of text, the experimental scientific article, a hybrid between the age-old style of biblical exegesis—which has previously been applied only to the Scriptures and classical texts—and *the new instrument that produces new inscriptions*. From this point on, witnesses will pursue their discussions around the air pump in its enclosed space, discussions about the meaningful behaviour of nonhumans. The old hermeneutics will persist, but it will add to its parchments *the shaky signature of scientific instruments*" (pp. 23–24, emphasis added). Here Latour extends the realm of the phenomena James is describing from psychical research to all experimental science, suggesting that laboratory instruments are in essence elaborate writing instruments—pen and paper writ large.

31. Richard Maurice Bucke, who popularized the phrase advocated here by James in his 1901 volume *Cosmic Consciousness: A Study in the Evolution of the Human Mind*, found it in turn in the work of Edward Carpenter, fellow Whitman enthusiast. According to Linda Dalrymple Henderson, Carpenter "referred . . . to a higher 'fourth-dimensional consciousness to whose gaze the interiors of solid bodies are exposed like mere surfaces' in his 1889 *Civilization: Its Cause and Cure*," but only "termed it cosmic consciousness" in 1892 ("Mysticism," p. 35). In "A Four-Dimensional Trio" Henderson discusses Stein in relation to contemporary claims for "a fourth dimension of space" (p. 106).

32. Gerald Myers thus observes that although "according to most commentators, James was chronically introspective[,] there are two important respects in which he was not. . . . First, he did not try to manage negative feelings by paying them introspective attention. Whereas some therapists contend that troublesome feelings are best handled by intense scrutiny, James counseled otherwise. . . . Negative states of consciousness, he claimed, are more effectively dissipated by strategic behavior than by introspective scrutiny. Second, James did not practice introspective self-diagnosis or self-analysis as Freud did, for example, in *The Interpretation of Dreams*. One of the most remarkable aspects of James's numerous references to his own problems is that he never attempted a sustained introspective analysis of their underlying causes. . . . James was to an extent an introspectionist in psychology, but he seldom used introspection to discover the causes of his own psychic states, nor did he advocate any systematic method by which people could locate the causes of their psychological troubles" (pp. 47–48).

33. This procedure is central to what David Lodge calls Stein's "experimental metonymic writing," in which the "natural emphasis" of prose on "syntagmatic continuity" is replaced by an "emphasis on paradigmatic similarity" more appropriate to lyric poetry (p. 155). Here Lodge draws on the linguistic distinction between a paradigm ("a set of words with the same grammatical function") and a syntagma (a combination of "linguistic entities" into a "linguistic unit . . . of a higher degree of complexity") as well as on the distinction between metonymic language ("association by contiguity") and metaphoric language ("association by similarity") employed by Roman Jakobson in "Two Aspects of Language and Two Types of Aphasic Disturbances" (Lodge, pp. 73–75). In this classic essay Jakobson proposed that different forms of the language disorder aphasia may be understood as involving difficulties with the selection of language and with its combination— that is, along the metaphoric and metonymic axes of linguistic activity. Although there is nothing wrong with characterizations like Lodge's, they run the risk of creating the illusion that something has been *explained* when all that has really been provided is a new *description*. Thus, in observing that Stein's writing "oscillated violently between the metonymic and metaphoric poles, pushing out in each direction to points where she began to exhibit symptoms of Jakobson's two types of aphasia," Lodge may appear to have *explained* Stein's writing as exhibiting "symptoms" of aphasia, when all that he has actually done is to *redescribe* the writing, as oscillating "violently" between the two poles (p. 144). James himself discusses "association by contiguity" and "association by similarity" in considerable detail, despite questioning the accuracy of these "well-worn phrase[s]" (PR, pp. 529, 545 [BC, pp. 244, 255]).

34. In BC James substitutes *want* for *emptiness* in an otherwise identical passage (p. 163).

35. In an important essay on what he calls "generic *seeds* or *kernels*, possibilities of expression *sprouting* and *exfoliating* into new literary phenomena," Northrop Frye distinguishes riddle from charm as follows: "The rhetoric of charm

is dissociative and incantatory: it sets up a pattern of sound so complex and repetitive that the ordinary processes of response are short-circuited. . . . The riddle is essentially a charm in reverse: it represents the revolt of the intelligence against the hypnotic power of commanding words. In the riddle a verbal trap is set, but if one can 'guess,' that is, point to an outside object to which the verbal construct can be related, the something outside destroys it as a charm, and we have sprung the trap without being caught in it. . . . Charms and riddles, however, are psychologically very close together, as the unguessed or unguessable riddle is or may be a charm" (pp. 123, 126, 137–38, emphasis added). Frye goes on to observe that "in modern times, at least, a poet interested in charm techniques is likely to be interested in riddle techniques also," and offers Stein as his principal example. She "came to be thought of as the very type of the dissociative writer, was often ridiculed or caricatured on that basis, and of course it is true that she was greatly interested in dissociative techniques. . . . But many of the vignettes of *Tender Buttons* are riddles of a fairly conventional type, with the solution, as often happens, provided in the title" (p. 142). The portrait of Picasso similarly serves as charm and riddle in one.

36. For a description of Basic English (which consisted of approximately a thousand words that could be used in combination to replace all other English words), see Brower's interview with Richards in *I. A. Richards: Essays in His Honor*, especially pp. 33–36, as well as the essay by Empson in the same volume. "There are three chief reasons why Basic is important," Empson observed in another essay, first "as an 'auxiliary' international language[,] secondly as a first step in the direction of full English which gives the right feeling about the words[,] thirdly as a test of a bit of writing for the Englishman himself, a way of separating statement from form and feeling." "But for a word or two in 'quotes,'" Empson added, "this [particular] bit of writing is in Basic, and the better for its limits" (*Argufying*, pp. 230–31).

37. The associations were not entirely impossible to follow, however. Much recent criticism of Stein, beginning with Bridgman and Gass, has been concerned with developing just such personal associations. The point that needs to be made is that this is exactly what Stein was *not* doing. She was rigorously, even ruthlessly, trying to make them irrelevant, inoperative—trying to make their operations irrelevant. Decoding her compositions is certainly not pointless, but it unavoidably misses the point of writing this way at all.

38. See Ruddick for an account of the consistent identification with dirt in Stein's early writing—from "Melanctha" (etymologically, "black earth") to "the solid dirt" of MA.

39. See James's chapters on "Association" in PR and BC as well as Abrams, Christensen, and Richards (*Imagination*) on Coleridge's anti-associationism.

40. See Abrams for the classic account of Coleridge's distinction between the "mechanical fancy" and the "organic imagination." Laplanche and Pontalis, who cite Freud to the effect that "'when conscious purposive ideas (*Zielvorstellungen*)

are abandoned, concealed purposive ideas assume control of the current of ideas,'"
note as well that the psychoanalytic practice of free association "is meant to bring
out a determinate order of the unconscious" (p. 170). Needless to say, "the fore-
most difficulty confronting a rigorously necessitarian theory of association," whether
Hartleian or Freudian, is "to account for its own writing" (Christensen, p. 28).

41. In the manuscript of the 1932 *Stanzas in Meditation*, Stein listed "Meditations in Stanzas" as an alternative title for the work.

42. Arthur Danto makes a similar suggestion when he comments in a recent
essay that if "we are structured as texts, then criticism is preemptive psychology
and even now the strategies evolved for addressing literary texts have application
to us" (p. 382). Supposing that "texts, as literary artifacts, are projections and
extensions of the unifying structures of a self or of a life," and that "the principles,
whatever they are, that enable us to tell and follow stories, to construct and read
poetry, are the principles that bind lives into unities," then criticism (as "the theory
of texts") would be "the paradigm human science" and "the matrix for understanding the physiology and ultimately the molecular biology of human cognition"
(pp. 384, 381, 385). As it happens, Danto contributed the foreword to a one-
volume abridgment of Langer's masterful study of the interinanimation of "mind"
and "human feeling," calling it "one of the most audacious philosophical visions
of recent times" (M, p. vi).

Chapter 6

1. Emerson's statement (from "The Poet") echoes the "one 'standard'
quotation," as Stephen Jay Gould would have it, of the great eighteenth-century
naturalist Georges-Louis Leclerc, comte de Buffon, who in the "inaugural address
following his election as one of the 'forty immortals' of the Académie Française"
proposed that "*le style c'est l'homme même*" (p. 83). Interestingly, in his own 1903
"Address at the Emerson Centenary in Concord," James alluded to both Emerson's
statement *and* Buffon's when he proposed that Emerson's "loyalty to his own
personal type"—that of the scholar, or "perceiver of pure truth"—and to his
"mission," as "the reporter in worthy form of each perception," was his "*first
half*[,] *but only half*; for genius, as he said, is insatiate for expression, and truth
has to be clad in the right verbal garment." "The form of the garment," James
continued, "was so vital with Emerson that it is impossible to separate it from the
matter. They form a chemical combination—thoughts which would be trivial
expressed otherwise, are important through the nouns and verbs to which he
married them. *The style is the man, it has been said*; the man Emerson's mission
culminated in his style" (pp. 20–22, emphasis added). The same year, William's
brother Henry alluded in a particularly ingenious manner to Buffon's remark in his
biography of Emerson's contemporary William Wetmore Story. Concerning "the
puerility of any pretended estimate of property in *subject*" (that is, of any claims

made for treating subject-matter as a form of property), Story's biographer observed that "a subject is never anything but his who can make something of it, and it is the thing made that becomes the property. But as between the thing made and the making the distinction is not to be seized, it is to the treatment alone that the fact of possession attaches—from which it is superfluous to warn us off. *The treatment—it was long ago said in another way—is the man himself*, whom we may be left free to plagiarise if we are able" (II, pp. 234–35, emphasis added).

2. It is presumably this perspective that links Jamesian pragmatism and the "new pragmatism" of Stanley Fish et al., with its affinities to reader-response criticism.

3. Recently "the hard problem," as David Chalmers has labeled it—"the problem of experience," of explaining "why and how . . . experience arises from a physical basis"—has begun to receive a great deal of attention from philosophers as well as from neurophysiologists; see Shear for a wide range of responses to Chalmers's own "candidates for the psychophysical principles that might go into a theory of consciousness" (pp. 11, 22). Also see Searle's critique.

4. This passage occurs on the last page of Volume 1 of the 1890 edition of PR, which was published in two volumes.

5. James distinguished the "physical phenomenon" of "retention" (which nullifies the "mysterious storing up of an 'idea' in an unconscious state") from the "psychophysical phenomenon" of "recall or recognition" (PR, pp. 617 [BC, p. 276]). Although *recall* possesses physical *and* psychological aspects, he did not attempt to explain the connection between them; as far as the science of psychology was concerned, it was a genuine rather than a bogus mystery.

6. See CBM for a superb overview of James's psychological investigations in the last two decades of his life.

7. For a meticulous reconstruction of the lectures, see Taylor (*Exceptional Mental States*).

8. James cites Pierre Janet on "l'automatisme psychologique" as well as articles by Alfred Binet "in the Chicago *Open Court*, for July 25, August 1, and November 7, 1889. Also in the *Revue Philosophique* for 1889 and '90" (PR, p. 201).

9. See Reed for an extended consideration of "the 'psychologist's fallacy' par excellence," as James labeled it—clearly, a variant of Whitehead's "fallacy of misplaced concreteness" (PR, p. 195).

10. Unpublished letter to Stein in YCAL, with Stein's response drafted on the back. Buss, a New England journalist and acquaintance of Ezra Pound, published her *Studies in the Chinese Drama* with the Four Seas Company in Boston, and later persuaded Stein to place GP with the same firm. Stein's 1930 portrait of her, "To Kitty Or Kate Buss," is included in PP.

11. See CBM on "the Myerian subliminal" as well as the account, in Frank Turner's important study of "the reaction to scientific naturalism in late Victorian England," of Myers's "quest for the immortal part" (CBM, p. 78; *Between Science and Religion*, p. 104).

12. The editors of ML give the date of this "Fragment of a Lecture on Exceptional Mental Phenomena" as 1895 or 1896. As Taylor notes, it follows James's outline for the second of the Lowell Lectures "almost exactly" (*Exceptional Mental States*, p. 35). For example, the material quoted addresses the question posed in the lecture, "But *where* is the part ruled out?" (ML, p. 67). There is nothing comparable in James's published work until certain passages in VAR.

13. See Hobson for a fascinating recent study that takes its lead from James's formulation here, with "the organization of mental life" understood "as an orderly sequence of conscious states," and in particular of the physiological states of waking, sleeping, and dreaming (p. viii).

14. Examples of James's use of these phrases in VAR include: "The most important consequences of having a strongly developed *ultra-marginal life* of this sort is that one's ordinary fields of consciousness are liable to incursions from it of which the subject does not guess the source" (p. 234); "incursions from beyond the *transmarginal region*" (p. 478); "The exploration of the *transmarginal field* has hardly yet been seriously undertaken" (p. 511); "difficulties present themselves as soon as we . . . ask how far *our transmarginal consciousness* carries us if we follow it on its remoter side" (p. 513); "The *subconscious self* is nowadays a well-accredited psychological entity" (p. 511); "The *subliminal region*, whatever else it may be, is at any rate a place now admitted by psychologists to exist" (p. 236).

15. The articles by Miller appeared in *The Philosophical Review* 2 (July 1893) and *The Psychological Review* 2 (November 1895). In 1896 James suggested that he regarded Miller, a former student of his who went on to teach at Bryn Mawr, Harvard, and Columbia, as his "most penetrating critic and intimate enemy." (The remark occurred in a letter James wrote to Miller; it is cited by Simon, who also reprints Miller's 1917 memoir of James.) I have taken the course descriptions from the Harvard Course Catalogue for 1895–96.

16. See Copeland for a discussion of the compositional relation between *Q.E.D.* and "Melanctha." In dozens of parallel passages like the following pair, Stein translated an unstable triangle of privileged, deracinated white women into a tale of failed, mostly heterosexual love among African Americans. "Adele spent much of their time together," begins one passage in *Q.E.D.*, which directly addresses the subject of self-quotation, "in announcing with great interest the result of her endless meditations. She would criticize and examine herself and her ideas with tireless interest. 'Helen,' she said one day, 'I always had an impression that you talked a great deal but apparently you are a most silent being. What is it? Do I talk so hopelessly much that you get discouraged with it as a habit? . . . really Helen why don't you talk more to me?' 'Because you know well enough that you are not interested in my ideas, in fact that they bore you. It's always been very evident. You know' Helen continued affectionately, 'that you haven't much talent for concealing your feelings and impressions.' Adele smiled, 'Yes you are certainly right about most of your talk, it does bore me,' she admitted. 'But that is because it's about stuff that you are not really interested in. You don't really care about general ideas and art values and musical development and surgical operations and

Heaven knows what all and naturally your talk about those things doesn't interest me. No talking is interesting that one hasn't hammered out oneself. I know I always bore myself unutterably when I talk the thoughts that I hammered out some time ago and that are no longer meaningful to me, for quoting even oneself lacks a flavor of reality, but you, you always make me feel that at no period did you ever have the thoughts that you converse with. Surely one has to hit you awfully hard to shake your realler things to the surface' (TL, pp. 221–22). The figure of Adele is transparently discoursing in a high Emersonian mode here, even going so far as to revise the line from "Experience," "I know that the world I converse with in the city and in the farms is not the world I *think*." Language used by Emerson to keep his two worlds apart is rudely conflated—Helen "converse[s] with," or by means of, her notably unoriginal "thoughts"—yet the worlds themselves remain distinct. When she rewrote the exchange between Adele and Helen in "Melanctha" two years later, Stein retained practically everything except the prefabricated pairs of nouns and adjectives ("general ideas and art values and musical development and surgical operations") *and the remark on self-quotation*: "Jeff Campbell had not got over his way of talking to her all the time about all the things he was always thinking. Melanctha never talked much, now, when they were together. Sometimes Jeff Campbell teased her about her not talking to him. 'I certainly did think Melanctha you were a great talker from the way Jane Harden and everybody said things to me, and from the way I heard you talk so much when I first met you. Tell me true Melanctha, why don't you talk more now to me, perhaps it is I talk so much I don't give you any chance to say things to me, or perhaps it is you hear me talk so much you don't think so much now of a whole lot of talking. Tell me honest Melanctha, why don't you talk more to me.' 'You know very well Jeff Campbell,' said Melanctha. 'You certainly do know very well Jeff, you don't think really much, of my talking. You think a whole lot more about everything than I do Jeff, and you don't care much what I got to say about it. You know that's true what I am saying Jeff, if you want to be real honest, the way you always are when I like you so much.' Jeff laughed and looked fondly at her. 'I don't say ever I know, you ain't right, when you say things like that to me, Melanctha. You see you always like to be talking just what you think everybody wants to be hearing from you, and when you are like that, Melanctha, honest, I certainly don't care very much to hear you, but sometimes you say something that is what you are really thinking, and then I like a whole lot to hear you talking'" (TL, p. 94). Both the Penguin edition of *Three Lives* and the Library of America selection of Stein's writing helpfully reprint *Q.E.D.* along with "Melanctha."

17. For a pair of allusions by Stein to the characteristically piecemeal nature of her writing, see Bridgman, who uses "Why cannot you speak in pieces and say no matter" and "I master pieces of it" (from "Why Cannot You Speak In Pieces" and "Saints and Singing" respectively) as epigraphs to his comprehensive, if often uncomprehending, study of Stein's corpus.

18. Interestingly enough, this noncontradictory combination, of states of mind "co-existing" in paragraphs, closely parallels Empson's seventh type of poetic

ambiguity—which he limited, however, to conflicting states of mind that exist simultaneously in a single person.

19. For discussions of Jamesian panpsychism, see Griffin et al. and Rorty ("Dewey").

20. Cited from the jacket copy of GP, in which Stein describes herself as "translat[ing] the rhythm of the spoken personality as directly as possible, using every form that she can invent to translate the repeated story of everybody doing what, what they are being." For the compositional history of this passage, see Chapter 4 above as well as my article on Stein's literary criticism in the *Cambridge History of Literary Criticism*.

21. In praising Myers as "an enormous collector," James set him in the same lineage as Louis Agassiz. Several years earlier, he had eulogized Agassiz (whose widow still presided over Radcliffe while Stein was a student there) as a pioneering naturalist whose "habit of collecting . . . knew no bounds save those that separate the things of Nature from those of human art." Agassiz, he added, was "one of those naturalists in the unlimited sense, one of those folio copies of mankind, like Linnaeus and Cuvier, who aim at nothing less than *an acquaintance with the whole of animated Nature*" and whose "genius for classifying was simply marvelous" ("Louis Agassiz," pp. 4, 6, emphasis added).

22. "Postlogic" is Elizabeth Sewell's term, introduced in *The Orphic Voice*, her valuable study of poetry and natural history. The distinction between heterogeneous and homogeneous dialectics, and between postlogic and formal logic, offers a particularly telling context for comparing Myers's idealizations in his early volume on Wordsworth (1880) with those in Maurice Bucke's 1883 study of Whitman—as well as the ways that these idealizations carry over into their respective masterworks, *Human Personality and Its Survival of Bodily Death* and *Cosmic Consciousness*.

23. I hope elsewhere to give a fuller account of this isomorphism between Stein's writing practices and Edelman's "theory of neuronal group selection" (or TNGS). For some preliminary remarks, see the conclusion to the present study. In any case, the earliest human writing may well have consisted of the use of marks to indicate directions, whether of home, danger, or prey, long antedating pictures such as those at Lascaux, which, as representational figures, exhibit the rudiments of writing even if they are not what we normally construe as texts. See Chatwin for a fascinating investigation of one contemporary version of aboriginal writing, and both Donald and Deacon for compelling accounts of writing's origins in terms drawn from the emerging discipline of evolutionary anthropology.

Chapter 7

1. James made this statement in the course of acknowledging the effect that Bergson had in persuading him definitively to "renounce the intellectualistic

method and the current notion that logic is an adequate measure of what can or cannot be" (pp. 264, 225). Although James characterized his philosophy as "bergsonian" (having "already in 1895," as he put it with reference to the landmark article "The Knowing of Things Together," which appeared in the second volume of *The Psychological Review*, been "far advanced toward my present bergsonian position"), Bergson appealed to him chiefly to the extent that he could be framed in Emersonian terms (p. 344). This becomes especially clear when one attends to the repeated echoes of Emerson's directive to "place yourself in the middle of the stream of power and wisdom which animates all whom it floats, and you are without effort impelled to truth, to right, and a perfect contentment" throughout the section of *A Pluralistic Universe* I am citing from here. "Out of no amount of discreteness can you manufacture the concrete," James announced in "Bergson and His Critique of Intellectualism." "But," he continued, *"place yourself at a bound, or d'emblée, as M. Bergson says, inside of the living, moving, active thickness of the real, and all the abstractions and distinctions are given into your hand. . . . Get at the expanding centre of a human character, the* élan vital *of a man, as Bergson calls it, by living sympathy, and at a stroke you see how it makes those who see it from without interpret it in such diverse ways. . . . Place yourself similarly at the centre of a man's philosophic vision and you understand at once all the different things it makes him write and say. . . .* What really exists is not things made but things in the making. Once made, they are dead, and an infinite number of alternative conceptual decompositions can be used in defining them. But *put yourself in the making by a stroke of intuitive sympathy with the thing and, the whole range of possible decompositions coming at once into your possession, you are no longer troubled with the question which of them is the more absolutely true. . . . Once adopt the movement of this life in any given instance and you know what Bergson calls the* devenir réel *by which the thing evolves and grows"* (pp. 261–64, emphasis added). It was immediately following this last remark that James proceeded to distinguish philosophy from science exactly as Stein would a quarter of a century later in LIA, when she contrasted her *scientific* concerns in MA with the newly *philosophical* concerns of TB. Philosophy, James wrote, "should seek this kind of living understanding of the movement of reality, not follow science in vainly patching together fragments of its dead results" (p. 264).

2. Letter to Virgil Thomson, dated February 23, 1929, in YCAL.

3. Cited from a letter to Carl Van Vechten, dated April 15, 1929, in Burns and Dydo, I, p. 193 ("We are leaving for our Belley house in a couple of weeks," Stein wrote, "we bought ourselves a white caniche [poodle] of two months which we call Basket to go with it and with us and I am working making sentences about the sentence"), and from the letter to Thomson dated February 23, 1929, in YCAL.

4. Wittgenstein introduces the notion of "family resemblance" in remark #67 of PI (p. 32e).

5. "In a certain sense," Wittgenstein wrote, "one cannot take too much care in handling philosophical mistakes, they contain so much truth" (*Zettel*, p. 82e).

6. Additional investigations dating from this period have been collected in *Remarks on the Philosophy of Psychology* and *Last Writings on the Philosophy of Psychology*.

7. Wittgenstein concluded another set of remarks composed in the late 1940s, regarding James's suggestion that "the emotion consists in the bodily feeling," with the instruction, "Compare fear and anxiety with care," and then added, "What sort of description is this: '*Ewiges Dustere steigt herunter . . .*'? / One might describe a pain like that; even paint it" (RPP, I, pp. 132e–133e). Joachim Schulte has observed, in the most thorough account of Wittgenstein's readings of James to date, that "the original German word translated as care is 'Sorge.' And Wittgenstein continues by asking himself what sort of description is given by words like 'Ewiges Dustere steigt herunter,' translated as 'Perpetual cloud descends.' These words are spoken by the figure of Sorge in the last act of Goethe's *Faust*" (p. 128). Schulte is quite right in proposing that Wittgenstein invokes *Sorge* here because it is an emotion typically "without a clear cause or object," by contrast with fear and anxiety. Yet, surely, it does not follow that the emotion is unaccompanied by "strong . . . physical feelings," as Schulte asserts; rather, regardless of the intensity, the feelings are less likely to be due to immediate external influences—*impacts*, in Langer's terminology. None of this is inconsistent with James's theory of emotion. Moreover, through the reference to *Sorge* Wittgenstein connects his early interest in the James of *The Varieties of Religious Experience* to his subsequent engagement with the author of *The Principles of Psychology*, and to the theorist of emotion in particular. For additional discussions of Wittgenstein and James, centered around the James-Lange theory, see Terwee and Budd.

8. "Most people," Stein wrote, "are more predetermined as to what is the human form and the human face than they are as to what are flowers, landscapes, still lifes"—most people, but "not everybody" (PCW, p. 40). Interestingly, she used the same, almost Blakean, phrase when she described Francis Picabia's "way of achieving the disembodied" in ABT. There, he is said to struggle "with the problem that a line should have the vibration of a musical sound and that this vibration should be the result of conceiving *the human form and the human face* in so tenuous a fashion that it would induce such vibration in the line forming it." "It was this idea," Stein added, giving agency to the idea rather than to the artist, "that conceived mathematically influenced Marcel Duchamp and produced his The Nude Descending the Staircase" (p. 210, emphasis added).

9. One of Wittgenstein's most expressly physiognomic remarks follows on the heels of the proposition that "meaning is a physiognomy" and concerns an alleged parallel between psychology and physics. In quite correctly disputing the parallel, he nevertheless neglected the *physiological* components of psychology and attributed a perspective to the psychologist that remained at a far greater remove from the subject under investigation than those available either to himself or to the physicist in their respective spheres of inquiry:

571. Misleading parallel: psychology treats of processes in the psychical sphere, as does physics in the physical.

Seeing, hearing, thinking, feeling, willing, are not the subject of psychology *in the same sense* as that in which the movements of bodies, the phenomena of electricity, etc., are the subject of physics. You can see this from the fact that the physicist sees, hears, thinks about, and informs us of these phenomena, and the psychologist observes the *external relations* (the behaviour) of the subject. (PI, p. 151e)

Apparently, Wittgenstein believed that James was a victim of this misleading analogy between psychology and physics himself; and many remarks of James's doubtless lend credence to this impression. Yet to attribute such a perspective to him is to ignore the fact that he directed precisely the same critique at his own thought, in the course of further refining his theory of emotion in the two decades that followed the publication of PR. In a sense, Wittgenstein's failure to acknowledge the development of James's thought beyond the conceptual framework of PR is beside the point, since the chief interest that James's textbook held for him lay in the thoroughness with which it mined the implications of common conceptions of psychology. It was the grammar of these ordinary conceptions, or misconceptions, that Wittgenstein was concerned to describe. That James might have come up with an explanatory framework for human experience that managed to avoid many of the pitfalls of typical psychological explanation would not have had much weight for Wittgenstein so long as it remained impossible to confirm such a theory experimentally, to determine an *"experimentum crucis* which could decide for or against the theory."* Recent advances in neurophysiology, both technological and theoretical, begin to make such experimental confirmation conceivable. In addition, one can also argue that Stein's radically experimental writing provides an extended *experimentum crucis*, which, if it doesn't exactly "decide for or against the theory," does succeed, I believe, in making James's radical empiricism more plausible—if not, to everyone's taste, more palatable.

Chapter 8

1. The photograph appeared in the January 30, 1950, issue of *Life*. Mili, a pioneer in the use of strobe photography in journalism, narrated "the course of [Picasso's] action as the image progresses from beginning to end" in his 1970 study *Picasso's Third Dimension*. First, Picasso "describes a small hook and swings upward to delineate the left arm, then the head and horns, the right arm and then the spine; at frantic speed—which is shown by the thinness of the line—he scribbles two wavering hind legs before he slows down, almost to a stop, while drawing the soft curve of the underbelly. As if he suddenly remembers there is more to do, he swiftly shoots straight up to fill in the facial structures and without breaking the

flow, signs off with a flourish." Aside from the fanciful subject matter, what distinguishes the photo from others taken during the same shoot is that "in this instance" Mili "fired a flash [as soon as] the camera was opened," making Picasso "visible as he started to draw in the dark" (p. 16).

2. Hobson probably didn't conjure the phrase out of thin air, as the heading of the *Life* article reads: "Picasso tries new art form, drawing in thin air with light" (p. 11).

3. Hobson briefly considers an account proposed by Roger Penrose and Stuart Hameroff, locating global binding at the level of brain microtubules, "intracellular circulation system[s] possessed by all neurons." According to the Penrose-Hameroff theory, the unity of conscious experience derives from "quantum oscillations" that occur within these protein transport mechanisms. The emergence among large quantities of microtubules of "quantum coherence . . . for relevant time periods" elicits an *orchestrated* "self-collapse" (whereby the "transient superposition of slightly different space-time geometries," which exist coherently, or simultaneously, reduces to "a single universe state"). "What would our mentor, William James, have said about orchestrated objective reduction theory?" Hobson asks. "Would it, I wonder, have inspired in him—as it does in me—something like his reaction to Sigmund Freud speaking on psychoanalysis at Worcester in 1907 [actually, 1909]? Recognizing Freud's genius and keen rhetorical skills, but wary of Freud's arrogance, James pointed out that the concept of a dynamic unconscious that could not be seen directly was exceedingly dangerous for psychology" (pp. 126–27). Aligning himself in this respect with Stein no less than with James, Hobson cautions against accepting the blatantly non-empirical claim that "it is the state of atoms and subatomic particles *that we can't see or even measure in functioning brains* that determines the state of the mind" (p. 125, emphasis added). Additional proposals for solving "the binding problem" include the one put forward by Crick, who speculates that "synchronized [neuronal] firing on, or near, the beat of a gamma oscillation (in the 35- to 70-Hertz range) might be the neural correlate of visual awareness," and another by Varela who, like Hobson, sets "resonance binding" in a broadly *physiological* rather than a reductively *physical* environment (Crick, pp. 208, 245; Varela, "The Reenchantment of the Concrete," p. 333).

4. Stein's practice of linguistic self-discipline involved the development of organic mechanisms similar to those lauded by James in "The Energies of Men," his 1906 presidential address to the American Philosophical Association, as well as by Hobson, ninety years later, under the rubric of "relaxation techniques" and the "conscious control of consciousness" (pp. 235, 49). Of "the Yoga system in Hindustan," which he regarded as the "most venerable" of the ascetic disciplines designed "to keep the deeper levels [of vital energy] constantly in reach," James observed, "From time immemorial . . . Hindu aspirants to perfection have trained themselves, month in and out for years. The result claimed, and certainly in many cases accorded by impartial judges, is strength of character, personal power,

unshakability of soul." In the version of the address that Stein would have read, he summarized "the experience with 'Hatha Yoga' of a very gifted European friend of mine who, by persistently carrying over for several months its methods of fasting from food and sleep, its exercises in breathing and thought-concentration, and its fantastic posture-gymnastics, seems to have succeeded in waking up deeper and deeper levels of will and moral and intellectual power in himself" (p. 679). When Stein resumed work on MA shortly after the appearance of James's article in the *American Magazine*, she did so with renewed vigor as well as with a marked change both in the perspective informing the work and in its writing style. Whatever the immediate causes of this shift, it took the form of just the sort of "methodical ascetic discipline" described by James, only within the medium of writing rather than in a more obviously spiritual or corporeal guise.

5. In a notebook entry, Stein observed sometime between 1906 and 1908 that "*real thinking* is conceptions aiming and aiming again always getting fuller, that is the difference between creative thinking and theorizing"; see notebook NB-N among the unpublished notebooks and working notes for MA in YCAL. At this stage, she continued to model writing after consciousness (and after James) rather than, as she would begin to do in the first portraits three or four years later, modeling consciousness after writing. Her conceptualization was still limited to notions of "real thinking," "conceptions," "theorizing," and "creative thinking," and what she would later call "the idea of the recreation of the word" is notably absent, as is any clear awareness of the role of language, and writing, in thought (TI, p. 18). The shift in emphasis was fully in place by 1913, however, when, shortly before composing her first play, Stein wrote to Mabel Dodge about Richard Strauss's *Elektra*, which she had just seen in London. The opera had produced a "deeper impression" on her, she reported, "than anything since Tristan in my youth . . . [Strauss] has made *real conversation* and he does it by intervals and relations directly without machinery" (Everett, p. 174, emphasis added). Some twenty years later, Stein described the experience in nearly identical terms, recalling that "for a long time" after moving to Paris, she "did not go to the theatre at all. I forgot the theatre, I never thought of the theatre at all. I did sometimes think about the opera. I went to the opera once in Venice and I liked it and then much later Strauss' Electra made me realise that in a kind of a way there could be a solution to the problem of conversation on the stage" (LIA, p. 117).

6. The letter and essay are both in YCAL.

7. In 1905, Owen Wister (author of the best-selling *The Virginian*) extolled Henry James's "later books" in a letter to the Philadelphia psychiatrist S. Weir Mitchell. Wister's delineation of James differs strikingly from King's description of him, yet taken together, their remarks establish an underlying homology between Stein's compositional practices and those of James, as well as the persistence of the concerns that motivated Stein throughout her career. "Henry James is in essence inscrutable," Wister wrote, "but one thing of him I know: our language has no artist more serious or austere at this moment. I explain to myself his bewildering

style thus: he is attempting the impossible with it—a certain very particular form of the impossible, namely, to produce upon the reader, as a painting produces upon the gazer, a number of superimposed, simultaneous impressions. He would like to put several sentences on top of each other so that you could read them all at once, and get all at once the various shadings and complexities, instead of getting them consecutively as the mechanical nature of his medium compels. This I am sure is the secret of his involved parenthesis, his strangely injected adverbs, the whole structure, in short, of his twisted syntax" (cited by Rosenzweig, p. 254, from Burr, II, pp. 322–23). Like Stein, James is said to resist the purportedly "mechanical nature of his medium" by opting for grammatical and syntactical superposition in lieu of consecutiveness; or, as Stein herself put it in a passage already cited in Chapter 3, his "whole paragraph was detached what it said from what it did, what it was from what it held, and over it all something floated not floated away but just floated" (LIA, p. 53). Here Stein was articulating the sense she shared with both King and Wister of the living, vibratory quality of James's language as it inhered in his sentences and paragraphs.

8. Like Stein, Robert Frost and Marianne Moore also investigated the correlations between intonation and understanding in the context of PR. Besides labeling PR one of the books that "did most to shape her vocational attitude and philosophy of life," Moore was a classmate and close friend of James's daughter, Peggy, at Bryn Mawr. In the early essay "The Accented Syllable," which appeared in *The Egoist* in 1916, Moore proposed that in certain instances, as in the lines "Then Louisa went into the kitchen and cried for it is exasperating to be unjustly accused" and "It is true enough to say that everybody is selfish provided we add, and unselfish" (cited respectively from August Strindberg's *Easter and Other Plays* and Richard C. Cabot's *What Men Live By*), the "pleasure" experienced in reading a given statement derives from "tone of voice" and not from any particular meaning. By *tone of voice*, she understood "intonation in which the accents which are responsible for it are so unequivocal as to persist, no matter under what circumstances the syllables are read or by whom they are read." Consequently, if "an author's written tone of voice is distinctive," the "reader's speaking tone of voice will not obliterate it," whatever the reader happens to feel about the state-ment's validity—however ironically one may choose to read the "group of words" in question (*Complete Prose*, pp. 31–32). About the time that Moore was distinguishing "written" from "speaking" tones of voice, and Stein was making the transition from rhythmic to dissociative writing, Frost was formulating a corresponding theory of "the sound of sense" in an important series of letters composed between 1913 and 1915. (For a compelling account of Frost's notion of "sentence sounds" in the context of Wittgenstein's grammatical investigations, see Guetti. Also see Poirier's discussion, in *Robert Frost: The Work of Knowing*, of James's "extensive influence" on the version of the poem "Design" that Frost completed in 1912, while he was teaching BC and James's 1899 volume, *Talks to Teachers on Psychology: and to Students on Some of Life's Ideals* [p. 249]. Frost

first read *The Will to Believe* during the summer of 1898, and the following academic year—his second, and last, at Harvard—he encountered BC in an introductory philosophy course.) "The best place to get the abstract sound of sense," Frost instructed a former student in the earliest of the letters on the "posture proper" to sentences in poetry, "is from voices behind a door that cuts off the words. Ask yourself how these sentences would sound without the words in which they are embodied: // You mean to tell me you can't read? / I said no such thing. / Well read then. / You're not my teacher." Or: "He says it's too late. / Oh, say! / Damn an Ingersoll watch anyway" (Barry, p. 59). On the basis of his concept of the *sentence sound*, which "often says more than the words" strung on it, Frost sought to "establish the distinction between the grammatical sentence and the vital sentence," that is, "the living part of a poem[,] . . . the intonation entangled some- how in the syntax idiom and meaning of a sentence" (pp. 66–67, 61). As for "the grammatical sentence," he added, it "is merely accessory to the other and chiefly valuable as furnishing a clue to the other." The account of the reader's experience in PR would have struck Frost, no less than Moore and Stein, as overly mechanical and out of sync with James's subsequent, more fully developed, radical empiricism. All three writers conceived of writing as expressing itself in certain instances *through* the "reader's speaking tone of voice," not *by means* of it, and hence as capable of communicating knowledge of acquaintance (whether in the mode of "the author's written tone of voice" or "the sound of sense" or "composition as explanation") beyond the capacity of a reader who merely possesses a "sense of at least the form of the sentence yet to come . . . fused with his consciousness of the present word."

9. King's twice-repeated characterization of the language of "Melanctha" as "colorless" is particularly striking in the context of Stein's emphasis on color in the work, at the level of theme as well as of image. (In a blurb prepared for a trial dustjacket for *Three Lives*, now in YCAL, King hardly ignored the "situation" of the "young coloured girl": "Everyone in the story is coloured, the whole world, with all its preoccupations and potentialities; the reader himself, for the time, is a coloured person too.") The sense of colorlessness may also correspond, in a differ- ent register, to the use of "deaccentuation" as a way of conveying depression, and as such serves as a particularly appropriate formal device for portraying the melancholy embodied in the figure of Melanctha.

10. Alternate characterizations of speech by Bolinger include the "stream of melody," "vocal stream," "speech stream," and "pitch stream" (pp. 28, 215, 273).

11. In addition, Bolinger introduces several variants (CA, CB, AC, CAC) that "combine more than one effective position." By contrast, each of the primary profiles is limited to "a single effective position"—with "the accents in A and B" always being "*above* certain other material in their configurations," while the accent in C is always below (INT, p. 155).

12. For an extended consideration of Stein's writing in 1928, and of this passage in particular, see Dydo ("*Landscape Is Not Grammar*").

13. Davidson's failure is implicitly contrasted in ABT with the experience of Janet Scudder, author of the 1925 autobiographical volume *Modeling My Life*. In Toklas's introduction of her, as in her introduction *to* Toklas, Scudder's most salient feature is her voice. "Jo Davidson too sculpted Gertrude Stein at this time," Toklas remarks. "There," in Davidson's studio, "all was peaceful, Jo was witty and amusing and he pleased Gertrude Stein. I cannot remember who came in and out, whether they were real or whether they were sculptured but there were a great many. There were among others Lincoln Steffens and in some queer way he is associated with the beginning of our seeing a great deal of Janet Scudder but I do not well remember just what happened.

"I do however remember very well the first time I ever heard Janet Scudder's voice. It was way back when I first came to Paris and my friend and I had a little apartment in the rue Notre-Dame-des-Champs. My friend in the enthusiasm of seeing other people enthusiastic had bought a Matisse and it had just been hung on the wall. Mildred Aldrich was calling on us, it was a warm spring afternoon and Mildred was leaning out of the window. I suddenly heard her say, Janet, Janet come up here. What is it, said a very lovely drawling voice. I want you to come up here and meet my friends Harriet and Alice and I want you to come up and see their new apartment. Oh, said the voice. And then Mildred said, and they have a new big Matisse. Come up and see it. I don't think so, said the voice.

"Janet did later see a great deal of Matisse when he lived out in Clamart. And Gertrude Stein and she had always been friends, at least ever since the period when they first began to see a good deal of each other"—some fifteen years after Toklas's initial encounter with Scudder (or more to the point, with her voice) on Notre-Dame-des-Champs. "Like Doctor Claribel Cone," the reminiscence concludes, "Janet, always insisting that she understands none of it, reads and feels Gertrude Stein's work and reads it aloud understandingly" (pp. 204–5).

14. Two LPs that include material from the January 30, 1935, recital have been released commercially. "Gertrude Stein Reads From Her Works" (Caedmon 1050; also CDL 51050, since reissued on tape) contains several passages from MA as well as the entire "Matisse," "If I Told Him. A Completed Portrait of Picasso," "Idem the Same. A Valentine to Sherwood Anderson," and "Madame Recamier. An Opera." Volume 1 of the "Spoken Arts Treasury of 100 Modern American Poets" (SA 1040) collects several pieces from PP: "A Description of The Fifteenth of November. A Portrait of T. S. Eliot," "Christian Berard," "Matisse" again, and "She Bowed To Her Brother." In his invaluable chronology of Stein's lecture tour, William Rice notes that a "recording on aluminum discs [was] made in Milbank Hall, Columbia University, for their collection of speech records," and that later the same day the works were re-recorded for "the National Council of Teachers of English at the Erpi Studios, in the Aeolian Hall Building, 250 West 57th Street" (p. 345).

15. The sense of sentences as *self*-motivated, that is to say, as singing or diagramming *themselves*, presumably involves some variant of the experience of

multiple correlations occurring among diverse modalities, discussed earlier in this chapter. After all, any sense of *self* requires heterogeneous correlations. In particular, sentences like Stein's raise "the problem of the relation of seeing and hearing," which she identified as central to her theatrical investigations and which I have argued was central to all her writing following the transitional works of 1911–12 (LIA, p. 104). Shades of Chaplin's criticism of the spoken voice, and of its tendency to regularize shifts in the visual rhythm of film, may perhaps be detected in Stein's remark in EA that "as yet they have not yet done any of mine *without music to help them*. They could though and it would be interesting but no one has yet" (p. 200, emphasis added). The immediate occasion for this mild rebuke was a 1934 production of *Four Saints in Three Acts* in Chicago, the first time she actually saw a work of hers staged, and she also had in mind the upcoming London production of *A Wedding Bouquet*. This "ballet with chorus" was based on her 1931 play "They Must. Be Wedded. To Their Wife," with music by Gerald Berners and choreography by Frederick Ashton. At the end of EA, she returned to the Berners/Ashton production as well as to the question of whether "sometime they will do one as a play" (p. 328). In bringing the current installment of her Life to a close in the immediate present—"now it is to-day" are the work's final words—the events being narrated coincide for once with the act of narration. Already, four pages prior to this open-ended conclusion, Stein was observing that "now it is spring and next Friday we go to London to see The Wedding Bouquet put on"; she then proceeded to mix tenses freely, as in the sentence "We went to the country for the day and night before watching the rehearsal, I have never seen a rehearsal and it will be very exciting" (pp. 324, 326). Clearly designed to convey a visceral sense of her own uncertainty in anticipation of opening night ("And so to-morrow is going to be the day"), the confusion ceases with the actual performance, which is described entirely in the past tense: "It was to-morrow which was yesterday and it was exciting, it was the first time I had ever been present when anything of mine had been played for the first time. . . . it all went so very well, each time a musician does something with the words it makes it do what they never did do, this time it made them do as if the last word had heard the next word and the next word had heard not the last word but the next word. / After all why not. / I like anything that a word can do. And words do do all they do and then they can do what they never do do. / This made listening to what I had done and what they were doing most exciting. / And then gradually it was ending . . . / I guess it was a great success. / I hope sometime they will do one as a play. I wonder can they" (pp. 326–28, virgules indicating new paragraphs). However muted, Stein's ambivalence is unmistakable. The genuine pleasure she experienced from public success—"it is a peaceful thing to be one succeeding"—did not erase the fact that in this case her words had been *made to succeed one another* by the music, with each word, in effect, conveying the impression that it had already heard the one following it (p. 328). Although "They Must. Be Wedded. To Their Wife" had been composed by Stein in the strictly aperiodic style of "Winning His Way"—see Chapter 2—Berners and Ashton chose instead to "produce [a] steadfastly legible and conventional" setting for the work (Kavanagh, p. 204). The difference is graphically displayed in the published score, "Music by LORD BERNERS, / Words by GERTRUDE STEIN." The words are Stein's, but the punctuation has been thoroughly normalized. For example, the opening line ("Any name. Of which. One. Has known. At least two") is rewritten as "A-ny name of which one has known at least two," and in a particularly egregious bowdlerization, the deliberately rough edges of "Also. / It would be well. If. No. Hail fell. / To *hurt*. The other things. That have been planted" are smoothed over as "Al-so it would be well if no hail fell to *spoil* the o-ther things that have been plant-ed" (OP, p. 160; Berners, pp. 1, 6, emphasis added). Anything *plant-ed*—that is to say, any *plant*—capable of being hurt, possesses ipso facto a capacity for feeling, but Berners has perfunctorily removed this Shelleyan train of thought from his score. Stein may indeed have found the tension "most exciting" between what Berners achieved with his ever-forward-looking music and what she herself had sought to accomplish with her excessive punctuation; yet the politeness of that *most* gives the game away, as does the intonationally impossible-to-misinterpret *I guess it was a great success.* (Note how the juxtaposition of *most* and *exciting* removes the wind from each term's sails.) As Stein discovered when she actually saw the production (somewhere between pp. 326 and 327 of EA), *her* words, the words embedded in a host of conjunctive and disjunctive relations in "They Must. Be Wedded. To Their Wife," were never really present in *A Wedding Bouquet*. Instead, they were experienced mediately, following the music's lead. It was that kind of a success.

16. "English grammar is interesting because it is so simple," Stein remarked in "The Gradual Making of The Making of Americans." "Once you really know how to diagram a sentence really know it, you know practically all you have to know about English grammar. In short any child thirteen years old properly taught can by that time have learned everything there is to learn about English grammar. So why make a fuss about it. However one does" (LIA, pp. 146–47).

17. See Fisher for a recent broad-ranging meditation on the potential for "wonder" in "ordered recognition," including all manner of philosophical and scientific investigation.

18. Here are some additional remarks of Bolinger's on C and A profiles: The C profile is "in most ways, the mirror image [of A]—that is to say, the opposite—in its functions. Where A tends to play up, to emphasize, to suggest contrast or newness, C plays down, deemphasizes, and often implies foreknowledge. If to accent something is to give it force, then the accent in C can be thought of as a reverse accent: the speaker needs to make the item stand out—figure against ground—but has opposite feelings about it. . . . The C profile is inherently contradictory, for it 'deaccents an accent'" (INT, p. 178). Bolinger sounds remarkably like William Empson in these comments, which suggests that their respective analyses of "the shapes of complete intonations" and "the structure of complex words" might usefully be compared.

19. Rorty uses the phrase *taking time seriously*, typically in quotation marks, in both of his early essays on Whitehead. In conversation, he has remarked that he might have been quoting his teacher Charles Hartshorne, who supervised his M.A. thesis at the University of Chicago on Whitehead's theory of eternal objects.

20. The two most prominent of these notions in the paper by Gilbert, Opitz, and Raff are *morphogenetic fields* and *homologies of process*. "From the 1920s through the middle of the 1930s," they explain, "embryology experienced a Renaissance"; and "the basic paradigm, . . . the idea that gave it structure and coherence, was *the morphogenetic field*," which provided "an alternative to the gene as the unit of ontogeny," or individual development. A "web of interactions" was envisioned, such that any given cell could be defined "by its position within its respective field." Gilbert and his coauthors cite the following definition of such a field, from Needham, as exemplary: "A morphogenetic field is a system of order such that the positions taken up by unstable entities in one part of the system bear a definite relation to the position taken up by other unstable entities in other parts of the system. The field effect is constituted by their several equilibrium positions. A field is bound to a particular substratum from which a dynamic pattern arises. It is heteroaxial and heteropolar, has recognizably distinct districts, and can, like a magnetic field, maintain its pattern when its mass is either reduced or increased. It can fuse with a similar pattern entering with new material if the axial orientation is favorable" (pp. 359–60). As for *homology*, the term was introduced a hundred and fifty years ago by Richard Owen, in his *Lectures on the Comparative Anatomy and Physiology of the Invertebrate Animals*, to refer to "the same organ in different animals under every variety of form and function"; subsequently, it was expanded to include all structures "trace[able] to a particular condition that originated once in a common ancestor" (Donoghue, pp. 171, 173). By definition, homologous structures are contrasted with *analogous* ones, similarities that can't be accounted for genetically. In speaking of "the *rediscovery* of homology," Gilbert et al. allude to what they also characterize as "a newly discovered and fascinating realm of homology—*the homology of process*" (pp. 362, 364, emphasis added). Traditionally viewed as an attribute of structure ("be it of skeleton or genes"), homology in its new incarnation "goes into the very mechanisms of development." Instead of "look[ing] at the similarities between entities," it addresses "the similarities of dynamic interactions," with the result that "although organs (such as the vertebrate and arthropod eye, the vertebrate and arthropod leg, etc.) can be structurally analogous, they may be formed by processes that are homologous!" (p. 364). To the extent that the concept of homology has had to be reconfigured along more radical empiricist lines (in order to account, for instance, for newly observed features of "the genes responsible for homeotic transformations," as when one type of insect segment mutates into discontinuous types), a hitherto unsuspected realm, itself mutant, has been *discovered*; yet, by the same token, the preexisting concept merely had to be *rediscovered* (p. 363). Furthermore, what is one to make in this context of Emerson's claim, discussed in Chapter 3, as to the "perfect

correspondence" of man and muskrat? Doesn't this already presume some notion of homologous *processes*—of "similarities of dynamic interactions" between organism and ambient, which permit the muskrat to be viewed as "man modified to live in a mud-bank"—even as Owen was coining the term in order to refer to homologous *structures?*

21. I should probably state, for the record, that I am *not* drawing an analogy between literary criticism (in relation to its object of study) and scientific investigations of the natural and biological world. Wendy Steiner persuasively argues in a recent article against the belief informing her own early study of Stein's portraiture, that "criticism should model itself on science" ("Practice Without Principle," p. 80). Here Steiner takes aim at the tendency Richard Poirier has decried, of "professionalist members of literature departments . . . increasingly want[ing] to demonstrate that the study of literature has created a field of knowledge little different from a science, with its own chronologies of discovery and progress, and its own technical jargon, which has now become all by itself a subject of study" (*Poetry and Pragmatism*, p. 141). Yet, when Steiner goes on to propose that "the analogy between the Two Cultures is growing ever more tenuous," she too quickly substitutes "literary criticism as a conventional literary discipline" for literary culture at large (pp. 86–87). If the analogy between the Two Cultures *is* growing increasingly tenuous, this is because it is premised on an erroneous claim—that two distinct cultures, one literary and one scientific, ever existed—and not because literary and scientific studies (including works of literature) are moving ever more perceptibly apart.

22. "Reading in Slow Motion" is the title Reuben Brower gave his introduction to *In Defense of Reading*, the 1962 volume that he coedited with Richard Poirier of essays by teachers of the Harvard General Education course "The Interpretation of Literature" (or "Hum 6"). As a method of encouraging students to "enter into, or rather engage in, experiences of imaginative literature" and so "make themselves readers of imagination," Brower advised "slowing down the process of reading to observe what is happening, in order to attend very closely to the words, their uses, and their meanings" (p. 4). The convergence with Stein's compositional practices is obvious. In a retrospective essay on "Hum 6," Poirier cites Wittgenstein to similar effect: "I really want my copious punctuation marks to slow down the speed of reading. Because I should like to be read slowly. (As I myself read.)" (*Poetry and Pragmatism*, p. 209; cited from *Culture and Value*, p. 16).

23. In a recent essay, Clark proposes that in speaking of "human brains, trained in a sea of words and text," there is "a real sense in which the cognitive agent" isn't just "the bare biological organism . . . co-opt[ing] and exploit[ing] surrounding structures (say, pen and paper)," but is "an extended entity incorporating brain, body, and some aspects of the local environment." Just as (in Clark's example) a bluefish tuna "actively creates . . . whorls and vortices" in its aquatic environment that become so "integral to [its] cognitive routines as to count as part of the cognitive machinery itself," so human beings "generate 'whirlpools and

vortices' of external, symbol-laden media," resulting in an "explosion" of language-based wideware (pp. 271–74). *Wideware*, a neologism of Clark, refers to "states, structures, or processes [that] play a functional role as part of an extended cognitive process," despite being "in some intuitive sense environmental" (p. 268). In line with this vision of "cognitive extension," Clark calls for the "develop[ment of] new tools and techniques capable of investigating the brain (literally) in action" within "normal ecological context[s]," as in the case of the "repeated loops into the environment" that come into play in "the process of writing an academic paper." He also envisions "explanatory strategies that better reflect and accommodate" the "dense interanimation" of brain, body, and "the ubiquitous devices of language, speech, and text" (pp. 271, 273–75).

24. Here Edelman offers the sort of "dynamical, process-based way of under-standing key terms like 'representation' and 'computation'" envisioned by Clark (p. 275). Sacks makes the crucial observation as well that reentry is to be distin-guished from all feedback or homeostatic processes. "Simple feedback loops," he observes, "are crucial in the nervous system, where they are used for control of all the body's automatic functions. . . . But at higher levels, where flexibility [is] all-important[,] one requires a mechanism that can construct, not just control or correct" (p. 108). The term *feedback* is often used indiscriminately for both sorts of process, constructive and corrective, making it appear that all nervous functions are ultimately automatic, unconscious. One unfortunate consequence of this ambiguity is that it is often translated, perhaps most egregiously in the case of Daniel Dennett, into an argument that consciousness is merely epiphenomenal. It is to protect against this confusion that Edelman distinguishes reentrant signaling from feedback loops, reserving the latter designation for all automatic processes of control and correction, and the former for any process that involves the least degree of consciousness, or to put it another way, the slightest emotional coloring, any experience that calls for "flexibility" or creativity. "Confusingly," Sacks notes, "the very term 're-entrant' has occasionally been used in the past to denote such feedbacks," as in Warren McCulloch's "early papers on automata" (p. 119). In describing reentry in terms of feedback, Posner and Raichle are recalling the earlier usage; confusion only ensues when they attribute a similar understanding to Edel-man. Still, the confusion is telling, since they expressly locate their own empiricist project of "analyzing thought processes into constituent elements" in a lineage stemming from "the efforts [in the late 1950s] to develop artificial intelligence," when "the idea of breaking down complex activities into their constituent parts was advanced substantially" (pp. 11–12). It is directly against the vision that emerged with the "pioneer[ing] explorations of logical automata and nerve nets" (namely, the prospect of "a brave new world in which ever more powerful compu-ters would be able to mimic, and even take over, the chief functions of brain and mind") that Sacks situates Edelman's radical empiricist account of how "brain functions are built [through] a selectionist process . . . in accord with the facts of evolution and development"—and, in particular, "how embodiment of mind takes

place," thus "connect[ing] cognition to biology" ("A New Vision," p. 101; BABF, pp. 82, 152). *Embodiment of mind* is McCulloch's own phrase, which Edelman puts to a very different use in conjunction with "the radical new meaning" he supplies for *reentry* ("A New Vision," p. 119).

25. Even unapologetic reductionists find the prospect of visualizing brain activity in some form of writing irresistible. "Imagine the following experiment," E. O. Wilson instructs the reader of *Consilience*, his recent brief for "the unity of knowledge": "A team of scholars—led perhaps by color-challenged Mary—has constructed an iconic language from the visual patterns of brain activity." (Mary has previously been described by Wilson as a "neurobiologist two centuries hence who understands all the physics of color and all the brain's circuitry giving rise to color vision," but who has been "cloistered all her life in a black-and-white room.") "The result resembles a stream of Chinese ideograms, each one representing an entity, process, or concept. The new writing—call it 'mind script'—is translated into other languages. As the fluency of its readers increases, the mind script can be read directly by brain imaging." "In the silent recesses of the mind," Wilson continues, "volunteer subjects recount episodes, summon adventures in dreams, recite poems, solve equations, recall melodies, and while they are doing this the fiery play of their neuronal circuitry is made visible by the techniques of neurobiology. The observer reads the script unfolding not as ink on paper but as electric patterns in live tissue. At least some of the thinker's subjective experience—his feeling—is transferred. The observer reflects, he laughs or weeps. And from his own mind patterns he is able to transmit the subjective responses back. The two brains are linked by perception of brain activity" (pp. 127–29). The brilliance of Wilson's fantasy, and at the same time the source of its logical inconsistency, lies in the likening of the brain's iconic language to Chinese calligraphy. Although one might be tempted to accuse him of picturing language as a stream of dissociated words when he speaks of "a stream of Chinese ideograms, each representing an entity . . . ," Wilson actually provides a far richer account than that, in citing the following description of the calligraphic experience. "The silk or paper used for calligraphy," Simon Leys observed in a 1996 review of Jean François Billeter's *The Chinese Art of Writing*, "has an absorbent quality: the lightest touch of the brush, the slightest drop of ink, registers at once—irretrievably and indelibly. The brush acts like a seismograph of the mind, answering every pressure, every turn of the wrist. Like painting, Chinese calligraphy addresses the eye and is an art of space; like music, it unfolds in time; like dance, it develops a dynamic sequence of movements, pulsating in rhythm" (p. 129). This is an experience of writing truly comparable to Stein's; the only problem is that it cannot be reconciled with Wilson's own alternate sense of writing as reducible to "the transmission of information": readily translatable, that is, "into other languages" and capable of being "read directly by brain imaging" in the form of "electric patterns in live tissue." If, as I have argued, transmitting information is actually a function of the communication of feeling, and not the other way around, then the empiricist

picture of writing as essentially a stream of entities, processes, and concepts—a stream of *nouns*—fails to do justice to the massively interconnected nature of this profoundly biological phenomenon, which renders the transmission of information possible only through the "transmi[ssion of] tones and flourishes" (pp. 128–29).

26. Despite a similar concern with the role played by objects in emotional experience, the radical empiricist account of an "affective tone originating from things whose relevance is given" couldn't be further from the behaviorism inherent in T. S. Eliot's influential proposal that "the only way of expressing emotion in the form of art is by finding an 'objective correlative'; in other words, a set of objects, a situation, a chain of events which shall be the formula of that *particular* emotion; such that when the external facts, which must terminate in sensory experience, are given, the emotion is immediately evoked" (AI, p. 176; *The Sacred Wood*, p. 100). In describing herself as seeking to "destroy associational emotion" in order to achieve "exactitude in the description of inner and outer reality," Stein was positioning herself directly against deterministic conceptions of emotion such as Eliot's (ABT, p. 211).

27. See Poirier's discussion, in *Poetry and Pragmatism*, of the significance of James's efforts on behalf of "the reinstatement of the vague to its proper place in our mental life" (PR, p. 246 [BC, p. 164]).

Abrams, M. H. *The Mirror and the Lamp: Romantic Theory and the Critical Tradition*. New York: Oxford University Press, 1953.

Albright, Daniel. *Quantum Poetics: Yeats, Pound, Eliot, and the Science of Modernism*. Cambridge: Cambridge University Press, 1997.

Aldrich, Mildred. *A Hilltop on the Marne*. London: Constable, 1915.

Allen, Gay Wilson. "A New Look at Emerson and Science." In *Literature and Ideas in America: Essays in Memory of Harry Hayden Clark*, ed. Robert Falk. Columbus: Ohio University Press, 1975.

——. *Waldo Emerson: A Biography*. New York: The Viking Press, 1981.

Ambrose, Alice, ed. *Wittgenstein's Lectures, Cambridge, 1932–1935*. Totowa, N.J.: Rowman and Littlefield, 1979.

Armstrong, Tim. *Modernism, Technology and the Body: A Cultural Study*. New York: Cambridge University Press, 1998.

The American Heritage Dictionary. 2d College Edition. Boston: Houghton Mifflin, 1985.

Ashton, Jennifer. "Gertrude Stein for Anyone." *ELH* 64 (1997): 289–331.

Auden, W. H. *Collected Poems*. Ed. Edward Mendelson. London: Faber and Faber, 1976.

Baer, Ulrich. "Photography and Hysteria: Toward a Poetics of the Flash." *The Yale Journal of Criticism* 7, no. 1 (Spring 1994): 41–77.

Barker, Lewellys F. *The Nervous System and Its Constituent Neurones*. New York: D. Appleton, 1899.

——. *Time and the Physician*. New York: G. P. Putnam, 1942.

Barry, Elaine, ed. *Robert Frost on Writing*. New Brunswick: Rutgers University Press, 1973.

Battersby, Christine. *Gender and Genius: Towards a Feminist Aesthetics*. Bloomington: Indiana University Press, 1989.

Baxter, Charles. "Stillness." In *Burning Down the House: Essays on Fiction*. Saint Paul, Minn.: Graywolf Press, 1997.

Beard, George Miller. *American Nervousness, Its Causes and Consequences*. New York: Putnam, 1881.

————. *The Nature and Diagnosis of Neurasthenia.* New York: 1879.

Beer, Gillian. *Open Fields: Science in Cultural Encounter.* Oxford: Oxford University Press, 1996.

Beizer, Janet. *Ventriloquized Bodies: Narratives of Hysteria in Nineteenth-Century France.* Ithaca, N.Y.: Cornell University Press, 1994.

Bell, Ian. *Critic as Scientist: The Modernist Poetics of Ezra Pound.* London: Methuen, 1981.

Belloli, Lucy. "The Evolution of Picasso's Portrait of Gertrude Stein." *The Burlington Magazine* 141 (January 1999): 12–18.

Bercovitch, Sacvan, and Myra Jehlen, eds. *Ideology and Classic American Literature.* Cambridge, England: Cambridge University Press, 1986.

Bernard, Claude. *An Introduction to the Study of Experimental Medicine.* Trans. Henry Copley Green. New York: Henry Schuman, 1949 [1865].

Berners, Gerald Hugh Tyrwhitt-Wilson, Baron. *A Wedding Bouquet. Piano Score.* London: J. & W. Chester, 1938.

Bernheimer, Charles, and Claire Kahane, eds. *In Dora's Case: Freud—Hysteria—Feminism.* New York: Columbia University Press, 1985.

Bidart, Frank. "Thinking Through Form." In *Ecstatic Occasions, Expedient Forms,* ed. David Lehman. New York: Macmillan, 1987.

Bloom, Harold. "Introduction: The Crystal Man." In *Selected Writings.* See Pater.

Bolinger, Dwight. *Intonation and Its Parts: Melody in Spoken English.* Stanford: Stanford University Press, 1986.

————. *Intonation and Its Uses: Melody in Grammar and Discourse.* Stanford: Stanford University Press, 1989.

Booth, Wayne C. *The Rhetoric of Fiction.* 2d edition. Chicago: University of Chicago Press, 1983.

Boring, E. G. *Sensation and Perception in the History of Experimental Psychology.* New York: Appleton-Century-Crofts, 1942.

Bowers, Jane Palatini. *"They Watch Me As They Watch This": Gertrude Stein's Metadrama.* Philadelphia: University of Pennsylvania Press, 1991.

Brakhage, Stan. "Gertrude Stein: Meditative Literature and Film." *Millennium Film Journal* 25 (Summer 1991): 100–107.

Bridgman, Richard. *Gertrude Stein in Pieces.* New York: Oxford University Press, 1970.

Brooks, Cleanth. "Implications of an Organic Theory of Poetry." In *Literature and Belief: English Institute Essays, 1957,* ed. M. H. Abrams. New York: Columbia University Press, 1958.

————. "Irony and 'Ironic' Poetry." *College English* 9, no. 5 (February 1948): 231–37.

————. "The Poem as Organism: Modern Critical Procedure." In *English Institute Annual: 1940.* New York: Columbia University Press, 1941.

Brower, Reuben A., Helen Vendler, and John Hollander, eds. *I. A. Richards: Essays in His Honor.* New York: Oxford University Press, 1973.

————, and Richard Poirier, eds. *In Defense of Reading.* New York: E. P. Dutton, 1962.

Brown, Lee Rust. "The Emerson Museum." *Representations* 40 (Fall 1992): 57–80.

Bryher. *The Heart to Artemis: A Writer's Memoirs.* London: Collins, 1963.

Bucke, Richard Maurice. *Cosmic Consciousness: A Study in the Evolution of the Human Mind.* New York: Penguin, 1991 [1901].

————. *Walt Whitman.* Philadelphia: D. McKay, 1883.

Budd, Malcolm. *Wittgenstein's Philosophy of Psychology.* London: Routledge, 1989.

Buell, Lawrence. *The Environmental Imagination: Thoreau, Nature Writing, and the Formation of American Culture.* Cambridge, Mass.: Harvard University Press, 1995.

Burke, Carolyn. "Gertrude Stein, the Cone Sisters and the Puzzle of Female Friendship." *Critical Inquiry* 8, no. 3 (Spring 1982): 543–64.

Burns, Edward, ed. *The Letters of Gertrude Stein and Carl Van Vechten 1913–1946.* 2 vols. New York: Columbia University Press, 1986.

————, and Ulla E. Dydo, eds., with William Rice. *The Letters of Gertrude Stein and Thornton Wilder.* New Haven: Yale University Press, 1996.

Burr, Anna R. *Weir Mitchell. His Life and Letters.* 2 vols. New York: Duffield, 1930.

Bush, Clive. *Halfway to Revolution: Investigation and Crisis in the Work of Henry Adams, William James and Gertrude Stein.* New Haven: Yale University Press, 1991.

Cabot, James Elliot. *A Memoir of Ralph Waldo Emerson.* 2 vols. London: Macmillan, 1887.

Calvin, William H. *The Cerebral Symphony: Seashore Reflections on the Structure of Consciousness.* New York: Bantam Books, 1990.

Canguilhem, Georges. "John Brown's System: An Example of Medical Ideology." In *Ideology and Rationality in the History of the Life Sciences.* Cambridge, Mass.: MIT Press, 1988.

————. "On the History of the Life Sciences Since Darwin." In *Ideology and Rationality.*

————. "The Question of Normality in the History of Biological Thought." In *Ideology and Rationality.*

Caramello, Charles. *Henry James, Gertrude Stein, and the Biographical Act.* Chapel Hill: University of North Carolina Press, 1996.

Carnap, Rudolf. "Scientific Empiricism; Unity of Science Movement." In *Dictionary of Philosophy*, ed. Dagobert D. Runes. New York: Philosophical Library, 1983 [1942].

Cash, Arthur H. *Laurence Sterne: The Later Years.* London: Methuen, 1986.

Cavell, Stanley. *Conditions Handsome and Unhandsome: The Constitution of Emersonian Perfectionism.* Chicago: University of Chicago Press, 1990.

————. "Emerson, Coleridge, Kant (Terms as Conditions)." In *In Quest of the Ordinary: Lines of Skepticism and Romanticism*. Chicago: University of Chicago Press, 1988.

————. "Emerson's Constitutional Amending: Reading 'Fate.' " In *Philosophical Passages: Wittgenstein, Emerson, Austin, Derrida*. Cambridge, Mass.: Blackwell, 1995.

————. "Finding as Founding: Taking Steps in Emerson's 'Experience.' " In *This New Yet Unapproachable America: Lectures after Emerson after Wittgenstein*. Albuquerque: Living Batch Press, 1989.

————. "Thinking of Emerson." In *The Senses of Walden*. Expanded edition. San Francisco: North Point Press, 1981.

————. "What Is the Emersonian Event? A Comment on Kateb's Emerson." *New Literary History* 25 (1994): 951–58.

Chalmers, David. "Facing Up to the Problem of Consciousness." In *Explaining Consciousness—The "Hard Problem."* See Jonathan Shear.

Changeux, Jean-Pierre. *Neuronal Man: The Biology of Mind*. New York: Pantheon Books, 1983.

Chatwin, Bruce. *The Songlines*. New York: Penguin, 1987.

Chessman, Harriet Scott. *The Public Is Invited to Dance: Representation, the Body, and Dialogue in Gertrude Stein*. Stanford: Stanford University Press, 1989.

Christensen, Jerome. *Coleridge's Blessed Machine of Language*. Ithaca, N.Y.: Cornell University Press, 1981.

Church, Ralph. *An Analysis of Resemblance*. London: Allen and Unwin, 1952.

————. *Bradley's Dialectic*. Ithaca, N.Y.: Cornell University Press, 1942.

————. *An Essay in Critical Appreciation*. London: Allen and Unwin, 1938.

————. *Hume's Theory of Understanding*. London: Allen and Unwin, 1935.

————. "A Note on the Writing of Gertrude Stein." *transition* 14 (Fall 1928): 164–68.

————. *A Study in the Philosophy of Malebranche*. London: Allen and Unwin, 1931.

Clark, Andy. "Where Brain, Body, and World Collide." *Dædalus* 127, no. 2 (Spring 1998): 257–80.

Clark, Harry Hayden. "Emerson and Science." *Philological Quarterly* 10 (July 1931): 225–60.

Clark, T. J. *Farewell to an Idea: Episodes from a History of Modernism*. New Haven: Yale University Press, 1999.

Coates, Robert M. *The View from Here*. New York: Harcourt, Brace, 1960.

Cobb, John B., Jr., and David Ray Griffin, eds. *Mind in Nature: Essays on the Interface of Science and Philosophy*. Washington, D.C.: University Press of America, 1978.

Coleridge, Samuel Taylor. *Biographia Literaria; or, Biographical Sketches of My Literary Life and Opinions*. Vol. 1, ed. James Engell and W. Jackson Bate. Princeton: Princeton University Press, 1984.

———. "Theory of Life." In *Shorter Works and Fragments*, Vol. 1, ed. H. J. Jackson and J. R. de J. Jackson. Princeton: Princeton University Press, 1995.

The Compact Edition of the Oxford English Dictionary. Oxford: Oxford University Press, 1971.

Conrad, Peter. *The History of English Literature: One Indivisible, Unending Book*. Philadelphia: University of Pennsylvania Press, 1987.

Coope, Christopher, Peter Geach, Timothy Potts, and Roger White. *A Wittgenstein Workbook*. Berkeley: University of California Press, 1970.

Cope, Karin. "Painting After Stein." *Diacritics* 24, no. 2–3 (Summer–Fall 1994): 190–203.

Copeland, Carolyn F. *Language & Time & Gertrude Stein*. Iowa City: University of Iowa Press, 1976.

Crary, Jonathan. *Techniques of the Observer: On Vision and Modernity in the Nineteenth Century*. Cambridge, Mass.: MIT Press, 1992.

———, and Sanford Kwinter, eds. *Incorporations*. New York: Zone, 1992.

Crawford, T. Hugh. *Modernism, Medicine, and William Carlos Williams*. Norman: University of Oklahoma Press, 1993.

Crick, Francis. *The Astonishing Hypothesis: The Scientific Search for the Soul*. New York: Simon and Schuster, 1994.

Crosby, Elizabeth C., Tryphena Humphrey, and Edward W. Lauer, eds. *Correlative Anatomy of the Nervous System*. New York: Macmillan, 1962.

Damasio, Antonio R. *Descartes' Error: Emotion, Reason, and the Human Brain*. New York: G. P. Putnam, 1994.

———. *The Feeling of What Happens: Body and Emotion in the Making of Consciousness*. New York: Harcourt, Brace, 1999.

Damasio, Hanna. *Human Brain Anatomy in Computerized Images*. New York: Oxford University Press, 1995.

Dant, Elizabeth A. "Composing the World: Emerson and the Cabinet of Natural History." *Nineteenth-Century Literature* 44, no. 1 (June 1989): 18–44.

Danto, Arthur. "Beautiful Science and the Future of Criticism." In *The Future of Literary Theory*, ed. Ralph Cohen. New York: Routledge, 1989.

Danziger, Kurt. *Constructing the Subject: Historical Origins of Psychological Research*. Cambridge, England: Cambridge University Press, 1990.

Darwin, Charles. *The Expression of the Emotions in Man and Animals*. Chicago: The University of Chicago Press, 1965 [1870].

Deacon, Terrence W. *The Symbolic Species: The Co-Evolution of Language and the Brain*. New York: Norton, 1997.

DeKoven, Marianne. *A Different Language: Gertrude Stein's Experimental Writing*. Madison: University of Wisconsin Press, 1983.

De Man, Paul. "Form and Intent in the American New Criticism." *Blindness and Insight: Essays in the Rhetoric of Contemporary Criticism*. Minneapolis: University of Minnesota Press, 1983 [1971].

————. "The Resistance to Theory." In *The Resistance to Theory*. Minneapolis: University of Minnesota Press, 1986.

————. "Time and History in Wordsworth." In *Romanticism and Contemporary Criticism: The Gauss Seminar and Other Papers*, ed. E. S. Burt, Kevin Newmark, and Andrzej Warminski. Baltimore: Johns Hopkins University Press, 1993.

————. "Wordsworth and the Victorians." In *The Rhetoric of Romanticism*. New York: Columbia University Press, 1984.

De Selincourt, Ernest, ed. *The Letters of William and Dorothy Wordsworth*. 2d edition, rev. Chester L. Shaver. 8 vols. Oxford: Oxford University Press, 1967.

Dennett, Daniel C. *Consciousness Explained*. Boston: Little, Brown, 1991.

————. "When HAL Kills, Who's to Blame? Computer Ethics." In *HAL's Legacy: 2001's Computer as Dream and Reality*, ed. David G. Stork. Cambridge, Mass.: MIT Press, 1997.

Detweiler, Robert. "Emerson and Zen." *American Quarterly* 14, no. 3 (Fall 1962): 422–38.

Devlin, Keith. *Mathematics: The Science of Patterns*. New York: Scientific American Library, 1994.

Dewey, John. "The Development of American Pragmatism." In *The Later Works, 1925–1953*. Vol. 2, *Nineteen Twenty-Five to Nineteen Twenty-Seven*, ed. Jo Ann Boydston and Bridget Walsh. Carbondale: University of Southern Illinois Press, 1984.

"Diagnosis: The Doctor Makes an Analysis of Gertrude Stein." *Newsweek* (December 8, 1934): 24.

Diamond, M. C., A. B. Scheibel, and L. M. Elson. *The Human Brain Coloring Book*. New York: Harper Collins, 1985.

Dibbell, Julian. "The Race to Build Intelligent Machines." *Time* (March 25, 1996): 57.

Dickinson, Emily. *The Complete Poems of Emily Dickinson*. Ed. Thomas H. Johnson. Boston: Little, Brown, 1976.

Diderot, Denis. *Rameau's Nephew / D'Alembert's Dream*. London: Penguin, 1966 [1769].

Donald, James, Anne Friedberg, and Laura Marcus, ed. *Close Up 1927–1933: Cinema and Modernism*. Princeton: Princeton University Press, 1998.

Donald, Merlin. *Origins of the Modern Mind: Three Stages in the Evolution of Culture and Cognition*. Cambridge, Mass.: Harvard University Press, 1991.

Donoghue, Michael J. "Homology." In *Keywords in Evolutionary Biology*, ed. Evelyn Fox Keller and Elisabeth A. Lloyd. Cambridge, Mass.: Harvard University Press, 1992.

Drabble, Margaret, ed. *The Oxford Companion to English Literature*. Oxford: Oxford University Press, 1985.

Drury, Maurice O'C. "Ludwig Wittgenstein: A Symposium: Assessments of the Man and the Philosopher, II." In *Ludwig Wittgenstein*. See K. T. Fann.

———. "Some Notes on Conversations with Wittgenstein." In *Ludwig Wittgenstein: Personal Recollections*, ed. Rush Rhees. Totowa, N.J.: Rowman and Littlefield, 1981.

Duncan, Robert. "For a muse meant." In *Letters*. Highlands, N.C.: The Jargon Society, 1958.

———. "Deconstruction a Discussion." In *Notebook Poems: 1953*. San Francisco: The Press in Tuscany Alley / San Francisco State University, 1991.

Dydo, Ulla E. "*Landscape Is Not Grammar*: Gertrude Stein in 1928." *Raritan* 7, no. 1 (Summer 1987): 97–113.

———. "*Stanzas in Meditation*: The Other Autobiography." *Chicago Review* 35, no. 2 (Winter 1985): 4–20.

———, ed. *A Stein Reader*. Evanston, Ill.: Northwestern University Press, 1993.

Edelman, Gerald M. *Bright Air, Brilliant Fire: On the Matter of the Mind*. New York: Basic Books, 1992.

———. "Building a Picture of the Brain." *Dædalus* 127, no. 2 (Spring 1998): 37–69.

Edmundson, Mark. *Towards Reading Freud: Self-Creation in Milton, Wordsworth, Emerson, and Sigmund Freud*. Princeton: Princeton University Press, 1990.

Eldredge, Niles, and Stephen Jay Gould. "Punctuated Equilibria: An Alternative to Phyletic Gradualism." In *Models in Paleobiology*, ed. T. J. M. Schopf. San Francisco: Freeman, Cooper, 1972.

Eliot, George [Mary Ann Evans]. *Middlemarch*. Ed. W. J. Harvey. New York: Penguin Books, 1985 [1871–72].

———. *The Mill on the Floss*. Ed. Sally Shuttleworth. Routledge: London, 1991 [1860].

Eliot, T. S. *Collected Poems: 1909–1962*. New York: Harcourt, Brace and World, 1970.

———. *The Sacred Wood: Essays on Poetry and Criticism*. London: Routledge, 1989 [1920].

———. *Selected Prose*. Ed. Frank Kermode. New York: Harcourt Brace, 1988 [1975].

———. *The Waste Land: A Facsimile and Transcript of the Original Drafts Including the Annotations of Ezra Pound*. Ed. Valerie Eliot. New York: Harcourt Brace Jovanovich, 1971.

Ellison, Julie. *Emerson's Romantic Style*. Princeton: Princeton University Press, 1984.

Ellsworth, Phoebe C. "William James and Emotion: Is a Century of Fame Worth a Century of Misunderstanding?" *Psychological Review* 101, no. 2 (April 1994): 222–29.

Elms, Alan C. "Skinner's Dark Year and *Walden Two*." In *Uncovering Lives: The Uneasy Alliance of Biography and Psychology*. New York: Oxford University Press, 1994.

Emerson, Ralph Waldo. *Collected Poems and Translations*. New York: The Library of America, 1994.

————. *Essays and Lectures*. New York: The Library of America, 1983.

————. "Lord Bacon." In *The Early Lectures of Ralph Waldo Emerson*, Vol. 1, ed. Stephen E. Whicher and Robert E. Spiller. Cambridge, Mass.: Harvard University Press, 1961.

————. *Natural History of Intellect and Other Papers*. Boston: Houghton, Mifflin, 1909 [1893].

————. "Poetry and Imagination." In *Ralph Waldo Emerson*, ed. Richard Poirier. New York: Oxford University Press, 1990.

————. *Representative Men*. Ed. Pamela Schirmeister. New York: Marsilio Publishers, 1995 [1850].

Empson, William. *Argufying: Essays on Literature and Culture*. Ed. John Haffenden. Iowa City: University of Iowa Press, 1987.

————. *Donne and the New Philosophy*. Vol. 1 of *Essays on Renaissance Literature*, ed. John Haffenden. Cambridge: Cambridge University Press, 1993.

————. *Seven Types of Ambiguity*. New York: New Directions, 1947 [1930].

————. *Some Versions of Pastoral*. Norfolk, Conn.: New Directions, n.d. [1935].

————. *The Structure of Complex Words*. Cambridge, Mass.: Harvard University Press, 1989 [1951].

Evans, Martha Noel. *Fits and Starts: A Genealogy of Hysteria in Modern France*. Ithaca, N.Y.: Cornell University Press, 1991.

Everdell, William R. *The First Moderns: Profiles in the Origins of Twentieth-Century Thought*. Chicago: The University of Chicago Press, 1997.

Everett, Patricia R., ed. *A History Of Having A Great Many Times Not Continued To Be Friends: The Correspondence Between Mabel Dodge & Gertrude Stein, 1911–1934*. Albuquerque: University of New Mexico Press, 1996.

Fann, K. T., ed. *Ludwig Wittgenstein: The Man and His Philosophy*. New York: Dell, 1967.

————. *Wittgenstein's Conception of Philosophy*. Berkeley: University of California Press, 1969.

Farnes, Patricia. "Women in Medical Science." In *Women of Science: Righting the Record*, ed. G. Kass-Simon and Patricia Farnes. Bloomington: Indiana University Press, 1990.

Finger, Stanley. *Origins of Neuroscience: A History of Explorations into Brain Function*. New York: Oxford University Press, 1994.

Firkins, O. W. *Ralph Waldo Emerson*. Boston: Houghton Mifflin, 1915.

Fish, Stanley. *Doing What Comes Naturally: Change, Rhetoric, and the Practice of Theory in Literary and Legal Studies*. Durham, N.C.: Duke University Press, 1989.

————. *Is There a Text in This Class? The Authority of Interpretive Communities*. Cambridge, Mass.: Harvard University Press, 1980.

Fisher, Philip. *Wonder, the Rainbow, and the Aesthetics of Rare Experiences*. Cambridge, Mass.: Harvard University Press, 1998.

Fletcher, Angus. *Colors of the Mind: Conjectures on Thinking in Literature.* Cambridge, Mass.: Harvard University Press, 1991.

———. " 'Positive Negation': Threshold, Sequence, and Personification in Coleridge." In *New Perspectives on Coleridge and Wordsworth: English Institute Essays.* New York: Columbia University Press, 1972.

Freedman, David H. *Brainmakers: How Scientists Are Moving Beyond Computers to Create a Rival to the Human Brain.* New York: Simon and Schuster, 1994.

Freud, Sigmund. *Introductory Lectures on Psychoanalysis.* New York: Norton, 1966.

———. *The Psychopathology of Everyday Life.* New York: Norton, 1989.

Froula, Christine. *Modernism's Body: Sex, Culture, and Joyce.* New York: Columbia University Press, 1996.

Frye, Northrop. "Charms and Riddles." In *Spiritus Mundi: Essays on Literature, Myth, and Society.* Bloomington: Indiana University Press, 1976.

Fye, W. Bruce. *The Development of American Physiology: Scientific Medicine in the Nineteenth Century.* Baltimore: Johns Hopkins University Press, 1987.

Gacek, Richard R. "Anatomy of the Central Vestibular System." In *Neurotology,* ed. Robert K. Jackler and Derald E. Brackman. St. Louis: Mosby-Year Book, 1994.

Galison, Peter. *Image and Logic: A Material Culture of Microphysics.* Chicago: University of Chicago Press, 1997.

Gallup, Donald, ed. *The Flowers of Friendship: Letters Written to Gertrude Stein.* New York: Octagon Books, 1979 [1953].

———. "Gertrude Stein and the *Atlantic.*" *The Yale University Library Gazette* 28, no. 3 (January 1954): 109–28.

———. *The Journals of Thornton Wilder, 1939–1961.* New Haven: Yale University Press, 1985.

Gardner, Howard. "Green Ideas Sleeping Furiously." *The New York Review of Books* (March 23, 1995): 32–38.

Gass, William. "Gertrude Stein and the Geography of the Sentence." In *The World Within the Word.* Boston: David Godine, 1979.

Gazzaniga, Michael S., Richard B. Ivry, and George R. Mangun. *Cognitive Neuroscience: The Biology of the Mind.* New York: W. W. Norton, 1998.

Gibson, James J. *The Ecological Approach to Visual Perception.* Hillsdale, N.J.: Lawrence Erlbaum, 1986 [1979].

———. "The Uses of Proprioception and the Detection of Propriospecific Information." In *Reasons for Realism: Selected Essays of James J. Gibson,* ed. Edward Reed and Rebecca Jones. Hillsdale, N.J.: Lawrence Erlbaum, 1982.

Giesenkirchen, Michaela. "Where English Speaks More Than One Language: Accents in Gertrude Stein's 'Accents in Alsace.' " *The Massachusetts Review* 34, no. 1 (Spring 1993): 45–62.

Gifford, Don. *The Farther Shore: A Natural History of Perception.* New York: Vintage Books, 1991.

Gilbert, Scott F. "Induction and the Origins of Developmental Genetics." In *A Conceptual History of Modern Embryology*, ed. Gilbert. Baltimore: Johns Hopkins University Press, 1991.

———, John M. Opitz, and Rudolf A. Raff. "Resynthesizing Evolutionary and Developmental Biology." *Developmental Biology* 173 (1996): 357–72.

Gödel, Kurt. *On Formally Undecidable Propositions in "Principia Mathematica" and Related Systems.* Trans. B. Melzer. New York: Dover, 1992 [1962].

Goethe, Johann Wolfgang von. *Scientific Studies.* Ed. Douglas Miller. Princeton: Princeton University Press, 1995.

———. *Selected Poems.* Ed. Christopher Middleton. London: John Calder, 1983.

Goldstein, Jan. "The Uses of Male Hysteria: Medical and Literary Discourse in Nineteenth-Century France." *Representations* 34 (Spring 1991): 134–65.

Goodwin, Brian. *How the Leopard Changed Its Spots: The Evolution of Complexity.* New York: Simon and Schuster, 1994.

Gould, Stephen Jay. "The Man Who Invented Natural History" [Review of *Buffon*, by Jacques Roger]. *The New York Review of Books* (October 22, 1998): 83–90.

———, and Richard C. Lewontin. "The Spandrels of San Marco and the Panglossian Paradigm: A Critique of the Adaptationist Programme." *Proceedings of the Royal Society, London* 205: 581–98.

Greenberg, Valerie D. *Freud and His Aphasia Book: Language and the Sources of Psychoanalysis.* Ithaca, N.Y.: Cornell University Press, 1997.

Griffin, David Ray, ed. *Physics and the Ultimate Significance of Time.* Albany: State University of New York Press, 1986.

———, ed. *The Reenchantment of Science: Postmodern Proposals.* Albany: State University of New York Press, 1988.

———, John B. Cobb, Jr., Marcus P. Ford, Pete A. Y. Gunter, and Peter Ochs, eds. *Founders of Constructive Postmodern Philosophy: Peirce, James, Bergson, Whitehead, and Hartshorne.* Albany: State University of New York Press, 1993.

Groth, Janet, and David Castronovo, eds. *From the Uncollected Edmund Wilson.* Athens: Ohio University Press, 1995.

Guetti, James. *Wittgenstein and the Grammar of Literary Experience.* Athens: University of Georgia Press, 1993.

Guttmann, Giselher, and Inge Scholz-Strasser, eds. *Freud and the Neurosciences: From Brain Research to the Unconscious.* Vienna: Verlag der Österreichischen Akademie der Wissenschaften, 1998.

Haas, Robert Bartlett, ed. *A Primer for the Gradual Understanding of Gertrude Stein.* Los Angeles: Black Sparrow Press, 1971.

Halpern, Richard. "The Lyric in the Field of Information: Autopoiesis and History in Donne's *Songs and Sonnets.*" *The Yale Journal of Criticism* 6, no. 1 (1993): 185–215.

Haraway, Donna. *Crystals, Fabrics, and Fields: Metaphors of Organicism in Twentieth-Century Developmental Biology*. New Haven: Yale University Press, 1976.

———. *Modest_Witness@Second_Millennium.FemaleMan©_Meets_OncoMouse™*. New York: Routledge, 1997.

Hardy, J. P., ed. *Johnson's Lives of the Poets: A Selection*. Oxford: Oxford University Press, 1971.

Harris, Roy. *Language, Saussure and Wittgenstein: How to Play Games with Words*. London: Routledge, 1988.

———. *Reading Saussure: A Critical Commentary on the "Cours de linguistique generale."* La Salle: Open Court, 1987.

Hartman, Geoffrey H. "A Touching Compulsion." In *The Unremarkable Wordsworth*. Minneapolis: University of Minnesota Press, 1987.

Hartshorne, Charles. "Whitehead's Concept of Prehension." In *Creativity in American Philosophy*. Albany: State University of New York Press, 1984.

Havelock, Eric A. *The Muse Learns to Write: Reflections on Orality and Literacy from Antiquity to the Present*. New Haven: Yale University Press, 1986.

Hayles, N. Katherine. "Narratives of Artificial Life." In *FutureNatural: Nature, Science, Culture*, ed. George Robertson, Melinda Mash, Lisa Tickner, Jon Bird, Barry Curtis, and Tim Putnam. London: Routledge, 1996.

Hellerstein, David. "Plotting a Theory of the Brain." *The New York Times Magazine* (May 22, 1988): 16–19, 27–28, 55, 61, 64.

Helmholtz, Hermann von. "On Goethe's Scientific Researches" and "Goethe's Presentiments of Coming Scientific Ideas." In *Science and Culture: Popular and Philosophical Essays*, ed. David Cahan. Chicago: University of Chicago Press, 1995.

Hendelman, Walter J. *Student's Atlas of Neuroanatomy*. Philadelphia: W. B. Saunders, 1994.

Henderson, Linda Dalrymple. "Mabel Dodge, Gertrude Stein, and Max Weber: A Four-Dimensional Trio." *Arts Magazine* 57 (September 1982): 106–11.

———. "Mysticism as the 'Tie That Binds': The Case of Edward Carpenter and Modernism." *Art Journal* 46 (Spring 1987): 29–37.

Henry, Michel. *The Genealogy of Psychoanalysis*. Stanford: Stanford University Press, 1993.

Hertz, Neil. "Lurid Figures." In *Reading de Man Reading*, ed. Lindsay Waters and Wlad Godzich. Minneapolis: University of Minnesota Press, 1989.

———. "Medusa's Head: Male Hysteria under Political Pressure" [with responses by Catherine Gallagher and Joel Fineman]. In Hertz, *The End of the Line: Psychoanalysis and the Sublime*. New York: Columbia University Press, 1985.

Hill, Geoffrey. " 'The Conscious Mind's Intelligible Structure': A Debate." *Agenda* (Autumn/Winter 1971–72): 14–23.

———. *The Lords of Limit: Essays on Literature and Ideas*. New York: Oxford University Press, 1984.

Hirst, R. J. "Realism." In *The Encyclopedia of Philosophy*, Vol. 7, ed. Paul Edwards. New York: Macmillan, 1967.

Hobson, J. Allan. *Consciousness*. New York: Scientific American Library, 1999.

Hodder, Alfred. *The Adversaries of the Sceptic; or, The Specious Present: A New Inquiry into Human Knowledge*. New York: Macmillan, 1901.

Hoffman, Michael J., ed. *Critical Essays on Gertrude Stein*. Boston: G. K. Hall, 1986.

———. *The Development of Abstractionism in the Writings of Gertrude Stein*. Philadelphia: University of Pennsylvania Press, 1965.

Hollander, John, ed. *American Poetry: The Nineteenth Century*. Vol. 2. New York: The Library of America, 1993.

Holms, J. F. Review of *Composition as Explanation*. *The Calendar of Modern Letters* (1927). Reprinted in *Towards Standards of Criticism*, ed. F. R. Leavis. London: Wishart, 1976 [1933].

Horowitz, Helen Lefkowitz. *The Power and Passion of M. Carey Thomas*. New York: Alfred A. Knopf, 1994.

Howe, Susan. *My Emily Dickinson*. Berkeley: North Atlantic Books, 1988.

Hubbell, Lindley. "A Letter to Gertrude Stein." *Pagany: A Native Quarterly* 1, no. 2 (April–June 1930): 37. Reprinted in *A Gertrude Stein Companion*, ed. Bruce Kellner.

Humphreys, Nicholas. *A History of the Mind: Evolution and the Birth of Consciousness*. New York: HarperCollins, 1992.

Hurley, Patrick J. "Time in the Earlier and Later Whitehead." In *Physics and the Ultimate Significance of Time*, ed. David R. Griffin.

———. "Whitehead's *Relational Theory of Space*—Text, Translation, and Commentary." *Philosophy Research Archives* 5 (1979): 676–777.

Hylan, J. B. "Fluctuations of the Attention (I)." *The Psychological Review* 3, no. 1 (January 1896): 56–63.

Jakobson, Roman. "Two Aspects of Language and Two Types of Aphasic Disturbances." In *Language and Literature*, ed. Krystyna Pomorska and Stephen Rudy. Cambridge, Mass.: Harvard University Press, 1987.

James, Henry. "The Figure in the Carpet." In *The Lesson of the Master and Other Tales*. London: Macmillan, 1922.

———. *William Wetmore Story and His Friends*. 2 vols. London: W. Blackwood, 1903.

James, William. "Address at the Emerson Centenary in Concord." In *Memories and Studies*.

———. *Collected Essays and Reviews*. New York: Russell and Russell, 1969 [1920].

———. "Confidences of a 'Psychical Researcher.'" In *Essays in Psychical Research*.

———. "Does 'Consciousness' Exist?" In *Writings 1902–1910*.

———. "The Energies of Men." In *Memories and Studies*, reprinted in *The Writings of William James*.

————. *Essays in Psychical Research*. Cambridge, Mass.: Harvard University Press, 1986.

————. *Essays in Radical Empiricism*. New York: Longmans, Green, 1912.

————. "The Feeling of Effort." In *Collected Essays and Reviews*.

————. "Fragment of a Lecture on Exceptional Mental Phenomena." In *Manuscript Lectures*.

————. "Frederic Myers's Service to Psychology." In *Essays in Psychical Research*.

————. "Human Immortality: Two Supposed Objections to the Doctrine." In *Writings: 1878–1899*.

————. "Is Life Worth Living?" In *Writings 1878–1899*.

————. "Louis Agassiz." In *Memories and Studies*.

————. *Manuscript Lectures*. Cambridge, Mass.: Harvard University Press, 1988.

————. *The Meaning of Truth: A Sequel to "Pragmatism."* In *Writings 1902–1910*.

————. *Memories and Studies*. New York: Longmans, Green, 1911.

————. "On a Certain Blindness in Human Beings." In *Writings: 1878–1899*.

————. "The Physical Basis of Emotion." In *Collected Essays and Reviews*.

————. "The Place of Affectional Facts in a World of Pure Experience." In *Writings 1902–1910*.

————. *A Pluralistic Universe*. In *Writings 1902–1910*.

————. *The Principles of Psychology*. Cambridge, Mass.: Harvard University Press, 1983.

————. *Psychology: Briefer Course*. In *Writings 1878–1899*.

————. "Review of *Human Personality and Its Survival of Bodily Death*, by Frederic W. H. Myers." In *Essays in Psychical Research*.

————. "The Sentiment of Rationality." In *The Writings of William James*.

————. *The Varieties of Religious Experience*. Ed. Martin E. Marty. New York: Penguin Books, 1982.

————. "What Is an Emotion?" In *Collected Essays and Reviews*.

————. *The Will to Believe and Other Essays in Popular Philosophy*. In *Writings 1878–1899*.

————. "A World of Pure Experience." In *Writings 1902–1910*.

————. *Writings 1878–1899*. New York: The Library of America, 1992.

————. *Writings 1902–1910*. New York: The Library of America, 1987.

————. *The Writings of William James: A Comprehensive Edition*. Ed. John J. McDermott. Chicago: University of Chicago Press, 1977.

Janet, Pierre. *L'automatisme psychologique: essai de psychologie expérimentale sur les formes inférieures de l'activité humaine*. Paris: Alcan, 1889.

Jehlen, Myra. *American Incarnation: The Individual, the Nation, and the Continent*. Cambridge, Mass.: Harvard University Press, 1986.

Joyce, James. *Stephen Hero*. Ed. John J. Slocum and Herbert Cahoon. New York: New Directions, 1944.

Kadlec, David. "Marianne Moore, Immigration, and Eugenics." *Modernism/Modernity* 1.2 (April 1994): 21–49.

Kalupahana, David J. *The Principles of Buddhist Psychology*. Albany: State University of New York Press, 1987.

Katz, Leon. "Weininger and *The Making of Americans*." In *Twentieth Century Literature* 24, no. 1 (Spring 1978): 8–26.

Kavanagh, Julie. *Secret Muses: The Life of Frederick Ashton*. New York: Pantheon, 1996.

Kayman, Martin. *The Modernism of Ezra Pound: The Science of Poetry*. New York: St. Martin's Press, 1986.

Keller, Evelyn Fox. *A Feeling for the Organism: The Life and Work of Barbara McClintock*. New York: W. H. Freeman, 1983.

———. *Refiguring Life: Metaphors of Twentieth-Century Biology*. New York: Columbia University Press, 1995.

Kellner, Bruce, ed. *A Gertrude Stein Companion: content with the example*. New York: Greenwood Press, 1988.

Kermode, Frank. *Romantic Image*. London: Routledge and Kegan Paul, 1986 [1957].

Kerr, John. *A Most Dangerous Method: The Story of Jung, Freud, and Sabina Spielrein*. New York: Alfred A. Knopf, 1993.

Kline, George L., ed. *Alfred North Whitehead: Essays on His Philosophy*. Englewood Cliffs: Prentice-Hall, 1963.

Knapp, Steven, and Walter Benn Michaels. "Against Theory." *Critical Theory* 9 (1982/83): 723–42.

———. "Reply to John Searle." *New Literary History* 25, no. 3 (1994): 669–75.

Koutstaal, Wilma. "Skirting the Abyss: A History of Experimental Explorations of Automatic Writing in Psychology." *Journal of the History of the Behavioral Sciences* 28 (January 1992): 5–27.

Krieger, Murray. *A Reopening of Closure: Organicism Against Itself*. New York: Columbia University Press, 1989.

Langer, Susanne K. *Feeling and Form: A Theory of Art*. New York: Scribner's, 1953.

———. "Living Form." In *Problems of Art: Ten Philosophical Lectures*. New York: Scribner's, 1957.

———. *Mind: An Essay on Human Feeling*. Abridged by Gary Van Den Heuvel. Baltimore: Johns Hopkins University Press, 1988 [1967, 1972, 1982].

———. *Philosophy in a New Key: A Study in the Symbolism of Reason, Rite, and Art*. New York: New American Library, 1954 [1942].

Laplanche, J., and J.-B. Pontalis. *The Language of Psycho-Analysis*. New York: W. W. Norton, 1973.

Latour, Bruno. "Do Scientific Objects Have a History? Pasteur and Whitehead in a Bath of Lactic Acid." *Common Knowledge* 5, no. 1 (Spring 1996): 76–91.

———. *We Have Never Been Modern*. Cambridge, Mass.: Harvard University Press, 1993.

Lawrence, D. H. *Fantasia of the Unconscious*. In *Fantasia of the Unconscious and Psychoanalysis and the Unconscious*. New York: Penguin Books, 1977 [1923].

Lenoir, Timothy. *Instituting Science: The Cultural Production of Scientific Disciplines*. Stanford: Stanford University Press, 1997.

———. "Was the Last Turn the Right Turn? The Semiotic Turn and A.-J. Greimas." *Configurations* 2 (1994): 119–36.

Leon, Philip W. *Walt Whitman and Sir William Osler: A Poet and His Physician*. Toronto: ECW Press, 1995.

Lettvin, J. Y., H. R. Maturana, W. S. McCulloch, and W. H. Pitts. "What the Frog's Eye Tells the Frog's Brain." *Proceedings of the Institute for Radio Engineers* 47, no. 11 (November 1959): 1940–51.

Levin, Jonathan. "The Esthetics of Pragmatism." *American Literary History* 6, no. 4 (Winter 1994): 658–83.

Levine, George, ed. *Realism and Representation: Essays on the Problem of Realism in Relation to Science, Literature, and Culture*. Madison: University of Wisconsin Press, 1993.

Levinson, Ronald B. "Gertrude Stein, William James, and Grammar." *The American Journal of Psychology* 54, no. 1 (January 1941): 124–28.

Lewis, Sinclair. *Arrowsmith*. Afterword by Mark Schorer. New York: Penguin Books, 1980 [1925].

Lewis, Wyndham. *Time and Western Man*. Ed. Paul Edwards. Santa Rosa: Black Sparrow Press, 1993 [1927].

Lewontin, Richard C. "A La Recherche du Temps Perdu" [Review of *Higher Superstition*, by Paul Gross and Norman Levitt, and *On Looking into the Abyss* by Gertrude Himmelfarb]. *Configurations* 2 (1995): 257–65.

Lieberman, Philip. *Eve Spoke: Human Language and Human Evolution*. New York: W. W. Norton, 1998.

Livingston, Ira. *Arrow of Chaos: Romanticism and Postmodernity*. Minneapolis: University of Minnesota Press, 1997.

Lodge, David. *The Modes of Modern Writing: Metaphor, Metonymy, and the Typology of Modern Literature*. Ithaca, N.Y.: Cornell University Press, 1977.

Loeb, Jacques. *The Mechanistic Conception of Life*. Ed. Donald Fleming. Cambridge, Mass.: Harvard University Press, 1964 [1912].

———. *The Organism as a Whole: From a Physico-Chemical Viewpoint*. New York: Putnam, 1916.

Lowe, Victor. *Alfred North Whitehead: The Man and His Work*. 2 vols. Baltimore: Johns Hopkins University Press, 1985, 1990. Vol. 2, ed. J. B. Schneewind.

———. *Understanding Whitehead*. Baltimore: Johns Hopkins University Press, 1962.

Loy, Mina. "Gertrude Stein." In *transatlantic review* 2 (October 1924): 305.

———. "Phenomenon in American Art." In *The Last Lunar Baedeker*. Ed. Robert L. Conover. Highlands, N.C.: The Jargon Society, 1982.

————. "Songs to Joannes I." In *The Lost Lunar Baedeker*. Ed. Roger L. Conover. New York: Farrar Straus Giroux, 1996.

Luhan, Mabel Dodge. *European Experiences*. New York: Harcourt, Brace, 1935.

————. *Movers and Shakers*. New York: Harcourt, Brace, 1936.

————. "Speculations, or Post-Impressionism in Prose." In *Critical Essays on Gertrude Stein*. See Michael J. Hoffman.

Lutz, Tom. *American Nervousness, 1903: An Anecdotal History*. Ithaca, N.Y.: Cornell University Press, 1991.

MacGowan, Kenneth, and Robert Edmond Jones. *Continental Stagecraft*. New York: Harcourt, Brace, 1922.

Maienschein, Jane. "Cell Theory and Development." In *Companion to the History of Modern Science*. See Olby et al.

Malin, Shimon. "A Whiteheadian Approach to Bell's Correlations." *Foundations of Physics* 18, no. 10 (October 1988): 1035–44.

Margulis, Lynn. "Big Trouble in Biology: Physiological Autopoiesis versus Mechanistic Neo-Darwinism." In *Slanted Truths: Essays on Gaia, Symbiosis, and Evolution*, ed. Lynn Margulis and Dorion Sagan. New York: Copernicus, 1997.

————, and Dorion Sagan. *What Is Life?* New York: Simon and Schuster, 1995.

Marin, Louis. "Frontiers of Utopia: Past and Present." *Critical Inquiry* 19 (Winter 1993): 397–420.

————. *Utopics: Spatial Play*. Atlantic Highlands: Humanities Press, 1984.

Maturana, Humberto R., and Francisco J. Varela. *Autopoiesis and Cognition: The Realization of the Living*. Dordrecht, Holland: D. Reidel, 1980.

————. *The Tree of Knowledge: The Biological Roots of Human Understanding*. Boston: Shambhala, 1992.

Mayr, Ernst. *The Growth of Biological Thought: Diversity, Evolution, and Inheritance*. Cambridge, Mass.: Harvard University Press, 1982.

Mays, Wolfe. "Recollections of Wittgenstein." In *Ludwig Wittgenstein*. See K. T. Fann.

McGuinness, Brian, and G. H. von Wright, eds. *Ludwig Wittgenstein: Cambridge Letters: Correspondence with Russell, Keynes, Moore, Ramsey and Sraffe*. Oxford: Blackwell, 1995.

————. *Wittgenstein: A Life. Young Ludwig: 1889–1921*. London: Duckworth, 1988.

————, ed. *Wittgenstein and the Vienna Circle: Conversation Recorded by Frederich Waismann*. New York: Barnes and Noble Books, 1979.

McMaster, Philip D., and Michael Heidelberger, eds. *Florence Rena Sabin: 1871–1953*. New York: Columbia University Press, 1960.

Mellow, James R. *Charmed Circle: Gertrude Stein & Company*. New York: Avon, 1974.

Melville, Herman. *Redburn, White-Jacket, Moby-Dick*. New York: The Library of America, 1983.

Merrill, James. *The Changing Light at Sandover*. New York: Alfred A. Knopf, 1993.

Meyer, Steven. "Gertrude Stein." In *Cambridge History of Literary Criticism*. Vol. 7, *Modernism and the New Criticism*, ed. A. Walton Litz, Louis Menand, and Lawrence Rainey. Cambridge: Cambridge University Press, 2000.

———. "Gertrude Stein Shipwrecked in Bohemia: Making Ends Meet in the *Autobiography* and After." *Southwest Review* (Winter 1992): 12–33.

———. "Introduction." *The Making of Americans*. See Gertrude Stein.

Micale, Mark S. *Approaching Hysteria: Disease and Its Interpretations*. Princeton: Princeton University Press, 1995.

———. "Charcot and the Idea of Hysteria in the Male: Gender, Mental Science and Medical Diagnosis in Late Nineteenth-Century France." *Medical History* 34 (October 1990): 363–411.

———. "Hysteria Male / Hysteria Female: Reflections on Comparative Gender Construction in Nineteenth-Century France and Britain." In *Science and Sensibility: Essays on Gender and Scientific Enquiry, 1780–1945*, ed. Marina Benjamin. London: Basil Blackwell, 1991.

Mili, Gjon. *Picasso's Third Dimension*. New York: Triton, 1970.

———. Photographs in "Speaking of Pictures." *Life* 28, no. 5 (January 30, 1950): 10–12.

Miller, Dickinson Sargeant. "A Memory of William James." In *William James Remembered*. See Simon.

Miller, Jonathan. "Going Unconscious." In *Hidden Histories of Science*. See Silvers.

Miller, Rosalind S. *Gertrude Stein: Form and Intelligibility*. New York: The Exposition Press, 1949.

Modrak, Deborah K. W. *Aristotle: The Power of Perception*. Chicago: University of Chicago Press, 1987.

Moers, Ellen. *Literary Women*. New York: Doubleday, 1976.

Monk, Ray. *Ludwig Wittgenstein: The Duty of Genius*. New York: The Free Press, 1990.

Moody, William Vaughn, and Robert Morss Lovett. *A First View of English Literature*. New York: Scribner, 1905.

Moore, Marianne. "Poetry" [longer version]. In *Complete Poems*. New York: Macmillan, 1981 [1967].

———. *Complete Prose*. Ed. Patricia C. Willis. New York: Viking Penguin, 1986.

Myers, Frederic William Henry. *Human Personality and Its Survival of Bodily Death*. 2 vols. London: Longmans, Green, 1903.

———. *Wordsworth*. New York: Harper, 1881 [1880].

Myers, Gerald E. *William James: His Life and Thought*. New Haven: Yale University Press, 1986.

Myerson, Joel. *Ralph Waldo Emerson: A Descriptive Bibliography*. Pittsburgh: University of Pittsburgh Press, 1982.

Nagy, Gregory. *Poetry as Performance: Homer and Beyond*. Cambridge: Cambridge University Press, 1996.

Nauta, Walle J. H., and Michael Feirtag. *Fundamental Neuroanatomy*. New York: W. H. Freeman, 1986.

Neagoe, Peter, ed. *Americans Abroad: An Anthology*. The Hague: Servire Press, 1932.

Nedo, Michael, ed. *Wiener Ausgabe / Vienna Edition [of the works of Ludwig Wittgenstein]. Einführung/Introduction*. Vienna: Springer-Verlag, 1993.

Needham, Joseph. *Biochemistry and Morphogenesis*. Cambridge: Cambridge University Press, 1950.

———. "S. T. Coleridge as a Philosophical Biologist." *Science Progress* 80 (April 1926): 692–702.

Neuman, Shirley, and Ira B. Nadel, eds. *Gertrude Stein and the Making of Literature*. Boston: Northeastern University Press, 1988.

Nichols, Herbert. "The Psychological Laboratory at Harvard." *McClure's Magazine* 1 (1893): 399–409.

Nuland, Sherwin B. *Doctors: The Biography of Medicine*. New York: Vintage Books, 1995 [1988].

Nussbaum, Martha C. *Love's Knowledge: Essays on Philosophy and Literature*. New York: Oxford University Press, 1990.

Olby, R. C., G. N. Cantor, J. R. R. Christie, and M. J. S. Hodge, eds. *Companion to the History of Modern Science*. London: Routledge, 1990.

Ong, Walter. *Orality and Literacy: The Technologizing of the Word*. London: Routledge, 1989 [1982].

Owen, Richard. *Lectures on the Comparative Anatomy and Physiology of the Invertebrate Animals*. London: Longman, Brown, Greene, and Longmans, 1843.

Packer, B. L. *Emerson's Fall: A New Interpretation of the Major Essays*. New York: Continuum, 1982.

Passmore, John. *A Hundred Years of Philosophy*. New York: Basic Books, 1967.

Pater, Walter. *Selected Writings*. Ed. Harold Bloom. New York: New American Library, 1974.

———. *Marius the Epicurean: His Sensations and Ideas*. London: The Soho Book Company, 1985 [1885].

———. *The Renaissance: Studies in Art and Poetry*. Ed. Adam Phillips. New York: Oxford University Press, 1986 [1888].

Pauly, J. P. *Controlling Life: Jacques Loeb and the Engineering Ideal in Biology*. Oxford: Oxford University Press, 1987.

Pearsall Smith, Logan. "Four Romantic Words." In *Logan Pearsall Smith: An Anthology*, ed. Edward Burman. London: Constable, 1989 [1925].

Peele, Talmage L. *The Neuroanatomic Basis for Clinical Neurology*. 3d edition. New York: McGraw-Hill, 1977.

Perelman, Bob. *The Trouble with Genius: Reading Pound, Joyce, Stein, and Zukofsky*. Berkeley: University of California Press, 1994.

Perloff, Marjorie. "Poetry as Word-System: The Art of Gertrude Stein." In *The Poetics of Indeterminacy: Rimbaud to Cage*. Princeton: Princeton University Press, 1981.

———. *Wittgenstein's Ladder: Poetic Language and the Strangeness of the Ordinary*. Chicago: University of Chicago Press, 1996.

Perry, Ralph Barton, ed. *The Thought and Character of William James*. 2 vols. Boston: Little, Brown, 1935.

Pickstone, John V. "Physiology and Experimental Medicine." In *Companion to the History of Modern Science*. See Olby et al.

Pierce, Constance. "Gertrude Stein and her Thoroughly Modern Protégé." *Modern Fiction Studies* 42, no. 3 (Fall 1996): 607–25.

Pierpont, Claudia Roth. "The Mother of Confusion." *The New Yorker* (May 11, 1998): 80–89.

Pinker, Steven. *The Language Instinct: How the Mind Creates Language*. New York: William Morrow, 1994.

Poirier, Richard. *A World Elsewhere: The Place of Style in American Literature*. Madison: University of Wisconsin Press, 1985 [1966].

———. *Poetry and Pragmatism*. Cambridge, Mass.: Harvard University Press, 1992.

———. "The Question of Genius." In *The Renewal of Literature: Emersonian Reflections*. New Haven: Yale University Press, 1988.

———. *Robert Frost: The Work of Knowing*. Stanford: Stanford University Press, 1990 [1977].

Pollack, Robert. *Signs of Life: The Language and Meanings of DNA*. Boston: Houghton Mifflin, 1994.

Pondrom, Cyrena N. "Influence? or Intertextuality? The Complicated Connection of Edith Sitwell with Gertrude Stein." In *Intertextuality in Literary History*, ed. Jay Clayton and Eric Rothstein. Madison: University of Wisconsin Press, 1991.

Posner, Michael I., and Marcus E. Raichle. *Images of Mind*. New York. W. H. Freeman, 1994.

Posnock, Ross. "Reading Poirier Pragmatically." *The Yale Review* 80, no. 3 (July 1992): 156–69.

Pound, Ezra. *Machine Art & Other Writings*. Ed. Maria Luisa Ardizzone. Durham, N.C.: Duke University Press, 1996.

Preston, John Hyde. "A Conversation." *The Atlantic Monthly* 156, no. 1 (August 1935): 187–94.

Price, Lucien. *Dialogues of Alfred North Whitehead*. Boston: Little, Brown, 1954.

Putnam, Hilary. "A Half Century of Philosophy, Viewed From Within." *Daedalus: Journal of the American Academy of Arts and Sciences* 126, no. 1 (Winter 1997): 175–208.

———. "James's Theory of Perception." In *Realism with a Human Face*, ed. James Conant. Cambridge, Mass.: Harvard University Press, 1990.

Quartermain, Peter. *Disjunctive Poetics: From Gertrude Stein and Louis Zukofsky to Susan Howe*. Cambridge: Cambridge University Press, 1992.

Quine, W. V. O. "Two Dogmas of Empiricism." In *From a Logical Point of View: Nine Logico-Philosophical Essays*. 2d edition. Cambridge, Mass.: Harvard University Press, 1980 [1953].

Rabinbach, Anson. "Neurasthenia and Modernity." In *Incorporations*, ed. Jonathan Crary and Sanford Kwinter. New York: Zone, 1992.

Radner, Daisie. "Heterophenomenology: Learning about the Birds and Bees." *The Journal of Philosophy* 91, no. 8 (August 1994): 389–403.

Ramachandran, V. S., and Sandra Blakeslee. *Phantoms in the Brain: Probing the Mysteries of the Human Mind*. New York: William Morrow, 1998.

Reed, Edward S. *From Soul to Mind: The Emergence of Psychology, from Erasmus Darwin to William James*. New Haven: Yale University Press, 1997.

———. *James J. Gibson and the Psychology of Perception*. New Haven: Yale University Press, 1988.

———. *The Necessity of Experience*. New Haven: Yale University Press, 1996.

———. "The psychologist's fallacy as a persistent framework in William James's psychological theorizing." *History of the Human Sciences* 8, no. 1 (1995): 61–72.

Restak, Richard. *Brainscapes: An Introduction to What Neuroscience Has Learned about the Structure, Function, and Abilities of the Brain*. New York: Hyperion, 1995.

Rewald, John. *Cézanne and America: Dealers, Collectors, Artists and Critics, 1891–1921*. Princeton: Princeton University Press, 1989.

Rice, William. "Gertrude Stein's American Lecture Tour." In *The Letters of Gertrude Stein and Thornton Wilder*. See Burns and Dydo.

Richards, I. A. *Coleridge on Imagination*. New York: Harcourt, Brace, 1935.

———. *The Philosophy of Rhetoric*. New York: Oxford University Press, 1965 [1936].

———. *Poetries and Sciences: A Reissue of* Science and Poetry *(1926, 1935) with Commentary*. London: Routledge and Kegan Paul, 1970.

Richardson, Joan. "Emerson's Sound Effects." *Raritan* 16, no. 3 (Winter 1997): 83–101.

Richardson, Robert D., Jr. *Emerson: The Mind on Fire*. Berkeley: University of California Press, 1995.

Riddel, Joseph N. "Stein and Bergson." In *The Turning Word: American Literary Modernism and Continental Theory*, ed. Mark Bauerlein. Philadelphia: University of Pennsylvania Press, 1996.

Riding, Laura, and Robert Graves. *A Survey of Modernist Poetry*. St. Clair Shores: Scholarly Press, 1972 [1927].

Risse, Gunter B. "The Brownian System of Medicine: Its Theoretical and Practical Implications." *Clio Medica* 5 (1970): 45–51.

————. "The Quest for Certainty in Medicine: John Brown's System of Medicine in France." *Bulletin of the History of Medicine* 44, no. 1 (January–February 1971): 1–12.

Ritchie, A. D. *The Natural History of Mind*. London: Longmans, Green, 1936.

Robinson, David. "Emerson's Natural Theology and the Paris Naturalists: Toward a Theory of Animated Nature." *Journal of the History of Ideas* 41, no. 1 (January–March 1980): 69–88.

————. "Fields of Investigation: Emerson and Natural History." In *American Literature and Science*, ed. Robert J. Scholnick. Lexington: University Press of Kentucky, 1992.

Rorty, Richard. "Dewey between Hegel and Darwin." In *Rorty and Pragmatism*. See Herman J. Saatkamp, Jr.

————. "Holism, Intrinsicality, and the Ambition of Transcendence." In *Dennett and His Critics: Demystifying Mind*, ed. Bo Dahlbom. Oxford: Basil Blackwell, 1993.

————. "Inquiry as Recontextualization: An Anti-Dualist Account of Interpretation." In *Objectivity, Relativism, and Truth*. Cambridge: Cambridge University Press, 1991.

————. "Introduction." *The Linguistic Turn: Recent Essays in Philosophical Method*. Chicago: University of Chicago Press, 1967.

————. "Matter and Event." In *The Concept of Matter*, ed. Ernan McMullin. Notre Dame: University of Notre Dame Press, 1963.

————. "Mind as Ineffable." In *Mind in Nature*, ed. Richard Q. Elvee. Nobel Conference 17. San Francisco: Harper and Row, 1982.

————. "Philosophy and the Future." In *Rorty and Pragmatism*. See Herman J. Saatkamp, Jr.

————. "Pragmatism as Anti-Representationalism." Introduction to *Pragmatism: From Peirce to Davidson*, by John P. Murphy. Boulder: Westview Press, 1990.

————. "The Subjectivist Principle and the Linguistic Turn." In *Alfred North Whitehead: Essays on His Philosophy*. See George L. Kline.

Rosenfield, Israel. *The Invention of Memory: A New View of the Brain*. New York: Basic Books, 1988.

————. *The Strange, Familiar, and Forgotten: An Anatomy of Consciousness*. New York: Alfred A. Knopf, 1992.

Rosenzweig, Saul. "The Jameses' Stream of Consciousness." *Contemporary Psychology* 3, no. 9 (September 1958): 250–57.

Rothfield, Lawrence. " 'A New Organ of Knowledge': Medical Organicism and the Limits of Realism in *Middlemarch*." In *Vital Signs: Medical Realism in Nineteenth-Century Fiction*. Princeton: Princeton University Press, 1992.

Royce, Josiah. *The Spirit of Modern Philosophy: An Essay in the Form of Lectures*. Boston: Houghton Mifflin Company, 1892.

Rubin, William, ed. *Pablo Picasso: A Retrospective*. New York: Museum of Modern Art, 1980.

Ruddick, Lisa. *Reading Gertrude Stein: Body, Text, Gnosis*. Ithaca, N.Y.: Cornell University Press, 1990.

Rupke, Nicolaas. *Richard Owen: Victorian Naturalist*. New Haven: Yale University Press, 1995.

Russell, Bertrand. *The Autobiography of Bertrand Russell: 1914–1944*. Boston: Little, Brown, 1968.

———. "Knowledge by Acquaintance and Knowledge by Description." In *Mysticism and Logic and Other Essays*. London: George Allen and Unwin, 1951 [1917].

———. *Logic and Knowledge: Essays 1901–1950*. Ed. Robert Charles Marsh. New York: G. P. Putnam's Sons, 1956.

———. "Logical Positivism." In *Logic and Knowledge*.

———. *My Philosophical Development*. New York: Simon and Schuster, 1959.

———. *Our Knowledge of the External World as a Field for Scientific Method in Philosophy*. New York: Routledge, 1993 [1914].

———. *Portraits from Memory*. New York: Simon and Schuster, 1956.

Saatkamp, Herman J., Jr., ed. *Rorty and Pragmatism: The Philosopher Responds to His Critics*. Nashville: Vanderbilt University Press, 1995.

Sabin, Florence R. *An Atlas of the Medulla and Midbrain: A Laboratory Manual*. Ed. Henry McE. Knower. Baltimore: Friedenwald, 1901.

———. *Franklin Paine Mall: The Story of a Mind*. Baltimore: Johns Hopkins University Press, 1934.

———. "Model of the Medulla, Pons and Midbrain of a New Born Babe." In *Johns Hopkins Hospital Reports*. Vol. 9, *Contributions to the Science of Medicine*. Baltimore: Johns Hopkins University Press, 1900.

Sacks, Oliver. "A New Vision of the Mind." In *Nature's Imagination: The Frontiers of Scientific Vision*, ed. John Cornwell. Oxford: Oxford University Press, 1995.

———. *Awakenings*. New York: E. P. Dutton, 1983 [1973].

———. "Making Up the Mind." *The New York Review of Books* (April 8, 1993): 42–49.

———. "Scotoma: Forgetting and Neglect in Science." In *Hidden Histories of Science*. See Silvers.

———. "The Case of the Colorblind Painter." In *An Anthropologist on Mars: Seven Paradoxical Tales*. New York: Vintage Books, 1995.

Samsell, R. L. "Paris Days with Ralph Church." In *Fitzgerald / Hemingway Annual 1972*, ed. Matthew J. Bruccoli and C. E. Frazer Clark, Jr. Washington, D.C.: 145–56.

Saussure, Ferdinand de. *Course in General Linguistics*. Trans. Roy Harris. La Salle: Open Court, 1983.

Sayre, Henry M. "The Artist's Model: American Art and the Question of Looking Like Gertrude Stein." In *Gertrude Stein and the Making of Literature*. See Neuman and Nadel.

Schmitz, Neil. *Of Huck and Alice: Humorous Writing in American Literature*. Minneapolis: University of Minnesota Press, 1983.

Schoenberg, Bruce S. "Gertrude Stein's Neuroanatomic Investigations: Roses or Thorns?" *Southern Medical Journal* 81, no. 2 (February 1988): 250–58.

Schorer, Mark. "Afterword." In *Arrowsmith*. See Sinclair Lewis.

Schulte, Joachim. *Experience and Expression: Wittgenstein's Philosophy of Psychology*. Oxford: Clarendon Press, 1993.

Seamon, David, and Arthur Zajonc, eds. *Goethe's Way of Science: A Phenomenology of Nature*. Albany: State University of New York Press, 1998.

Searle, John R. *The Mystery of Consciousness*. New York: The New York Review of Books, 1997.

Serres, Michel, with Bruno Latour. *Conversations on Science, Culture, and Time*. Ann Arbor: University of Michigan Press, 1995.

Sewell, Elizabeth. *The Orphic Voice: Poetry and Natural History*. New Haven: Yale University Press, 1960.

Shear, Jonathan, ed. *Explaining Consciousness—The "Hard Problem."* Cambridge, Mass.: MIT Press, 1997.

Shepherd, Gordon M. *Foundations of the Neuron Doctrine*. New York: Oxford University Press, 1991.

Sherrington, Charles S. *Goethe on Nature and on Science*. Cambridge: Cambridge University Press, 1942.

———. *The Integrative Action of the Nervous System*. New Haven: Yale University Press, 1906.

Shimony, Abner. "Quantum Physics and the Philosophy of Whitehead." In *In Search for a Naturalistic World View*. Vol. 2, *Natural Science and Metaphysics*. Cambridge: Cambridge University Press, 1993.

Shortt, S. E. D. *Victorian Lunacy: Richard M. Bucke and the Practice of Late Nineteenth-Century Psychiatry*. New York: Cambridge University Press, 1986.

Shusterman, Richard. *Pragmatist Aesthetics: Living Beauty, Rethinking Art*. Cambridge, Mass.: Blackwell, 1992.

———. *Practicing Philosophy: Pragmatism and the Philosophical Life*. New York: Routledge, 1997.

Shuttleworth, Sally. *George Eliot and Nineteenth-Century Science: The Make-Believe of a Beginning*. New York: Cambridge University Press, 1984.

Sidis, Boris. *The Psychology of Suggestion: A Research into the Subconscious Nature of Man and Society*. New York: D. Appleton, 1898.

———, and Simon Goodhart. *Multiple Personality: An Experimental Investigation into the Nature of Human Individuality*. New York: D. Appleton, 1905.

Silvers, Robert B., ed. *Hidden Histories of Science*. New York: The New York Review of Books, 1995.

Simmons, Nancy Craig. "Arranging the Sibylline Leaves: James Elliot Cabot's Work as Emerson's Literary Executor." In *Studies in the American Renaissance 1983*, ed. Joel Myerson. Charlottesville: University Press of Virginia, 1983.

Simon, Linda, ed. *Gertrude Stein: A Composite Portrait*. New York: Avon Books, 1974.

———, ed. *William James Remembered*. Lincoln: University of Nebraska Press, 1996.

Sitney, P. Adams. *Modernist Montage: The Obscurity of Vision in Cinema and Literature*. New York: Columbia University Press, 1990.

Skinner, B. F. "Has Gertrude Stein a Secret?" In *Critical Essays on Gertrude Stein*. See Michael J. Hoffman.

———. *Verbal Behavior*. Englewood Cliffs: Prentice-Hall, 1957.

Smith, Henry Nash. *Virgin Land: The American West as Symbol and Myth*. Cambridge, Mass.: Harvard University Press, 1950.

Smith-Rosenberg, Carroll. "The Hysterical Woman: Sex Roles and Role Conflict in Nineteenth-Century America." In *Disorderly Conduct: Visions of Gender in Victorian America*. New York: Alfred A. Knopf, 1985.

Solomons, L. M. "The Saturation of Colors." *The Psychological Review* 3, no. 1 (January 1896): 50–56.

Southam, B. C. *A Student's Guide to* The Selected Poems of T. S. Eliot. 5th ed. London: Faber and Faber, 1990.

Spillmann, Jutta, and Lothar Spillmann. "The Rise and Fall of Hugo Münsterberg." *Journal of the History of the Behavioral Sciences* 29 (October 1993): 322–38.

Sprigge, Elizabeth. *Gertrude Stein: Her Life And Work*. New York: Harper, 1957.

Stapp, Henry P. *Mind, Matter, and Quantum Physics*. Berlin: Springer-Verlag, 1993.

Stein, Barry E., and M. Alex Meredith. *The Merging of the Senses*. Cambridge, Mass.: MIT Press, 1993.

Stein, Gertrude. "American Language and Literature." In *Gertrude Stein and the Making of Literature*. See Shirley Neuman.

———. *An Acquaintance with Description*. In *A Stein Reader*. See Dydo.

———. "An American and France." In *What Are Masterpieces*.

———. *The Autobiography of Alice B. Toklas*. New York: Vintage Books, 1990 [1933].

———. *Bee Time Vine and Other Pieces [1913–1927]*. Vol. 3 of *The Yale Edition of the Unpublished Writings of Gertrude Stein*. New Haven: Yale University Press, 1953.

———. [Comment concerning reprint of *Tender Buttons*]. *transition* 14 (Fall 1928): 13.

———. "Composition as Explanation." In *What Are Masterpieces*.

———. *Everybody's Autobiography*. Cambridge: Exact Change, 1993 [1937].

————. *Fernhurst, Q.E.D., and Other Early Writings.* Ed. Donald Gallup. New York: Liveright, 1973.

————. *Four in America.* New Haven: Yale University Press, 1947.

————. "Genuine Creative Ability." In *A Primer for the Gradual Understanding of Gertrude Stein.* See Robert Bartlett Haas.

————. *The Geographical History of America or the Relation of Human Nature to the Human Mind.* Baltimore: Johns Hopkins University Press, 1995 [1936].

————. *Geography and Plays.* Madison: University of Wisconsin Press, 1993 [1922].

————. *How To Write.* Los Angeles: Sun and Moon Press, 1995 [1931].

————. *How Writing Is Written: Volume II of the Previously Uncollected Writings of Gertrude Stein.* Ed. Robert Bartlett Haas. Los Angeles: Black Sparrow Press, 1974.

————. *Last Operas and Plays.* Ed. Carl Van Vechten. New York: Rinehart, 1949.

————. *Lectures in America.* Boston: Beacon Press, 1985 [1935].

————. *Lucy Church Amiably.* New York: Something Else Press, 1969 [1930].

————. *The Making of Americans.* Normal, Ill.: The Dalkey Archive Press, 1995 [1925].

————. *Matisse Picasso and Gertrude Stein with Two Shorter Stories.* Barton, Vt.: Something Else Press, 1972 [1933].

————. "Message from Gertrude Stein." In *Selected Writings*, ed. Carl Van Vechten. New York: Vintage Books, 1972 [1946].

————. "Mildred's Thoughts." In *American Caravan: A Yearbook of American Literature*, ed. Alfred Kreymborg, Van Wyck Brooks, Lewis Mumford, and Paul Rosenfield. New York: Macaulay, 1927.

————. "More Grammar for a Sentence." In *A Stein Reader.* See Dydo.

————. "My Debt to Books." In *Primer.* See Robert Bartlett Haas.

————. *Narration.* Chicago: University of Chicago Press, 1935.

————. *Operas and Plays.* Barrytown, N.Y.: Station Hill Press, 1987 [1932].

————. *Painted Lace and Other Pieces [1914–1937].* Vol. 5 of *The Yale Edition of the Unpublished Writings of Gertrude Stein.* New Haven: Yale University Press, 1955.

————. *Paris France.* New York: Charles Scribner's Sons, 1940.

————. *Picasso: The Complete Writings.* Ed. Edward Burns. Boston: Beacon Press, 1970.

————. *Portraits and Prayers.* New York: Random House, 1934.

————. "Possessive Case." In *As Fine As Melanctha (1914–1930).* Vol. 4 of *The Yale Edition of the Unpublished Writings of Gertrude Stein.* New Haven: Yale University Press, 1954.

————. "The Radcliffe Manuscripts." In *Gertrude Stein: Form and Intelligibility.* See Rosalind S. Miller.

————. *Reflection on the Atomic Bomb.* Ed. Robert Bartlett Haas. Los Angeles: Black Sparrow Press, 1973.

————. "Sentences and Paragraphs." In *How To Write.*

————. *Stanzas in Mediation and Other Poems*. Vol. 6 of *The Yale Edition of the Unpublished Writings of Gertrude Stein*. New Haven: Yale University Press, 1956.

————. *Tender Buttons*. Los Angeles: Sun and Moon Press, n.d. [1914].

————. "Thoughts on an American Contemporary Feeling." In *Reflection on the Atomic Bomb*.

————. *Three Lives*. Introduction by Ann Charters. New York: Penguin Books, 1990 [1909].

————. "A Transatlantic Interview 1946." In *Primer*. See Robert Bartlett Haas.

————. *Two: Gertrude Stein and Her Brother and Other Early Portraits*. Vol. 1 of *The Yale Edition of the Unpublished Writings of Gertrude Stein*. New Haven: Yale University Press, 1951.

————. *Useful Knowledge*. Barrytown, N.Y.: Station Hill Press, 1988 [1928].

————. *Wars I Have Seen*. New York: Random House, 1945.

————. "What Are Master-pieces And Why Are There So Few Of Them." In *What Are Masterpieces*.

————. *What Are Masterpieces*. Los Angeles: The Conference Press, 1940.

Stein, Gertrude, and Leon M. Solomons. *Motor Automatism*. New York: The Phoenix Book Shop, 1969 [1896, 1898].

Stein, Leo. *Journey Into the Self: Being the Letters, Papers and Journals of Leo Stein*. Ed. Edmund Fuller. New York: Crown, 1950.

Steinberg, Leo. "The Algerian Women and Picasso at Large." In Steinberg, *Other Criteria*. New York: Oxford University Press, 1975.

Steiner, Wendy. *Exact Resemblance to Exact Resemblance: The Literary Portraiture of Gertrude Stein*. New Haven: Yale University Press, 1978.

————. "Practice without Principle: The Two Cultures, Out of Step." *The American Scholar* 68, no. 3 (Summer 1999): 77–87.

Stern, David G. *Wittgenstein on Mind and Language*. New York: Oxford University Press, 1995.

Sterne, Laurence. *The Life and Opinions of Tristram Shandy, Gentleman*. Ed. Ian Watt. Boston: Houghton Mifflin, 1965 [1759–67].

————. *A Sentimental Journey through France and Italy*. Ed. Graham Petrie. New York: Penguin, 1986 [1768].

Stimpson, Catharine R. "Gertrice/Altrude: Stein, Toklas, and the Paradox of the Happy Marriage." In *Mothering the Mind: Twelve Studies of Writers and Their Silent Partners*, ed. Ruth Perry and Martine Watson Brownley. New York: Holmes and Meier, 1984.

————. "Gertrude Stein and the Lesbian Lie." In *American Women's Autobiography: Fea(s)ts of Memory*, ed. Margo Culley. Madison: University of Wisconsin Press, 1992.

————. "Gertrude Stein and the Transposition of Gender." In *The Poetics of Gender*, ed. Nancy K. Miller. New York: Columbia University Press, 1986.

————. "Gertrude Stein: Humanism and Its Freaks." *boundary 2* 12, no. 3 and 13, no. 1 (Spring/Fall 1984): 301–19.

————. "The Mind, the Body, and Gertrude Stein." *Critical Inquiry* 3, no. 3 (Spring 1977): 489–506.

————. "The Somograms of Gertrude Stein." *Poetics Today* 6, nos. 1–2 (1985): 67–80.

Strauch, Carl F. "Emerson's Sacred Science." *PMLA* 73, no. 3 (June 1958): 237–50.

Suleiman, Susan. "A Double Margin: Women Writers and the Avant-Garde in France." In *Subversive Intent: Gender, Politics, and the Avant-Garde.* Cambridge, Mass.: Harvard University Press, 1990.

Sulloway, Frank J. *Freud, Biologist of the Mind: Beyond the Psychoanalytic Legend.* New York: Basic Books, 1983.

Sutherland, Donald. *Gertrude Stein: A Biography of Her Work.* New Haven: Yale University Press, 1951.

Taylor, Eugene. *William James on Consciousness Beyond the Margin.* Princeton: Princeton University Press, 1996.

————, ed. *William James on Exceptional Mental States.* New York: Scribner's, 1983.

Terwee, Sybe. "James' Theory of Emotion—A Wittgensteinian View." In *Epistemology and Philosophy of Science: Proceedings of the 7th International Wittgenstein Symposium*, ed. Paul Weingartner and Johannes Czermak. Vienna: Holder-Pichler-Tempsky, 1983.

Thomas, David Wayne. "Gödel's Theorem and Postmodern Theory." *PMLA* 110, vol. 2 (March 1995): 248–61.

Toklas, Alice B. *Staying on Alone.* Ed. Edward Burns. New York: Liveright, 1973.

————. *What Is Remembered.* Berkeley: North Point Press, 1985 [1963].

Turner, Frank Miller. *Between Science and Religion: The Reaction to Scientific Naturalism in Late Victorian England.* New Haven: Yale University Press, 1974.

Turner, Kay. *Baby Precious Always Shines: Selected Love Notes Between Gertrude Stein and Alice B. Toklas.* New York: St. Martin's Press, 1999.

Varela, Francisco J. "The Reenchantment of the Concrete." In *Incorporations.* See Jonathan Crary.

————, Evan Thompson, and Eleanor Rosch. *The Embodied Mind: Cognitive Science and Human Experience.* Cambridge, Mass.: MIT Press, 1991.

Vlastos, Gregory. "Organic Categories in Whitehead." In *Alfred North Whitehead: Essays on His Philosophy.* See George L. Kline.

Waismann, Frederich. *Wittgenstein and the Vienna Circle.* See Brian McGuinness.

Walker, Jayne. *The Making of a Modernist: Gertrude Stein from "Three Lives" to "Tender Buttons."* Amherst: University of Massachusetts Press, 1984.

Weekley, Ernest. *An Etymological Dictionary of Modern English.* New York: Dover Publications, 1967 [1921].

Weininger, Otto. *Sex and Character.* New York: G. P. Putnam, 1906.

Weissmann, Gerald. "Gertrude Stein on the Beach." In *The Doctor with Two Heads.* New York: Knopf, 1990.

W. G. S. "Notes on New Books: *The Nervous System and Its Constituent Neurones*. By Lewellys F. Barker." *Johns Hopkins Hospital Bulletin* 10, no. 105 (December 1899): 234–35.

White, Ray Lewis, ed. *Sherwood Anderson / Gertrude Stein*. Chapel Hill: University of North Carolina Press, 1972.

Whitehead, Alfred North. *Adventures of Ideas*. New York: The Free Press, 1967 [1933].

———. *An Enquiry Concerning the Principles of Natural Knowledge*. 2d edition. New York: Dover Publications, 1982 [1925].

———. *Essays in Science and Philosophy*. New York: Philosophical Library, 1947.

———. *The Function of Reason*. Princeton: Princeton University Press, 1929.

———. "Historical Changes." In *Essays in Science and Philosophy*.

———. *Modes of Thought*. New York: The Free Press, 1968 [1938].

———. *Nature and Life*. Chicago: University of Chicago Press, 1934.

———. "Process and Reality." In *Essays in Science and Philosophy*.

———. *Process and Reality*. Corrected edition, ed. David Ray Griffin and Donald W. Sherburne. New York: The Free Press, 1978 [1929].

———. *Religion in the Making*. New York: Fordham University Press, 1996 [1926].

———. *Science and the Modern World*. New York: The Free Press, 1967 [1925].

———. *Symbolism: Its Meaning and Effect*. New York: Fordham University Press, 1985 [1927].

Wilder, Thornton. *Journals*. See Donald Gallup.

Williams, William Carlos. *Autobiography*. New York: New Directions, 1951.

———. *The Embodiment of Knowledge*. Ed. Ron Loewinsohn. New York: New Directions, 1974.

———. *Kora in Hell*. In *Imaginations*, ed. Webster Schott. New York: New Directions, 1970.

———. "The Work of Gertrude Stein." In *Selected Essays*. New York: Random House, 1954.

Wilson, Edmund. "A. N. Whitehead and Bertrand Russell." In *From the Uncollected Edmund Wilson*. See Janet Groth.

———. "A. N. Whitehead: Physicist and Prophet." In *From the Uncollected Edmund Wilson*. See Janet Groth.

———. *Axel's Castle: A Study in the Imaginative Literature of 1870–1930*. New York: Norton, 1984 [1931].

———. "Modern Literature: Between the Whirlpool and the Rock." In *From the Uncollected Edmund Wilson*. See Janet Groth.

———. *Upstate: Records and Recollections of Northern New York*. New York: Farrar, Straus and Giroux, 1971.

Wilson, Edward O. *Consilience: The Unity of Knowledge*. New York: Random House, 1998.

Wimsatt, W. K. "Genesis: An Argument Resumed." In *Day of the Leopards*. New Haven: Yale University Press, 1976.

Wineapple, Brenda. *Sister Brother: Gertrude and Leo Stein*. New York: G. P. Putnam, 1996.

Wittgenstein, Ludwig. *Culture and Value*. Ed. G. H. von Wright. Chicago: University of Chicago Press, 1980.

———. *Last Writings on the Philosophy of Psychology*. Vol. 1, *Preliminary Studies for Part II of "Philosophical Investigations."* Ed. G. H. von Wright and Heikki Nyman. Chicago: University of Chicago Press, 1990.

———. *Last Writings on the Philosophy of Psychology*. Vol. 2, *The Inner and the Outer, 1949–1951*. Ed. G. H. von Wright and Heikki Nyman. Oxford: Blackwell, 1992.

———. *Philosophical Grammar*. Ed. Rush Rhees. Berkeley: University of California Press, 1978.

———. *Philosophical Investigations*. 3d edition. Ed. G. E. M. Anscombe and Rush Rhees. New York: Macmillan, 1958.

———. "Philosophy." In *Philosophical Occasions: 1912–1951*, ed. James C. Klagge and Alfred Nordmann. Indianapolis: Hackett, 1993.

———. *Remarks on Colour*. Ed. G. E. M. Anscombe. Berkeley: University of California Press, 1978.

———. *Remarks on the Philosophy of Psychology*. Vol. 1, ed. G. E. M. Anscombe and G. H. von Wright. Vol. 2, ed. G. H. von Wright and Heikki Nyman. Chicago: University of Chicago Press, 1980.

———. *The Blue and Brown Books: Preliminary Studies for the "Philosophical Investigations."* New York: Harper and Row, 1965 [1958].

———. *Zettel*. Ed. G. E. M. Anscombe and G. H. von Wright. Berkeley: University of California Press, 1970.

Wordsworth, Dorothy. *Selections from the Journals*. Ed. Paul Hamilton. New York: NYU Press, 1992.

Wordsworth, William. "Essays on Epigraphs." In *Wordsworth's Literary Criticism*.

———. "Preface of 1815." In *Wordsworth's Literary Criticism*.

———. *The Prelude: 1799, 1805, 1850*. Ed. Jonathan Wordsworth, M. H. Abrams, and Stephen Gill. New York: W. W. Norton, 1979.

———. *Selected Poems and Prefaces*. Ed. Jack Stillinger. Boston: Houghton Mifflin, 1965.

———. *Wordsworth's Literary Criticism*. Ed. W. J. B. Owen. London: Routledge and Kegan Paul, 1974.

———, and Samuel Taylor Coleridge. *Lyrical Ballads*. 2d edition. Ed. R. L. Brett and A. R. Jones. New York: Routledge, 1991.

Zajonc, Arthur. *Catching the Light: The Entwined History of Light and Mind*. New York: Oxford University Press, 1993.

Zeki, Semir. *A Vision of the Brain*. Oxford: Blackwell Scientific Publications, 1993.

Žižek, Slavoj. "Otto Weininger, or, 'Woman Doesn't Exist.'" *New Formations* 23 (Summer 1994): 97–113.

367; on "arithmetical addition," 175, 177, 183; mentioned, xviii, 10, 13, 55, 285. *See also titles of individual works*

Emotion, 11, 18, 58, 190, 292, 294, 319, 397, 399; James's account of, 22–27, 112, 116, 192, 278–81, 335–36, 386–87; and sensation, 23–26, 126, 271, 279–81, 336; and movement, 23–24, 272, 283, 325; expression of, 23, 279–80, 399; T. S. Eliot on, 33, 151; Stein on, 62, 115, 203; and obstruction, 192, 271; in paragraphs and sentences, 254–55, 262, 271–76, 279, 281–83; communication of, 279, 318. *See also* Non sequitur

Emphasis, 53, 235, 297, 299, 301, 308; and repetition, 123, 182–83, 209, 237, 301, 303, 328

Empiricism, 3, 18, 25, 36, 293, 321, 336–37, 342, 371, 397–99; empirical limits of, 6, 22, 214, 371, 376; eighteenth-century, 11, 36, 39; naïve, 12, 24, 215, 336, 371; and rationalism, 200, 214, 373; and radical empiricism, 11–13, 18, 20, 36, 215–16, 224, 292, 323, 373, 397

Empson, William, 21, 217, 220–21, 339, 373, 379, 383–84, 394

Encephalitis, 51, 53–54, 295. *See also* Sleep

"Energies of Men, The" (W. James), 354, 388–89

England, *see* America

Enjoyment, xvii, 16, 105, 296

Enquiry Concerning the Principles of Natural Knowledge, An (Whitehead), 178–85 *passim*, 204–5, 364

Entity, 113–14, 117, 124–26, 128, 145, 147, 364, 396–97; consciousness as, 216, 243, 245, 318

Environment, 7, 9, 32, 35f, 115, 234, 246, 248, 260, 268, 292, 326, 388; and organism, 46, 133–35, 185, 356, 396–97; as background, 47, 117, 133, 282–83, 292; and identity, 48, 178, 348; and definition, 116–17, 137. *See also* Conditions; Organism/ambient relation

Equilibrium, 135, 140. *See also* Proprioception

Error, 20, 271–73, 286–89, 321; deliberate, 99, 101, 104–6, 190f. *See also* Waywardness

Essays in Radical Empiricism (W. James), 319, 372

Eternal, 105, 124, 134, 210, 304, 342, 362; objects, 254, 363, 395; endless thought, 254, 276

Eternity, 9, 39, 183, 209

Everybody's Autobiography, 6, 8, 63

Evolution, 10, 35, 131, 174, 209f, 213, 246, 327, 334, 384f; co-, 116, 132–33, 319

Exactitude, 62, 184, 219–20, 233, 316–17, 399; of meaning, 229, 231, 252, 282–83

Excitement, 22–23, 25, 124, 170, 174, 203–4, 209f, 301f, 304, 344, 394; of creation, 10, 117, 197; words "excitedly feeling themselves," 106, 137; "intrinsically exciting," 115, 117

Experience, 19, 22, 27, 33, 37, 42, 186f, 188f, 211; past and present, 7–8, 13, 17; and radical empiricism, 12–13, 20, 33, 215f; immediate, 12, 15, 39, 42, 219–20, 371; James on, 15, 25–27, 216–19; of writing, 15, 28, 43–44, 48, 61, 128, 242, 276; emotional, 23–24, 26, 189, 293, 336, 399; second-order, 23–24, 47; physical basis of, 24, 34, 291, 381; and expression, 28–29, 136, 155, 178; reductive accounts of, 65, 200–201; Whitehead on, 173–74, 188–93, 363

"Experience" (Emerson), 13, 131, 140f, 168, 217, 219, 383

Experimentation, 19, 21, 115, 194, 203, 278, 326, 339–40, 369, 387; Stein's radically experimental writing, xx–xxi, 3, 36–37, 53, 101, 224, 226, 387; writing and, 34, 46, 64, 75, 82f, 99, 240; thought experiments, 43, 341

Explanation, 10, 20, 37, 74, 187, 200, 210, 378. *See also* Composition as explanation

Expression, 22–23, 181, 183f, 206, 252, 269–70, 279–80, 296–98, 302–3, 360–61; and writing, xv, 32, 52, 391; and experience, 28–30, 44, 136, 155, 178; and thought, 64, 169–70, 172; self-, 209, 241–42, 250–51, 295, 380

External/internal relation, 40, 101, 185f, 217, 234, 280, 284, 293, 325f, 350, 386; "the problem of the external and the internal," 45–48, 233; external and internal milieus, 82, 115–16; "description of inner and outer reality," 220, 399; "mixing the outside with the inside," 232, 253, 262; "the inside as seen from the outside," 232, 253, 342

WRITING SCIENCE

Helmut Müller-Sievers, *Self-Generation: Biology, Philosophy, and Literature Around 1800*

Karen Newman, *Fetal Positions: Individualism, Science, Visuality*

Peter Galison and David J. Stump, eds., *The Disunity of Science: Boundaries, Contexts, and Power*

Niklas Luhmann, *Social Systems*

Hans Ulrich Gumbrecht and K. Ludwig Pfeiffer, eds., *Materialities of Communication*